MANAGEMENT
An Introduction

PEARSON
mymanagementlab

INSTANT ACCESS TO INTERACTIVE LEARNING

With your purchase of a new copy of this textbook, you received a Student Access Kit to **MyManagementLab** for *Management: An Introduction*, Fifth Edition, by David Boddy with Steve Paton.

MyManagementLab gives you access to an unrivalled suite of online resources. It provides a variety of tools to enable you to assess and progress your own learning, including questions, tests and learning aids for each chapter of the book. You will benefit from a personalised learning experience, where you can:

- Complete a diagnostic 'pre-test' to generate your own Study Plan, which adapts to your strengths and weaknesses and enables you to focus on the topics where your knowledge is weaker.
- Improve your understanding through a variety of practice activities that match the chapters of *Management: An Introduction*.
- Measure your progress with a follow-up 'post-test' that ensures you have mastered key learning objectives – and gives you the confidence to move on to the next chapter.
- Study on the go and refer to pages from an e-book version of this text.
- Watch and learn from a wealth of video clips and case studies and analyse how top managers at a wide range of organisations talk about real life situations that relate to management.
- Revise by listening to audio summaries of the key concepts in each chapter.
- Check your understanding using a comprehensive glossary of key terms, with flashcards to check your knowledge.

See the Guided Tour of **MyManagementLab** on page xxii for more details.

To activate your pre-paid subscription go to **www.pearsoned.co.uk/mymanagementlab**. Follow the instructions on-screen to register as a new user and see your grades improve!

PEARSON

We work with leading authors to develop the
strongest educational materials in management,
bringing cutting-edge thinking and best learning
practice to a global market.

Under a range of well-known imprints, including
Financial Times Prentice Hall, we craft high-quality
print and electronic publications which help readers
to understand and apply their content, whether
studying or at work.

To find out more about the complete range of our
publishing, please visit us on the World Wide Web at:
www.pearsoned.co.uk

David B

MA NT

A Edition

With **Steve**

**Financial Times
Prentice Hall
is an imprint of**

PEARSON

Harlow, England • London • New York • Boston • San Francisco • Toronto • Sydney • Singapore • Hong Kong
Tokyo • Seoul • Taipei • New Delhi • Cape Town • Madrid • Mexico City • Amsterdam • Munich • Paris • Milan

4843

Pearson Education Limited
Edinburgh Gate
Harlow
Essex CM20 2JE
England

and Associated Companies around the world

Visit us on the World Wide Web at:
www.pearsoned.co.uk

First published 1998 under the Prentice Hall Europe imprint
Second edition published 2002
Third edition published 2005
Fourth edition published 2008
Fifth edition published 2011

© Prentice Hall Europe 1998
© Pearson Education Limited 2002, 2011

ISBN: 978-0-273-73896-1

British Library Cataloguing-in-Publication Data
A catalogue record for this book is available from the British Library.

Library of Congress Cataloging-in-Publication Data

Boddy, David.
  Management : an introduction / David Boddy ; with Steve Paton. – 5th ed.
    p. cm.
  Includes bibliographical references and index.
  ISBN 978-0-273-73896-1 (pbk. : alk. paper)   1. Management.   I. Paton, Steve.
  II. Title.

  HD31.B583 2011
  658 – dc22   2010031597

10 9 8 7 6 5 4 3 2
14 13 12

Typeset in 10.5/12.5 pt Minion by 73
Printed and bound by Rotolito Lombarda, Italy

BRIEF CONTENTS

CONTENTS

PART 1
AN INTRODUCTION TO MANAGEMENT

PART 2
THE ENVIRONMENT OF MANAGEMENT

PART 3
PLANNING

PART 4
ORGANISING

PART 5
LEADING

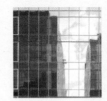

PART 6
CONTROLLING

MANAGEMENT: AN INTRODUCTION, FIFTH EDITION

SUPPORTING RESOURCES

MyManagementLab for students and instructors

PEARSON
mymanagementlab

www.pearsoned.co.uk/mymanagementlab

Every new copy of this textbook comes with an access kit for **MyManagementLab**, giving access to an unrivalled suite of online resources that relate directly to the content of *Management: An Introduction,* Fifth Edition.

Within a flexible course management platform, instructors can:

- Assess student progress through homework quizzes and tests that are easily set using the extensive pre-prepared question bank.
- Assign short answer, discussion and essay questions from each chapter for student homework or tutorial preparation.
- Track student activity and performance using detailed reporting capabilities.
- Communicate with students and teaching staff using e-mail and announcement tools.

Students will benefit from a personalised learning experience, where they can:

- Complete a diagnostic 'pre-test' to generate a personal self-study plan that enables them to focus on the topics where their knowledge is weaker.
- Improve their understanding through a variety of practice activities including: revision flashcards, e-book reading assignments, short answer questions, audio downloads and video cases.
- Measure their progress with a follow-up 'post-test' that ensures they have mastered key learning objectives – and gives them the confidence to move on to the next chapter.

A dedicated team is available to give you all the assistance you need to get online and make the most of **MyManagementLab**. Contact your sales representative for further details.

Additional instructor resources

- Complete, downloadable Instructor's Manual, which includes teaching tips, examples and solutions to discussion questions and other exercises within the text.
- Customisable testbank of question material.
- Downloadable PowerPoint slides of useful content and Figures in the book.

These lecturer resources can be downloaded from the lecturer website at **www.pearsoned.co.uk/boddy**. Click on the cover of *Management: An Introduction*, Fifth Edition, and select lecturer resources. Any content that includes answers will be password protected.

PREFACE TO THE FIRST EDITION

This book is intended for readers who are undertaking their first systematic exposure to the study of management. Most will be first-year undergraduates following courses leading to a qualification in management or business. Some will also be taking an introductory course in management as part of other qualifications (these may be in engineering, accountancy, law, information technology, science, nursing or social work) and others will be following a course in management as an element in their respective examination schemes. The book should also be useful to readers with a first degree or equivalent qualification in a non-management subject who are taking further studies leading to Certificate, Diploma or MBA qualifications.

The book has the following three main objectives:

- to provide newcomers to the formal study of management with an introduction to the topic;
- to show that ideas on management apply to most areas of human activity, not just to commercial enterprises; and
- to make the topic attractive to students from many backgrounds and with diverse career intentions.

Most research and reflection on management has focused on commercial organisations. However, there are now many people working in the public sector and in not-for-profit organisations (charities, pressure groups, voluntary organisations and so on) who have begun to adapt management ideas to their own areas of work. The text reflects this wider interest in the topic. It should be as useful to those who plan to enter public or not-for-profit work as to those entering the commercial sector.

European perspective

The book presents the ideas from a European perspective. While many management concepts have developed in the United States, the text encourages readers to consider how their particular context shapes management practice. There are significant cultural differences that influence this practice, and the text alerts the reader to these – not only as part of an increasingly integrated Europe but as part of a wider international management community. So the text recognises European experience and research in management. The case studies and other material build an awareness of cultural diversity and the implications of this for working in organisations with different managerial styles and backgrounds.

Integrated perspective

To help the reader see management as a coherent whole, the material is presented within an integrative model of management and demonstrates the relationships between the many academic perspectives. The intention is to help the reader to see management as an integrating activity relating to the organisation as a whole, rather than as something confined to any one disciplinary or functional perspective.

While the text aims to introduce readers to the traditional mainstream perspectives on management which form the basis of each chapter, it also recognises that there is a newer body of ideas which looks at developments such as the weakening of national boundaries and the spread of information technology. Since they will affect the organisations in which readers will spend their working lives, these newer perspectives are introduced where appropriate. The text also recognises the more critical perspectives that some writers now take towards management and organisational activities. These are part of the intellectual world in which management takes place and have important practical implications for the way people interpret their role within organisations. The text introduces these perspectives at several points.

Relating to personal experience

The text assumes that many readers will have little if any experience of managing in conventional organisations, and equally little prior knowledge of relevant evidence and theory. However, all will have experience of being managed and all will have managed activities in their domestic and social lives. Wherever possible the book encourages readers to use and share such experiences from everyday life in order to explore the ideas presented. In this way the book tries to show that management is not a remote activity performed by others, but a process in which all are engaged in some way.

Most readers' careers are likely to be more fragmented and uncertain than was once the case and many will be working for medium-sized and smaller enterprises. They will probably be working close to customers and in organisations that incorporate diverse cultures, values and interests. The text therefore provides many opportunities for readers to develop skills of gathering data, comparing evidence, reflecting and generally enhancing self-awareness. It not only transmits knowledge but also aims to support the development of transferable skills through individual activities in the text and through linked tutorial work. The many cases and data collection activities are designed to develop generic skills such as communication, teamwork, problem solving and organising – while at the same time acquiring relevant knowledge.

PREFACE TO THE FIFTH EDITION

This fifth edition takes account of helpful comments from staff and students who used the fourth edition, and the suggestions of reviewers (please see below). The book retains the established structure of six parts, and the titles of the 20 chapters are substantially as they were before. Within that structure each chapter has been updated where necessary, and several also provide readers with additional academic material and/or a clearer sequence. The main changes of this kind are:

Chapters:

Chapter 3 (Organisation cultures and contexts) – a new section on corporate governance.

Chapter 4 (Managing internationally) – same (updated) material but clearer structure.

Chapter 8 (Managing strategy) – fuller discussion of the process of forming strategy.

Chapter 9 (Managing marketing) – same (updated) material but clearer structure.

Chapter 12 (Information technology and e-business) – substantial revision, beginning with current developments in social networking and co-creation.

Chapter 13 (Managing change and innovation) – latter half on innovation completely new.

Chapter 17 (Teams) – same (updated) material but clearer structure using 'inputs, processes, outcomes' model.

Chapter 18 (Managing operations and quality) – substantially re-written.

Chapter 19 (Performance measurement and control) – substantially re-written.

Chapter 20 (Finance and budgetary control) – substantially re-written.

The order of these last three chapters (forming Part 6) has also been changed.

Academic content: This remains substantially as before, but has been extended and updated where appropriate. Examples include new material on corporate governance in Chapter 3, more on biases in decision making in Chapter 7, a new section on the processes of managing strategy in Chapter 8, a fuller treatment of innovation in Chapter 13, and more on managing service operations in Chapter 18.

Integrating themes – NEW and stronger: The concluding 'current themes and issues' section of each chapter has been re-titled, and while the 'internationalisation' theme remains, the others reflect two current themes – 'sustainable performance' and 'governance and control' respectively. The section aims to relate aspects of the chapter to each theme, bringing each chapter to a consistent close. In addition, I have strengthened the potential value of this feature by including it as an item in the chapter objectives, in the chapter summary and in the review questions.

Teachers may wish to use this feature by, for example, setting a class project or assignment on one of the themes (such as sustainable performance) and inviting students to draw on the multiple perspectives on the topic which each chapter provides. For example:

Chapter 3 (Section 3.9) provides material on sustainability from the Stern report.

Chapter 6 (Section 6.9) shows how one company is planning to work more sustainably.

Chapter 10 (Section 10.10) relates the familiar dilemma of centralisation/de-centralisation to sustainability.

Chapter 15 (Section 15.8) links motivation to sustainability and illustrates it with a company which includes measures of sustainability in the management reward system.

Chapter 18 (Section 18.8) argues that all waste is the result of a failure in operations, which therefore needs to be the focus of improving sustainable performance.

Cases: These have been revised and updated – and seven are completely new; Crossrail (Chapter 6), IKEA (Chapter 7, was Chapter 15), HMV Group (Chapter 8), Apple (Chapter 14), The Eden Project (Chapter 15), Facebook (Chapter 16), Zara (Chapter 18) and an NHS Foundation Hospital (Chapter 19).

MyManagementLab: With every purchase of a new copy of this textbook, the reader receives a Student Access Kit that allows them to make use of MyManagementLab, an unrivalled suite of online resources that accompany this textbook. It provides a variety of tools to enable students to assess and progress their own learning, including audio summaries, questions, tests and learning aids for each chapter of the book, as well as material for instructors to assign, including video case studies. (See pages i and xxii–xxv for a more detailed outline of the content and functionality of MyManagementLab.) To encourage students to use this resource, each of the companies which features in the video clip also features in some way in the book itself. The Eden Project is the Chapter Case in Chapter 15 (Motivation) while the others provide Management in Practice features in several chapters.

Features: Many of the Management in Practice features have been updated and renewed, as have some Key Ideas. There are over 180 new references and additional suggestions for Further Reading. Several of the Case Questions and Activities have been revised to connect more closely with the theories being presented. The Learning Objectives provide the structure for the Summary section at the end of each chapter.

Critical thinking: At the end of the first chapter I continue to present ideas on the components of critical thinking: assumptions, context, alternatives and limitations. These themes are used systematically to frame many of the learning objectives, and structure the Critical Reflection feature at the end of each chapter.

Web-based activities: Each chapter concludes with a list of the websites of companies that have appeared in the chapter, and a suggestion that students visit these sites (or others in which they have an interest) to find some information and seek information on some of the themes in the chapter. This should add interest and help retain the topicality of the cases.

Each part continues to conclude with several skills development activities, drawing on and in some cases integrating ideas from several of the chapters in that part.

List of reviewers

I would like to express thanks to the original reviewers and review panel members who have been involved in the development of this book. I am extremely grateful for their insight and helpful recommendations.

Reviewers of the second edition

John Clark (London Metropolitan University)
James Edgar (Queens University, Belfast)
Olaf Sigurjonsson (Reykjavik University, Iceland)
Eddie Pargeter (Birmingham College of Food, Tourism and Creative Study)
Bart Bossink (Vrije University, Amsterdam)
Ian Parkinson (Hull College)
Nicky Metcalf (St Martin's College, Lancaster)
Jackie Shaw (Macclesfield College)
Jos Weel (Hogeschool van Amsterdam)
Peter Williams (Leeds Metropolitan University)
Iraj Tavakolo (Brighton University)
Ray Rogers (Coventry)
John Chamberlain (Derby)
Siobhan Tiernan (University of Limerick)
Andrew Godley (University of Reading)

Reviewers of the third edition

Peter Falconer (Glasgow Caledonian University)
Ad van Iterson (Maastricht University)
Gail Shepherd (Coventry University)
Abby Cathcart (University of Sunderland)
Paschal McNeill (University College, Dublin)

Reviewers of the fourth edition

Paul Dudley
Dearbhla Finn
Bobby Mackie
Howard Weston
Colin Combe
Joyce Liddle
Matyna Siiwa
Paul Griseri
Nerys Fuller Love
Frank van Luix
Boon Tan

Reviewers of the fifth edition

Hadyn Bennett, University of Ulster
John Clark, London Metropolitan University
Colin Combe, Glasgow Caledonian University
John Middleton, Bath Spa University
Martijn van Velzen, University of Twente

GUIDED TOUR

PART 4
ORGANISING

Introduction

Part 4 examines how management creates the structure within which people work. Alongside planning the direction of the business, managers need to consider how they will achieve the direction chosen. A fundamental component of that is the form of the organisation. This is a highly uncertain area of management as there are conflicting views about the kind of structure to have and how much influence structure has on performance.

Chapter 10 describes the main elements of organisation structure and the contrasting forms they take. Chapter 11 deals with one aspect of organisation structure, namely its human resource management policies. These are intended to ensure that employees work towards organisational objectives.

Chapter 12 focuses on information technology and e-business, showing how information technologies have deep implications for organisations and their management. Chapter 13 looks at some of the issues that arise in implementing organisational change and in stimulating innovation.

The Part case is The Royal Bank of Scotland, which has gone from being a highly regarded and innovative bank, to one that came close to failure. Now majority owned by the UK government, it is trying to rebuild its reputation.

The book is divided into six parts each of which opens with an **introduction** helping you to orientate yourself within the book.

CHAPTER 10
ORGANISATION STRUCTURE

Aim

To introduce terms and practices that show the choices managers face in shaping organisational structures.

Objectives

By the end of your work on this chapter you should be able to outline the concepts below in your terms and:

1 Outline the links between strategy, structure and performance

2 Give examples of how managers divide and co-ordinate work, with their likely advantages and disadvantages

3 Compare the features of mechanistic and organic structures

4 Summarise the work of Woodward, Burns and Stalker, Lawrence and Lorsch and John Child, showing how they contributed to this area of management

5 Use the 'contingencies' believed to influence choice of structure to evaluate the structure unit

6 Explain and illustrate the features of a learning organisation

7 Show how ideas from the chapter add to your understanding of the integrating themes

Chapter openers provide a brief introduction to chapter **aims** and **objectives**.

Key terms

This chapter introduces the following ideas:

organisation structure	divisional structure
organisation chart	matrix structure
formal structure	network structure
informal structure	mechanistic structure
vertical specialisation	organic structure
horizontal specialization	contingencies
formal authority	technology
responsibility	differentiation
delegation	integration
span of control	contingency approaches
centralisation	determinism
decentralisation	structural choice
formalisation	learning organisation
functional structure	

Each is a term defined within the text, as well as in the Glossary at the end of the book.

A list of **key terms** introduces the main ideas covered in the chapter

Case study Oticon www.oticon.com

Oticon is a small Danish company which competes successfully with larger firms – in part because of its unusual organisation structure. It employs about 1,200 staff in Denmark in its research and production facilities, which supply high-tech devices to the rapidly growing number of people with hearing difficulties. Competition intensified during the 1980s and the company began to lose market share to larger rivals such as Siemens. Lars Kolind was appointed chief executive in 1988. In 1990 he concluded that a new approach was needed to counter the threats from larger competitors that were becoming stronger. Oticon's only hope for survival was to be radical in all aspects of the business. Kolind intended the changes to turn Oticon from an *industrial* organisation into a service organisation with a physical product.

He organised product development around projects. The project leader was appointed by the management team and recruited staff from within the firm to do the work: they chose whether or not to join – and could only do so if their current project leader agreed. Previously most people had a single skill; they were now required to be active in at least three specialties – one based on professional qualification and two others unrelated to the first. A chip designer could develop skills in customer support and advertising, for example. These arrangements allowed the company to respond quickly to unexpected events and use skills fully.

Previously Oticon had a conventional hierarchical structure, and a horizontal structure of separate functional departments. The only remnant of the hierarchy is the ten-person management team, each member of which acts as an 'owner' to the many projects through which work is done. Kolind refers to this as 'managed chaos'. The company tries to overcome the dangers of this by developing a strong and clear mission – 'to help people with X problem to live better with X'; and a common set of written values. Examples include: 'an assumption that we only employ adults (who can be expected to act responsibly)', and 'an assumption that staff want to know what and why they are doing it', so all information is available to everyone (with a few legally excepted areas).

There are no titles – people do whatever they think is right at the time. The potential for chaos is averted

Oticon

by building the flexible organisation on a foundation of clearly defined business processes, setting out essential tasks:

The better your processes are defined, the more flexible you can be.

The absence of departments avoids people protecting local interests and makes it easier to cope with fluctuations in workload.

Oticon was one of the earliest companies to redesign the workplace to maximise disturbance. This was most visible in the 'mobile office', in which each workstation was a desk without drawers (nowhere to file paper). There were no installed telephones, although everyone had a mobile. The workstations were equipped with powerful PCs through which people worked (staff had a small personal trolley for personal belongings which they wheeled to wherever they were working that day). Although common today, this arrangement was revolutionary at the time

Sources: Based on Bjorn-Andersen and Turner (1994); Rivard et al. (2004); and company website.

Case questions 10.1
- What factors persuaded management to change the structure at Oticon?
- How would you expect staff to react to these changes?

Case studies throughout the book engage student interest and encourage critical analysis. They also come with some questions to help you test your understanding.

Networks

A network structure is when tasks required by one company are performed by other companies with expertise in those areas.

Network structures refer to situations in which organisations remain independent but agree to work together to deliver products or services. Sometimes this happens when managers arrange for other companies to undertake certain non-core activities on their behalf. The remaining organisation concentrates on setting strategy direction and managing the core units. Electronic companies often do this: Dell's products are made under contract by companies that specialise in such work. The arrangement is becoming common in personal services – such as when Care UK runs schools for disturbed children for local government, and in Community Health Partnerships (see the following Management in Practice).

Management in practice Community Health Partnerships (CHP)
www.communityhealthpartnerships.co.uk

Many social and health problems are caused by a range of conditions which have traditionally been the responsibility of distinct public bodies – health, social work, education, housing and police. Many practitioners believe that effective solutions depend on these independent agencies working together to offer a more comprehensive service than any agency could do alone.

A prominent example is Community Health Partnerships (CHP), an independent company, wholly owned by the UK Department of Health. It aims to deliver innovative ways to improve health and local authority services through the Local Improvement Finance Trust (LIFT) initiative which provides modern premises for health and social authority services in England.

It has established 48 LIFT partnerships, covering two-thirds of England's population, and is responsible for more than 250 buildings that are either open or under construction. More recently, CHP has developed new models of public–private partnership, such as Community Ventures and Social Enterprises, to improve health and social care.

The different backgrounds, priorities and cultures of the organisations taking part make such ventures challenging to manage.

Sources: Company website; other published sources.

Mixed forms

Large organisations typically combine functional, product and geographical structures within the same company – see for example BP (Part 2 Case) or RBS (Part 4 Case).

The counterpart of dividing work is to co-ordinate it, or there will be confusion and poor performance.

Activity 10.4 Comparing structures

Think of an organisation you have worked in or about which you can gather information.
- Which of the five structural forms did it correspond to most closely?
- What were the benefits and disadvantages of that approach?
- Compare your conclusions with colleagues on your course, and use your experience to prepare a list of the advantages and disadvantages of each type of structure.

Management in practice boxes provide real-world examples and encourage students to identify and engage with managerial issues and challenges.

Activities enable students to personally engage and investigate managerial theory and practice.

Information systems

Information systems help to ensure that people who need to work in a consistent way have common information, so that they can co-ordinate their activities. Computer systems and internet applications enable different parts of an organisation, as well as suppliers and customers, to work from common information, making co-ordination much easier (see Chapter 12).

Key ideas Co-ordinating sales and marketing

Large organisations typically create separate sales and marketing departments, which must then co-ordinate their work to ensure co-operation, customer satisfaction and profitability. Homburg et al. (2008) concluded (from a survey of German firms in financial services, consumer goods and chemicals) that the best performance was in firms where managers had:

- developed strong structural links between the two functions, especially by using teams, and requiring staff to plan projects jointly; and
- ensured that staff in both functions had high market knowledge, by rotating them between other functions in the firm to develop knowledge about customers and competitors, which then helped the two functions to work effectively together.

Source: Homburg et al. (2008).

Most companies purchase goods and services electronically, ensuring that orders and payments to suppliers flow automatically to match current demand. This co-ordinates a laborious task where mistakes were common.

Direct personal contact

The most human form of co-ordination is when people talk to each other. Mintzberg (1979) found that people use this method in both the simplest and the most complex situations. There is so much uncertainty in the latter that information systems cannot cope – only direct contact can do this, by enabling people to making personal commitments across business units (Sull and Spinosa, 2005) (see the above Key Ideas and the following Management in Practice).

Management in practice Co-ordination in a social service

The organisation cares for the elderly in a large city. Someone who had worked there for several years reflected on co-ordination:

Within the centre there was a manager, two deputies, an assistant manager, five senior care officers (SCOs) and 30 care officers. Each SCO is responsible for six care officers, allowing daily contact between the supervisor and the subordinates. While this defines job roles quite tightly, it allows a good communication structure to exist. Feedback is common as there are frequent meetings of the separate groups, and individual appraisals of the care officers by the SCOs. Staff value this opportunity for praise and comments on how they are doing.

Contact at all levels is common between supervisor and care officers during meetings to assess the needs of clients, for whom the care officers have direct responsibility. Frequent social gatherings and functions within the department also enhance relations and satisfy social needs. Controls placed on the behaviour of the care officers come from senior management, often derived from legislation such as the Social Work Acts or the Health and Safety Executive.

Source: Private communication.

Key ideas are short vignettes which illustrate how developments in management thought influence practice today.

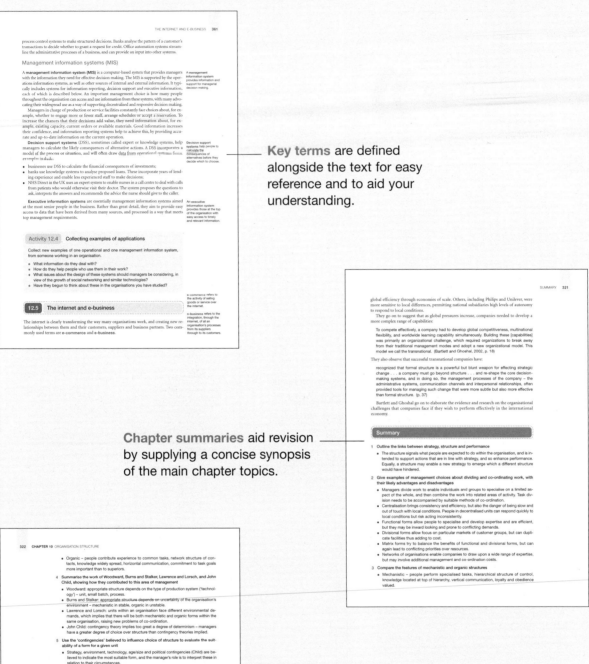

Key terms are defined alongside the text for easy reference and to aid your understanding.

Chapter summaries aid revision by supplying a concise synopsis of the main chapter topics.

Review questions enable students to check their understanding of the main themes and concepts.

7   If contingency approaches stress the influence of external factors on organisational structures, what is the role of management in designing organisational structures?
8   What is the main criticism of the contingency approaches to organisation structure?
9   What examples can you find of organisational activities that correspond to some of the features of a learning organisation identified by Pedler et al. (1997)?
10 Summarise an idea from the chapter that adds to your understanding of the integrating themes.

Concluding critical reflection

Think about the structure and culture of your company or one with which you are familiar. Review the material in the chapter, and perhaps visit some of the websites identified. Then make notes on the following questions:

*   What examples of the themes discussed in this chapter are currently relevant to your company? What type of structure do you have – centralised or decentralised; functional or divisional, etc? Which of the methods of co-ordination identified do you typically use? Which form of culture best describes the one in which you work? What structural or cultural issues are that are not mentioned here?
*   In responding to issues of structure, what assumptions about the nature of organisations appear to guide your approach? If the business seems too centralised or too formal, why do managers take that approach? What are their assumptions, and are they correct?
*   What factors in the context of the company appear to shape your approach to organising – what kind of environment are you working in, for example? To what extent does your structure involve networking with people from other organisations, and why is that?
*   Have you seriously considered whether the present structure is right for the business? Do you regularly compare your structure with that in other companies to look for **alternatives**? How do you do it?
*   What **limitations** can you identify in any of the ideas and theories presented here? For example, how helpful is contingency theory to someone deciding whether to make the organisation more or less mechanistic?

Further reading

Burns, T. and Stalker, G.M. (1961), *The Management of Innovation*, Tavistock, London.

Lawrence, P. and Lorsch, J.W. (1967), *Organization and Environment*, Harvard Business School Press, Boston, MA.

Woodward, J. (1965), *Industrial Organization: Theory and practice*, Oxford University Press, Oxford. Second edition 1980.

> These influential books give accessible accounts of the research process, and it would add to your understanding to read at least one of them in the original. The second edition of Woodward's book (1980) is even more useful, as it includes a commentary on her work by two later scholars.

Bartlett, C.A. and Ghoshal, S. (2002), *Managing Across Borders: The transnational solution* (2nd edn) Harvard Business School Press, Boston, MA.

> Applies ideas on organisations and their structure to international management.

Concluding critical reflections are a series of questions intended to develop critical thinking skills and analysis of key debates.

Further reading

Bernoff, J. and Li, C. (2008), 'Harnessing the power of the oh-so-social web', *MIT Sloan Management Review*, vol. 49, no. 3, pp. 36–42.

Boulding, W., Staelin, R. and Ehret, M. (2005), 'A customer relationship management roadmap: What is known, potential pitfalls, and where to go', *Journal of Marketing*, vol. 69, no. 4, pp. 155–166.

Bozarth, C. (2006), 'ERP implementation efforts at three firms', *International Journal of Operations & Production Management*, vol. 26, no. 11, pp. 1223–1239.

> Three recent empirical studies of the organisational aspects of managing information systems.

Iyer, B. and Davenport, T. H. (2008), 'Reverse engineering Google's innovation machine', *Harvard Business Review*, vol. 86, no. 4, pp. 58–68.

> Many insights into the company.

Laudon, K.C. and Laudon, J.P. (2004), *Management Information Systems: Organization and technology in the networked enterprise*, Prentice Hall, Harlow.

> This text, written from a management perspective, focuses on the opportunities and pitfalls of information systems.

Phillips, P. (2003), *E-Business Strategy: Text and cases*, McGraw-Hill, Maidenhead.

> A comprehensive European perspective on internet developments relevant to business and strategy.

Tapscott, E. and Williams, A.D. (2006), *Wikinomics: How mass collaboration changes everything*, Viking Penguin, New York.

> Best-selling account of the rise of co-creation.

Weblinks

These websites are those that have appeared in the chapter:

www.google.com
www.connectingforhealth.nhs.uk
www.bbc.co.uk
www.selectminds.com
www.renault.com
www.siemens.com
www.Yahoo.com
www.amazon.com
www.moneyfacts.com
www.tesco.com
www.irisnation.com
www.nestle.com
www.buckman.com

Visit two of the business sites in the list, or any others that interest you, and answer the following questions:

*   If you were a potential employee, how well does it present information about the company and the career opportunities available? Could you apply for a job online?

Further reading and weblinks provide a starting point for further research and project work.

PART 4
SKILLS DEVELOPMENT

To help you develop your skills, as well as knowledge, this section includes tasks that relate the key themes covered in the Part to your daily life. Working through these will help you to deepen your understanding of the topic, and develop skills and insights which you can use in many situations.

Task 4.1   Analysing a department or organisation

While every organisation is unique, all are made up of the elements shown in Figure 1.3. These form the internal context within which managers operate, and shape the demands which the manager faces. A useful skill is that of being able to use this model to identify and analyse significant features of an organisation or business unit. This exercise invites you to analyse just four of the elements – select more if they seem relevant to the situation.

Analyse a department or organisation with which you are familiar, by making a few notes in response to these questions:

*   What is the main objective or mission of the department or organisation?
*   What is the structure?
*   What are the main characteristics of the people?
*   What technologies (and in what layout) do people use to meet the objectives? This includes all kinds of physical facilities, including computer systems.

Consider a recent large change. What were the direct and indirect effects on each of these components? What difficulties, if any, had to be managed?

Compare your answers with those prepared by another student, to further increase your skills of analysis, and of identifying key organisational features.

Task 4.2   Distinguishing mechanistic from organic structures

Chapter 10 distinguished between mechanistic and organic forms. Since these greatly affect how people work, a manager needs to be able to identify each type, and the practices which can, whether intended or not, lead an organisation towards one or the other.

Analyse a department or organisation with which you are familiar by making a few notes in response to the following questions:

*   Identify a department that is mainly mechanistic, and indicate the features or practices that illustrate it.
*   Identify a department that is mainly organic, and indicate the features or practices that illustrate that.
*   Why do you think each takes the form they do?

Skills development sections include tasks which allow students to relate key managerial themes to personal experience.

GUIDED TOUR OF MyManagementLab

The fifth edition of *Management: An Introduction* comes with **MyManagementLab**. **MyManagementLab** is a personalised and innovative online study and testing resource which provides a variety of tools to enable you to assess and progress your own learning.

To get started take your **access kit**, which is included inside this book. This access kit will enable you to register online.

Register and log in

Go to **www.pearsoned.co.uk/mymanagementlab** and click on the option to register as a student user. Enter your course ID if you have already been given this by your lecturer. If you don't have a course ID then search for the author and book title to register and login and follow the instructions on screen using the code in your access kit. The login screen will look like this:

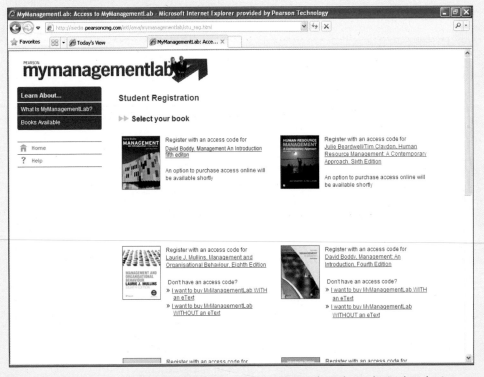

Now you should be registered with your own password and ready to log in to your own course.

When you log in to your course for the first time, the course home page will look like this:

Now follow the steps below for the chapter you are studying:

Step 1: Take a diagnostic test

There is a diagnostic test for each chapter. This will enable you to test yourself to see how much you already know about a particular topic and will then identify the areas in which you need practice.

Step 2: Review your study plan

The results of the diagnostic test you have taken will be incorporated into your study plan, showing you what sections you have mastered and what sections you need to study further – helping you make the most efficient use of your self-study time.

Step 3: Have a go at an exercise

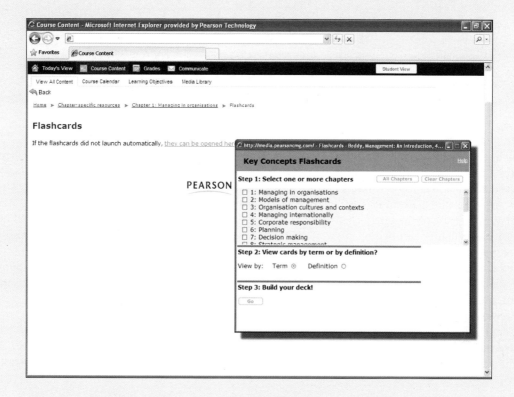

From the study plan, click on the section of the book you are studying and have a go at the interactive **Exercises**.

If you are struggling with a question, you can click on the **e-book** link to read the relevant part of your textbook again.

Good luck getting started with **MyManagementLab**.

ACKNOWLEDGEMENTS

This book has benefited from the comments, criticisms and suggestions of many colleagues and reviewers of the fourth edition. It also reflects the reactions and comments of students who have used the material and earlier versions of some of the cases. Their advice and feedback have been of immense help.

Most of the chapters were written by the author, who also edited the text throughout. Chapter 11 (Human resource management) was created by Professor Phil Beaumont and then developed by Dr Judy Pate and Sandra Stewart: in this edition it was revised by the author. Chapter 18 (Managing operations and quality) was created by Professor Douglas Macbeth and developed in the fourth edition by Dr Geoff Southern: in this

edition it was rewritten by Dr Steve Paton. Chapter 20 (Financial and budgetary control) was created by Douglas Briggs: in this edition it was rewritten by Dr Steve Paton. Dr Paton has also revised and added new material to Chapters 13 and 19 – and also helped in other ways in preparing this edition. Errors and omissions are my responsibility.

Finally, I gratefully acknowledge the support and help that my wife, Cynthia, has provided throughout this project.

David Boddy
University of Glasgow, April 2010

Publisher's acknowledgements

We are grateful to the following for permission to reproduce copyright material:

Figures

Figure 2.2 from *Becoming a master manager* (Quinn, R. E., Faerman, S.R., Thompson, M. P. and McGrath, M. R. 2003) Copyright © 2003 John Wiley & Sons, Inc. Reproduced with permission of John Wiley & Sons, Inc.; Figure 2.3 after GREENBERG, JERALD; BARON, ROBERT A., *BEHAVIOR IN ORGANIZATIONS*, 6th Edition © 1997, p. 13. Reprinted by permission of Pearson Education, Inc., Upper Saddle River, NJ; Figure 2.7 from *Chaos, Management and Economics: The implications of non-linear thinking, Hobart Paper 125*, Institute of Economic Affairs, London (Parker, D. and Stacey, R. 1994) First published by the Institute of Economic Affairs, London,1994; Figure 3.4 Reprinted with the permission of The Free Press, a Division of Simon & Schuster, Inc., from *COMPETITIVE STRATEGY: Techniques for Analyzing Industries and Competitors* by Michael E. Porter, Copyright © 1980, 1998 by The Free Press. All rights reserved; Figure 4.4 from Clustering countries on attitudinal dimensions: A review and synthesis, Academy of Management journal by S. Ronen and O. Shenkar. Copyright 1985 by ACADEMY OF MANAGEMENT (NY). Reproduced with permission of

ACADEMY OF MANAGEMENT (NY) in the format Textbook via Copyright Clearance Center; Figure 4.5 adapted from YIP, GEORGE S., *TOTAL GLOBAL STRATEGY II*, 2nd Edition © 2003, p. 10. Reprinted by permission of Pearson Education, Inc., Upper Saddle River, NJ; Figure 5.3 from Carroll, A. B., Corporate social responsibility, *Business and Society*, vol. 38, no. 3, pp. 268–95 (1999), Copyright © 1999 by Sage Publications. Reprinted by permission of SAGE Publications; Figure 5.5 from Does it pay to be green? A systematic overview, The Academy of Management perspectives by S. Ambec and P. Lanoie, vol. 22, no. 4, pp. 45–62. Copyright 2008 by ACADEMY OF MANAGEMENT (NY). Reproduced with permission of ACADEMY OF MANAGEMENT (NY) in the format Textbook via Copyright Clearance Center; Figure 5.6 from Vodafone Corporate Responsibility Report for the year ended 31 March 2009, reproduced with permission; Figure 5.7 from 'Implicit' and 'Explicit' CSR: A conceptual framework for a comparative understanding of corporate social responsibility, The Academy of Management review by D. Matten and J. Moon, vol. 33, no. 2, pp. 404–424. Copyright 2008 by ACADEMY OF MANAGEMENT (NY). Reproduced with permission of ACADEMY OF MANAGEMENT (NY) in the format Textbook via Copyright Clearance Center; Figure 6.6

from *Managing Information Systems: Strategy and Organisation*, 3 ed., Financial Times/Prentice Hall (Boddy, D., Boonstra, A., & Kennedy, G. 2009), reproduced with permission; Figure 7.4 from ROBBINS, STEPHEN P.; COULTER, MARY, MANAGEMENT, 8th Edition, © 2005, p. 144. Reprinted by permission of Pearson Education, Inc., Upper Saddle River, NJ; Figure 7.5 from *Making Management Decisions*, 2 ed., Prentice Hall (Cooke, S. and Slack, N. 1991) Reproduced with permission; Figure 8.2 from *The rise and fall of strategic planning*, Prentice Hall International (Mintzberg, H. 1994) with permission from Prentice Hall and the author; Figure 7.8 from Figure 9.1 Decision-Process Flow Chart from *Leadership and Decision-Making*, and the taxonomy used in the figure is from Table 2.1 Decision Method for Group and Individual Problems from *Leadership and Decision-Making*, by Victor H. Vroom and Philip W. Yetton, © 1973. Reprinted by permission of the University of Pittsburgh Press; Figure 8.3 from Strategic planning in a turbulent environment: evidence from oil majors, *Strategic Management Journal*, vol 24, no. 6, pp. 491–517 (Grant, R. M. 2003), reproduced with permission from John Wiley & Sons Ltd.; Figure 8.4 from Closing the gap between strategy and execution, *MIT Sloan Management Review*, vol. 48, no. 4, pp. 30–38 (Sull, D. N. 2007) © 2010 from MIT Sloan Management Review/Massachusetts Institute of Technology. All rights reserved. Distributed by Tribune Media Services; Figure 8.5 from Reprinted with the permission of The Free Press, a Division of Simon & Schuster, Inc., from *COMPETITIVE ADVANTAGE: Creating and Sustaining Superior Performance by Michael E. Porter*, Copyright © 1985, 1998 by Michael E. Porter. All rights reserved; Figure 8.8 adapted from *Exploring Corporate Strategy*, 7ed., FT/Prentice Hall (Johnson, G., Scholes, K. and Whittington, R. 2006), where it was adapted from Chapter 6 of H. I. Ansoff, *Corporate Strategy*, pub. Penguin, 1988, reproduced with permission from Prentice Hall and the Ansoff Family Trust; Figure 8.9 *reprinted with the permission of The Free Press, a Division of Simon & Schuster, Inc., from COMPETITIVE ADVANTAGE: Creating and Sustaining Superior Performance by Michael E. Porter*, Copyright © 1985, 1998 by Michael E. Porter. All rights reserved; Figure 9.6 from KOTLER, PHILIP; ARMSTRONG, GARY, *PRINCIPLES OF MARKETING*, 13th ed. © 2010, p. 52. Reprinted by permission of Pearson Education, Inc., Upper Saddle River, NJ; Figure 10.2 from www. baesystems.com, http://www.baesystems.com/ContactUs/index.aspx, reproduced with permission; Figure 10.10 from *The learning company: A strategy for sustainable development*, 2 ed., McGraw-Hill Publishing Company (Pedler, M., Burgoyne, J. and Boydell, T. 1997) reproduced with the kind permission of the McGraw-Hill

Publishing Company; Figure 11.1 from *Managing human assets*, Macmillan (Beer, M., Spector, B., Lawrence, P. R. and Quinn Mills, D. 1984), reproduced with permission from Professor Michael Beer; Figure 11.3 adapted from *Developments in the Management of Human Resources*, Blackwell (Storey, J. 1992) reproduced with permission; Figure 11.4 adapted from *Successful selection interviews*, Blackwell (Anderson, N. and Shackleton, V. 1993) reproduced with permission; Figures 12.1, 12.4 and 16.2 from *Managing information systems: An organisational perspective*, 2 ed., FT/Prentice Hall (Boddy, D., Boonstra, A. and Kennedy, G. 2005) reproduced with permission; Figure 12.2 from *Managing Information Systems: Strategy and Organisation*, FT/Prentice Hall (Boddy, D., Boonstra, A., & Kennedy, G. 2009) p. 62, reproduced with permission; Figure 12.9 adapted and reprinted by permission of Harvard Business Review. Exhibit adapted from Strategy and the Internet, *Harvard Business Review*, vol. 79, no. 3, pp. 63–78 by M. E. Porter, Copyright © 2001 by Harvard Business School Publishing Corporation; all rights reserved; Figure 13.4 from *Project Management* 9 ed., Gower, Aldershot (Lock, D. 2007), © Ashgate Publishing Ltd., reproduced with permission; Figure 13.8 adapted from *Managing Innovation: Integrating Technological, Market and Organisational Change*, Wiley, Chichester (Tidd, J. & Bessant, J. 2009), reproduced with permission; Figure 14.3 from NHS Institute for Innovation and Improvement, 2005. NHSLeadership qualities framework, http://www.nhsleadershipqualities.nhs.uk, reproduced with permission; Figure 14.5 reprinted by permission of Harvard Business Review. Exhibit adapted from How to choose a leadership pattern: should a manager be democratic or autocratic – or something in between?, *Harvard Business Review*, vol. 37, no. 2, pp. 95–102 by R. Tannenbaum and W. H. Schmidt, Copyright © 1973 Harvard Business School Publishing Corporation; all rights reserved; Figure 14.7 from *Leadership skills,* CIPD (Adair, J. 1997), with the permission of the publisher, the Chartered Institute of Personnel and Development, London (www.cipd.co.uk); Figure 15.3 adapted from The Psychology of the Employment Relationship: An Analysis Based on the Psychological Contract, *Applied Psychology*, vol. 53, no. 4, pp. 541–555 (Guest, D. E. 2004), Reproduced with permission of Blackwell Publishing Ltd.; Figure 15.5 reprinted by permission of Harvard Business Review. Exhibit from One more time: How do you motivate employees?, *Harvard Business Review*, vol. 65, no. 5, pp. 109–120 by F. Herzberg, Copyright © 1987 Harvard Business School Publishing Corporation, all rights reserved; Figure 15.7 adapted from Development of the job diagnostic survey, *Journal of Applied Psychology*, vol. 60, no. 2, pp. 159–170, American Psychological Association (Hackman, J. R. and

Oldham, G. R. 1975), adapted with permission; Figure 16.4 from The selection of communication media as an executive skill, The Academy of Management executive by R.H. Lengel and R.L. Daft, vol. 11, no. 3, pp. 225–232. Copyright 1988 by ACADEMY OF MANAGEMENT (NY). Reproduced with permission of ACADEMY OF MANAGEMENT (NY) in the format Textbook via Copyright Clearance Center; Figure 16.5 was published in Group Processes by Berkowitz, L., 'Communication networks fourteen years later', Shaw, M. E., copyright Elsevier, 1978; Figure 16.8 from The strategic communication imperative, *MIT Sloan Management Review*, vol. 46, no. 3, pp. 83–89 (Argenti, P. A., Howell, R. A. and Beck, K. A. 2005) © 2010 from MIT Sloan Management Review/Massachusetts Institute of Technology. All rights reserved. Distributed by Tribune Media Services; Figure 17.5 from *New patterns of management*, The McGraw-Hill Companies, Inc. (Lickert, R. 1961), reproduced with permission; Figure 18.4 adapted and reprinted by permission of Harvard Business Review. Exhibit adapted from Link Manufacturing Process and Product Lifecycles, *Harvard Business Review*, vol. 57, no. 1, pp. 133–140 by R. H. Hayes and S. C. Wheelwright, Copyright © 1979 Harvard Business School Publishing Corporation; all rights reserved.

Tables

Table on page 69 adapted from Innocent's website, reproduced with permission from Innocent Ltd.; Table on page 625 from Tesco Annual Report and Accounts 2009 from Tesco's website, reproduced with permission from Tesco Stores Limited; Table 1.4 adapted from Anderson & Krathwohl, *A TAXONOMY FOR LEARNING, TEACHING AND ASSESSING*, Table 3.3: 'The Six Categories of the Cognitive Process Dimension and Related Cognitive Process' p. 31, © 2001 by Addison Wesley Longman, Inc. Reproduced by permission of Pearson Education, Inc.; Table 2.3 adapted and reprinted from *Long Range Planning*, vol. 40, no. 6, pp. 574–593, Macmillan, E. and Carlisle, Y., Strategy as order emerging from chaos: A public sector experience, Copyright (2007), with permission from Elsevier; Table 9.5 from *Financial Times*, 22 April 2009, with permission from Bowen Craggs & Co.; Table 11.1 from Human resource management and industrial relations, *Journal of Management Studies*, vol. 24, no. 5, pp. 502–521 (Guest, D. E. 1987), Reproduced with permission of Blackwell Publishing Ltd.; Table 12.2 from *Case studies in knowledge management*, CIPD (Scarborough, H. and Swan, J. 1999) with the permission of the publisher, the Chartered Institute of Personnel and Development, London (www.cipd.co.uk); Table on pages 450–1 from *Organizational Behaviour*, 6 ed., FT/Prentice Hall (Buchanan, D.A. and Huczynski, A.A. 2007), reproduced with permission from the author; Table 17.1 from *Groups that work (and those that don't)*, Jossey-Bass, San Francisco, CA (Hackman, J. R. 1990), p. 489, Reprinted with permission of John Wiley & Sons, Inc.; Table 17.6 adapted from *Groups that work (and those that don't)*, Jossey-Bass, San Francisco, CA (Hackman, J. R. 1990), Reprinted with permission of John Wiley & Sons, Inc.; Table 19.4 adapted from *Operations management*, FT/Prentice Hall (Slack, N., Chambers, S. and Johnston, R. 2007), reproduced with permission; Table on page 603 from BASF Group, Company annual report 2008–2009, reproduced with permission; Table on page 607 from Marks and Spencer plc Annual Report 2009, www.marksandspencer.com, reproduced with permission; Table on page 610 from BASF Group, reproduced with permission.

Text

Case Study on page 202 from IKEA's founder warns: we must cut more jobs, *The Guardian*, 07/07/2009 (Graeme Wearden), Copyright Guardian News & Media Ltd 2009; Case Study on page 225 adapted from HMV Group website, with permission from HMV UK Ltd.; Box on page 504 from WHETTEN, DAVID A.; CAMERON, KIM S., *DEVELOPING MANAGEMENT SKILLS*, 6th Edition © 2005, p. 216. Reprinted by permission of Pearson Education, Inc., Upper Saddle River, NJ.

Photographs

Alamy Images: Purestock 105; © BASF Aktiengesellschaft: 603; © BMW Group: 327; BP plc: 160; Courtesy of Cisco Systems, Inc. Unauthorised use not permitted: 513; Copyright © Inditex: 551; Corbis: Bettmann 135, Kim Komenich / San Francisco Chronicle 483, Thierry Tronnel 5, KIMBERLY WHITE / Reuters 419; Courtesy of Nokia: 77; By kind permission, Crossrail: 169; Eden Project: 449; Getty Images: Getty Images News 579; Photo courtesy Google UK: 351; By kind permission, HMV: 225; © Inter IKEA Systems BV 2006: 193; Innocent Ltd: Innocent Ltd 67; Oticon: 293; Press Association Images: Kin Cheung / AP 255; Reproduced by kind permission of New Lanark Conservation Trust www.newlanark.org: New Lanark Conservation Trust 35; © The Royal Bank of Scotland Group plc: 410; © Tesco PLC: 624; Visual Media: 284; © Vodafone 2007: 381; Courtesy of W. L. Gore & Associates UK Ltd. © 2007 W. L. Gore & Associates: 541.

In some instances we have been unable to trace the owners of copyright material, and we would appreciate any information that would enable us to do so.

PART 1

AN INTRODUCTION TO MANAGEMENT

Introduction

This part considers why management exists and what it contributes to human wealth and well-being. Management is both a universal human activity and a distinct occupation. We all manage in the first sense, as we organise our lives and deal with family and other relationships. As employees and customers we experience the activities of those who manage in the second sense, as members of an organisation with which we deal. This part offers some ways of making sense of the complex and contradictory activity of managing.

Chapter 1 clarifies the nature and emergence of management and the different ways in which people describe the role. It explains how management is both a universal human activity and a specialist occupation. Its purpose is to create wealth by adding value to resources, which managers do by influencing others – the chapter shows how they do this. It concludes with some ideas about managing your study of the topic. You are likely to benefit most by actively linking your work on this book to events in real organisations, and the chapter includes some suggestions.

Chapter 2 sets out the main theoretical perspectives on management and shows how these can complement each other despite the apparently competing values about the nature of the management task. Be active in relating these theoretical perspectives to real events as this will help you to understand and test the theory.

The Part case is Innocent Drinks, an innovative company which was established by three graduates in 1998, and has established a leading position in the smoothies market. The founders have some original and stimulating ideas on managing, which link many themes in this part.

CHAPTER 1
MANAGING IN ORGANISATIONS

Aim

To introduce the tasks, processes and context of managerial work in organisations.

Objectives

By the end of your work on this chapter you should be able to outline the concepts below in your own terms and:

1   Explain that the role of management is to add value to resources in diverse settings
2   Give examples of management as a universal human activity, and as a distinct role
3   Compare the roles of general, functional, line, staff and project managers, and of entrepreneurs
4   Compare how managers influence others to add value to resources through:
    a. the process of managing
    b. the tasks (or content) of managing and
    c. the contexts within which they and others work
5   Explain the elements of critical thinking and use some techniques to develop this skill
6   Suggest what implications the integrating themes of the book have for managing organisations.

Key terms

This chapter introduces the following ideas:

entrepreneur	general managers
innovation	functional managers
organisation	line managers
tangible resources	staff managers
intangible resources	project managers
competences	entrepreneurs
value	stakeholders
management as a universal human activity	creativity
manager	networking
management	management tasks
management as a distinct role	critical thinking
role	sustainable performance

Each is a term defined within the text, as well as in the Glossary at the end of the book.

Case study Ryanair www.ryanair.com

In 2010 Ryanair, based in Dublin, was Europe's largest low-fare airline and, despite the recession, it carried almost 66 million passengers in the 12 months to the end of February: a record for that period. In 1985 the company began offering services between Dublin and London, in competition with the established national carrier, Aer Lingus. In the early years the airline changed its business several times – initially a conventional competitor for Aer Lingus, then a charter company, at times offering a cargo service. The Gulf War in 1990 discouraged air travel and deepened the company's financial problems. In 1991 senior managers decided to focus the airline as a 'no-frills' operator, in which many traditional features of air travel (free food, drink, newspapers and allocated seats) were no longer available. It aimed to serve a group of flyers who wanted a functional and efficient service, not luxury.

In 1997 changes in European Union regulations enabled new airlines to enter markets previously dominated by established national carriers such as Air France and British Airways. Ryanair quickly took advantage of this, opening new routes between Dublin and continental Europe. Although based in Ireland, 80 per cent of its routes are between airports in other countries – in contrast with established carriers that depend heavily on passengers travelling to and from the airline's home country (Barrett, 2009, p. 80).

Managers were quick to spot the potential of the internet, and in 2000 opened Ryanair.com, a booking site. Within a year it sold 75 per cent of seats online and now sells almost all seats this way. It also made a long-term deal with Boeing to purchase 150 new aircraft over the next eight years.

Several factors enable Ryanair to offer low fares:

- Simple fleet – using a single aircraft type (Boeing 737 – most of which are quite new) simplifies maintenance, training and crew scheduling.
- Secondary airports – using airports away from major cities keeps landing charges low, sometimes as little as £1 per passenger against £10 at

© Thierry Tronnel/Corbis

a major airport; it also avoids the delays and costs caused by congestion at major airports.
- Fast turnrounds – staff typically turn an aircraft round between flights in 25 minutes, compared with an hour for older airlines. This enables aircraft to spend more time in the air, earning revenue (11 hours compared with seven at British Airways).
- Simplified operations – not assigning seats at check-in simplifies ticketing and administrative processes, and also ensures that passengers arrive early to get their preferred seat.
- Flying directly between cities avoids transferring passengers and baggage between flights, where mistakes and delays are common.
- Cabin staff collect rubbish before and after landing, saving the cost of cleaning crews which established carriers choose to use.

Source: *Economist*, 10 July 2004; O'Connell and Williams (2005); Doganis (2006); and other published information.

Case questions 1.1

- What did 'management' contribute to the growth of the airline?
- Give examples of three points at which managers changed what the organisation does and how it works.

1.1 Introduction

An **entrepreneur** is someone with a new venture, project or activity, and is usually associated with creative thinking, driving innovation and championing change.

Innovation is usually concerned with product or service development.

The Ryanair case illustrates several aspects of management. A group of **entrepreneurs** saw an opportunity in the market, and created an organisation to take advantage of it. They bring resources together and transform them into a service which they sell to customers. They differ from their competitors by using different resources (e.g. secondary airports) and different ways to transform these into outputs (e.g. short turnrounds). They have been innovative in the way they run the business, such as in identifying what some customers valued in a flight – cost rather than luxury – and carried a record 65 million passengers in 2009.

Entrepreneurs such as Michael O'Leary of Ryanair are always looking for ways to **innovate** and make the most of new opportunities. Other managers face a different challenge – more demand with less resources. Those managing the United Nations World Food Programme struggle to raise funds from donor countries – aid is falling while hunger is increasing. In almost every public healthcare organisation, managers face a growing demand for treatment, but have fewer resources with which to provide it.

Organisations of all kinds – from rapidly growing operations such as Facebook to established businesses such as Royal Dutch Shell or Marks & Spencer – depend on people at all levels who can run the current business efficiently and also innovate. This book is about the knowledge and skills that enable people to meet these expectations, and so build a satisfying and rewarding management career.

Figure 1.1 illustrates the themes of this chapter. It represents the fact that people draw resources from the external environment and manage their transformation into outputs that they hope are of greater value. They pass these back to the environment, and the value they obtain in return (money, reputation, goodwill, etc.) enables them to attract new resources to continue in business (shown by the feedback arrow from output to input). If the outputs do not attract sufficient resources, the enterprise will fail.

The chapter begins by examining the significance of managed organisations in our world. It then outlines what management means, and introduces theories about the nature of managerial work. Finally, it introduces ideas on studying management.

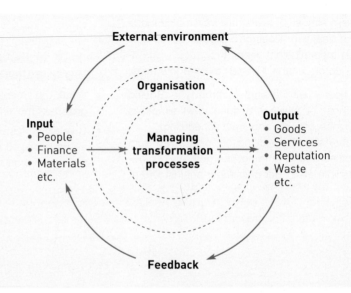

Figure 1.1
Managing organisation and environment

Activity 1.1   **What is management?**

Write a few notes summarising what you think 'management' means.

- You may find it helpful to think of instances in which you have encountered 'management' – such as when you have been managed in your school or university.
- Alternatively, reflect on an occasion when you have managed something, such as a study project. Keep the notes so you can refer to them.

1.2 Managing to add value to resources

We live in a world of managed **organisations**. We experience many every day – domestic arrangements (family or flatmates), large public organisations (the postal service), small businesses (the newsagent), well-known private companies (the jar of coffee) or a voluntary group (the club we attended). They affect us and we judge their performance. Did the transaction work smoothly or was it chaotic? Was the service good, reasonable or poor? Will you go there again?

> An **organisation** is a social arrangement for achieving controlled performance towards goals that create value.

Key ideas   Joan Magretta on the innovation of management

What were the most important innovations of the past century? Antibiotics and vaccines that doubled, or even tripled, human life spans? Automobiles and aeroplanes that redefined our idea of distance? New agents of communication, such as the telephone, or the chips, computers and networks that are propelling us into a new economy?

All of these innovations transformed our lives, yet none of them could have taken hold so rapidly or spread so widely without another. That innovation is the discipline of management, the accumulating body of thought and practice that makes organisations work. When we take stock of the productivity gains that drive our prosperity, technology gets all of the credit. In fact, management is doing a lot of the heavy lifting.

Source: Magretta (2002), p. 1.

As human societies become more specialised, we depend more on others to satisfy our needs. We meet some of these by acting individually or within family and social groups: organisations provide the rest. Good managers make things work – so that aid is delivered, roads are safe, shops have stock, hospitals function and all the rest. They do not do the work themselves, but build an organisation with the resources *and* competences to deliver what people need (Johnson *et al.*, 2008, pp. 95–6). **Tangible resources** are physical assets such as plant, people and finance – things you can see and touch. **Intangible resources** are non-physical assets such as information, reputation and knowledge.

To transform these resources into valuable goods and services people need to work together. They need to know what to do, understand their customers, deal with enquiries properly and generally make the transaction work well. Beyond that, they look for opportunities to improve, be innovative and learn from experience. Good managers bring out the best in their staff so that they willingly 'go the extra mile': together they develop effective ways of working that become second nature. These 'ways of working' are **competences** – skills, procedures or systems that enable people to use resources productively. The managers role is to secure and retain resources and competences so that the organisation adds **value** – it is producing an output that is more valuable than the resources it has used.

> **Tangible resources** are the physical assets of an organisation such as plant, people and finance.
>
> **Intangible resources** are non-physical assets such as information, reputation and knowledge.
>
> **Competences** are the skills and abilities by which resources are deployed effectively – systems, procedures and ways of working.
>
> **Value** is added to resources when they are transformed into goods or services that are worth more than their original cost plus the cost of transformation.

Well-managed organisations create value in many ways. If you buy a ticket from Ryanair, you can easily measure the tangible value of a cheap flight. In other purchases the value is intangible, as people judge a product by its appearance, what it feels or smells like, how trendy it is or whether it fits their image. Others value good service, or a clear set of instructions. Good managers understand what customers value and build an organisation to satisfy them.

Management in practice   Creating value at DavyMarkham   www.davymarkham.com

Kevin Parkin is Managing Director (and part-owner) of DavyMarkham, a small engineering company. Although the company has a long history, by the mid-1990s it was making regular losses, and its survival was in doubt. Since Mr Parkin joined the company he has returned it to profit, and in 2009 was predicting a 10 per cent increase in sales the following year. He has concentrated on identifying what the company is good at, and then using tough management and financial discipline to make sure staff follow the recipe for success. Mr Parkin has removed poor managers, walks the shop floor twice a day to check on progress, and engages with the workforce.

It's been essential to tell people the truth about the business, whether it's good or bad, and giving them the enthusiasm they require to make them want to succeed . . . I also ask [my 'mentors' – people I have known in previous jobs] about key strategic decisions, people issues, market penetration, capital spending and general business solutions.

Source: From an article by Peter Marsh and Andrew Bounds, *Financial Times*, 27 May 2009.

Commercial organisations of all kinds (business start-ups, small and medium-sized enterprises (SMEs), online firms and international enterprises) aim to add value and create wealth. So do voluntary and not-for-profit organisations – by educating people, counselling the troubled or caring for the sick. There are about 190,000 charities in England and Wales, with annual incoming resources of over £50 billion (equal to about 3 per cent of gross domestic product), and employing over 660,000 staff (Charities Commission Annual Report for 2008–9, at **www.charitycommission.gov.uk**). Managing a large charity is at least as demanding a job as managing a commercial business, facing similar challenges of adding value to limited resources. Donors and recipients expect them to manage resources well so that they add value to them.

Theatres, orchestras, museums and art galleries create value by offering inspiration, new perspectives or unexpected insights. Other organisations add value by serving particular interests – such as Unison, a trade union that represents workers in the UK public sector, or the Law Society, which defends the interests of lawyers. Firms in most industries create trade organisations to protect their interests by lobbying or public relations work.

While organisations aim to add value, many do not do so. If people work inefficiently they will use more resources than customers will pay for. They may create pollution and waste, and so destroy wealth. Motorway builders create value for drivers, residents of by-passed villages, and shareholders – but destroy value for some people if the route damages an ancient woodland rich in history and wildlife. The idea of creating value is subjective and relative.

Managers face some issues that are unique to the setting in which they operate (charities need to maintain the support of donors) and others which arise in most organisations (business planning or ensuring quality). Table 1.1 illustrates some of these diverse settings, and their (relatively) unique management challenges – which are in addition to challenges that are common to all.

Table 1.1 Where people manage

Setting – industry or type	Examples in this book	'Unique' challenges
Business start-ups	Innocent Drinks in the early days – Part 1 case	Securing funding to launch and enough sales of an unknown product to sustain cash-flow. Building credibility
Small and medium-sized enterprises (SMEs)	DavyMarkham – MIP feature above	Generating enough funds to survive, innovate and enter new markets
Professional business services	Hiscox (insurance) – MIP feature in Chapter 11	Managing highly-qualified staff delivering customised, innovative services
Voluntary, not-for-profit organisations and charities	Eden Project – Chapter 15 case	Providing an experience which encourages visitors to return, raising funds for educational work, fulfilling mission
Public sector organisations	Crossrail – Chapter 6 case	Managing high-profile political and commercial interests
Large private businesses	Virgin Media – Part 4 case	Controlling diverse activities
Online firms	Google – Chapter 12 case; Apple – Chapter 14 case	Maintaining constant innovation in rapidly changing market
International businesses	Starbucks – Chapter 4 case Zara – Chapter 19 case	Managing diverse activities across many cultures; balancing central control and local initiative

Note: MIP = Management in Practice

Whatever its nature, the value an organisation creates depends on how well those who work there develops its capabilities.

Activity 1.2 **Focus on management settings**

Choose ONE of the settings in Table 1.1 which interests you. Gather information about an organisation of that type (using, for example, case studies in this book or someone you know who works in that setting) so you can:

- Name one organisation in that setting.
- Identify how it adds value to resources, and the main management challenges it faces.
- Collect evidence about the managing in that setting.
- Compare your evidence with someone who has gathered data about a different setting, and summarise similarities or differences in the management challenges.

1.3 Meanings of management

Management as a universal human activity

Management as a universal human activity occurs whenever people take responsibility for an activity and consciously try to shape its progress and outcome.

As individuals we run our lives and careers: in this respect we are managing. Family members manage children, elderly dependants and households. Management is both a **universal human activity** and a distinct occupation. In the first sense, people manage an infinite range of activities:

> When human beings 'manage' their work, they take responsibility for its purpose, progress and outcome by exercising the quintessentially human capacity to stand back from experience and to regard it prospectively, in terms of what will happen; reflectively, in terms of what is happening; and retrospectively, in terms of what has happened. Thus management is an expression of human agency, the capacity actively to shape and direct the world, rather than simply react to it. (Hales, 2001, p. 2)

A **manager** is someone who gets things done with the aid of people and other resources.

Management is the activity of getting things done with the aid of people and other resources.

Rosemary Stewart (1967) expressed this idea when she described a **manager** as someone who gets things done with the aid of people and other resources, which defines **management** as the activity of getting things done with the aid of people and other resources. So described, management is a universal human activity – domestic, social and political – as well as in formally established organisations.

In pre-industrial societies people typically work alone or in family units, controlling their time and resources. They decide what to make, how to make it and where to sell it, combining work and management to create value. Self-employed craftworkers, professionals in small practices, and those in a one-person business do this every day. We all do it in household tasks or voluntary activities in which we do the work (planting trees or selling tickets for a prize draw) and the management activities (planning the winter programme).

Activity 1.3 Think about the definition

Choose a domestic, community or business activity you have undertaken.

- What, specifically, did you do to 'get things done with the aid of people and other resources'?
- Decide if the definition accurately describes 'management'.
- If not, how would you change it?

Management as a distinct role

Management as a distinct role develops when activities previously embedded in the work itself become the responsibility not of the employee but of owners or their agents.

Human action can also separate the 'management' element of a task from the 'work' element, thus creating 'managers' who are in some degree apart from those doing the work. **Management as a distinct role** emerges when external parties, such as a private owner of capital, or the state, gain control of a work process that a person used to complete themselves. These parties may then dictate what to make, how to make it and where to sell it. Workers become employees selling their labour, not the results of their labour. During industrialisation in Western economies, factory owners took control of the physical and financial means of production. They also tried to control the time, behaviour and skills of those who were now employees rather than autonomous workers.

The same evolution occurs when someone starts an enterprise, initially performing the *technical* aspects of the work itself – writing software, designing clothes – and also more *conceptual* tasks such as planning which markets to serve or deciding how to raise money.

If the business grows and the entrepreneur engages staff, he or she will need to spend time on *interpersonal* tasks such as training and supervising their work. The founder progressively takes on more management roles – a **role** being the expectations that others have of someone occupying a position. It expresses the specific responsibilities and requirements of the job, and what someone holding it should (or should not) do.

A **role** is the sum of the expectations that other people have of a person occupying a position.

This separation of management and non-management work is not inevitable or permanent. People deliberately separate the roles, and they can also bring them together. As Henri Fayol (1949) (of whom you will read more in Chapter 2) observed:

> Management . . . is neither an exclusive privilege nor a particular responsibility of the head or senior members of a business; it is an activity spread, like all other activities, between head and members of the body corporate. (p. 6)

Key ideas   **Tony Watson on separating roles**

All humans are managers in some way. But some of them also take on the formal occupational work of being managers. They take on a role of shaping . . . work organisations. Managers' work involves a double . . . task: managing others and managing themselves. But the very notion of 'managers' being separate people from the 'managed', at the heart of traditional management thinking, undermines a capacity to handle this. Managers are pressured to be technical experts, devising rational and emotionally neutral systems and corporate structures to 'solve problems', 'make decisions', 'run the business'. These 'scientific' and rational–analytic practices give reassurance but can leave managers so distanced from the 'managed' that their capacity to control events is undermined. This can mean that their own emotional and security needs are not handled, with the effect that they retreat into all kinds of defensive, backbiting and ritualistic behaviour which further undermines their effectiveness.

Source: Watson (1994), pp. 12–13.

Someone in charge of part of, say, a production department will usually be treated as a manager and referred to as one. The people who operate the machines will be called something else. In a growing business such as Ryanair, the boundary between 'managers' and 'non-managers' is likely to be very fluid, with all staff being ready to perform a range of tasks, irrespective of their title. Hales' (2006) research shows how first-line managers now hold some responsibilities traditionally associated with middle managers. They are still responsible for supervising subordinates, but often also have to deal with costs and customer satisfaction – previously a middle manager's job.

1.4   **Specialisation between areas of management**

As an organisation grows, senior managers usually create separate functions and a hierarchy, so that management itself becomes divided (there are exceptions such as W.L. Gore Associates – see Chapter 17 – but these are still a small minority).

Functional specialisation

General managers typically head a complete unit of the organisation, such as a division or subsidiary, within which there will be several functions. The general manager is responsible for the unit's performance, and relies on the managers in charge of each function. A small

General managers are responsible for the performance of a distinct unit of the organisation.

Functional managers are responsible for the performance of an area of technical or professional work.

Line managers are responsible for the performance of activities that directly meet customers' needs.

organisation will have only one or two general managers, who will also manage the functions. At Shell UK the most senior general manager in 2010 was James Smith, the Chairman.

Functional managers are responsible for an area of work – either as line managers or staff managers. **Line managers** are in charge of a function that creates value directly by supplying products or services to customers: they could be in charge of a retail store, a group of nurses, a social work department or a manufacturing area. Their performance significantly affects business performance and image, as they and their staff are in direct contact with customers or clients. At Shell, Mike Hogg was (in 2010) the General Manager of Shell Gas Direct, while Melanie Lane was General Manager, UK Retail.

Management in practice   The store manager – fundamental to success

A manager with extensive experience of retailing commented:

The store manager's job is far more complex that it may at first appear. Staff management is an important element and financial skills are required to manage a budget and the costs involved in running a store. Managers must understand what is going on behind the scenes – in terms of logistics and the supply chain – as well as what is happening on the shop floor. They must also be good with customers and increasingly they need outward-looking skills as they are encouraged to take high-profile roles in the community.

Source: Private communication from the manager.

Staff managers are responsible for the performance of activities that support line managers.

Staff managers are in charge of activities such as finance, personnel, purchasing or legal affairs which support the line managers, who are their customers. Staff in support departments are not usually in direct contact with external customers, and so do not earn income directly for the organisation. Managers of staff departments operate as line managers within their unit. At Shell, in 2010 Bob Henderson was Head of Legal, and Kate Smith was Head of UK Government Relations.

Project managers are responsible for managing a project, usually intended to change some element of an organisation or its context.

Project managers are responsible for a temporary team created to plan and implement a change, such as a new product or system. Mike Buckingham, an engineer, managed a project to implement a new manufacturing system in a van plant. He still had line responsibilities for aspects of manufacturing, but worked for most of the time on the project, helped by a team of technical specialists. When the change was complete he returned to full-time work on his line job.

Entrepreneurs are people who are able to see opportunities in a market which others have overlooked. They quickly secure the resources they need, and use them to build a profitable business. John Scott (Managing Director of Scott Timber, now the UK's largest manufacturer of wooden pallets – **www.scott-timber.co.uk**) recalls the early days – 'I went from not really knowing what I wanted to do . . . to getting thrown into having to make a plant work, employ men, lead by example. We didn't have an office – it was in my mum's house, and she did the invoicing. The house was at the top of the yard, and the saw mill was at the bottom' (*Financial Times*, 11 July 2007, p. 18).

Management hierarchies

As organisations grow, senior managers usually create a hierarchy of positions. The amount of 'management' and 'non-management' work within these positions varies, and the boundaries between them are fluid (Hales, 2006).

Performing direct operations

People who perform direct operations do the manual and mental work to make and deliver products or services. These range from low-paid cleaners or shop workers to highly-paid pilots or lawyers. The activity is likely to contain some aspects of management work, although in lower-level jobs this will be limited. People running a small business combine management work with direct work to meet customer requirements.

Supervising staff on direct operations

Sometimes called supervisors or first-line managers, they typically direct and control the daily work of a group or process,

> framed by the requirement to monitor, report and improve work performance. (Hales 2005, p. 484)

They allocate and co-ordinate work, monitor the pace and help with problems. Sometimes they become involved with middle managers in making operational decisions on staff or work methods. Examples include the supervisor of a production team, the head chef in a hotel, a nurse in charge of a hospital ward or the manager of a bank branch. They may continue to perform some direct operations, but they will spend less time on them than subordinates.

Management in practice   Leading an army platoon

In the British Army an officer in charge of a platoon is responsible for 30 soldiers. Captain Matt Woodward, a platoon commander, describes the job:

> As a platoon commander at a regiment you're looking after up to 30 soldiers, all of whom will have a variety of problems you'll have to deal with – helping them [sort out financial difficulties], one of them might need to go to court for something, and you might go and represent them in court, try and give them a character reference, help them as best you can. Or a soldier who has got a girl pregnant, or a soldier who has just got family problems and needs some help. Somebody else may want to take a posting back to England if they're based in Germany, or indeed if they're in England they might want to go to Germany. That's your job to try and help them out as best you can, to help manage their career to find them the best job they can but also in the place they want to be. And obviously as well as welfare and family and discipline problems we lead soldiers in the field and on operations.

Source: Based on an interview with Matt Woodward.

Managing supervisors or first-line managers

Usually referred to as middle managers, they – such as an engineering manager at Ryanair – are expected to ensure that first-line managers work in line with company policies. They translate strategy into operational tasks, mediating between senior management vision and operational reality. They may help to develop strategy by presenting information about customer expectations or suggesting alternative strategies to senior managers (Floyd and Wooldridge, 2000; Currie and Proctor, 2005). They provide a communication link – telling first-line managers what they expect, and briefing senior managers about current issues. Others face the challenge of managing volunteers. Charities depend on their time and effort, yet commonly face problems when they don't turn up, or work ineffectively – but cannot draw on the systems commonly used to reward and retain paid staff (Boezeman and Ellemers, 2007).

Managing the business

Managing the business is the work of a small group, usually called the board of directors. They establish policy and have a particular responsibility for managing relations with people and institutions in the world outside, such as shareholders, media or elected representatives. They need to know broadly about internal matters, but spend most of their time looking to the future or dealing with external affairs. Depending on local company law, the board usually includes non-executive directors – senior managers from other companies who should bring a wider, independent view to discussions. Such non-executive directors can enhance the effectiveness of the board, and give investors confidence that the board is acting in their interests. They can

> both support the executives in their leadership of the business and monitor and control executive conduct. (Roberts *et al.*, 2005, p. 36)

by challenging, questioning, discussing and debating issues with the executive members. The board will not consider operational issues.

1.5 Influencing through the process of managing

Stakeholders are individuals, groups or organisations with an interest in, or who are affected by, what the organisation does.

Whatever their role, people add value to resources by influencing others, including internal and external **stakeholders** – those parties who affect, or who are affected by, an organisation's actions and policies. The challenge is that stakeholders will have different priorities, so managers need to influence them to act in ways they believe will add value.

They do this directly and indirectly. Direct methods are the interpersonal skills (see Chapter 14) which managers use – persuading a boss to support a proposal, a subordinate to do more work, or a customer to change a delivery date. Managers also influence others indirectly through:

- the process of managing;
- the tasks of managing (Section 1.6); and
- shaping the context (Section 1.7).

| Key ideas | Rosemary Stewart – how managers spend their time |

What are managers' jobs like? Do they resemble an orderly, methodical process – or a constant rush from one problem to the next? One of the best-known studies was conducted by Rosemary Stewart (1967) of Oxford University, who asked 160 senior and middle managers to keep a diary for four weeks. This showed that they typically worked in a fragmented, interrupted fashion. Over the four weeks they had, on average, only nine periods of 30 minutes or more alone, with 12 brief contacts each day. They spent 36 per cent of their time on paperwork (writing, dictating, reading, calculating) and 43 per cent in informal discussion. They spent the remainder on formal meetings, telephoning and social activities.

The research team also found great variety between managers, identifying five distinct profiles based not on level or function but on how they spent their time:

- **Emissaries** spent most time out of the organisation, meeting customers, suppliers or contractors.
- **Writers** spent most time alone reading and writing, and had the fewest contacts with other managers.
- **Discussers** spent most time with other people and with their colleagues.
- **Troubleshooters** had the most fragmented work pattern, with many brief contacts, especially with subordinates.
- **Committee members** had a wide range of internal contacts, and spent much time in formal meetings.

Source: Stewart (1967).

Henry Mintzberg – ten management roles

Mintzberg (1973) observed how (five) chief executives spent their time, and used this data to create a frequently quoted model of management roles. Like Stewart he noted that managers' work was varied and fragmented (see Key Ideas), and contained ten roles in three categories – informational, interpersonal and decisional. Managers can use these roles to influence other people. Table 1.2 describes them, and illustrates each with a contemporary example provided by the manager of a school nutrition project.

Informational roles

Managing depends on obtaining information about external and internal events, and passing it to others. The *monitor role* involves seeking out, receiving and screening information to understand the organisation and its context. It comes from websites and reports, and especially from chance conversations – such as with customers or new contacts at conferences

Table 1.2 Mintzberg's ten management roles

Category	Role	Activity	Examples from a school nutrition project
Informational	Monitor	Seek and receive information, scan reports, maintain interpersonal contacts	Collect and review funding applications; set up database to monitor application process
	Disseminator	Forward information to others, send memos, make phone calls	Share content of applications with team members by email
	Spokesperson	Represent the unit to outsiders in speeches and reports	Present application process at internal and external events
Interpersonal	Figurehead	Perform ceremonial and symbolic duties, receive visitors	Sign letters of award to successful applicants
	Leader	Direct and motivate subordinates, train, advise and influence	Design and co-ordinate process with team and other managers
	Liaison	Maintain information links in and beyond the organisation	Become link person for government bodies to contact for progress reports
Decisional	Entrepreneur	Initiate new projects, spot opportunities, identify areas of business development	Use initiative to revise application process and to introduce electronic communication
	Disturbance handler	Take corrective action during crises, resolve conflicts among staff, adapt to changes	Holding face-to-face meetings with applicants when the outcome was negative; handling staff grievances
	Resource allocator	Decide who gets resources, schedule, budget, set priorities	Ensure fair distribution of grants nationally
	Negotiator	Represent unit during negotiations with unions, suppliers, and generally defend interests	Working with sponsors and government to ensure consensus during decision making

Source: Based on Mintzberg (1973) and private communication from the project manager.

and exhibitions. Much of this information is oral (gossip as well as formal meetings), or building on personal contacts. In the *disseminator role* the manager shares information by forwarding reports, passing on rumours or briefing staff. As a *spokesperson* the manager transmits information to people outside the organisation – speaking at a conference, briefing the media or giving the department's view at a company meeting. Michael O'Leary at Ryanair is renowned for flamboyant statements to the media about competitors or officials in the European Commission with whose policies he disagrees.

Interpersonal roles

Interpersonal roles arise directly from a manager's formal authority and status, and shape relationships with people within and beyond the organisation. In the *figurehead role* the manager is a symbol, representing the unit in legal and ceremonial duties such as greeting a visitor, signing legal documents, presenting retirement gifts or receiving a quality award. The *leader role* defines the manager's relationship with other people (not just subordinates), including motivating, communicating and developing their skills and confidence – as one commented:

> I am conscious that I am unable to spend as much time interacting with staff members as I would like. I try to overcome this by leaving my door open whenever I am alone, as an invitation to staff to come in and interrupt me, and encourage them to discuss any problems.

The *liaison role* focuses on contacts with people outside the immediate unit. Managers maintain a network in which they trade information and favours for mutual benefit with clients, government officials, customers and suppliers. For some managers, particularly chief executives and sales managers, the liaison role takes a high proportion of their time and energy.

Management in practice   Strengthening interpersonal roles

A company restructured its regional operations, closed a sales office in Bordeaux and transferred the work to Paris. The sales manager responsible for south-west France was now geographically distant from her immediate boss and the rest of the team. This caused severe problems of communication and loss of teamwork. She concluded that the interpersonal aspects of the role were vital as a basis for the informational and decisional roles. The decision to close the office had broken these links.

She and her boss agreed to try the following solutions:

- A 'one-to-one' session of quality time to discuss key issues during monthly visits to head office.
- Daily telephone contact to ensure speed of response and that respective communication needs were met,
- Use of fax and email at home to speed up communications.

These overcame the break in interpersonal roles caused by the location change.

Source: Private communication.

Decisional roles

Creativity is the ability to combine ideas in a unique way or to make unusual associations between ideas.

In the *entrepreneurial role* managers demonstrate **creativity** and initiate change. They see opportunities and create projects to deal with them. Managers play this role when they introduce a new product or create a major change programme – as when Lars Kolind became chief executive of Oticon (Chapter 10 case), determined to change an established and inflexible business, unable to deal with new competition. Managers play the *disturbance-handler role* when they deal with problems and changes that are unexpected.

Management in practice   Handling disturbance www.bt.com

In early 2009, Ian Livingston, BT's chief executive, surprised financial markets by reporting a pre-tax loss for the first quarter. The main cause was in Global Services, which supplies telecoms networks to international companies and public bodies, but also to severe competition and the recession – the share price fell 60 per cent in the past year. To recover, Global Services will be split up, each of the three new units aiming at one market; capital spending across the group will be cut; and 15,000 jobs will go in 2009–10.

Source: *Financial Times*, 30 April 2009.

The *resource-allocator role* involves choosing among competing demands for money, equipment, personnel and other resources. How much of her budget should the housing manager, quoted on page 22, spend on different types of project? What proportion of the budget should a company spend on advertising a product? The manager of an ambulance service regularly decides between paying overtime to staff to replace an absent team member, or letting service quality decline until a new shift starts. This is close to the *negotiator role*, in which managers seek agreement with other parties on whom they depend. Managers at Ryanair regularly negotiate with airport owners to agree on the services and fees for a subsequent period.

Activity 1.4   Gather evidence about Mintzberg's model

Recall a time when you were responsible for managing an activity. Alternatively draw on your experience of being managed, and use your then manager as the focus for the activity.

- Do the ten roles cover all of the roles you performed, or did you do things that are not included in his list? What were they?
- Give examples of what you did under (say) five of the roles.
- Were there any of these roles to which you should have given more time? Or less?
- If possible compare your results with other members of your course.
- Decide if the evidence you have collected supports or contradicts Mintzberg's theory.

Mintzberg proposed that every manager's job combines these roles, with their relative importance depending on the manager's level and type of business. Managers usually recognise that they use many of the roles as they influence others.

Case study   Ryanair – the case continues www.ryanair.com

The company has continued to grow rapidly, announcing that it had carried almost 66 million passengers in the 12 months to the end of February. It now referred to itself as 'the world's largest international scheduled airline', and continued to seek new bases from which to operate its growing European network.

The airline's success depends on balancing low costs, fare levels and load factors (Malighetti *et al.,* 2009). Airline seats are what is known as a perishable good – they have no value if they are not used on the flight, so companies aim to maximise the proportion of seats sold on a flight. Ryanair uses a technique known as dynamic pricing, which means that prices change with circumstances. Typically, fares rise the nearer the passenger is to the departure date, although if a flight is under-booked, the company encourages late sales by very low fares.

Ryanair also earns a growing proportion of revenue from charges and services such as refreshments, and in 2009 it sharply increased the cost of checked-in bags: it prefers customers to carry hand baggage into the cabin. Each time a passenger rents a car or books a hotel room on the Ryanair website, it earns a commission. It sells scratch cards on board, offers in-flight gambling and online gaming over its website: the chief executive thinks that gambling could double Ryanair's profits over the next decade. The company expects revenue from ancillary activities will continue to grow more rapidly than passenger revenue.

Sources: *Economist*, 10 July 2004; *Independent*, 7 October 2006; *Financial Times*, 7 June 2006; Kumar (2006); Malighetti *et al.* (2009); and company website.

Case questions 1.2

- Which of Mintzberg's management roles can you identify being exercised in the latest stage of the Ryanair case?

- Decide which two of these roles are likely to be most critical in the next stage of the company's development, and explain why.

Managers often highlight two roles missing from Mintzberg's list – manager as subordinate and manager as worker. Most managers have subordinates but, except for those at the very top, they are subordinates themselves. Part of their role is to advise, assist and influence their boss – over whom they have no formal authority. Managers often need to persuade people higher up the organisation of a proposal's value or urgency. A project manager recalled:

> This is the second time we have been back to the management team, to propose how we wish to move forward, and to try and get the resources that are required. It is worth taking the time up front to get all members fully supportive of what we are trying to do. Although it takes a bit longer we should, by pressure and by other individuals demonstrating the benefits of what we are proposing, eventually move the [top team] forward.

Many managers spend time doing the work of the organisation. A director of a small property company helps with sales visits, or an engineering director helps with difficult technical problems. A lawyer running a small practice performs both professional and managerial roles.

Key ideas	Managerial work in small businesses

O'Gorman *et al.* (2005) studied the work of ten owner-managers of small growth-oriented businesses to establish empirically if the nature of their work differs from those in the large businesses studied by Mintzberg. They concluded that managerial work in these businesses is in some ways similar to that in large organisations, finding brevity, fragmentation and variety; mainly verbal communication; and an unrelenting pace.

Another observation was that managers moved frequently between roles, switching from, say, reviewing financial results to negotiating prices with a customer. They were constantly receiving, reviewing and giving information, usually by telephone or in unscheduled meetings. They reacted immediately to live information by redirecting their attention to the most pressing issues, so that their days were largely unplanned, with frequent interruptions. They spent only a quarter of their time in scheduled meetings compared with Mintzberg's finding that managers in large organisations spent almost 60 per cent of their time in this way. Finally, the owners of these small businesses spent 8 per cent of their time in non-managerial activities – twice that of those in Mintzberg's study.

The research shows that the nature of managerial work in small growth-oriented businesses is in some ways similar to, and in others different from, that in large organisations. There is the same brevity and fragmentation, but more informal communication.

Source: O'Gorman *et al.* (2005).

Managers as networkers

Does the focus of a manager's influencing activities affect performance? Mintzberg's study gave no evidence on this point, but work by Luthans (1988) showed that the relative amount of time spent on specific roles did affect outcomes. The team observed 292 managers in four organisations for two weeks, recording their behaviours in four categories – communicating, 'traditional management', networking, and human resource management. They also distinguished between levels of 'success' (relatively rapid promotion) and 'effectiveness' (work-unit performance and subordinates' satisfaction). They concluded that *successful* managers spent much more time networking (socialising, politicking, interacting with outsiders) than the less successful. *Effective* managers spent most time on communication and human resource management.

Wolff and Moser (2009) confirmed the link between **networking** and career success, showing building, maintaining and using internal and external contacts was associated with current salary, and with salary growth. Effective networkers seek out useful connections and contacts, and use the information and ideas they gather to create something valuable. They also look critically at their networks – are they dealing too often with people like themselves and with a similar professional background? And a network that is too extensive may take more time and energy than it is worth.

> **Networking** refers to behaviours that aim to build, maintain and use informal relationships (internal and external) that may help work-related activities.

| 1.6 | **Influencing through the tasks of managing** |

A second way in which managers influence others is when they manage the transformation of resources into more valuable outputs. Building on Figure 1.1, this involves the **management tasks** of planning, organising, leading and controlling the transformation of resources. The amount of each varies with the job and the person, and they do not perform them in sequence: they do them simultaneously, switching as the situation requires.

Figure 1.2 illustrates the elements of this definition. It expands the central 'transforming' circle of Figure 1.1 to show the tasks that together make up the transformation process.

> **Management tasks** are those of planning, organising, leading and controlling the use of resources to add value to them.

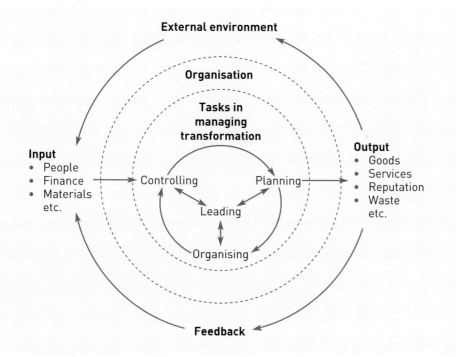

Figure 1.2
The tasks of managing

People draw inputs (resources) from the environment and transform them through the tasks of planning, organising, leading and controlling. This results in goods and services that they pass as output into the environment. The feedback loop indicates that this output is the source of future resources.

External environment

Organisations depend on the external environment for the tangible and intangible resources they need to do their work. So they depend on people in that environment being willing to buy or otherwise value their outputs. Commercial firms sell goods and services, and use the revenue to buy resources. Public bodies depend on their sponsors being sufficiently satisfied with their performance to provide their budget. Most managers are now facing the challenge of how they manage their organisations to ensure that they use natural resources not just efficiently but also sustainably. Part 2 of the book deals with the external environment.

Planning

Planning sets out the overall direction of the work to be done. It includes forecasting future trends, assessing resources and developing performance objectives. It means deciding on the scope and direction of the business, the areas of work in which to engage and how to use resources. Managers invest time and effort in developing a sense of direction for the organisation, or their part of it, and express this in a set of objective. Part 3 deals with planning.

Management in practice   **Planning major rail projects**   www.networkrail.co.uk

More than most civil engineering projects, rail projects depend on extensive and detailed advance planning. In 2010 the UK government announced the preferred route for the first stage of a high-speed West Coast railway line. The first stage will run from London to Birmingham, but construction is not expected to begin until 2015 at the earliest, with completion about four years later. The Crossrail project in London (see Chapter 6 case) also illustrates the scale and complexity of the planning required to build a large railway through (and below) the centre of London.

Source: Company website.

Organising

Organising moves abstract plans closer to reality by deciding how to allocate time and effort. It includes creating a structure for the enterprise, developing policies for human resource management (HRM), deciding what equipment people need, and how to implement change. Part 4 deals with organising.

Management in practice   **Chris Thompson, serial entrepreneur** www.express-group.co.uk

Chris Thompson's grandfather was a shipyard worker on Tyneside and his father a draughtsman who set up Express Engineering, an engineering business, in the 1970s. While working as an apprentice toolmaker in the company, Chris Thompson also sold jeans on a market stall, and turned oil drums into barbecues in his spare time. He took over Express Engineering in 1986, and since then has created more than 40 new businesses. He has sold some to management or third parties, while remaining closely involved with about 20 of them as an investor, director or chairman, many grouped under the brand name Express Group.

The companies are in manufacturing, product development, consultancy, training and property, with many customers in relatively resilient economic sectors such as oil and gas, aerospace and defence. A senior colleague from another company says of Mr Thompson:

> **He is clear and decisive. He is very considered; doesn't jump to conclusions but makes decisions very quickly. He could have simply continued with the business his father started and been very successful: he is a great example, a great role model.**

As well as being closely involved with about 20 of the companies he has founded, he also takes on public sector roles, notably as deputy chair of the regional development agency:

> **I enjoy the good things in life, but I'm conscious of the disparity between the haves and the have-nots.**

Source: From an article by Chris Tighe and Peter March, *Financial Times*, 17 June 2009, p.12.

Leading

Leading is the activity of generating effort and commitment – influencing people of all kinds, generating commitment and motivation, and communicating – whether with individuals or in teams. These activities are directed at all of the other tasks – planning, organising and controlling – so they are placed in the middle of Figure 1.2. Part 5 deals with this topic.

Controlling

Control is the task of monitoring progress, comparing it with plan and taking corrective action. For example, managers set a budget for a housing department, an outpatients' clinic or for business travel. They then ensure that there is a system to collect information regularly on expenditure or performance – to check that they are keeping to budget. If not, they need to decide how to bring actual costs back into line with budgeted costs. Are the outcomes consistent with the objectives? If so, they can leave things alone. But if by Wednesday it is clear that staff will not meet the week's production target, then managers need to act. They may deal with the deviation by a short-term response – such as authorising overtime. Control is equally important in creative organisations. Ed Catmull, cofounder of Pixar comments:

> Because we're a creative organization, people [think that what we do can't be measured]. That's wrong. Most of our processes involve activities and deliverables that can be quantified. We keep track of the rates at which things happen, how often something had to be reworked, whether a piece of work was completely finished or not when it was sent to another department . . . Data can show things in a neutral way, which can stimulate discussion. (Catmull, 2008, p. 72)

The discussion to which Catmull refers is the way to learn from experience – an essential contributor to performance. Good managers create and use opportunities to learn from what they are doing, as the Management in Practice feature on a charity illustrates. Part 6 deals with control.

Management in practice   **A charity which encourages learning**

The organisation is a national charity that runs residential homes for people with severe learning disabilities. It has a high reputation for the quality of the care it gives and for the way it treats the carers. Managers take whatever opportunities they can to help staff gain confidence in the difficult and often stressful work. An example:

> **Staff in one area described how their manager supported their studies by creating a file for them containing information on relevant policies and legislation. The same manager recognised that a night shift**

worker doing a qualification was not getting the range of experience necessary to complete college assessments: 'So she took me to a review last week and also took me to a referral for a service user. I'd never seen that side before – but now I can relate to the stuff that will come up at college. It's about giving you the fuller picture, because sometimes the night shift can be quite isolating.'

Source: Unpublished research.

The tasks in practice

Managers typically switch between tasks many times a day. They deal with them intermittently and in parallel, touching on many different parts of the job, as this manager in a not-for-profit housing association explains:

> My role involves each of these functions. Planning is an important element as I am part of a team with a budget of £8 million to spend on promoting particular forms of housing. So planning where we will spend the money is very important. Organising and leading are important too, as staff have to be clear on which projects to take forward, as well as being clear on objectives and deadlines. Controlling is also there – I have to compare the actual money spent with the planned budget and take corrective action as necessary.

And a manager in a professional services firm:

> As a manager in a professional firm, each assignment involves all the elements to ensure we carry it out properly. For example, I have to set clear objectives for the assignment, organise the necessary staff and information to perform the work, supervise staff and counsel them if necessary, and evaluate the results. All the roles interrelate and there are no clear stages for each one.

Activity 1.5   Gather evidence about the tasks of managing

- Do the four tasks of managing cover all of your work, or did you do things that are not included? What were they?
- Give an example of something which you did in each of the tasks.
- Were there any of these to which you should have given more time? Or less?
- If possible, compare your results with other members of your course.

1.7   Influencing through shaping the context

A third way in which managers influence others is through changing aspects of the context in which they work. Changing an office layout, people's reporting relationships, or the rewards they obtain, alter their context and perhaps their actions. The context is both an influence on the manager and a tool with which to influence others (Johns, 2006):

> It is impossible to understand human intentions by ignoring the settings in which they make sense. Such settings may be institutions, sets of practices, or some other contexts created by humans – contexts which have a history, within which both particular deeds and whole histories of individual actors can and have to be situated in order to be intelligible. (Czarniawska, 2004, p. 4)

Managers continually aim to create contexts that they hope will influence others to act in ways that meet their objectives.

Dimensions of context

Internal context

Figures 1.1 and 1.2 show the links between managers, their organisation and the external environment. Figure 1.3 enlarges the 'organisation' circle to show more fully the elements that make up the internal environment within which managers work. Any organisation contains these elements – they represent the immediate context of the manager's work. For example, as Jorma Ollila built Nokia into a major business, he and his team made many changes to technology, business processes – and, indeed, to all the elements shown in the figure (Steinbock, 2001), which later chapters examine:

- **culture** (Chapter 3) – norms, beliefs and underlying values of a unit;
- **objectives** (Chapters 6 and 8) – a desired future state of an organisation or unit;
- **structure** (Chapter 10) – how tasks are divided and co-ordinated to meet objectives;
- **technology** (Chapter 12) – facilities and equipment to turn inputs into outputs;
- **power** (Chapter 14) – the amount and distribution of power with which to influence others;
- **people** (Chapter 15) – their knowledge, skills, attitudes and goals;
- **business processes** (Chapter 18) – activities to transform materials and information; and
- **finance** (Chapter 20) – the financial resources available;

Models such as this show that managers work within constraints – they are to some degree helped or hindered by the elements in Figure 1.3. Effective managers do not accept their context passively – they initiate change to create the combination of elements to meet their objectives (Chapter 13).

Historical context

Managing takes place within the flow of history, as what people do now reflects past events and future uncertainties. Managers typically focus on current issues, ensuring that things

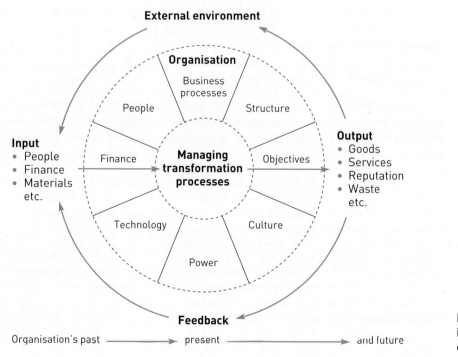

Figure 1.3 The internal and external context of management

run properly, and that the organisation works. At the same time, history influences them through the structure and culture they work within, and which affects how people respond to proposals.

Effective managers also look to the future, questioning present systems and observing external changes. Are we wasting resources? What are others doing? The arrow at the foot of Figure 1.3 represents the historical context.

External context

Chapter 3 shows that the external context includes an immediate competitive (micro) environment and a general (or macro) environment. These affect performance and part of the manager's work is to identify, and adapt to, external changes. Managers in the public sector are expected to deliver improved services with fewer resources, so they seek to influence people to change the internal context (such as how staff work) in order to meet external expectations. They also seek to influence those in the external context about both expectations and resources.

Table 1.3 summarises the last two sections and illustrates how managers can influence others as they perform tasks affecting internal, micro and macro contexts.

Managers and their context

Managers use one of three theories (even if subconsciously) of the link between their context and their action – determinism, choice or interaction.

Determinism

This describes the assumption that factors in the external context determine an organisation's performance – micro and macro factors such as the industry a company is in, the amount of competition, or the country's laws and regulations. Managers adapt to external changes and have little independent influence on the direction of the business. On this view, the context is an independent variable, as shown in Figure 1.4(a).

Table 1.3 Examples of managing tasks in each context

	Internal (organisational)	Micro (competitive)	Macro (general)
Planning	Clarifying the objectives of a business unit and communicating them clearly to all staff	Reducing prices in the hope of discouraging a potential competitor from entering the market	Lobbying for a change in a trade agreement to make it easier to enter an overseas market
Organising	Changing the role of a business unit	Reducing the number of suppliers in exchange for improved terms	Lobbying government to change planning laws to enable longer trading hours
Leading	Redesigning tasks and training staff to higher levels to improve motivation	Arranging for staff to visit customers so that they understand more fully what the customer's need	Sending staff to work in an overseas subsidiary to raise awareness of different markets
Controlling	Ensuring the information system keeps an accurate output record	Implementing an information system directly linked to customers and suppliers	Lobbying for tighter procedures to ensure all countries abide by trade agreements

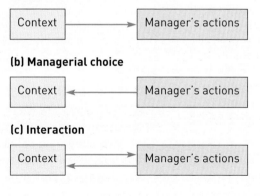

Figure 1.4
Alternative models of managers and their context

Choice

An alternative assumption is that people are able to influence events and shape their context. Those in powerful positions choose which businesses to enter or leave, and in which countries they will operate. Managers in major companies lobby to influence taxation, regulations and policy generally, in order to serve their interests. On this view, the context is a dependent variable, as shown in Figure 1.4(b).

Interaction

The interaction approach expresses the idea that people are influenced by, and themselves influence, the context. They interpret the existing context and act to change it to promote personal, local or organisational objectives. A manager may see a change in the company's external environment, and respond by advocating that it responds by entering the market with a product that meets a perceived demand. Others interpret this proposal in the light of *their* perspective – existing suppliers may lobby government to alter some regulations to protect them from this new competitor – the players try to influence decisions in a way that best suits their interests. The outcomes from these interactions affect the context (the company enters the market or the regulations deter them from doing so) – which now provides the historical background to future action. The essential idea is that the relation between the manager and the context works both ways, as shown in Figure 1.4(c). People shape the context, and the context shapes people. Throughout the book there are examples of managers interacting with their context.

Case study   Ryanair – the case continues   www.ryanair.com

The company depends on securing agreements with airport operators, and also approvals from aviation authorities in the countries to which it flies. This often leads it into public disputes with airport operators and/or with the European Commission over subsidies.

In 2009 it withdrew its flights from Manchester airport when it was unable to reach agreement with the airport's owners over landing charges. Michael O'Leary takes a deliberately aggressive stance to these controversies, believing that:

> as long as its not safety-related, there's no such thing as bad publicity.

He is dismissive of traditional high-cost airlines, the European Commission, airport operators, travel agents and governments that try to protect established airlines from competition.

The Open Skies agreement reached between the European Union and the US in 2008 is intended to increase the number of flights between Europe and the US (Barrett, 2009). This offers new possibilities for Ryanair to extend the successful model from short to long flights – especially given the many people of Irish descent who live in the US.

Sources: *Business Week*, 8 May 2006; *Independent*, 7 October 2006; and other sources.

Case questions 1.3

- Which aspects of the external general environment have affected the company?

- How has the company affected these environments?

- In 2010 the company faced a strategic decision on whether to offer flights to the US. Evaluate the extent to which the factors that have supported its success would be present on these new routes.

1.8 Critical thinking

Managers continually receive data, information and knowledge – but they cannot take what they receive at face value. They must test it by questioning the underlying assumptions, relating it to context, considering alternatives and recognising limitations. These are the skills of critical thinking.

Critical thinking

Brookfield (1987) stresses the benefits of thinking critically, in that it:

> involves our recognizing the assumptions underlying our beliefs and behaviors. It means we can give justifications for our ideas and actions. Most important, perhaps, it means we try to judge the rationality of these justifications . . . by comparing them to a range of varying interpretations and perspectives. (p. 13)

Critical thinking identifies the assumptions behind ideas, relates them to their context, imagines alternatives and recognises limitations.

Critical thinking is positive activity that enables people to see more possibilities, rather than a single path. Critical thinkers 'are self-confident about their potential for changing aspects of their worlds, both as individuals and through collective action' (Brookfield, 1987, p. 5). He identifies four components of critical thinking.

Identifying and challenging assumptions

Critical thinkers look for the assumptions that underlie taken-for-granted ideas, beliefs and values, and question their accuracy and validity. They are ready to discard those that no longer seem valid guides to action, in favour of more suitable ones. Managers who present a well-supported challenge to a theory of marketing that seems unsuitable to their business, or who question the need for a new business division, are engaging in this aspect of critical thinking.

Recognising the importance of context

Critical thinkers are aware that context influences thought and action. Thinking uncritically means assuming that ideas and methods that work in one context will work equally well in others. What we regard as an appropriate way to deal with staff reflects a specific culture: people in another culture – working in another place or at a different time – will have other expectations. Critical thinkers look for such approaches suitable for the relevant context.

Imagining and exploring alternatives

Critical thinkers develop the skill of imagining and exploring alternative ways of managing. They ask how others have dealt with a situation, and seek evidence about the effectiveness of different approaches. This makes them aware of realistic alternatives, and so increases the range of ideas which they can adapt and use.

Seeing limitations

Critical thinking alerts people to the limitations of knowledge and proposals. Critical thinkers recognise that because a practice works well in one situation it does not ensure it will work in another. They are sceptical about research whose claims seem over-sold, asking about the sample or the analysis. They are open to new ideas, but only when supported by convincing evidence and reasoning.

Key ideas   Techniques to help develop your ability to think critically

1. Identifying and challenging assumptions:
   - Reflect on recent events which worked well or not-so-well; describing what happened and your reactions to it may help to identify assumptions that were confirmed or challenged by events.
   - Do the same for an achievement of which you are most proud.
   - Imagine that you have decided to leave your job and are advising the committee who will appoint your replacement: list the qualities they should look for in that person. That may indicate the assumptions you hold about the nature of your job, and what it takes to do it well.

2. Recognising the importance of context:
   - Select a practice which people in your organisation take for granted; ask people in other organisations how they deal with the matter, and see if the differences relate to context.
   - Repeat that with people who have worked in other countries.

3. Imagining and exploring alternatives:
   - Brainstorming – trying to think of as many solutions to a problem as you can in a short period, by temporarily suspending habitual judgements.
   - Gather evidence about how other businesses deal with an aspect of management that interest you: the more alternatives you find, the easier it may become to think of alternatives that could work for you.

4. Seeing limitations:
   - Acknowledging the limited evidence behind a theory or prescription.
   - Asking if it has been tested in different settings or circumstances.

Source: Based on Brookfield (1987) and Thomas (2003), p. 7.

Thinking critically will deepen your understanding of management. It does not imply a 'do-nothing' cynicism, 'treating everything and everyone with suspicion and doubt' (Thomas, 2003, p. 7). Critical thinking lays the foundation for a successful career, as it helps to ensure that proposals are supported by convincing evidence and reasoning.

Managing your studies

Studying management is itself a task to manage. Each chapter sets out some learning objectives. The text, including the activities and case questions, help you work towards these objectives, and you can check your progress by using the review questions at the end of each chapter. The questions reflect objectives of varying levels of difficulty (Anderson and Krathwohl, 2001), which Table 1.4 illustrates. Working on these will help develop your confidence to think critically in your studies and as a manager.

Table 1.4 Types of Learning Objective in the Text

Type of objective	Typical words associated with each	Examples
Remember – retrieve relevant knowledge from memory	Recognise, recall	State or write the main elements and relationships in a theory
Understand – construct meaning from information	Interpret, give examples, summarise, compare, explain, contrast	Compare two theories of motivation; contrast two strategies, and explain which theory each reflects
Apply – use a procedure in a specified situation	Demonstrate, calculate, show, experiment, illustrate, modify	Use (named theory) to show the issues which managers in the case should consider
Analyse – break material into parts, showing relation to each other and to wider purpose	Classify, separate, order, organise, differentiate, infer, connect, compare, divide	Collect evidence to support or contradict (named theory); which theory is reflected in (example of practice)?
Evaluate – make judgements based on criteria and standards	Decide, compare, check, judge	Decide if the evidence presented supports the conclusion; should the company do A or B?
Create – put parts together into a coherent whole; reorganise elements	Plan, make, present, generate, produce, design, compose	Present a marketing plan for the company; design a project proposal

Source: Adapted from Anderson and Krathwohl (2001), p. 31.

Studying is an opportunity to practice managing. You can plan what you want to achieve, organise the resources you need, generate personal commitment and check your progress. The book provides opportunities to improve your skills of literacy, reflection (analysing and evaluating evidence before acting), critical thinking, communicating, problem solving and teamwork.

The most accessible sources of ideas and theory are this book, (including the 'further reading' and websites mentioned), your lectures and tutorials. Draw on the experience of friends and relatives to help with some of the activities and questions. As you go about your educational and social lives you are experiencing organisations, and in some cases helping to manage them. Actively reflecting on these experiences will support your studies.

1.9   Integrating themes

Each chapter concludes with a section relating the topic to three integrating themes:

- achieving environmentally sustainable performance;
- meeting expectations about standards of governance and control;
- working in an increasingly international economy.

Sustainable performance

'Sustainability' features regularly in media discussion, is on the legislative agenda of most national governments, and is the subject of the Kyoto Agreement which aims to secure international action to avert climate change. Most managers are aware of the issues, and consider how changes in public opinion and legislation will affect their organisation – what are the implications for the competitive landscape, what threats and opportunities are arising, what should they do to deal with issues of sustainability so that they enhance performance? Managers in the public sector face similar pressures, being expected to provide better services with the same or fewer resources. The interest in **sustainable performance** is driven mainly by legislation, consumer concerns and employees' interest, while barriers include a lack of information on what to do, perceived difficulty in making the business case for such expenditure, and poor implementation of such proposals as are agreed (Hopkins, 2009).

Amory Lovins (Hawken *et al.,* 1999) is an influential advocate of running organisations in a sustainable way, believing that it is wrong to see it as a cost that business will need to bear. Drawing on years of advisory experience at the Rocky Mountain Institute which he helped to found, he maintains that companies who make productive use, not only of financial and physical resources but also of human and natural ones, do well. They turn waste into profit – for example, by taking a radical approach to energy efficiency in buildings, processes and vehicles, and by designing products and services so that they avoid waste.

He also acknowledges that 'turning waste into profit' does not happen easily – it needs thought and careful planning, and will change the way people throughout the organisation do things. It is no different, he suggests, from any other management innovation – people have to pay attention to the problem to find and implement a workable solution. This is likely to involve new capabilities such as being able to work on a whole system, rather than isolated parts; working with colleagues in other units; developing a culture which encourages long-term thinking; and engaging with external stakeholders. These are all part of the work of managing in organisations.

> **Sustainable performance** refers to economic activities that meet the needs of the present population while preserving the environment for the needs of future generations.

Governance and control

The shareholders of commercial companies expect to receive a return on the investment they have made in the business: unless they can be reasonably sure that a business is financially sound they will not lend money or buy shares. They can find some basic information relevant to this in the published Annual Reports, but these are inherently historical documents and cannot cover all aspects of the business. High-profile corporate collapses (see Table 5.1 on page 137 for more details) have occurred despite their Annual Reports giving the impression that all was well. There has also been widespread criticism over the pay and pensions of senior executives, especially in banks. These scandals have damaged investors and employees – and public confidence in the way managers were running these and other large companies.

Many questioned how such things could happen. Why could such apparently successful businesses get into such difficulties so quickly? Were there any warning signals that were ignored? What can be done to prevent similar events happening again? How can public confidence in these businesses be restored? These questions are all linked to corporate governance:

> a lack of effective corporate governance meant that such collapses could occur; good corporate governance can help prevent [them] happening again. (Mallin, 2007, p. 1)

Corporate governance is also relevant in the public sector. There too have been scandals about the poor delivery of service, losses of personal data, failures by staff supposed to be protecting vulnerable people, and examples of dubious expense claims and criminal charges when people award public contracts to business associates. Again people ask how this could happen, who was in charge and what can be done to put things right?

A narrow definition of corporate governance expresses it in essentially financial terms – such that it deals with the ways in which the suppliers of finance to corporations assure themselves of getting a return on their investment. Many now interpret the topic more broadly, to cover the interests of people other than shareholders, and also to include public and not-for-profit organisations. A broader view of the topic is that it is concerned with ensuring that internal controls adequately balance the needs of those with a financial interest in the organisation, and that these are balanced with the interests of other stakeholders.

Governance is an essential mechanism helping the organisation to meet its objectives, by monitoring performance towards them. It does so by:

- helping to ensure there are adequate systems of control to safeguard assets;
- preventing any single individual from becoming too powerful;
- reviewing relationships between managers, directors, shareholders and other stakeholders; and
- ensuring transparency and accountability in transactions.

Internationalisation

Developments in communications technology and changes in the regulations governing international trade have helped to steadily increase the amount of trade that crosses national borders. Managing the international activities of an organisation has become a common feature of the work of many managers – whether working as an expatriate manager in another country, being part of an international team with colleagues from many countries, or managing in an international business which works in many countries.

The international dimension is a pervasive theme of management, with implications for each of the tasks of managing – how to lead in an international environment, and the implications of an increasingly dispersed business for planning, organising and controlling the organisation. These issues will be explored not just in Chapter 4 but also as an integrating theme throughout the book.

Summary

1 **Explain that the role of management is to add value to resources in diverse settings**

- Managers create value by transforming inputs into outputs of greater value: they do this by developing competences within the organisation which, by constantly adding value (however measured) to resources, is able to survive and prosper. The concept of creating value is subjective and open to different interpretations. Managers work in an infinite variety of settings, and Table 1.1 suggests how each setting raises relatively unique challenges.

2 **Give examples of management as a universal human activity and as a distinct role**

- Management is an activity that everyone undertakes to some extent as they manage their daily lives. In another sense, management is an activity within organisations, conducted in varying degrees by a wide variety of people. It is not exclusive to people called 'managers'. People create the distinct role when they separate the management of work from the work itself and allocate the tasks to different people. The distinction between management and non-management work is fluid and is the result of human action.

3 **Compare the roles of general, functional, line, staff and project managers, and of entrepreneurs**

- General managers are responsible for a complete business or a unit within it. They depend on functional managers who can be either in charge of line departments meeting customer needs, such as manufacturing and sales, or in staff departments such as finance which provide advice or services to line managers. Project managers are in charge of temporary activities usually directed at implementing change. Entrepreneurs are those who create new businesses to exploit opportunities they have seen in a market

4 **Explain how managers influence others to add value to resources**

- The processes of managing. Rosemary Stewart drew attention to the fragmented and interrupted nature of management work, while Mintzberg identified ten management roles in three groups which he labelled informational, interpersonal and decisional. Luthans, and more recently Moser, have observed that successful managers were likely to be those who engaged in networking with people inside and outside of the organisation.

- The tasks (or content) of managing. Planning is the activity of developing the broad direction of an organisation's work, to meet customer expectations, taking into account internal capabilities. Organising is the activity of deciding how to deploy resources to meet plans, while leading seeks to ensure that people work with commitment to achieve plans. Control monitors activity against plans, so that people can adjust either if required.

- Contexts within which they and others work. The organisational context consists of eight elements which help or hinder the manager's work – objectives, technology, business processes, finance, structure, culture, power and people. The historical context also influences events, as does the external context made up from the competitive and general environments.

5 **Explain the elements of critical thinking and use some techniques to develop this skill**

- Critical thinking is a positive approach to studying, as it encourages people to develop the skills of identifying and challenging assumptions; recognising the importance of context; imagining and exploring alternatives; and seeing the limitations of any idea or proposal.

6 **Evaluate a manager's approach to the role by analysing how they influence others**

- You can achieve this objective by arranging with a manager to discus their role, and organise your questions or discussion around the theories of the processes, contents and contexts of managerial work outlined in the chapter. If possible, compare your results with others on your course and try to explain any differences which you find.

7 **Current themes and issues**

Managers are expected to:

- achieve environmentally sustainable performance;
- meet expectations about governance and control;
- work in an increasingly international economy.

Review questions

1 Apart from delivering goods and services, what other functions do organisations perform?

2 What is the difference between management as a general human activity and management as a specialised occupation? How has this division happened and what are some of its effects?

3 What examples are there in the chapter of this boundary between 'management' and 'non-management' work being changed and what were the effects?

4 Describe, with examples, the differences between general, functional, line, staff and project managers.

5 Give examples from your experience or observation of each of the four tasks of management.

6 How does Mintzberg's theory of management roles complement that which identifies the tasks of management?

7 What is the significance to someone starting a career in management of Luthans' theory about roles and performance?

8 How can thinking critically help managers do their job more effectively?

9 Review and revise the definition of management that you gave in Activity 1.1.

Concluding critical reflection

Think about the way managers in your company, or one with which you are familiar, go about their work. If you are a full-time student, draw on any jobs you have held, or on the management of your studies at school or university. Review the material in the chapter and make notes on the following questions:

- Which of the issues discussed in this chapter are most relevant to the way you and your colleagues manage?
- What **assumptions** about the role of management appear to guide the way you, or others, manage? Are these assumptions supported by the evidence of recent events – have they worked or not? Which aspects of the content and process of managing are you expected to focus on – or are you unsure? Does your observation support, or contradict, Luthans' theory?
- What aspects of the historical or current **context** of the company appear to influence how you, and others, interpret your management role? Do people have different interpretations?
- Can you compare and contrast your role with that of colleagues on your course? Does this suggest any plausible **alternative** ways of constructing your management role, in terms of where you devote your time and energy? How much scope do you have to change it?
- What **limitations** can you see in the theories and evidence presented in the chapter? For example, how valid might Mintzberg's theory (developed in large commercial firms) be for those managing in a small business or in the public sector? Can you think of ways of improving the model – e.g. by adding elements to it, or being more precise about the circumstance to which it applies?

Further reading

Alvesson, M. and Wilmott, H. (1996), *Making Sense of Management*, Sage, London.

Discusses management from a critical perspective.

Currie, G. and Proctor, S.J. (2005), 'The Antecedents of Middle Managers' Strategic Contribution: The Case of a Professional Bureaucracy', *Journal of Management Studies*, vol. 42, no. 7, pp. 1325–1356.

An empirical study comparing how middle managers contributed to strategy in three hospitals, showing the ambiguities in their changing roles, and how contextual factors affected performance.

Drucker, P. (1999), *Management Challenges for the 21st Century,* Butterworth/Heinemann, London.

Worth reading as a collection of insightful observations from the enquiring mind of this great management theorist.

Finkelstein, S. (2003), *Why Smart Executives Fail: And what you can learn from their mistakes*, Penguin, New York.

Analysis of failure, giving valuable insights into the complexities of managing.

Hales, C. (2006), 'Moving down the line? The shifting boundary between middle and first-line management', *Journal of General Management*, vol. 32, no. 2, pp. 31–55.

Reviews the growing pressure on managers as additional responsibilities are added to their role.

Handy, C. (1988), *Understanding Voluntary Organisations,* Penguin, Harmondsworth.

A valuable perspective on management in the voluntary sector.

Hopkins, M.S. (2009), 'What Executives Don't Get About Sustainability', *MIT Sloan Management Review,* vol. 51, no. 1, pp. 35–40.

Brief introduction to sustainability from a manager's perspective, including an interview with one of the authors of *Natural Capitalism* (Hawken *et al.,* 1999).

Magretta, J. (2002), *What Management Is (and Why it is Everyone's Business),* Profile Books, London.

This small book by a former editor at the *Harvard Business Review* offers a brief, readable and jargon-free account of the work of general management.

Weblinks

These websites have appeared in the chapter:

www.ryanair.com
www.charitycommission.gov.uk
www.davymarkham.com
www.shell.co.uk
www.scott-timber.co.uk
www.networkrail.co.uk
www.express-group.co.uk

Visit two of the business sites in the list, or those of other organisations in which you are interested, and navigate to the pages dealing with recent news, press or investor relations.

- What are the main issues which the organisation appears to be facing?
- Compare and contrast the issues you identify on the two sites.
- What challenges may they imply for those working in, and managing, these organisations?

For video case studies, audio summaries, flashcards, exercises and annotated weblinks related to this chapter, visit **www.pearsoned.co.uk/mymanagementlab**

CHAPTER 2
MODELS OF MANAGEMENT

Aim

To present the main theoretical perspectives on management and to show how they relate to each other.

Objectives

By the end of your work on this chapter you should be able to outline the concepts below in your own terms and:

1   Explain the value of models of management, and compare unitary, pluralist and critical perspectives

2   State the structure of the competing values framework and evaluate its contribution to our understanding of management

3   Summarise the rational goal, internal process, human relations and open systems models, and evaluate what each can contribute to managers' understanding of their role

4   Use the model to classify the dominant form in two or more business units, and to gather evidence about the way this affects the roles of managing in those units

5   Show how ideas from the chapter add to your understanding of the integrating themes

Key terms

This chapter introduces the following ideas:

model (or theory)
metaphor
scientific management
operational research
bureaucracy
administrative management
human relations approach
system

open system
system boundary
feedback
subsystem
socio-technical system
complexity theory
non-linear systems

Each is a term defined within the text, as well as in the Glossary at the end of the book.

Robert Owen – an early management innovator www.newlanark.org.uk

Robert Owen (1771–1856) was a successful manufacturer of textiles, who ran mills in England and at New Lanark, about 24 miles from Glasgow, in Scotland. David Dale built the cotton-spinning mills at New Lanark in 1785 – which were then the largest in Scotland. Since they depended on water power Dale had built them below the Falls of Clyde – a well-known tourist attraction throughout the eighteenth century. Many people continued to visit both the Falls and New Lanark, which combined both manufacturing and social innovations.

Creating such a large industrial enterprise in the countryside meant that Dale (and Owen after him) had to attract and retain labour – which involved building not only the mill but also houses, shops, schools and churches for the workers. By 1793 the mill employed about 1,200 people, of whom almost 800 were children, aged from 6 to 17: 200 were under 10 (McLaren, 1990). Dale provided the children with food, education and clothing in return for working 12 hours each day: visitors were impressed by these facilities.

One visitor was Robert Owen, who shared Dale's views on the benefits to both labour and owner of good working conditions. By 1801 Dale wanted to sell New Lanark to someone who shared his principles and concluded that Owen (who had married his daughter) was such a man. Owen had built a reputation for management skills while running mills in England, and did not approve of employing children in them.

Having bought the very large business of New Lanark, Owen quickly introduced new management and production control techniques. These included daily and weekly measurements of stocks, output and productivity; a system of labour costing; and measures of work-in-progress. He used a novel control technique: a small, four-sided piece of wood, with a different colour on each side, hung beside every worker. The colour set to the front indicated the previous day's standard of work – black indicating bad. Everyone could see this measure of the worker's performance, which overseers recorded to identify any trends in a person's work:

> **Every process in the factory was closely watched, checked and recorded to increase labour productivity and to keep costs down.** (Royle, 1998, p. 13)

Reproduced with kind permission of New Lanark Conservation Trust. www.newlanark.org

Most adult employees, at this stage of the Industrial Revolution, had no experience of factory work, or of living in a large community such as New Lanark. Owen found that many 'were idle, intemperate, dishonest [and] devoid of truth' (quoted in Butt, 1971). Evening patrols were introduced to stop drunkenness, and there were rules about keeping the residential areas clean and free of rubbish. He also had 'to deal with slack managers who had tolerated widespread theft and embezzlement, immorality and drunkenness' (Butt, 1971).

During Owen's time at the mill it usually employed about 1,500 people, and soon after taking over he stopped employing children under 10. He introduced other social innovations: a store at which employees could buy goods more cheaply than elsewhere (a model for the Co-operative Movement), and a school which looked after children from the age of one – enabling their mothers to work in the mills.

Sources: Butt (1971); McLaren (1990); Donachie (2000).

Case questions 2.1

- What management issues was Owen dealing with at New Lanark?
- What assumptions guided his management practices?

2.1   Introduction

The brief sketch of Robert Owen illustrates three themes that run through this book. First, he devised management systems to control the workforce and improve mill performance. Second, Owen engaged with the wider social system: he criticised the effects of industrialisation and tried to influence local and national policy to end the use of child labour. Third, he was managing at a time of transition from an agricultural to an industrial economy, and many of the practices he invented were attempts to resolve the tensions between those systems – as we now face tensions between industrial and post-industrial systems.

Owen was an entrepreneur. His attempts to change worker behaviour were innovative, and he was equally creative in devising management systems and new ways of working. Managers today cope with similar issues. HMV needs to recruit willing and capable people for its stores, and ensure that their work creates value. Many share Owen's commitment to responsible business practice: Cooperative Financial Services make a point of stating, and working to, clear ethical principles throughout its business, and doing so in a way that still brings healthy profits. Most see that working conditions affect family life – and try to balance the two by subsidising child care and offering flexible hours to those with family responsibilities.

They also operate in a world experiencing changes equal to those facing Owen. In the newer industrial countries of Eastern Europe and Asia the transition is again from agriculture to industry. Everywhere the internet is enabling people to organise economic activity in new ways, equivalent to the industrial revolution of which Owen was part. Sustainability is now on the agendas of most management teams, as is the move to a more connected international economy.

In coping with such changes, managers, such as Owen before them, search for ways to manage their enterprises to add value. They make assumptions about the best way to do things – and through trial and error develop methods for their circumstances. Managers today can build on these methods when deciding how to deal with their problems. No single approach will suit all conditions – managers need to draw critically and selectively on several perspectives.

The next section introduces the idea of management models, and why they are useful. Section 2.3 presents the competing values framework – a way of seeing the contrasts and complementarities between four theoretical perspectives – and the following sections outline the major ideas within each approach. The final section indicates some of the issues facing managers today – and new models that may represent these conditions.

2.2   Why study models of management?

A **model (or theory)** represents a complex phenomenon by identifying the major elements and relationships.

A **model (or theory)** represents a more complex reality. Focusing on the essential elements and their relationship helps to understand that complexity, and how change may affect it. Most management problems can only be understood by examining them from several perspectives, so no model offers a complete solution. Those managing a globally competitive business require flexibility, quality and low-cost production. Managers at Ford or Daimler-Chrysler want models of the production process that help them to organise it efficiently from a technical perspective. They also want models of human behaviour that will help them to organise production in a way that encourages enthusiasm and commitment. The management task is to combine both approaches into an acceptable solution.

Managers act in accordance with their model (or theory) of the task. To understand management action we need to know the models available and how people use them, although Pfeffer and Sutton (2006) suggest why people frequently ignore such evidence: see Key Ideas.

Key ideas	Pfeffer and Sutton on why managers ignore evidence

In a paper making the case for evidence-based management Pfeffer and Sutton (2006) observe that experienced managers frequently ignore new evidence relevant to a decision and suggest that they:

- trust personal experience more than they trust research;
- prefer to use a method or solution which has worked before;
- are susceptible to consultants who vigorously promote their solutions;
- rely on dogma and myth – even when there is no evidence to support their value;
- uncritically imitate practices that appear to have worked well for famous companies.

Their paper outlines the benefits of basing practice on sound evidence – similar to the ideas of critical thinking presented in Chapter 1.

Source: Pfeffer and Sutton (2006).

Models identify the variables

Models (theories) aim to identify the main variables in a situation, and the relationships between them: the more accurately they do so, the more useful they are. Since every situation is unique, many experienced managers doubt the value of theory. Magretta's answer is that:

> without a theory of some sort it's hard to make sense of what's happening in the world around you. If you want to know whether you work for a well-managed organization – as opposed to whether you like your boss – you need a working theory of management. (Magretta, 2002, p. 10)

We all use theory, acting on (perhaps implicit) assumptions about the relationships between cause and effect. Good theories help to identify variables and relationships, providing a mental toolkit to deal consciously with a situation. The perspective we take reflects the assumptions we use to interpret, organise and makes sense of events – see Alan Fox in Key Ideas.

Key ideas	Alan Fox and a manager's frame of reference

Alan Fox (1974) distinguished between unitary, pluralist or radical perspectives on the relationship between managers and employees. Which assumption a person holds affects how they interpret the tasks of managing. Fox argued that those who take a:

- **unitary perspective** believe that organisations aim to develop rational ways of achieving common interests. Managerial work arises from a technical division of labour, and managers work to achieve objectives shared by all members.
- **pluralist perspective** believe that the complex division of labour in modern organisations creates groups with distinctive interests. Some conflict over ends and/or means is inevitable, and managerial work involves gaining sufficient consent to meet all interests in some mutually acceptable way.
- **radical perspective** challenge both unitary and pluralist models, arguing that they ignore the fact that the horizontal and vertical division of labour sustains unequal social relations within capitalist society. As long as these exist managers and employees will be in conflict.

Source: Fox (1974).

As managers influence others to add value they use their mental model of the situation to decide where to focus effort. Figure 2.1 develops Figure 1.3 (the internal context within which managers work) to show some variables within each element: 'structure' could include more specific variables such as roles, teams or control systems. In 2010 Willie Walsh, Chief Executive

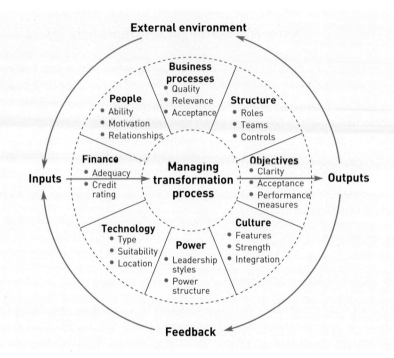

Figure 2.1
Some variables
within the internal
context of
management

of British Airways, was continuing with one of his objectives (set by his predecessor) to raise operating profits to 10 per cent of sales. Figure 2.1 suggests ways of meeting this:

- *objectives* – retaining a reputation for premium travel (a different market than Ryanair);
- *people* – continuing to reduce the number of employees;
- *technology* – reducing capacity at London City Airport, and focusing more flights on Terminal 5 at Heathrow;
- *business processes* – negotiating new working practices with cabin staff.

In each area there are theories about the variables and their relationships – and about which changes will best add value. A change in one element affects others – reducing staff risks hindering the aim of providing a premium service. Any change would depend on available *finance* – and on the chief executive's *power* to get things done. External events (Chapter 3) such as rising fuel prices or changes in economic conditions shape all of these.

Managers need to influence people to add value: people who are aware, thinking beings, with unique experiences, interests and objectives. This affects what information they attend to, the significance they attach to it and how they act. There is an example in Chapter 3 of a retail business in which senior managers, store managers and shop-floor staff attached different meanings to the culture in which they worked. People interpret information subjectively, which makes it hard to predict how they will react: the following MIP feature illustrates two managers' contrasting assumptions about how to deal with subordinates.

| Management in practice | Practice reflects managers' theories |

These examples illustrate contrasting theories about motivation.

Motivating managers: Tim O'Toole, who became Chief Executive of London Underground in 2003, put in a new management structure, appointing a general manager for each line to improve accountability.

> Now there's a human being who is judged on how that line is performing and I want them to feel that kind of intense anxiety in the stomach that comes when there's a stalled train and they realise that it's their stalled train.

Source: From an article by Simon London, *Financial Times*, 20 February 2004.

Supporting staff: John Timpson, Chairman of the shoe repair and key cutting chain, believes the most important people in the company are those who cut customers' keys and re-heel their shoes:

> You come back for the service you get from the people in the shops. They are the stars . . . we need to do everything to help them to look after you as well as possible. [A bonus based on shop takings] is fundamental to the service culture I want. It creates the adrenalin. That is the reason why people are keen to serve you if you go into one of our shops. And why they don't take long lunch breaks.

Source: *Financial Times*, 3 August 2006.

Case questions 2.2

- Give examples of the variables in Figure 2.1 which Robert Owen was attempting to influence?
- Which of the variables were influencing the performance of his mill?
- Is there a conflict between the need to control workers and Owen's creative approach to management?

Models reflect their context

People look for models to deal with the most pressing issues they face. In the nineteenth century, skilled labour was scarce and unskilled labour plentiful: managers were hiring workers unfamiliar with factories to meet growing demand, so wanted ideas on how to produce more efficiently. They looked for ways to simplify tasks so that they could use less-skilled employees, and early management theories gave priority to these issues. People often refer to this focus on efficiency as a manufacturing mindset.

Peter Drucker (1954) observed that customers do not buy products, but the satisfaction of needs: what they value may be different from what producers think they are selling. Manufacturing efficiency is necessary but not sufficient. Managers, Drucker argued, should develop a marketing mindset, focused on what customers want and how much they will pay. Now, as managers try to meet changing customer needs quickly and cheaply, they seek models of flexible working. As business becomes more global, they seek theories about managing across the world.

A **metaphor** is an image used to signify the essential characteristics of a phenomenon.

Key ideas	Gareth Morgan's images of organisation

Since organisations are complex creations, no single theory can explain them adequately. We need to see them from several viewpoints, each of which will illuminate one aspect or feature – while also obscuring others. Gareth Morgan (1997) shows how alternative mental images and **metaphors** can represent organisations. Metaphors are a way of thinking about a phenomenon, attaching labels which vividly indicate the image being used. Images help understanding – but also obscure or distort understanding if we use the wrong image. Morgan explores eight ways of seeing organisations as:

- **Machines** – mechanical thinking and the rise of the bureaucracies.
- **Organisms** – recognising how the environment affects their health.
- **Brains** – an information-processing, learning perspective.
- **Cultures** – a focus on beliefs and values.
- **Political systems** – a view on conflicts and power.
- **Psychic prisons** – how people can become trapped by habitual ways of thinking.
- **Flux and transformation** – a focus on change and renewal.
- **Instruments of domination** – over members, nations and environments.

Critical thinking helps improve our mental models

The ideas on critical thinking in Chapter 1 suggest that working effectively depends on being able and willing to test the validity of any theory, and to revise it in the light of experience by:

- identifying and challenging assumptions;
- recognising the importance of context;
- imagining and exploring alternatives;
- seeing limitations.

As you work through this chapter, there will be opportunities to practise these components of critical thinking.

2.3   The competing values framework

Quinn *et al.* (2003) believe that successive models of management (which they group according to four underlying philosophies – 'rational goal', 'internal process', 'human relations' and 'open systems') complement, rather than contradict, each other. They are all:

> symptoms of a larger problem – the need to achieve organizational effectiveness in a highly dynamic environment. In such a complex and fast-changing world, simple solutions become suspect . . . Sometimes we needed stability, sometimes we needed change. Often we needed both at the same time. (p. 11)

While each adds to our knowledge, none is sufficient. The 'competing values' framework integrates them by highlighting their underlying values – see Figure 2.2.

The vertical axis represents the tension between flexibility and control. Managers seek flexibility to cope with rapid change. Others try to increase control – apparently the opposite of flexibility. The horizontal axis distinguishes an internal focus from an external one. Some managers focus on internal issues, while others focus on the world outside. Successive models of management relate to the four segments.

The labels within the circle indicate the criteria of effectiveness which are the focus of models in that segment, shown around the outside. The human relations model, upper left in the figure, stresses the human criteria of commitment, participation and openness. The open systems model (upper right) stresses criteria of innovation, adaptation and growth. The rational goal model in the lower right focuses on productivity, direction and goal clarity. The internal process model stresses stability, documentation and control, within a hierarchical structure. Finally, the outer ring indicates the values associated with each model – the dominant value in the rational goal model is that of maximising output, while in human relations it is developing people. Successive sections of the chapter outline theories associated with each segment.

Management in practice   **Competing values at IMI?** www.imiplc.com

When Martin Lamb took control of IMI (a UK engineering group which in 2010 employed 14,000 staff in 30 countries) he introduced significant changes to make the company profitable. He decided to concentrate the business on five sectors of engineering, each associated with high-value products and a strong chance of growth in the next few years. He moved much of the manufacturing to low-cost countries, encouraged close links with key customers and aimed to boost innovation. Mr Lamb says:

> This is a fundamental transition, aimed at moving IMI away from an old-established manufacturing enterprise to a company focused on product development and applications of knowledge.

Someone who knew the company well commented:

I always had the feeling . . . that IMI was a bit introverted and anything that (makes) the company more aggressive on the sales side is to be applauded.

The IMI Academy is a forum within which Key Account Managers (staff responsible for major customers) develop their skills of managing customer relationships within an entrepreneurial, customer-focused culture. It includes cross-company courses and web-based discussions, enabling staff to share knowledge, strategy and tactics.

Source: Extracts from an article in *Financial Times*, 4 February 2004; company website.

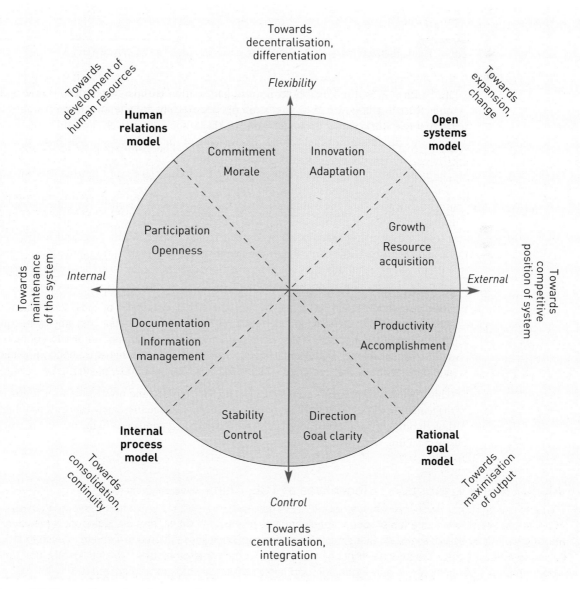

Figure 2.2 Competing values framework

Source: Quinn *et al*. (2003), p. 13.

Activity 2.1   Critical reflection on the model

Using the model to reflect on IMI:

- Which of the competing values would probably have been dominant in the company ten years ago, and which is dominant now?
- What practices can you find in the case which correspond to the Open Systems model?

Using the model to reflect on your organisation:

- Which of the competing values are most dominant in, say, three separate departments?
- What evidence can you find of how that affects the way people manage?
- Does your evidence support or contradict the model?

2.4   Rational goal models

Adam Smith (1776), the Scottish economist, had written enthusiastically about how a pin manufacturer in Glasgow had broken a job previously done by one man into several small steps. A single worker now performed one of these steps repetitively, and this greatly increased the output. Smith believed that this was one of the main ways in which the new industrial system was increasing the wealth of the country.

The availability of powered machinery during the Industrial Revolution enabled business owners to transform manufacturing and mining processes. These technical innovations encouraged, but were not the only reason for, the growth of the factory system. The earlier 'putting-out' system of manufacture, in which people worked at home on materials supplied and collected by entrepreneurs, allowed great freedom over hours, pace and methods of work, and agents had little control over the quantity and quality of output. Emerging capitalist entrepreneurs found that they could secure more control if they brought workers together in a factory. Having all workers on a single site meant that:

> coercive authority could be more easily applied, including systems of fines, supervision . . . the paraphernalia of bells and clocks, and incentive payments. The employer could dictate the general conditions of work, time and space; including the division of labour, overall organisational layout and design, rules governing movement, shouting, singing and other forms of disobedience. (Thompson and McHugh, 2002, p. 22)

This still left entrepreneurs across Europe and later the US (and now China – see following Management in Practice) with the problem of how to manage these new factories profitably. Although domestic and export demand for manufactured goods was high, so was the risk of business failure.

Management in practice   Incentives at TCL, China www.tcl.com

TCL Corporation is one of the top producers of electronics products in China, and management is proud of the long hours that employees work. Signs posted next to production lines encourage workers to push themselves to do even more. 'If you don't diligently work today', one warns ominously, 'you'll diligently look for work tomorrow.' The company is growing rapidly and has won many awards for design and quality.

Source: Based on 'Bursting out of China', *Business Week*, 17 November 2003, pp. 24–25; company website.

Key ideas	Charles Babbage

Charles Babbage supported and developed Adam Smith's observations. He was an English mathematician better known as the inventor of the first calculating engine. During his work on that project he visited many workshops and factories in England and on the Continent. He then published his reflections on 'the many curious processes and interesting facts' that had come to his attention (Babbage, 1835). He believed that 'perhaps the most important principle on which the economy of a manufacture depends is the division of labour amongst the persons who perform the work' (p. 169).

Babbage also observed that employers in the mining industry had applied the idea to what he called 'mental labour'. 'Great improvements have resulted . . . from the judicious distribution of duties . . . amongst those responsible for the whole system of the mine and its government' (p. 202). He also recommended that managers should know the precise expense of every stage in production. Factories should also be large enough to secure the economies made possible by the division of labour and the new machinery.

Source: Babbage (1835).

Frederick Taylor

The fullest answer to the problems of factory organisation came in the work of Frederick W. Taylor (1856–1915), always associated with the ideas of **scientific management**. An American mechanical engineer, Taylor focused on the relationship between the worker and the machine-based production systems that were in widespread use:

> the principal object of management should be to secure the maximum prosperity for the employer, coupled with the maximum prosperity for each employee. The words 'maximum prosperity' . . . mean the development of every branch of the business to its highest state of excellence, so that the prosperity may be permanent. (Taylor, 1917, p. 9)

Scientific management: the school of management called 'scientific' attempted to create a science of factory production.

He believed that the way to achieve this was to ensure that all workers reached their state of maximum efficiency, so that each was doing 'the highest grade of work for which his natural abilities fit him' (p. 9). This would follow from detailed control of the process, which would become the managers' primary responsibility: they should concentrate on understanding the production systems, and use this to specify every aspect of the operation. In terms of Morgan's images, the appropriate image would be the machine. Taylor advocated five principles:

- use scientific methods to determine the one best way of doing a task, rather than rely on the older 'rule of thumb' methods;
- select the best person to do the job so defined, ensuring that their physical and mental qualities were appropriate for the task;
- train, teach and develop the worker to follow the defined procedures precisely;
- provide financial incentives to ensure people work to the prescribed method; and
- move responsibility for planning and organising from the worker to the manager.

Taylor's underlying philosophy was that scientific analysis and fact, not guesswork, should inform management. Like Smith and Babbage before him, he believed that efficiency rose if tasks were routine and predictable. He advocated techniques such as time and motion studies, standardised tools and individual incentives. Breaking work into small, specific tasks would increase control. Specialist managerial staff would design these tasks and organise the workers:

> The work of every workman is fully planned out by the management at least one day in advance, and each man receives in most cases complete written instructions, describing in detail the task which he is to accomplish, as well as the means to be used in doing the work . . . This task specifies not only what is to be done but how it is to be done and the exact time allowed for doing it. (Taylor, 1917, p. 39)

Taylor also influenced the development of administrative systems such as record keeping and stock control to support manufacturing.

Management in practice	Using work study in the 1990s

Oswald Jones recalls his experience as a work study engineer in the 1990s, where he and his colleagues were deeply committed to the principles of scientific management:

> Jobs were designed to be done in a mechanical fashion by removing opportunities for worker discretion. This had dual benefits: very simple jobs could be measured accurately (so causing less disputes) and meant that operators were much more interchangeable which was an important feature in improving overall efficiency levels. (Jones, 2000, p. 647)

Managers in industrialised economies adopted Taylor's ideas widely: Henry Ford was an enthusiastic advocate. When he introduced the assembly line in 1914, the time taken to assemble a car fell from over 700 hours to 93 minutes. Ford also developed systems of materials flow and plant layout, a significant contribution to scientific management (Biggs, 1996; Williams *et al.*, 1992).

Increased productivity often came at human cost (Thompson and McHugh, 2002). Trade unions believed that Taylor's methods increased unemployment, and vigorously opposed them. Many people find that work on an assembly line is boring and alienating, devoid of much meaning. In extreme cases, the time taken to complete an operation is less than a minute, and uses few human abilities.

Management in practice	Ford's Highland Park plant

Ford's plant at Highland Park, completed in 1914, introduced predictability and order 'that eliminates all questions of how work is to be done, who will do it, and when it will be done. The rational factory, then, is a factory that runs like a machine' (Biggs, 1996, p. 6). Biggs provides abundant evidence of the effects of applying rational production methods:

> The advances made in Ford's New Shop allowed the engineers to control work better. The most obvious and startling change in the entire factory was, of course, the constant movement, and the speed of that movement, not only the speed of the assembly line, but the speed of every moving person or object in the plant. When workers moved from one place to another, they were instructed to move fast. Laborers who moved parts were ordered to go faster. And everyone on a moving line worked as fast as the line dictated. Not only were workers expected to produce at a certain rate in order to earn a day's wages but they also had no choice but to work at the pace dictated by the machine. By 1914 the company employed supervisors called pushers (not the materials handlers) to 'push' the men to work faster.
>
> The 1914 jobs of most Ford workers bore little resemblance to what they had been just four years earlier, and few liked the transformation. . . . As early as 1912, job restructuring sought an 'exceptionally specialized division of labor [to bring] the human element into [the] condition of performing automatically with machine-like regularity and speed'. (Biggs, 1996, p. 132)

Frank and Lillian Gilbreth

Frank and Lillian Gilbreth (1868–1924 and 1878–1972) worked as a husband and wife team, and were advocates for scientific management. Frank Gilbreth had been a bricklayer, and knew why work was slow and output unpredictable. He filmed men laying bricks and used this to set out the most economical movements for each task. He specified exactly what the employer should provide, such as trestles at the right height and materials at the right time. Supplies of mortar and bricks (arranged the right way up) should arrive at a time that did not interrupt work. An influential book (Gilbreth, 1911) gave precise guidance on how to reduce unnecessary actions (from 18 to 5) and hence fatigue. The rules and charts would help apprentices:

> [They] will enable the apprentice to earn large wages immediately, because he has . . . a series of instructions that show each and every motion in the proper sequence. They eliminate the 'wrong' way [and] all experimenting. (Quoted in Spriegel and Myers, 1953, p. 57)

Lillian Gilbreth focused on the psychological aspects of management, and on the welfare of workers. She also advocated scientific management, believing that, properly applied, it would enable individuals to reach their full potential. Through careful development of systems, careful selection, clearly planned training and proper equipment, workers would build their self-respect and pride. In *The Psychology of Management* (1914) she argued that if workers did something well, and that was made public, they would develop pride in their work and in themselves. She believed workers had enquiring minds, and that management should explain the reasons for work processes:

> Unless the man knows why he is doing the thing, his judgment will never reinforce his work . . . His work will not enlist his zeal unless he knows exactly why he is made to work in the particular manner prescribed. (Quoted in Spriegel and Myers, 1953, p. 431)

Activity 2.2   **What assumptions did they make?**

What assumptions did Frederick Taylor and Lillian Gilbreth make about the interests and abilities of industrial workers?

Operational research

Another practice within the rational goal model is **operational research** (OR). This originated in the early 1940s, when the UK War Department faced severe management problems – such as the most effective distribution of radar-linked anti-aircraft gun emplacements, or the safest speed at which convoys of merchant ships should cross the Atlantic (see Kirby (2003) for a non-technical introduction to the topic). To solve these it formed operational research teams, which pooled the expertise of scientific disciplines such as mathematics and physics. These produced significant results: Kirby points out that while at the start of the London Blitz 20,000 rounds of ammunition were fired for each enemy aircraft destroyed:

Operational research is a scientific method of providing (managers) with a quantitative basis for decisions regarding the operations under their control.

> by the summer of 1941 the number had fallen . . . to 4,000 as a result of the operational research (teams) improving the accuracy of radar-based gun-laying. (Kirby 2003, p. 94)

After the war, managers in industry and government saw that operational research techniques could also help to run complex civil organisations. The scale and complexity of business were increasing, and required new techniques to analyse the many interrelated variables. Mathematical models could help, and computing developments supported increasingly sophisticated models. In the 1950s, the steel industry needed to cut the cost of transporting iron ore: staff used OR techniques to analyse the most efficient procedures for shipping, unloading and transferring it to steelworks.

The method is widely used in both business and public sectors, where it helps planning in areas as diverse as maintenance, cash flow, inventory and staff scheduling in call centres (e.g. Taylor, 2008). Willoughby and Zappe (2006) illustrate how a university used OR techniques to help allocate students to seminar groups.

Table 2.1 Modern applications of the rational goal model

Principles of the rational goal model	Current applications
Systematic work methods	Work study and process engineering departments develop precise specifications for processes
Detailed division of labour	Where staff focus on one type of work or customer in manufacturing or service operations
Centralised planning and control	Modern information systems increase the scope for central control of worldwide operations
Low-involvement employment relationship	Using temporary staff as required, rather than permanent employees

OR cannot take into account human and social uncertainties, and the assumptions built into the models may be invalid, especially if they involve political interests. The technique clearly contributes to the analysis of management problems, but it is only part of the solution.

Current status

Table 2.1 summarises principles common to rational goal models and their modern application.

Examples of aspects of the rational goal approaches are common in manufacturing and service organisations – but note that companies will often use only one of the principles that suits their business. The following Management in Practice feature gives an example from a very successful service business with highly committed and involved members of staff – which wishes to give the same high-quality experience wherever the customer is. It uses the principle of systematic work methods to achieve this.

Management in practice   **Making a sandwich at Pret a Manger** www.pret.com

It is very important to make sure the same standards are adhered to in every single shop, whether you're in Crown Passage in London, Sauchiehall Street in Glasgow, or in New York. The way we do that is by very, very detailed training. So, for example, how to make an egg mayonnaise sandwich is all written down on a card that has to be followed, and that is absolutely non-negotiable. When somebody joins Pret they have a 10-day training plan, and on every single day there is a list of things that they have to be shown, from how to spread the filling of a sandwich right to the edges (that is key to us), how to cut a sandwich from corner to corner, how to make sure that the sandwiches look great in the box and on the shelves. So every single detail is covered on a 10-day training plan. At the end of that 10-days the new team member has to pass a quiz, it's called the big scary quiz, it is quite big and it is quite scary, and they have to achieve 90 per cent on that in order to progress.

Source: Interview with a senior manager at the company.

Case questions 2.3

- Which of the ideas in the rational goal model was Owen experimenting with at New Lanark?
- Would you describe Owen's approach to management as low involvement?
- What assumptions did he make about the motivation of workers?

The methods are also widely used in the mass production industries of newly industri- alised economies such as China and Malaysia. Gamble *et al.* (2004) found that in such plants:

> Work organization tended to be fragmented (on Taylorist lines) and routinised, with con- siderable surveillance and control over production volumes and quality. (p. 403)

Human resource management policies were consistent with this approach – the recruit- ment of operators in Chinese electronics plants was:

> often of young workers, generally female and from rural areas. One firm said its operators had to be 'young farmers within cycling distance of the factory, with good eyesight. Edu- cation is not important'. (p. 404)

Activity 2.3   Finding current examples

Try to find an original example of work that has been designed on rational goal prin- ciples. There are examples in office and service areas as well as in factories. Compare your examples with those of colleagues.

2.5   Internal process models

Max Weber

Max Weber (1864–1920) was a German social historian who drew attention to the significance of large organisations, noting that, as societies became more complex, they concentrated responsibility for core activities in large specialised units. These government departments and large industrial or transport businesses were hard to manage, a difficulty which those in charge overcame by creating systems ('institutionalising the management process') – rules and regulations, hierarchy, precise division of labour and detailed procedures. Weber observed that **bureaucracy** brought routine to office operations just as machines had to production.

Bureaucratic management has the characteristics shown in the following Key Ideas box.

Bureaucracy is a system in which people are expected to follow precisely defined rules and procedures rather than to use personal judgement.

Key ideas   The characteristics of bureaucratic management

- **Rules and regulations:** the formal guidelines that define and control the behaviour of employees. Follow- ing these ensures uniform procedures and operations, regardless of an individual's wishes. They enable top managers to co-ordinate middle managers and, through them, first-line managers and employees. Managers leave, so rules bring stability.
- **Impersonality:** rules lead to impersonality, which protects employees from the whims of managers. Although the term has negative connotations, Weber believed it ensured fairness, by evaluating subordinates objec- tively on performance rather than subjectively on personal considerations. It limits favouritism.
- **Division of labour:** managers and employees work on specialised tasks, with the benefits originally noted by Adam Smith – such as that jobs are relatively easy to learn and control.
- **Hierarchical structure:** Weber advocated a clear hierarchy in which jobs were ranked vertically by the amount of authority to make decisions. Each lower position is under the control of a higher position.
- **Authority structure:** a system of rules, impersonality, division of labour and hierarchy forms an authority structure – the right to make decisions of varying importance at different levels within the organisation.
- **Rationality:** this refers to using the most efficient means to achieve objectives. Managers should run their organisations logically and 'scientifically' so that all decisions help to achieve the objectives.

Activity 2.4   Bureaucratic management in education?

Reflect on your role as a student and how rules have affected the experience. Try to identify one example of your own to add to those below or that illustrates the point specifically within your institution:

- Rules and regulations – the number of courses you need to pass for a degree.
- Impersonality – admission criteria, emphasising previous exam performance, not friendship.
- Division of labour – chemists not teaching management and vice versa.
- Hierarchical structure – to whom your lecturer reports and to whom they report.
- Authority structure – who decides whether to recruit an additional lecturer.
- Rationality – appointing new staff to departments that have the highest ratio of students to staff.

Compare your examples with those of other students and consider the effects of these features of bureaucracy on the institution and its students.

Weber was aware that, as well as creating bureaucratic structures, managers were using scientific management techniques to control production and impose discipline on factory work. The two systems complemented each other. Formal structures of management centralise power, while hierarchical organisation aids functional specialisation. Fragmenting tasks, imposing close discipline on employees and minimising their discretion ensures controlled, predictable performance (Thompson and McHugh, 2002).

Weber stressed the importance of a career structure clearly linked to a person's position. This allowed him/her to move up the hierarchy in a predictable and open way, which would increase his/her commitment to the organisation. Rules about selection and promotion brought fairness at a time when favouritism was common. Weber also believed that officials should work within a framework of rules. The right to give instructions was based on a person's position in the hierarchy, and a rational analysis of how staff should work. This worked well in large public and private organisations, such as government departments and banks.

While recognising the material benefits of these methods, Weber saw their costs:

> Bureaucratic rationalization instigates a system of control that traps the individual within an 'iron cage' of subjugation and constraint . . . For Weber, it is instrumental rationality, accompanied by the rise of measurement and quantification, regulations and procedures, accounting, efficiency that entraps us all in a world of ever-increasing material standards, but vanishing magic, fantasy, meaning and emotion. (Gabriel, 2005, p. 11)

Activity 2.5   Gathering evidence on bureaucracy

Rules often receive bad publicity, and we are all sometimes frustrated by rules that seem obstructive. To evaluate bureaucracy, collect some evidence. Think of a job that you or a friend has held, or of the place in which you work.

- Do the supervisors appear to operate within a framework of rules, or do they do as they wish? What are the effects?
- Do clear rules guide selection and promotion procedures? What are the effects?
- As a customer of an organisation, how have rules and regulations affected your experience?
- Check what you have found, preferably combining it with that prepared by other people on your course. Does the evidence support the advantages, or the disadvantages, of bureaucracy?

Henri Fayol

Managers were also able to draw on the ideas of **administrative management** developed by Henri Fayol (1841–1925). While Taylor focused on production systems, Fayol devised management principles that would apply to the whole organisation. Like Taylor, Fayol was an engineer, who in 1860 joined Commentry–Fourchambault–Decazeville, a coal mining and iron foundry company combine. He rose rapidly through the company and became managing director in 1888 (Parker and Ritson, 2005). When he retired in 1918 it was one of the success stories of French industry. Throughout his career he kept detailed diaries and notes, which in retirement he used to stimulate debate about management in both private and public sectors. His book *Administration, industrielle et générale* became available in English in 1949 (Fayol, 1949).

> **Administrative management** is the use of institutions and order rather than relying on personal qualities to get things done.

Fayol credited his success to the methods he used, not to his personal qualities. He believed that managers should use certain principles in their work – listed in the following Key Ideas box. The term 'principles' did not imply they were rigid or absolute:

> It is all a question of proportion . . . allowance must be made for different changing circumstances . . . the principles are flexible and capable of adaptation to every need; it is a matter of knowing how to make use of them, which is a difficult art requiring intelligence, experience, decision and proportion. (Fayol, 1949, p. 14)

In using terms such as 'changing circumstances' and 'adaptation to every need' in setting out the principles, Fayol anticipated the contingency theories which were developed in the 1960s (see Chapter 10). He was also an early advocate of management education:

> Elementary in the primary schools, somewhat wider in the post-primary schools, and quite advanced in higher education establishments. (Fayol, 1949, p. 16)

Key ideas   Fayol's principles of management

1. **Division of work:** if people specialise, they improve their skill and accuracy, which increases output. However, 'it has its limits which experience teaches us may not be exceeded'.
2. **Authority and responsibility:** the right to give orders derived from a manager's official authority or his/her personal authority. 'Wherever authority is exercised, responsibility arises.'
3. **Discipline:** 'Essential for the smooth running of business . . . without discipline no enterprise could prosper.'
4. **Unity of command:** 'For any action whatsoever, an employee should receive orders from one superior only' – to avoid conflicting instructions and resulting confusion.
5. **Unity of direction:** 'One head and one plan for a group of activities having the same objective . . . essential to unity of action, co-ordination of strength and focusing of effort.'
6. **Subordination of individual interest to general interest:** 'The interests of one employee or group of employees should not prevail over that of the concern.'
7. **Remuneration of personnel:** 'Should be fair and, as far as possible, afford satisfaction both to personnel and firm.'
8. **Centralisation:** 'The question of centralisation or decentralisation is a simple question of proportion . . . [the] share of initiative to be left to [subordinates] depends on the character of the manager, the reliability of the subordinates and the condition of the business. The degree of centralisation must vary according to different cases.'
9. **Scalar chain:** 'The chain of superiors from the ultimate authority to the lowest ranks . . . is at times disastrously lengthy in large concerns, especially governmental ones.' If a speedy decision were needed, it was appropriate for people at the same level of the chain to communicate directly. 'It provides for the usual exercise of some measure of initiative at all levels of authority.'
10. **Order:** materials should be in the right place to avoid loss, and the posts essential for the smooth running of the business filled by capable people.

11 **Equity:** managers should be both friendly and fair to their subordinates – 'equity requires much good sense, experience and good nature'.

12 **Stability of tenure of personnel:** a high employee turnover is not efficient – 'Instability of tenure is at one and the same time cause and effect of bad running.'

13 **Initiative:** 'The initiative of all represents a great source of strength for businesses . . . and . . . it is essential to encourage and develop this capacity to the full. The manager must be able to sacrifice some personal vanity in order to grant this satisfaction to subordinates . . . a manager able to do so is infinitely superior to one who cannot.'

14 **Esprit de corps:** 'Harmony, union among the personnel of a concern is a great strength in that concern. Effort, then, should be made to establish it.' Fayol suggested doing so by avoiding sowing dissension among subordinates, and using verbal rather than written communication when appropriate.

Source: Fayol (1949).

Current status

Table 2.2 summarises some principles common to the internal process models of management and indicates their modern application.

'Bureaucracy' has had many critics, who believe that it stifles creativity, fosters dissatisfaction and hinders motivation. Others credit it with bringing fairness and certainty to the workplace, where it clarifies roles and responsibilities, makes work effective – and so helps motivation. Adler and Borys (1996) sought to reconcile this by distinguishing between bureaucracy which is:

- enabling – designed to enable employees to master their tasks; and that which is
- coercive – designed to force employees into effort and compliance.

Table 2.2 Modern applications of the internal process model

Some principles of the internal process model	Current applications
Rules and regulations	All organisations have these, covering areas such as expenditure, safety, recruitment and confidentiality
Impersonality	Appraisal processes based on objective criteria or team assessments, not personal preference
Division of labour	Setting narrow limits to employees' areas of responsibility – found in many organisations
Hierarchical structure	Most company organisation charts show managers in a hierarchy – with subordinates below them
Authority structure	Holders of a particular post have authority over matters relating to that post, but not over other matters
Centralisation	Organisations balance central control of (say) finance or online services with local control of (say) pricing or recruitment
Initiative	Current practice in many firms to increase the responsibility of operating staff
Rationality	Managers are expected to assess issues on the basis of evidence, not personal preference

They studied one aspect of bureaucracy – workflow formalisation (the extent to which an employee's tasks are governed by written rules, etc) – in companies such as Ford, Toyota and Xerox. They concluded that if employees helped to design and implement a procedure, it was likely that they would accept the new rules, and that these would help them to work effectively. This 'enabling bureaucracy' had a positive effect on motivation, while rules that were imposed by management (coercive bureaucracy) had a negative effect. There is a similar example in the W.L. Gore case in Part 5.

Bureaucratic methods are widely used (Walton, 2005) especially in the public sector, and in commercial businesses with geographically dispersed outlets – such as hotels, stores and banks. Customers expect a predictable service wherever they are, so management design centrally controlled procedures and manuals – how to recruit and train staff, what the premises must look like and how to treat customers. If managers work in situations that require a degree of change and innovation that even an enabling bureaucracy will have trouble delivering, they need other models.

2.6   Human relations models

In the early twentieth century, several writers such as Follett and Mayo recognised the limitations of the scientific management perspective as a complete answer.

Mary Parker Follett

Mary Parker Follett (1868–1933) graduated with distinction from Radcliffe College (now part of Harvard University) in 1898, having studied economics, law and philosophy. She took up social work and quickly acquired a reputation as an imaginative and effective professional. She realised the creativity of the group process, and the potential it offered for truly democratic government – which people themselves would have to create.

She advocated replacing bureaucratic institutions by networks in which people themselves analysed their problems and implemented their solutions. True democracy depended on tapping the potential of all members of society by enabling individuals to take part in groups organised to solve particular problems and accepting personal responsibility for the result. Such ideas are finding renewed relevance today in the work of institutions such as community action and tenants' groups.

Key ideas   Mary Parker Follett on groups

Follett saw the group as an intermediate institution between the solitary individual and the abstract society, and argued that it was through the institution of the group that people organised co-operative action. In 1926 she wrote:

> Early psychology was based on the study of the individual; early sociology was based on the study of society. But there is no such thing as the 'individual', there is no such thing as 'society'; there is only the group and the group-unit – the social individual. Social psychology must begin with an intensive study of the group, of the selective processes which go on within it, the differentiated reactions, the likenesses and the unlikenesses, and the spiritual energy which unites them.

Source: Graham (1995), p. 230.

In the 1920s, Follett became involved in the business world, when managers invited her to investigate business problems. She again advocated the self-governing principle that would facilitate the growth of individuals and the groups to which they belonged. Conflict was inevitable if people brought valuable differences of view to a problem: the group must then resolve the conflict to create what she called an integrative unity among the members.

She acknowledged that organisations had to optimise production, but did not accept that the strict division of labour was the right way to achieve this (Follett, 1920), as it devalued human creativity. The human side should not be separated from the mechanical side, as the two are bound together. She believed that people, whether managers or workers, behave as they do because of the reciprocal responses in their relationship. If managers tell people to behave as if they are extensions of a machine, they will do so. She implied that effective managers would not manipulate their subordinates, but train them to use power responsibly:

managers should give workers a chance to grow capacity or power for themselves.

Graham (1995) provides an excellent review of Follett's work.

Elton Mayo

Elton Mayo (1880–1949) was an Australian who taught logic, psychology and ethics at the University of Queensland. In 1922 he moved to the US, and in 1926 became Professor of Industrial Research at Harvard Business School, applying psychological methods to industrial conflict. He was an accomplished speaker, and his ideas were arousing wide interest in the academic and business communities (Smith, 1998).

In 1924 managers of the Western Electric Company initiated a series of experiments at their Hawthorne plant in Chicago to discover the effect on output of changing defined factors in the physical environment. The first experiments studied the effect of lighting. The researchers established a control and an experimental group, varied the level of illumination and measured the output. As light rose, so did output. More surprisingly, as light fell, output continued to rise: it also rose in the control group, where conditions had not changed. The team concluded that physical conditions had little effect and so set up a more comprehensive experiment to identify other factors.

They assembled a small number of workers in a separate room and altered variables in turn, including working hours, length of breaks and providing refreshments. The experienced workers were assembling small components to make telephone equipment. A supervisor was in charge and there was also an observer to record how workers reacted to the experiments. Great care was taken to prevent external factors disrupting the effects of the variables under investigation. The researchers were careful to explain what was happening and to ensure that the workers understood what they were expected to do. They also listened to employees' views of working conditions.

The researchers varied conditions every two or three weeks, while the supervisor measured output regularly. This showed a gradual, if erratic, increase – even when the researchers returned conditions to those prevailing at an earlier stage, as Figure 2.3 shows.

> **Activity 2.6   Explaining the trend**
>
> Describe the pattern shown in Figure 2.3. Compare in particular the output in periods 7, 10 and 13. Before reading on, how would you explain this?

In 1928 senior managers invited Mayo to present the research to a wider audience (Smith, 1998; Roethlisberger and Dickson, 1939; Mayo, 1949). They concluded from the relay-assembly test room experiments that the increase in output was not related to the physical changes, but to the change in the social situation of the group:

the major experimental change was introduced when those in charge sought to hold the situation humanly steady (in the interests of critical changes to be introduced) by getting

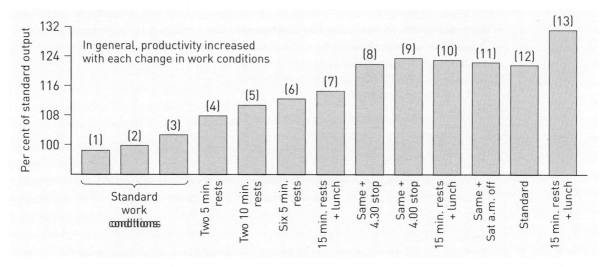

Figure 2.3 The relay assembly test room – average hourly output per week (as percentage of standard) in successive experimental periods

Source: After GREENBERG, JERALD; BARON, ROBERT A., *BEHAVIOR IN ORGANIZATIONS*, 6th Edition © 1997, p. 13. Reprinted by permission of Pearson Education, Inc., Upper Saddle River, NJ.

the co-operation of the workers. What actually happened was that 6 individuals became a team and the team gave itself wholeheartedly and spontaneously to co-operation in the environment. (Mayo, 1949, p. 64)

The group felt special: managers asked for their views, were involved with them, paid attention to them and they had the chance to influence some aspects of the work.

The research team also observed another part of the factory, the bank wiring room, which revealed a different aspect of group working. Workers here were paid according to a piece-rate system, in which management pays workers a set amount for each item, or piece, that they produce. Such schemes reflect the assumption that financial incentives will encourage staff to work. The researchers observed that employees regularly produced less than they could have done. They had developed a sense of a normal rate of output, and ensured that all adhered to this rate, believing that if they produced, and earned, too much, management would reduce the piece-rate. Group members exercised informal sanctions against colleagues who worked too hard (or too slowly), until they came into line. Members who did too much were known as 'rate-busters', while those who did too little were 'chisellers'. Anyone who told the supervisor about this was a 'squealer'. Sanctions included being 'binged' – tapped on the shoulder to let them know that what they were doing was wrong. Managers had little or no control over these groups, who appointed their leader.

Finally, the research team conducted an extensive interview programme. They began by asking employees about the working environment and how they felt about their job, and then some questions about their life in general. The responses showed that there were often close links between work and domestic life. Work affected people's wider life much more than had been expected, and domestic circumstances affected their feelings about work. This implied that supervisors needed to think of a subordinate as a complete person, not just as a worker.

Activity 2.7   **A comparison with Taylor**

Compare this evidence with Frederick Taylor's belief that piece-rates would be an incentive to individuals to raise their performance. What may explain the difference?

Mayo's reflections on the Hawthorne studies drew attention to aspects of human behaviour that practitioners of scientific management had neglected. He introduced the idea of 'social man', in contrast to the 'economic man' who was at the centre of earlier theories. While financial rewards would influence the latter, group relationships and loyalties would influence the former, and may outweigh management pressure.

On financial incentives, Mayo wrote:

> Man's desire to be continuously associated in work with his fellows is a strong, if not the strongest, human characteristic. Any disregard of it by management or any ill-advised attempt to defeat this human impulse leads instantly to some form of defeat for management itself. In [a study] the efficiency experts had assumed the primacy of financial incentive; in this they were wrong; not until the conditions of working group formation were satisfied did the financial incentives come into operation. (Mayo, 1949, p. 99)

People had social needs that they sought to satisfy – and how they did so may support management interests or oppose them.

Later analysis of the experimental data by Greenwood *et al.* (1983) suggested that the team had underestimated the influence of financial incentives. Becoming a member of the experimental group in itself increased the worker's income. Despite possible inaccurate interpretations, the findings stimulated interest in social factors in the workplace. Scientific management stressed the technical aspects of work. The Hawthorne studies implied that management should give at least as much attention to human factors, leading to the **human relations approach**. This advocates that employees will work more effectively if management shows some interest in their well-being, such as by having more humane supervision.

Human relations approach is a school of management which emphasises the importance of social processes at work.

> ### Key ideas · Peters and Waterman – *In Search of Excellence*
>
> In 1982 Peters and Waterman published their best-selling book *In Search of Excellence*. As management consultants with McKinsey & Co., they wanted to understand the success of what they regarded as 43 excellently managed US companies. One conclusion was that they had a distinctive set of philosophies about human nature and the way that people interact in organisations. They did not see people as rational beings, motivated by fear and willing to accept a low-involvement employment relationship. Instead, the excellent companies regarded people as emotional, intuitive and creative social beings who like to celebrate victories and value self-control – but who also need the security and meaning of achieving goals through organisations. From this, Peters and Waterman deduced some general rules for treating workers with dignity and respect, to ensure that people did quality work in an increasingly uncertain environment.
>
> Peters and Waterman had a significant influence on management thinking: they believed that management had relied too much on analytical techniques of the rational goal models, at the expense of more intuitive and human perspectives. They developed the ideas associated with the human relations models and introduced the idea of company culture – discussed in the next chapter.
>
> Source: Peters and Waterman (1982).

> ## Case questions 2.4
> - Which of the practices that Robert Owen used took account of workers' social needs?
> - Evaluate the extent to which he anticipated the conclusions of the Hawthorne experiments.

Current status

The Hawthorne studies have been controversial, and the interpretations questioned. Also, the idea of social man is itself now seen as an incomplete picture of people at work. Providing good supervision and decent working environments may increase satisfaction but not necessarily productivity. The influences on performance are certainly more complex than Taylor assumed – and also more complex than the additional factors that Mayo identified.

Other writers have followed and developed Mayo's emphasis on human factors. McGregor (1960), Maslow (1970) and Alderfer (1972) have suggested ways of integrating human needs with those of the organisation as expressed by management. Some of this reflected a human relations concern for employees' well-being. A much stronger influence was the changing external environments of organisations, which have become less predictable since the time of Taylor and Mayo. These changes encouraged scholars to develop open systems models.

| **2.7** | **Open systems models** |

The open systems approach builds on earlier work in general systems theory, and has been widely used to help understand management and organisational issues. The basic idea is to think of the organisation not as a **system**, but as an **open system**.

The open systems approach draws attention to the links between the internal parts of a system, and to the links between the whole system and the outside world. The system is separated from its environment by the **system boundary**. An open system imports resources such as energy and materials, which enter it from the environment across this boundary, undergo some transformation process within the system, and leave the system as goods and services. The central theme of the open systems view of management is that organisations depend on the wider environment for inputs if they are to survive and prosper. Figure 2.4 (based on Figure 1.1) is a simple model of the organisation as an open system.

The figure shows input and output processes, conversion processes and feedback loops. The organisation must satisfy those in the wider environment well enough to ensure that they continue to provide resources. The management task is to sustain those links if the organisation is to thrive. **Feedback** refers to information about the performance of the system. It may be deliberate, through customer surveys, or unplanned, such as the loss of business to a competitor. Feedback enables those managing the system to take remedial action.

A **system** is a set of interrelated parts designed to achieve a purpose.

An **open system** is one that interacts with its environment.

A **system boundary** separates the system from its environment.

Feedback (in systems theory) refers to the provision of information about the effects of an activity.

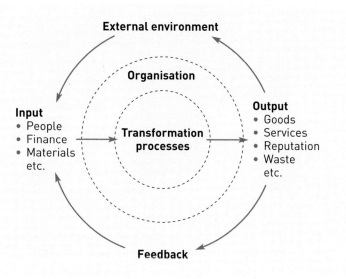

External environment

Organisation

Input
- People
- Finance
- Materials
etc.

Transformation processes

Output
- Goods
- Services
- Reputation
- Waste
etc.

Feedback

Figure 2.4
The systems model

Subsystems are the separate but related parts that make up the total system.

Another idea is that of **subsystems**. A course is a subsystem within a department or faculty, the faculty is a subsystem of a university, the university is a subsystem of the higher education system. This in turn is part of the whole education system. A course itself will consist of several systems – one for quality assurance, one for enrolling students, one for teaching, another for assessment and so on. In terms of Figure 2.1, each of the organisational elements is itself a subsystem – there is a technical subsystem, a people subsystem, a finance subsystem and so on, as Figure 2.5 shows.

These subsystems interact with each other, and how well people manage these links affects the functioning of the whole system: when a university significantly increases the number of students admitted to a popular course, this affects many parts of the system – such as accommodation (*technology*), teaching resources (*people*) and examinations (*business processes*).

A systems approach emphasises the links between systems, and reminds managers that a change in one will have consequences for others. For example, Danny Potter, Managing Director of Inamo (**www.inamo-restaurant.com**) a new London restaurant where customers place their order directly to the kitchen from an interactive ordering system on their table explains:

> I think the greatest challenge that we faced is communicating our ideas down through the business about what we're trying to achieve. There is a big overlap between essentially the computer software side and the actual restaurant side, to unite those in a way that people [new staff, suppliers, etc.] understand has proven rather tricky.

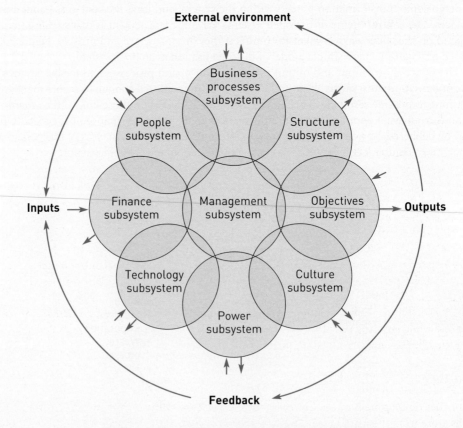

Figure 2.5
Interacting subsystems in organisations

→ = Input/output flow of materials, energy, information

Case study   Robert Owen – the case continues   www.newlanark.org.uk

Owen actively managed the links between his business and the wider world. On buying the mills he quickly became part of the Glasgow business establishment, and was closely involved in the activities of the Chamber of Commerce. He took a prominent role in the social and political life of the city. He used these links in particular to argue the case for reforms in the educational and economic systems, and was critical of the effect that industrialisation was having upon working-class life.

Owen believed that education in useful skills would help to release working-class children from poverty. He provided a nursery for workers' children over one-year old, allowing both parents to continue working, and promoted the case for wider educational provision. He also developed several experiments in co-operation and community building, believing that the basis of his successful capitalist enterprise at New Lanark (education, good working conditions and a harmonious community) could be applied to society as a whole.

These attempts to establish new communities (at New Harmony in Indiana, the US, and at Harmony in Hampshire, England) cost him a great deal of money, but soon failed (Royle, 1998), because of difficulties over admission, finance and management processes.

More broadly, he sought new ways of organising the economy to raise wages and protect jobs, at a time of severe business fluctuations. In 1815 he persuaded allies in Parliament to propose a bill making it illegal for children under the age of 10 to work in mills. It would also have limited their working hours to 10 a day. The measure met strong opposition from mill owners and a much weaker measure became law in 1819.

Sources: Butt (1971); Royle (1998).

Case questions 2.5

- Draw a systems diagram detailing the main inputs, transformation and outputs of Robert Owen's mill.

- What assumptions did Owen make about the difference between running a business and running a community?

Socio-technical systems

An important variant of systems theory is the idea of the **socio-technical system**. The approach developed from the work of Eric Trist and Ken Bamforth (1951) at the Tavistock Institute in London. Their most prominent study was of an attempt in the coal industry to mechanise the mining system. Introducing what were in essence assembly line technologies and methods at the coalface had severe consequences for the social system that the older pattern of working had encouraged. The technological system destroyed the social system, and the solution lay in reconciling the needs of both.

> A **socio-technical system** is one in which outcomes depend on the interaction of both the technical and social subsystems.

This and similar studies showed the benefits of seeing a work system as a combination of a material technology (tools, machinery, techniques) and a social organisation (people, relationships, constitutional arrangements). Figure 2.6 shows that an organisation has technical and social systems: it is a socio-technical system. Each affects the other, so people need to manage both.

A socio-technical analysis aims to integrate the social and technical components: optimising one while ignoring the other is likely to be unproductive. Cherns (1987) developed a set of principles for re-designing organisations on socio-technical principles.

Contingency management

A further development of the open systems view is the contingency approach (Chapter 10). This arose from the work of Woodward (1958) and Burns and Stalker (1961) in the UK, and of Lawrence and Lorsch (1967) in the US. The main theme is that to perform well managers must adapt the structure of the organisation to match external conditions.

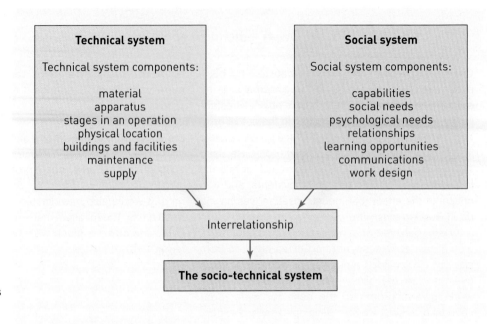

Figure 2.6
The organisation as
a socio-technical
system

The contingency approach implies that managers consciously look out for aspects of their environment which they need to take into account in shaping their organisation – see the Management in Practice feature.

Management in practice   **Hong Kong firms adapt to the environment in China**

Child *et al.* (2003) studied the experience of Hong Kong companies managing affiliated companies in China, predicting that successful firms would be those that adapted their management practices to suit those conditions. Because the business environment at the time was uncertain and difficult for foreign companies, they proposed that a key aspect of management practice in these circumstances would be the extent to which affiliated companies are controlled by, and integrated with, the parent company.

Their results supported this – in this transitional economy successful firms kept their mainland affiliates under close supervision, maintained frequent contact and allowed them little power to make decisions.

Source: Child *et al.* (2003).

As the environment becomes more complex, managers can use contingency perspectives to examine what structure best meets the needs of the business. Contingency theorists emphasise creating organisations that can cope with uncertainty and change, using the values of the open systems model: they also recognise that some functions need work in a stable and predictable way, using the values of the internal process model.

Complexity theory

A popular theme in management thinking is that of managing complexity, which arises from feedback between the parts of linked systems. People in organisations, both as individuals and as members of a web of working relationships, react to an event or an attempt to influence them. That reaction leads to a further response – setting off a complex feedback process. Figure 2.7 illustrates this for three individuals, X, Y and Z.

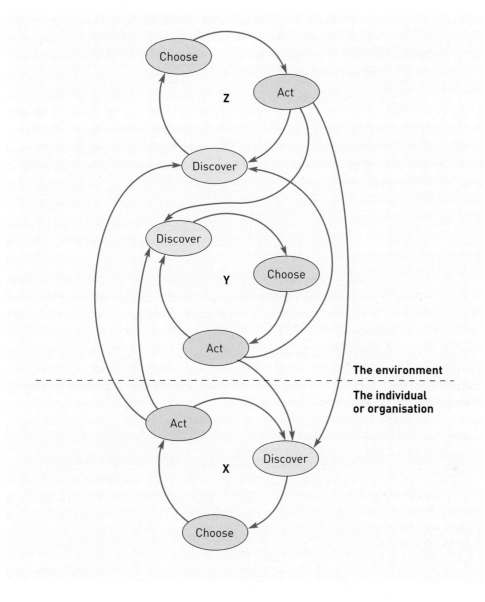

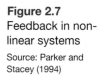

Figure 2.7
Feedback in non-
linear systems
Source: Parker and
Stacey (1994)

If we look at the situation in Figure 2.7 from the perspective of X, then X is in an environ-ment made up from Y and Z. X discovers what Y and Z are doing, chooses how to respond and then acts. That action has consequences for Y and Z, which they discover. This leads them to choose a response, which has consequences that X then discovers and acts on. This contin-ues indefinitely. Every act by X feeds back to have an impact on the next acts of Y and Z – and the same is true of Y and Z. Successive interactions create a feedback system – and the sequence shown for the individuals in the figure also occurs between organisations. These then make up complex systems:

> In contrast to simple systems, such as the pendulum, which have a small number of well-understood components, or complicated systems, such as a Boeing jet, which have many components that interact through predefined coordination rules . . . complex sys-tems typically have many components that can autonomously interact through emergent rules. (Amaral and Uzzi, 2007, p. 1033)

In management, complex systems arise whenever agents (people, organisations or communities) act on the (limited) information available to them without knowing how these actions may affect other (possibly distant) agents, nor how the action of those agents may affect them. There is no central control system to co-ordinate their actions, so the separate agents organise themselves spontaneously, creating new structures and new behaviours as they respond to themselves and their environment: in other words, they change themselves. **Complexity theory** tries to understand how these complex, changing (dynamic) systems learn and adapt from their internal experiences and from their interactions with similar systems.

Complexity theory is concerned with complex dynamic systems that have the capacity to organise themselves spontaneously.

These ideas on self-organising systems have implications for management, especially for how they cope with change and innovation (see Chapter 13). An example would be when senior managers in, say, a pharmaceutical firm such as GlaxoSmithKline or a technology company such as Apple create teams to work with a high degree of autonomy (to encourage creativity) on discrete parts of a larger project. The team members will work creatively within a network of informal contacts and exchanges relevant to their part of the task. These webs of human interactions lead to stable or unstable behaviour, and the skill is to balance these extremes. If an organisation is too stable it will stifle innovation, but if it is too unstable it will disintegrate:

> Successful organisations work between these two conditions. [In changing environments], rather than seeking to control their organisations to maintain equilibrium . . . [managers] need to embrace more flexible and adaptive models of change and innovation. (McMillan and Carlisle, 2007, p. 577)

Table 2.3 contrasts approaches to change suggested by traditional and complexity perspectives.

Non-linear systems are those in which small changes are amplified through many interactions with other variables so that the eventual effect is unpredictable.

This way of thinking about organisations sometimes uses the terms 'linear' and **'non-linear' systems**. 'Linear' describes a system in which an action leads to a predictable reaction. If you light a fire in a room, the thermostat will turn the central heating down. Non-linear systems are those in which outcomes are less predictable. If managers reduce prices they will be surprised if sales match the forecast – they cannot predict the reactions of competitors, changes in taste, or new products. Circumstances in the outside world change in ways that management cannot anticipate, so while short term consequences of an act are clear, long run ones are not.

Current status

Although theories of management develop at particular times in response to current problems, this does not mean that newer is better. While new concerns bring out new theories, old concerns usually remain. While recently developed ideas seek to encourage flexibility and change, some businesses, and some parts of highly flexible businesses, still require control. Rather than thinking of theoretical development as a linear process, see it as circular or iterative

Table 2.3 Traditional and complexity inspired approaches to change

Management practice	Traditional	Complexity inspired
Who initiates change?	Devised at the top	Emerges lower down
Who forms teams to plan and implement change?	Managers appoint members to formal teams	Teams form spontaneously, perhaps after call for volunteers
Who allocates roles?	Managers say who does what	Team members decide
Who sets out authority to act?	Managers empower members	Team empowers individuals
Who controls activities?	Managers either control directly or steer indirectly	Team acts within boundaries, influenced by management

Source: Based on McMillan and Carlisle (2007), p. 577.

Table 2.4 Summary of the models within the competing values framework

Features/model	Rational goal	Internal process	Human relations	Open systems
Main exponents	Taylor Frank and Lillian Gilbreth	Fayol Weber	Mayo Follett Barnard Peters and Waterman	Trist and Bamforth Woodward Burns and Stalker Lawrence and Lorsch Stacey and Parker
Criteria of effectiveness	Productivity, profit	Stability, continuity	Commitment, morale, cohesion	Adaptability, external support
Means/ends theory	Clear direction leads to productive outcomes	Routinisation leads to stability	Involvement leads to commitment	Continual innovation secures external support
Emphasis	Rational analysis, measurement	Defining responsibility, documentation	Participation, consensus building	Creative problem solving, innovation
Role of manager	Director and planner	Monitor and coordinator	Mentor and facilitator	Innovator and broker

in which familiar themes recur as new concerns arise. The competing values approach captures the main theoretical developments in one framework and shows the relationships between them – see Table 2.4.

The emerging management challenges come from many sources. One is the widely accepted need to develop a more sustainable economic system. Another is the need to balance innovation and creativity with closer governance and control, especially in financial services. Deregulation of many areas of activity is allowing new competitors to enter previously protected markets (airlines, financial services). Still another is the closer integration between many previously separate areas of business (telecommunications, consumer electronics and entertainment). There is also the growing internationalisation of business. Managers today look for radical solutions – just as Robert Owen did in the early days of the industrial revolution.

Case study   Robert Owen – the case continues www.newlanark.org.uk

The mills at New Lanark continued to operate after Owen's departure in 1825. Competition from new sources of supply meant that the mills eventually became unprofitable and they closed in 1968, threatening the survival of the village community. There had been little new building since Owen left, so the site (with its high mills and rows of workers' cottages) represented a time capsule of industrial and social history. The New Lanark Conservation Trust was created to restore it as a living community, and as a lasting monument to Owen and his philosophies.

Visitors can see the mills and examples of the machinery they contained, visit many of the communal buildings Owen created (such as the store which was the inspiration for the worldwide co-operative movement), and some of the workers housing. New Lanark is not just a tourist destination – it is a living community with most of the houses occupied by people who work elsewhere in the area.

Sources: Published sources and www.newlanark.org.uk

> ### 2.8   Integrating themes

Sustainable performance

Current attention to sustainability is an example of the values associated with the open systems model – a recognition, in this case, that human and natural systems interact with each other in complex and often unpredictable ways. Senge *et al.* (2008) present a valuable explanation of the idea that not only do businesses have a duty to society to act sustainably, but that it is in their business interest to do so. Reducing a company's carbon footprint not only reduces environmental damage but also reduces costs and makes the business more efficient. Renewable energy is not just better for the planet than fossil fuels – it may often be cheaper.

In 2002 General Electric began making alternative energy technologies (such as desalination systems) when oil was $25 a barrel. As oil prices have risen to several times that amount, the company is reaping large profits as demand for non-oil energy systems has risen sharply. Customers too played a role – the authors quote the GE chief executive:

> When society changes its mind, you better be in front of it and not behind it, and this is an issue on which society has changed its mind. As CEO, my job is to get out in front of it, or you're going to get ploughed under.

Governments and other institutions are developing policies to try to limit the damage that almost all scientists believe human activities are causing. This work tends to reflect values of order, regulation and control – values associated with the internal process model. Distinct sets of people are working on the same problem, sustainability, from two distinct perspectives: how they reconcile these two approaches will have significant effects on progress towards a more sustainable economy.

Governance and control

Theories of corporate governance, like those of management, continue to evolve in response to evidence that current arrangements are no longer suitable for the job. Much corporate governance focuses on protecting shareholders from potential fraud or dishonesty by senior managers, and that aspect is unlikely to diminish.

An additional theme is to consider whether those responsible for governance and control of an organisation could usefully be more forthright in challenging managers over the quality of their decisions. Pfeffer and Sutton (2006) present the case for basing management actions on substantiated theories and relevant evidence. They acknowledge the difficulties of putting that into practice, given that the demands for decisions are relentless and that information is incomplete. They also acknowledge that evidence-based management depends on being willing to put aside conventional ways of working.

Nevertheless they identify practices which could help those conducting corporate governance responsibilities to foster an evidence-based approach:

> If you ask for evidence of efficacy every time a change is proposed, people will sit up and take notice. If you take the time to parse the logic behind that evidence, people will become more disciplined in their own thinking. If you treat the organization like an unfinished prototype and encourage trial programs, pilot studies, and experimentation – and reward learning from these activities, even when something new fails – your organization will begin to develop its own evidence base. And if you keep learning while acting on the best knowledge you have and expect your people to do the same – if you have what has been called 'the attitude of wisdom' – then your company can profit from evidence-based management. (p. 70)

Pfeffer and Sutton's advice to demand evidence, examine logic, be willing to experiment and to embrace the attitude of wisdom would bring substantial change to the way in which many organisations operate.

Internationalisation

The theories outlined here were developed when most business was conducted within national boundaries, although of course with substantial foreign trade in certain products and services. They take little direct account of the explosion in global trade, and the way in which many organisations are reorganising themselves as international or global businesses. However, the competing values framework provides a useful starting point, by highlighting the importance of underlying assumptions behind a theory, and how this relates to particular contexts. The fact that a theory based on, say, open systems values works well in some economies, does not necessarily mean that it will be suitable in others. As Chapters 3 and 4 show, cultural factors affect performance, yet it is still unclear how multiple national cultures interact with the corporate culture of an international business.

Summary

1 **Explain the value of models of management, and compare unitary, pluralist and critical perspectives**

- Models represent more complex realities, help to understand complexity and offer a range of perspectives on the topic. Their predictive effect is limited by the fact that people interpret information subjectively in deciding how to act.
- A unitary perspective emphasises the common purpose of organisational members, while the pluralist draws attention to competing interest groups. Those who take a critical perspective believe that organisations reflect deep divisions in society, and that attempts to integrate different interests through negotiation ignore persistent differences in the distribution of power.

2 **State the structure of the competing values framework and evaluate its contribution to our understanding of management**

- A way of integrating the otherwise confusing range of theories of management. Organisations experience tensions between control and flexibility, and between an external and internal focus. Placing these on two axes allows theories to be allocated to one of four types – rational goal, internal process, human relations and open systems.

3 **Summarise the rational goal, internal process, human relations and open systems models and evaluate what each can contribute to a managers understanding of their role**

- Rational goal (Taylor, the Gilbreths and operational research):
  - clear direction leads to productive outcomes, with an emphasis on rational analysis and measurement.
- Internal process (Weber, Fayol):
  - routinisation leads to stability, so an emphasis on defining responsibility and on comprehensive documentation and administrative processes.
- Human relations (Follett, Mayo):
  - people are motivated by social needs, and managers who recognise these will secure commitment. Practices include considerate supervision, participation and seeking consensus.
- Open systems (socio-technical, contingency and complexity):
  - Continual innovation secures external support, achieved by creative problem solving.

These theories have contributed to the management agendas in these ways:

- Rational goal – through techniques such as time and motion study, work measurement and a variety of techniques for planning operations; also the narrow specification of duties, and the separation of management and non-management work.

- Internal process – clear targets and measurement systems, and the creation of clear management and reporting structures. Making decisions objectively on the basis of rules and procedures, rather than on favouritism or family connections.
- Human relations – considerate supervision, consultation and participation in decisions affecting people.
- Open systems – understanding external factors and being able and willing to respond to them through individual and organisational flexibility especially in uncertain, complex conditions characterised by the idea of non-linear systems. While a linear system is one in which a relatively stable environment makes some planning feasible, a non-linear system is strongly influenced by other systems. This means that actions lead to unexpected consequences.

4 **Use the model to classify the dominant form in two or more business units, and to gather evidence about the way this affects the roles of managing in those units**

- You can achieve this objective by asking people (perhaps others on your course) to identify which of the four cultural types in the Competing Values Framework most closely correspond to the unit in which they work. Ask them to note ways in which that cultural type affects their way of working. Compare the answers in a systematic way and review the results.

5 **Show how ideas from the chapter add to your understanding of the integrating themes**

- Increased attention to sustainability is an example of the values associated with the open systems model, while attempts to regulate and control activities are perhaps associated with internal process values.
- Pfeffer and Sutton's ideas on evidence-based management offer a model which those seeking more effective governance and control could use – challenging managers to back-up ideas with more rigorous evidence and analysis to reduce risk.
- The alternative models at the heart of the competing values framework is a reminder that values that shape management practice in one country do not necessarily have the same influence in others.

Review questions

1 Name three ways in which theoretical models help the study of management.
2 What are the different assumptions of the unitary, pluralist and critical perspectives on organisations?
3 Name at least four of Morgan's organisational images and give an original example of each.
4 Draw the two axes of the competing values framework, and then place the theories outlined in this chapter in the most appropriate sector.
5 List Taylor's five principles of scientific management and evaluate their use in examples of your choice.
6 What was the particular contribution that Lillian Gilbreth made concerning how workers' mental capacities should be treated?
7 What did Follett consider to be the value of groups in community as well as business?
8 Compare Taylor's assumptions about people with those of Mayo. Evaluate the accuracy of these views by reference to an organisation of your choice.
9 Compare the conclusions reached by the Hawthorne experimenters in the relay assembly test room with those in the bank wiring room.
10 Is an open system harder to manage than a closed system and, if so, why?
11 How does uncertainty affect organisations and how do non-linear perspectives help to understand this?
12 Summarise an idea from the chapter that adds to your understanding of the integrating themes.

Concluding critical reflection

Think about the way your company, or one with which you are familiar, approaches the task of management, and the theories that seem to lie behind the way people manage themselves and others. Review the material in the chapter, and perhaps visit some of the websites identified. Then make notes on the following questions:

- What examples of the issues discussed in this chapter are currently relevant to your company?
- In responding to these issues, what **assumptions** about the nature of management appear to guide what people do? Do they reflect rational goal, internal process, human relations or open systems perspectives? Or a combination of several? Do these assumptions reflect a unitary or pluralist perspective and, if so, why?
- What factors such as the history or current **context** of the company appear to have influenced the prevailing view? Does the approach appear to be right for the company, its employees and other stakeholders?
- Have people put forward **alternative** ways of managing the business, or even a small part of it, based on evidence about other companies? Does the competing values model suggest other approaches to managing, in addition to the current pattern? How might others react to such alternatives?
- What **limitations** can you see in the theories and evidence presented in the chapter? For example, how valid might the human relations models be in a manufacturing firm in a country with abundant supplies of cheap labour, competing to attract overseas investment? Will open systems models be useful to those managing a public bureaucracy?

Further reading

Drucker, P. (1954), *The Practice of Management*, Harper, New York.

Still the classic introduction to general management.

Fayol, H. (1949), *General and Industrial Management*, Pitman, London.

Taylor, F.W. (1917), *The Principles of Scientific Management*, Harper, New York.

The original works of these writers are short and lucid. Taylor (1917) contains illuminating detail that brings the ideas to life, and Fayol's (1949) surviving ideas came from only two short chapters, which again are worth reading in the original.

Biggs, L. (1996), *The Rational Factory*, The Johns Hopkins University Press, Baltimore, MD.

A short and clear overview of the development of production systems from the eighteenth to the early twentieth centuries in a range of industries, including much detail on Ford's Highland Park plant.

Gamble, J., Morris, J. and Wilkinson, B. (2004), 'Mass production is alive and well: the future of work and organization in east Asia', *International Journal of Human Resource Management*, vol. 15, no. 2, pp. 397–409.

Graham, P. (1995), *Mary Parker Follett: Prophet of management*, Harvard Business School Press, Boston, MA.

The contribution of Mary Parker Follett has been rather ignored, perhaps overshadowed by Mayo's Hawthorne studies – or perhaps it was because she was a woman. This book gives a full appreciation of her work.

McMillan, E. and Carlisle, Y. (2007), 'Strategy as Order Emerging from Chaos: A Public Sector Experience', *Long Range Planning*, vol. 40, no. 6, pp. 574–593.

Shows how complexity theory was used to generate a major change at The Open University.

Mumford, E. (2006), 'The story of socio-technical design: reflections on its successes, failures and potential', *Information Systems Journal*, vol. 16, no. 4, pp. 317–342.

A review of socio-technical design from one of its leading practitioners.

Smith, J.H. (1998), 'The Enduring Legacy of Elton Mayo', *Human Relations*, vol. 51, no. 3, pp. 221–249.

Walton, E.J. (2005), 'The Persistence of Bureaucracy: A Meta-analysis of Weber's Model of Bureaucratic Control', *Organization Studies*, vol. 26, no. 4, pp. 569–600.

Two papers which show the continued application in successful business of early theories of management.

Weblinks

These websites have appeared in the chapter:

www.newlanark.org.uk
www.imiplc.com
www.pret.com
www.tcl.com
www.inamo-restaurant.com

Visit two of the business sites in the list, or those of other organisations in which you are interested, and navigate to the pages dealing with recent news, press or investor relations.

- What are the main issues which the organisation appears to be facing?
- Compare and contrast the issues you identify on the two sites.
- What challenges may they imply for those working in, and managing, these organisations?

For video case studies, audio summaries, flashcards, exercises and annotated weblinks related to this chapter, visit **www.pearsoned.co.uk/mymanagementlab**

PART 1 CASE

INNOCENT DRINKS

www.innocent.com

Richard Reed, Jon Wright and Adam Balon founded innocent Drinks in 1998. They had known each other since they met during their first week at Cambridge University in 1991 where they became instant friends. After graduating, Reed worked in advertising, while Balon and Wright worked for (different) firms of management consultants. They also organised events in London (which they had already done while in Cambridge) – such as a music festival called Jazz on the Green in 1997 and 1998. Although following different careers, they often joked about starting a company together – and during a winter sports trip in March 1998 the topic came up again:

> We'd had this conversation so many times. One of us said: 'We either have to stop talking about this, or get on with it, otherwise we'll drive ourselves nuts.' So on that trip we made a simple commitment to each other: by the end of the weekend either we would come up with a business idea that we were excited by, or we would drop the topic for good. (Germain and Reed, 2009)

They considered several ideas, talking about their lifestyles in London – working long hours followed by late nights. They wanted to be healthy but didn't have much time. What about healthier food or drinks? They realised a lot of people were in the same position; so that became the problem they wanted to solve – to make it easy for people to do themselves some good. Having identified the need, they thought of 'smoothies' – natural fruit crushed and put into bottles that people could buy on their way to work.

They had hit on the idea which led to the creation of one of the UK's most successful entrepreneurial companies

The juice and smoothie market

Smoothies are blends of fruit that include the fruit's pulp and sometimes contain dairy products such as yogurt. They tend to be thicker and fresher than ordinary juice. While some smoothies are made on demand at a juice bar, this was not the market for which Innocent aimed. It focused on the market for pre-packaged smoothies, which has a premium and a standard segment. Premium smoothies contain no water or added sugar and command a higher price than the standard product.

Most smoothies were sold though three channels – supermarkets, cafés and sandwich shops, and impulse retail (convenience stores and petrol stations).

Innocent Ltd

Early decisions at Innocent

They saw the fact that other brands were already available in 1998 (principally PJ) as a positive sign, showing that a market existed – but the challenge was to make a better alternative. They decided to focus on offering only pure, fresh fruit, with nothing added or taken away.

They also decided how to divide the roles needed to build the business. Reed, with advertising experience, took care of marketing. Balon, who had recent experience of selling Virgin Cola, took on sales, while Wright (who had studied manufacturing engineering at Cambridge) was in charge of operations. They agreed that rather than have one chief executive all three would jointly lead the company.

They used their August 1998 Jazz on the Green festival to do some market research. They prepared a quantity of smoothies using borrowed equipment and set up a stall. In a move that has become part of the company's distinctive image they put a sign above two bins for empty bottles (marked Yes and No) asking the question: 'Should we give up our day jobs to make these smoothies?' By the end of the weekend they had sold all their smoothies, and the 'Yes' bin was full. They were still nervous about giving up good jobs, so agreed to toss a coin – 'heads we go back to work'. They each called tails, and tossed the same coin three times – each time it came up tails. They took that as a sign to stop dithering, and resigned their jobs the next day (Germain and Reed, 2009, p. 29).

A vital decision was price. Their main competitor (PJ) sold smoothies made with concentrate. Innocent planned to make a higher-quality product in that it would be fresher and more natural. This made it more expensive, and the founders doubted if customers would pay the premium required when compared with the cost of a 330ml PJ bottle. The solution came when a designer suggested a 250 ml bottle – risky, but marking Innocent as different from the established brand.

Another issue was whether to build their own juice factory, or work with someone else's. At first they had assumed they would have to build their own factory, but soon realised that it would be smarter to work with a manufacturing partner:

- their own factory would cost millions of pounds to establish and maintain;
- they had no experience of manufacturing;
- it would distract them from the core tasks of growing the business and building the brand; and
- it would make them less flexible – for example, a decision to change from bottles to cartons would be harder to implement in their own factory than with their suppliers.

Although there were no smoothie manufacturers in Britain with the facilities to make the fresh smoothies the team wanted, they came across a small supplier who was keen to diversify away from his current major customers. He also got on well with the Innocent team, and agreed to work for them. Partnering with other manufacturers has enabled the company to attain a rapid increase in sales without needing a large amount of capital. They believe that if they had tried to build their own squeezing and bottling sites, the company would not be the size it is today.

Finally, they had to raise capital to finance their growth. Conventional sources were reluctant to invest, but eventually Maurice Pinto, a private investor, put in £235,000 in return for a 20 per cent stake in the company. A critical matter in any business which wants to grow is that it continues to have access to the cash needed to finance expansion. Launching a new product or entering a new geographical market inevitably drains cash for a period, even if the venture is eventually profitable. They realised that continental Europe was a major potential market, but that in each country they would be entering into competition with large established companies, who could spend money on advertising and other tactics to defend their position.

So in September 2008 they launched a fund-raising process: Coca-Cola invested £30 million in return for 20 per cent of the shares in the company. This was controversial with a small number of customers, who believed that selling a share in the business ran counter to the values of the company. The company argues that the three founders remain in charge of the business, and that Coke have no decision-making powers over the way the business operates. The deal enabled the company to continue growing rapidly, and also gave it access, if required, to the larger company's distribution systems in Europe.

The Innocent brand

An old friend of the founders, Dan Germain, joined the business in the summer of 1999. They discussed packaging and came up with the idea of printing off-beat messages on the smoothie labels. These became one of the hallmarks of the Innocent brand, as the tone was off-beat, honest, irreverent and distinctly non-corporate. Germain began to take over as the unofficial voice of the brand – writing most of the labels, a newsletter and customer communications.

As the company grew it incorporated more traditional marketing approaches, such as bus and London Underground advertisements. One manager noted:

> We have to balance Big Brand with Little Brand – the former being a row of cartons on a supermarket shelf, the latter being an Innocent fridge covered with grass in a café next door.

An experienced marketing consultant commented:

> They have a really astute understanding of what makes a young metropolitan audience tick. It's almost anti-marketing.

Company growth

The formula which the company had adopted was highly successful and sales grew rapidly. The original outside investor advised the founders that, despite this success, they should start thinking about opportunities for further growth. Two options were whether to expand in Europe, or to extend the brand to other products (such as ice cream) in the UK. They decided not to diversify, but to concentrate on geographic expansion of the core range. By 2009 they were operating in most European countries, and were planning to enter the others soon. The table summarises their growth.

	1999	2010
Number of employees	3	250
Number of different products on sale	3	36
Market share	0%	80%
Turnover	£0	over £100 million each year
Number of retailers	1 (on first day)	Over 10,000
Number of smoothies sold	20 (on first day)	Two million a week

Source: Innocent's website. Reproduced with permission from Innocent Ltd.

Since 1999, 11 competing brands have been launched and all have withdrawn – their original main competitor (PJ) was bought by PepsiCo. Several major companies have offered to buy Innocent, but all have been refused. The trio are 69committed to staying with the company for at least the next few years.

Despite the fun image, they run the business very firmly, and are not afraid to fire employees who do not pull their weight. Growth means that they have brought in professional managers from established companies to complement their skills.

Innocent ethics

They want to prove that business can be a force for good. They say:

> We want to leave things a little better than we found them. Our strategy for doing so is simple – firstly, only ever make 100 per cent natural products that are 100 per cent good for people. Secondly, procure our ingredients ethically. Thirdly, use ecologically sound packaging materials. Fourth, reduce and offset our carbon emissions across our entire business system. Fifth, lead by example at Fruit Towers by doing good things. And, finally, give 10 per cent of our profits each year to charities in countries (such as Rainforest Alliance) where our fruit comes from.

Where next?

Founded in 1999, the founders run one of the best-loved and fastest growing businesses in Britain. They have no chief executive, give 10 per cent of profits to charity, and have a constant dialogue with customers – 40,000 of who have signed up to receive a weekly email. The company is growing so fast that finding the right staff is one factor that is slowing them down. As one experienced management observer noted:

> Consumers are looking for businesses to trust, and they want to reward that trustworthiness. Innocent is a model of the values all businesses should aspire to.

Sources: Based on material from 'Innocent Drinks', a case prepared by William Sahlman (2004), Harvard Business School, Case No. 9-805-031; *Sunday Times*, 24 September 2006; Germain and Reed (2009); company website.

Part case questions

- How does the management approach of the Innocent founders differ from that of Ryanair and Robert Owen respectively?
- Can you see any similarities?
- Visit the website and check on the latest news about developments in the company.
- In what ways are managers at Innocent adding value to the resources they use?
- What seems to you unusual about their approach to managing a business?
- In what ways will further growth pose new problems for the company, especially in Europe?
- In what ways, if at all, are the models in the competing values framework supported by the Innocent case?

PART 1
SKILLS DEVELOPMENT

To help you develop your skills as well as knowledge, this section includes tasks which relate the key themes covered in the Part to your daily life. Working through these will help you to deepen your understanding of the topic, and develop skills and insights which you can use in many situations.

Task 1.1   Managing your time

Managers often say that they do not have enough time to do their job as well as they would like. People often find that reflecting carefully on how they, and others, spend time helps to improve the way they use it: 'when one is very busy and under pressure, it is difficult to find the time to take stock of the way one works. Yet the effort is worthwhile. Those who do usually find they can organise more effectively both what they do and how they do it' (Stewart, 1967).

To help you begin this reflective process think back over your recent work, and then:

- list examples of time being badly used, and identify what led to that;
- list examples of time being well used, and identify what led to that;
- list examples of time being spent in activities that involve creativity.

Form a group of three or four colleagues, and exchange information about what you have found. Identify any common themes, and agree at least one practice that you will try to use to improve the way you use your time, either as a student or in an organisation.

Task 1.2   Understanding your roles

The term 'role' refers to the set of expectations which others have of someone occupying a position. The task below should help relate these ideas to your situation.

Part A – creating a role map

The aim of this exercise is to help you identify those people or groups (stakeholders) who have expectations of you in your role as a student *or* in an organisation. What do they expect of you, and what does that mean for where you spend time and energy?

1 Draw a circle in the middle of a page – this represents you in your studying or managing role.
2 Around the sheet draw other circles, each with the name of a person or group (stakeholder) that has expectations of you. Your map should include, among others:
- the organisation or the boss – respresenting what people formally expect;
- colleagues – the people who work for you or with you;
- families and others beyond the immediate role.

Place those where the links are particularly strong nearer the centre, and those that are less critical nearer the edge.

Part B – analysing expectations

Lay out a sheet of paper with the headings below across the top, and a deep row for each main stakeholder. Select three of the stakeholders you identified in Part A, list them in the left-hand column, and make notes on each of the questions in the other columns.

	[1]	[2]	[3]	[4]
Other person or institution (stakeholder)	What are they expecting of you, and you of them?	In view of (1), what are the three or four study or management tasks you must do well?	Are there situations where the expectations in (1) cause difficulty?	How did you resolve this, or how might you do so?

Part C – comparing with others

Using the role analysis you have carried out, work in pairs or trios with other colleagues on your course. In turn, outline your maps and your analysis in Part B. Your objective is to clarify your awareness of your role, by explaining to your partner(s) what you have written, and then revising it if necessary. Also seek their ideas on the column headed (4).

Part D – connecting theory and practice

Refer to Mintzberg's theory of management roles in Chapter 1. Which (several) of the roles he identified may be most important in helping you to meet the main expectations that others have of you?

Task 1.3   Managing your career

If you have not yet begun your management career, this activity may help you to think about the options and opportunities. Visit major online career websites, such as:

- www.monster.co.uk
- www.fish4jobs.co.uk
- www.prospects.ac.uk

You will be asked to enter a search word for jobs that interest you such as 'marketing' or 'information technology', or to choose a term from a list. This will probably return many possible opportunities – select three and print the job description. Compile a list of the educational and experience requirements, and of aspects of the job that appeal to you, or which you find unattractive.

Another exercise is to select three of the companies featured on the site, or that are mentioned in this part, or that interest you. Go to their website and then to the section on 'careers' or 'jobs with us' – again identify some possible jobs, and do as in the previous exercise.

What clues can you find in the information about how the job requirements relate to the tasks of managing (planning, organising, leading and controlling)?

Task 1.4   Identifying what makes a manager effective

You will all have worked with or for people who were managing an activity, either in an organisation or in some other human activity. What makes some better managers than others? Form a group with three or four others on your course and share your experience of managers – good and bad. List what those who were good managers did, which led you to regard them favourably.

Then answer these questions.

- To which of the management tasks or roles identified in Chapter 1 do these seem to relate?
- Are there any which do not fit the theories?

How would you judge your skills in dealing with the tasks and roles you identified? Be ready to share your conclusions in class.

PART 2
THE ENVIRONMENT OF MANAGEMENT

Introduction

Management takes place within a context, and this part examines the external context of organisations. Managers need to be familiar with that external environment, although they do not have to accept it passively. They try to influence it by lobbying powerful players, by reaching agreement with competitors or by shaping public opinion. Nevertheless, since the organisation draws its resources from the external world, it needs to deliver goods or services well enough to persuade people in that environment to continue their support. This is most obvious in commercial organisations. It is equally relevant in the public service: if a department set up to deliver care is managed badly it will not deliver. Taxpayers or clients will press their elected representatives to improve performance, and they in turn will demand improved performance from management and staff. If they do not, the enterprise will fail.

Chapter 3 examines the most immediate aspect of the manager's context – the culture of the organisation – and then offers tools for analysing systematically the competitive and general environments, and stakeholder expectations. Chapter 4 reflects the international nature of much business today, by examining international features of the general environment – political developments such as the European Union, international economic factors and differences in national cultures.

Pressure from interest groups and some consumers has encouraged many companies to take a positive approach to issues of corporate responsibility. There are conflicting interests here, and Chapter 5 presents some concepts and tools that help to consider these issues in a coherent and well-informed way.

The Part case is BP – a leading player in the world oil business. The business itself is inherently international, being affected by political and economic developments around the world. The case also raises issues of responsibility in safety and environmental matters.

CHAPTER 3
ORGANISATION CULTURES AND CONTEXTS

Aim

To identify the cultures and contexts within which managers work, and to outline some analytical tools.

Objectives

By the end of your work on this chapter you should be able to outline the concepts below in your own terms and:

1 Compare the cultures of two organisational units, using Quinn's or Handy's typologies

2 Use Porter's five forces model to analyse an organisation's competitive environment

3 Collect evidence to make a comparative PESTEL analysis for two organisations

4 Compare environments in terms of their complexity and rate of change

5 Give examples of stakeholder expectations

6 Explain the meaning and purposes of corporate governance

7 Show how ideas from the chapter add to your understanding of the integrating themes

Key terms

This chapter introduces the following ideas:

competitive environment
general environment
external environment (or context)
culture
power culture
role culture

task culture
person culture
five forces analysis
PESTEL analysis
corporate governance

Each is a term defined within the text, as well as in the Glossary at the end of the book.

Case study   Nokia   www.nokia.com

Nokia is the world's leading manufacturer of mobile phones. With an almost 40 per cent share of the market, it sold twice as many handsets in 2009 as second-placed Motorola and many times the number of other rivals such as Samsung and Ericsson. A Finnish company, founded in 1895 as a paper manufacturer, Nokia grew into a conglomerate with interests including electronics, cable manufacture, rubber, chemicals, electricity generation and, by the 1960s, telephone equipment. In the early 1990s senior managers decided to focus on the new mobile phone industry.

Two factors favoured this move. First, the Finnish government had taken a lead in telecoms deregulation and Nokia was already competing vigorously with other manufacturers supplying equipment to the national phone company. Second, the European Union (EU) adopted a single standard – the Global System for Mobile Telephony (GSM) – for Europe's second generation (digital) phones. Two-thirds of the world's mobile phone subscribers use this standard. Finland's links with its Nordic neighbours also helped, as people in these sparsely populated countries adopted mobile phones enthusiastically.

Nokia has strong design skills, but above all managers were quick to recognise that mobile phones are not a commodity but a fashion accessory. By offering smart designs, different ring tones and coloured covers Nokia became the 'cool' mobile brand for fashion-conscious people. Nokia has also mastered the logistics of getting millions of phones to customers around the world.

While many competitors subcontract the manufacture of handsets, Nokia assembles most of its own, with factories in many countries across the world. Managers believe this gives them a better understanding of the market and the manufacturing process. Nokia buys about 80 billion components a year, and has close relationships with its most important suppliers.

While all of these factors helped Nokia, managers believe there was a further reason. Although competitors such as Motorola and Ericsson already had advantages of scale, experience and distribution networks, the arrival of the new digital technology

Courtesy of Nokia

changed the rules of the game, forcing all players to start from scratch. Managers acknowledge that some external factors helped Nokia, but comment that 'good luck favours the prepared mind'.

The company's leading position in the industry owes much to Jorma Ollila, who became chief executive in 1992. He helped to shape the mobile phone industry by pursuing his vision of a mass market for voice communication while on the move. As he prepared to hand over to a new chief executive (Olli-Pekka Kallasvuo) in 2006, he observed that the next challenge would be to enable users to access the internet, videos, music, games and emails through a new generation of 'smart' phones and hand-held devices.

Source: Based on *The Economist*, 16 June 2001; *Financial Times*, 29 June 2001 and 10 October 2005.

Case questions 3.1

- How has the environment favoured the development of Nokia?

- How could the same factors turn to the disadvantage of the company?

- Visit Nokia's website and read its most recent trading statement (under investor relations). What have been the main developments in the last year?

3.1 Introduction

Nokia's success depends on the ability of its managers to spot and interpret signals from consumers in the mobile phone market, and to ensure that the organisation responds more effectively than competitors. It also depends on identifying ideas emerging within the organisation (such as from the research laboratories) that have commercial potential – and working to ensure that consumers are aware of and receptive to the idea when it is incorporated into the next generation of products. The early success of the company was helped by recognising that many users see a mobile as a fashion item, and by using its design skills to meet that need. It also gained when the EU established common standards for mobile telephony, which the Finnish government supported.

All managers work within a context which both constrains and supports them. How well they understand, interpret and interact with that context affects their performance. Finkelstein (2003) (especially pp. 63–68) shows how Motorola, an early market leader in mobile communications, failed to take account of changes in consumer preferences (for digital rather than the older analogue mobile phones). By the time managers realised the new environment, Nokia had a commanding lead in the market. Each business is unique, so the forces with which they interact differ: those who are able to identify and shape them (Nokia) will perform better than those who are not (Motorola).

The **internal environment (or context)** consists of elements within the organisation such as its technology, structure or business processes.

Figure 3.1 shows four environmental forces. The inner circle represents the organisation's **internal environment (or context)** – which Chapter 1 introduced. That includes its culture,

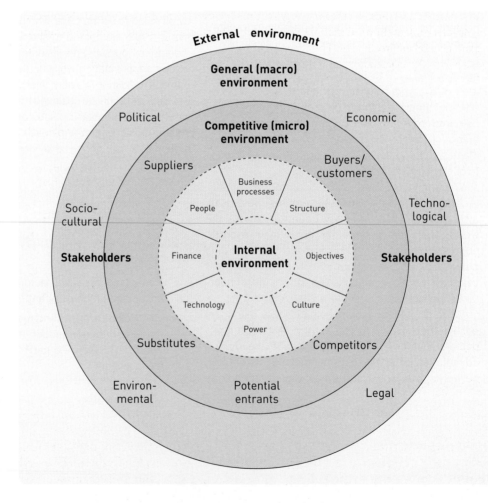

Figure 3.1
Environmental influences on the organisation

which many now regard as a major contextual feature. Beyond that is the immediate **competitive environment (or context),** sometimes known as the micro-environment. This is the industry-specific environment of customers, suppliers, competitors and potential substitute products. The outer circle shows the **general environment (or context)**, sometimes known as the macro-environment – political, economic, social, technological, (natural) environmental and legal factors that affect all organisations. Forces in the internal and competitive environments usually have more impact on, and are more open to influence by, the organisation than those in the general environment.

Together these make up an organisation's **external environment (or context)** – a constantly changing source of threats and opportunities: how well people cope with these affects performance.

Forces in the external environment do not affect practice of their own accord. They become part of the agenda only when internal or external stakeholders act to place them on the management agenda. In terms of Figure 3.1, they are a fourth force. Managers (who are themselves stakeholders) balance conflicting interpretations of their context. They work within an internal context, and look outside for actual and potential changes that may affect the centre of Figure 3.1. The figure implies a constant interaction between an organisation's culture and its external environment.

Managers do not passively accept their business environment, but try to shape it by actively persuading governments and other agencies to act in their favour (known as 'lobbying'). Car makers and airlines, for example, regularly seek subsidies, cheap loans or new regulations to help their businesses, while most industry bodies (such as the European Automobile Manufacturers' Association – **www.acea.be**) lobby international bodies such as the European Commission – often employing a professional lobbying business to support their case.

The next section presents ideas on organisational culture, which is an immediate aspect of a manager's context. Beyond that managers need to interact intelligently with their competitive and general environments. The chapter contrasts stable and dynamic environments, outlines stakeholder expectations and introduces ideas on governance and control.

> A **competitive environment (or context)** is the industry-specific environment comprising the organisation's customers, suppliers and competitors.

> The **general environment (or context)** (sometimes known as the macro-environment) includes political, economic, social technological, (natural) environmental and legal factors that affect all organisations.

> The **external environment (or context)** consists of elements beyond the organisation – it combines the competitive and general environments.

Activity 3.1   Which elements of the business environment matter?

- Write a few notes summarising aspects of the business environment of which you are aware. You may find it helpful to think of a manager you have worked with, or when you have been managing an activity.
- Identify two instances when they (or you) were discussing aspects of the wider context of the job – such as the culture of the organisation or the world outside.
- How did this aspect of the context affect the job of managing?
- How did the way people dealt with the issue affect performance?

3.2   Cultures and their components

Developing cultures

Interest in organisation **culture** has grown as academics and managers have come to believe that it influences behaviour. Several claim that a strong and distinct culture helps to integrate individuals into the team or organisation (Deal and Kennedy, 1982; Peters and Waterman, 1982). Deal and Kennedy (1982) refer to culture as 'the way we do things around here' and Hofstede (1991) sees it as the 'collective programming of the mind', distinguishing one

> **Culture** is a pattern of shared basic assumptions that was learned by a group as it solved its problems of external adaptation and internal integration, and that has worked well enough to be considered valid and transmitted to new members (Schein, 2004, p. 17).

group from another. They claim that having the right culture explains the success of high-performing organisations.

Someone entering a department or organisation for the first time can usually sense and observe the surface elements of the culture. Some buzz with life and activity, others seem asleep; some welcome and look after visitors, others seem inward looking; some work by the rules, while others are entrepreneurial and risk taking; some have regular social occasions while in others staff rarely meet except at work.

Management in practice   A culture of complaint in a bank

John Weeks (2004) spent six years working in a UK bank (believed to be NatWest, which the Royal Bank of Scotland acquired in 2000) as part of his doctoral research. He observed and recorded the bank's distinctive culture – which he described as one of 'complaint'.

No-one liked the culture – from the most senior managers to the most junior counter staff – people spent much of their time complaining about it. Weeks realised that this was a ritual, a form of solidarity among the staff: complaining about the culture *was* the culture. He noticed that most complaints were directed at other parts of the bank – not at the unit in which the complainer worked. He noted:

> Local sub-cultures are sometimes described positively – usually to contrast them with the mainstream – but I never heard anyone [describe the bank's culture in positive terms]. It is described as too bureaucratic, too rules driven, not customer-focused enough, not entrepreneurial enough, too inflexible, too prone to navel gazing, too centralized. (p. 53)

His detailed narrative shows, with many examples, how people in the bank made sense of their culture – using it to achieve their goals, while others did the same to them.

Source: Weeks (2004).

Figure 3.2 illustrates how a distinctive culture develops; as people develop and share common values they use these to establish beliefs and norms which guide their behaviour towards each other and to outsiders. Positive outcomes reinforce their belief in the values underlying their behaviour, which then become a stronger influence on how people should work and relate to each other: should people have job titles? How should they dress? Should meetings be confrontational or supportive?

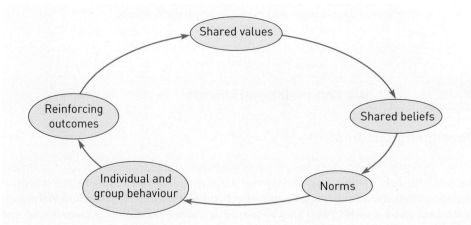

Figure 3.2
The stages of cultural formation

A shared culture provides members with guidelines about how they can best contribute. The more they work on these issues to develop a common understanding, the better they will perform.

Components of cultures

Schein (2004) identifies three levels of a culture, 'level' referring to the degree to which the observer can see its components.

- **Artifacts** represent the visible level – elements such as the language or etiquette which someone coming into contact with a culture can observe:

  - architecture (open-plan offices without doors or private space)
  - technology and equipment
  - style (clothing, manner of address, emotional displays)
  - rituals and ceremonies (leaving events, awards ceremonies and away-days)
  - courses (to induct employees in the culture as well as the content).

  While it is easy to observe artifacts, it is difficult for outsiders to decipher what they mean to the group, or what underlying assumptions they reflect. That requires an analysis of beliefs and values.

- **Espoused beliefs and values** are the accumulated beliefs that members hold about their work. As a group develops, members refine their ideas about what works in this business: how people make decisions, how teams work together, and how they solve problems. Practices that work become the accepted way to behave:

  - 'Quality pays.'
  - 'We should stick to our core business.'
  - 'Cultivate a sense of personal responsibility.'
  - 'We depend on close team work.'
  - 'Everyone is expected to challenge a proposal – whoever made it.'

  Some companies codify and publish their beliefs and values, to help induct new members and to reinforce them among existing staff. Such beliefs and values shape the visible artifacts, though companies vary in the degree to which employees internalise them. The extent to which they do so depends on how clearly they derive from shared basic underlying assumptions.

- **Basic underlying assumptions** are deeply held by members of the group as being the way to work together. As they act in accordance with their values and beliefs, those that work become embedded as basic underlying assumptions. When the group strongly holds these, members will act in accordance with them, and reject actions based on others:

  - 'We need to satisfy customers to survive as a business.'
  - 'Our business is to help people with X problem live better with X problem.'
  - 'People can make mistakes, as long as they learn from them.'
  - 'We employ highly motivated and competent adults.'
  - 'Financial markets worry about the short term: we are here for the long term.'

  Difficulties arise when people with assumptions developed in one group work with people from another. Mergers sometimes experience difficulty when staff who have to work together realise they are from different cultures.

| **Management in practice** | **A strong culture at Bosch**   www.bosch.com |

Franz Fehrenbach is chief executive of Bosch, Germany's largest privately owned engineering group, and the world's largest supplier of car parts. In 2009 he said:

> **The company culture, especially our high credibility, is one of our greatest assets. Our competitors cannot match us on that because it takes decades to build up.**

The cultural traditions include a rigid control on costs, an emphasis on team thinking, employees taking responsibility for their errors, cautious financial policies, and long-term thinking. For example, to cope with the recession in 2009 Mr Fehrenbach explained that:

We have to cut costs in all areas. We will reduce spending in the ongoing business, but we will not cut back on research and development for important future projects.

Source: Based on an article by Daniel Schaefer, *Financial Times*, 2 March 2009, p. 16.

Activity 3.2 **Culture spotting**

- Identify as many components of culture (artifacts, beliefs and values, underlying assumptions) in an organisation or unit as you can.
- What may the artifacts suggest about the deeper beliefs and values, or underlying assumptions?
- Gather evidence (preferably by asking people) about how the culture affects behaviour, and whether they think it helps or hinders performance.
- Analyse your results and decide which of the four types in the competing values framework most closely reflects that organisation's culture.

3.3 Types of culture

This section outlines three ways of describing and comparing cultures.

Competing values framework

The competing values model developed by Quinn *et al.* (2003) reflects inherent tensions between flexibility or control and between an internal or an external focus. Figure 3.3 (based on Figure 2.2) shows four cultural types.

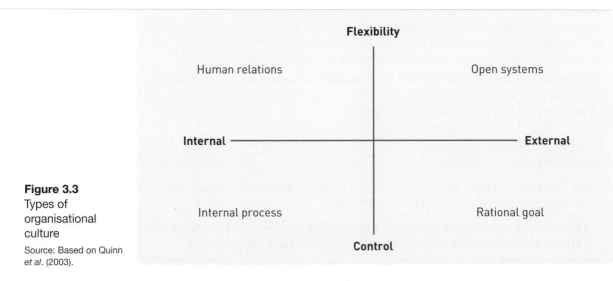

Figure 3.3
Types of organisational culture
Source: Based on Quinn *et al.* (2003).

Open systems

This represents an open systems view, in which people recognise that the external environment plays a significant role, and is a vital source of ideas, energy and resources. It also sees the environment as complex and turbulent, requiring entrepreneurial, visionary leadership and flexible, responsive behaviour. Key motivating factors are growth, stimulation, creativity and variety. Examples are start-up firms and new business units – organic, flexible operations.

Rational goal

Members see the organisation as a rational, efficiency-seeking unit. They define effectiveness in terms of production or economic goals that satisfy external requirements. Managers create structures to deal with the outside world. Leadership tends to be directive, goal-oriented and functional. Key motivating factors include competition and the achievement of goals. Examples are large, established businesses – mechanistic.

Internal process

Here members focus on internal matters. Their goal is to make the unit efficient, stable and controlled. Tasks are repetitive and methods stress specialisation, rules and procedures. Leaders tend to be cautious and spend time on technical issues. Motivating factors include security, stability and order. Examples include utilities and public authorities – suspicious of change.

Human relations

People emphasise the value of informal interpersonal relations rather than formal structures. They try to maintain the organisation and nurture its members, defining effectiveness in terms of their well-being and commitment. Leaders tend to be participative, considerate and supportive. Motivating factors include attachment, cohesiveness and membership. Examples include voluntary groups, professional service firms and some internal support functions.

Charles Handy's cultural types

Charles Handy (1993) distinguished four cultures – **power**, **role**, **task** and **person**.

Power

A dominant central figure holds power: others follow the centre's policy and interpret new situations in the way the leader would. Many entrepreneurial firms operate in this way, with few rules but with well-understood, implicit codes on how to behave and work. The firm relies on the individual rather than on seeking consensus through discussion.

Role

Typical characteristics of this culture are the job description or the procedure. Managers define what they expect in clear, detailed job descriptions. They select people for a job if they meet the specified requirements. Procedures guide how people and departments interact. If all follow the rules, co-ordination is straightforward. People's position in the hierarchy determines their power.

Task

People focus on completing the task or project rather than their formal role. They value each other for what they can contribute and expect everyone to help as needed. The emphasis is on getting the resources and people for the job and then relying on their commitment and enthusiasm. People will typically work in teams, to combine diverse skills into a common purpose.

A **power culture** is one in which people's activities are strongly influenced by a dominant central figure.

A **role culture** is one in which people's activities are strongly influenced by clear and detailed job descriptions and other formal signals as to what is expected from them.

A **task culture** is one in which the focus of activity is towards completing a task or project using whatever means are appropriate.

A **person culture** is one in which activity is strongly influenced by the wishes of the individuals who are part of the organisation.

Person

The individual is at the centre and any structure or system is there to serve them. The form is unusual – small professional and artistic organisations are probably closest to it, and perhaps experiments in communal living. They exist to meet the needs of the professionals or the members, rather than some larger organisational goal.

Activity 3.3   Cultural examples

For each of Handy's four cultural types, identify an example from within this text that seems to correspond most closely to that form.

● What clues about the company have you used to decide that allocation?
● Why do you think that culture is suitable for that organisation?
● What evidence would you seek to decide if that culture was suitable?
● Compare the similarities and differences in the competing values and Handy models.

Multiple cultures

Martin (2002) proposed that organisations have not one, but several cultures: observers take one of three perspectives towards a culture:

● **Integration** – a focus on identifying consistencies in the data, and using those common patterns to explain events.
● **Differentiation** – a focus on conflict, identifying different and possibly conflicting views of members towards events.
● **Fragmentation** – a focus on the fluid nature of organisations, and on the interplay and change of views about events.

Ogbonna and Harris (1998, 2002) provided empirical support for this view, based on interviews with staff in a retail company. They found that a person's position in the hierarchy determined his/her perspective on the culture (see Table 3.1). As consensus on culture was unlikely, they advised managers to recognise the range of sub-cultures within their oganisation, and

Table 3.1 Hierarchical position and cultural perspectives

Position in hierarchy	Cultural perspective	Description	Example
Head office managers	Integration	Cultural values should be shared across the organisation. Unified culture both desirable and attainable	'If we can get every . . . part of the company doing what they should be doing, we'll beat everybody'
Store managers	Differentiation	Reconciling conflicting views of head office and shop floor. See cultural pluralism as inevitable	'People up at head office are all pushing us in different directions. Jill in Marketing wants customer focus, June in Finance wants lower costs'
Store employees	Fragmented	Confused by contradictory nature of the espoused values. See organisation as complex and unpredictable	'One minute it's this, the next it's that. You can't keep up with the flavour of the month'

Source: Based on Ogbonna and Harris (1998).

only seek to reconcile those differences that were essential to policy. They also observed that culture remains a highly subjective idea, largely in the eye of the beholder

> and is radically different according to an individual's position in the hierarchy. (Ogbonna and Harris, 1998, p. 45)

Culture and performance

Peters and Waterman (1982) believed that an organisation's culture affected performance, and implied that managers should try to change their culture towards a more productive one. Others are more skeptical about the effects on performance and question whether, even if a suitable culture has a positive effect, managers can consciously change it. Kotter and Heskett (1992) studied 207 companies to assess the link between culture and economic performance. Although they were positively correlated, the relationship was much weaker than advocates of culture as a factor in performance had predicted.

Thompson and McHugh (2002), while also critical of much writing on the topic, observe the potential benefits which a suitable culture can bring to not-for-profit organisations:

> Creating a culture resonant with the overall goals is relevant to any organisation, whether it be a trade union, voluntary group or producer co-operative. Indeed, it is more important in such consensual groupings. Co-operatives, for example, can degenerate organisationally because they fail to develop adequate mechanisms for transmitting the original ideals from founders to new members and sustaining them through shared experiences. (pp. 208–209)

Case study   Nokia – the case continues   www.nokia.com

In March 2010 Nokia estimated that it had maintained its market share at 34 per cent of total device sales of 1.14 billion units. It is continuing to add value to its devices, by integrating them with innovative services providing music, maps, apps and email. It also believes that its wide range of handsets means it will be able to meet demand if customers begin to prefer cheaper handsets. It also saw growth opportunities in areas of the world, such as the US and Korea, where it had little or no market share, and in smartphones where the company's products had been weak.

The company had also been reducing its reliance on selling handsets, by diversifying into new growth areas. In 2006 it reached a deal with Siemens to merge their network businesses, creating the world's third largest network equipment supplier. In 2008 it concluded that success depended not just on good quality handsets, but also on the quality of the services and applications. It therefore grouped all handset products into a Device Unit, while applications and services became part of a new Mobile Services and Software unit. Both were supported by a Marketing unit which provided sales, marketing and operational support.

One factor in the company's sustained success appears to have been a culture which encourages co-operation within teams, and across internal and external boundaries. Jorma Ollila, CEO until 2006, believed that Nokia's innovative capacity springs from multi-functional teams working together to bring new insights to products and services. Staff in the four divisions work in teams which may remain constant for many years – but sometimes combine with other teams to work on a common task.

Informal mentoring begins as soon as someone steps into a new job. Within a few days, the employee's manager lists the people in the organisation whom it would be useful for the employee to meet. He/she also reviews what topics the newcomer should discuss with the suggested contact, and why establishing a relationship with each one is important. The gift of time – in the form of hours spent on coaching and building networks – is a crucial part of the collaborative culture.

Nokia also encourages a culture of communication by creating small groups from around the company to work on a strategic issue for four months. This helps them to build ties with many parts of the company – some of which continue during later work. The induction process for new employees also encourages team-building and co-operation: the newcomer's manager must introduce him/her to at least 15 people within and outside the team.

Sources: Grattan and Erickson (2007); Doz and Kosonen (2008); company website

> ### Case questions 3.2
> - Which of the cultural types identified by Quinn *et al.* (2003) would you expect to find within Nokia's handset business?
> - How will the practices to encourage communication help a culture to develop? (Refer to Figure 3.2.)

As managers work within an organisational culture, they also work within an external context – whose members will have expectations from the organisation. They need some tools with which to analyse that external world.

3.4 The competitive environment – Porter's five forces

Five forces analysis is a technique for identifying and listing those aspects of the five forces most relevant to the profitability of an organisation at that time.

Managers are most directly affected by forces in their immediate competitive environment. According to Porter (1980a, 1985), the ability of a firm to earn an acceptable return depends on five forces – the ability of new competitors to enter the industry, the threat of substitute products, the bargaining power of buyers, the bargaining power of suppliers and the rivalry among existing competitors. Figure 3.4 shows Porter's **five forces analysis**.

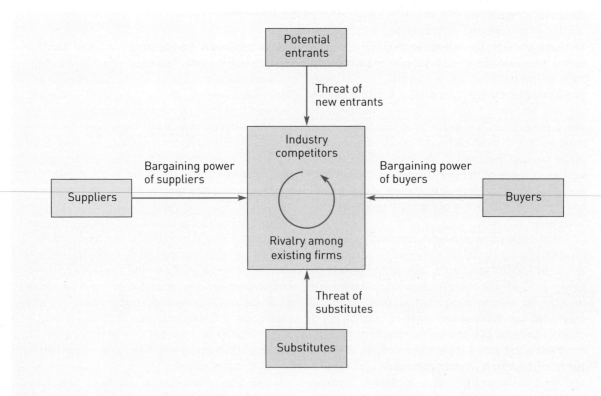

Figure 3.4 The five forces of industry competition

Porter believes that the *collective* strength of the five forces determines industry profitability, through their effects on prices, costs and investment requirements. Buyer power influences the prices a firm can charge, as does the threat of substitutes. The bargaining power of suppliers determines the cost of raw materials and other inputs. The greater the collective strength of the forces, the less profitable the industry: the weaker they are, the more profitable they are. Managers can use their knowledge of these forces to shape strategy.

Threat of new entrants

The extent of this threat depends on how easily new entrants can overcome barriers such as:

- the need for economies of scale (to compete on cost), which are difficult to achieve quickly;
- high capital investment required;
- lack of distribution channels;
- subsidies which benefit existing firms at the expense of potential new entrants;
- cost advantages of existing firms, such as access to raw materials or know-how;
- strong customer loyalty to incumbent companies.

Nokia faces competition from new entrants to the mobile phone industry especially Apple and Research in Motion (BlackBerry) at the top end of the market. The Chinese ZTE Corporation is supplying cheap mobiles to consumers in emerging markets.

Intensity of rivalry among competitors

Strong competitive rivalry lowers profitability, and occurs when:

- there are many firms in an industry;
- there is slow market growth, so companies fight for market share;
- fixed costs are high, so firms use capacity and overproduce;
- exit costs are high; specialised assets (hard to sell) or management loyalty (in old family firms) deter firms from leaving the industry, which prolongs excess capacity and low profitability;
- products are similar, so customers can easily switch to other suppliers.

A highly competitive market will also be one in which the threat of new entrants is high. While Nokia still dominated the mobile phone industry in 2010, it continued to face pressure from established competitors Motorola, Siemens and Ericsson, and from new entrants in Asia.

Management in practice   Competition amongst Chinese brewers

SABMiller and Anheuser-Busch both sought to enter the Chinese market by buying an existing major player, Harbin (with Anheuser-Busch quickly winning the contest). They were attracted by the fact that China is the world's largest market for beer, growing at 6–8 per cent a year. However, it is also fiercely competitive as there are over 400 brewers competing for sales: this keeps prices down, and profits are on average less than 0.5 per cent of sales.

Source: *The Economist*, 15 May 2004.

Power of buyers (customers)

Buyers (customers) seek lower prices or higher quality at constant prices, thus forcing down prices and profitability. Buyer power is high when:

- the buyer purchases a large part of a supplier's output;
- there are many substitute products, allowing easy switching;

- the product is a large part of the buyers' costs, encouraging them to seek lower prices;
- buyers can plausibly threaten to supply their needs internally.

Management in practice   Wal-Mart's power as a buyer   www.walmart.com

Wal-Mart (which owns Asda in the UK) is the world's largest company, being three times the size of the second largest retailer, the French company Carrefour. Growth has enabled it to become the largest purchaser in America, controlling much of the business done by almost every major consumer-products company. It accounts for 30 per cent of hair care products sold, 26 per cent of toothpaste, 20 per cent of pet food, and 20 per cent of all sales of CDs, videos and DVDs. This gives it great power over companies in these industries, since their dependence on Wal-Mart reduces their bargaining power.

Source: *Business Week*, 6 October 2003, pp. 48–53; and other sources.

Bargaining power of suppliers

Conditions that increase the bargaining power of suppliers are the opposite of those applying to buyers. The power of suppliers relative to customers is high when:

- there are few suppliers;
- the product is distinctive, so that customers are reluctant to switch;
- the cost of switching is high (e.g. if a company has invested in a supplier's software);
- suppliers can plausibly threaten to extend their business to compete with the customer;
- the customer is a small or irregular purchaser.

Threat of substitutes

In Porter's model, substitutes refer to products in other industries that can perform the same function, e.g. using cans instead of bottles. Close substitutes constrain the ability of firms to raise prices, and the threat is high when buyers are able and willing to change their habits. Technological change and the risk of obsolescence pose a further threat: online news services (such as that freely available from the BBC) and recruitment sites threaten print newspapers.

Analysing the forces in the competitive environment enables managers to seize opportunities, counter threats and generally improve their position relative to competitors. They can consider how to alter the strength of the forces to improve their position by, for example, building barriers to entry or increasing their power over suppliers or buyers. Chapter 8 (Strategy) examines how managers can position their organisation within the competitive environment.

Activity 3.4   Critical reflection on the five forces

Conduct a five forces analysis for an organisation with which you are familiar. Discuss with a manager of the organisation how useful he/she finds the technique.

- Evaluate whether it captures the main competitive variables in his/her industry?
- Compare your analysis with one done for Nokia, and present a summary of similarities and differences in the forces affecting the companies.

3.5   The general environment – PESTEL

Forces in the wider world also shape management policies, and a **PESTEL analysis** (short for political, economic, socio-cultural, technological, environmental and legal) helps to identify these – which Figure 3.5 summarises. When these forces combine their effect is more pronounced – pharmaceutical companies face problems located in slower progress in transferring scientific knowledge into commercial products, more risk-averse regulators who require longer and more costly trials, challenges from companies making cheap generic alternatives to patented drugs, and governments trying to reduce the costs of drugs supplied to citizens.

PESTEL analysis is a technique for identifying and listing the political, economic, social, technological, environmental and legal factors in the general environment most relevant to an organisation.

Political factors

Political systems vary between countries and often shape what managers can and cannot do. Governments often regulate industries such as power supply, telecommunications, postal services and transport by specifying, among other things, who can offer services, the conditions they must meet and what they can charge. Regulations differ between countries and are a major factor in managers' decisions.

When the UK and most European governments altered the law on financial services, non-financial companies such as Virgin and Sainsbury's quickly began to offer banking services. Deregulating air transport stimulated the growth of low-cost airlines, especially in the US

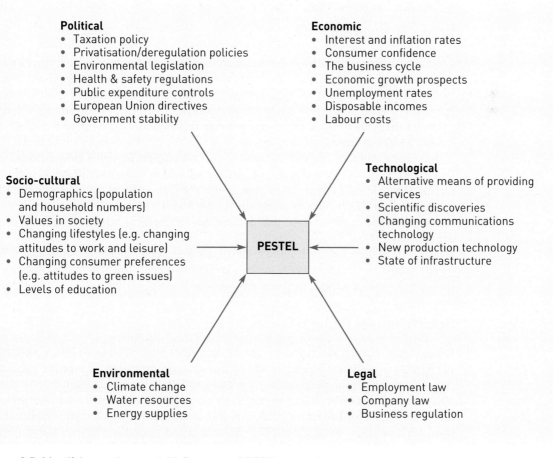

Political
- Taxation policy
- Privatisation/deregulation policies
- Environmental legislation
- Health & safety regulations
- Public expenditure controls
- European Union directives
- Government stability

Economic
- Interest and inflation rates
- Consumer confidence
- The business cycle
- Economic growth prospects
- Unemployment rates
- Disposable incomes
- Labour costs

Socio-cultural
- Demographics (population and household numbers)
- Values in society
- Changing lifestyles (e.g. changing attitudes to work and leisure)
- Changing consumer preferences (e.g. attitudes to green issues)
- Levels of education

Technological
- Alternative means of providing services
- Scientific discoveries
- Changing communications technology
- New production technology
- State of infrastructure

PESTEL

Environmental
- Climate change
- Water resources
- Energy supplies

Legal
- Employment law
- Company law
- Business regulation

Figure 3.5 Identifying environmental influences – PESTEL analysis

(e.g. Southwest Airlines), Europe (easyJet), Australia (Virgin Blue) and parts of Asia (Air Asia), although as the Ryanair case in Chapter 1 shows, these companies still work in a political environment. The EU is developing regulations to try to manage the environmentally friendly disposal of the millions of personal computers and mobile phones that consumers scrap each year.

Managers aim to influence these political decisions by employing professional lobbyists, especially at international institutions. The European Commission (which performs the detailed analysis behind EU policy) relies on contributions from interested parties to inform its decisions, and lobbying firms provide this. They focus on those people who have decision-making power, often members of the European parliament.

Management in practice   **VT Group depends on government** www.vtplc.com

The UK government is the biggest customer of VT Group, the defence, education and engineering out-sourcer. Current contracts include broadcasting the BBC's World Service and managing the Metropolitan Police's vehicle fleet. Contracts with the UK public sector represented 67 per cent of VT's revenues in 2008, and the US public sector made up much of the rest. The company sees both danger and opportunity in this. While shifts in demand for an existing service are usually gradual and predictable, future government policy is often unknown – especially before elections. Paul Lester, who in 2009 was chief executive of the group, maintains close contact with government ministers and leading members of the main opposition party.

Source: *Financial Times*, 29 June 2009.

Economic factors

Economic factors such as wage levels, inflation and interest rates affect an organisation's costs. During the 2009 recession Unilever (**www.unilever.com**) detected significant changes in shopping habits, with many doing without expensive bubble baths, body moisturisers and upmarket cleaning products in favour of less expensive purchases. The consumer goods company said that sales of stock cubes were growing very rapidly as more people 'cooked from scratch' instead of buying prepared meals.

Increasing competition and the search for cost advantages drive globalisation. Ford (**www.ford.com**) has invested in plant to make small cars in India, where demand is growing rapidly as people there become more prosperous. The same economic trend encouraged Tata (**www.tata.com**), the Indian conglomerate, to launch a low-cost car, the Nano: Renault/Nissan (**www.renault.com**) expect to be selling more cars in emerging markets than in developed countries by 2015.

The state of the economy is a major influence on consumer spending, which affects firms meeting those needs. Managers planning capital investments follow economic forecasts: if these suggest slower growth, they may postpone the project.

Socio-cultural factors

Demographic change affects most organisations, apart from those most clearly affected by the ageing population – healthcare and pharmaceuticals businesses. A growing number of single people affects the design of housing, holidays and life assurance. Demographic change affects an organisation's publicity to ensure, for example, that advertising acknowledges racial diversity. Leading banks develop investment and saving schemes that comply with *sharia* law, to attract devout Muslim investors. The growth in spending on live music encouraged HMV Group (**www.hmv.com**) to enter this market in addition to selling music through the stores (see Chapter 8 Case).

Management in practice   Changing tastes challenge pubs

Across Europe people are drinking more alcohol at home and less in pubs. The trend is particularly marked in Britain, where in 2009 about 40 pubs were closing each week. They are gradually being usurped as the biggest sellers of beer in the UK, with supermarkets supplying most ale and lager. Many pub managers have adapted to this change by selling more food, some of whom have become gastro-pubs – offering high-quality food in the simple 'public house' environment. A manager at a company with several gastro-pubs said:

> Our pubs are doing really well and we want to raise our exposure to this market. The new pubs are in good areas such as west London where people are going to eat out two or three times a week, and want a relaxed place where they can meet their friends without [having to spend too much].

Source: *Financial Times*, 26 August 2008; and other sources.

Consumer tastes and preferences change. Commenting on a decision to increase the number of healthier products, the chief executive of Nestlé said:

> I think this shows you where the future direction of the company is. This emphasis on (healthier products) is a strategic decision, reflecting changing economic and demographic conditions.

Key ideas   *Grown Up Digital*

In his latest book (subtitled *How the Net Generation is Changing your World*) Don Tapscott (2009) proposes that senior managers need to understand what he calls the 'net generation' – people born between 1977 and 1997 – sometimes called 'generation Y'. His research team interviewed thousands of 16-to-19-year-olds in 12 countries, as well as holding comparative interviews with older people. He notes that the net generation grew up using a wider range of media than its parents: they typically spend hours on their computer – while also talking on the phone, listening to music, doing homework and reading. Technology is shaping their minds to access information in a different way. Rather than absorb information sequentially from a limited number of sources, they are more likely to 'play' with information by clicking, cutting, pasting and linking to interesting material.

Tapscott suggests that this challenges established educational methods, and also media companies whose established products may not match the way young people expect to interact with information.

Source: Tapscott (2009).

Technological factors

Companies pay close attention to the physical infrastructure – such as the adequacy of power supplies and transport systems. Even more, they monitor advances in information technology, which are dramatically changing the business environment of many companies. Advances in technology do not only affect data systems. Computers traditionally handled data, while other systems handled voice (telephones) and pictures (film and video). These components of the information revolution are familiar as separate devices, but their use of common digital technology greatly increases their ability to exchange information. Digitisation – the packaging of images and sounds into digital form – has profound implications for many industries, as Table 3.2 illustrates.

Table 3.2 Examples of digital technologies affecting established businesses

Technology	Application	Businesses affected
Digital Versatile Discs (DVDs)	Store sound and visual images	Sales of stereophonic sound systems decline sharply
IPOD, MP3 and smartphones	Digital downloads of talking books	New markets created for talking books, with titles to suit new audience
Broadband services delivering online content	Enables advertisers to use online media rather than print or television	Media companies (some of whom have now moved online – NewsCorp acquired MySpace)
Voice over Internet Protocol (VoIP)	Enables telephone calls over the internet at very low cost	Threat to revenues of traditional phone companies
Digital photography	Enables people to store pictures electronically and order prints online	Photographic retailers such as Jessops lose significant part of business

Bernoff and Li (2008) show how social networking (Facebook) and user-generated content sites (YouTube) change the technological context – to which companies are in turn responding: see Chapter 12.

Case study Nokia – the case continues www.nokia.com

While Nokia, like all mobile phone companies, regularly introduces more technically sophisticated devices, these account for a small proportion of the units which the industry sells each year. However, the 'smartphone' segment of the market is growing rapidly, with almost 55 million units sold in the first quarter of 2010 – a 57 per cent increase on the same quarter of 2009. Observers expected that, as prices for phones and services continue to drop, demand for more basic devices will continue to grow rapidly in the large markets of China, India, Brazil and Russia.

Nokia has been particularly successful in meeting this demand, making great efforts to secure first-time buyers and then build lifelong loyalty to the brand. Moreover, status-conscious buyers in the third world disdain unknown brands:

> Brazilians want brand names and are willing to pay a bit more for Nokia or Motorola (Quoted in *Business Week,* 7 November 2005, p. 21)

More than any other handset maker, the Finnish company has connected with consumers in China and India. Greater China (the mainland, Hong Kong and Taiwan) is the company's biggest market: in 2005 it supplied 31 per cent of all sets sold there, well ahead of the 10 per cent from second-place Motorola. It has about 60 per cent of the market in India, which it expects will be the company's biggest market by 2010. It owes its strong position in both countries in part to a decentralised organisation which can spot local sales trend very quickly, together with an ability to produce sets tailored to local tastes and languages.

It also competes at the top end of the market: in October 2008 it launched a new service – Comes With Music (CWM) as a rival to Apple's iPhone. The CWM devices consist of a mobile handset which also includes a year's free unlimited subscription to Nokia's music catalogue. The company pays music publishers and artists a share of handset sales, depending on the amount of music downloaded.

Chief executive Olli-Pekka Kallasvuo set a target of 300 million users of its mobile services by the end of 2011. This is part of the company's wider strategy to offer mobile services, investing large sums in buying companies to support that – such as Navteq, a digital maps company. Such a move would help it gain higher margins from the sales of these more expensive handsets.

Sources: *Business Week*, 27 March 2006; *Financial Times*, 17 July 2009; International Data Corporation, 7 May 2010.

Case questions 3.3

Gather some information about current developments in the mobile phone industry. Also collect information on Nokia.

- Use Porter's five forces model to outline the competitive environment of the industry.
- Which of these factors may have contributed to Nokia's success?
- Which PESTEL factors are most affecting the development of the industry?

Environmental factors

The natural resources available in an economy – including minerals, agricultural land and the prevailing climate – affect the kind of businesses that managers create: the mills at New Lanark (Chapter 2 case) were built beside a source of water power.

Many senior managers know that climate change will have major implications for their organisations, and are working out how best to respond. It will put most businesses at risk, with the probability of more droughts, floods, storms and heat waves – less rainfall in some places, more in others. For some it represents a threat – insurance companies, house builders and water companies are only the most visible examples of companies that are being affected. For others, sustainability brings opportunities – alternative energy suppliers, emission control businesses and waste management companies are all seeing more interest in their products and services.

Legal factors

Governments create the legal framework within which companies operate, most obviously in areas such as health and safety, employment, consumer protection and pollution control. They also create the legal basis for business – such as when the UK parliament passed the Joint Stock Companies Act in 1862. Previously people were discouraged from putting their money into a business as they were personally liable for the whole of a company's debts if it failed. The Act of 1862 limited their liability to the value of the shares they held in the company – they could lose their investment, but not the rest of their wealth. This stimulated company formation and other countries soon passed similar legislation, paving the way for the countless 'limited liability' companies that exist today (Micklethwait and Wooldridge, 2003).

The PESTEL analysis is just as relevant to public and voluntary sector organisations. Many public service organisations are in business to do things that the market does not, so a PESTEL analysis can identify emerging issues that need attention. An example is the age structure of the population: a country with growing numbers of elderly people has to finance changes in community care services, social services and hospitals. Public sector organisations are often unable to expand their operations where new problems or needs are identified, but the results can be used to lobby for increased funding or to target their existing budgets.

The PESTEL framework is a useful starting point for analysis if managers use it to identify factors that are relevant to their business and how they are changing.

3.6   Types of environment and stakeholders

Perceptions of environments

The axes in Figure 3.6 show two variables (Duncan, 1972) which affect how people see their environment – the degree of complexity and the degree of dynamism. Complexity refers to the number and similarity of factors which people take into consideration when making a decision – the more of these, and the more different they are, the more complex the situation. Dynamism refers to the degree to which these factors remain the same or change.

To consider only the most contrasting cells in Figure 3.6, those who perceive themselves to be in a *simple-static* environment will experience little uncertainty. Competitors offer similar products, newcomers rarely enter the market and there are few technological breakthroughs. Examples could include routine legal work such as house sales and wills, or trades such as joinery. The information required for a decision is likely to be available, so people can assess

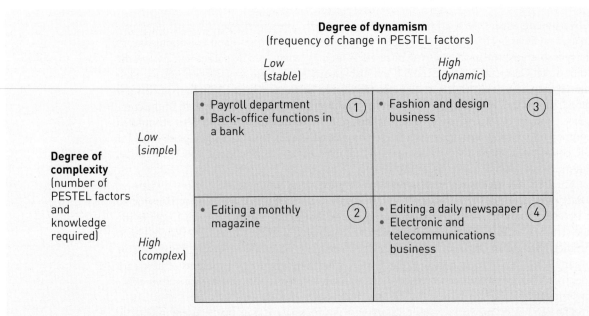

Figure 3.6 Types of environment

the outcome of a decision quickly and accurately. They can use past trends to predict the future with a reasonable degree of confidence. Some aspects of health and education, where demand is driven largely by demographic change, may also fit this pattern: the capacity needed in primary and secondary schools is easy to predict several years ahead.

Key ideas   Donald Sull – active waiting in unpredictable markets

Donald Sull (2005) has studied more than 20 pairs of comparable companies in unpredictable industries such as airlines, telecommunications and software development. By comparing similar companies he was able to show how they responded differently to unforeseen threats and opportunities. Successful companies regularly responded more effectively to unexpected shifts in regulation, technology, competitive or macro-environments. They did this by what he termed 'actively waiting', using techniques which included:

- Keeping priorities clear to avoid dissipating energy and resources.
- Conducting reconnaissance to identify gaps in the market.
- Keeping a reserve of cash to fund major opportunities when they emerge.
- Using lulls to push through operational improvements.
- Declare that an opportunity is the company's main effort to seize it faster than rivals.

Source: Based on Sull (2005).

At the other extreme, those working in complex-dynamic environments face great uncertainty. They have to monitor many diverse and changing factors. Companies in the mobile phone or entertainment industries are like this. Multinationals such as Shell and BP experience great complexity, operating across diverse political, legal and cultural systems. Eric Schmidt (Chief Executive of Google) has said that in many high tech and other industries:

> the environment is changing so fast that it requires improvisation in terms of strategy, products and even day-to-day operations. Just when you think you understand the technology landscape, you see a major disruption.

Activity 3.6   Critical reflection on type of environment

Use Figure 3.6 to analyse the environment in which your unit of the organisation works. Then try to do the same analysis for one or two other units of the organisation.

- Compare the nature of these environments.
- What are the implications of that for managing these departments, and for the organisation?

Most managers claim to work in dynamic and complex situations. This implies that they face great uncertainty over how the future will unfold. In these circumstances historical analysis is likely to be a less useful guide to the future and managers need to develop different ways of anticipating what may lie ahead.

Case question 3.4

- How would you classify the environment in which Nokia operates? Which factors contributed to your answer?

Stakeholders

All managers need to deal with stakeholders – individuals, groups or other organisations with an interest in, or who are affected by, what the enterprise does (Freeman, 1984). Organisations depend on their micro and macro environments (see Figure 3.1) for the resources they need. Stakeholders in these environments make resources available or withhold them, depending on their view of the organisation. Managers in any sector need to pay attention to stakeholder expectations, and meet these to an acceptable degree to ensure a positive view.

Stakeholders may be internal (employees, managers, different departments or professional groups, owners, shareholders) or external (customers, competitors, bankers, local communities, members of the public, pressure groups and government). The challenge is that:

> Different stakeholders do not generally share the same definition of an organization's 'problems', and hence, they do not in general share the same 'solutions.' As a result, the typical approaches to organizational problem solving, which generally pre-suppose prior consensus or agreement among parties, cannot be used; they break down. Instead a method is needed that builds off a starting point of disagreement . . . (Mitroff, 1983, p. 5)

Stakeholders have expectations of organisations and managers choose whether or not to take account of these. Nutt (2002) shows the dangers of ignoring them: he studied 400 strategic decisions and found that half of them 'failed' – in the sense that they were not implemented or produced poor results – largely because managers failed to attend to stakeholders.

Faced with evidence of excessive risk-taking in banks, shareholders have begun to become more active in criticising directors over the pay and bonus systems through which they reward senior managers in their companies. This has led to changes in corporate governance arrangements.

Figure 3.7 indicates what stakeholders may expect.

Case study   Nokia – the case continues   www.nokia.com

The manufacture of components for mobile phones is being moved rapidly out of the Nordic country to low-cost locations. Early in 2006 three of its subcontractors announced that they were cutting more than 1,100 jobs in Finland, underlining the dramatic shift in the global telecoms business, in which a rapidly growing share of revenue comes from cost-conscious emerging markets.

This is leading the Finns to reassess their high dependence on the industry. An economist at the Bank of Finland slated:

> Nokia's profits, and the tax revenues they have generated for Finland, have exceeded our wildest dreams in the past ten years. But it is disappointing that the production has not provided the highly-paid, large-scale source of employment we hoped for.

The company is also collaborating on long-term technical projects with Intel, whose microprocessors run about 80 per sent of the world's computers. They plan to create a type of mobile computing device beyond today's smartphones and netbooks. Kai Oistamo, Nokia's vice-president in charge of devices said:

> The mobile and computing industries are coming together, and we as leaders in our respective industries, are taking the responsibility to really be the enablers to create this brave new world.

Source: *Financial Times*, 13 March 2006 and 24 June 2009.

Case questions 3.5

- Who are the main stakeholders in Nokia?
- What are their interests in the success of the company?
- How can management ensure it maintains the support of the most important stakeholders?

Shareholders
- Growth in dividend payments
- Growth in share price
- Growth in asset value

Customers
- Competitive price
- Quality product or service
- Guarantee provisions

Suppliers
- Timely payment of debt
- Adequate liquidity
- Integrity of directors
- Trustworthy purchasing manager

Employees
- Good pay and benefits
- Job security
- Sense of purpose in the job
- Opportunities for personal development

Government
- Adhering to the country's laws
- Paying taxes
- Providing employment
- Value for money in using public funds

Lenders
- Financial strength of the company
- Quality of management
- Quality of assets available for security
- Ability to repay interest and capital

Figure 3.7
Examples
of possible
stakeholder
expectations

| 3.7 | **Corporate governance** |

Why have governance systems?

Scandals and failures in prominent organisations lead people to question the adequacy of their systems of **corporate governance**. They show that senior managers cannot always be trusted to act in the best interests of the company and the shareholders. To reduce this risk, owners have developed rules and processes which are intended to guide and control those responsible for managing public and private organisations, ensuring that they act in the interests of influential stakeholders. Governance systems are based on the principle that those managing an organisation are accountable for their actions, and create mechanisms to do that.

In capitalist economies, ownership typically becomes separated from control. The founder provides the initial capital but growth requires further finance – which investors provide in exchange for an income. They cannot supervise management decisions, but need to be confident that the business is secure before they provide further funds.

Berle and Means (1932) highlighted the dilemma facing owners who become separated from the managers they appoint to run the business:

> The corporation is a means by which the wealth of innumerable individuals has been concentrated into huge aggregates and whereby control over this wealth has been surrendered to a unified direction . . . The direction of industry other than by persons who have ventured their wealth has raised the question . . . of the distribution of the returns from business enterprise. (p. 4)

Their observations led others to develop what is now termed 'agency theory', which seeks to explain what happens when one party (the principal) delegates work to another party (the agent). In this case the shareholders (principals) have financed, and own, the business, but they delegate the work of running it to managers (agents). The principals then face the risk that managers may not act in their (the principals') best interests: they may take excessive investment risks, or withhold information so that the state of the business appears to be better than it is. The principal is then at a disadvantage to the agent, who may use this to personal advantage. Failures at major financial institutions, caused in part by lending money to risky borrowers in the hope of high returns, show that the separation of ownership from management, of principal from agent, is as relevant as ever.

Corporate governance refers to the rules and processes intended to control those responsible for managing an organisation.

Management in practice	The interests of managers and shareholders

While senior managers often claim to be trying to align their interests with those of shareholders, the two often conflict. Mergers often appear to benefit senior managers and their professional advisers rather than shareholders. Acquiring companies often pay too much for the target, but executives inside the enlarged company receive higher pay. Professional advisers (investment bankers) make money on both the merger and the break-up.

Using company money to buy the company's shares in the market uses money that can't be spent on dividends. From the vantage point of many CEOs, paying dividends is about the last thing they would want to do with corporate earnings. In theory, a CEO is carrying out shareholder wishes. In practice, as the spate of recent scandals has shown, the interests of chief executives and their shareholders can widely diverge.

Source: Based on extracts from an article by Robert Kuttner, *Business Week,* 9 September 2002.

Similar issues arise in the public sector, where elected members are nominally in charge of local authorities, health boards and other agencies – and who appoint professional managers to run the organisation on behalf of the citizens. Elected members face the risk that the people they have appointed act in their narrow professional or personal interests, rather than of those of the electorate. Hartley *et al.* (2008) point out:

> a new awareness of the social, economic and cultural contribution of government, public organizations and public services has resulted in a significant period of reform and experimentation. At the heart of these initiatives is the idea that improvements to the way public services can be governed, managed and delivered will produce improved outcomes for citizens. (p. 3)

Stakeholder theory is also relevant, as it tries to explain the evolving relationship between an organisation and its stakeholders. Many believe that governance systems should take account of the interests of this wider group, as well as those of shareholders with only a financial interest.

The substance of corporate governance

Mallin (2007) suggests that to provide an adequate oversight of managers, governance systems should have:

- an adequate system of internal controls which safeguards assets;
- mechanisms to prevent any one person having too much influence;
- processes to manage relationships between managers, directors, shareholders and other stakeholders;
- the aim of managing the company in the interests of shareholders and other stakeholders; and
- the aim of encouraging transparency and accountability, which investors and many external stakeholders expect.

Proposals to deal with these issues affect the context in which managers work, and this book will examine the topic as an integrating theme at the end of each chapter.

3.8	Integrating themes

Sustainable performance

Nicholas Stern advises the UK government on climate change, and his latest book (Stern, 2009) calls for urgent action to mitigate the effects. The paragraphs below summarise some of his points.

Climate change is not a theory struggling to maintain itself in the face of problematic evidence. The opposite is true: as new information comes in, it reinforces our understanding across a whole spectrum of indicators. The subject is full of uncertainty, but there is no serious doubt that emissions are growing as a result of human activity and that more greenhouse gases will lead to further warming.

The last 20 years have seen special and focused attention from the Intergovernmental Panel on Climate Change (IPCC) (**www.ipcc.ch**), which has now published four assessments, the most recent in 2007. With each new report, the evidence on the strength and source of the effects, and the magnitude of the implications and risks, has become stronger. The basic scientific conclusions on climate change are very robust and for good reason. The greenhouse effect is simple science: greenhouse gases trap heat, and humans are emitting ever more greenhouse gases. There will be oscillations, there will be uncertainties. But the logic of the greenhouse effect is rock-solid and the long-term trends associated with the effects of human emissions are clear in the data.

In 2010 a report by the UK Meteorological Office (Stott, 2010) confirmed these conclusions, saying that the evidence was stronger now than when the IPCC carried out its last assessment in 2007. The analysis assessed 110 research papers on the subject, concluding that the earth is changing rapidly, probably because of greenhouse gases. The study found that changes in Arctic sea ice, atmospheric moisture, saltiness of parts of the Atlantic Ocean and temperature changes in the Antarctic are consistent with human influence on our climate.

Governance and control

This chapter has examined the culture of organisations and their external contexts: governance links the two. There are high-profile examples of organisations whose culture has encouraged managers and staff to act in their interests, rather than in the interests of those they were expected to serve. This has focused attention on corporate governance arrangements, which are part of the context within which managers of all organisations work: most of the time these will be far in the background, but they become visible at times of difficulty.

The Cadbury Report (1992) has influenced the development of corporate governance systems around the world, including the UK. Set up following a series of UK financial scandals it made recommendations about the operation of the main board, the establishment and operation of board committees, the roles of non-executive directors, and on reporting and control mechanisms. These recommendations have been combined with the outcomes of related reports into what is known as the Combined Code – the latest version of which was published in 2006 (Financial Reporting Council, 2006). This is a voluntary Code of Best Practice, with which the boards of all companies listed on the London Stock Exchange are expected to comply – or to explain why they have not done so. It includes guidance on matters such as:

The Board. Every company should be headed by an effective board, which is collectively responsible for the success of the company;

Chairman and chief executive. There should be a clear division of responsibilities . . . between the running of the board and the executive responsible [for running the business]. No one individual should have unfettered powers of decision.

Board balance. The board should include a balance of executive and [independent] non-executive directors so that no individual or small group can dominate the board's decision taking

Board appointments. There should be a formal, rigorous and transparent procedure for appointing new directors to the board.

Internationalisation

Models of national culture (see Chapter 4) are highly generalised summaries of diverse populations. Their value is to give some clues about broad differences between the places in which those managing internationally will be working. They encourage people to be ready to adapt the way they work to local circumstances. Others take a more robust view of cultural differences and try to eliminate their influence within the organisation. Steve Chang founded Trend Micro, an anti-virus software company operating in many countries:

> The curse is that national cultures are very different. We have to figure out how to convert everybody to one business culture – no matter where they're from. (*Business Week*, 22 September 2003)

The following Management in Practice feature shows how Iris, a rapidly growing advertising agency with a very strong and distinctive company culture AND many global clients, seeks to gain the benefits of the diversity of its international staff and combine this to add more value for the client.

Management in practice   Gaining from cultural differences www.irisnation.com

Iris was founded in 1999 and has established a distinctive position as an independent media and advertising agency, with a growing international business. An innovative technique which is very popular with global clients is 'Project 72'. Steve Bell, chief executive of Iris London, and one of the founding partners, explains:

> Project 72 is a very simple concept, and probably the purest way of bringing different agencies in the group together as one with a common goal and a common vision. [Suppose] Iris Miami is working on a brief for a client: they say 'right, let's engage a Project 72 on this one'. So the brief will go to the other agencies around the world, it will be handed to London, for example, we will work on it for 12 hours, we will then [hand the baton] to Sydney, they will work on it for 12 hours, baton change to Singapore, so you can see how within 72 hours we've got the best freshest brains working on a brief to the common goal of developing the best creative work that we possibly can do. It's been fantastic . . .
>
> Project 72 benefits hugely from the cultural differences, and when I say cultural differences I don't mean within the agency but the societal cultural differences that happen within different areas around the world. So tapping into the fact that Singapore has a certain view around mobile telecomms enables us to look at things in a slightly different way, so it just allows fresh thinking, fresh outlooks, fresh cultures to inject some pace and some innovation around a particular brief at a given time.

Source: Interview with Steve Bell.

Summary

1 **Identify the main elements of the environments in which organisations work**
   - They include the immediate competitive environment, the wider general (or macro) environment and the organisation's stakeholders.

2 **Compare the cultures of two organisational units, using Quinn's or Handy's typologies**
   - Quinn *et al.* (2003) – open systems, rational goal, internal process and human relations.
   - Handy (1993) – power, role, task and person.

3 **Use Porter's five forces model to analyse the competitive environment of an organisation**
   - This identifies the degree of competitive rivalry, customers, competitors, suppliers and potential substitute goods and services.

4 **Collect evidence to make a comparative PESTEL analysis for two organisations**
   - The PESTEL model of the wider external environment identifies political, economic, social, technological, environmental and legal forces.

5 Compare perceptions of environments, and give examples of stakeholder expectations
   - Environments can be evaluated in terms of their rate of change (stable/dynamic) and complexity (low/high).
   - These are shown in Figure 3.7

6 Explain the meaning and purpose of corporate governance
   - Corporate governance frameworks are intended to monitor and control the performance of managers to ensure they act in the interests of organisational stakeholders, and not just of the managers themselves.

7 Show how ideas from the chapter add to your understanding of the integrating themes
   - A major feature of the natural environment relevant to managers is the accumulating evidence that climate change is due to human activities, leading to pressure for organisations and people to work and live more sustainably.
   - Some organisational cultures encouraged staff to take excessive risks, gravely damaging companies and economies: this is leading stakeholders to press for tighter governance and control mechanisms to reduce the chances of similar events happening again.
   - While culture has a powerful effect on what people do in an organisation, when they operate internationally it provides an opportunity to benefit from diverse perspectives.

Review questions

1 Describe an educational or commercial organisation that you know in terms of the competing values model of cultures.

2 What is the significance of the idea of 'fragmented cultures' for those who wish to change a culture to support performance?

3 Identify the relative influence of Porter's five forces on an organisation of your choice and compare your results with a colleague's. What can you learn from that comparison?

4 How should managers decide which of the many factors easily identified in a PESTEL analysis they should attend to? If they have to be selective, what is the value of the PESTEL method?

5 Since people interpret the nature of environmental forces from unique perspectives, what meaning can people attach to statements about external pressures?

6 Illustrate the stakeholder idea with an example of your own, showing their expectations of an organisation.

7 Explain at least two of the mechanisms which Mallin (2007) recommends should be part of a corporate governance system.

8 Summarise an idea from the chapter that adds to your understanding of the integrating themes.

Concluding critical reflection

Think about the culture which seems to be dominant in your company, and how managers deal with the business environment and with stakeholders. Alternatively take another company with which you are familiar, and find what you can about its culture, and how it monitors and assesses the external environment. Review the material in the chapter and make notes on the following questions:

   - Which of the issues discussed in this chapter are most relevant to the way you and your colleagues manage? What **assumptions** appear to guide the culture, and the factors in the external environment which managers believe have most effect on the business? Do you all attach the same significance to them or do views vary? Why is that? How do these views affect your tasks as managers and, indeed, the nature of your organisation?

● What factors in the **context** appear to have shaped the prevailing view about which changes in the environment will most affect the business? Why do they think that? Do people have different interpretations?

● Can you compare your business environment with that of colleagues on your course, especially those in similar industries? Does this show up any **alternative** ways of seeing the context, and of dealing with stakeholders?

● What are the **limitations** of the ideas on culture and stakeholders which the chapter has presented. For example, are the cultural types transferable across nations, or how may they need to be adapted to represent different ways of managing?

Further reading

Hawken, P., Lovins, A.B. and Lovins. L.H. (1999), *Natural Capitalism: The next industrial revolution*, Earthscan, London.

> Generally positive account of the environmental challenges facing us all, and what organisations are doing about it.

Johns, G. (2006), 'The essential impact of context on organizational behavior', *Academy of Management Review*, vol. 31, no. 2, pp. 386–408.

> An overview of the many ways in which writers have expressed the idea of 'context', and how it affects organisational behaviour and research. It proposes two ways of thinking about context; one grounded in journalistic practice and the other in classic social psychology.

Frooman, J. (1999), 'Stakeholder influence strategies', *Academy of Management Review*, vol. 24, no. 2, pp. 191–205.

Pajunen, K. (2006), 'Stakeholder influences on organizational survival', *Journal of Management Studies*, vol. 43, no. 6, pp. 1261–1288.

> These two articles provided a comprehensive theoretical background to case studies of stakeholder management.

Steinbock, D. (2001), *The Nokia Revolution*, American Management Association, New York.

> This is an authoritative account of the development of the company, and its interaction with the external environment.

Tapscott, E. and Williams, A.D. (2006), *Wikinomics: How Mass Collaboration Changes Everything*, Viking Penguin, New York.

> Best-selling account of the radical changes which convergent technologies bring to society, especially the relationship between producers and consumers.

Weblinks

These websites have appeared in the chapter:

www.nokia.com
www.acea.be
www.walmart.com

www.bosch.com
www.vtplc.com
www.unilever.com
www.ford.com
www.tata.com
www.renault.com
www.hmv.com
www.ipcc.ch
www.irisnation.com

Visit some of these, or any other companies which interest you, and navigate to the pages dealing with recent news, press or investor relations.

- What can you find about their culture?
- What are the main forces in the external environment which the organisation appears to be facing?
- What assessment would you make of the nature of that environment?
- Compare and contrast the issues you identify on the two sites.
- What challenges may they imply for those working in, and managing, these organisations?

For video case studies, audio summaries, flashcards, exercises and annotated weblinks related to this chapter, visit **www.pearsoned.co.uk/mymanagementlab**

CHAPTER 4
MANAGING INTERNATIONALLY

Aim

To outline the factors shaping the work of managing internationally.

Objectives

By the end of your work on this chapter you should be able to outline the concepts below in your own terms and:

1 Contrast the ways in which organisations conduct international business

2 Explain, with examples, how PESTEL factors affect the decisions of those managing internationally

3 Summarise at least one aspect of EU policy (or of an international trade agreement) which is of interest to you for your career

4 Explain and illustrate the evidence on national cultures, and evaluate the significance of Hofstede's research for managers working internationally

5 Compare and contrast the features of national management systems

6 Summarise the forces stimulating the growth of international business

7 Show how ideas from the chapter add to your understanding of the integrating themes

Key terms

This chapter introduces the following ideas:

outsourcing	pervasiveness (of corruption)
foreign direct investment	arbitrariness (of corruption)
licensing	high-context cultures
franchising	low-context cultures
joint venture	power distance
multinational company	uncertainty avoidance
transnational company	individualism
global companies	collectivism
theory of absolute advantage	masculinity
political risk	femininity
ideology	globalisation

Each is a term defined within the text, as well as in the Glossary at the end of the book.

Case study   Starbucks   www.starbucks.com

Starbucks sells coffee, pastries, confectionery and coffee-related accessories through over 16,000 retail stores – about 12,000 in the US and 4,000 in more than 50 countries. In the financial year to the end of September 2009 its total revenue amounted to $9.8 billion, and profits to almost $900 million.

Three entrepreneurs created the company in 1971 to sell coffee in Seattle, and by 1981 they had five stores. The owners decided to sell the business in 1987 and Howard Schultz (a former employee) bought the company, which he then expanded rapidly, so that by 1991 there were 114 Starbucks stores. The company was also innovative with new products to attract customers – such as introducing low-fat iced coffee for the diet conscious. It grew by about 20 per cent a year during the 1990s, but some believed that the market in the US would become saturated.

To maintain rapid growth, the company began to expand overseas, through Starbucks Coffee International, a wholly owned subsidiary. By September 2009 it had 4,000 stores (30 per cent of the total) outside the US. It entered the Asia Pacific rim first, as the eagerness of young people there to imitate Western lifestyles made them attractive markets for Starbucks. The company used joint ventures, licensing or wholly owned subsidiaries to enter new markets. Initially it opened a few stores in trendy parts of the country, with the company's managers from Seattle handling the operation. Local *baristas* (brew masters) were trained in Seattle for 13 weeks, to ensure consistent standards across the world. Similar products were stocked, and all stores were 'No Smoking'.

The company's managers adapted the business to local tastes – such as offering curry puffs and meat buns in Asia, where people prefer to eat something while having coffee. In the Middle East the coffee shops had segregated sections for ladies. In 1998 the company opened in Europe, with stores in the UK, Switzerland, Germany and Greece. The company believed that it was successful not because it was selling coffee, but because it was selling an experience. In many markets it faces local competition and is subject to the same economic conditions as other businesses of its type.

It has attracted criticism in some overseas markets – in common with many US businesses. In

Purestock/Alamy

Starbucks' case this also focused on the sources of its coffee. Advocates of fair trade argued that big coffee buyers such as Starbucks should do more to ensure that they buy coffee at fair prices from growers who do not exploit workers.

Source: Based on published sources.

Case questions 4.1

- What encouraged managers at Starbucks to expand overseas, and what influenced their choice of countries in which to operate?

- What are the main risks that Starbucks faces in expanding rapidly in overseas markets?

- What does the case so far suggest about the management issues it will face in operating internationally?

4.1 Introduction

Managers at Starbucks decided to expand their business overseas, and in doing so are likely to face common problems in moving to a global operation. Having expanded rapidly in their home market, they believe that the best way to maintain their growth is building the business overseas. 'Going international' will bring new and unfamiliar problems – how to create a strategy for a global business and how to implement it.

Others face the same issues. Retailers such as Tesco (Part 6 case) and Ikea (Chapter 7 case) are extending their international operations, despite the problems of understanding different customer tastes, and of obtaining government permission to open stores in some countries. Managers in companies such as Marlborough and H&M, with large overseas sales, balance the consistency of the global brand with what local customers expect.

Manufacturers such as BMW and service providers such as Lloyds TSB have transferred many types of work to low-wage countries such as China and India. That raises new management problems when managing operations in unfamiliar countries: Ford is working out how to manage a joint venture with the Chong Qing Group in China to manufacture a compact family car. When Kraft, the US food group, bought Cadbury's in 2010 it acquired a brand with strong historical associations: these are part of the context as it re-structures the operation to reduce costs. Managers investing overseas consider not only the economic or market aspects, but also whether the legal system will protect their investments and whether the country is politically stable. Many overseas ventures fail: those managing them have not added value but destroyed it.

There has been international trade since the earliest times. The merchants who created the East India Company in London in 1599 to trade with the spice islands in South-East Asia (in close and violent competition with the Dutch East India Company, founded in 1602), were formalising established practice, and by the nineteenth century there were many worldwide trading companies. International operations are inherent in transport and mineral businesses. Federal Express and Maersk move products around the world for their customers; BP and Rio Tinto Zinc necessarily secure resources in some parts of the world and sell them in others.

What is new is the high proportion of production that crosses national boundaries, much of it through businesses operating on a regional or global scale. One-third of all trade takes place within transnational companies, quite apart from external sales of foreign subsidiaries. Rapid economic development in China, India and other Asian countries is transforming them into major players in world trade. High-value/low-weight products are traded across the world, increasing growth – and providing opportunities for the shipping business – see the following Management in Practice.

Management in practice   **Maersk and global trade**   www.maersk.com

Maersk is the world's largest container shipping line, and it's growth has reflected that of world trade. Doug Bannister, Managing Director of Maersk Line (UK and Ireland) explained:

We're involved in the transportation sector, about 90 per cent of world trade is done by sea-borne transportation, it is an incredible industry to be associated with: our primary mission is to create opportunities in global commerce.

The scale of containerised shipping is enormous. Container shipping has been around for 40 years, and it's had incredible growth, 8 to 10 per cent a year. The types of stuff we bring in are anything from lamps, to furniture, to bananas, about 90 per cent of anything that you'd see in any room was transported in by one of our ships.

Several external factors have really played into Maersk Line's growth, globalisation probably being the primary one, and the explosion of world trade has been incredible. This is down to efficient transport solutions, as well as offshoring of production to low-cost areas such as China.

Source: Interview with Doug Bannister.

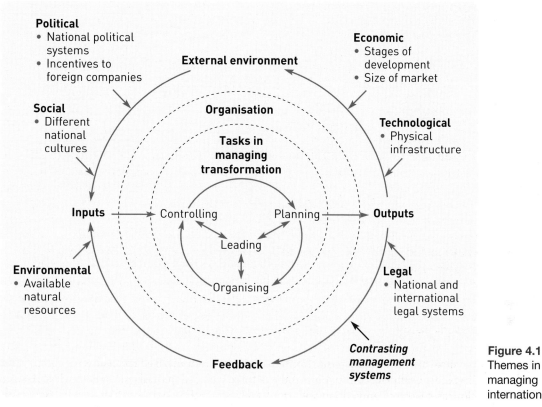

Figure 4.1
Themes in
managing
internationally

From a career point of view, **international management** (managing business operations in more than one country) can mean:

- working as an *expatriate manager* in another country;
- joining or managing an *international team* with members from several countries;
- managing in a *global organisation* whose employees, systems and structures are truly international in that they no longer reflect its original, national base.

International management is the practice of managing business operations in more than one country.

This chapter begins by showing how companies conduct business internationally, and then introduces ideas on the context of international business, with separate sections on trade agreements and culture. It shows the differences between national management systems and examines why international trade develops. The final section links these ideas to the integrating themes. Figure 4.1 shows a plan of the chapter.

  4.2   Ways to conduct business internationally

Companies which conduct international business use one or more of the following methods.

Outsourcing

Outsourcing (sometimes called 'offshoring') happens when managers decide to transfer some activities to countries that will do them more cost-effectively. This began when companies in developed Western economies transferred routine manufacturing activities to low-wage developing countries. The practice is now more diverse, with the internet enabling companies to transfer routine administrative activities (such as payroll or accounting) to overseas centres. Companies in India now outsource some work to emerging economies where staff are cheaper or more plentiful.

Outsourcing (offshoring) is the practice of contracting out defined functions or activities to companies in other countries that can do the work more cost-effectively.

Exporting and importing

The longest established way of dealing with overseas customers and suppliers is by transporting physical products (raw materials or finished goods) or delivering services (a retail shop, consultancy or legal advice) across national boundaries. If the final distribution of exports is arranged through a dealer or agent in the receiving country, the implications for people in the exporting company are limited, apart from those directly involved in managing the transactions.

Foreign direct investment

Foreign direct investment (FDI) is the practice of investing shareholder funds directly in another country, by building or buying physical facilities, or by buying a company.

Foreign direct investment (FDI) is when a firm builds or acquires facilities in a foreign country, and manages them directly. Motor companies often do this – Nissan manufactures at several sites in the UK, while General Motors built a plant in India to make the Chevrolet Spark. If the venture is a wholly owned subsidiary, profits, stay within the company, which retains control over expertise, technology and marketing. In these examples the companies have built and managed the facilities themselves – in others, such as Kraft's purchase in 2010 of Cadbury's, managers buy the assets of an existing business. Chung and Bruton (2008) provide an informative review of the scale and diversity of FDI in China.

Licensing

Licensing is when one firm gives another firm the right to use assets such as patents or technology in exchange for a fee.

Licensing occurs when a business grants the right (licenses) to a firm in another country (the licensee) to produce and sell its products for a specified period – such as the deal between Imperial Tobacco and a Chinese group to produce and distribute Imperial brands in the world's largest cigarette market. The licensing firm receives a payment for each unit sold (usually called a royalty payment), while the licensee takes the risk of investing in manufacturing and distribution facilities.

Franchising is the practice of extending a business by giving other organisations, in return for a fee, the right to use your brand name, technology or product specifications.

Franchising is similar, commonly used by service businesses (such as Starbucks) that wish to expand rapidly beyond their home market. The expanding firm sells the right (the franchise) to a company which allows them (the franchisee) to use the brand name and product design to build a business in the target market. The seller usually imposes tight conditions on matters such as quality and working procedures: many fast-food outlets are run by franchisees.

Joint ventures

A **joint venture** is an alliance in which the partners agree to form a separate, independent organisation for a specific business purpose.

Joint ventures enable firms in two or more countries to share the risks and resources required to do business internationally. Most joint ventures involve a foreign firm linking with one in the host country to take advantage of its distribution arrangements and knowledge of local customs, politics and ways of working. Both firms agree their respective investment in the venture and how they will share the profits. Starbucks typically uses joint ventures in overseas markets: in Germany this is with KarstadtQuelle, a department store group. Royal Dutch Shell has a joint venture with Shenhua Group, China's largest coal company, to study the possibility of creating a coal-to-liquids facility in western China. The hazards of joint ventures include cultural differences between the partners, and misunderstanding what each expects.

Wholly owned subsidiary

Managers who want to retain close control over their company's international activities can create a subsidiary in another country. This is costly, but if the venture works all profits stay within the company. It retains control over its expertise, technology and marketing, and can secure local knowledge by employing local staff to run the subsidiary. The company may establish the subsidiary as a new entity, or, if time is scarce, it may acquire an existing company – which still brings the problem of managing different cultures.

Which route to take (if any) is a significant management decision, as many international ventures fail: their managers have destroyed value. Johnson and Tellis (2008) relate the success or otherwise of attempts by firms to enter the Chinese and/or Indian markets to the extent to which the firm is able to retain control over the process. Exporting (cheap) gives very little control, as managers cannot control how their products are distributed and sold once they are sent. A wholly owned subsidiary (expensive) gives high control, as the company can deploy further resources such as finance or marketing knowledge if it believes this will support the strategy. They found that firms which retained a high degree of control were consistently more successful than those who did not. Early entrants were more successful than latecomers, and smaller companies were more successful than large.

Companies also develop different forms of organisation through which to conduct their international business – multinational, transnational and global.

Management in practice	A Chinese company aims to become a global player
	www.tcl.com

TCL Corporation is one of the top producers of electronics products in China and, having become one of the most prominent brands at home, the company's entrepreneurial management wants to make the company a global player. In November 2003 it formed a joint venture with French electronics maker Thomson to create the world's largest producer of televisions. For TCL, Thomson's brand names – which include RCA and Thomson – were key to the deal. TCL also wants to use Thomson's distribution system to extend its reach.

Source: Based on 'Bursting out of China', *Business Week*, 17 November 2003.

Multinational companies are based in one country, but have significant production and marketing operations in many others – perhaps accounting for more than a third of sales. Managers in the home country make the major decisions.

> **Multinational companies** are managed from one country, but have significant production and marketing operations in many others.

Transnational companies also operate in many countries but decentralise many decisions to local managers. They use local knowledge to build the business, while still projecting a consistent company image.

> **Transnational companies** operate in many countries and delegate many decisions to local managers.

Global companies work in many countries, securing resources and finding markets in whichever are most suitable. Production or service processes are performed, and integrated, across many global locations – as are ownership, control and top management. Trend Micro, an anti-virus software company, needed to organise so that staff can respond rapidly to new viruses that appear anywhere and spread very quickly. Trend's financial headquarters is in Tokyo; product development is in Taiwan (a good source of staff with a PhD); and the sales department is in California – inside the huge US market. Nestlé is another example: although headquarters are in Switzerland, 98 per cent of sales and 96 per cent of employees are not. Such businesses are often organised by product, with those in charge of each unit securing resources from whichever country gives best value.

> **Global companies** work in many countries, securing resources and finding markets in whichever country is most suitable.

Management in practice	An Indian supplier to Wal-Mart www.walmart.com

Deep in the Punjab heartland, in the town of Barnala, Rajinder Gupta is a star supplier to the world's biggest company – Wal-Mart. Gupta's Abhishek Industries exports textiles and has twice been judged the Wal-Mart International Supplier of the year. He says:

> We've grown with Wal-Mart since we first began supplying to them five years ago. Now we've created a dedicated capacity for them, with systems geared to their needs.

From tanneries in Kanpur and rug weavers in Mumbai to shirt manufacturers in Tirupur, Wal-Mart has zeroed in on 142 low-cost quality manufacturing units across India, which will supply to its stores in the US and 12 other countries . . . It recently set up Wal-Mart Global Procurement Company in Bangalore where a staff of 54 are working towards further expanding business with India. A company official said:

Indian suppliers are capable, qualified and quality-focused and we intend to grow India as a source of supply, especially in categories like textiles, shoes, jewellery and gift items.

Source: Based on 'Wal-Mart Effect', *Times of India Corporate Dossier*, 28 May 2004.

Activity 4.1   Choosing between approaches

Consider the different ways of expanding a business internationally.

- For each of the methods outlined above, note the advantages and disadvantages.
- Identify a company with international operations, and gather evidence to help you decide which method it has used and why.
- Compare your research with colleagues on your course, and prepare a short presentation summarising your conclusions.

Case questions 4.2

- Which of the modes of entry outlined above has Starbucks used?
- Would you classify Starbucks as a multinational, transnational or global firm?

4.3   The contexts of international business – PESTEL

People managing international operations pay close attention to the international aspects of the general business environment outlined in Chapter 3: the PESTEL framework becomes international, as shown in Figure 4.2. Section 4.3 outlines four of these (beginning, for clarity, with the economic context), and Sections 4.4 and 4.5 present the socio-cultural and legal contexts.

Economic context

One area of economic theory is that which aims to understand why nations trade with each other, rather than being self-sufficient. It uses the idea of the specialisation of effort, from which comes the **theory of absolute advantage**. This states that by specialising in the production of those goods which they can produce more cheaply than other countries, and trade them with others, nations will increase their economic well-being. If countries use the resources in which they have an advantage (such as fertile land, rich raw materials or efficient methods) to produce goods and services, and then exchange them with countries for things in which *they* are most efficient, they will collectively add more value than if everyone were self-sufficient. While being self-sufficient sounds attractive, it is more costly than buying things which someone else can produce more cheaply.

The **theory of absolute advantage** is a trade theory which proposes that by specialising in the production of goods and services which they can produce more efficiently than others, nations will increase their economic well-being.

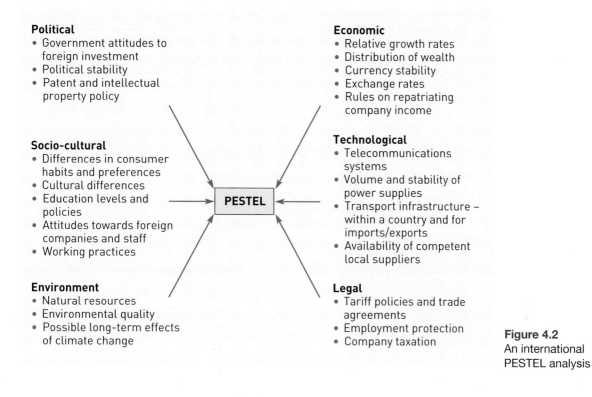

Political
- Government attitudes to foreign investment
- Political stability
- Patent and intellectual property policy

Socio-cultural
- Differences in consumer habits and preferences
- Cultural differences
- Education levels and policies
- Attitudes towards foreign companies and staff
- Working practices

Environment
- Natural resources
- Environmental quality
- Possible long-term effects of climate change

Economic
- Relative growth rates
- Distribution of wealth
- Currency stability
- Exchange rates
- Rules on repatriating company income

Technological
- Telecommunications systems
- Volume and stability of power supplies
- Transport infrastructure – within a country and for imports/exports
- Availability of competent local suppliers

Legal
- Tariff policies and trade agreements
- Employment protection
- Company taxation

Figure 4.2
An international
PESTEL analysis

The theory is, of course, a great deal more complex (see Chapter 6 in Rugman and Hodgetts (2003) for a fuller treatment of this topic) – but even this simple account begins to explain why nations trade with each other, even though each could make the traded goods themselves.

Evidence which supports this theory is evident in the rapid internationalisation of productions since the 1960s. At that time many firms in the developed world realised that labour intensive manufacturing and service operations in their home country was a costly way of working. This was especially the case in electrical and electronic goods, clothing, footwear and toys, which faced growing competition from cheaper imports. Managers looked for new sources of supply, and received a positive response from a small group of Asian countries – Taiwan, Hong Kong, South Korea and especially Singapore. These took the opportunity over the next 30 years to become major 'outsourcing' centres, supplying goods and components to companies around the world. They also developed their education systems so that they can now do work of higher value, widening their product range – including a growing trade in services such as software development and the back-office functions of airlines and banks. Table 4.1 gives some examples.

Companies sometimes find that operations in remote locations require more management time than they expected, thus reducing the cost advantage. Some also find that customers object to talking to a call centre operator in a distant country, who may lack the local knowledge to conduct a transaction smoothly. They are then likely to 'repatriate' the outsourced activities.

The internationalisation of markets happens when companies from the wealthier countries see market opportunities in less developed ones. Car companies expect emerging economies to buy more than half of their output by 2015, as people in these countries become richer and seek greater personal mobility. Consumer products companies (especially tobacco makers such as British American Tobacco or Phillip Morris) see good prospects in developing countries such as Malaysia and South Africa, whose high birth rates ensure more young consumers. Hong Kong Disneyland reflects the company's belief that Asia's media and entertainment

Table 4.1 Examples of the internationalisation of production

Company	Work transferred	Reasons given
BT www.bt.com	Opened call centres in India, replacing the jobs of 2,000 staff in the UK	'To meet cost-saving targets and remain competitive'
Gillette www.gillette.com	Closed three factories (two UK and one German) and transferred work to new factory in eastern Europe	'Significantly reduce costs and improve operating efficiency'
Dyson www.dyson.co.uk	Moved production of vacuum cleaners and washing machines from UK to Malaysia	'Reduce manufacturing costs help protect UK jobs in design and development'

market will grow rapidly. The Chinese government agreed, taking a 57 per cent stake in the project. Disney hopes this will help it win good terms for other ventures there – TV, films, advertising and consumer products.

Case study   Starbucks – the case continues www.starbucks.com

In 2007 the company's presence within Beijing's Forbidden City was threatened, amid complaints that the presence of the chain in the former imperial palace constitutes an 'affront to Chinese culture'. China's official media said that a low-key Starbucks' outlet near the rear of the sprawling Palace Museum site might be removed following online protests sparked by a patriotic polemic published by a TV anchorman on his personal blog. The controversy surrounding Starbucks' presence in the Forbidden City highlights the risks to foreign companies of offending nationalist sentiment.

It was also experiencing some problems elsewhere, with rivals often charging less for similar products, while others offered a higher quality experience. By January 2008 the company was in severe trouble, which many blamed on too rapid an expansion. Former employee Howard Schultz returned as Chief Executive in that month (he had remained as Chairman after giving up as CEO in 2000) and acted quickly to turn the business round. It closed 600 underperforming stores, improved internal processes to cut costs, improved customer service, which had declined in the preceding years, and improved the coffee and food.

In March 2010 the company appeared to be recovering, although sales and profits were both slightly below the level of the previous year. Speaking to a conference of store managers, he congratulated them on one of the most historic turnrounds in corporate history, but warned staff against complacency:

> We can't allow mediocrity to creep back into the business. The worst thing we could do is not understand what happened three years ago.

Source: *Financial Times*, 19 January 2007; 22 March 2010; Starbucks Corporation *Annual Report 2009* (on website).

The economic context of a country includes its stage of development as well as levels of inflation, exchange rates or levels of debt. The measure of economic development usually used is income per head of population – a measure of a country's total production, adjusted for size of population. Lower-income countries are concentrated in the southern hemisphere and include many in Asia, Africa and South America. The richer, developed countries tend to be in the northern hemisphere, where most international firms are located.

> **Key ideas** The complex forces behind China's transition to capitalism
>
> Doug Guthrie (2006) presents a valuable insight into one of the major business developments in recent years – the transition of China from a state-run towards a market-based system. A distinctive feature of his analysis is the emphasis he places on the links between political, social, cultural and economic forces:
>
> > Economic institutions and practices are deeply embedded in political, cultural and social systems, and it is impossible to analyze the economy without analyzing the way it is shaped by politics, culture and the social world. The perspective is essential for understanding the complex processes of economic and social reform in any transforming society, but it is especially critical for understanding China's reform path and trajectory. This position may seem obvious to some, but . . . for years, economists from the World Bank, the IMF [International Monetary Fund], and various reaches of academia have operated from a different set of assumptions: they have assumed that a transition to markets is a simple and, basically, apolitical process . . . In other words, 'don't worry about the complexities of culture or pre-existing social or political systems; if you put the right capitalist institutions in place (i.e. private property), transition to a market economy will be a simple process'. **The perspective I present here is that the standard economic view of market transitions that defined a good deal of policy for the IMF and the World Bank in the late twentieth century could not be more simplistic or more wrong.**
>
> Source: Guthrie (2006), pp.10–11.

Political context

Whatever economic theory may predict about the patterns of trade, political factors – such as the institutions and processes of the political system, the extent of government involvement in the economy, whether it aims to influence market behaviour, and a nation's laws regarding corruption. These factors also shape the **political risk** a company faces in a country – the risk of losing assets, earning power or managerial control due to political events or the actions of host governments. During the 1990s, east European countries offered large incentives to attract Western companies to build, for example, power plants in their territories: now they are members of the EU these incentives may be judged as illegal state aid, so the investing companies risk losing money.

Political risk is the risk of losing assets, earning power or managerial control due to political events or the actions of host governments.

The political system in a country influences business, and managers adapt to the prevailing **ideology**. Political ideologies are closely linked to economic philosophies and attitudes towards business. In the US the political ideology is grounded in a constitution which guarantees the rights of people to own property and to have wide freedom of choice. This laid the foundations of a capitalist economy favourable to business. While countries such as Australia or the UK are equally capitalist in outlook, others such as Brazil or France have political ideologies which give more emphasis to social considerations.

An **ideology** is a set of integrated beliefs, theories and doctrines that helps to direct the actions of a society.

There are close links between political and economic systems – especially in how they allocate resources and deal with property ownership. Governments of all forms set the rules that establish what commercial activity takes place within their jurisdiction, and how it can be conducted – whether in a fundamentally capitalist way, in a centrally controlled way, or a mix of the two. Differences in political systems affect business life through:

- the balance between state-owned and privately owned enterprises;
- the amount of state intervention in business through subsidies, taxes and regulation;
- policies towards foreign companies trading in the country, with or without local partners (India is reluctant to allow foreign retailers such as Ikea to enter the country);
- policies towards foreign companies acquiring local firms;
- policies on employment practices, working conditions and job protection (in 2010 the French government ordered Renault to make the new Clio in France, rather then move production to Turkey).

All states are affected to some degree by corruption – when politicians or officials abuse public power for private benefit. Coping with this is part of the job of managers operating internationally, but as Rodriguez *et al.* (2005) point out

> while corruption is everywhere . . . it is not the same everywhere. (p. 383)

Rodriguez *et al.* (2005) introduce a two-dimensional framework to help understand the different forms of corruption, and its implications for business – based on its **pervasiveness** and **arbitrariness**. Pervasiveness is the extent to which a firm is likely to encounter (and so have to deal with) corruption in the course of normal transactions with state officials. Arbitrariness is the degree of ambiguity associated with corrupt transactions in a given state. When corruption is arbitrary, officials apply laws and rules capriciously and haphazardly – perhaps enforcing them strictly in some areas of the country but ignoring them elsewhere. Figure 4.3 illustrates this.

Pervasiveness (of corruption) represents the extent to which a firm is likely to encounter corruption in the course of normal transactions with state officials.

Arbitrariness (of corruption) is the degree of ambiguity associated with corrupt transactions.

Technological context

Infrastructure includes all of the physical facilities that support economic activities – ports, airports, surface transport and, increasingly, telecommunications facilities. Companies operating abroad, especially in less developed countries, are closely interested in the quality of this aspect of a country as it has a huge effect on the cost and convenience of conducting business in the area.

Management in practice — Power shortages benefit Aggreko — www.aggreko.com

Many developing economies regularly experience severe shortages of power, as demand for electricity exceeds their generating capacity. This provides opportunities for Aggreko, a company with about 2,000 staff, which rents power generation and temperature control equipment in 29 countries around the world. In 2009 it reported that its strongest-performing division that year had been its International Power Projects Division, which provides long-term power generation capacity to countries without sufficient installed capacity. For example, the company provides almost half of Uganda's electricity, and also supplies Bangladesh and Kenya.

Source: Company website.

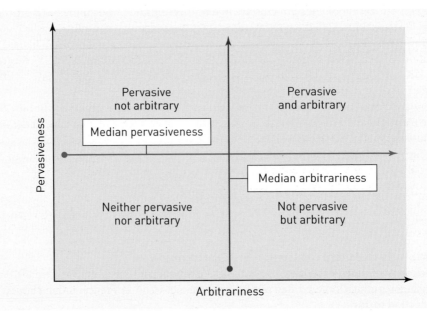

Figure 4.3
Two dimensions of corruption: pervasiveness and arbitrariness

Source: Based on Rodriguez *et al.* (2005).

A poor infrastructure is an opportunity for those supplying such facilities. European water companies have contracts to apply their expertise to providing water and sanitation services to many developing countries.

Developments in information technology stimulate international trade in two ways. The electronics industry requires billions of high-value, low-weight components, which are produced in globally dispersed factories and transported to assembly plants – from which finished products are in turn transported to consumers around the world. These movements have been a major driver of the growth of world trade. In addition, companies of all kinds use the internet to help them control international operations. The efficiency this brings encourages them to continue extending these.

Environmental context

The natural environment is a further aspect of the business context. One aspect is the natural resources available in an economy – oil, coal and other minerals, agricultural land and the prevailing climate. A key distinction in considering natural resources is between those that are renewable and those that are not: land can be used for several purposes in succession; timber is renewable – but oil is not. Water supplies are increasingly scarce and a major concern to international food production companies.

These considerations affect the kind of businesses that people create in different countries, and on the pattern of world trade. Technological developments enable the discovery of previously unknown resources (new oil reserves in Central Asia) and the fuller use of some that were previously uneconomic. This benefits the countries concerned, and the companies who agree to exploit the resources.

The process is also controversial, as when foreign mining or oil companies come into conflict with local populations whose land they occupy, or over the commercial terms of the concessions.

Management in practice   **Insurgency that may threaten business growth**

Just as India is emerging as an economic powerhouse on the world stage, landless revolutionaries committed to the class struggle and the destruction of the state are gaining control of large areas of the country. Maoist groups are estimated by the government to be running parallel administrations, including legal systems, in one-quarter of India's 600 districts, and are imposing high costs on the country's ability to attract investment in mineral-rich states such as Orissa and Jharkand. Manmohan Singh, India's Prime Minister, identifies the Maoists, motivated by resentment at generations of social injustice and the inequitable distribution of the country's new wealth, as the single greatest threat to India's security.

Source: From an article by Jo Johnson, *Financial Times*, 26 April 2006, p. 13.

Activity 4.2   **Reflecting on contexts**

Go to the website of a large company (such as BAE systems (**www.bae.com**) and see what examples you can find of managers responding to the factors in this section.

Alternatively, if you have worked in a company operating internationally, which of the contextual factors in this section have had most effect on the management of the venture?

- Within each heading, which items had most impact and why?
- Which items that are NOT listed had a significant impact and why?
- Evaluate the usefulness of the model as a guide to those managing internationally.

Some object to the environmental degradation associated with timber or mineral exploitation, whose effects spread widely (such as when rivers are polluted in one country before flowing to another). Economic development itself causes pollution – a problem for people in the area, and an opportunity for foreign businesses that specialise in environmental remediation.

4.4   Legal context – trade agreements and trading blocs

Managers planning to enter an overseas market need to ensure that they are familiar with local laws and regulations affecting business practice: they also need to satisfy themselves that the legal system there will protect them in the event of disputes with customers or suppliers. Beyond conditions in an individual country, international managers are closely interested in trade agreements and regional economic alliances.

GATT and the World Trade Organisation

The General Agreement on Tariffs and Trade (GATT) reduces the propensity of national governments to put tariffs on physical goods to protect domestic companies. Its main tool is tariff concessions, whereby member countries agree to limit the level of tariffs they impose on imports. GATT has also sponsored a series of international trade negotiations aimed at reducing restrictions on trade – one of which established the World Trade Organisation (WTO). This is a permanent global institution, which monitors international trade, and arbitrates in disputes between countries over the interpretation of tariffs and other barriers to trade. It is also seeking a world agreement on rules governing foreign investment – both to encourage it and, where thought necessary, to control it.

European Union

Since the leaders of the original member states signed the Treaty of Rome in 1959, the aim of the EU has been to eliminate tariffs and other restrictions that national governments use to protect domestic industries. This was broadly achieved by 1968, and it led to further work to integrate the economies of the member states. This culminated in the Single European Act of 1986 that aimed to create a single internal market within the EU. Introducing the euro as a common currency for many of the members encouraged further changes in the European economy by unifying capital markets and making price comparisons more transparent. In 2010 the EU was the world's biggest economy, and the world's biggest single trading bloc.

The European Commission (responsible for proposing and implementing policy) is encouraging this liberalisation by proposing changes in national laws to make cross-border trade easier. One project will make it easier for investment businesses to sell investment products across Europe – most currently operate only in their home country. This and similar deals have encouraged a rapid growth in trade within the region. Car companies such as BMW and DaimlerChrysler have plants in several countries, specialising in particular components or models. They simultaneously import and export these between the countries as part of a region-wide production system.

Enlargement has long been a feature of the EU agenda, the greatest single enlargement being in 2004 when 10 new members (many from Eastern Europe) joined: discussions continue about the accession of Turkey.

Simultaneously, with enlargement the EU continues to deepen integration through the internal market, to enable the free movement of goods and services. The intention is to extend the range of issues affecting competition that are covered by European policies, to improve efficiency within the EU. Areas covered include:

- harmonising technical regulations between member states;
- common industrial policy (such as subsidies for local businesses and/or foreign investment);
- liberalising services (such as postal services) across the Union;
- harmonising rules on employment and environmental protection;
- facilitating cross-border mergers; and
- recognising professional qualifications (e.g. in medicine and dentistry) between member states to enable freer movement of labour.

The EU is also developing common policies on monetary and political matters, in the hope that it will be able to speak with a single voice on matters as diverse as interest rates, foreign affairs and security. The Lisbon Treaty (2009) aims to enable the enlarged EU to work more effectively. It created a full-time President of the European Council, appointed by national governments for a period of two and a half years, replacing the system of six-monthly Presidencies. It also creates a 'High Representative of the Union for Foreign Affairs and Security Policy' who will conduct the EU's Common Foreign and Security Policy.

It also extends Qualified Majority Voting (QMV) to new policy areas, which supporters hope will streamline decision making in a number of technical areas (e.g. appointments to the European Central Bank's executive board). The UK has always insisted on maintaining national control in areas of justice and home affairs, social security, tax, foreign policy and defence. The Lisbon Treaty clarifies this position for the UK. Supporters of the treaty believe that the impact of QMV under the Lisbon Treaty will be significantly less than, for example, under the Single European Act or the Treaty of Maastricht.

Management in practice   Business opportunities in eastern Europe

Austria's banks are among the market leaders in eastern Europe, having spotted the market potential early. In 2006 the chief executive of the recently privatised post office foresaw huge potential for growing his business, as the state-owned post offices in the accession states were sold to private investors and the postal markets opened to new services:

> The privatization process hasn't started, [but] I think it will. It will probably be different in each case. It's a highly political issue, but it will open the door for us.

Source: *Financial Times* 19 April 2006.

Activity 4.3   Access the European Union website
http://ec.europa.eu

Access the EU website, and navigate to areas that interest you, such as those on European Policies or on Jobs at the Commission.

Alternatively, gather information that provides you with specific examples or evidence about one of the topics in this chapter, which you could use in an essay or assignment.

Make notes on what you have found and compare them with a colleague on your course.

4.5 Socio-cultural context

Culture is distinct from human nature (features which all human beings have in common) and from an individual's personality (the person's unique way of thinking, feeling and acting). It is a collective phenomenon, shared with people in the common social environment in which it was learned. Hofstede and Hofstede (2005) describe it as the unwritten rules of the social game:

> the collective programming of the mind which distinguishes one group or category of people from others (in which 'group' means a number of people in contact with each other, and a 'category' means people who have something in common, such as people born before 1940). (pp. 4, 377)

While humans share common biological features, those in a particular society, nation or region develop a distinct culture. As a business becomes more international, its managers balance a similar approach to business across the world with the unique cultures of the places in which they operate.

Cultural diversity and evolution

Hofstede and Hofstede (2005) note the wide diversity of cultures between human societies, even though people have evolved from common ancestors. There are recognisable differences between people in geographically separate areas in how they communicate with each other, how they respond to authority, when they go to work – and in countless other aspects of social life. Societies develop these practices as they adapt to their natural environment, experience military or religious conquest, or exploit scientific discoveries in agriculture and industry. These societal developments are usually overlaid by the relatively recent creation of nations:

> strictly speaking, the concept of a common culture applies to societies, not to nations . . . yet rightly or wrongly, properties are ascribed to the citizens of certain countries: people refer to 'typically American,' 'typically German,' 'typically Japanese' behaviour. Using nationality is a matter of expediency. (pp. 18–19)

Nations develop distinct institutions – governments, laws, business systems and so on. Some argue that these in themselves account for differences in behaviour between countries, implying that institutions (such as a legal or banking system) that work in one country will do so elsewhere. A counter view is that institutions reflect the culture in which they developed: something that works well in one country, may fail in another:

> Institutions cannot be understood without considering culture, and understanding culture presumes insight into institutions. (Hofstede and Hofstede, 2005, p. 20)

Managers and those who work for them are part of a nation, and to understand and work with them we need to understand their respective cultures – what types of personality are common, how they see work in relation to family life, their dominant values, and what they regard as important.

Management in practice   Cultural variety in the early days of the European Commission

Marcello Burattini was head of protocol for the European Commission. On the fortieth anniversary of the Treaty of Rome he recalled the early days:

> At the beginning of the 1960s the rules, based on the principles of Franco-Prussian administration, were strict, formal modes of address, and ties were de *rigueur* . . . Then certain political leaders decided

to enlarge [the Community]. Thus the British and the Irish arrived, bringing with them the English language, humour, simplicity in human relations, many original ideas – for example, pragmatism – somewhat softening the rigorous orthodoxy. The Danes taught us to be less formal, and were astonished by our way of doing things – and by the fact that secretaries made coffee for their bosses.

Source: *The European*, 27 March 1997.

Activity 4.4   **Comparing cultures**

Form a group among your student colleagues, made up of people from different countries.

- Identify the main characteristics of the respective cultures in your group.
- Gather any evidence about how members think they affect the work of managing.
- Compare your evidence on cultural differences with that from Hofstede's research (see Section 4.6).

High-context and low-context cultures

Hall (1976) distinguished between high- and low-context cultures. A **high-context culture** is one in which information is implicit, and can only be fully understood in conjunction with shared experience, assumptions and various forms of verbal codes. High-context cultures occur when people live closely with each other, where deep mutual understandings develop, that then provide a rich context within which communication takes place. In a **low-context culture** information is explicit and clear. These cultures occur where people are typically psychologically distant from each other, and so depend more on explicit information to communicate:

High-context cultures are those in which information is implicit and can only be fully understood by those with shared experiences in the culture.

Low-context cultures are those where people are more psychologically distant so that information needs to be explicit if members are to understand it.

> Japanese, Arabs and Mediterranean people, who have extensive information networks among family, friends, colleagues and clients and who are involved in close personal relationships, are examples of high context cultures. Low context peoples include Americans, Germans, Swiss, Scandinavians and other northern Europeans; they compartmentalise their personal relationships, their work and many aspects of day-to-day life. (Tayeb, 1996, pp. 55–56)

Attitude to conflict and harmony

Disagreements and conflicts arise in all societies. The management interest is in how various societies have developed different ways of handling conflict. Individualistic cultures such as those of the US or the Netherlands see conflict as healthy, on the basis that all people have a right to express their views. People are encouraged to bring contentious issues into the open and discuss conflicts rather than suppress them. Other cultures place greater value on social harmony and on not disturbing the way things are:

> The notion of harmony is central in almost all East Asian cultures, such as Korea, Taiwan, Singapore and Hong Kong, through their common Confucian heritage. In . . . Korea the traditional implicit rules of proper behaviour provide appropriate role behaviour for individuals in the junior and subordinate roles of an interpersonal relationship. (Tayeb, 1996, p. 60)

Key ideas	Overemphasising diversity?

This chapter has illustrated the diversity of national cultures. There is another view that the underlying fundamentals of management outweigh cultural variations in detailed processes. One powerful constraint on diversity is the economic context of an essentially capitalist economic system. This places similar requirements on managers wherever they are. They have to provide acceptable returns, create a coherent organisational structure, maintain relations with stakeholders and try to keep control.

Further, if managers work in a multinational organisation that has developed a distinctive corporate culture (Chapter 3), will that influence their behaviour more than the local national culture?

Another constraint is the use of integrated information systems across companies (and their suppliers) operating internationally, which can place common reporting requirements on managers irrespective of their location. This ties units more closely together, and may bring more convergence in the work of management.

These are unresolved questions: look for evidence as you work on this chapter that supports or contradicts either point of view.

Several scholars have developed formal instruments to classify and compare national cultures, notably Trompenaars (1993), House *et al.* (2004) and Hofstede (2001). Hofstede's work has been the most widely used and replicated in management research (Kirkman *et al.*, 2006), and the following section outlines it.

4.6	Hofstede's comparison of national cultures

Geert Hofstede is a Dutch academic who has conducted widely quoted studies of national cultural differences. The second edition of his research (Hofstede, 2001) extends and refines the conclusions of his original work, which was based on a survey of the attitudes of 116,000 IBM employees, one of the earliest global companies. The research inspired many empirical studies with non-IBM employees in both the original countries in which IBM operated and in places where they did not. Kirkman *et al.* (2006) reviewed many of these and concluded that "most of the country differences predicted by Hofstede were supported" (p. 308), and Hofstede and Hofstede (2005, pp. 25–28) make a similar point and also provide an accessible account of the research method.

Hofstede (2001), as already noted, defined culture as a collective programming of people's minds, which influences how they react to events in the workplace. He identified five dimensions of culture and sought to measure how people in different countries vary in their attitudes to them.

Power distance

Power distance is the extent to which the less powerful members of organisations within a country expect and accept that power is distributed unevenly.

Power distance (PD) as 'the extent to which the less powerful members of . . . organisations within a country expect and accept that power is distributed unevenly' (Hofstede and Hofstede, 2005, p. 46). One of the ways in which countries differ is in how power and authority are distributed. Related to this is how people view the resultant inequality. In some the existence of inequality in boss/subordinate relationships is seen as undesirable while in others people see it as part of the natural order of things. The questionnaire allowed the researchers to calculate scores for PD, countries with a high PD being those where people accepted inequality. Those with high scores included Malaysia, Mexico, Venezuela, Arab countries, China, France and Brazil. Those with low PD scores included Australia, Germany, Great Britain, Sweden, and Norway.

Uncertainty avoidance

Uncertainty avoidance is 'the extent to which the members of a culture feel threatened by ambiguous or unknown situations' (Hofstede and Hofstede, 2005, p. 167). People in some cultures tolerate ambiguity and uncertainty quite readily – if things are not clear they will improvise or use their initiative. Others are reluctant to move without clear rules or instructions. High scores, indicating low tolerance of uncertainty, were obtained in the Latin American, Latin European and Mediterranean countries, and for Japan and Korea. Low scores were recorded in the Asian countries other than Japan and Korea, and in most of the Anglo and Nordic countries – such as the US, Great Britain, Sweden and Denmark.

> **Uncertainty avoidance** is the extent to which members of a culture feel threatened by uncertain or unknown situations.

Individualism/collectivism

Hofstede and Hofstede (2005) distinguish between **individualism** and **collectivism:**

> Individualism pertains to societies in which the ties between individuals are loose: everyone is expected to look after himself or herself and his or her immediate family. Collectivism as its opposite pertains to societies in which people, from birth onwards, are integrated into strong, cohesive in-groups which throughout people's lifetime continue to protect them in exchange for unquestioning loyalty. (p. 76)

Some people live in societies in which the power of the group prevails: there is an emphasis on collective action and mutual responsibility, and on helping each other through difficulties. Other societies emphasise the individual, and his/her responsibility for his/her position in life. High scores on the individualism dimension occurred in wealthy countries such as the US, Australia, Great Britain and Canada. Low scores occurred in poor countries such as the less developed South American and Asian countries.

> **Individualism** pertains to societies in which the ties between individuals are loose.
>
> **Collectivism** 'describes societies in which people, from birth onwards, are integrated into strong, cohesive in-groups which . . . protect them in exchange for unquestioning loyalty' (Hofstede, 1991, p. 51).

Activity 4.5   Implications of cultural differences

- Consider the implications of differences on Hofstede's first two dimensions of culture for management in the countries concerned. For example, what would Hofstede's conclusions lead you to predict about the method that a French or Venezuelan manager would use if he/she wanted a subordinate to perform a task, and what method would the subordinate expect his/her manager to use?
- How would your answers differ if the manager and subordinates were Swedish?

Masculinity/femininity

> A society is called **masculine** when emotional gender roles are clearly distinct: men are supposed to be assertive, tough and focused on material success, whereas women are supposed to be more modest, tender and concerned with the quality of life. A society is called **feminine** when emotional gender roles overlap (i.e. both men and women are supposed to be modest, tender and concerned with the quality of life). (Hofstede and Hofstede, 2005, p. 120)

Hofstede's research showed that societies differ in the desirability of assertive behaviour (which he labels as masculinity) and of modest behaviour (femininity). Many societies expect men to seek achievements outside the home, while women care for things within the home. Masculinity scores were not related to economic wealth: 'we find both rich and poor masculine countries, and rich and poor feminine countries' (Hofstede and Hofstede, 2005, p. 120). The most feminine countries were Sweden, Norway, the Netherlands and Denmark. Masculine countries included Japan, Austria, Germany, China and the US.

> **Masculinity** pertains to societies in which social gender roles are clearly distinct.
>
> **Femininity** pertains to societies in which social gender roles overlap.

Integrating the dimensions

These four dimensions describe the overall culture of a society, and each culture is unique. They also have similarities – for example the UK, Canada and the US all have high individualism, moderately high masculinity, low power distance, and low uncertainty avoidance. In these nations managers expect workers to take the initiative and assume responsibility (high individualism), rely on the use of individual (not group) rewards to motivate staff (moderate masculinity), treat their employees as valued people whom they do not treat officiously (low power distance) and keep bureaucracy to a minimum (low uncertainty avoidance). A systematic analysis of Hofstede's data for all the countries in his survey revealed that most of them (the exceptions being Brazil, Japan, India and Israel) fall into a particular cultural cluster. Figure 4.4 illustrates this.

Long-term and short-term orientation

In their 2005 work, Hofstede and Hofsted added this fifth dimension to their account, describing it thus:

> Long-term orientation (LTO) stands for the fostering of virtues oriented towards future rewards – in particular perseverance and thrift. Its opposite pole, short-term orientation, stands for the fostering of virtues related to the past and present – in particular respect for tradition, preservation of 'face', and fulfilling social obligations. (Hofstede and Hofstede, 2005, p. 210)

Countries with high LTO scores include China, Hong Kong, Taiwan and Japan. Great Britain, Australia, New Zealand, the US and Canada have a short-term orientation, in which many people see spending, not thrift, as a virtue

Limitations of Hofstede's work

Other scholars have drawn attention to some limitations of Hofstede's work, including:

- the small (and so possibly unrepresentative) number of respondents in some countries;
- reducing a phenomenon as complex as a nation's culture to five dimensions;

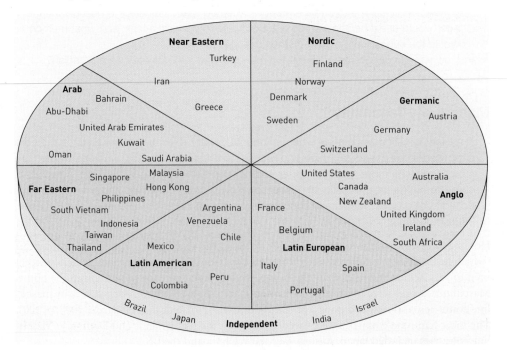

Figure 4.4
A synthesis of country clusters

Source: Ronen and Shenkar (1985).

- basing the original sample on the employees of a single multinational;
- the possibility that cultures change over time;
- the variety of cultures within a country (e.g. between religious or ethnic groups); and
- the likelihood of differences of culture within IBM (McSweeney, 2002).

Even if the precision of the results is questionable, they are a useful starting point for those working internationally to think about the culture in which they operate, and to reflect on their own cultural biases. People operating internationally need to develop an ability to deal with the different cultural contexts.

Case questions 4.3

Below are some of the countries in which Starbucks operates. If Hofstede's analysis is accurate, what may be the implications for managing the business in each of those countries, and for a manager who needs to work with colleagues in each? Check the text for the cultural features which Hofstede identified for each country, and then compare them:

- US
- Japan
- France
- UK.

Activity 4.6   Critical reflection on cultural differences

If you have worked in an organisation with international operations, reflect on whether your experience leads you to agree or disagree with the ideas in this section. For example:

- can you recognise the differences in national cultures identified by Hofstede?
- if so, in what ways did they affect the way people worked?
- how did company culture and national culture interact?

4.7   Contrasting management systems

Despite the growth of international trade and the growing interdependence of business across the world, countries vary substantially in the way that they organise economic activities. There are major differences in the way businesses are organised in different countries – even though all are capitalist economies. As Whitley (1999) explains:

> Different patterns of industrialization developed in contrasting institutional contexts and led to contrasting institutional arrangements governing economic processes becoming established in different market economies . . . Partly as a result, the structure and practices of state agencies, financial organizations and labour-market actors (in different) countries continue to diverge and to reproduce distinctive forms of economic organization. (p. 5)

Table 4.2 illustrates his ideas in relation to the US and Europe. There are significant differences between countries within Europe, and in some respects the UK is closer to the US model than to the rest of Europe.

Table 4.2 Contrasting business systems, of the US and Europe

	US	Europe
Power of state	Relatively limited, with more scope for discretion by companies to provide employee and social benefits	Relatively strong, with more engagement in economic activity through nationalisation, etc.
Financial system	Stock market central source of finance for companies, with shareholdings dispersed. Corporations expected to be transparent and accountable to investors	Corporations in network of relations with small number of larger investors. Non-shareholders often play equal role to shareholders
Education and labour system	Corporations have developed policies; relatively local and decentralised labour relations and collective bargaining	Publicly led training and labour market policies, in which corporations participated; national collective bargaining
Cultural systems	Traditions of participation, philanthropy, wary of government, moral value of capitalism; ethic of giving back to society	Preference for representative organisations – political parties, trade unions, trade associations, state

Source: Based on Whitley (1999, 2009).

He also examines the Japanese model with networks of interdependent relations, and a tradition of mutual ownership between different but friendly business units. Companies have close financial and obligational links with each other and the Ministry of Industry actively supports and guides the strategic direction of major areas of business. Firms create a network of mutually dependent organisations and decide strategy by negotiation with their stakeholders – other companies and financial institutions.

At the other extreme, firms in the US and UK are more isolated, raising most of their funds from the capital markets. Some observers believe that investors in US and UK companies expect steadily increasing returns from the companies they invest in, which in turn leads those managing the companies to focus on short-term profits at the expense of the long-term health of the business. The collapse of some financial institutions in 2008–2009 was in part blamed on executives taking excessive risks to meet capital market expectations.

Management in practice   The Italian private/public model

Managerial capitalism is taking root in Italy – but the country's tradition of public companies controlled by powerful founding families is not yet ready to bow out. It is almost impossible to exaggerate the importance for the Italian economy of a model widely known as the 'Italian private/public company' – a group of large, publicly quoted companies managed and controlled by founding families.

Italian corporate dynasties have traditionally controlled their industrial and financial groups via a complex structure involving a cascade of holding companies, often quoted, with minimum capital outlay. They further strengthened their hold on their groups through friendly shareholder syndicates and cross-shareholdings based on the principle of 'don't hurt me and I won't hurt you'. . . .

The tenacity of the family business culture in Italy is such that even Silvio Berlusconi, the prime minister, was unable to resolve a conflict of interest between his extensive business empire . . . and his political office.

Source: Extracts from an article by Paul Betts, *Financial Times*, 24 March 2003.

| 4.8 | Forces driving globalisation |

The globalisation of markets?

If you travel to another country, you immediately see many familiar consumer products or services – things that epitomise the idea that global brands are steadily displacing local products. In several industries identical products (Canon cameras, Sony Walkman, Famous Grouse whisky) are sold across the globe without modification. Theodore Levitt observed this trend towards **globalisation** – see Key Ideas.

> **Globalisation** refers to the increasing integration of internationally dispersed economic activities.

Key ideas   The globalisation of markets

Theodore Levitt, a Professor at Harvard Business School, argued that advances in communications technology were increasingly inspiring consumers around the world to want the same things. 'The world's needs and desires have been irrevocably homogenized. This makes the multinational corporation obsolete and the global corporation absolute' (p. 93). He believed therefore that international companies should cease to act as 'multinationals' that customised their products to fit local markets and tastes. Instead they should become 'global' by standardising the production, distribution and marketing of their products across all countries. Sameness meant efficiency and would be more profitable than difference. From economies of scale would flow competitive advantage.

Source: Based on Levitt (1983).

Practice in many global businesses soon appeared to support Levitt's theory. In the mid-1980s British Airways developed an advertisement ('The world's favourite airline') and (after dubbing it into 20 languages) showed it in identical form in all 35 countries with a developed TV network. Consumer companies such as Coca-Cola and McDonald's began promoting themselves as identical global brands, with standard practices and a centralised management structure.

What has led to this increasingly global business world? Yip (2003) developed a model (Figure 4.5) of the factors that drive globalisation in particular industries – managers (such as those at Starbucks) can use such a model to analyse the global potential of a business. Market factors were probably the most significant in Starbucks' case – such as the transferability of brands and advertising, and the ability to develop international distribution channels. In other industries cost factors are more prominent drivers – in motor manufacture this is especially true, with the economies of scale in manufacturing, and the ability to buy components around the world. In other cases government incentives for companies to relocate manufacturing facilities away from their home base have added to globalisation. Developments in information and communication technologies drive globalisation in many industries, by enabling the efficient flow of data on which international operations depend.

There is also evidence of resistance to the apparent inevitability of Yip's model. Local companies develop new products, and customers may find that they offer better value – so global brands offering standard products regardless of local tastes, lose market share. Therefore rather than 'going global' companies began to 'go local' – Coca-Cola, for instance, owns not one brand but 200, many of them in only one or two markets; Starbucks and McDonald's vary their offerings to suit local tastes; Nestlé has about 200 varieties of its instant coffee. Two examples from the motor industry show contrasting approaches – see the following Management in Practice.

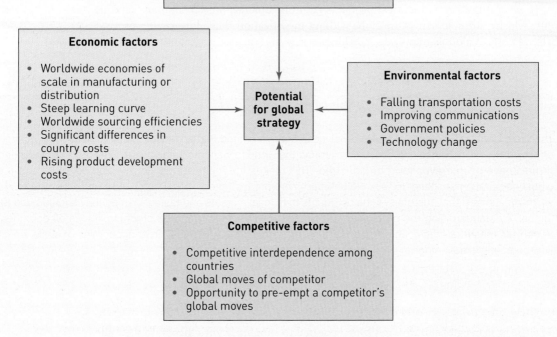

Figure 4.5 Factors driving globalisation in an industry

Source: Adapted from YIP, GEORGE S., *TOTAL GLOBAL STRATEGY II*, 2nd Edition © 2003, p. 10. Reprinted by permission of Pearson Education, Inc., Upper Saddle River, NJ.

Management in practice   Contrast Ford (www.Ford.com) with VW (www.VW.com)

In 2008 Ford announced that it was trying to break down the 'regional fiefdoms' which managers of the company's businesses around the world had developed. Designers, engineers and marketing staff focused primarily on their parts of the world producing, for example, a Ford Focus in Europe that was quite different from that sold in the US. Alan Mulally, Ford's chief executive (who had joined the company from Boeing) saw this as inefficient:

> We didn't make different 737s for France and China.

Under his plan, by 2015 all cars of each model will share a common platform, irrespective of where they are sold, believing this will produce great economies of scale for it and its suppliers.

In the same year Martin Winterkorn, chief executive of Volkswagen said that the days of building one car for the whole world were over:

> We will make the VW group the world's most international car maker. The days of a 'world car' are dead and buried. Our customers in China or India expect us, as a global player, to offer entirely different solutions than we do in the US or western Europe.

Source: *Financial Times*, 14 March 2008 and 25 July 2008.

Alan Rugman has noted that rather than becoming globalised, the world has divided into three regions – North America, the EU and Japan/East Asia – see Key Ideas. He notes that almost three-quarters of exports from EU members went to other EU countries, concluding that what we are seeing is not so much globalisation as regionalisation:

> Only in a few sectors is globalization a successful firm strategy . . . For most manufacturers and all services, regionalization is much more relevant than globalization.' (Rugman, 2005, p. 18)

Key ideas   Alan Rugman – the myth of globalisation

'It is widely accepted that multinationals drive globalisation. The top 500 multinationals dominate international business, accounting for over 90 per cent of the world's FDI and nearly half its trade. But globalisation, as commonly understood, is a myth. Far from taking place in a single global market, business activity by most large multinationals takes place within any one of the world's three great trading blocs – North America, Europe and Asia-Pacific.

Of the world's 500 multinationals, in 2001 428 were in the US, the EU and Japan. Only a handful – 9 – were by my definition truly global. These took at least a fifth of their sales from each of the three regions, but less than half from any one region. Most – 320 out of 380 – were stay-at-home multinationals, deriving on average four-fifths of their sales from their home regions.

Source: Rugman (2005), p. 6.

Concerns about globalisation

Supporters of more liberal world trade argue that it brings benefits of wider access to markets, and cheaper goods and services. The growth in trade that follows benefits both consumers and workers by encouraging innovation and investment. It has given many consumers a much wider choice of goods, by being able to attract supplies from around the world, often much more cheaply than those produced locally. Others take a much more critical view, pointing out that moves towards liberalisation through bodies such as the WTO are driven by the rich countries. They believe the agreements reached serve the interests of multinational businesses and richer economies rather than indigenous producers in local economies.

Case study   Starbucks – the case continues   www.starbucks.com

The company has not only faced some setbacks in its global expansion plans (although business in China was said to be growing rapidly again in 2010), but also criticism from activists in several countries. Some criticise it for an apparently relentless expansion, offering a similar global brand that tends to push out local companies, reducing the variety of local shopping areas.

Others have cast doubt on its claims to treat coffee growers fairly. It has taken these criticisms seriously, and has for 10 years been working with Conservation International to help farmers grow coffee in ways that are better for people and for the planet. The goal is that 100 per cent of coffee will be responsibly gown and ethically traded – at present about 75 per cent meets that standard. It also has targets that by 2015 all of the cups will be reusable or recyclable, and that it will contribute more than one million community service hours each year.

It expects all suppliers to comply with the conditions set out in a detailed statement of social responsibility standards, covering matters such as transparency, worker health and safety, worker treatment and rights, hours and pay, and environmental protection.

Sources: *Fortune*, 13 November 2006; company website; Argenti (2004).

> **Activity 4.7**   **Debating globalisation**
>
> Arrange a debate or discussion on these questions:
>
> - Has globalisation increased people's power as consumers, or diminished their power as employees?
> - Has it lifted millions out of poverty, or has it widened the gap between rich and poor?
> - Has it widened consumer choice, or has it encouraged levels of industrialisation and consumption which make unsustainable demands on the Earth's natural resources?
> - Does globalisation heighten aesthetic awareness of different cultures, or does it expose people to a stream of superficial images?
> - Does it enable more people to experience diversity, or does it lead to a bland homogenisation of local cultures into a global view?

All of these developments imply much greater patterns of contact between managers in different countries. Legislative changes and treaties remove some barriers to trade, but they do not solve the management problems of making those economic activities work efficiently. Above all, they bring many managers face to face with the need to manage cultural differences.

4.9   Integrating themes

Sustainable performance

Businesses will respond to government incentives to reduce the impact of climate change, provided it is in their interests to do so: they cannot be expected to do otherwise (except in a marginal, low-cost way), as they would then be unable to compete with companies that chose not to bear those costs. Effective action to combat climate change depends on political action – and given the global nature of the problem, that means that effective global policies must be in place. The core of the proposals put forward by Lord Stern (2009) is that global emissions of greenhouse gas must peak in the next 15 years, and then fall by at least 50 per cent, relative to 1990 levels, by 2050, when global emissions must on average be 2 tons per head.

Any set of policies to achieve this must be effective, efficient and equitable. The most difficult of these criteria to meet in this context is that of equity, principally between the developed (who emitted three-fifths of the stock of man-made greenhouse gases) and developing countries (who wish to develop their economies, which will mean more emissions). Persuading developing countries to accept binding limits even in 2020 is bound to be hard, given the gross inequity of the starting point.

While this is all very uncertain, the implication for business is that:

> both climate change, and ever tightening climate change policies by governments and international bodies, are realities. Managers should plan their long-term investments and their research and development priorities in this light. (Based on an article by Martin Wolf in a *Financial Times Supplement on Climate Change*, Part 3, 2 December 2008)

Governance and control

Mallin (2007) points out that while the work of Berle and Means (1932) (highlighting the implications of the separation of ownership from control in modern corporations) has been highly influential in protecting shareholders, countries' different legal systems lead them to achieve this aim in different ways.

The US and the UK have legal systems which generally give good protection to shareholders, which encourages a widely diversified shareholder base. Other countries have different ownership systems – family firms or a small number of large dominant shareholders, are more common in Continental Europe than in the UK. Banks often play a much bigger role in financing companies, and are likely to exercise control *via* seats on the board. This implies that governance arrangements in these countries will be adapted to suit the institutional arrangements in the local context.

Mallin (2007) summarises the arrangements in many parts of the world. In Continental Europe, for example, she finds that governance arrangements have developed idiosyncratically – for example, in the German dual board structure, employees are represented on the supervisory board which appoints, and oversees the working of, the management board, and banks are influential in the governance system. However, she believes that there appears to be convergence on certain key features, for example on the need for:

> more transparency and disclosure, accountability of the board, and the independence of at least a portion of the directors. (Mallin, 2007, p. 182)

Internationalisation

As business becomes increasingly international, do managers respond passively to aspects of the environment in the countries where they do business, or do they also try to shape it? The first view stresses how features of the political or other environments can constrain choice, especially in economies with a tradition of significant government involvement in business. It sees managers as having a passive role, reacting to pressures from their environment. An alternative view regards managers as proactive, influencing policies which are part of their context: the Management in Practice feature reports a study which gives some empirical support for the proactive view.

Management in practice   MNCs and environmental policy in China and Taiwan

In a study of the interaction between companies and government institutions over environmental policy, Child and Tsai compared the experience of companies in China and Taiwan. They examined three multinational corporations (MNCs) in the chemicals sector, each with plants in China and Taiwan – which have different environmental policies. In examining how these policies affected companies, and how companies affected the policies, they found that:

- MNCs took a broad view of the stakeholders to whom they paid attention, including suppliers, customers, local communities and especially non-governmental agencies (NGOs) who could affect public opinion.
- Non-governmental organisations (NGOs) played a major role in mobilising public concerns.
- MNCs engaged in proactive political action, often in conjunction with NGOs, to influence environmental policy.

Source: Based on Child and Tsai (2005).

Summary

1 **Contrast the ways in which organisations conduct international business**

- Exporting, licensing, joint ventures, wholly owned subsidiaries.
- Multinational (independent operations in many countries, run from centre); transnational (independent operations in many countries, decentralised); global (linked and interdependent operations in many countries, closely co-ordinated).

2 **Explain, with examples, how PESTEL factors affect the decisions of those managing internationally**

- This would involve gathering data and information about political, economic, socio-cultural, technological, environmental and legal.

3 **Explain and illustrate the evidence on national cultures, and evaluate the significance of Hofstede's research for managers working internationally**

- This would involve gathering evidence (as in the Activities) on differences in national culture (using Hofstede or a similar model), and on whether the cultural differences had a noticeable effect on the task of managing.
- Low-context – information explicit and clear; high-context – information is implicit and can only be understood through shared experience, values and assumptions.
- Hofstede distinguished between cultures in terms of power distance (acceptance of variations in power); uncertainty avoidance (willingness to tolerate ambiguity); individualism/collectivism (emphasis on individual or collective action); and masculinity/femininity (preferences for assertive or modest behaviour); and long-short-term orientation.

4 **Compare and contrast the features of national management systems**

- These shape the way people interpret generic activities of management:
  - US – individualistic, rational approach, contingent design of organisations.
  - Europe – collective, rational approach, pragmatic.
  - Japan – collective responsibility, trust of subordinates, consensus building.

5 **Summarise the forces stimulating the growth of international business**

- Yip proposes that these factors are market, economic, environmental and competitive.

6 **Show how ideas from the chapter add to your understanding of the integrating themes**

- Reducing global emissions of greenhouse gases depends on regulations by governments and international bodies; while the shape of these is still uncertain, managers should plan their long-term investments in ways that anticipate these changes.
- Governance arrangements vary between countries, reflecting the evolution of distinctive national systems.
- Managers are often active in influencing government policy and regulations in the countries in which they would like to do business.

Review questions

1 What factors are stimulating the growth in world trade?

2 Compare internationalisation and globalisation. Give a specific example of a company of each type about which you have obtained some information.

3 Outline the difference between a high- and a low-context culture and give an example of each from direct observation or discussion.

4 Explain accurately to another person Hofstede's four dimensions of national cultures. Evaluate his conclusions on the basis of discussions with your colleagues from any of the countries in his study. Evaluate the limitations and criticisms of his study.

5 Give some illustrations of your own about the way in which the history of a country has affected its culture, and how that in turn affects the management of organisations there.

6 What are the distinctive features of Japanese, European and US management systems?

7 Compare the implications of globalisation for (a) national governments, (b) their citizens, (c) the management of global companies, and (d) the environment.

8 What factors does Yip believe have encouraged the growth of international business likely to affect management functions?

9 Summarise an idea from the chapter that adds to your understanding of the integrating themes.

Concluding critical reflection

Think about the way managers in your company, or one with which you are familiar, deal with the international aspects of business. Review the material in the chapter and make notes on the following questions:

- Which of the issues discussed in this chapter are most relevant to the way you and your colleagues manage? For example, what structure(s) do you use to manage the international aspects of the business? Which of the PESTEL factors have most effect in your situation?

- What **assumptions** appear to guide the way people manage internationally? Do they assume that cultural factors are significant or insignificant? Do they see globalisation as a benefit or a threat? Do they acknowledge any responsibilities to those who may be damaged by it?

- What aspects of the historical or current **context** of the company appear to influence your company's approach to internationalisation and globalisation? Do people see it as a threat or an opportunity and why? Are there different views on how you should deal with this aspect of the business?

- Can you compare your approach with that of other companies in which colleagues on your course work? Does this suggest any plausible **alternative** ways of managing internationally? How much scope do you have to change this?

- What **limitations** can you see in the theories and evidence presented? For example, is Hofstede's analysis of different cultures threatened by the increasingly international outlook and interests of young people?

Further reading

Chen, M. (2004), *Asian Management Systems*, Thomson, London.

Comparative review of the management systems in Japan, mainland China, overseas Chinese and Korean. These are compared with Western approaches to management.

Chung, M.L. and Bruton, G.D. (2008), 'FDI in China: What we know and what we need to study next', *Academy of Management Perspectives*, vol. 22, no. 4, pp. 30–44.

Excellent study of FDI in China, with many ideas that are also relevant to other countries.

Daniels, J.D., Radebaugh, L.H. and Sullivan, D.P. (2004), *International Business: Environments and operations* (10th edn), Pearson/Prentice Hall, Upper Saddle River, NJ.

Provides a comprehensive exposure to many aspects of international business, combining a strong theoretical base with many current examples.

Friedman, T. (2005), *The World is Flat: A brief history of the globalized world in the 21st century*, Penguin/Allen Lane, London.

Best-selling account of the forces that are driving globalisation, and enabling greater collaboration between companies wherever they are. The same forces that assist company networks also assist terrorist networks.

Guthrie, D. (2006), *China and Globalization: The social, economic and political transformation of Chinese society*, Routledge, London.

An excellent review of China's transition towards a market economy, showing how the visible economic changes depend on supportive social, cultural and political changes.

Moore, F. (2005), *Transnational Business Cultures: Life and work in a multinational corporation*, Ashgate Publishing, Aldershot.

An excellent (and rare) ethnographic study of people working in a German bank with offices in Frankfurt and London, which explores the complex emerging cultures combining local, global and corporate elements.

Pinder, J. (2001), *The European Union: A very short introduction*, Oxford University Press, Oxford.

As the title implies, a concise account of the development of the EU.

Weblinks

These websites have appeared in the chapter:

www.starbucks.com
www.maersk.com
www.tcl.com
www.walmart.com
www.bt.com
www.gillette.com
www.dyson.co.uk
www.aggreko.com
www.genpact.com
www.bae.com
http://ec.europa.eu
www.irisnation.com
www.Ford.com
www.VW.com

Visit two of the sites in the list, or others which interest you, and navigate to the pages dealing with recent news, press or investor relations.

● What signs are there of the international nature of the business, and what are the main issues in this area that the business appears to be facing?

● Compare and contrast the issues you identify on the two sites.

● What challenges may they imply for those working in, and managing, these organisations?

 **WWW** For video case studies, audio summaries, flashcards, exercises and annotated weblinks related to this chapter, visit **www.pearsoned.co.uk/mymanagementlab**

CHAPTER 5

CORPORATE RESPONSIBILITY

Aims

To introduce the dilemmas of ethical and responsible behaviour that managers face, and offer some analytical tools to help manage them.

Objectives

By the end of your work on this chapter you should be able to outline the concepts below in your own terms and:

1 Give examples of controversial, and philanthropic, business practices
2 Distinguish criteria that people use to evaluate individual and corporate actions
3 Use a model of ethical decision making to explain behaviour
4 Show how stakeholders, strategies and responsible behaviour interact
5 Evaluate an organisation's methods for managing corporate responsibility
6 Show how ideas from the chapter can add to your understanding of the integrating themes

Key terms

This chapter introduces the following ideas:

philanthropy
enlightened self-interest
corporate responsibility
social contract
ethical decision-making models

ethical relativism
ethical investors
ethical consumers
ethical audit

Each is a term defined within the text, as well as in the Glossary at the end of the book.

Case study   The Ford Pinto

In the late 1960s Lee Iacocca, then president of Ford, sought to improve the company's market position by having a new car, the Ford Pinto, on the market by the 1971 model year. This would be a basic vehicle selling for $2,000, which meant that it had to be produced very cheaply, with a small margin between production costs and selling price.

The designers placed the petrol tank at the back of the car, 6 inches from a flimsy rear bumper. Bolts were placed just 3 inches from the tank. Other sharp metal edges surrounded the tank, and the filler pipe tended to break loose from the tank in low-speed crashes. These features could have been redesigned, but the extra expense would go against Iacocca's aim of 'a 2,000 pound car for $2,000'.

In testing its new design, Ford found that when it was struck from behind at 20 mph the bumper would push the bolts into the tank, causing it to rupture. This posed a significant risk to those inside and contravened proposed legislation which required cars to withstand an impact at 30 mph without fuel loss. No one informed Iacocca of these findings, for fear of being fired. He was fond of saying 'safety doesn't sell'.

The car went on sale and in 1976 a magazine exposed the dangers of the Pinto petrol tank. This prompted the National Highway Traffic Safety Administration (NHTSA) to launch an investigation, which in 1977 identified 28 rear-end crashes in which petrol had leaked and caused a fire: 27 occupants had died and 24 suffered burns.

Feeling some pressure to fix the tank, Ford officials devised a polythene shield to prevent it from being punctured by the bolts, and a jacket to cushion it against impact. The engineers calculated that these improvements would cost $11 per car, and had to decide whether to recall the cars to make these repairs. They conducted a cost–benefit analysis. Using NHTSA figures for the cost to society of death or serious injury, and an estimate of the likely number of future deaths and serious injuries, Ford's calculations were:

Benefits of altering design
Savings: 180 deaths; 180 serious injuries; 2,100 vehicles
Unit cost: $200,000 per death; $67,000 per serious injury; $700 per vehicle
Total benefit: $49.5 million

© Bettmann/Corbis

Costs of altering the design
Sales: 11 million cars; 1.5 million light trucks
Unit cost: $11 per car; $11 per truck
Total cost: $137.5 million

Since the costs of recalling and altering the cars outweighed the benefits they decided not to do so, continuing to produce the Pinto in its original form. They reasoned that the current design met federal safety standards at the time. While it did not meet proposed legislation, it was as safe as current competing models.

In 1977 the proposed fuel tank legislation was adopted and Ford decided to recall all 1971–1976 Pintos to modify their fuel tanks. A month before the recall began three people in a Pinto were struck from behind in a low-speed crash and burned to death. A $120 million lawsuit followed, but Ford escaped on a technicality. Ford won the lawsuit, but its reputation suffered badly.

Source: Based on Shaw (1991) and Nutt (2002).

Case questions 5.1

- As a marketing or production manager at Ford at the time, what dilemmas would you face?

- How would you express these dilemmas within the company?

5.1   Introduction

Ford managers dealing with the Pinto chose to put profit before safety. Yet they did not act illegally, and customers then were not as interested in safety features as they are today. A manager who tried to delay the model launch would have damaged his career, his family economy – and the livelihood of other Ford workers. But the managers' decisions led to death and injury.

Most people are only aware of corporate responsibility (or lack of) when there is a controversy about (say) food safety or the use of child labour. They also take note of events such as the collapse of Enron (Swartz and Watkins, 2002) and Arthur Andersen (Toffler and Reingold, 2003). The high salary and pension paid to Fred Goodwin, whose leadership almost destroyed The Royal Bank of Scotland in 2008 until the UK government saved it, increase distrust of corporate bodies.

While such situations seem clear-cut, they are often ambiguous:

> there is no consensus on what constitutes virtuous corporate behavior. Is sourcing overseas to take advantage of lower labor costs responsible? Are companies morally obligated to insist that their contractors pay a 'living wage' rather than market wages? Are investments in natural resources in poor countries with corrupt governments always, sometimes or never irresponsible? (Vogel, 2005, pp. 4–5)

Should BP be praised for acknowledging climate change before many of its competitors, or criticised for its poor safety record? Is Shell acting responsibly by extracting oil in Nigeria which supports the nation's development, but which may damage local communities?

These issues arise at each stage of the value-adding chain. They arise over:

- inputs (e.g. whether to use existing staff or to outsource work);
- transformation (e.g. treatment of employees, use of energy, transport and other resources); and
- outputs (e.g. waste and pollution, honest treatment of customers).

The chapter begins with examples of contrasting business behaviour, and asks whether these can be resolved by universal prescriptive theories, or by considering the context within which people choose their actions. The second section outlines ideas on universal prescriptions, and those which follow outline three 'contextual' perspectives – ethical decision making models, stakeholders and strategy. A further section illustrates practices which organisations use to implement and support their policies on corporate responsibility.

Management in practice   Bernard Madoff – the biggest fraud ever?

In 2009 Bernard Madoff (71) was sentenced to 150 years in prison for running a fraudulent investment scheme in the US that took £39 billion from thousands of investors around the world. He attracted investors by offering unusually large returns and by cultivating an image of competence and trustworthiness – clients were eager for him to accept their money. Instead of investing it, he used it to pay dividends to earlier investors – so the scheme depended on continually attracting new ones. When the world economic decline began in 2008 many asked for their money back – revealing that it was no longer there. Individuals and charitable foundations lost large amounts of money.

A remarkable feature of the story was that regulatory bodies set up after previous financial frauds failed to see what Madoff was doing: the agency responsible for regulating that part of the financial services industry was understaffed, and never inspected his accounts.

Sources: *Financial Times* 24 and 30 June 2009.

5.2   Contrasts in business practice

The Pinto case is a prominent example of questionable corporate actions, and Table 5.1 notes some recent cases – some of which were illegal while others, although dubious, were not.

There is an equally long tradition of ethical behaviour in business: Robert Owen (Chapter 2 case) campaigned against the employment of children in the mines and mills of nineteenth-century Britain. From the start of the Industrial Revolution some entrepreneurs acted philanthropically:

1803–1876	Titus Salt	Textiles	Employee welfare; Saltaire Village
1830–1898	Jeremiah Coleman	Mustard	Charities; Salvation Army; YMCA
1839–1922	George Cadbury	Chocolate	Employee welfare; Bournville Village
1836–1925	Joseph Rowntree	Chocolate	Employee welfare; New Earswick Village
1851–1925	William Lever	Soap	Employee welfare; Port Sunlight Village

They recognised the social impact of industry and tried to use its potential to improve social conditions. By fostering an ethos of care, these industrialists offered an unconventional

Table 5.1 Recent financial scandals at major companies

Company	Incident	Outcome
Bernard Madoff, 2009, US investment company	Fraudulent investment company, paying early investors dividends with money raised from new ones	Thousands of investors, including charities, lost money. Madoff sentenced to 150 years in jail
The Royal Bank of Scotland, 2008, UK Bank	Used short-term borrowing to fund high-risk investments. The investments failed, and the company almost collapsed	UK government buys majority stake. Fred Goodwin, chief executive, retires with £800,000 annual pension
Volkswagen, 2007, German car manufacturer	Former head of personnel admits illegal payments to trade union leaders, managers and prostitutes	Initially denies involvement, then resigns and pleads guilty; receives short jail sentence. Trade union leaders charged
Ahold, 2006, Dutch retailer	Conceals documents about joint ventures from auditors, so that revenues appeared higher than they should have been	Chief executive and chief financial officer convicted for fraud. Shareholder groups criticised lenient sentences
Parmalat, 2003, Italian dairy company	Managers claimed assets in bank accounts that did not exist, to cover liabilities. CEO accused of diverting £600 million to his own use	Senior managers convicted of fraud and admitted misleading investors. Company continues to trade under new management
Enron, 2001, a US trading company	Company collapsed in 2001, amid allegations of accounting practices that artificially inflated earnings and share prices, to benefit top managers	Employees lost jobs and pensions, directors received large financial benefits. Founder Ken Lay and CEO Jeff Skilling convicted of fraud in May 2006
Arthur Andersen, 2002, accounting and consulting firm, worked for Enron	Shredded thousands of documents to hide malpractice at Enron	Found guilty of obstructing justice, CEO resigns, firm collapses

Sources: *Business Week*, 12 January 2004; *Financial Times*, 20 February 2004, 23 May 2006, 26 May 2006, 18 January 2007; other published sources.

Philanthropy is the practice of contributing personal wealth to charitable or similar causes.

Enlightened self-interest is the practice of acting in a way that is costly or inconvenient at present, but which is believed to be in one's best interest in the long term.

Corporate responsibility refers to the awareness, acceptance and management of the wider implications of corporate decisions.

business model and showed society what was possible. Their **philanthropy** helped to position **enlightened self-interest** as a viable approach to business.

Some of today's business leaders give substantial donations to charities. Bill Gates (founder of Microsoft) gives very large sums to health and educational causes, and Jeff Skoll (ex-president of eBay) gave £5 million to the Said Business School at Oxford University. Lord Sainsbury, former head of the UK supermarket chain, is the UK's most generous charitable donor: he has put £400 million into his Gatsby Charitable Foundation and plans to give another £600 million before he dies. Sir Tom Hunter (founder of JJB Sports and, in 2009, Scotland's richest man) has made many large donations to help young people, and pledged a further £1 billion.

Between these extremes of often illegal behaviour and unstinting philanthropy are many ambiguous issues of **corporate responsibility**. This is a broad term, which refers here to the awareness, acceptance and management of the wider implications of corporate decisions. These can arise throughout an organisation, at any stage of the value chain – Table 5.2 lists examples of the topics which managers face, and how they may choose to deal with them in a responsible way.

Public interest has encouraged more companies to manage issues of corporate responsibility, and report publicly on how they do so. Business in the Community (**www.bitc.org.uk**) encourages organisations of all kinds to respond to this interest, and publicises their achievements.

Table 5.2 Common topics of corporate responsibility: content and process

Content (or substance) of corporate responsibility

Topics	Examples
Inputs and resource supplies	Dealing fairly with producers and suppliers, sustainable sourcing of raw materials and supplies, avoiding exploitation of labour by suppliers in poor countries
Workforce activities	Promoting diversity, equality, health and safety, work–life balance and other elements of the employment relationship; reward and risk – fair pay, bonus and pension schemes
Operations	Help the environment by reducing energy in production and transport, using resources efficiently to reduce waste (e.g. less packaging)
Product and service impacts	Responsible customer relations, including advertising and promotion (drink responsibly), protecting children, limit harmful ingredients, clear and accurate labels, product accessibility
Community activities	Education, employability and regeneration in communities – donations, employee volunteering, gifts in kind, being a good neighbour

Processes of corporate responsibility

Leadership	Defining commitment to responsible action, resourcing it, identifying roles and reporting relationships, monitoring compliance with policies and codes
Stakeholder engagement	Mapping stakeholders and their main concerns, consulting them

---

Activity 5.1   Looking for responsible business activity

Collect two examples of organisations that seem to be taking the matter seriously by introducing explicit policies on environmental, social or ethical matters. You could check company websites to find what they say about responsible corporate behaviour – see Section 5.7 for some award-winning sites, or go to the Business in the Community website for examples.

- What aspects of the business (e.g. inputs, transformation, outputs, communities) does the policy cover?
- How did management develop the policy (e.g. which people or groups took part in forming it)?
- How do they ensure that people follow the policy, and that it has the expected effects?
- Compare what you find with colleagues on your course and present a short summary, with questions for further research.

5.3   Perspectives on individual actions

Before looking at some tools for managing these corporate dilemmas, use Activity 5.2 to locate your ethical position.

Activity 5.2   Reflecting on your ethics

- You are walking down the street. There is no one nearby and you see: (a) a 50 pence piece, (b) a £5 note, (c) a £50 note, (d) a £100 note, (e) £1,000. Do you keep it? Yes or no?
- The money you find was actually in a wallet with the owner's name and address in it. Does this make a difference?
- That name indicates to you that it belongs to: (a) a wealthy person, (b) a pensioner of modest means, (c) a single parent. Does this make a difference?
- Suppose there were some people nearby. Does this make a difference?
- Explore your reasons for each of your decisions.

Three domains of human action

'Ethics' refers to a code of moral principles and values that guide human action by setting standards of what is acceptable. We can understand this more clearly if we compare ethics with actions that are governed by law and by free choice (see Figure 5.1). Some actions are the subject of legislation which can be enforced in the courts: it is illegal to steal. At the other extreme are actions in the domain of free choice – anyone can apply for another job.

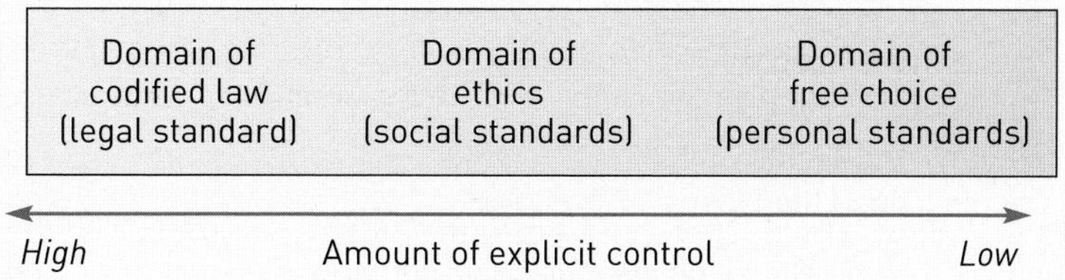

Domain of codified law (legal standard)	Domain of ethics (social standards)	Domain of free choice (personal standards)

High ←   Amount of explicit control   → *Low*

Figure 5.1
Three domains of human action

Source: From *Management*, 5th edition by Daft (2000). © Copyright 2000, South-Western, a division of Thomson Learning.

In between are acts that have an ethical dimension. Laws do not prescribe action, but nor are people free to act as they wish: they are constrained by shared principles and values about acceptable behaviour in the circumstances. An ethically acceptable action is one that is legal *and* meets a society's ethical standards – which raises the question of how people form and express those standards: a standard that you think should be respected may be ignored by others.

Ethical dilemmas arise when an action which benefits one person or group will harm others, such as if you:

- believe that a parent has given inaccurate information to secure a place for his/her child at a popular school – should you tell?
- see a golfer surreptitiously move his/her ball to improve his/her chance of winning a prize – should you tell?
- see someone steal a valuable item from a small shop while the owner is attending to an elderly customer – should you tell?

People may disagree on which answer is right, which probably means they are using different criteria: what might they be?

Four criteria for evaluating an action

Philosophers have identified four principles that people use to evaluate whether an action is ethical – moral principle, utilitarianism, human rights and individualism. Understanding these may help to understand what people expect of others.

- **Moral principle** People use this criterion when they evaluate an action against a moral principle – the rules that societies develop and which members generally accept as valid guides to behaviour (e.g. people do not steal, cheat or deliberately injure each other). If someone acts in a way that conforms to these principles, it is right: if not, it is wrong.
- **Utilitarianism** People use this criterion when they evaluate an action against its effect, not on individual pleasure and pain but on the total balance of pleasure and pain in society. An act is right if it brings pleasure to more people than it hurts. An act is wrong if the amount of pain is greater than the amount of pleasure.
- **Human rights** People use this criterion when they evaluate an action against its effect on human rights which a society recognises (such as privacy, free speech or fair treatment). An act is right if it supports the human rights of those whom it affects, and wrong if it damages them.
- **Individualism** People use this criterion when they evaluate an action against its effect on their interests. An act is right if they can show that it serves a person's interests. This may seem strange, but Adam Smith used it in his book *The Wealth of Nations* (1776) to justify a free enterprise economy, on the grounds that apparently selfish behaviour would actually help society as a whole: entrepreneurs acting selfishly would only benefit if their actions benefitted others – producing things that people wanted to buy, for example.

Activity 5.3   Justifying actions

Think of actions which you have justified on the grounds that:

- it was fair to those affected;
- it was the right thing to do;
- it was the best option for yourself;
- more people gained than lost.

Explain which of the ethical philosophies outlined above matches each reason.

Table 5.3 Questions within each philosophy

Philosophy	Questions
Moral principle	Who determines that a moral principle is 'generally accepted'? What if others claim that a principle leading to a different decision is equally 'accepted'?
Utilitarianism	Who determines the majority, and the population of which it is the greatest number? Is the benefit assessed over the short term or long term?
Human rights	Actions usually involve several people – what if the decision would protect the rights of some but breach the rights of others? How to balance them?
Individualism	Whose self-interest comes first? What if the action of one damages the self-interest of another?

These tools from moral philosophy may show the reasoning behind someone's decision on an ethical issue – although Table 5.3 shows that others could challenge each of these criteria.

Figure 5.2 shows why people often find it difficult to agree on whether or not a decision is ethical. It shows that the people (B, C, D . . .) who observe an action by A, and the criteria that A uses to justify it, will themselves be evaluating the action *and* the criteria. Their diverse personalities, backgrounds and experiences make it likely that they will attach different meanings to what they see, and so make different judgements.

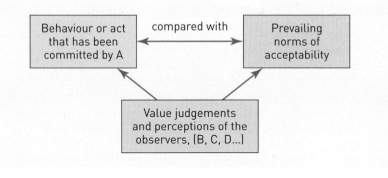

Figure 5.2
Making ethical judgements
Source: Adapted from Carroll (1989).

5.4 Perspectives on corporate actions

Figure 5.3 shows four responsibilities which managers can take into account as they develop their decisions, ranging from economic on the left-hand side to discretionary on the right: this builds on Figure 5.1, and locates ethical issues between legal and discretionary responsibilities.

Legal responsibilities

Society expects managers to obey the law – by not misleading investors, exploiting staff or selling faulty goods. These are among countless issues upon which nations create laws regulating company behaviour. Some companies take these responsibilities seriously – but go no

Figure 5.3
A range of
corporate
responsibilities
Source: Carroll (1999).

further. Their only criterion is that what they do is legal: as long as a decision meets that test they will take it, even if it has damaging consequences for others. Managers involved with the Pinto scandal took this view, as did, more recently, many of those involved in trading complex financial instruments which contributed to the financial crisis of 2008.

Economic responsibilities – Milton Friedman

Here managers focus on serving the economic interests of the company and its shareholders. Milton Friedman was clear that:

> [In a free economy] there is one and only one social responsibility of business – to use its resources and engage in activities designed to increase its profits so long as it stays within the rules of the game, which is to say, engages in open and free competition, without deception or fraud. (Friedman, 1962, p. 133)

As an economist, Friedman believed that operating business 'without deception or fraud' provided sufficient social benefit through the creation of wealth or employment. In terms of Figure 5.3, managers should concern themselves only with the two left-hand boxes – legal and economic responsibilities. For a business to give money to charitable purposes was equivalent to self-imposed taxation. He argued that the board of directors in charge of a business should concentrate on generating wealth for shareholders and distributing it to them. Shareholders could then decide if they wished to use that income for charitable purposes.

Many agree, claiming that stringent environmental or other regulations increase costs for a business, and make it less competitive (Stavins, 1994). Spending money on socially responsible but unprofitable ventures will damage the firm and be unsustainable. An example of this was when Burberry's, the luxury goods retailer, decided to close one of its few remaining UK factories. The finance director was questioned by the media about the decision, and she commented:

> Ultimately if a factory isn't commercially viable you have to take the decision to close . . . that's what your obligations to your shareholders dictate. When you know you've made the right decision commercially, you have to stay true to that. These are the facts – commercial realities reign. (*Financial Times*, 15 February 2007, p. 3)

Ethical responsibilities

The **social contract**
consists of the mutual
obligations that society
and business recognise
they have to each other.

Some claim that while society depends on business for goods and services, business in turn depends on society. It requires inputs – employees, capital and physical resources – and the socially created institutions that enable business to operate – such as a legal and education system. This is part of the moral case for corporate responsibility – namely that it reflects this interdependency: society and business have mutual obligations within a **social contract**.

Actions in this area are not specified by law, and may not serve a company's narrow economic interests. Managers take these actions because they believe they meet some wider social interest, such as discouraging tobacco consumption, protecting the natural environment or supporting a socially disadvantaged group. They may also do so in the belief that it will help meet their economic responsibilities by enhancing their reputation with customers.

Discretionary responsibilities

This covers actions which are entirely voluntary, not being shaped by economic legal or ethical considerations. They include anonymous donations with no expectation or possibility of a pay-back, sponsorship of local events and contributions to charities – the actions are entirely philanthropic. The decision by Innocent Drinks (Part 1 case) to donate 10 per cent of profits to charities such as the Rainforest Alliance is an example (**www.innocent.com**).

Friedman believed that managers' responsibilities are to do what is best for the business and the shareholders. Those advocating a more inclusive view of corporate responsibility believe that recognising wider interests is enlightened self-interest, in the sense that it can satisfy both economic *and* moral expectations. Managers may add more value (and serve their shareholders better) if they meet ethical and discretionary responsibilities, in ways that benefit the business. Both consider stakeholders, but in different ways.

Activity 5.4   Gathering views on the role of business

Gather information from people you know who work in a business about which of the above four views:

- they personally favour
- they believe has most influence on practice in their company.

If you work in an organisation

- which of the two views guides policy?
- use Table 5.2 to gather examples of topics on which the organisation has deliberately acted as part of a corporate responsibility agenda.

Compare your examples with colleagues on your course.

Case question 5.2

- Did Ford act unethically at that time? Should the law be the only influence on a corporation's actions? What responsibilities do you think a major company has?
- Ford used cost–benefit analysis to decide what to do – could this have been improved? Was it a useful decision tool in this case?
- Imagine you were a Ford manager at this time. What would you have done and why? List the social costs and benefits to the company and society of the alternatives to help you determine your answer.
- Imagine you worked for Ford as an engineer and were aware of this potential design fault. What would you do? What, if any, are your responsibilities to the customer and/or your employer?

What factors influence managers' decisions? The next section introduces an ethical decision-making model.

5.5 An ethical decision-making model

Trevino and Weaver (2003) note that attempts to develop universal guidelines for responsible behaviour in business have a long history: Aristotle commented on the ethical propriety of commercial practices. They also find much of the commentary on modern scandals – suppliers bribing government officials to secure contracts or banks paying their staff high salaries – is essentially normative, in that it prescribes what people should and should not do. They continue:

> important as it is to engage in the normative study of what is, and is not, ethically proper in business, it is just as important to understand the organizational and institutional context within which ethical issues, awareness and behavior are situated. (p. xv)

They find little empirical research into why managers decide to adopt such practices, or into their effects on performance or any other variable.

Figure 5.4 shows a simple **ethical decision-making model** (there is a complex one with more variables in Trevino, 1986). The figure predicts that an individual's choice of behaviour when faced with an ethical dilemma depends on factors unique to the individual and on factors within his/her context.

The individual factors are:

- **Stage of moral development** – the extent to which the person can distinguish between right and wrong; the higher this is, the more likely the person is to act ethically.
- **Ego strength** – the extent to which people are able to resist impulses and follow their convictions; the greater this is, the more likely each person will do what he/she thinks is right.
- **Locus of control** – the extent to which the person believes he/she has control over his/her life, rather than this being determined by others; the more a person sees him/herself as having control, the more likely he/she is to act ethically

The contextual factors are:

- **Work-group norms** – the beliefs within the work group about how to behave in a situation.
- **Incentives** – such as management policies on rewards and disciplines.
- **Rules and regulations** – management policies about relevant ethical dilemmas.

Ethical decision-making models examine the influence of individual characteristics and organisational policies on ethical decisions.

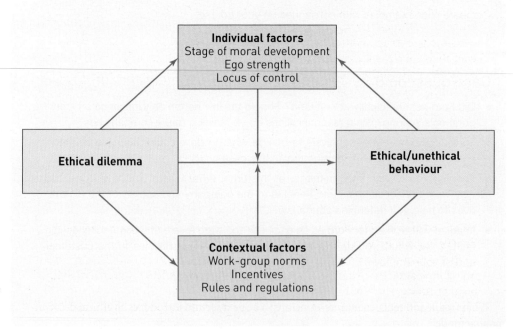

Figure 5.4 A simple model of ethical decision making

The figure also shows that behaviour has consequences that feed back to, and possibly change, the individual and his/her context – which shape the way the person responds to future dilemmas. Many other factors could be added, but in this context the purpose of the figure is to indicate the type of factors that influence ethical choices as a guide to management action.

Pierce and Snyder (2008) illustrate this by showing that the willingness of staff to commit fraud varied with their employer's policies. They analysed vehicle testing records in a state over two years, during which time some testers moved between employers (typically small workshops). They found that testers' leniency varied with their employer – norm of behaviour and incentives at their current workshop encouraged them to behave ethically (making decisions in line with regulations) or unethically (passing vehicles that should fail). Many believe that the 2008 financial crises was caused by senior managers in some banks encouraging a culture of risk. This rewarded staff for taking risks – bringing financial gain to themselves but financial ruin to others.

Case study   The Ford Pinto – the case continues

Court records showed that Ford's top managers knew that the Pinto was unsafe, but concluded that it was cheaper to incur the losses from lawsuits than to fix the cars. Production staff also knew of the risks, but they were never given the opportunity to tell top management about them. Fords' 'profit drives principle' philosophy of the time discouraged staff from drawing attention to risks. Actions were guided by the original aim for the Pinto – '2,000 pounds for $2,000' – and a 'safety doesn't sell' mindset. Insiders believed they were acting in line with company values. Richard Pascale (1990) noted that during the 1970s:

> The company was financially focussed. Cost accounting drove suboptimal design decisions at the front edge of the product development process. In the factories, a system tied a large percentage of plant managers' compensation to volume, driving plants to build cars as rapidly as possible and worry about the defects later. (Pascale, 1990, pp. 116–117)

These practices were rooted in the distant past, and did not address the issues the company was facing in the late 1970s, when consumers were more concerned about safety and less concerned about price.

When a new chief executive took over, he went to great lengths to consult with top managers about major decisions. He wanted to break away from the previously autocratic 'do as I say' style of management, in order to encourage debate and discussion: which may enable people to raise ethical issues early in the decision-making process.

Sources: Pascale (1990); Nutt (2002).

Case question 5.3

- Does the ethical decision-making model help explain the decisions made by Ford at that time?
- How did the style of the new chief executive alter the likelihood of a similar scandal arising?

Activity 5.5   Evaluating decisions at The Royal Bank of Scotland

Read the Part 4 case on The Royal Bank of Scotland, and make notes on the following questions:

- What evidence is there of organisational practices which encouraged some staff to behave in the ways which led to the bank's difficulties?
- Gather evidence from news reports or other sources (such as friends or family) about ethical or unethical behaviour, and any organisational practices that influenced people.
- Compare and discuss your evidence, and use it to evaluate the model in Figure 5.4.

Figure 5.4 also illustrates the dilemma some people face when working in countries with different views on giving and taking bribes to influence management decisions. On the universal perspective, people should act in an ethically consistent way irrespective of where they are. **Ethical relativism** suggests taking account of the local context, and incorporating prevailing norms and values when deciding issues with an ethical dimension: if local and home country norms conflict, people should follow the local norms. For international companies ethical relativism is a convenient philosophy, but causes difficulties for individual managers if their personal views are more universal than relative.

> **Ethical relativism** is the principle that ethical judgements cannot be made independently of the culture in which the issue arises.

5.6 Stakeholders and corporate responsibility

Stakeholder priorities – balancing trade-offs

Chapter 3 explains that organisations have internal and external stakeholders with an interest in what the organisation does. Table 5.4 lists the main groups, and illustrates the issues to which they are likely to give priority.

Each stakeholder category will express conflicting views. Multinationals deal with the governments (national and local) in many countries, which inevitably expect different things. Communities within one country will show similar diversity – managers can satisfy one only at the expense of another. Scottish and Southern Energy wants to increase the amount of power it generates from wind farms, which will help to meet the UK government's renewable energy target. Some stakeholders object that building wind farms, and the associated distribution lines, will damage landscapes, endanger migrating birds, and require large subsidies which could be used for other public services. Local authorities wishing to dump less waste want to build incinerators, but face objections from residents about traffic flows or pollution. Devinney (2009) addresses this, believing that advocates of corporate responsibility ignore the conflicts between what he terms the virtues and vices of organisations – see Key Ideas.

Table 5.4 Stakeholders and interests in relation to corporate responsibility (CR)

Stakeholders	Expectations
Employees	Employment, security, safe working conditions, rewarding work, fairness in promotion, security and pay
Shareholders	Financially centred investors: high return on investment **Ethical investors:** strong CR policies and reputation
Suppliers	Fair terms, prompt payment, long-term relationships
Customers	Majority: price, quality, durability and safety Minority (ethical consumers): fair trade sources, fair treatment of staff, care for environment
Communities	Employment; income; limits on pollution and noise
Competitors	Fair competition, follow the norms of behaviour in the industry
Governments	Pay taxes, obey laws, provide economic opportunities
Environmental campaigners	Minimise pollution, emissions, waste and assist recycling
Charities and causes	Donations and gifts in kind

> **Ethical investors** are people who only invest in businesses that meet specified criteria of ethical behaviour.

> ### Key ideas   Timothy Devinney – the myth of the socially responsible firm
>
> Devinney (2009) questions the feasibility of the 'socially responsible firm' since, in his view:
>
> > CSR is no free lunch [as] corporations, by their very nature, have conflicting virtues and vices that ensure that they will never be truly socially responsible by even the narrowest of definitions.
>
> He makes it clear that he is not saying that people and organisations do not have values and incentives intended to behave in a responsible, ethical way. His point is that:
>
> > any position taken by a firm and its management, social, ethical or otherwise, has trade-offs that cannot be avoided. Corporations can be made more 'virtuous' on some dimensions . . . but this will inevitably involve a price on other dimensions . . . [corporate responsibility], like most aspects of life, has very few, if any, win/win outcomes.
>
> Source: Devinney (2009).

Almost any major decision involves trade-offs, in the sense that a benefit in one area is likely to bring a disadvantage somewhere else: this applies to decisions aimed at promoting responsibility as much as in any other areas of management action. As much as an organisation does to satisfy one set of stakeholders, others are likely to object.

> ## Case questions 5.3
>
> - What did customers of Ford expect of the Pinto at that time?
> - Would customers today have different expectations?
> - Does that affect your view of the company's actions?
> - What other stakeholders would have been affected by Ford's decisions?

Stakeholders influence managers

Stakeholders vary in their influence over managers. If the most powerful expect a company to follow a Friedmanite position, managers will deliver that, perhaps with some public commitment to socially acceptable practice. Other companies have powerful shareholders who, while expecting a financial return, are willing to take a longer view: they believe their managers can best deliver long-term returns by meeting, to some degree, the expectations of other stakeholders.

> Firms with this perspective will invest in social initiatives because they believe that such investments will result in increased profitability. (Peloza, 2006)

Many companies differentiate themselves less by their products than by the ideas, emotions and images that their brand conveys – they value their reputation. Managers who allow their brand to become associated with hostility to people, communities or the natural environment risk their reputation and profits. Adopting responsible practices enables a firm to imbue the brand with positive themes that coincide with the beliefs of many customers. A positive reputation has value

> precisely because (developing one) takes considerable time and depends on a firm making stable and consistent investments. (Roberts and Dowling, 2002)

This valuable asset can be damaged if activists target the company. Companies such as Nike, Shell, McDonald's and Starbucks have all faced well-organised campaigns.

Managers influence stakeholders – the lobbying business

Consistent with the interaction model, managers also influence their context by, for example, lobbying powerful interest groups to make decisions in their favour. Companies and industry associations invest substantial resources protecting their interests against legislation which they believe is against their interests – the Management in Practice feature illustrates how the European motor industry does this.

Management in practice   Lobbying for the motor industry   www.acea.ch

Ivan Hodac is chief executive of the European Automobile Manufacturers' Association, and many regard him as one of the most successful of the 15,000 lobbyists who influence EU decisions. Automakers are fighting for survival, and Mr Hodac's talents are often called for. In December 2008 his organisation was credited with delaying environmental legislation which would have forced automakers to cut vehicle carbon dioxide emissions 18 per cent by 2012. Now they have until 2015 and the penalties for failure will be less severe. Environmental groups were furious, but Mr Hodac argued that it was a reasonable compromise for an industry on its knees and with little cash for research and development.

Source: *Financial Times*, 16 June 2009.

  Corporate responsibility and strategy

Will responsible behaviour pay? If it does not, how will the responsible organisation survive? David Vogel (2005) believes that responsible corporate action is only sustainable if it yields a financial return – otherwise less responsible players may gain a competitive advantage over the more responsible – see Key Ideas. There are three ways in which responsible action can support wider strategy and bring a financial return: as their mission, to meet customer needs and by being integral to strategy.

Key ideas   David Vogel on responsibility and strategy

Vogel (2005) examines the claims for and against the idea that corporations should act responsibly, by analysing the forces driving the corporate responsibility (CR) movement. He concludes that while the managers of businesses which are prominent advocates of CR (The Body Shop or Co-operative Financial Services among many others) are genuinely motivated by a commitment to social goals, CR is only sustainable if 'virtue pays off'. He acknowledges that not every business expenditure or policy needs to directly increase shareholder value, and that many of the benefits of responsible action are difficult to quantify. But ultimately responsible action is both made possible and constrained by market forces.

Market forces encourage and also limit responsible corporate action. Encouraging forces include demand for responsibly made products, consumer boycotts, challenges to a firm's reputation by NGOs such as Greenpeace, pressure from ethical investors and the values of managers and employees. This has led many firms to accept that they need to be accountable to a broad community of stakeholders. Virtuous behaviour can make business sense for some firms in some areas in some circumstances:

> Many of the proponents of (CR) mistakenly assume that because some companies are behaving more responsibly in some areas, (more) firms can be expected to behave responsibly in more areas. This assumption is misinformed. There *is* a place in the market economy for responsible firms. But there is also a large place for their less responsible competitors. (p. 3)

While some companies can benefit from acting responsibly, market forces alone cannot prevent others from acting in less responsible ways and profiting from doing so.

Source: Vogel (2005).

Responsible action as the corporate mission

Some companies position corporate responsibility at the heart of their business, reflecting the beliefs and values of founders and senior managers. An early example was The Body Shop (founded by the late Anita Roddick) which became a major retailing group by, among many other things, taking a strong ethical position on issues such as testing cosmetics on live animals. Its unique position was gradually eroded – partly by its own success. Animal testing of cosmetics (one of the firm's early campaigns) was stopped, and more people are aware of environmental issues. So a strategically valuable position, benefiting those it aimed to help, came under competitive threat – the company is now owned by the French cosmetics group, L'Oreal.

Management in practice   The Co-operative   www.co-operative.coop

Established in the early nineteenth century, the Co-op is now Britain's fifth largest retail chain, with a strong financial services business. It is run democratically by its members, who twice a year receive a share of the profits, based on how much they have spent in the business, and how much profit the business made in the year.

Working in line with ethical principles has always been part of the Co-op's mission and way of working – so it has been quick to take into account current concerns of corporate responsibility, such as climate change and world poverty. The company produces an annual sustainability report, outlining what the group has done throughout the business to manage it in a more sustainable way. The fund managers in its investment businesses, for example, take a distinctive approach to investing, in that they consider environmental, social and governance issues alongside financial measures.

The company website gives more information about all the group's activities supporting responsible corporate behaviour.

Source: Company website.

Responsible action to meet customer needs

Other companies, while not focused on responsibility as a mission, focus on meeting the needs of **ethical consumers** – those who take ethical issues into account when making a purchase, and try to avoid buying products from companies that damage the environment, deal with oppressive regimes, have a poor record on animal rights or pay low wages. Such consumers have supported the growth of the Fair Trade scheme, under which companies guarantee that suppliers in poor countries receive higher prices for their products than they would from market forces alone. Café Direct, Green and Black Chocolate are examples of such products.

Ethical consumers are those who take ethical issues into account in deciding what to purchase.

Not all customers share the concerns of ethical consumers, but there are enough of them to encourage some companies to try to meet their requirements. Doing so does not necessarily add to costs. Hawken *et al.* (1999) provide many examples of companies finding that environmentally friendly practices are cost-neutral: by looking carefully at supply, manufacture and distribution, they work out how to make responsible practices pay. In 2010 Marks & Spencer (**www.marksandspencer.com**) announced that it aims to become the world's most sustainable retailer by 2015 (see Chapter 6, Section 6.9 for more information).

Management in practice   **Red – Bono and Aids in Africa**   www.joinred.com

In 2006 Bono announced the creation of his new brand – Red – which will dedicate some of its revenue to fight Aids in Africa. The effort will include a series of joint ventures with companies such as American Express, Georgio Armani and Gap to sell products under the brand (for example, go to **www.gap.com** and you will see the Red brands featured). They will be marketed first in the UK to an estimated 1.5 million 'conscience consumers' who are seen as more likely to buy products associated with a social benefit. Other products available will include Converse sports shoes made with African mud-cloth, a new line of Gap vintage T-shirts and wraparound Armani sunglasses.

'I think doing the Red thing, doing good, will turn out to be good business for them', said Bono, who has long been associated with campaigns on African debt relief, Aids, and unfair trading rules that hurt the continent's poor. This and similar efforts are being supported by big companies worried that television advertising is losing its punch. The idea is that using good works or services will gain consumer attention – what some call 'corporate social opportunity'.

Sources: *Financial Times,* 26 January 2006; *Independent*, 13 May 2006; U2 and Red websites.

Responsible action as part of strategy

Others follow responsible practices towards, for example, their use of resources, because they fit their business strategy. Using energy efficiently, avoiding waste and treating staff with respect are established daily practices in many companies – some of which now present such practices as part of a responsible image. In 2009 Mars, the world's biggest confectioner, announced that its entire cocoa supply will be produced sustainably by 2020. It will achieve this by working with the Rainforest Alliance, which encourages farmers to preserve their environment. Cadbury announced that all the cocoa in Dairy Milk, Britain's biggest-selling chocolate, would be certified by Fair Trade, the organisation that works to ensure a minimum price for farmers. Both companies have substantial business reasons for their actions: they are worried about how much cocoa will be available a decade from now, as world production is falling.

Management in practice   **Sustainable coffee**   www.kraft.com

Kraft Foods, which buys about 10 per cent of the world's coffee, has agreed to blend sustainably produced beans into its main European brands, which include Kenco, Jacobs and Carte Noire. The deal with the non-profit Rainforest Alliance is the most serious attempt by a big coffee purchaser to tackle the crisis that has pushed down the commodity price, which is often below the cost of production. This threatens the livelihood of 25 million coffee farmers, and the long-term supply of beans. Said a senior Kraft commodity manager:

> We need to make sure we can get the coffees we need 20 years from now. This is not philanthropy. This is about incorporating sustainable coffee into our mainstream brands as a way to have a more efficient and competitive way of doing business.

Kraft will buy £5 million of Rainforest Alliance-certified coffee in the first year, paying farmers a premium of 20 per cent. The company also plans to introduce a brand of coffee aimed at the away-from-home market, which includes universities and other institutions seen as sensitive to issues of global equity.

Coffee brokers said the deal would send a signal to the entire supply chain, particularly producers, that roasters are concerned about more than just the purity of the coffee and may pay more to know that the beans have been produced using good environmental practices by workers who are adequately paid.

Source: *Financial Times*, 7 October 2003; company website.

Does responsible action affect performance?

The evidence is not clear. One review found a positive relationship between responsible corporate behaviour and financial performance (Orlitzky *et al.,* 2003). Ambec and Lanoie (2008) identified seven mechanisms which firms use to improve environmental *and* economic performance (see Figure 5.5).

They propose that, under pressure from stakeholders, some firms use responsible practices to increase revenue (gaining better access to markets; differentiating products; or selling pollution control technologies) and/or reduce costs (risk management; lower costs of materials, energy, capital and labour). Their examples appear to show that companies can both act responsibly and perform well economically.

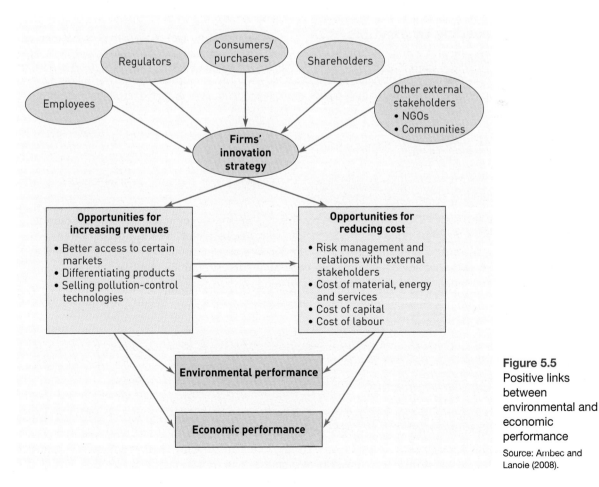

Figure 5.5
Positive links between environmental and economic performance

Source: Ambec and Lanoie (2008).

Vogel (2005) is more sceptical. He found studies that showed a positive relationship between, for example, the level of emission reduction and financial performance, but the direction of causality was unclear – perhaps profitable firms could afford to invest in equipment to reduce emissions. Another possibility was that factors not included in the research affected both variables. Overall he found an inconclusive picture of the relationship between responsibility and profitability, perhaps due to limitations in the studies:

- different measures of financial performance (one review of 95 studies found that they had 49 different accounting measures);
- different measures of corporate responsibility (95 studies used 27 different data sources);
- questionability validity of some measures (some rankings only included the views of executives in the industry).

His overall conclusion is that the relationship between responsible behaviour and performance must be treated with caution.

> just as firms that spend more on marketing are not necessarily more profitable than those that spend less, there is no reason to expect more responsible firms to outperform less responsible ones. (p. 33)

5.8 Managing corporate responsibility

Managers use several methods to promote responsible behaviour, including: leading by example; codes of practice; ethical structures and reporting; and inclusion in the FTSE4Good Index.

Leading by example

Senior managers set the tone for an organisation by their actions. If others they are acting in line with stated ethical principles, their credibility will rise and others are likely to follow. Leaders known to be engaging in malpractice are likely to encourage it to spread throughout the business.

Management in practice   **Strict ethics at Wipro**   www.wipro.com

Wipro (Chapter 7 case) is one of India's leading hi-tech businesses, and in the early days its founder, Azim Premji took a firm stand on ethics. Steve Hamm (2007) writes:

> In the late 1960s and early 1970s corruption was rampant in the Indian economy. Government officials asked for kickbacks. Farmers bribed clerks to tamper with weighing machines . . . Premji set a zero-tolerance policy for bribes and any form of corruption or corner-cutting – from top managers to labourer . . . 'We said anybody committing a breach of integrity would lose their job. It's open and shut and black and white,' Premji says. It took several firings before people believed it. But finally they did. The company stood out, and not just from the local Indian outfits. Some of the multinationals had fallen into the trap of paying bribes as well. (p. 35)

Source: Hamm (2007).

Codes of practice

A code of practice is a formal statement of the company's values, setting out general principles on matters such as quality, employees or the environment. Others set out procedures for situations – such as conflicts of interest or the acceptance of gifts. Their effectiveness depends on the extent to which top management supports them with sanctions and rewards.

Corporate responsibility structures and reporting

These are the formal systems and roles that companies create to support responsible behaviour. This may include staff with direct responsibilities for developing and implementing company policies and practices, together with procedures for regular monitoring and reporting, both within the company and to external stakeholders. Most companies now include a corporate responsibility statement in their Annual Report, and may include in this an **ethical audit** profiling current practice. The Management in Practice feature describes aspects of Vodafone's approach.

Ethical audits are the practice of systematically reviewing the extent to which an organisation's actions are consistent with its stated ethical intentions.

Management in practice   Corporate responsibility at Vodafone www.vodafone.com

Chris Burgess is Director of Corporate Responsibility at Vodafone, and heads a team that reports to the Director of Group External Affairs, who is a member of the Executive Committee. The CR team is responsible for supporting the development of policies and for global CR management. It works closely with local CR managers, since they have a vital role in implementing the Group's CR policies.

The company conducts extensive research, and close engagement with stakeholders, to identify the CR issues that are 'most material' to the business – summarised in the 'materiality matrix' (see Figure 5.6). This guides the work of the CR team, who report progress to the Group Executive Committee, and in the annual CR Report.

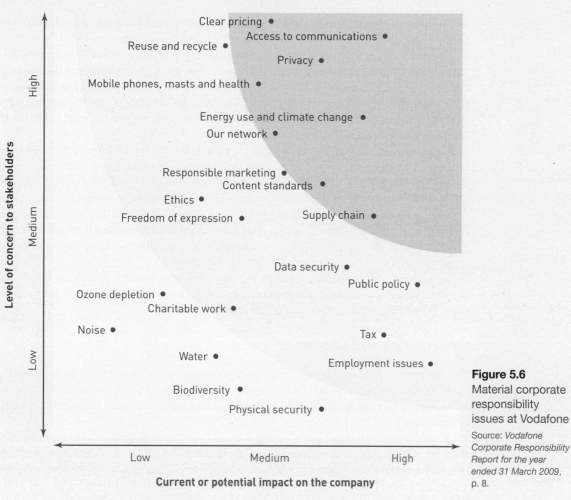

Figure 5.6
Material corporate responsibility issues at Vodafone

Source: *Vodafone Corporate Responsibility Report for the year ended 31 March 2009*, p. 8.

Inclusion in the FTSE4Good Index Series www.FTSE4Good.com

The FTSE4Good Index Series guides investors on companies that meet defined criteria of corporate responsibility. These are developed in consultation with NGOs, governments and other players: to be part of the Index companies need to show they are working towards:

- environmental management;
- climate change mitigation and adaptation;
- countering bribery;
- upholding human and labour rights; and
- supply chain labour standards.

Simon Sproule, Corporate Vice President at Nissan comments:

Trust is fast becoming one of the most valued assets in any organization. Without the trust of our stakeholders, the sustainability of our business is at risk. Being included in the FTSE4Good index is a key element for Nissan to demonstrate its commitment to a sustainable business that inspires trust from all our stakeholders.

5.9   Integrating themes

Sustainable performance

As part of a worldwide effort to reduce greenhouse gases, governments and international bodies are developing policies to slow the release of carbon dioxide emissions, such as emission trading schemes. These enable companies to buy or sell Certified Emission Reductions (CERs) in the market which, Kolk and Pinkse (2005) point out, gives companies some clear strategic choices in how they respond to the problem. They can change their processes to reduce emissions (an 'innovation' approach); they can buy emissions certificates from other companies (a 'compensation' approach); or they can do both. Any of these approaches can be done by the company acting alone, or in conjunction with others.

A company that takes the innovative approach would try to improve its operating processes to reduce emissions, or it could develop new products (such as Shell investing in systems to produce solar energy). If it reduced emissions sufficiently, it could earn CERs which it could then sell to other companies. These could be companies which were big energy users, or which found it hard to change their processes quickly. It might then be more profitable for them to retain their existing processes much as they are, and compensate for this by buying CERs in the market, which would give them the right to continue operating.

Such schemes are in their early stages, but they illustrate a broader point from this chapter that management decisions on corporate responsibility can best be understood by relating them to the wider strategic interests of the company.

Governance and control

People expect a responsible organisation to introduce policies and ways of working that make its activities more sustainable. Many do so, such as by investing in equipment to reduce emissions or by signing up to certification schemes which monitor their environmental performance.

A valid question about such schemes is whether they actually affect sustainability. Schaefer (2007) studied the experience of three water companies as they introduced various environmental management schemes (EMS) – sets of standards which specify the procedures and practices that an organisation must follow if it is to achieve and retain accreditation to the standard. Managers have several motives for introducing such systems, such as maintaining the goodwill of customers or improving performance (on cost or environmental measures).

Her long-term study showed that being keen to maintain the goodwill of customers was the main motivation in these cases, while improvements in environmental performance played a small role. Although this had improved, there was no evidence that this was due to introducing EMS: it was just as likely to have been due to more capital spending on equipment. Shaeffer concludes:

> If one is to take the sustainability challenge seriously the implications are worrying. The adoption of a management innovation that improves companies' environmental legitimacy without doing much to tackle their (wider) environmental performance may give a false sense of achievement and [inhibit] more far-reaching improvement. (Schaefer, 2007, p. 531)

Boiral (2007) reached a similar conclusion in a study on the use of the ISO 14001 standard by nine Canadian companies. The standard is intended to improve environmental performance, by ensuring that people throughout the organisation take environmental issues seriously in the way they do their jobs. Despite being certified as meeting the standards, Boiral concluded:

> daily management practices remained decoupled from the prescriptions of the ISO 14001 system, of which employees generally had only a vague understanding. (p. 127)

Internationalisation

Matten and Moon (2008) observed that activity relating to corporate responsibility is much more visible in the US than in Europe. They note that 'Comparative research in CSR between Europe and the United States has identified remarkable differences between companies on each side of the Atlantic' (p. 404). These included evidence that:

- US companies were significantly more likely than French or Dutch companies to mention CSR explicitly on their websites;
- of 15 voluntary codes of conduct established by corporations in the coffee industry, only two were from Europe, with 13 from the US; and
- the value of voluntary community contributions by US companies was more than 10 times greater than their UK counterparts.

They ask if this means that US companies have taken the issue more seriously than those elsewhere, or is this due to differences in the respective business contexts? They support the latter view, explaining the apparent difference by using Whitley's (1999) model of differences in national business systems, (see Chapter 4, Section 4.7). This shows how differences in political, financial, education/labour and cultural systems between countries lead to differences in the nature of the firm, in how markets are organised and how companies are governed.

Matten and Moon (2008) show that in the US CR is embedded in a culture of individualism and democratic pluralism, in which corporations have more discretion, and often incentive, to engage publicly in explicit CSR activities. In Europe, CSR activities are embedded in established process of industrial relations, labour law and corporate governance.

Figure 5.7 illustrates their suggestion that differences in national business systems shape the nature of CSR between countries. Institutions that encourage individualism and provide discretion to private economic activities in liberal markets would encourage CSR as an explicit aspect of corporate policies – as is the case in the US. In contrast, European institutions have a more co-ordinated approach to economic and social governance through a partnership of representative actors led by government.

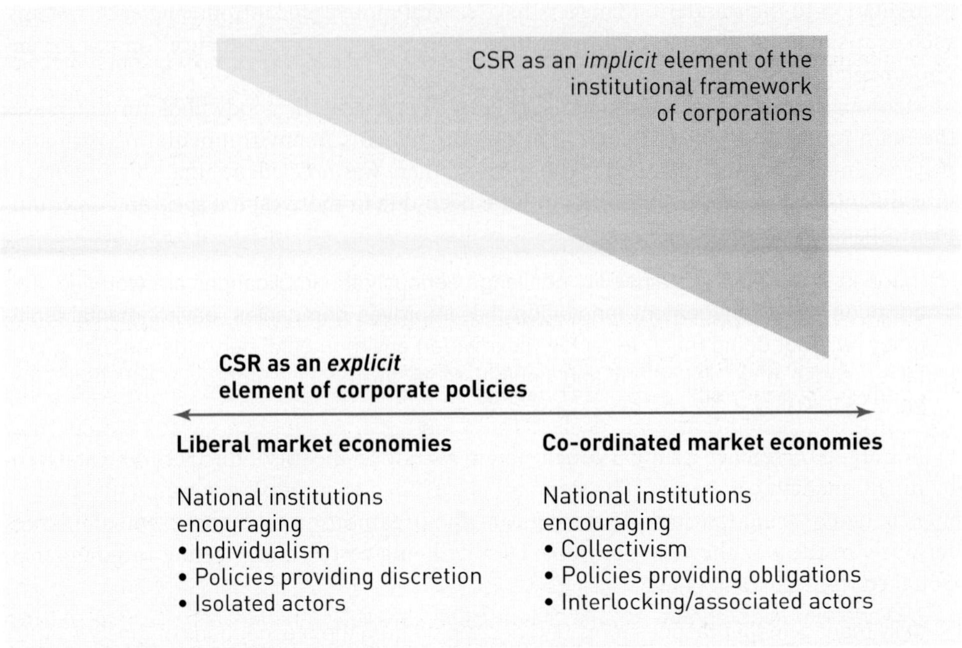

CSR as an *implicit* element of the institutional framework of corporations

CSR as an *explicit* element of corporate policies

Liberal market economies	Co-ordinated market economies
National institutions encouraging • Individualism • Policies providing discretion • Isolated actors	National institutions encouraging • Collectivism • Policies providing obligations • Interlocking/associated actors

Figure 5.7
Implicit and explicit CSR

Source: Matten and Moon (2008).

Summary

1 **Give examples of controversial, and of philanthropic, business practices**

 • Negative examples include poor treatment of suppliers or staff, wasteful uses of energy and other resources during transformation, and unfair treatment of customers. Reputations are also damaged by cases of senior management fraud or high compensation to failed managers.

 • In contrast there are many examples of philanthropy, in which people give to charities and other causes without expecting any specific benefit in return.

2 **Distinguish criteria that people use to justify individual and corporate actions**
 Individual

 • Moral principle – the decision is consistent with generally accepted principles.

 • Utilitarianism – the decision that benefits the greatest number of people is the right one to take.

 • Human rights – decisions that support one of several human rights (such as privacy) are right.

 • Individualism – decisions that serve the individual's self-interest are right; in the long run they will benefit society as well.

 Corporate

 • Legal responsibilities – obey the law

 • Economic responsibilities – Friedman's view that the only function of business is to act legally in the interests of shareholders.

 • Ethical responsibilities – that business has wider responsibilities, since it depends on aspects of the society in which it operates.

 • Discretionary – actions that are entirely philanthropic.

3 **Use a model of ethical decision making to explain behaviour**

 • Figure 5.4 shows a simple model of individual and contextual factors that shape ethical or unethical behaviour.

4 Show how stakeholders, strategies and responsible behaviour interact

- Stakeholders' expectations and relative power will influence how managers interpret responsible behaviour, bearing in mind Vogel's point that this is only sustainable if it supports strategy. The chapter shows how this happens – when corporate responsibility is part of the mission, meets customer needs or otherwise supports strategy

5 Evaluate an organisation's methods for managing corporate responsibility

- These include leading by example, codes of practice, CR structures and reporting mechanisms, and inclusion in the FTSE4Good Index Series.

6 Show how ideas from the chapter add to your understanding of the integrating themes

- One set of schemes to reduce emissions are carbon trading schemes, in which industries with heavy emissions can buy permits to continue to do so from companies that use less than their allowed level. Although still imperfect, these schemes illustrate how companies can relate aspects of corporate responsibility (in this case sustainability) to their strategy.
- There is evidence that some companies use environmental management schemes, intended to act as form of governance and control, more to impress customers and regulators than to change daily practice.
- Variations in corporate responsibility reporting between countries may have more to do with the traditions of national management systems than with differences in practice.

Review questions

1 Identify two recent examples of dubious corporate behaviour (including one from the public sector) and two of philanthropic behaviour. What were their effects?

2 Describe in your own terms each of four schools of ethical theory mentioned in the chapter, and illustrate each with an example of how it has been used to justify a decision.

3 Summarise the four responsibilities which corporations may choose to meet (or not), illustrating each with an example.

4 Sketch the ethical decision making model, and use it to analyse the Pinto case – that is, to explain why managers acted as they did.

5 How can managers take account of the diverse interest of stakeholders?

6 Why is it important, in Vogel's view, to link corporate responsibility to strategy?

7 Illustrate each of the ways in which organisations do this with a current example.

8 Visit a website of your choice, and try to find out which practices the organisation uses to promote and monitor responsible behaviour.

9 Summarise an idea from the chapter that adds to your understanding of the integrating themes.

Concluding critical reflection

Think about the way your company, or one with which you are familiar, approaches issues of corporate responsibility. Review the material in the chapter, and perhaps visit some of the websites identified. Then make notes on the following questions:

- What examples of the issues discussed in this chapter are currently relevant to your company?
- In responding to these issues, what **assumptions** about the role of business in society appear to have guided what people have done? Are they closer to the Friedmanite or the social responsibility view?

- What factors such as the history or current **context** of the company appear to have influenced the prevailing view? Does the approach appear to be right for the company, its employees and other stakeholders? Have any stakeholders tried to challenge company policy?

- Have people put forward **alternative** ways of dealing with these issues, based on evidence about other companies? If you could find such evidence, how may it affect company practice?

- What **limitations** do you find in the ideas and theories presented here? For example, while it is easy to advocate that a company should act responsibly, Vogel points out that that managers' willingness to do so is constrained by the potential threat of competitors who act less responsibly – perhaps offering cheaper products from less sustainable sources. Can you find evidence for and against Vogel's view?

Further reading

Ackroyd, S. and Thompson, P. (1999), *Organizational Misbehaviour,* Sage, London.

> Looks at the larger corporate view of 'organisational misbehaviour'.

Ambec, S. and Lanoie, P. (2008), 'Does it pay to be green? A systematic overview', *Academy of Management Perspectives*, vol. 22, no. 4, pp. 45–62.

> Clear analysis of how companies have acted to reduce their impact on the environment, and to become more profitable. The paper contains many examples of successful practice.

Bartlett, D. (2003), 'Management and business ethics: A critique and integration of ethical decision-making models', *British Journal of Management,* vol. 14, no. 3, pp. 223–235.

> Useful as an overview of recent attempts to resolve the dilemmas between organisational and individual approaches to ethical questions.

Blowfield, M. and Murray, A. (2008), *Corporate Responsibility: A critical introduction*, Oxford University Press, Oxford.

> Comprehensive account of the topic with many examples from practice, and activities to illustrate the themes.

Clarke, F.L. (2003), *Corporate Collapse: Accounting, regulatory and ethical failure,* Cambridge University Press, Cambridge.

Jackall, R. (1998), *Moral Mazes: The world of corporate managers,* Oxford University Press, Oxford.

> Focuses on the managerial role in tackling the complexity of ethical issues.

Megone, C. and Robinson, S.J. (2002), *Case Histories in Business Ethics*, Routledge, London.

Vogel, D. (2005), *The Market for Virtue: The potential and limits of corporate social responsibility*, Brookings Institution Press, Washington, DC.

> Places issues of corporate responsibility within a wider consideration of company strategy. Many current examples support the discussion.

Weblinks

These websites have appeared in the chapter:

www.bitc.org.uk
www.innocentdrinks.co.uk
www.co-operative.coop

www.joinred.com
www.kraft.com
www.gap.com
www.wipro.com
www.vodafone.com
www.FTSE4Good.com
www.bitc.org.uk

Visit two of the sites in the list, and navigate to the pages dealing with corporate responsibility, sustainability or corporate governance.

- What are the main concerns that they seem to be addressing?
- What information can you find about their policies?
- Compare and contrast the concerns and policies expressed on the sites.
- Gather information from the media or pressure group websites which relate to these companies. What differences are there between these perspectives? What dilemmas does that imply that managers in these companies are dealing with?

For video case studies, audio summaries, flashcards, exercises and annotated weblinks related to this chapter, visit **www.pearsoned.co.uk/mymanagementlab**

PART 2 CASE

BP

www.bp.com

In 2009 BP was one of the world's largest international oil and natural gas producers, having grown in the early 2000s through mergers and joint ventures. By its nature it is engaged in international business, with a strong interest in managing the political, economic and technological environments. Some criticise the oil industry for contributing to climate change – though the companies can point out that they are meeting the growing demand that people in all countries have for energy.

BP is a British registered company, but 40 per cent of its assets are in the US, and it is that country's largest gas producer. It does 80 per cent of its business outside the UK, and is inevitably involved with political considerations. With so much business in the US, the company is also sensitive to policy in that country – such as US policy on the Middle East.

The search for new supplies

The company is what is termed an 'integrated' oil company, which earns revenue by extracting oil and by selling refined oil products to end-users. Both parts of the business are becoming more difficult. On the production side, the company faces access problems, as governments are less been to bring in foreign companies to develop their resources. Countries with large reserves (those with over 30 years' supply) are all members of OPEC, the oil producing countries' cartel. All accept investment by foreign oil companies such as BP, but impose strict conditions as a way of supporting their national energy companies.

The company has invested heavily in gaining access to oil reserves not only by exploration but also by acquisitions and joint ventures, such as TNK-BP. This was a strategically important deal as it opened the way to redevelop Russia's large but ageing oil and gas fields. It also fitted a wider political strategy of reducing the West's dependence on Middle Eastern supplies. Securing more oil reserves continues to be the major strategic challenge facing the company. On a positive note, Thunderhorse, a new production platform in the Gulf of

Mexico was, by the end of 2009, exceeding expectations and producing the equivalent of 300,000 barrels a day of oil and gas (but see below). It also has new supplies from oil fields in Azerbaijan, Egypt, Angola and Indonesia. In July 2009 it reached an agreement with Iraq to rehabilitate the giant Rumaila oil field. Some analysts were unsure that the terms of the deal would benefit BP,

BP plc.

but acknowledged that the risks could be worthwhile, by giving the company a presence in a country with the world's third-largest known oil reserves.

The search for new demand

It also faces challenges on the sales side, as demand for oil in the developed countries may have peaked. BP's former Chief Executive, Tony Hayward believed it unlikely that the company will ever again sell as much conventional petrol in the US as it did in the first half of 2008. Energy efficiency measures such as tighter fuel economy standards, and the growth of biofuels, mean that the total market for oil-derived products is likely to shrink. For a company such as BP, which earns about 40 per cent of its revenue in the US, that is a worrying prospect. It will be hard to replace this demand by entering rapidly growing markets such as China and

India: they have national oil companies which are keen to protect their position.

A trading culture

Although the company refines some 4 million barrels of oil a day, it sells almost 6 million through its 23,000 service stations and other distribution systems around the world. It buys refined products from other companies to satisfy its needs. One observer noted:

> most of the majors trade oil to balance their own systems, BP is far more ambitious. They look on trading as a profit-generating centre.

A unique trading culture has developed within the company, fuelled by above-average incentives for traders, which has its roots in the company's origin as Anglo-Persian Oil in 1909. The company then produced oil in what is now Iran, but had few outlets to refine and market it. So it created a trading operation to sell the oil, and remains the most active energy trader among major oil companies.

Oil and the environment

Dealing head on with the industry's impact on the environment became one of the principles of John Browne's leadership (he was chief executive until 2007):

> These are issues of tremendous complexity. Do you want a clean environment or do you want hydrocarbons? False trade-off. You have to ask if you want both, and in the service of gaining both usually comes technology and better ways of doing things. The industry hasn't handled it well. Consumers want to consume more, they recognise the consequences of consumption, they don't want to shoulder the burden of that themselves, so they transfer it on to the shoulders of the oil and gas companies . . . The reality is it's a shared responsibility. We can do a lot but so must consumers.

John Browne made significant investments in alternative sources of energy such as biofuels, wind farms and solar power. Some believe that these ventures distract the company from its core oil and gas businesses, but Tony Hayward retained them, and increased spending on renewables and low-carbon energy, which now amount to about 5 per cent of annual capital spending. He says:

> Alternative energy is expected to be a major part of the global energy mix, and energy is our business.

Safety failures

The company's reputation suffered in March 2005 when an explosion at the Texas City refinery, its biggest in the US, killed 15 people and injured about 500, making it the deadliest US refinery accident in more than a decade. An investigation by the Department of Labor uncovered more than 300 violations at the refinery. An internal BP report found that senior managers at the plant had ignored advice to spend money on safety improvements, although boasting internally that the plant had just had its most profitable year.

There was further damage a year later when a pipeline spilled 270,000 gallons of crude oil onto the Alaskan Tundra, from North America's largest oilfield. The Alaska Department of Environmental Conservation blamed corrosion for the spill, something which workers had for years complained that managers were neglecting. BP denied this, saying that its expenditure on corrosion inspection and maintenance had increased. The authorities began criminal investigations into aspects of the company's Alaskan operations, after representations on behalf of workers who complained about the company's Corrosion Inspection and Control Division.

Browne's successor, Tony Hayward, stressed on his appointment that that his priority was simple and clear:

> BP had to implement strategy by focusing like a laser on safe and reliable operations.

In April 2010 an explosion on the Deepwater Horizon drilling rig in the Gulf of Mexico killed 11 workers and released a flow of oil from fractured pipes into the sea. This damaged the waters of the Gulf which in turn caused economic hardship to coastal communities which made a living from fishing and tourism. The flow was eventually brought under control when the damaged well was capped in early August 2010.

The episode also damaged BP's reputation, with American political leaders calling for severe penalties against the company (which did not own the rig, but leased it from another business). BP suspended dividend payments to shareholders, and set aside some $25 billion dollars to cover likely compensation claims: it would raise the funds by selling assets.

The company also decided that Mr. Hayward should resign as Chief Executive. It appointed Bob Dudley to replace him who said:

> BP will hold itself to a higher standard in understanding process safety . . . putting it in the culture so that we ensure this never happens again.

A new chairman

In June 2009 the company appointed a new Chairman to replace Peter Sutherland, who had overseen the dramatic growth of the company since 1997. He is Carl-Henric Svanberg, who was previously chief executive of the Swedish company Ericsson, where he developed a deep knowledge of the world's emerging countries. He says of them:

> Telecommunications plays probably as important a role as energy does in a country. Of the four or five matters on an agenda in an emerging market, telecoms is one of those. So I met a lot of those people that I think I will come across again.

Ericsson has been a particular success in China:

> We are the biggest infrastructure builder there. But so we are in Russia, so we are in India, so we are in sub-Saharan Africa

He also believes that the pace of growth of car ownership and air travel are unsustainable.

With a normal growth rate, the world's gross domestic product will triple by 2050, and we will probably see another 2 billion people in the world. If we continue to do things in the same way, it will not be easy for this planet to cope with that. So we have to find more intelligent solutions, and the energy industry is in the centre of that. BP is actively searching for alternative energy sources.

Sources: *Financial Times*, 14 August, 2006, 6 February 2008, 29 April 2009, 11 June 2009, 26 June 2009, 27 July 2010; BP; and other sources.

Part case questions

- The case mentions 'culture' at several points. What sub-cultures can you identify, and what may this imply for senior management's attempts to establish a unified image of the business.
- Analyse the five forces acting on BP. Which present the greatest threat to the company?
- Construct a PESTEL analysis to establish the main aspects of the environment that affect BP.
- In what ways will managing in BP, with such an international exposure, be different from managing in a national company with no international business? List the three most significant ones.
- What evidence is there in the case about the company's priorities in the area of corporate responsibility?
- Do you agree with Lord Browne's comments on the responsibilities of the consumer in reducing energy consumption? From your experience, do you think that consumers are likely to play this role? What might encourage them to do so?
- The new Chairman has no experience of the oil industry. Why do you think the Board chose him?

PART 2
SKILLS DEVELOPMENT

To help you develop your skills, as well as knowledge, this section includes tasks that relate the key themes covered in the part to your daily life. Working through these will help you to deepen your understanding of the topic, and develop skills and insights that you can use in many situations.

Task 2.1 Dimensions of the competitive environment

Select an industry in which you have an interest (perhaps for a potential career), and write a one to two page paper describing the main competing players in that industry, and the major issues the industry is facing. Identify the companies in which you are interested by checking articles about the industry in sources such as **www.hoovers.com**, **www.ft.com** or **www.economist.com** (these sites are subscription only once you get beyond the headlines) and then go to the companies' websites for more detailed information.

Task 2.2 Dimensions of the general environment

Changes in a country's demography have significant implications for managers, as they affect the resources available as inputs to organisations, the outputs that are likely to be in demand, and aspects of the transformation process (such as the growing desire for flexible working times). Information about these trends is available from official websites – such as (in the UK) **www.statistics.gov.uk**

Go to that site, or the equivalent in your country, and find out: (1) the total number of people in the country now, and the predictions for five and ten years on; (2) the changing age distribution; (3) the number of people with internet access; (4) other data which interest you as a student of management.

What implications may your results have for business in five years time?

Task 2.3 Comparing industry environments

While all organisations face opportunities and threats from their competitive and general environments, these differ. Summarise the work you have done in the earlier activities so that you can set out the main threats and opportunities facing one industry. Then compare your conclusions with another student who has studied a different industry. List those factors which are the same, and those which are different.

Task 2.4   Tracking multinationals

Since an increasing amount of business is done through multinational businesses, it pays to become familiar with some of them. Select three businesses that have a major international presence (preferably not limited to the most obvious ones) and go to their websites. Find out about their main products and services, the countries in which they operate, the broad structure of the organisation, and their statements about social responsibility. You could also check their careers page.

Compare what you have found with a colleague, identifying what is similar about the companies, and what is different.

Task 2.5   Country studies for a multinational

Suppose that one of the companies you have worked with in Task 4 is considering launching a valuable new product in one of the following countries: Malaysia, Singapore, Brazil, or Australia. One issue in their decision will be the status of regional trading alliances affecting these countries. Use the internet to establish whether these countries are part of any such alliances. If so, compile a one-page report on that alliance for presentation to the company. The managers of the company would also like information on the main PESTEL factors in each country. Prepare a one-page report outlining the main PESTEL factors for one of the countries identified. They are also interested in what environmental constraints they may face in that country – try to include a commentary on this aspect, as in some industries it will be critical part of an investment decision, if you can find adequate information.

PART 3
PLANNING

Introduction

This part examines the generic management activities of planning and decision making, and then looks at two substantive applications of these ideas – to strategy and marketing respectively. Both areas depend on understanding the environment of the business and the stakeholders within it. They also both depend on building an internal capability to deliver whatever direction management decides upon.

Chapter 6 provides an overview of planning in organisations, setting out the purposes of planning, the types of plan and the tasks of planning. While all these tasks are likely to be part of the process, their shape will always depend on the circumstances for which a plan is being made.

Decision making is closely linked to planning, made necessary by finite resources and infinite demands. People in organisations continually decide on inputs, transformation processes and outputs – and the quality of those decisions affects organisational performance. Chapter 7 therefore introduces the main decision making processes, and contrasts several theories of decision making in organisations.

Chapter 8 outlines the strategy process, and introduces techniques that managers use to analyse the options facing businesses of all kinds. This analysis can then lead to clearer choices about future direction.

Central to that is the market the organisation chooses to serve. Chapter 9 presents some marketing methods, and shows how they are closely linked to strategy. Like strategy, they use external and internal analysis to establish a way forward, and like strategy it depends on the support of other units to meet customer expectations profitably.

The Part case is The Virgin Group, illustrating the interaction of the external environment with the developing corporate and marketing strategies.

CHAPTER 6
PLANNING

Aim

To describe the purposes of planning in organisations, and illustrate the iterative tasks in the planning cycle

Objectives

By the end of your work on this chapter you should be able to outline the concepts below in your own terms and:

1 Explain the purposes of planning and the content of different types of plan
2 Compare alternative planning processes, and evaluate when each may be most suitable
3 Outline the seven iterative steps in planning, and describe techniques used in each
4 Use theory to evaluate the motivational effect of the goals stated in a plan
5 Use a framework to evaluate whether a plan is sufficiently comprehensive
6 Evaluate the context that will affect the ability of managers to implement a plan
7 Show how ideas from the chapter can add to your understanding of the integrating themes

Key terms

This chapter introduces the following ideas:

planning
goal (or objective)
business plan
strategic plan
strategic business unit
operational plans
enterprise resource planning
planning system
SWOT analysis

critical success factors
optimism bias
strategic misrepresentation bias
sensitivity analysis
scenario planning
stated goals
real goals
organisational readiness

Each is a term defined within the text, as well as in the Glossary at the end of the book.

Crossrail is a new railway for London and the south-east of England which will connect the City, Canary Wharf, the West End and Heathrow Airport to commuter areas east and west of the capital. It aims to be a world-class, affordable railway, with high-frequency, convenient and accessible services across the capital. The plans are intended to:

- relieve congestion on many Underground and rail lines;
- provide new connections and new services;
- bring modern trains;
- provide eight new stations in central London.

By kind permission, Crossrail

It will add 10 per cent to London's overall transport capacity and provide 40 per cent of the extra rail capacity London needs. Main construction of the railway will begin in 2010, with services commencing in 2017. Crossrail will make travelling in the area easier and quicker, and reduce crowding on London's transport network. It will operate with main-line-size trains, each carrying more than 1,500 passengers.

It is the largest civil engineering project in the UK and the largest single addition to the London transport network for over 50 years. It will run 118 km from Maidenhead and Heathrow in the west, through new twin-bore 21 km tunnels under Central London out to Shenfield and Abbey Wood in the east, joining the Great Western and Great Eastern railway networks.

The project has a long history – it was first proposed in 1990, but amidst considerable opposition from other players it was cancelled in 1996. Pressure continued to build the line as a contribution to solving London's transport problems, and the company claims wide support for Crossrail among UK businesses and business organisations such as the CBI, London First and the London Chamber of Commerce and Industry.

Political conditions changed again, and Royal Assent was given to the Crossrail Act in July 2008 giving authority for the railway to be built. In December 2008 the government and the Mayor of London signed the key funding agreements for Crossrail.

By March 2010 the overall plan was turning into reality as many of the smaller elements were implemented. For example, the company announced the award of contracts for what it calls enabling work such as various pieces of complex demolition work at several stations and their surrounding area. The company also announced that the Learning & Skills Council had agreed to provide £5 million towards the cost of a new tunnelling and underground construction academy. A senior manager said:

> This is great news for the programme and great news for the tunnelling and underground construction industry. This decision means we can now progress our plans to build this fantastic training facility, which the industry so urgently needs.

Construction would commence soon and the facility is expected to be fully operational by the end of 2010.

Source: Company website and other published sources.

Case questions 6.1

Visit the Crossrail website (see above).

- What are the main items of recent news about the progress of the project?
- From what you read, what are the main challenges the managers face in planning the project?
- What kind of environment do you think the company is operating in (Chapter 3, Section 3.6)?

6.1 Introduction

Crossrail is an example of a major project which managers can only achieve by a substantial investment in planning. From the early political processes to secure support from many interested parties (Glaister and Travers, 2001) – some in favour of the project, some against – through raising capital and securing public consent, managers have engaged in a continual planning process. That now continues, as it turns to the very detailed planning required to drive a new railway through a crowded capital city. The case will illustrate how Crossrail's managers deal with these challenges, some of which are still unforeseen.

Brews and Purahit (2007) show empirically that, as business conditions become more unstable, companies do more planning. Change creates uncertainty, and planning helps people adapt to this by clarifying objectives, specifying how to achieve them, and monitoring progress. Plans include both ends (what to do) and means (how to do it).

Informal plans (not written down, nor widely shared) work perfectly well in many situations, but as the number of people involved in an activity increases they need something more to guide them. That is the focus here – on more formal plans – which put into writing the goals of a business or unit, and who will do what to achieve them. When senior managers at Hiscox, a small but rapidly growing insurance company, decided to add an online service to its traditional way of doing business through insurance brokers, it needed not only a plan for the website, but also a plan to reassure the brokers that they would still have a role. When two entrepreneurs decided to create the City Inn hotel chain they planned in detail the kind of hotels they would be: contemporary, city centre, newly built, 'active and open' atmosphere, and a consistent room design across the group. Plans like this can then be communicated to relevant players, to ensure they act consistently.

Figure 6.1 provides an overview of the themes. At the centre are seven generic tasks in planning – but people vary the order, and how much attention they give to each. The chapter outlines the benefits of planning and distinguishes the content of plans. Later sections examine the process of planning, and its seven generic steps – stressing throughout that these take place iteratively, and that their form depends on circumstances.

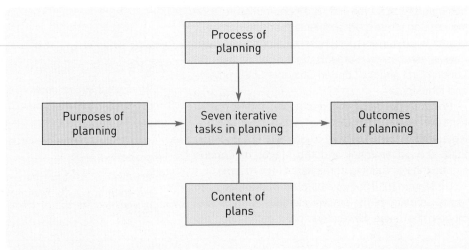

Figure 6.1 An overview of the chapter

6.2 Purposes of planning

A planner is an individual who contemplates future actions: the activity of **planning** involves establishing the **goals** (or **objectives**) for the task, specifying how to achieve them, implementing the plan and evaluating the results. Goals are the desired future state of an activity or organisational unit, and planning to meet them typically includes allocating resources and specifying what people need to do to meet the goals.

> **Planning** is the iterative task of setting goals, specifying how to achieve them, implementing the plan and evaluating the results.
>
> A **goal** (or **objective**) is a desired future state for an activity or organisational unit.

Planning, if done well:

- clarifies direction;
- motivates people;
- uses resources efficiently; and
- increases control, by enabling people to measure progress against targets.

The act of planning may in itself add value, by ensuring that people base decisions on a wider range of evidence than if there was no planning system. Giraudeau (2008) shows how the planning process in one of Renault's divisions enhanced debate among managers, and stimulated their strategic imagination. Closely observing the company's planners as they developed their plan to build a plant in Brazil, the author shows how providing detailed draft plans to other managers (many of whom were unfamiliar with that country) led them to visualise opportunities they had not considered. If done badly, planning has the opposite effect, leading to confusion and waste.

Good plans give direction to the people whose work contributes to their achievement. If everyone knows the purpose of a larger activity and how their task contributes, they can work more effectively. They adjust their work to the plan (or vice versa), and co-operate and co-ordinate with others. It helps them to cope with uncertainty: if they know the end result they can respond to unexpected changes, without waiting to be told. People like to know how their task fits the bigger picture, as it adds interest and enables them to take more responsibility.

Management in practice Maersk – planning key to strategy www.maersk.com

Maersk is the world's largest container operator, and depends on planning. Mark Cornwall, Operations Manager, explains:

Maersk operates 470 container ships with 1.9 million individual containers that are all travelling around the world, and our job is to build efficiencies into the system – moving the cargo to the customer on time.

Part of our strategy is to deliver unmatched reliability, and operations is key to that. From the top of the company right down to the clerks on the desk, everybody's focused on meeting deadlines and the requirements of the customer every step of the way. So whether it's a ship arriving in a port on time, or a container loading on a ship on time, or a truck delivery to a warehouse, everybody's focused all the way through the chain on making sure that everything happens against the deadline as planned.

Efficiency's all about making the best use of your assets, so whether it's putting as many containers as possible on a ship, or maximising your utilisation of a particular train, or getting as many miles out of a truck as you can during a shift, it's all about planning your assets to get the biggest use out of them during that period.

Source: Interview with Mark Cornwall.

Planning reduces overlap and at the same time ensures that someone is responsible for each activity. A plan helps people co-ordinate their separate tasks, so saving time and resources; without a plan they may work at cross-purposes. If people are clear on the goal they can spot inefficiencies or unnecessary delays and act to fix them.

| Key ideas | **Does planning help entrepreneurial behaviour and new ventures?** |

Delmar and Shane (2003) studied whether planning helps new ventures, by gathering data from over 200 new firms in Sweden. They hypothesised that planning would support new ventures by:

- enabling quicker decisions;
- providing a tool for managing resources to minimise bottlenecks;
- identifying actions to achieve broader goals in a timely manner.

They gathered extensive data from the firms at their start-up in 1998, and then at regular intervals for three years. The results supported each of their hypotheses, leading them to conclude that planning did indeed support the creation of successful new ventures.

Source: Delmar and Shane (2003).

Setting final and interim goals lets people know how well they are progressing, and when they have finished. Comparing actual progress against the intended progress enables people to adjust the goal or change the way they are using resources.

Preparing a plan may also perform a ceremonial function. Kirsch *et al.* (2009) in a study of entrepreneurs seeking funding from venture capitalists found that:

> neither the presence of business planning documents nor their content serve a communicative role for venture capitalists [in the sense of conveying information that influences the funding decision]. With some qualifications, we find that business planning documents may serve a limited ceremonial role [in the sense of showing that the presenter understands how the target expects them to behave].

The content of a plan is the subject – *what* aspect of business it deals with: strategic, business unit, operational, tactical or special purpose. The next section deals with those topics, and the one which follows focuses on *how* – the planning process.

| Activity 6.1 | **Reflection on the purpose of plans** |

Find an example of a plan that someone has prepared in an organisation – preferably for one of the types listed in the next section.

- Ask someone what its purpose is, and whether it achieves that.
- Ask whether the plan is too detailed, or not detailed enough.
- What do they regard as the strengths and weaknesses of the planning process?
- Refer to your notes as you work on this chapter.

6.3 The content of plans

A **business plan** is a document that sets out the markets the business intends to serve, how it will do so and what finance is required.

People starting a new business or expanding an existing one prepare a **business plan** – a document that sets out the markets the business intends to serve, how it will do so and what finance is required (Sahlman, 1997; Blackwell, 2004). It does so in considerable detail (see Part 3

Skills Development), as it needs to convince potential investors to lend money. Managers seeking capital investment or other corporate resources need to convince senior managers to allocate them – which they do by presenting a convincing plan. People in the public sector do the same: a director of roads, for example, needs to present a plan to convince the chief executive or elected members that planned expenditure on roads will be a better use of resources than competing proposals from (say) the director of social work. Service managers inevitably compete with each other for limited resources, and develop business plans to support their case.

Strategic plans apply to the whole organisation. They set out the overall direction and cover major activities: markets and revenues, together with plans for marketing, human resources and production. Strategy is concerned with deciding what business an organisation should be in, where it wants to be and how it is going to get there. These decisions involve major resource commitments and usually require a series of consequential operational decisions.

> A **strategic plan** sets out the overall direction for the business, is broad in scope and covers all the major activities.

In a large business there will be divisional plans for each major unit. If subsidiaries operate as autonomous **strategic business units** (SBUs) they develop their plans with limited inputs from the rest of the company, as they manage distinct products or markets.

Strategic plans usually set out a direction for several years, although in businesses with long lead times (energy production or aircraft manufacture) they look perhaps 15 years ahead. Ryanair plans to grow capacity to meet demand, and makes a plan showing the financial and other implications of enlarging the fleet, recruiting staff and opening new routes. Such plans are not fixed: managers regularly update them to take account of new conditions, so they are sometimes called 'rolling plans'.

> A **strategic business unit** consists of a number of closely related products for which it is meaningful to formulate a separate strategy.

Management in practice British Airways plans survival www.ba.com

In 2009 British Airways reported that it expected to lose money for the second successive year, and said it was planning more cost reductions to help it survive an expected two-year recession. It was shrinking operations at Gatwick Airport reducing the aircraft fleet based there from 32 to 24.

Other plans included:

- cutting thousands of jobs across the business;
- negotiating a merger with Spain's Iberia to create Europe's third-largest aviation group;
- reducing absenteeism among staff;
- negotiating more efficient working practices for cabin staff;
- reducing capacity at London City Airport by a further 17 per cent from an earlier plan.

Source: *Financial Times*, 6 March 2009.

Operational plans detail how managers expect to achieve the strategic objectives. They are narrower in scope, indicating what departments or functions should do to support the strategy. So there may be a family of related plans forming a hierarchy: a strategic plan for the organisation and main divisions, and several operational plans for departments or teams. An example is when Sainsbury announced an aggressive expansion plan in 2009, with the aim of opening 50 new supermarkets and extending another 50, over the next two years. Justin King, chief executive, said that it would concentrate the expansion in areas where it was weak, such as the west of England, Wales and Scotland. Such plans will contain linked objectives and will become more specific as they move down the organisation – eventually dealing with small activities that need to be dealt with for each new store – but aiming to be consistent with the wider expansion strategy. Table 6.1 shows this hierarchical arrangement, and how the character of plans changes at each level.

> **Operational plans** detail how the overall objectives are to be achieved, by specifying what senior management expects from specific departments or functions.

Table 6.1 A planning hierarchy

Type of plan	Strategic	Operational	Activity
Level	Organisation or business unit	Division, department, function or market	Work unit or team
Focus	Direction and strategy for whole organisation	Functional changes or market activities to support strategic plans	Actions needed to deliver current products or services
Nature	Broad, general direction	Detail on required changes	Specific detail on immediate goals and tasks
Timescale	Long term (2–3 years?)	Medium (up to 18 months?)	Very short term (hours to weeks?)

Case study   Crossrail – the case continues www.crossrail.co.uk

The company has published its outline plans for the station and tunnelling work to be done – making it clear that as detailed design and development of the scheme progresses there will be increasing certainty over the exact times that works will start and finish at each location. The information below gives the assumed timings (early 2010) for main construction works at key locations.

At some locations enabling works (such as the diversion of utilities like gas mains, and demolition of existing buildings) will need to take place before main works. The sites may also be required after main works, for example to support fitting out of stations and tunnels.

Stations

The following table of station start and completion dates reflects the start of construction (main civil contract works) and when enabling works begin. Note that only the first four station sites are shown here.

Location	Enabling works start	Construction starts	Works complete
Canary Wharf	December 2008	May 2009	2016
Tottenham Court Road	January 2009	Early 2010	2016
Farringdon	July 2009	August 2010	2017
Custom House	Early 2012	Late 2012	2014

Tunnelling works

The completion dates shown in the following table refer to the completion of the tunnel. Fit out will take place beyond these dates. Note that only the first three tunnels to be bored are shown here.

Location of tunnel drive	Boring begins	Tunnel drive complete
Royal Oak to Framlington (X)	October 2011	March 2013
Limmo to Farringdon (Y)	April 2012	April 2014
Plumstead to North Woolwich (H)	September 2012	October 2014

On network works

Work on stations and tracks on the existing surface, railway which will be served by Crossrail, will be carried out by Network Rail. These are expected to start in mid 2010. The exact start and duration will vary by location and more detail on the programme will be published when it is available.

Source: Company website.

Case questions 6.2

● How are the strategic plans for the project being turned into operational plans?

● Visit the company website and look for information about developments which may affect these plans.

Most organisations prepare annual plans that focus on finance and set budgets for the coming year – these necessarily include sales, marketing, production or technology plans as well. Activity plans are short-term plans which deal with immediate production or service delivery – a sheet scheduling which orders to deliver next week, or who is on duty tomorrow. Standing plans specify how to deal with routine, recurring issues such as recruitment or customer complaints. Some use a method called **enterprise resource planning (ERP)** to integrate the day-to-day work of complex production systems – Chapter 12 describes this technique in Section 12.6.

Figure 6.2 contrasts specific and directional plans. Specific plans have clear, quantified objectives with little discretion in how to achieve them. When Tesco opens a new store, staff follow defined procedures detailing all the tasks required to ensure that it opens on time and within the budget. Where there is uncertainty about what needs to be done to meet the objective, managers will use a directional plan, setting the objective but leaving staff to decide how they achieve it. Hamm (2007) describes how in the early days of Wipro (a successful Indian information technology company) the founder, Azim Premji, held weekly telephone conversations with his regional managers, in which he set their targets for the following week – but they decided how to meet them. They were accountable for meeting the target, not for how they did so, provided they met his high ethical standards.

> **Enterprise resource planning (ERP)** is a computer-based planning system which links separate databases to plan the use of all resources within the enterprise.

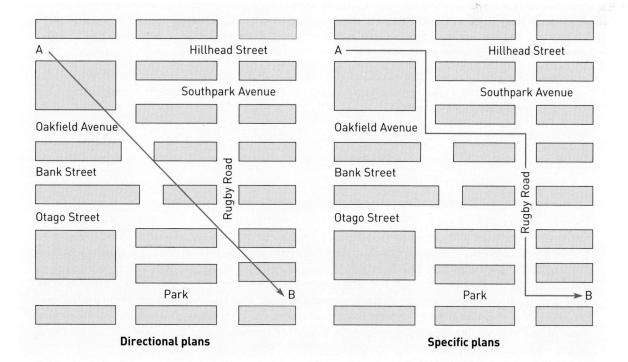

Directional plans   **Specific plans**

Figure 6.2 Specific and directional plans

Managers also prepare special purpose plans. They may have plans for disaster recovery (after, say, a major computer failure or terrorist action), and project plans to organise and implement specific changes, such as introducing a new computer system or launching a new product. When The Royal Bank of Scotland (RBS) took over NatWest Bank, managers quickly developed over 160 interlocking plans to incorporate NatWest operations into those of RBS (Kennedy *et al.*, 2006).

6.4 The process of planning

The process of planning refers to the way plans are produced – are they developed from the top of the organisation or from the bottom up? How frequently are they revised? Who creates them? A **planning system** organises and co-ordinates the activities of those involved: the process shapes the quality and value of a plan. Designing and maintaining a suitable planning system is part of the planning task.

Participation is one issue – who is involved in making the plan? One approach is to appoint a group of staff specialists to be responsible for producing plans, with or without consultation with the line managers or staff concerned. Others believe the quality of the plan, and especially the ease of implementing it, will be increased if staff familiar with local conditions help to create the plan.

A **planning system** refers to the processes by which the members of an organisation produce plans, including their frequency and who takes part in the process.

Management in practice   A new planning process at Merck www.merck.com

In the early 1990s, Merck was the world's leading pharmaceutical company, but by 2006 it was ranked only eighth. Dick Clark, the new chief executive, was charged with reviving a company: one of his first actions was to make radical changes in the company's planning process. Teams of employees were asked to present the business cases to senior managers to test possible directions for the company – such as whether to build a generic drugs business. This process was vital, said Mr Clark, as it showed the 200 senior executives that Merck would now operate in an atmosphere where assumptions would be openly questioned by anyone. He has also changed the way the company sets its earnings projections. Formerly set by top managers, projections are now set by lower-level teams.

> It wasn't like Dick Clark said 'We're going to have double-digit growth, go out and find it!' We tested it and tweaked it . . . but it was legitimate and we believe in it, so let's go public with it. And that's the first time we'd done that as a company.

Source: From an article by Christopher Bowe, *Financial Times*, 27 March 2006, p. 10.

Key ideas   The benefits of participation and communication

Ketokivi and Castañer (2004) studied the strategic planning process in 164 manufacturing plants, in five countries and three industries (automotive supplies, machinery and electronics). It has long been recognised that organisational members tend to focus on the goals of their unit or function, rather than on those of the enterprise – known as 'position-bias'. The study sought to establish empirically whether position bias existed, and, more importantly, whether strategic planning reduced this. The evidence confirmed the tendency to position-bias. It also showed that having employees participate in strategic planning, and communicating the outcome to them, significantly diminishes it. If top management wants to reduce position bias, they should incorporate participation and communication into the strategic planning process.

Source: Ketokivi and Castañer (2004).

Figure 6.3
Seven iterative
tasks in making
a plan

A related debate (see Chapter 8, Section 8.7) is between those who advocate a rational approach to planning, and those who favour what are variously called learning or emergent approaches. They argue that when a company is in dynamic context, plans must be essentially temporary and provisional, so that managers can adapt them to suit changing circumstances, drawing on new information from the frequent interaction of a wide range of participants (Fletcher and Harris, 2002; Papke-Shields *et al.*, 2006). Andersen (2000) sought to reconcile these views by studying the use of strategic planning and autonomous action in three industries with different external conditions. He concluded that strategic planning was associated with superior organisational performance in all industrial settings. Whether industries were complex and dynamic or stable and simple, companies that planned performed better than those that did not. In addition, he found that in complex dynamic industries a formal planning process was accompanied by autonomous actions by managers, which further enhanced performance.

Planning and doing may seem like separate activities, and in stable conditions that may be true. In volatile conditions, with markets or technologies changing quickly, people conduct them almost simultaneously. In their study of strategic planning, Whittington *et al.* (2006) conclude that, far from strategising and organising being separate activities

> they become very similar, or even common: in the heat of the moment practitioners may be unable to distinguish the two. (p. 618)

Jennings (2000) shows how companies change their approach to planning as conditions change. A study of the UK electricity generating company PowerGen (now owned by the German company E.on) which was privatised in 1991 traced the evolution since then of the company's corporate planning process. It had retained a formal process with a five-year planning horizon, but it is more devolved. A small central team focuses on overall strategy while business units develop local plans, quickly completing the planning cycle. These changes created a more adaptive style of planning which suited the (new) uncertainty of the business. Grant (2003) also shows how planning systems of large oil companies have changed to deal with uncertainty.

Figure 6.3 shows the seven generic tasks which people can perform when they make a plan. They use them iteratively, often going back to an earlier stage when they find new information that implies, say, that they need to reshape the original goals. And of course they may miss a stage, or spend too little or too much time on them: the figure only indicates a way of analysing the stages of planning.

6.5 Gathering information

Any plan depends on information – including informal, soft information gained from casual encounters with colleagues, as well as formal analyses of economic and market trends.

Chapter 3 outlines the competitive and general environments, and planners usually begin by drawing on information about these. External sources include government economic and demographic statistics, industry surveys and general business intelligence services. Managers also commission market research on, for example, individual shopping patterns, attitudes towards particular firms or brand names, and satisfaction with existing products or services. Many firms use focus groups to test consumer reaction to new products (for more on this see Chapter 9).

Management in practice — Inamo – planning the start-up www.inamo-restaurant.com

Danny Potter, Managing Director, explained the information they needed before they started:

Well, in terms of market research, we looked into what other interactive ordering restaurants and concepts there might be, a lot of research on the world wide web and just going round London to various restaurants. We also looked at good guides which give you a quick summary. Also meeting people in the industry, going to shows and exhibitions are quick ways of learning a great deal. Also a few brainstorming sessions to get feedback on what people thought of the concept – one piece of feedback from that was that this would not fit a formal French dining environment, for example. We came to the conclusion that Oriental fusion was the appropriate cuisine type.

We spent a great deal of time finding the right location. We went through the government statistics database and built a database of our own, analysing demographics of the whole of London. What we found was that a very small area around central London is really where all the buzz happens, where all of the restaurants want to be. And then focused on finding the right location in this area.

Source: Interview with Danny Potter.

SWOT analysis

A **SWOT analysis** is a way of summarising the organisation's strengths and weaknesses relative to external opportunities and threats.

At a strategic level, planning will usually combine an analysis of external environmental factors with an internal analysis of the organisation's strengths and weaknesses. A **SWOT analysis** does this, bringing together the internal strengths and weaknesses and the external opportunities and threats. Internally, managers would analyse the strengths and weaknesses of the resources within, or available to, the organisation (Grant, 1991), such as a firm's distinctive research capability, or its skill in integrating acquired companies. The external analysis would probably be based on PESTEL and Porter's (1980a) five forces model (see Chapter 3). These tools help to identify the main opportunities and threats that people believe could affect the business.

While the method appears to be a rational way of gathering information, its usefulness depends on recognising that it is a human representation of reality: participants will differ about the significance of factors – a debate which may itself add value to the process (Hodgkinson *et al.*, 2006).

Activity 6.2 — Conducting a SWOT analysis

Choose one of the companies featured in the text (or any that interests you).

- Gather information from the company's website and other published data to prepare a SWOT analysis.
- Compare your analysis with that of a colleague on your course.
- Identify any differences between you in terms of the factors identified, and the significance given to them. What do those differences tell you about the value of the SWOT method?

Given the diversity and complexity of organisational environments it is easy to have too much information. Managers needs to focus on the few trends and events that are likely to be of greatest significance. De Wit and Meyer (2004) report that planners at Royal Dutch/Shell focus on critical factors such as oil demand (economic), refining capacity (political and economic), the likelihood of government intervention (political) and alternative sources of fuel (technological).

Critical success factors analysis

In considering whether to enter a new market, a widely used planning technique is to assess the **critical success factors** (Leidecker and Bruno, 1984) in that market. These are the things which customers in that particular market most value about a product or service – and they therefore play a key role as people plan whether to move into a line of business. Some value price, others quality, others some curious aspect of the product's features. But in all cases they are things that a company must be able to do well in order to succeed in that market.

Critical success factors are those aspects of a strategy that *must* be achieved to secure competitive advantage.

Forecasting

Forecasts or predictions of the future are often based on an analysis of past trends in factors such as input prices (wages, components, etc.), sales patterns or demographic characteristics. All forecasts are based on assumptions. In relatively simple environments people can reasonably assume that past trends will continue, but in uncertain conditions they need alternative assumptions. A new market might support rapid sales growth, whereas in a saturated market (e.g. basic foods, paid-for newspapers) it might be more realistic to assume a lower or nil growth rate.

Forecasting is big business, with companies selling analyses to business and government, using techniques such as time-series analysis, econometric modelling and simulation. However, because forecasts rely heavily on extrapolating past trends, they are of little value as conditions become uncertain. Grant (2003) reports that oil companies have significantly reduced the resources they spend on preparing formal forecasts of oil demand and prices, preferring to rely on broader assumptions about possible trends. Forecasts of cost and demand in major public sector projects are also unreliable (see Key Ideas).

Optimism bias refers to a human tendency to judge future events in a more positive light than is warranted by experience.

Strategic misrepresentation is where competition for resources leads planners to underestimate costs and overestimate benefits, to increase the likelihood that their project gains approval.

Key ideas   The planning fallacy in large projects

Large public infrastructure projects regularly cost more and deliver less than their promoters promised: Flyvbjerg (2008) quotes research showing that the average cost inaccuracy for rail projects is 44 per cent, for bridges and tunnels 34 per cent, and for roads 20 per cent. He then draws on work by Daniel Kahneman (Lovallo and Kahneman, 2003) which identified a systematic fallacy in planning, whereby people underestimate the costs, completion times and risks of planned actions, whereas they overestimate their benefits. This became known as the 'planning fallacy', which has two sources:

- **optimism bias** – a human tendency to judge future events in a more positive light than is warranted by actual experience; and
- **strategic misrepresentation** – where competition for scarce resources leads forecasters and planners deliberately to underestimate costs and overestimate benefits, to increase the likelihood that their project, not competing ones, gains approval and funding.

Kahneman believes these biases lead planners to take an 'inside view', focusing on the constituents of the plan, rather than an 'outside view' focusing on the outcomes of similar plans that have been completed.

Source: Flyvbjerg (2008).

Sensitivity analysis

A sensitivity analysis tests the effect on a plan of several alternative values of the key variables.

One way to test assumptions is to make a **sensitivity analysis** of key variables in a plan. This may assume that the company will attain a 10 per cent share of a market within a year: what will be the effect on the calculations if they secure 5 per cent or 15 per cent? What if interest rates rise, increasing the cost of financing the projects? Planners can then compare the robustness of the options and assess the relative risks. Johnson *et al.* (2008) give a worked example (pp. 378–379).

Scenario planning

An alternative to forecasting is to consider possible scenarios. Cornelius *et al.* (2005) note:

> scenarios are not projections, predictions or preferences; rather they are coherent and credible stories about the future.

Scenario planning is an attempt to create coherent and credible alternative stories about the future.

Scenario planning typically begin by considering how external forces such as the internet, an ageing population or climate change might affect a company's business over the next five–ten years. Doing so can bring managers new ideas about their environment, enabling them to consider previously unthinkable possibilities. Advocates (Van der Heijden, 1996) claim two benefits. The first is that it discourages reliance on 'single-point forecasting' – a single view of the future; second, it encourages managers to develop alternatives – plans to cope with outcomes that depart from the scenario. Few companies use the technique systematically, as it is time consuming and costly. An exception is at Shell, where:

> Scenario thinking now underpins the established way of thinking at Shell. It has become a part of the culture, such that people throughout the company, dealing with significant decisions, normally will think in terms of multiple, but equally plausible futures to provide a context for decision making. (Van der Heijden, 1996, p. 21)

A combination of PESTEL and five forces analysis should ensure that managers recognise major external factors. Forecasting and scenario planning can help them to consider possible implications for the business.

Management in practice DSM – business strategy dialogue www.dsm.com

DSM is a Dutch chemical company which has developed a planning process that requires each Business Group to conduct a business strategy dialogue (BSD) every three years. This ensures a consistent method and terminology for the planning process across the company. The reviews have five phases:

- **Characterising the business situation** Collecting information on what business you are in, the competitors, how attractive is the industry (growth, profitability), how do you compare with competitors?
- **Analysing the business system (macro)** Analysing the industry in which the group competes, using Porter's Five Forces model.
- **Analysing the business system (micro)** The internal processes of the business, including its value chain, and strengths and weaknesses.
- **Options and strategic choice** This uses the earlier phases to allow the business managers to choose which strategic option to pursue and what it requires.
- **Action planning and performance measurement** The chosen strategy is then turned into a plan and linked to performance measurement. The team sets performance indicators such as market share, new product development, customer satisfaction and cost per unit of output. These enable managers to monitor implementation.

Source: Based on Bloemhof *et al.*, 2004; company website.

| **6.6** | **Setting goals (or objectives)** |

A clear plan depends on being clear about the ultimate purpose of a task: whether it concerns the organisation or a unit. This seems obvious, but managers favour action above planning (Stewart, 1967) – especially the ambiguities of agreeing on goals (sometimes called objectives). Yet until people clarify goals they make little progress.

Goals (or objectives)

Goals give focus to a task: what will we achieve, by when? Setting goals is difficult as we have to look beyond a (relatively) known present to an unknown future. Bond *et al.* (2008) asked people to set objectives for a personally relevant task (finding a good job) – and they consistently omitted nearly half of the objectives that they later identified as important, when these were drawn to their attention. The researchers secured the same results in a software company.

Goals provide the reference point for other decisions, and the criteria against which to measure performance. At the business level they include quantified financial objectives – earnings per share, return on shareholders' funds and cash flow. At the project level the targets will be expressed in other ways (see Management in Practice).

| **Management in practice** | **Environmental targets at Heathrow Terminal 5** |

Building Terminal 5 was an opportunity to embed environmentally sustainable practices into every aspect of the terminal's operation. An environmental assessment group identified several sustainability focus areas, which evolved into the project requirements and then into environmental targets such as:

Aspect	Key performance indicator	Target
Water	Potable water use	70% cut in potable water use (more from other sources)
	Water consumption	25 litres/passenger
Pollution control	Total harmful emissions to water	Capture 25% of surface water runoff for re-use
Waste	Waste recycled/composted	40% by 2010, 80% by 2020
Resource use	Compliance with T5 materials	40% of coarse aggregate in concrete to be re-cycled

Source: Lister (2008).

| **Activity 6.3** | **Developing goals** |

- Go to the websites of some companies that interest you and collect examples of planning goals.
- Does the organisation or unit for which you work have stated planning goals? If so, how were they developed?
- Gather examples of goals at either organisational, operational or activity levels. If you can, ask those affected by them about the process by which they were set. Also ask if this has affected their attitudes towards them.

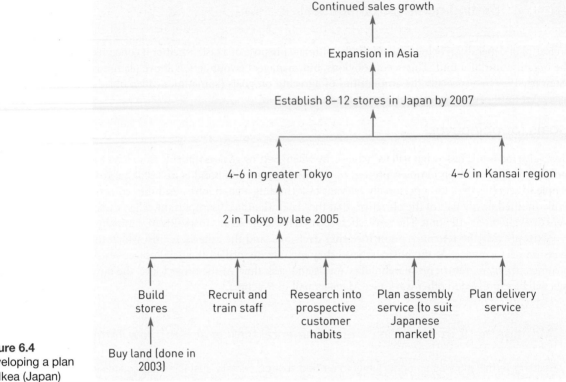

Figure 6.4
Developing a plan
for Ikea (Japan)

A hierarchy of goals

A way of relating goals to each other is to build them into a hierarchy, in which the overall goals are transformed into more specific goals for different parts of the organization, such as marketing, finance, operations and human resources. Managers in those areas develop plans setting out the actions they must undertake in order to meet the overall goal. Figure 6.4 illustrates this by using Ikea's plan to expand in Japan. To meet its planned sales growth, managers decided to open many stores across Asia, of which the first were to be in Japan. That evolved into a plan for their probable location, and then into a precise plan for two near Tokyo. That in turn led managers to develop progressively more detailed plans for the thousands of details that will need to be in good order if the venture is to succeed.

Plans such as this need to be flexible, as they will need to change between design and completion. Managers often stress their firm commitment to the highest-level goals – but leave staff with more discretion about how to achieve lower-level plans.

However convincingly set out, statements of goals only have value if they guide action. Effective goal setting involves balancing multiple goals, considering whether they meet the SMART criteria (see 'Criteria for assessing goals'), and evaluating their likely motivational effects.

Single or multiple goals?

Company statements of goals – whether long or short term – are usually expressed in the plural, since a single measure cannot indicate success or failure. Emphasis on one goal, such as growth, ignores another, such as dividends. Managers balance multiple, possibly conflicting goals: Gerry Murphy, who became chief executive of Kingfisher (a UK DIY retailer), recalled:

> Alan Sheppard, my boss at Grand Metropolitan and one of my mentors, used to say that senior management shouldn't have the luxury of single point objectives. Delivering growth without returns or returns without growth is not something I find attractive or acceptable. Over time we are going to do both. (*Financial Times*, 28 April 2004, p. 23)

As senior managers try to take account of a range of stakeholders, they balance their diverse interests. This can lead to conflict between **stated goals**, as reflected in public announcements, and the **real goals** – those to which people give most attention. The latter reflect senior managers' priorities, expressed through what they say and how they reward and discipline managers.

> **Stated goals** are those which are prominent in company publications and websites.
>
> **Real goals** are those to which people give most attention.

Criteria for assessing goals

The SMART acronym summarises some criteria for assessing a set of goals. What form of each is effective depends on circumstances (specific goals are not necessarily better than directional ones). The list simply offers some measures against which to evaluate a statement of goals.

- **Specific** Does the goal set specific targets? People who are planning a meeting can set specific goals for what they hope to achieve, such as:

  > By the end of the meeting we will have convinced them to withdraw their current proposal, and to have set a date (within the next two weeks) at which we will start to develop an alternative plan.

  Having a clear statement of what the meeting (or any other activity in a plan) is intended to achieve helps people to focus effort.
- **Measurable** Some goals may be quantified ('increase sales of product X by 5 per cent a year over the next three years') but others, equally important, are more qualitative ('to offer a congenial working environment'). Quantitative goals are not more useful than qualitative ones – what can be measured is not necessarily important. The important point is that goals be defined precisely enough to measure progress towards them.
- **Attainable** Goals should be challenging, but not unreasonably difficult. If people perceive a goal as unrealistic, they will not be committed. Equally, goals should not be too easy, as they too undermine motivation. Goal setting theory (see the following Key Ideas) predicts the motivational consequences of goal setting.
- **Rewarded** People need to see that attaining a goal will bring a reward – this gives meaning and help ensure commitment.
- **Timed** Does the goal specify the time over which it will be achieved, and is that also a reasonable and acceptable standard?

Key ideas   Practical uses of goal-setting theory

Goal theory offers some practical implications for those making plans:

- **Goal difficulty**: set goals for work performance at levels that will stretch employees but are just within their ability.
- **Goal specificity**: express goals in clear, precise and, if possible, quantifiable terms, and avoid setting ambiguous or confusing goals.
- **Participation**: where practicable, encourage staff to take part in setting goals to increase their commitment to achieving them.
- **Feedback**: provide information on the results of performance to allow people to adjust their behaviour and perhaps improve their achievement of future plans.

Source: Locke and Latham (2002).

Activity 6.4   **Evaluating a statement of goals**

- Choose a significant plan that someone has produced in your organisation within the last year. Is it SMART? Then try to set out how you would amend the goals to meet these criteria more fully. Alternatively, comment on how the criteria set out in the text could be modified, in the light of your experience with these goals.

6.7   Identifying actions and allocating resources

This part of the planning process involves deciding what needs to be done, who will do it and communicating that information. In a small activity such as planning a project in a club this would just mean listing the tasks and dividing them clearly among a few able and willing members. At the other extreme, Ford's plan to build a new car plant in China probably runs to several volumes.

Identifying what needs to be done – and by whom

Figure 1.3 (reproduced here again as Figure 6.5) provides a model to help envisage the implications of a goal, by enabling managers to ask what, if any, changes they need to be make to each element.

If the goal is to launch a new product, the plan could identify which parts of the organisation will be affected (structure), what investment is needed (finance), how production will fit with existing lines (business processes) and so on. New technology projects often fail because planners pay too much attention to the technological aspects, and too little to contextual

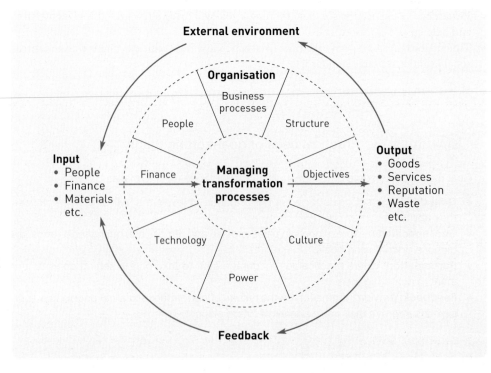

Figure 6.5
Possible action areas in a plan

elements such as structure, culture and people (Boddy *et al.* 2009b). Each main heading will require further actions that people can identify and assign.

Lynch (2003) points out that managers handle this aspect of planning comprehensively, incrementally or selectively.

- **Comprehensive (specific) plan** This happens if managers decide to make a clear-cut change in direction, in response to a reassessment of the market, a financial crisis or a technological development. They assume that success depends on driving the changes rapidly and in a co-ordinated way across the organisation – which implies a comprehensive plan.
- **Incremental (directional) plan** People use this approach in uncertain conditions, such as volatile markets or when direction depends on the outcomes of research and development. Tasks, times and even the objective are likely to change as the outcomes of current and planned activities become known; 'Important strategic areas may be left deliberately unclear until the outcomes of current events have been established' (Lynch, 2003, p. 633).
- **Selective plan** This approach may work when neither of the other methods is the best way forward, such as when managers wish to make a comprehensive change, but are unable to do so because of deep opposition in some area affected by the plan. They may then try to implement the major change in only some areas of the business which, while not their preferred choice, may enable them to make some progress towards the objectives.

Communicating the plan

In a small organisation or where the plan deals with only one area, communication in any formal way is probably unnecessary. Equally, those who have been involved in developing the objectives and plans will be well aware of it. However, in larger enterprises managers will probably invest time and effort in communicating both the objectives and the actions required throughout the areas affected. They do this to:

- ensure that everyone understands the plan;
- allow them to resolve any confusion and ambiguity;
- communicate the judgements and assumptions that underlie the plan;
- ensure that activities around the organisation are co-ordinated in practice as well as on paper.

6.8   Implementing plans and monitoring progress

However good the plan, nothing worthwhile happens until people implement it, acting to make visible, physical changes to the organisation and the way people work within it. Many managers find this the most challenging part of the process – when plans, however well developed, are brought into contact with the processes people expect them to change. Those implementing the plan then come up against a variety of organisational and environmental obstacles – and possibly find that some of the assumptions in the plan are incorrect.

Organisations are slower to change than plans are to prepare, so events may overtake the plan. Miller *et al.* (2004) tracked the long-term outcomes of 150 strategic plans to establish how managers put them into action and how that affected performance. They defined implementation as:

> all the processes and outcomes which accrue to a strategic decision once authorisation has been given to . . . put the decision into practice. (Miller *et al.*, 2004, p. 203)

Their intention was to identify the conditions in which implementation occurs, the managerial activities involved in putting plans into practice, and the extent to which they achieved the objectives. They concluded that success was heavily influenced by:

- managers' experience of the issue, and
- **organisational readiness** for a change.

> Having relevant experience of what has to be done . . . enables managers to assess the objectives [and to] specify the tasks and resource implications appropriately, leading [those affected to accept the process].' (Miller *et al.*, 2004, p. 206)

Readiness means a receptive organisational climate that enables managers to implement the change within a positive environment.

The statistical results were illustrated by cases that showed, for example, how managers in a successful company were able to implement a plan to upgrade their computer systems because they had *experience* of many similar changes. They were able to set targets, detail what needed doing and allocate the resources. That is, they could plan and control the implementation effectively. In another illustration, a regional brewer extending into the London area had no directly relevant experience, and so was not able to set a specific plan. But people in the organisation were very *receptive* to new challenges, and could implement the move with little formal planning.

The authors concluded that the activities of planning do not in themselves lead to success, but are a means for gaining acceptance of what has to be done when it is implemented. Planning helps by inducing confidence in the process, leading to high levels of acceptability:

> Planning is a necessary part of this approach to success, but it is not sufficient in itself. (Miller *et al.*, 2004, p. 210)

The final stage in planning is to set up a system that allows people to monitor progress towards the goals. This happens at all levels of planning – from a project manager monitoring and controlling the progress of a discrete project to a Board committee monitoring the progress of a broad strategic change that affects many parts of the business, such as integrating an acquisition or entering a new line of business. This is sometimes called a programme, and monitoring then focuses on the interdependencies between many smaller specific projects.

Project plans define and display every task and activity, but someone managing a programme of linked projects would soon become swamped with such detail. The programme manager needs to maintain a quick-to-understand snapshot of the programme. This should show progress to date, the main events being planned, interdependencies, issues and expected completion dates. This also helps the programme manager to communicate with senior executives and project managers. One way to do this is to create a single chart with a simplified view of each project on an indicative timeline. Figure 6.6 illustrates this. Details vary but the main features are usually:

- An indicative timeline, along which the individual projects are plotted.
- A simplified representation of the major milestones in each project or change area.
- Descriptions of progress made against that expected for each project.
- Indications of interdependencies between projects.

6.9 Integrating themes

Sustainable performance

Many companies are responding to the challenges posed by climate change, and are developing policies to reduce carbon emissions and other environmentally damaging practices. Such policy statements depend on the quality of the plans that managers develop – unless they make detailed plans, they will be no more than good intentions. In 2007 Marks & Spencer announced 'Plan A' – which by 2009 had delivered significant benefits to the environment (such as having diverted 20,000 tonnes of waste from landfill) and to the company (cost savings of about £50 million).

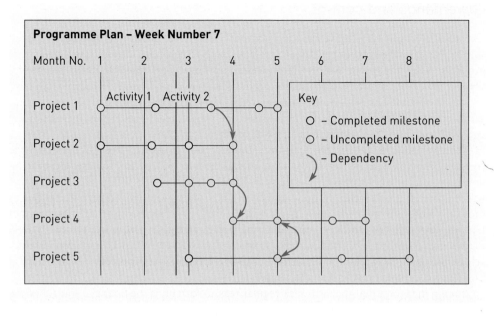

Figure 6.6
A programme overview chart
Source: Boddy *et al.* (2009a).

In March 2010 the company launched a programme to become the world's most sustainable retailer by 2015. To achieve this it will extend Plan A to cover all of its 36,000 product lines, so that each carries at least one sustainable or ethical quality, and to fully embed sustainability into the way the company and its suppliers do business. The new Plan A commitments are divided into seven areas:

1 **Customers and Plan A** – to help customers to live more sustainable lives.
2 **Make Plan A part of how we do business** – to accelerate our moves to make Plan A 'how we do business'.
3 **Tackling climate change** – make operations in the UK and Republic of Ireland carbon neutral.
4 **Packaging and waste** – stop sending waste to landfill from stores, offices and warehouses, reduce use of packaging and carrier bags, and find new ways to recycle and reuse the materials.
5 **Being a fair partner** – improve the lives of hundreds of thousands of people in the supply chain and local communities.
6 **Natural resources** – ensure that key raw materials come from the most sustainable source possible, in order to protect the environment and the world's natural resources.
7 **Health and well-being** – helping thousands of customers and employees to choose a healthier lifestyle.

Source: Company website (**www.marksandspencer.com**)

In each of these areas more detailed plans will be required to bring the plan into reality – including ensuring that suppliers also plan changes in the way that they operate.

Activity 6.5 Progress towards the goals of Plan A

- Visit the Marks & Spencer website and navigate to the Plan A pages. These explain the plan fully, and also include current information on progress towards the target.
- Identify a theme that interests you, and find out how Marks & Spencer is implementing the plan, and what progress it has made.

Governance and control

Glaister and Travers (2001) give a graphic account of the range of interests who have invested significant capital or other resources in Crossrail, and who are closely interested in its progress. While the broad project plan has been approved and construction is beginning, managers will face many decisions as the project is implemented, some of which could have serious consequences for one or more parties. They have therefore put in governance arrangements to ensure that, as far as possible, the project team acts in the interests of the Crossrail sponsors – whose interests may well conflict.

The most obvious of these mechanisms is the company structure. Crossrail Limited is the company charged with delivering Crossrail. It was created in 2001 to promote and develop new lines and is a wholly owned subsidiary of Transport for London (TfL). The ten members of the Crossrail Board include representatives of the project sponsors and partners, as well as those appointed for their relevant expertise in, say, finance or law. Sponsors are the Mayor of London (through TfL) and the Department of Transport. Other partners are Network Rail, British Airports Authority (BAA), The City of London, Canary Wharf Group (property developers) and Berkeley Homes (residential property developers). The executive team managing the project report regularly to the Main Board.

Among the issues that they will seek regular reassurance on is the financial control of the project. The Key Ideas feature on page 179 shows that infrastructure projects often cost more than expected. A function of the Main Board will be to monitor how executives manage the project to ensure it stays within budgeted costs, especially as public funds to cover any excess costs will be very hard to secure in the foreseeable financial climate.

Internationalisation

A theme in all international businesses is the extent to which they should plan the business on a global scale, or leave local managers with autonomy to adapt to local conditions. As Chapter 4 points out, the globalisation of markets was observed, and advocated, by Theodore Levitt, who noted the trend in the early 1980s for global brands to displace local products, with identical goods being sold across the globe without modification.

| Management in practice | Coca-Cola finds formula for India www.cocacola.com |

Coca-Cola India totally misjudged rural India, home to two-thirds of the country's 1 billion population, when it re-entered the country in 1993. It paid a high price for the then market leader, Thumbs Up, and then tried to kill it off in the mistaken belief that this would pave the way for Coca-Cola's rise. The approach failed – best illustrated by the fact that India is one of the few markets where Pepsi-Cola leads Coca-Cola. 'We were just not addressing the masses', admitted Sanjeev Gupta, Coca-Cola's operations chief. In 2000, management decided to change their approach, by focusing on the distinctive needs of the Indian rural consumer. This meant using smaller bottles, lower prices, more outlets and an advertising campaign (featuring Bollywood stars) that makes sense to villagers as well as city dwellers.

Source: Extracts from an article by Khozem Merchant, *Financial Times*, 18 June 2003.

This approach began to lose favour, so companies began adapting products to suit local tastes (see the above Management in Practice). The dilemma is how far to plan globally, and how much to leave to local managers. Managers typically identify some features that are important to the overall health of the brand, such as ingredients or design, and are likely to plan these issues at the global level. They leave other matters, such as choice of suppliers or methods of distribution, to local planners. Establishing that balance in planning is likely to affect the value they add.

Summary

1 **Explain the purposes of planning and the content of different types of plan**

- Effective plans can clarify direction, motivate people, use resources efficiently and allow people to measure progress towards objectives.
- Plans can be at strategic, tactical and operational levels, and, in new businesses, people prepare business plans to secure capital. Strategic business units also prepare plans relatively independently of the parent. There are also special-purpose or project plans, and standing plans. All can be either specific or directional in nature.

2 **Compare alternative planning processes and evaluate when each may be most suitable**

- Plans can be formal/rational/top down in nature, or they can be adaptable and flexible (logical incrementalism); accumulating evidence that a combination of approaches most likely to suit firms in volatile conditions.

3 **Outline the seven iterative steps in planning and describe techniques used in each**

- Recycling through the tasks of gathering information, developing a mission, setting goals, identifying actions and allocating resources, implementing plans, monitoring progress and evaluating results.
- Planners draw information from the general and competitive environments using tools such as Porter's Five Forces Analysis. They can do this within the framework of a SWOT analysis, and also use forecasting, sensitivity analysis, critical success factors and scenario planning techniques.

4 **Use theory to evaluate the motivational effect of the goals stated in a plan**

- Goal setting theory predicts that goals can be motivational if people perceive the targets to be difficult but achievable.
- Goals can also be evaluated in terms of whether they are specific, measurable, attainable, rewarded or timed.

5 **Use a framework to evaluate whether a plan is sufficiently comprehensive**

- The 'wheel' provides a model for recalling the likely areas in an organisation which a plan should cover, indicating the likely ripple effects of change in one area on others.

6 **Evaluate the context which will affect the ability of managers to implement a plan**

- The value of a plan depends on people implementing it, but Miller's research shows that that depends on the experience of those implementing it, and the receptivity of the organisation to change.

7 **Show how ideas from the chapter can add to your understanding of the integrating themes**

- Long-term sustainability depends on organisations making equally long-term plans, which many organisations, such as M&S, are beginning to do.
- Complex, one-off, projects such as those in construction and information technology, require effective high-level governance and control systems to ensure that the many diverse and possibly conflicting interests work together.
- Companies operating internationally increasingly try to customise their products for local markets to reflect varying customer preferences. This affects not only the product but also product advice, packaging and distribution methods – and is a significant planning activity in such firms.

Review questions

1 What types of planning do you do in your personal life? Describe them in terms of whether they are (a) strategic or operational, (b) short or long term, and (c) specific or directional.

2 What are four benefits that people in organisations may gain from planning?

3 What are the main sources of information that managers can use in planning? What models can they use to structure this information?

4 What are SMART goals?

5 In what ways can a goal be motivational? What practical things can people do in forming plans that take account of goal-setting theory?

6 What is meant by the term 'hierarchy of goals', and how can that idea help people to build a consistent plan?

7 Explain the term 'organisational readiness', and how people can use the idea in developing a plan that is more likely to work.

8 What are the main ways of monitoring progress on a plan, and why is this so vital a task in planning?

9 Summarise an idea from the chapter that adds to your understanding of the integrating themes.

Concluding critical reflection

Think about the way your company, or one with which you are familiar, makes plans. Review the material in the chapter, and perhaps visit some of the websites identified. Then make notes on the following questions:

● What examples of the themes discussed in this chapter are currently relevant to your company? What types of plans are you most closely involved with? Which of the techniques suggested do you and your colleagues typically use and why? What techniques do you use that are not mentioned here?

● In responding to these issues, what **assumptions** about the nature of planning in business appear to guide your approach? Are the prevailing assumptions closer to the planning or emergent perspectives? Why do you think that is?

● What factors in the **context** of the company appear to shape your approach to planning – what kind of environment are you working in, for example? To what extent does your planning process involve people from other organizations? Why is that?

● Have you compared your planning processes with those in other companies to check if they use **alternative** methods to yours? How do they plan?

● Have you considered the **limitations** of your approach – such as whether you plan too much, or too little? What limitations can you see in some of the ideas presented here – for example the usefulness of scenario planning or SWOT analyses?

Further reading

Grant, R.M. (2003), 'Strategic planning in a turbulent environment: Evidence from the oil majors', *Strategic Management Journal*, vol. 24, no. 6, pp. 491–517.

> Empirical study of the strategic planning systems in major international oil companies, and how these aim to cope with uncertainty in that industry.

Latham, G.P. and Locke, E.A. (2006), 'Enhancing the benefits and overcoming the pitfalls of goal setting', *Organizational Dynamics*, vol. 35, no. 4, pp. 332–340.

Leidecker, J.K. and Bruno, A.V. (1984), 'Identifying and using critical success factors', *Long Range Planning*, vol. 17, no. 1, pp. 23–32.

This useful article identifies eight possible sources for identifying critical success factors, gives examples, and suggests ways of assessing their relative importance.

Sahlman, W.A. (1997), 'How to write a great business plan', *Harvard Business Review*, vol. 75, no. 4, pp. 98–108.

Valuable guidance by an experienced investor, relevant to start-ups and established businesses.

Whittington, R., Molloy, E., Mayer, M. and Smith, A. (2006), 'Practices of strategising/organising: Broadening strategy work and skills', *Long Range Planning*, vol. 39, no. 6, pp. 615–629.

Weblinks

These websites have appeared in the chapter:

www.crossrail.co.uk
www.maersk.com
www.ba.com
www.sabmiller.com
www.merck.com
www.dsm.com
www.marksandspencer.com
www.inamo-restaurant.com
www.cocacola.com

Visit two of the sites in the list, and navigate to the pages dealing with corporate news or investor relations.

- What planning issues can you identify that managers in the company are likely to be dealing with?
- What kind of environment are they likely to be working in, and how will that affect their planning methods and processes?

 For video case studies, audio summaries, flashcards, exercises and annotated weblinks related to this chapter, visit **www.pearsoned.co.uk/mymanagementlab**

CHAPTER 7
DECISION MAKING

Aims

To identify major aspects of decision making in organisations and to outline alternative ways of making decisions.

Objectives

By the end of your work on this chapter you should be able to outline the concepts below in your own terms and:

1 Outline the (iterative) stages of the decision making process and the tasks required in each

2 Explain, and give examples of, programmed and non-programmed decisions

3 Distinguish decision-making conditions of certainty, risk, uncertainty and ambiguity

4 Contrast rational, administrative, political and garbage-can decision models

5 Give examples of common sources of bias in decisions

6 Explain the contribution of Vroom and Yetton, and of Irving Janis, to our understanding of decision making

7 Show how ideas from the chapter add to your understanding of the integrating themes

Key terms

This chapter introduces the following ideas:

decision	rational model of decision making
decision making	administrative model of
problem	decision making
opportunity	bounded rationality
decision criteria	satisficing
decision tree	incremental model
programmed decision	political model
procedure	heuristics
rule	prior hypothesis bias
policy	representativeness bias
non-programmed decision	optimism bias
certainty	illusion of control
risk	escalation of commitment
uncertainty	groupthink
ambiguity	

Each is a term defined within the text, as well as in the Glossary at the end of the book.

Case study   Ikea   www.ikea.com

In early 2010 there were over 300 Ikea home furnishing stores in 38 countries: the stores had generated sales of over 22 billion euros in 2009. This represented a slower rate of increase than usual, as the recession had affected demand. The company had also decided to slow the rate at which it would open new stores, and to reduce the 130,000 co-workers it employs by about 5,000.

The Ikea Concept is founded on a low-price offer in home furnishings. It aims to offer a wide range of well-designed home furnishing products at prices so low that as many people as possible can afford them. The way Ikea products are designed, manufactured, transported, sold and assembled contributes to transforming the Concept into reality.

The Concept began when Ingvar Kamprad, a Swedish entrepreneur, had the idea of offering well-designed furniture at low prices. He decided to achieve this not by cutting quality but by applying simple cost-cutting solutions to manufacture and distribution. Its first showroom opened in 1953 and until 1963 all the stores were in Sweden. In that year the international expansion began with a store in Norway: it has entered one new country in almost every year since then.

The objective of the parent company, Inter Ikea Systems BV, is to increase availability of Ikea products by the worldwide franchising of the Ikea Concept. It operates very large stores close to major cities. Ikea employs its own designers, although other companies manufacture most of the products. It is renowned for modern innovative design, and for supplying large products in a form that customers must assemble themselves. An example of its innovative approach is 'Children's Ikea', introduced in 1997. The company worked with child psychologists to develop products that would help children develop their motor skills, social development and creativity. Children helped to make the final selection of the range.

The company employs about 130,000 staff – whom it calls co-workers. In 1999 Ingvar Kamprad initiated the Big Thank You Event as a millennium reward for the co-workers. The total value of all sales on that day was divided equally among everyone in the company. For most it was more than a month's pay.

The company vision is to create a better everyday life for many people, and acknowledges that it is the co-workers who make that possible. They aim to give people the possibility to grow both as individuals and in their professional roles 'we are strongly committed to creating a better life for ourselves and our customers'. In its recruitment the company looks for people who share the company's values which include togetherness, cost-consciousness, respect and simplicity. The website explains that, as well as being able to do the job, the company seeks people with many other personal qualities such as a strong desire to learn, the motivation to continually do things better, simplicity and common sense, the ability to lead by example, efficiency and cost-consciousness:

These values are important to us because our way of working is less structured than at many other organisations.

Source: Company website.

Case questions 7.1

- Make a note of the decisions which have appeared in the story so far.
- How have they affected the development of the business?
- Visit the company's website and note examples of recent decisions which have shaped the company.

7.1 Introduction

The case recounts the recent history of one of Europe's biggest and most successful companies, which is now a global player in the home furnishing market. To develop the business from a Swedish general retailer to its present position, senior managers at Ikea needed to decide where to allocate time, effort and other resources. Over the years their decisions paid off and they now face new issues, such as how to attract customers and well-qualified staff against competition from established global companies. They also face critical comments from environmental campaigners about their sources of timber, and need to decide how to respond. How they do so will shape Ikea's future.

The performance of every organisation reflects (as well as luck and good fortune) the decisions that people make, and there are many studies of the activity – Buchanan and O'Connell (2006) provide a historical review. People at all levels of an organisation continually make choices as they see problems that need attention or ideas they may be able to use. Resources are limited, there are many demands and people have different goals. Choices relate to all aspects of the management task: inputs (how to raise capital, who to employ), outputs (what products to make, how to distribute them) and transformations (how to deliver a new service, how to manage the finances). Decisions affect how well the organisation uses resources, and whether it adds sufficient value to ensure survival.

> Like management itself, decision-making is a generic process that is applicable to all forms of organised activity. (Harrison, 1999, p. 8)

Choice brings tension as it makes us worry about 'what if' we had selected the other option (Schwartz, 2004). Speed is sometimes more important than certainty: the chief executive of Eli Lilly (pharmaceuticals) recalled that when he took over he realised the company needed to make decisions more quickly:

> We've had the luxury of moving at our own pace. Sometimes you can think for so long that your competitors pass you by. We need to act with 80 per cent, not 99.5 per cent, of the information.

He gives the example of a biotech company for which a rival company made a take-over offer, triggering a rapid and ultimately successful counter-bid from Lilly.

> We had them on our radar, and we had no premonition the other company would bid. But we were well-prepared and, within a couple of days, we convinced ourselves that we should get into the process. (From an article by John Lechleiter, *Financial Times*, 6 April 2009)

Figure 7.1 illustrates the themes of the chapter, showing that decision making involves:

- identifying the type of decision;
- identifying the conditions surrounding the decision;
- using one or more models to guide the approach;
- selecting a decision-making style;
- working through the process and implementing the decision.

This chapter outlines the iterative steps in any decision process, and explains the difference between decisions that are called 'programmed' and those that are 'non-programmed'. It identifies four 'conditions' surrounding a decision, compares four models of the process, shows how bias affects decisions and finally examines how managers can shape the context of decision making.

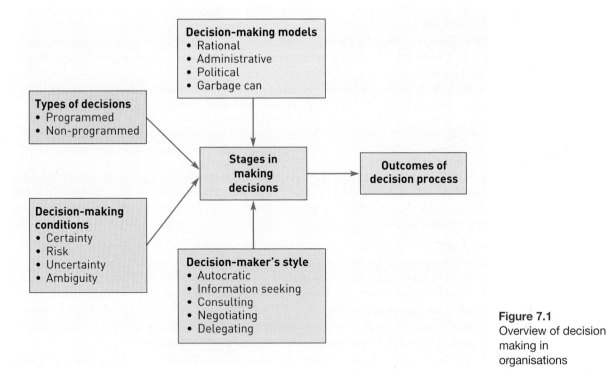

Figure 7.1
Overview of decision making in organisations

7.2   Stages in making decisions

A **decision** is a specific commitment to action (usually a commitment of resources). People make such choices at all levels: some affecting the business significantly (Barclay's Bank deciding during the 2008 banking crisis to raise capital privately, rather than accept support from the UK government – RBS and HBOS made the opposite decision). Others affect local operations: whether to recruit staff, how much to spend on advertising next week.

A **decision** is a specific commitment to action (usually a commitment of resources).

Others are made explicitly, by specifying criteria about which patients, or which conditions, are eligible for treatment. In the UK the National Institute for Clinical Excellence (NICE) decides which drugs or technologies are cost effective. It then gives explicit guidance to hospitals on whether, and in what circumstances, they should use them to treat patients.

The committees making these decisions include representatives of medical and patient interests, as well as those of the pharmaceutical industries. They make their (sometimes controversial) decisions public.

Sources: Published information; NICE website.

Decision making is the process of identifying problems and opportunities and then resolving them.

Such choices are part of a wider process of **decision making** – which includes identifying problems, opportunities and possible solutions, and involves effort before and after the actual choice. In deciding whether to select Jean, Bob or Rasul for a job, the manager would, among other things, have to:

- identify the need for a new member of staff;
- perhaps persuade his/her boss to authorise the budget;
- decide where to advertise the post;
- interview candidates;
- select the preferred candidate;
- decide whether or not to agree to his/her request for a better deal; and
- arrange their induction into the job so that they work effectively.

At each of these stages the manager may go back in the process to think again, or to deal with another set of decisions – such as who to include on the selection committee. In Nokia's case the choice of model would follow decisions about the target market and basic design concept, and lead to decisions about production volumes and price. A manager makes small but potentially significant decisions all the time: which of several urgent jobs to deal with next; whose advice to seek; which report to read; which customer to call. These shape the way that people use their time, and the issues which they decide are sufficiently important to place on the agenda.

As we make decisions we attend to the tasks shown in Figure 7.2. The arrows show the iterative nature of the process, as we move back and forwards between the tasks. As we move through an activity we find new information, reconsider what we are doing, go back a stage or two and perhaps decide on a different route. People may miss a stage, or give too much attention to one topic and too little to others. Giving just enough time to each stage is a decision-making skill.

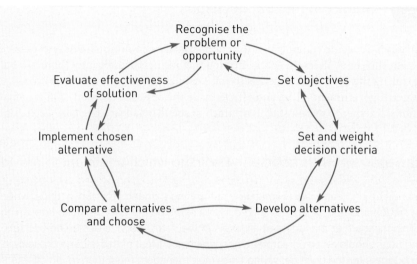

Figure 7.2
Stages in making decisions

Paul Nutt on 'idea discovery' and 'idea imposition'

Paul Nutt studied over 400 decisions involving major commitments of resources. He distinguished between an 'idea discovery process' which usually led to success, and an 'idea imposition process' which usually led to failure. Decision makers select tactics that push their process towards one or other of these types, and Nutt argues that, by being aware of these, managers have a better chance of success than failure.

Those following a discovery process spend time at the start looking beyond the initial claim that 'a problem has arisen that requires a decision': they spend time *understanding the claims* – by talking to stakeholders to judge the strength of their concerns and their views. This leads to a better-informed expression of the 'arena of action' on which to take a decision. They also identify at the outset the forces that may block them from *implementing the preferred idea*, as this helps to understand the interests of stakeholders whose support may be required.

These early actions enable decision makers *to set a direction* – an agreed outcome of the decision. Dealing thoroughly with these three stages makes the remaining stages – *uncovering and evaluating ideas* – comparatively easy, as they help build agreement on what the decision is expected to achieve.

Those following an idea imposition process

skip some stages . . . jump to conclusions and then try to implement the solution they have stumbled upon. This bias for action causes them to limit their search, consider very few ideas, and pay too little attention to people who are affected, despite the fact that decisions fail for just these reasons. (Nutt, 2002, p. 49)

Analysis of more decisions (Nutt, 2008) confirmed that decision makers were as likely to use the failure-prone 'idea imposition process' as they were to use the (usually more successful) 'discovery process'.

Sources: Nutt (2002, 2008).

Recognising a problem or opportunity

People make decisions which commit time and other resources towards an objective. They do so when they become aware of a **problem** – a gap between an existing and a desired state of affairs – or an **opportunity** – the chance to do something not previously expected. An example to illustrate the steps is a manager who needs to decide whether to buy new laptops for the sales team, who say that the machines they have are too slow and waste their time – so they are presenting the manager with a clear problem. Most situations are more ambiguous, and people will have different views about the significance of an event or a piece of information: labelling a problem as significant is a subjective, possibly contentious matter. Before a problem (or opportunity) gets onto the agenda, enough people have to be aware of it and feel sufficient pressure to act. Managers at Microsoft were slow to realise that Linux software was a serious threat to their growth, and this delay lost valuable time.

A **problem** is a gap between an existing and a desired state of affairs.

An **opportunity** is the chance to do something not previously expected.

The opportunity for Iris www.irisnation.com

Ian Millner explains the decision to start Iris:

We started about ten years ago, and we were essentially a group of friends all working within a really large advertising agency group, and we just decided that we could do it better. And then I guess one thing led to another and before we knew it we were having conversations with one of the clients that we had at the time, which was Eriksson. Once we had that conversation Iris was quite quickly born, and then over a period of months, myself and those friends, we sort of left the building and set Iris up.

> I think without doubt the biggest success that we've had is around momentum and being able to keep the momentum high and continue to change as we've gone from being a small company which is just defined by a group of friends, to a large company that is global, expanding really quickly and driving the strategic agenda of a lot of clients all over the world. We've always had a strong entrepreneurial streak, we've always been willing to try things and learn quickly.
>
> Source: Interview with Ian Millner.

Managers become aware of a problem as they compare existing conditions with the state they desire. If things are not as they should be – the sales reps are complaining that their slow laptops prevent them doing their jobs properly – then there is a problem. People are only likely to act if they feel pressure, such as a rep threatening to leave or a customer complaining. Pressure comes from many sources, and people differ in whether they pay attention: some react quickly, others ignore uncomfortable information and postpone a difficult (to them) decision.

Setting and weighting the decision criteria

Decision criteria define the factors that are relevant in making a decision.

To decide between options people need **decision criteria**: the factors that are relevant to the decision. Until people set these, they cannot choose between options: in the laptop case, criteria could include usefulness of features, price, delivery, warranty, compatibility with other systems, ease of use and many more. Some criteria are more important than others and the decision process needs to represent this in some way, perhaps by assigning 100 points between the factors depending on their relative importance. We can measure some of these criteria (price or delivery) quite objectively, while others (features, ease of use) are subjective.

Like problem recognition, setting criteria is subjective: people vary in the factors they wish to include, and the weights they give them. They may also have private and unexpressed criteria, such as 'will cause least trouble', 'will do what the boss wants' or 'will help my career'. Changing the criteria or their relative weights will change the decision: so the manager in the laptop case has to decide whether to set and weight the criteria him/herself, or to invite the views of the reps.

Developing alternatives

Another task is to identify solutions: in the laptop case this is just a list of available brands. In more complex problems the alternatives need to be developed but how many and at what cost? Too few will limit choice, but too many will be costly. Schwartz (2004) found that giving people more choices beyond a certain point is counter-productive as it leads to stress, frustration and anxiety about making the wrong decision (see Key Ideas).

Key ideas   Too many jams to choose

Iyengar and Lepper (2000) demonstrated that consumers protect themselves from the stress of too much choice by refusing to purchase. In an experiment conducted in a food store, they set up a tasting booth offering different types of jam. When 24 types were on display, about 60 per cent of passers-by stopped at the booth, compared with just 40 per cent when only six jams were shown. But when it came to choosing a pot of jam to buy, the proportions changed. Just 3 per cent of the visits to the 24-jam booth resulted in a purchase, while 30 per cent of those who visited the smaller display made a purchase. The limited selection was the most effective in converting interest into sales.

Source: Iyengar and Lepper (2000).

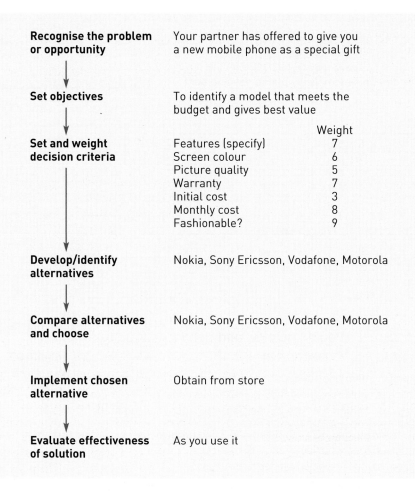

		Weight
Recognise the problem or opportunity	Your partner has offered to give you a new mobile phone as a special gift	
Set objectives	To identify a model that meets the budget and gives best value	
Set and weight decision criteria	Features (specify)	7
	Screen colour	6
	Picture quality	5
	Warranty	7
	Initial cost	3
	Monthly cost	8
	Fashionable?	9
Develop/identify alternatives	Nokia, Sony Ericsson, Vodafone, Motorola	
Compare alternatives and choose	Nokia, Sony Ericsson, Vodafone, Motorola	
Implement chosen alternative	Obtain from store	
Evaluate effectiveness of solution	As you use it	

Figure 7.3
Illustrating the decision-making tasks – a new mobile phone

Comparing alternatives and making a choice

As in daily life, management decisions need a system for comparing and choosing. Since criteria and weights are subjective, several people making a choice can easily end in argument.

Figure 7.3 illustrates the tasks in making a decision through a simple personal example. Although superficially simple, people find it difficult to set criteria, which are often subjective and so open to different interpretations – especially if several people take part.

Another way to structure a situation in which there are several alternative actions is to draw a **decision tree**. This helps to assess the relative suitability of the options by assessing them against identified criteria: successively eliminating the options as each relevant factor is introduced. Figure 7.8 is an example of a decision tree – it shows how a manager can decide the most suitable method of solving a problem by asking a succession of questions about the situation, leading to the most likely solution for those circumstances. The main challenge in using the technique is to identify the logical sequence of intermediate decisions and how they relate to each other.

A **decision tree** helps someone to make a choice by progressively eliminating options as additional criteria or events are added to the tree.

Key ideas   **Mintzberg's study of major decisions**

Henry Mintzberg and his colleagues studied 25 major, unstructured decisions in 25 organisations, finding that rational techniques could not cope with the complexity of strategic decisions. They concluded that:

- whether people recognised the need for a decision depended on the strength of the stimuli, the reputation of the source, and the availability of a potential solution;

- most decisions depended on designing a custom-made solution (a new organisation structure, a new product or a new technology); and
- the choice phase (see Figure 7.2), was less significant than the development phase: it was essentially ratifying a solution that was determined implicitly during development.

Source: Mintzberg *et al.* (1976).

Implementing the choice

In the laptop case this is a simple matter if the manager has conducted the process well. In bigger decisions this will be a much more problematic stage as it is during implementation that the decision commits scarce resources, and perhaps meets new objections. So implementation often takes longer than expected, and depends on people making other supportive decisions. It also shows the effects of the decision-making process: if the promoter involved others in the decision, they may be more willing to co-operate with the consequential changes, for example in the way they work.

Management in practice	Decide quickly, and don't be afraid to switch

www.wipro.com

Wipro is a very successful Indian information services company, competing around the world. It faces rapidly changing technical and business conditions, so needs to make decisions quickly. Wipro has evolved a management rhythm that is organised around the type of decisions managers have to make. There are:

- weekly meetings in each business unit about spotting and fixing problems, or exploiting opportunities;
- monthly IT management meetings to introduce and adjust tactics;
- quarterly strategy council meetings to decide longer-term issues.

In each of these meetings, the spirit of experimentation is pervasive. Managers are inclined to try things and get them going fast – essentially pilot projects. They track the projects closely, so if something doesn't work, they spot it quickly and make adjustments, or even pull the plug. (Hamm, 2007, p. 286)

Source: Hamm (2007).

Evaluating the decision

The final stage is evaluation: looking back to see if the decision has resolved the problem, and what can be learned. It is a form of control, which people are often reluctant to do formally, preferring to turn their attention to future tasks, rather than reflect on the past. That choice inhibits their ability to learn from experience.

Having given this simplified overview of the process, the following sections outline different types of decisions, and some models that seek to explain how people make them.

Activity 7.2	Critical reflection on making a decision

Work through the steps in Figure 7.3 for a decision you currently face, such as where to go on holiday, which courses to choose next year, or which job to apply for. Then do the same for a decision that involves several other people, such as which assignment to do in your study group or where to go for a night out together.

If you work in an organisation, select two business decisions as the focus of your work.

- How did working through the steps affect the way you reached a decision?
- Did it help you think more widely about the alternatives?
- How did the second decision, involving more people, affect the usefulness of the method?
- Then reflect on the technique itself: did it give insight into the decision process? What other tasks should it include?

7.3   Programmed and non-programmed decisions

Many decisions that managers face are straightforward and need not involve intense discussion, others require unique or novel solutions.

Programmed decisions

Programmed (or structured) decisions (Simon, 1960) deal with problems that are familiar and, where the information required is easy to define and obtain, the situation is well structured. If a store manager notices that a product is selling more than expected there will be a simple, routine procedure for deciding how much extra to order from the supplier. Decisions are structured to the extent that they arise frequently and can be dealt with routinely by following an established **procedure**: a series of related steps, often set out in a manual, to deal with a structured problem. They may also reach a decision by using an established **rule**, which sets out what someone can or cannot do in a given situation. They may also refer to a **policy**: a guideline that establishes some general principles for making a decision.

People make programmed decisions to resolve recurring problems: to reorder supplies when stocks drop below a defined level, to set the qualifications required for a job, or to decide whether to lend money to a bank customer. Once managers formulate procedures, rules or policies, others can usually make the decisions. Computers handle many decisions of this type, for example the checkout systems in supermarkets calculate the items sold and order new stock.

> A **programmed (or structured) decision** is a repetitive decision that can be handled by a routine approach.
>
> A **procedure** is a series of related steps to deal with a structured problem.
>
> A **rule** sets out what someone can or cannot do in a given situation.
>
> A **policy** is a guideline that establishes some general principles for making a decision.

Non-programmed decisions

Simon (1960) also observed that people make **non-programmed (unstructured) decisions** to deal with situations that are novel or unusual, and so require a unique solution. The issue has not arisen in quite that form, and the information required is unclear, vague or open to several interpretations. Major management decisions are of this type, such as the choice that managers at Marks and Spencer faced in deciding whether to launch their (2010) programme to become the world's most sustainable retailer by 2015. This will bring many benefits to the environment and the company, but will be challenging and time-consuming to introduce as it involves changing the way suppliers work. While the company will have done a lot of research before making the decision, no-one has made this commitment before, and it cannot be sure how customers and competitors will respond. Most issues of strategy are of this type, because they involve great uncertainty and many interests.

> A **non-programmed (unstructured) decision** is a unique decision that requires a custom-made solution when information is lacking or unclear.

Management in practice   Inamo – choosing a designer   www.inamo-restaurant.com

Inamo is a new London restaurant where customers place their order directly to the kitchen from an interactive ordering system on their table. Selecting the designer for such a novel idea was a big step. Noel Hunwick, Chief Operating Officer said:

An early and crucial decision we had to make was to select our interior design company. The way we've always worked is to make sure that we always [have] options from which to choose, so based on recommendations and on web research, and going to various shows and events, I put together a large portfolio of work . . . to get a rough price per square foot that these companies generally charged.

We then selected eight companies to give us a full design brief, and then cut that down to three – who came out with three entirely different concepts so I think that then allowed us to narrow it down to two and have a final showdown. [Given that our ordering system was so novel] I think that was a crucial decision – we had to make sure it wasn't an overload on the customer, so I think that was a very delicate and difficult business decision. We always want options. Every single decision, whether it's the cleaning company that we use, everything, we want three options at least. I think that's very important.

Source: Interview with Noel Hunwick.

People need to deal with programmed and non-programmed decisions in different ways. The former are amenable to procedures, routines, rules and quantitative analytical techniques such as those associated with operational research (see Chapter 2). They are also suitable for resolution by modern information systems. Non-programmed decisions depend on judgement and intuition.

Figure 7.4 relates the type of decision to the levels of the organisation. Those lower in the organisation typically deal with routine, structured problems, which they can resolve by applying procedures. As people move up the hierarchy they face more unstructured decisions: lower-level staff hand decisions that do not fit the rules to someone above them, while the latter pass routine matters to subordinates.

Case study   Ikea - the case continues   www.ikea.com

In mid-2009 the founder of Ikea warned that the Swedish retailer must lose more jobs after the recession squeezed sales of flat-pack furniture. Ingvar Kamprad believes that the 5,000 jobs that the company has already shed will not be enough to deal with the tougher economic climate:

We need to decrease the number of staff further, particularly within manufacturing and logistics. It's about adjusting to sales being a lot less and becoming more efficient.

The Swedish billionaire revealed that sales are running at about 7 per cent below target, adding that the company can no longer match its recent rate of expansion, when up to 20 stores would open every year. Kamprad said:

The forecast is that our margins and profits are decreasing substantially this year. This is proof that we have been too negligent in how we take care of our existing stores. Actually, I have long

tried to warn about our excessive focus on expansion, and now the board has decided to hit the brakes,

A spokeswoman confirmed that there may be further job cuts, but insisted that the company was also hiring at its new stores, and was committed to opening between ten and 15 stores a year. It had however suspended its investment in Russia, a major target, blaming the 'unpredictability of administrative processes'.

Source: IKEA's founder warns: we must cut more jobs, *The Guardian*, 07/07/2009 (Graeme Wearden), Copyright Guardian News & Media Ltd 2009.

Case questions 7.2

- Are these decisions programmed or non-programmed?
- What other insights does this part of the case give into decision making processes at Ikea?

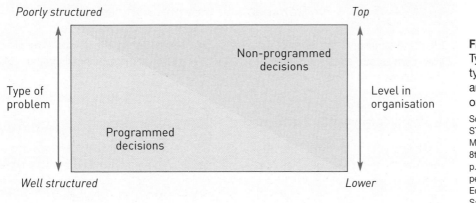

Figure 7.4
Types of decision,
types of problem
and level in the
organisation

Source: ROBBINS,
STEPHEN P.; COULTER,
MARY, *MANAGEMENT*,
8th Edition, © 2005,
p. 144. Reprinted by
permission of Pearson
Education, Inc. Upper
Saddle River, NJ.

Many decisions have elements of each type. Non-programmed decisions probably contain elements that can be handled in a programmed way.

Dependent or independent

Another way to categorise decisions is in terms of their links to other decisions. People make decisions in a historical and social context, and so are influenced by past and possible future decisions and the influence of other parts of the organisation. Legacy computer systems (the result of earlier decisions) frequently constrain how quickly a company can adopt new systems.

Some decisions have few implications beyond their immediate area, but others have significant ripples around the organisation. Changes in technology, for example, usually require consistent, supportive changes in structures and processes if they are to be effective. Although decisions on these areas are harder to make than those affecting the technology. More generally, local units may be limited in their decisions by wider company policies. Figure 7.5 illustrates this.

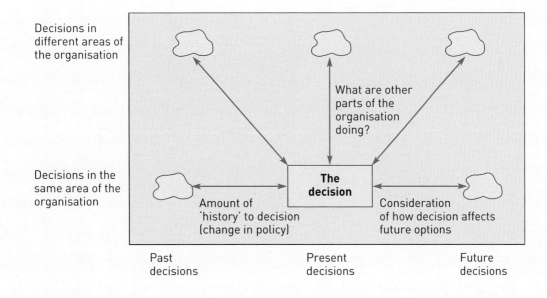

Figure 7.5 Possible relationships between decisions
Source: Cooke and Slack (1991), p. 24.

Activity 7.3   Programmed and non-programmed decisions

Identify examples of the types of decision set out above. Try to identify one example of your own to add to those below or that illustrates the point specifically within your institution:

- **Programmed decision** – whether to reorder stock
- **Non-programmed decision** – whether to launch a new service in a new market.

Compare your examples with those of other students and consider how those responsible made each decision. What examples of programmed and non-programmed decisions can you see in the Ikea case? How easy is it to divide decisions between these two categories? How useful are they as distinguishing characteristics?

7.4   Decision-making conditions

Certainty describes the situation when all the information the decision maker needs is available.

Risk refers to situations in which the decision maker is able to estimate the likelihood of the alternative outcomes.

Uncertainty is when people are clear about their goals, but have little information about which course of action is most likely to succeed.

Decisions arise within a wider context, and the conditions in this context, as measured by the degree of **certainty, risk, uncertainty** and **ambiguity** materially affect the decision process. Figure 7.6 relates the nature of the problem to the type of decision. Whereas people can deal with conditions of certainty by making programmed decisions, many situations are both uncertain and ambiguous. Here people need to be able to use a non-programmed approach.

Certainty

Certainty is when the decision makers have all the information they need; they are fully informed about the costs and benefits of each alternative. A company treasurer wanting to place reserve funds can readily compare rates of interest from several banks, and calculate exactly the return from each. Few decisions are that certain, and most contain risk and/or uncertainty.

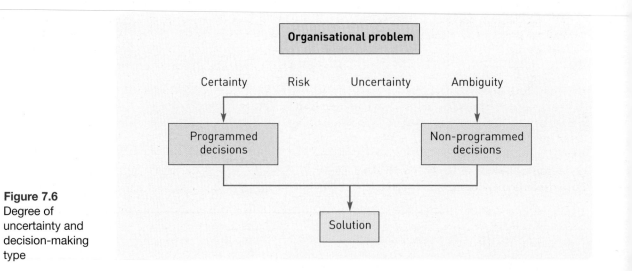

Figure 7.6
Degree of uncertainty and decision-making type

Risk

Risk refers to situations in which the decision maker can estimate the likelihood of the alternative outcomes, possibly using statistical methods. Banks have developed tools to assess credit risk, and so reduce the risk of the borrower not repaying the loan. The questions on an application form for a loan (home ownership, time at this address, employer's name, etc.) enable the bank to assess the risk of lending money to that person.

Uncertainty

Uncertainty means that people know what they wish to achieve, but they do not have enough information about alternatives and future events to estimate the risk confidently. Factors that may affect the outcomes of deciding to launch a new product (future growth in the market, changes in customer interests, competitors' actions) are difficult to predict.

Managers at GSK, the pharmaceutical group, experience great uncertainty in deciding how to allocate research funds. Scientists who wished to develop a new range of vaccines have to persuade the Board to divert resources to their project. Uncertainties include the fact that science is evolving rapidly, other companies are making competing discoveries, and it will be many years before the company receives income from the research results (if any).

Case study   Ikea - the case continues www.ikea.com

In June 2009 the company announced it was abandoning efforts to set up stores in India, afer failing to persuade the Indian government to ease restrictions on foreign investment. It has tried to do this for over two years, and had believed the change was imminent – but it did not happen. Ikea's Asia-Pacific retail manager said:

> We still face a very high level of uncertainty. It is a very sensitive political issue in India and it may take a new government more time to negotiate with the different parties and agree the changes that are required to open up and develop the retail sector.

More generally, managers in Ikea have placed great emphasis on developing a strong culture within the company, transmitting this to new employees and reinforcing it by events for existing ones. The belief is that if co-workers develop a strong sense of shared meaning of the Ikea concept, they deliver good service wherever in the group they are. As Edvardsson and Enquist (2002) observe,

> The strong culture in Ikea can give Ikea an image as a religion. In this aspect the *Testament of a Furniture Dealer* [written by Kamprad and given to all co-workers] is the holy script. The preface reads:

> Once and for all we have decided to side with the many. What is good for our customers is also good for us in the long run. After the preface the testament is divided into nine points: (1) The Product Range – our identity, (2) The Ikea Spirit: A Strong and Living Reality, (3) Profit Gives us Resources, (4) To Reach Good Results with Small Means, (5) Simplicity is a Virtue, (6) The Different Way, (7) Concentration of Energy – important to our success, (8) To Assume Responsibility – a privilege, (9) Most Things Still Remain to be Done. A Glorious Future! (p. 166)

Source: Edvardsson and Enquist (2002).

Case questions 7.3

- What implications may the Indian episode have for Ikea's next decisions about expansion?
- How may the culture described here affect decision-making processes in Ikea?

Ambiguity

Ambiguity is when people are uncertain about their goals and how best to achieve them.

Ambiguity describes a situation in which the intended goals are unclear, and so the alternative ways of reaching them are equally fluid. Ambiguity is by far the most difficult decision situation. Students would experience ambiguity if their teacher created student groups, told each group to complete a project, but gave them no topic, direction or guidelines. Ambiguous problems are often associated with rapidly changing circumstances, and unclear links between decision elements (see Management in Practice).

Management in practice   Ambiguity at EADS defers a decision   www.eads.com

EADS is the parent company of Airbus, and has experienced long-running conflicts between French and German shareholders. In 2007 the Board was under pressure to approve a cost-cutting plan proposed by the chief executive of Airbus, necessary because of the delays to the A380, which had increased losses at the company. It was also trying to launch a project to build a new fleet of aircraft to compete with Boeing's Dreamliner, but had been unable to agree how to divide the work between operations in France, Germany, Spain and the UK. National political conflicts at the highest level over this long-term issue were delaying the Board's decision on the short-term re-structuring issue.

Source: *Financial Times*, 20 February 2007.

Case questions 7.4

- Reflect on Ikea's decision to invest in Russia, and its attempts to enter India. What risks, uncertainties or ambiguities were probably associated with these situations?
- What dependencies may the moves have involved (use Figure 7.5 to help you structure your answer)?

7.5   Decision-making models

James Thompson (1967) distinguished decisions on two dimensions: agreement or disagreement over goals, and the beliefs that decision makers hold about the relationship between cause and effect. A decision can be mapped on these two dimensions: whether or not there is agreement on goals, and how certain people are about the consequences of their decisions. Figure 7.7 shows these, and an approach to making decisions that seems best suited to each cell.

Computational strategy – rational model

The **rational model of decision making** assumes that people make consistent choices to maximise economic value within specified constraints.

The **rational model of decision making** is based on economic assumptions. Traditional economic models suggested that the role of a manager was to maximise the economic return to the firm, and that they did this by making decisions on economically rational criteria. The assumptions underlying this model are that the decision maker:

- aims for goals that are known and agreed, and that the problem is structured;
- strives for conditions of certainty, gathering complete information and calculating the likely results of each alternative;
- selects the alternative that will maximise economic returns;
- is rational and logical in assigning values, setting preferences and evaluating alternatives.

Agreement on goals?

	High	Low
Certainty	I Computational strategy Rational model	III Compromise strategy Political model
Beliefs about cause-and-effect relationships Uncertainty	II Judgemental strategy Administrative, incremental and intuitional models	IV Inspirational strategy Garbage-can model

Figure 7.7
Conditions favouring different decision processes
Source: Based on Thompson (1967), p. 134.

The rational model is normative, in that it defines how a decision maker should act. It does not describe how managers make decisions. It aims to help decision makers act more rationally, rather than rely solely on intuition and personal preferences, and is most valuable for programmed decisions where there is little conflict. Where the information required is available and people can agree the criteria for choice, the approach can work well.

Key ideas   **Evidence-based management?**

Pfeffer and Sutton (2006) note that managers frequently make decisions without considering the evidence about what works, and what does not. They often base decisions on:

- experience (which may or may not fit current circumstances);
- solutions with which they are familiar;
- accepting commercially motivated claims about a technique;
- dogmas or beliefs for which there is no reliable evidence.

After enumerating the possible reasons for this, they advocate that evidence-based management could change the way every manager thinks and acts.

> We believe that facing the hard facts and truth about what works and what doesn't, understanding the dangerous half-truths that constitute so much conventional wisdom about management, and rejecting the total nonsense that too often passes for sound advice will help organizations perform better. (p. 74)

Source: Pfeffer and Sutton (2006).

Developments in technology enable computers to take some decisions traditionally made by people. Many early attempts to use what are known as artificial intelligence or decision support systems failed, but Davenport and Harris (2005) report successful modern examples. They work well when decisions require rapid analysis of large quantities of data, with complex relationships, such as in power supply, transport management and banking. Automated decision systems:

> sense online data or conditions, apply codified knowledge or logic and make decisions – all with minimal amounts of human intervention. (Davenport and Harris, 2005, p. 84)

Table 7.1 shows examples.

Table 7.1 Examples of the application of automated decision systems

Type of decision	Example of automated decision application
Solution configuration	Mobile phone operators who offer a range of features and service options: an automated programme can weigh all the options, including information about the customer, and present the most suitable option to the customer
Yield optimisation	Widely used in the airline industry to increase revenue by enabling companies to vary prices depending on demand. Spreading to other transport companies, hotels, retailing and entertainment
Fraud detection	Credit card companies, online gaming companies and tax authorities use automated screening techniques to detect and deter possible fraud
Operational control	Power companies use automated systems to sense changes in the physical environment (power supply, temperature or rainfall), and respond rapidly to changes in demand, by redirecting supplies across the network

Source: Based on Davenport and Harris (2005).

Such applications will continue to spread, supporting companies where many decisions can be handled by using rational, quantitative methods. When decisions are more complex and controversial, the rational approach itself will not be able to resolve a decision. It can play a part but only as one input to a wider set of methods.

Judgemental strategies – administrative, incremental and intuitional

Administrative models

The **administrative model of decision making** describes how people make decisions in uncertain, ambiguous situations.

Simon's (1960) **administrative model of decision making** aims to describe how managers make decisions in situations which are uncertain and ambiguous. Many management problems are unstructured and not suitable for the precise quantitative analysis implied by the rational model. People rely heavily on their judgement to resolve such issues.

Simon based the model on two concepts: bounded rationality and satisficing. **Bounded rationality** expresses the fact that people have mental limits, or boundaries, on how rational they can be. While organisations and their environments are complex and uncertain, people can process only a limited amount of information. This constrains our ability to operate in the way envisaged by the rational model, which we deal with by **satisficing**: we choose the first solution that is 'good enough'. While searching for other options may eventually produce a better return, identifying and evaluating them costs more than the benefits. Suppose we are in a strange city and need coffee before a meeting. We look for the first acceptable coffee shop that will do the job: we satisfice. In a similar fashion, managers may seek alternatives only until they find one they believe will work.

Bounded rationality is behaviour that is rational within a decision process which is limited (bounded) by an individual's ability to process information.

Satisficing is the acceptance by decision makers of the first solution that is 'good enough'.

Key ideas	A behavioural theory of decision making

Richard Cyert, James March and Herbert Simon (Simon, 1960; Cyert and March, 1963; March, 1988) developed an influential model of decision making. It is sometimes referred to as the behavioural theory of decision making since it treats decision making as an aspect of human behaviour. Also referred to as the administrative model, it recognises that in the real world people are restricted in their decision processes, and therefore have to accept what is probably a less than perfect solution. It introduced the concepts of 'bounded rationality' and 'satisficing' to the study of decision making.

The administrative model focuses on the human and organisational factors that influence decisions. It is more realistic than the rational model for non-programmed, ambiguous decisions. According to the administrative model, managers:

- have goals that are typically vague and conflicting, and are unable to reach a consensus on what to do – as indicated by the EADS example on page 206;
- have different levels of interest in the problems or opportunities facing the business, and interpret information subjectively;
- rarely use rational procedures, or use them in a way that does not reflect the full complexity of the issue;
- limit their search for alternatives;
- usually settle for a satisficing rather than a maximising solution; having both limited information and only vague criteria of what would be 'maximising'.

The administrative model is descriptive, aiming to show how managers make decisions in complex situations rather than stating how they should make them.

Management in practice   Satisficing in e-health projects

Boddy *et al.* (2009) studied the implementation of several 'e-health' projects, in which modern information and communication technologies assist clinicians in delivering care. These include applications such as remote diagnostic systems, in which a consultant, assisted by video-conferencing equipment, examines the condition of a patient in a clinic hundreds of miles away. Such methods offer significant savings in patient travel time, and in the better use of scarce consultants' time, especially in remote parts of the country. Despite this, uptake of e-health systems has been slow.

To secure the fullest benefits, managers and staff also need to make significant changes throughout the organisation. The processes for interacting with patients change, as does the work of consultants, nurses and other medical staff. These changes are harder to implement than a decision to buy the technology. Many small pilot projects are producing modest benefits, but nothing like those which could flow from a national programme. A reasonable conclusion is that managers have unconsciously decided to satisfice; they can show they are trying the new methods and producing benefits. To secure the full potential would require more effort than they are willing to give.

Source: Boddy *et al.* (2009b).

Incremental models

Charles Lindblom (1959) developed what he termed an **incremental model**, which he observed people used when they were uncertain about the consequences of their choice. In the rational model these are known, but people face many decisions in which they cannot know what the effects will be. Lindblom built on Simon's idea of bounded rationality to show that if people made only a limited search for options their chosen solution would differ only slightly from what already existed. Current choices would be heavily influenced by past choices – and would not move far from them.

On this view, policy unfolds not from a single event, but from many cumulative small decisions. Small decisions help people to minimise the risk of mistakes, and to reverse the decision

People use an **incremental model** of decision making when they are uncertain about the consequences. They search for a limited range of options, and policy unfolds from a series of cumulative small decisions.

if necessary. He called this incrementalism, or the 'science of muddling through'. Lindblom contrasted what he called the 'root' method of decision making with the 'branch' method. The root method required a comprehensive evaluation of options in the light of defined objectives. The branch method involved building out, step-by-step and by small degrees, from the current situation. He claimed that the root method is not suitable for complex policy questions, so the practical person must follow the branch approach: the science of muddling through. The incremental model (like the administrative one) recognises human limitations.

Intuitional models

George Klein (1997) studied how effective decision makers work, including those working under extreme time pressure such as surgeons, firefighters and nurses. He found that they rarely used classical decision theory to weigh the options: instead they used pattern recognition to relate the situation to their experience. They acted on intuition – a subconscious process of basing decisions on experience and accumulated judgement – sometimes called 'tacit knowledge'. Klein concluded that effective decision makers use their intuition as much as formal processes – perhaps using both as the situation demands. Experienced managers act quickly on what seems like very little information. Rather than formal analysis, they rely on experience and judgement to make their decisions. Woiceshyn (2009) provides experimental evidence that senior managers use rational and intuitive methods to decide between options, and Hodgkinson *et al.* (2009) quote the co-founder of Sony, Akio Mariata, who was the driving force behind one of the great entertainment innovations of the twentieth century:

> Creativity requires something more than the processing of information. It requires human thought, spontaneous intuition and a lot of courage. (p. 278)

Compromise strategy – political model

The **political model** is a model of decision making that reflects the view that an organisation consists of groups with different interests, goals and values.

The **political model** examines how people make decisions when managers disagree over goals and how to pursue them (Pfeffer, 1992b; Buchanan and Badham, 1999). It recognises that an organisation is not only a working system but also a political system, which establishes the relative power of people and functions. A decision will enhance the power of some people and limit that of others. People will pursue goals relating to personal and sub-unit interests, as well as those of the organisation as a whole. They will evaluate a decision in terms of its likely effects on those possible conflicting objectives.

They will often try to support their position by building a coalition with those who share their interest. This gives others the opportunity to contribute their ideas and enhance their commitment if the decision is adopted.

The political model assumes that:

- organisations contain groups with diverse interests, goals and values. Managers disagree about problem priorities and may not understand or share the goals and interests of other managers;
- information is ambiguous and incomplete. Rationality is limited by the complexity of many problems as well as personal interests; and
- managers engage in the push and pull of debate to decide goals and discuss alternatives – decisions arise from bargaining and discussion.

Inspirational strategy – garbage-can model

This approach is likely when those concerned are not only unclear about cause-and-effect relationships, but are also uncertain about the outcome they seek. James March observed that in this situation the processes of reaching a decision become separated from the decisions reached. In the other models there is an assumption that the processes which the decision makers pass through lead to a decision. In this situation of extreme uncertainty the elements that constitute the decision problem are independent of each other, coming together in random ways.

March argued that decisions arise when four independent streams of activities meet. When this happens will depend largely on accident or chance. The four streams are:

- **Choice opportunities** Organisations have occasions at which there is an expectation that a decision will be made – budgets must be set, there are regular management meetings, people meet by chance, etc.
- **Participants** A stream of people who have the opportunity to shape decisions.
- **Problems** A stream of problems that represent matters of concern to people: a lost sale, a new opportunity, a vacancy.
- **Solutions** A stream of potential solutions seeking problems – ideas, proposals, information – that people continually generate.

In this view, the choice opportunities (scheduled or unscheduled meetings) act as the container (garbage can) for the mixture of participants, problems and solutions. One combination of the three may be such that enough participants are interested in a solution, which they can match to a problem – and make a decision accordingly. Another group of participants may not have made those connections, or made them in a different way, thus creating a different outcome.

This may at first sight seem an unlikely way to run a business, yet in highly uncertain, volatile environments this approach may work. Creative businesses depend on a rapid interchange of ideas, not only about specified problems but on information about new discoveries, research at other companies, what someone heard at a conference. They depend on people bringing these solutions and problems together – and deliberately foster structures that maximise opportunities for face-to-face contact and rapid decisions. The practical implication is that encouraging frequent informal contact between creative people will improve decisions and performance.

Management in practice   Oticon builds a better garbage can www.oticon.com

Oticon, a leading maker of sophisticated hearing aids, underwent a massive transformation in the early 1990s, in which the chief executive, Lars Kolind, broke down all barriers to communication. He realised that the key to success in the face of severe competition was to ensure that the talents of staff in the company were applied to any problems that arose. In March's terms, problems were expressed as a project, for which a member of staff (a participant) took responsibility, depending on other staff to suggest or help develop a solution.

> Any and all measures were taken to encourage contact and informal communication between employees. Elevators were made inoperable so that employees would meet each other on the stairs, where they were more likely to engage in conversation. Bars were installed on all three floors where coffee was served and meetings could be organised – standing up. Rooms with circular sofas were provided, complete with small coffee tables, to encourage discussion. (Rivard et al., 2004, p. 170)

These discussions centred on reaching fast and creative decisions about problems and new product ideas. The arrangement is credited with helping the continuing success of the company.

Source: Rivard et al., (2004); see also Chapter 10 case.

Table 7.2 summarises these four models, which are complementary in that a skilful manager or a well-managed organisation will use all of them, depending on the decision and the immediate context. A new product idea may emerge from a process resembling the garbage-can model, but will then need a rational business investment case to persuade the Board to develop it.

Table 7.2 Four models of decision making

Features	Rational	Administrative/incremental	Political	Garbage can
Clarity of problem and goal	Clear problem and goals	Vague problems and goals	Conflict over goals	Goals and solutions independent
Degree of certainty	High degree of certainty	High degree of uncertainty	Uncertainty and/or conflict	Ambiguity
Available information on costs and benefits	Full information about costs and benefits of alternatives	Little information about costs and benefits of alternatives	Conflicting views about costs and benefits of alternatives	Costs and benefits unconnected at start
Method of choice	Rational choice to maximise benefit	Satisficing choice – good enough	Choice by bargaining among players	Choice by accidental merging of streams

---

 Activity 7.4   **Identify decision requiring one of these approaches**

Here are some decisions which Virgin (see Part case) has faced:

- Whether or not to order further airliners.
- How severely to cut services during the economic downturn.
- Whether to increase their sponsorship of the 2014 Olympics.
- Whether to become involved with Crossrail.

In each case, decide which of the four decision models best describes the situation, and explain why.

Compare your answers with colleagues on your course, and prepare a short report summarising your conclusions from this activity.

7.6   **Biases in making decisions**

Heuristics – simple rules or mental short cuts that simplify making decisions

Since people are subject to bounded rationality (limited capacity to process information) they tend to use **heuristics** – simple rules or short cuts, that help us to overcome our limited capacity to deal with information and complexity (Kahneman and Tversky, 1974). While these short cuts help us to make decisions, they expose us to the danger of biases: four of which are prior hypothesis, representativeness, illusion of control and escalating commitment (Schwenk, 1984): a fifth is emotional attachment (Finkelstein *et al.*, 2009a, 2009b).

Prior hypothesis bias

Prior hypothesis bias results from a tendency to base decisions on strong prior beliefs, even if the evidence shows that they are wrong.

People who have strong prior beliefs about the relationship between two alternatives base their decisions on those beliefs, even when they receive evidence that the beliefs are wrong. In doing so they fall victim to the **prior hypothesis bias**, which is strengthened by a tendency to use information consistent with their beliefs, and ignore that which is inconsistent. People recall vivid events more readily than others, and these bias their decisions, even if circumstances have changed.

Representativeness bias

This is the tendency to generalise from a small sample or single episode, and to ignore other relevant information. Examples of this **representativeness bias** are:

- predicting the success of a new product on the basis of an earlier success;
- appointing someone with a certain type of experience because a previous successful appointment had a similar background.

Representativeness bias results from a tendency to generalise inappropriately from a small sample or a single vivid event.

Optimism bias

Lovallo and Kahneman (2003) believe that a major reason for poor decisions is the 'planning fallacy' discussed in Chapter 6. This is when people systematically underestimate the costs and overestimate the benefits of a proposal. One source of this fallacy is what they call **optimism bias** – a human tendency to judge future events in a more positive light than is warranted by actual experience. People often exaggerate their talents and their role in success, leading them to make optimistic assessments.

Optimism bias is a human tendency to see the future in a more positive light than is warranted by experience.

Illusion of control

Other errors in making decisions result from the **illusion of control**, which is the human tendency to overestimate our ability to control activities and events. Those in senior positions, especially if they have a record of successes, are prone to this bias which causes them to overestimate the odds of a favourable outcome.

The *illusion of control* is a source of bias resulting from the tendency to overestimate one's ability to control activities and events.

Escalating commitment

Managers may also be influenced by the phenomenon known as the **escalation of commitment**, which is an increased commitment to a previous decision despite evidence that it may have been wrong (Drummond, 1996). People are reluctant to admit mistakes, and rather than search for a new solution, they increase their commitment to the original decision.

Escalation of commitment is a bias which leads to increased commitment to a previous decision despite evidence that it may have been wrong.

Management in practice   A study of escalation – Taurus at the Stock Exchange

Helga Drummond studied the attempt by management at the London Stock Exchange to implement a computerised system to deal with the settlement of shares traded on the Exchange. The project was announced in May 1986 and was due to be completed by 1989 at a cost of £6 million. After many crises and difficulties, the Stock Exchange finally abandoned the project in March 1993. By that time the Exchange had spent £80 million on developing a non-existent system. Drummond interviewed many key participants to explore the reasons for this disaster – which occurred despite the commitment of the system designers.

She concluded that the project suffered from fundamental structural problems, in that it challenged several powerful vested interests in the financial community, each of whom had their own idea about what should be done. Each new demand, reflecting this continuing power struggle, made the system more complicated. However, while many interests needed to work together, structural barriers throughout the organisation prevented this. There was little upward communication, so that senior managers were largely unaware of staff concerns about the timetable commitments being made.

Senior managers continued to claim that the project was on track until a few days before it was finally, and very publicly, terminated. The lack of proper mechanisms to identify pressing issues lulled those making decisions into a false sense of security about the state of the project.

Source: Drummond (1996).

Guler (2007) found exactly the same phenomenon in the venture capital industry, whose firms lend money to entrepreneurs starting and building a business. Investors provide money in instalments over several years, which allows them to limit their exposure to risk. Guler found that investors became less likely to terminate an investment as they participated in further rounds, despite evidence that returns were declining. This was influenced by three factors: social (losing face among colleagues), political (pressure from other investors) and institutional (damage to reputation if it pulled out of an investment).

Emotional attachment

A final source of bias is emotional attachments to people, ideas or places. Finkelstein *et al.* (2009a, 2009b) note that people are frequently influenced by emotional attachments to:

- family and friends;
- communities and colleagues;
- objects – things and places which have meaning for us.

Finkelstein and his colleagues suggest that these attachments (negative or positive), which bring us meaning and happiness, are bound to influence our decisions. Most of the effects are insignificant, but sometimes a manager's emotional attachments can lead him/her to make bad business decisions. They give examples such as Samsung's disastrous investment in car manufacturing (widely opposed as a poor use of resources, but initiated and supported by a chairman who liked cars); and the chairman who justified the retention of a small and unprofitable design consultancy because:

I like it! It's exciting. I enjoy it . . . So I'm keeping it! (Finkelstein *et al.,* 2009a, p. 87)

Activity 7.5   **Examples of bias**

- List the sources of bias on a screen or sheet of paper.
- Try to identify one example of each which you have personally experienced in your everyday discussions with friends, family or colleagues.
- What (be specific) did they (or you) say which led you to label it as being of that type?
- Compare your results, so that, if possible, you have a clear example of each type of decision bias.

7.7   **Group decision making**

While people often make decisions as individuals, they also do so within the context of a group. This section looks at two ideas: Vroom and Yetton's decision model and Irving Janis' identification of groupthink.

Vroom and Yetton's decision model

The idea behind Vroom and Yetton's (1973) contingency model of decision making is to influence the quality and acceptability of decisions. This depends on the manager choosing how best to involve subordinates in making a decision – and being willing to change his/her style to match the situation. The model defines five leadership styles and seven characteristics of problems. Managers can use these characteristics to diagnose the situation. They can find the recommended way of reaching a decision on that problem by using the decision tree shown in Figure 7.8. The five leadership styles defined are:

- **AI** (**Autocratic**) You solve the problem or make the decision yourself using information available to you at that time.
- **AII** (**Information-seeking**) You obtain the necessary information from your subordinate(s), then decide on the solution to the problem yourself. You may or may not tell your subordinates what the problem is when getting the information from them. The role played by your subordinates in making the decision is clearly one of providing the necessary information to you rather than generating or evaluating alternative solutions.
- **CI** (**Consulting**) You share the problem with relevant subordinates individually, getting their ideas and suggestions without bringing them together as a group. Then *you* make the decision that may or may not reflect your subordinates' influence.

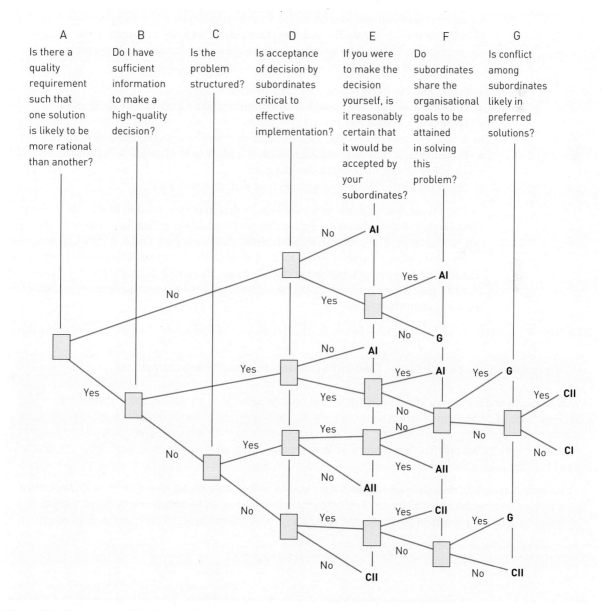

Figure 7.8 Vroom and Yetton's decision tree

Source: Figure 9.1 Decision-Process Flow Chart from *Leadership and Decision-Making*, and the taxonomy used in the figure is from Table 2.1 Decision Method for Group and Individual Problems from *Leadership and Decision-Making*, by Victor H. Vroom and Philip W. Yetton, © 1973. Reprinted by permission of the University of Pittsburgh Press.

- **CII (Negotiating)** You share the problem with your subordinates as a group, obtaining their collective ideas and suggestions. Then you make the decision that may or may not reflect your subordinates' influence.
- **G (Group)** You share the problem with your subordinates as a group. Together you generate and evaluate alternatives and attempt to reach agreement (consensus) on a solution. Your role is much like that of a chairperson. You do not try to influence the group to adopt 'your' solution, and you are willing to accept and implement any solution that has the support of the entire group.

The idea behind the model is that no style is in itself better than another. Some believe that consultative or delegating styles are inherently preferable to autocratic approaches, as being more in keeping with democratic principles. Vroom and Yetton argue otherwise. In some situations (such as when time is short or the manager has all the information needed for a minor decision) going through the process of consultation will waste time and add little value. In other situations, such as where the subordinates have the relevant information, it is essential to consult them. The point of the model is to make managers more aware of the range of factors to take into account in using a particular decision-making style.

The problem criteria are expressed in seven diagnostic questions:

- Is one solution likely to be better than another?
- Does the manager have enough information to make a high-quality decision?
- Is the problem structured?
- Is acceptance of the decision by subordinates critical to effective implementation?
- If the manager makes the decision alone, is it likely to be accepted by subordinates?
- Do subordinates share organisational goals?
- Is conflict likely among subordinates over preferred solutions?

The Vroom–Yetton decision model implies that managers need to be flexible in the style they adopt. The style should be appropriate to the situation rather than consistent throughout all situations. The problem with this is that managers may find it difficult to switch between styles, perhaps several times a day. Although the approach appears objective, it still depends on the manager answering the questions. Requiring a simple yes or no answer to complex questions is too simple, and managers often want to say 'it all depends' on other historical or contextual factors.

Management in practice   Decision making in a software company

This Swedish company was founded in 1998, and now concentrates on developing software for mobile phones, such as an application which sends text messages from a computer to a mobile. It sells the products mainly to the operating companies who use them to add value to their services. The business depends on teams of highly skilled software developers, able to produce innovative, competitive products very rapidly. The chief technology officer commented:

> As well as technical decisions we regularly face business decisions about where to focus development effort, or which customers to target. In this highly industrialised technocratic environment I am highly influenced by the experts in the team, and routinely consult them about the preferred course of action.

Source: Private communication from the chief technology officer.

Nevertheless the model is used in management training to alert managers to the style they prefer to use and to the range of options available. It also prompts managers to consider systematically whether that preferred style is always appropriate. They may then handle situations more deliberately than if they relied only on their preferred style or intuition.

Irving Janis and groupthink

Groupthink is a pattern of biased decision making that occurs in groups that become too cohesive. Members strive for agreement among themselves at the expense of accurately and dispassionately assessing relevant, and especially disturbing information. An influential analysis of how it occurs was put forward by the social psychologist Irving Janis. His research (Janis, 1972) began by studying major and highly publicised failures of decision making, looking for some common theme that might explain why apparently able and intelligent people were able to make such bad decisions, such as President Kennedy's decision to have US forces invade Cuba in 1961. One common thread he observed was the inability of the groups involved to consider a range of alternatives rationally, or to see the likely consequences of the choice they made. Members were also keen to be seen as team players, and not to say things that might end their membership of the group. Janis termed this phenomenon 'groupthink', and defined it as:

> . . . a mode of thinking that people engage in when they are deeply involved in a cohesive in-group, when the members' striving for unanimity overrides their motivation to realistically appraise alternative courses of action. (Janis, 1972, p. 9)

He identified eight symptoms of groupthink, shown in the Key Ideas.

Groupthink is 'a mode of thinking that people engage in when they are deeply involved in a cohesive in-group, when the members' striving for unanimity overrides their motivation to realistically appraise alternative courses of action' (Janis, 1972).

Key ideas — Irving Janis on the symptoms of groupthink

Janis (1977) identified eight symptoms that give early warning of groupthink developing. The more of them that are present, the more likely it is that the 'disease' will strike. The symptoms are:

- **Illusion of invulnerability** The belief that any decision they make will be successful.
- **Belief in the inherent morality of the group** Justifying a decision by reference to some higher value.
- **Rationalisation** Playing down the negative consequences or risks of a decision.
- **Stereotyping out-groups** Characterising opponents or doubters in unfavourable terms, making it easier to dismiss even valid criticism from that source.
- **Self-censorship** Suppressing legitimate doubts in the interest of group loyalty.
- **Direct pressure** Strong expressions from other members (or the leader) that dissent to their favoured approach will be unwelcome.
- **Mindguards** Keeping uncomfortable facts or opinions out of the discussion.
- **Illusion of unanimity** Playing down any remaining doubts or questions, even if they become stronger or more persistent.

Source: Based on Janis (1977).

Management in practice — Groupthink in medicine

An experienced nurse observed three of the symptoms of groupthink in the work of senior doctors:

- **Illusion of invulnerability** A feeling of power and authority leads a group to see themselves as invulnerable. Traditionally the medical profession has been very powerful and this makes it very difficult for non-clinicians to question their actions or plans.
- **Belief in the inherent morality of the group** This happens when clinical staff use the term 'individual clinical judgement' as a justification for their actions. An example is when a business manager is trying to reduce drug costs and one consultant's practice is very different from those of his colleagues. Consultants often reply that they are entitled to use their clinical judgement. This is never challenged by their colleagues, and it is often impossible to achieve change.

- **Self-censorship** Being a doctor is similar to being in a very exclusive club, and none of the members want to be excluded. Therefore doctors will usually support each other, particularly against management. They are also extremely unlikely to report each other for mistakes or poor performance. A government scheme to encourage 'whistle-blowing' was met with much derision in the ranks.

Source: Private communication.

When groupthink occurs, pressures for agreement and harmony within the group have the unintended effects of discouraging individuals from raising issues that run counter to the majority opinion (Turner and Pratkanis, 1998). An often-quoted example is *Challenger* disaster in 1986, when the space shuttle exploded shortly after take-off. Investigations showed that NASA and the main contractors, Morton Thiokol, were so anxious to keep the Shuttle programme on schedule that they ignored or discounted evidence that would slow the programme down. On a lighter note, Professor Jerry Harvey tells the story of how members of his extended family drove 40 miles into town on a hot day, to no obvious purpose – and everyone was miserable. Discussing the episode with the family later, each person admitted that they had not wanted to go, but went along to please the others. Harvey (1988) coined the term 'Abilene paradox' to describe this tendency to go along with others for the sake of avoiding conflict.

7.8   Integrating themes

Sustainable performance

As expectations of organisations' sustainability become more demanding and circumstances more volatile, the task of making decisions to promote sustainable performance are correspondingly more challenging. While some members of the management team will wish to promote strategies to enhance sustainable performance, either as strategically valuable or, at the very least, as enlightened self-interest, others may disagree, leading to a contested decision. Nutt (2002) identifies the causes of failure in decision making and point towards practices that he claims increase the chances of a successful outcome. His suggestions include:

- avoid making premature commitments – the hazard of grabbing hold of the first idea that comes up;
- maintaining an exploratory mind-set – keeping an open-mind towards other possibilities;
- letting go of the quick-fix – deferring choice until understanding has been gained;
- pausing to reflect – even if this means resisting demands for a quick fix;
- use resources to evaluate options, not just the preferred solution (or current quick fix);
- pay attention to both the rational and the political aspects of a decision process.

Adopting such practices would undoubtedly add to the quality of decision making: the challenge is whether they will be able to resist the pressures from others to deal with issues in a more risky way, especially if they are susceptible to bias or groupthink.

Governance and control

Several themes in this chapter highlight the traps that await decision makers, but also show how good governance arrangements can help to protect them and the organisation. The top level strategic decisions which shape an organisation's future are inherently unprogrammed, unstructured decisions which no-one has dealt with in quite that form. Senior managers make these decisions in conditions of risk, uncertainty and ambiguity – further placing at risk the assets and resources of the business. They are prone to any and all of the biases the chapter set out: a good example is the failure of the Taurus project at the London Stock Exchange, where those in charge continued to commit additional resources to the project, despite evidence that the project would not be able to deliver a solution acceptable to the main players. This was as much as anything a failure of governance.

More generally, the evidence on groupthink shows the delusions to which powerful senior managers are susceptible, as they come to believe in the soundness of their decisions, and are dismissive of those who question their views. This was evident in the 2008 banking crisis, where not enough, if any, of the non-executive directors were able and willing to provide the necessary challenges to the over-enthusiasm of executives taking too many risky decisions. Put another way, these companies had, on the face of it, put in place the governance procedures recommended in the Combined Code (see Chapter 3, Section 3.9), but those with the power to do so did not exercise those responsibilities.

Internationalisation

The structure of decision-making processes change as companies become international. Decisions will cross the boundaries between managers at global headquarters and those in local business units. Neither of the extreme possibilities is likely to work. If decision making tilts too far in favour of global managers at the centre, local preferences are likely to be overlooked, and local managers are likely to lack commitment to decisions in which they have had no say. Leaving too many decisions to local managers can waste opportunities for economies of scale or opportunities to serve global clients consistently.

A solution may be to identify the major ways in which the company adds value to resources, and align the decision-making processes to make the most of them. For example, if procurement is a critical factor *and* can best be done on a global scale, that would imply that those at the centre should make these decisions. Once supply contracts are agreed, however, responsibility for operating them could pass back to local level. Conversely, they might leave decisions on pricing or advertising expenditure to local managers. The central issue is to spend time on the difficult choices about the location of each set of decisions, to achieve an acceptable balance between global and local expectations.

Summary

1 **Outline the (iterative) stages of the decision making process and the tasks required in each**

- Decisions are choices about how to act in relation to organisational inputs, outputs and transformation processes. The chapter identifies seven *iterative* steps in the process:
- Recognise the problem – which depends on seeing and attending to ambiguous signals.
- Set and weight criteria – the features of the result most likely to meet problem requirements, and that can guide the choice between alternatives.
- Develop alternatives – identify existing or develop custom-built ways of dealing with the problem.
- Compare and choose – using the criteria to select the preferred alternative.
- Implement – the task that turns a decision into an action.
- Evaluate – check whether the decision resolved the problem.
- Most decisions affect other interests, whose response will be affected by how the decision process is conducted, in matters such as participation and communication.

2 Explain, and give examples of, programmed and non-programmed decisions

- Programmed decisions deal with familiar issues within existing policy – recruitment, minor capital expenditure, small price changes.
- Non-programmed decisions move the business in a new direction – new markets, mergers, a major investment decision.

3 Distinguish decision-making conditions of certainty, risk, uncertainty and ambiguity

- Certainty – decision makers have all the information they need, especially the costs and benefits of each alternative action.
- Risk – where the decision maker can estimate the likelihood of the alternative outcomes. These are still subject to chance, but decision makers have enough information to estimate probabilities.
- Uncertainty – when people know what they wish to achieve, but information about alternatives and future events is incomplete. They cannot be clear about alternatives or estimate their risk.
- Ambiguity – when people are unsure about their objectives and about the relation between cause and effect.

4 Contrast rational, administrative, political and garbage-can decision models

- Rational models are based on economic assumptions which suggest that the role of a manager is to maximise the economic return to the firm, and that they do this by making decisions on economically rational criteria.
- The administrative model aims to describe how managers actually make decisions in situations of uncertainty and ambiguity. Many management problems are unstructured and not suitable for the precise quantitative analysis implied by the rational model.
- The political model examines how people make decisions when conditions are uncertain, information is limited, and there is disagreement among managers over goals and how to pursue them. It recognises that an organisation is not only a working system, but also a political system, which establishes the relative power of people and functions.
- The garbage-can model identifies four independent streams of activities that enable a decision when they meet. When participants, problems and solutions come together in a relevant forum (a 'garbage can'), then a decision will be made.

5 Give examples of common sources of bias in decisions

- Sources of bias stem from the use of heuristics – mental short-cuts which allow us to cope with excessive information. Four biases are:
  - Representativeness bias – basing decisions on unrepresentative samples or single incidents.
  - Prior hypothesis bias – basing decisions on prior beliefs, despite evidence they are wrong.
  - Illusion of control – excessive belief in one's ability to control people and events.
  - Escalating commitment – committing more resources to a project despite evidence of failure.

6 Explain the contribution of Vroom and Yetton, and of Irving Janis, to our understanding of decision making in groups

- Vroom and Yetton introduced the idea that decision-making styles in groups should reflect the situation – which of the five ways of involving subordinates in a decision (autocratic, information-seeking, consulting, negotiating and delegating) to use depended on identifiable circumstances, such as whether the manager has the information required.
- Irving Janis observed the phenomenon of groupthink, and set out the symptoms which indicate that it is affecting a group's decision-making processes.

7 **Show how ideas from the chapter add to your understanding of the integrating themes**

- The analysis by Nutt (2002) of successful approaches to decision making, and that by Pfeffer and Sutton (2006) are highly relevant to situations in which managers are dealing with difficult decisions about how to improve the sustainability of their operations.
- The chapter shows the many traps and biases that afflict decision makers – good governance can protect them and their organisations from these by subjecting them to close external scrutiny. Groupthink is likely to have been present in many groups of senior managers as they made bad decisions which damaged their firms and the wider economy.
- Those managing internationally constantly search for the best balance between central and local decision making.

Review questions

1 Explain the difference between risk and ambiguity. How may people make decisions in different ways for each situation?

2 List three decisions you have recently observed or taken part in. Which of them were programmed and which unprogrammed?

3 What are the major differences between the rational and administrative models of decision making?

4 What is meant by satisficing in decision making? Can you illustrate the concept with an example from your experience? Why did those involved not try to achieve an economically superior decision?

5 What did Henry Mintzberg's research on decision making contribute to our understanding of the process?

6 List and explain three common biases in making decisions.

7 The Vroom–Yetton model describes five styles. How should the manager decide which style to use?

8 Recall four of the symptoms of groupthink, and give an example to illustrate each of them.

9 Summarise an idea from the chapter that adds to your understanding of the integrating themes.

Concluding critical reflection

Think about the ways in which your company, or one with which you are familiar, makes decisions. Review the material in the chapter, and perhaps visit some of the websites identified. Then make notes on these questions:

- What examples of the issues discussed in this chapter struck you as being relevant to practice in your company?
- Are people you work with typically dealing mainly with programmed or non-programmed decisions? What **assumptions** about the nature of decision making appear to guide their approach: rational, administrative, political or garbage can? On balance, do their assumptions accurately reflect the reality you see?
- What factors, such as the history or current **context** of the company, appear to influence people who are expected to reach decisions? Does the current approach appear to be right for the company in its context, or would a different view of the context lead to a different approach? (Perhaps refer to some of the Management in Practice features for how different contexts encourage different approaches.)
- Have people put forward **alternative** approaches to decision making, based on evidence companies? If you could find such evidence, how may it affect company practice?
- Can you identify **limitations** in the ideas and theories presented here, for example are you convinced of the garbage-can model of decision making? Can you find evidence that supports or challenges that view?

Further reading

Bazerman, M.H. (2005), *Judgment in Managerial Decision Making* (6th edn), John Wiley, New York.

Comprehensive and interactive account, aimed at developing the skill of judgement among students, and so enabling them to improve how they make decisions.

Buchanan, L. and O'Connell, A. (2006), 'A brief history of decision making', *Harvard Business Review*, vol. 84, no. 1, pp. 32–41.

Informative overview, placing many of the ideas mentioned in the chapter within a historical context. Part of a special issue of the *Harvard Business Review* devoted to decision making.

Finkelstein, S., Whitehead, J. and Campbell, A. (2009), 'How inappropriate attachments can drive good leaders to make bad decisions', *Organizational Dynamics*, vol. 38, no. 2, pp. 83–92.

Revealing insights into this source of bias in decision making.

Harrison, E.F. (1999), *The Managerial Decision-making Process* (5th edn), Houghton Mifflin, Boston, MA.

Comprehensive interdisciplinary approach to the generic process of decision making, with a focus on the strategic level. The author draws on a wide range of scholarly perspectives and presents them in a lucid and well-organised way.

Harvey, J.B. (1988), 'The abilene paradox: The management of agreement', *Organizational Dynamics*, vol. 17, no. 1, pp. 17–43.

First published in the same journal in 1974, this reprint also includes an epilogue by Harvey, and further commentaries on this classic paper by other management writers.

Schwartz, B. (2004), *The Paradox of Choice*, Ecco, New York.

An excellent study of decision making at the individual level. It shows how people in modern society face an ever-widening and increasingly bewildering range of choices, which is a source of increasing tension and stress. Many of the issues the author raises apply equally well to decision making in organisations.

Weblinks

These websites have appeared in the chapter:

www.ikea.com
www.nice.org.uk
www.wipro.com
www.pg.com
www.inamo-restaurant.com
www.eads.com
www.oticon.com

Visit two of the business sites in the list, or any other company that interests you, and navigate to the pages dealing with recent news or investor relations.

- What examples of decisions which the company has recently had to take can you find?
- How would you classify those decisions in terms of the models in this chapter?
- Gather information from the media websites (such as **www.FT.com**) which relate to the companies you have chosen. What stories can you find that indicate something about the decisions the companies have faced, and what the outcomes have been?

For video case studies, audio summaries, flashcards, exercises and annotated weblinks related to this chapter, visit **www.pearsoned.co.uk/mymanagementlab**

CHAPTER 8
MANAGING STRATEGY

Aim

To describe and illustrate the processes and content of managing strategy.

Objectives

By the end of your work on this chapter you should be able to outline the concepts below in your own terms and:

1. Explain why the process, content and context of strategy matters, and how the issues vary between sectors
2. Compare planning, learning and political views on strategy
3. Summarise evidence on how managers develop strategies
4. Explain how tools for external and internal analysis help managers to develop strategy
5. Use the product/market matrix to compare corporate level strategies
6. Use the generic strategies matrix to compare business-level strategies
7. Illustrate the alternative ways in which managers deliver a strategy
8. Show how ideas from the chapter add to your understanding of the integrating themes

Key terms

This chapter introduces these ideas:

strategy
competitive strategy
emergent strategy
unique resources
core competencies
dynamic capabilities

value chain
mission statement
cost leadership strategy
economies of scale
differentiation strategy
focus strategy

Each is a term defined within the text, as well as in the Glossary at the end of the book.

Case study   HMV Group   www.hmv.com

HMV and Waterstone's are two familiar retailing brands, specialising in music, films, games and books. The business began in 1921 when 'His Master's Voice' opened a store in London's Oxford Street: the HMV Group now has over 400 entertainment stores and websites in the UK, Ireland, Canada, Hong Kong and Singapore, and Waterstone's. This is the UK's only specialist bookchain, and includes most of the 130 Ottakar's stores acquired when it took over that company in 2006.

The music side of the business was part of EMI Group, but in 2002 the company demerged from that company to create a purely retail company, rather than being part of the diversified EMI Group, which also owned Dillon's, another bookselling chain. HMV Group then bought Waterstone's from WH Smith.

In 2006 the company itself faced a takeover threat from Permira, an investment company. The company rejected this bid, believing that it seriously undervalued the company. HMV had experienced severe losses the previous year, which gave Permira the opportunity to mount a takeover bid. HMV had suffered from the growth of illegal music downloads, and the consequent fall in sales of CDs. Management were confident that they could recover from a poor year's trading, but the bid is a constant reminder that if management does not meet investors' expectations, they will again be vulnerable to a takeover.

This episode prompted the management team, led by chief executive Simon Fox, to develop a transformation strategy for the group. This has three strands; *revitalising the HMV and Waterstone's stores; growing revenue* from new channels; and *becoming more efficient*. The next paragraphs outline the strategy for the stores: the other strands are on later pages.

In the HMV *stores* the company is changing the mix of products to offset the decline in physical music sales. They are stocking more games software and consoles, as well as introducing MP3/4 players and accessories. They expect market growth at Waterstone's to come mainly from non-book sales, so are extending the range of high-quality gift stationery, and concentrating on the book categories

By kind permission, HMV

that are growing most rapidly, such as fiction and children's books.

To help understand customers' needs and to encourage sales to the most loyal and high spending, the company launched the Pure HMV loyalty card. Customers can exchange the points earned – at Waterstone's for future purchases, and at HMV for entertainment-related rewards. It is also developing the HMV store format to become a more inspiring shopping venue, with more interactive features.

The recession which began in 2008 affected the industry: in 2008 music retailers Zavvi and Woolworth's collapsed, followed in 2009 by Borders Bookshops. HMV issued additional shares which enabled it to buy about 20 of the Zavvi stores.

Case questions 8.1

Visit an HMV or Waterstone's store and the group website (**www.hmvgroup.com**) – navigate to the section on 'the company'.

- Note the sales and profit performance in the most recent period compared with an earlier one.

- What do the chairman and chief executive write about the company's current strategy?

- What challenges do they say the company is facing?

Activity 8.1   **Describing strategy**

Before reading this chapter, write some notes on what you understand 'strategy' to be.

- Think of one organisation with which you have had contact, or about which you have read, in the last week.
- Make brief notes summarising what that company does and how it does it.
- What clues does that give you about the strategic decisions it has made?
- Record your ideas as you may be able to use them later.

8.1   Introduction

HMV illustrates the value of managing strategy. For many years it was a leading player in the UK music retailing industry, but in 2005 its performance declined. Management successfully resisted a hostile takeover bid, arguing that it undervalued the company and was not in the shareholders' interests. They then had to deliver on that promise: the board appointed a new chief executive, who set out a three-year strategic plan to improve performance. Managers know that entrepreneurs could again use any trading weakness as an opportunity to buy the company.

All organisations (not just those in trouble) face strategic issues. Established businesses such as BT are in a growing and diversifying telecommunications market, but they face new competition that threatens their core business. Should the company try to compete in all areas, or concentrate on one sector, as Vodafone has done? Should Virgin continue to extend the brand into ever more diverse areas of activity, or would it gain more by building profits in the existing areas, and achieving more synergies across the group? Some charities face declining income: should their managers continue as they are now, or will they serve their cause better by initiating a radical review of their strategy? Strategic management enables companies to be clear about how they will add value to resources, even though much is changing in their world. Strategy links the organisation to the outside world, where changes in the competitive (micro) and wider (macro) environment bring opportunities and threats. Table 8.1 gives some examples of organisations managing their strategies.

Table 8.1 Examples of organisations making strategic changes

Organisation and strategic issue	Strategic decisions or moves
MySpace – in 2010 facing competition from Facebook and a slow growth in advertising revenues. Owner (News Corporation) seeking better financial return. **www.MySpace.com**	New management abandon international expansion strategy, and close several overseas offices, making about 30 per cent of staff redundant. Also scrap plans for a new corporate campus in Los Angeles
Procter and Gamble (world's largest supplier of consumer goods, such as soap and toothpaste) – how to ensure long-term growth. **www.pg.com**	Changed from focus on people in rich economies to those in poor countries; affects R&D, market research and manufacturing to identify and make suitable products
Nestlé (global food and beverage company) – how to stimulate sales and profits in a mature business. **www.nestle.com**	Increased emphasis on healthy foods, by adapting current products and taking over companies with established reputations for healthy products

The first sections of the chapter give you some ideas about the strategy process: how managers develop their strategy, and the tools they use to analyse their external and internal environments. The following two sections then present models with which to analyse corporate and business unit strategies, followed by a presentation of the ways in which managers choose to deliver their strategy.

8.2 Strategy – process, content and context

What is strategy?

Strategy is about how people decide to organise major resources to enhance the performance of an enterprise. It is about resource decisions that are large, relatively long term, expensive and visible – with correspondingly large implications for performance: decisions that are not strategic are operational or tactical. Elaborating on the definition:

Strategy is about how people decide to organise major resources to enhance performance of an enterprise.

- **People** Strategy is typically the responsibility of senior management, but some believe that in conditions of rapid change enabling more people to contribute will improve the result.
- **Decide** In formal planning processes and/or informal conversations among managers.
- **Organise** How to divide and co-ordinate activities to add most value.
- **Major** Significant, expensive, visible – decisions with long-term implications.
- **Resources** Inputs the enterprise needs, including those in other organizations.
- **Enhance performance** The intended outcome of strategic decisions.
- **Enterprise** All types of organisations can benefit from managing their strategy.

The definition is consistent with the view of Johnson *et al.* (2007), who suggest that strategy is something people do (their strategy process) *and* that organisations have (their strategy content).

Process

People, usually senior managers, talk, email and argue about their present and future strategy: this is their strategy process. In this sense, strategy is something that people do (Johnson *et al.*, 2007). Understanding this perspective implies finding out who takes part in strategy formation, what information they gather and how they use the tools available. Do they work in formal settings leading to rationally based plans, or is the process more fluid and iterative? Are strategies set for years, or do they emerge, alter and disappear, sometimes very quickly? Sections 8.3 and 8.4 introduce ideas on strategic processes.

Content

The existing strategy is the starting point of, and the new one is the result of, the strategy process, so in this sense strategy is something that organisations have (Johnson *et al.,* 2007). Something stimulates managers to question current strategy (such as the takeover bid for HMV) or the emergence of a new service which customers may value, but which will require strategic investment. Most managers develop strategy to perform well against competitors. They try to identify what gives their enterprise an edge, so that they can define their **competitive strategy**. This includes deciding what to offer, to which markets, using what resources. Sections 8.5 and 8.6 will deal with these topics.

Competitive strategy explains how an organisation (or unit within it) intends to achieve competitive advantage in its market.

Context

Context here refers to the setting in which the organisation works, which affects the issues those managing it will face. Not-for-profit (NFP) or public sector organisations share some characteristics with commercial businesses (they need to attract and retain enthusiastic and capable staff) and differ in others (their performance criteria and sources of funding). Table 8.2 illustrates these differences between some familiar types of organisation.

Table 8.2 Strategic issues in different settings

Type of organisation	Distinctive strategic issues	Examples in this text
Large MNCs	Structure and control of global activities Allocating resources between units	Procter and Gamble (this chapter); BP (Part 2 case)
SMEs	Strongly influenced by founders or owners; lack of capital limits choices	Linn Products (Section 18.3)
Manufacturing	Relative contribution to competitive advantage of the manufacturing (physical product) or service aspect (delivery, customer support) of the offer	BMW (Chapter 11)
Firms in innovative sectors	Adding value depends on rapid innovation, so strategy aims to create a culture of questioning and challenge	Nokia (Chapter 3); Oticon (Chapter 10)
Public sector	Competing for resources, and so aim to demonstrate best value in outputs; most problems require co-operation between agencies, thus complicating strategy	Crossrail (Chapter 6)
Voluntary and NFP sector	Balancing ideology and values with interests of funding sources; balancing central control (consistency) with local commitment (volunteers and local staff).	The Eden Project (Chapter 15)

Whatever their context, strategists hope that their work will enhance performance by clarifying and unifying purpose, reducing uncertainty, linking short-term actions to long-term goals and providing control – since setting goals provides standards against which to measure performance.

Activity 8.2   **Think about the definition**

Reflect on an organisation you have worked in, or ask a friend or relative who works in an organisation to help.

- Can you/they identify examples of people in that organisation working on some or all of the items in the definition of strategy?
- Did you/they do other things that were seen as 'managing strategy' but which are not mentioned?
- Decide if the definition accurately describes 'strategy'.
- If not, how would you change it?

8.3   **Planning, learning and political perspectives on strategy**

Table 8.3 shows three perspectives on the strategy process, comparing their approach, content, nature and outcomes – and the context in which they may be suitable.

Planning

The 'planning view' is prescriptive and based on a belief that the complexity of strategic decisions requires an explicit and formalised approach to guide management through the

Table 8.3 Alternative perspectives on the strategy process

	Planning	Learning	Political
Approach	Prescriptive; assumes rationality	Descriptive; based on bounded rationality	Descriptive; based on bounded rationality
Content	Analytical tools and techniques; forecasting; search for alternatives, each evaluated in detail	Limited use of tools and techniques; limited search for options: time and resources don't permit	As learning view, but some objectives and options disregarded as politically unacceptable
Nature of process	Formalised, systematic, analytical; top down – centralised planning teams	Adaptive, learning by doing; top down and bottom up	Bargaining; use of power to shape strategies; top down and bottom up
Outcomes	Extensive plans made before work begins; plans assumed to be achieved with small changes	Plans are made but not all are 'realised'; some strategies are not planned but emerge in course of 'doing'	Plans may be left ambiguous to secure agreement; need interpretation during implementation; compromises
Context/environment	Stable environment; assumption that future can be predicted; if complex, use of more sophisticated tools	Complex, dynamic, future unpredictable	Stable or dynamic, but complex; stakeholders have diverging values, objectives and solutions

process. In the 1960s and 1970s a wide literature, most notably the work of Ansoff (1965), took this approach, presenting strategy development as a systematic process, following a pre-scribed sequence of steps and making extensive use of analytical tools and techniques (shown in Figure 8.1). Those favouring this perspective assume that events and facts can be expressed or observed objectively and that people respond rationally to information.

Those who challenge these assumptions of objectivity and rationality advocate two alternative views: the learning and the political (Brews and Hunt, 1999).

Learning

This sees strategy as an *emergent* or adaptive process. Mintzberg (1994a, 1994b) regards for-mal strategic planning as a system developed during a period of stability, and designed mainly for the centralised bureaucracies typical of the Western manufacturing industry in the

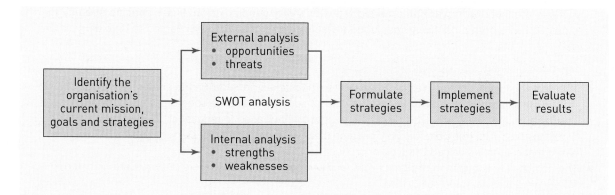

Figure 8.1 The planning view of strategy

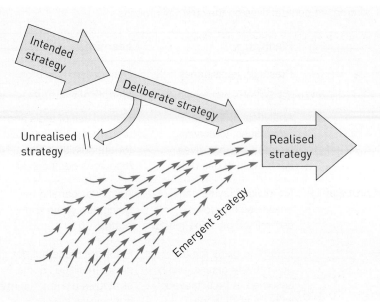

Figure 8.2
Forms of strategy

Source: Mintzberg
(1994a).

mid-twentieth century. This style of planning is appropriate for those conditions, but not for businesses in rapidly changing sectors: they require a more flexible approach.

Emergent strategies
are those that result from actions taken one by one that converge in time in some sort of consistency pattern.

He therefore distinguished between intended and **emergent strategy** (Figure 8.2). He acknowledges the validity of strategy as a plan, setting out intended courses of action, and recognises that some deliberate intentions may be realised. But it is also likely that some plans are not implemented (unrealised strategies) and that others which he describes as 'emergent strategies' were not expressly intended. They resulted from:

> actions taken one by one, which converged in time in some sort of consistency or pattern. (Mintzberg, 1994a, p. 25)

Management in practice   Emergent strategy at Ikea www.ikea.com

Barthélemy (2006) offers an insight into the strategy process at Ikea (Chapter 7 case). Ikea's strategy has clearly been highly successful, but how did it come about? A close examination of the company's history shows that many of the specifics of the strategy were not brought about through a process of deliberate formulation followed by implementation:

> Instead, the founder, Ingvar Kamprad started with a very general vision. Ikea's specific strategy then emerged as he both proactively developed a viable course of action and reacted to unfolding circumstances. (p. 81)

Examples include:

- The decision to sell furniture was an adaptation to the market, not a deliberate strategy – furniture was initially a small part of the retail business, but was so successful that he soon dropped all other products.
- The flat pack method which symbolises the group was introduced to reduce insurance claims on the mail order business – its true potential only became clear when the company started opening stores, and realised that customers valued this type of product.
- The company only began to design its own furniture because other retailers put pressure on established furniture companies not to sell to Ikea.

Source: Barthélemy (2006).

A flexible approach to strategy recognises that:

> the real world inevitably involves some thinking ahead of time as well as some adaptation *en route*. (Mintzberg, 1994a, p. 26)

The essence of the learning view is adaptation, reacting to unexpected events, experimenting with new ideas 'on the ground'. Mintzberg gives the example of a salesperson coming up with the idea of selling an existing product to some new customers. Soon all the other salespeople begin to do the same, and

> one day, months later, management discovers that the company has entered a new market. (Mintzberg, 1994a, p. 26)

This was not planned but learned, collectively, during implementation.

Political view

Strategy as an emergent process has much in common with political perspectives, since both draw on the concepts of bounded rationality and satisficing behaviour (Chapter 7). While the learning view reflects the logic that planning can never give complete foresight, the political view adds dimensions of power, conflict and ambiguity.

Drawing on his experience in the public policy sphere, Lindblom (1959) was an early proponent of the political view (see also Chapter 7). He drew attention to the way value judgements influence policy and to the way in which conflicting interests of stakeholders frustrate attempts to agree strategy. He concluded that strategic management is not a scientific, comprehensive or rational process, but is an iterative, incremental process, characterised by restricted analysis and bargaining between the players. Lindblom (1959) called this the method of 'successive limited comparisons' whereby 'new' strategy is made by marginal adjustments to existing strategy:

> Policy is not made once and for all; it is made and remade endlessly . . . [through] . . . a process of successive approximation to some desired objectives.

It is not a comprehensive, objective process but a limited comparison of options, restricted to those that are politically acceptable and possible to implement.

While advocating a learning view, Mintzberg also stresses the value of planning:

> Too much planning may lead us to chaos, but so too would too little, more directly. (Mintzberg, 1994a, p. 416)

The planning style suited the relative stability of the 1960s. Uncertain business conditions probably require a different approach, of which the next section provides some evidence.

Activity 8.3   Gather evidence about the three perspectives

Read one of these case studies – Crossrail (Chapter 6), Apple (Chapter 14), or any other organisation will be suitable for this activity.

- Identify two or three strategic moves made by the company, and write a brief note on each.
- Can you find evidence to show which of the three perspectives on strategy they used: planning, learning or political?
- On reflection, does that seem to have been the best method for the situation?
- Compare your answers with other students on your course, and try to identify any common or contrasting themes.

8.4   How do managers develop strategies?

Grant (2003) gives some insights into the way managers develop strategy from his study in eight major oil companies, especially how the greater uncertainty in their business environment had affected them. In the relatively stable conditions of the 1970s they had developed formal planning systems which were conducted by staff at corporate HQ, with much emphasis on analysis, detailed forecasts of energy demand and price, and documents setting out long-term plans for the businesses to follow.

At the time of Grant's study, all oil companies used a clear planning process – the details varied between them but Figure 8.3 shows the common components. Corporate HQ set the overall strategic direction, which provided a framework within which business unit staff developed their strategic proposals. They discussed these with corporate staff, and the revised plans then informed both the annual financial budget, and the corporate plan. After Board approval, the corporate plan formed the context for annual performance targets, and for appraising their achievement.

As expected, all the companies said that the more turbulent environment (volatile oil prices, economic uncertainty and competition) had changed the strategy process. There was now:

- less detailed forecasting, more broad scenario planning (see below), more making assumptions about significant variables;
- less formality and documentation, more face-to-face discussion between corporate and business unit staff;
- shorter planning meetings;
- a shift in responsibility from corporate to business management, and from planning staff to line management.

The content of strategic plans had also changed in that they now covered shorter periods, were more concerned with direction than with detail, and emphasised performance planning by setting:

- financial targets;
- operating targets;

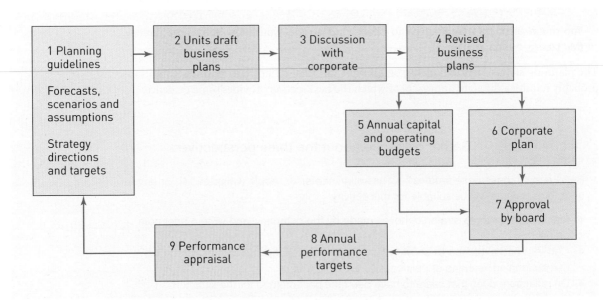

Figure 8.3 The generic strategic planning cycle among the oil majors
Source: Based on Grant (2003), p. 499.

- safety and environmental targets;
- strategic mileposts; and
- capital expenditure limits.

Grant's final conclusion was that the strategic planning processes in these companies were mainly concerned with co-ordinating the strategies emerging from the business units, and with monitoring and controlling their implementation:

> Strategic planning has become less about strategic decision making and more a mechanism for coordination and performance managing . . . permitting increased decentralization of decision making and greater adaptability and responsiveness to external change. (p. 515)

The eight oil companies are not typical organisations – but studies in other sectors of the economy present a similar picture of contemporary strategic planning as a process combining elements of formality and informality, of demanding targets and intelligent flexibility. Whittington *et al.* (2006) and Johnson *et al.* (2007) add to this with their view of 'strategy as practice', showing what people do as they craft strategy, and how their context influences this (see Key Ideas).

Key ideas   Strategy as practice

Whittington *et al.* (2006) conducted qualitative research in 10 organisations to examine how they developed their strategies. They conclude that in a world of accelerating change the linked activities of formulating strategy and designing organisation are best conducted as tightly linked practical activities. They focused on three specific tools; strategy workshops or away-days, strategic change projects, and symbolic artifacts (things that people develop to represent and communicate strategy). Their observations showed the transitory nature of strategies and organisational forms leading them to suggest that verbs ('strategising' and 'organising' respectively) capture the nature of the work people do as they work on strategy.

They also found that practical crafts of strategising and organising were as important as the formal tools of analysis:

> Formal strategy can be renewed by a greater appreciation of the everyday, practical, non-analytical skills required to carry it out [especially those of coordination, communication and control]. (p. 616) Strategists run workshops and video-conferences, draw flip-charts, design PowerPoints, manipulate spreadsheets, manage projects, write reports, monitor metrics and talk endlessly: their skills at these activities can mean success or failure for entire strategy processes. (p. 625)

Source: Whittington *et al.* (2006).

Hodgkinson *et al.* (2006) studied the use of strategy workshops, a common management practice in which senior managers take time out from daily activities to deliberate on the longer-term direction of the concern, especially on formulating and implementing changes in strategy. Their research showed that workshops did indeed play an important role in the strategic planning process, were more discursive than analytical, and were typically for top managers. They also found that:

- most companies held strategy workshops once a year, as part of their formal planning process, usually lasting between one and three days;
- most participants spent less than one day preparing for them – rather than detailed information gathering and analysis, they were designed to allow participants to share experience and ideas;
- tools most commonly used to help structure the discussion were SWOT analysis, stakeholder analysis, scenario planning, market segmentation, competence analysis, PESTEL and Value Chain Analysis; and
- top managers were more likely to attend than middle managers.

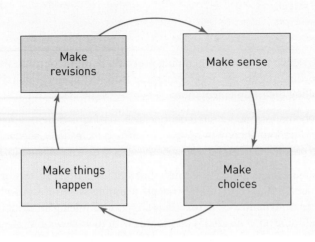

Figure 8.4
The strategy loop

Source: Closing the gap between strategy and execution, *MIT Sloan Management Review*, vol. 48, no. 4, pp. 30–38 (Sull, D. N. 2007) © 2010 from MIT Sloan Management Review/ Massachusetts Institute of Technology. All rights reserved. Distributed by Tribune Media Services.

They observed that since the main benefit of such workshops was to communicate and co-ordinate strategy, the absence of middle managers made this difficult to achieve.

Sull (2007) believes that since volatile markets throw out a steady stream of opportunities and threats, managers cannot predict the form, magnitude or timing of events. This makes the planning view of strategy inadequate, as it may deter people from incorporating new information into action. He therefore sees the strategy process as inherently iterative – a loop instead of a line:

> According to this view, every strategy is a work in progress that is subject to revision in light of ongoing interactions between the organization and its shifting environment. To accommodate those interactions, the strategy loop consists of four major steps: making sense of a situation, making choices on what to do (and what not to do), making those things happen and making revisions based on new information (p. 31).

Figure 8.4 shows the strategy loop, the most important feature of which is that it implies that managers incorporate and use new information as it becomes available, closely linking strategy formation and implementation.

Sull stresses the importance of conversations – formal and informal, short and long, one-on-one and in groups – as the key mechanism for co-ordinating activity inside a company. To put the strategy loop into practice, managers at every level must be able to lead discussions about the four steps. The following sections provide ideas and examples about each of these:

- making sense – using information about external and internal environments;
- making choices – deciding strategy at corporate and business unit levels;
- making things happen – ways to deliver strategy; and
- making revisions – reflecting on results, and taking in new information.

8.5   Making sense – external and internal analysis

Case study   **HMV – the case continues** www.hmv.com

The second strand in the new strategy is to *grow revenue* from new channels, instead of relying on physical purchases in the stores. HMV Group is therefore investing in both stores' online sites. Customers can purchase music through the hmv.com site, giving the choice of a digital download or a physical album. The company plans to extend the site to offer video downloads as soon as this becomes worthwhile to customers and the company. They are also planning to grow revenue from live music events and ticket sales.

On becoming *more efficient*, the company is changing major parts of the cost base. For example, Waterstone's had invested in a centralised book hub, to which all book suppliers deliver their products. These are then sorted and delivered to each store as a single daily delivery, rather than having several deliveries to a store each day by individual suppliers. They are also centralising their purchasing to reduce costs, and consolidating many back-office functions of the two store chains.

Source: Group website.

Case questions 8.2

- What developments in the external environment are reflected in the company's strategy?
- What internal changes do you think this may have led to in the way the company operates?

External analysis

Chapter 3 outlined Porter's five forces model, showing the forces which affect the profitability of an industry (see Key Ideas).

Key ideas   Using Porter's five forces in strategic analysis

Analysing the likely effects on a company of the five forces which Michael Porter (1980a, 2008) identified can show the action points which managers need to consider in their strategy.

- **Threat of entry**: what are the barriers that new entrants need to overcome if they are to compete successfully? High barriers are good for incumbents: they fear barriers that are becoming lower, as this exposes them to more competition. Government legislation in the 1980s reduced the barriers protecting banks from competition, and allowed other companies to enter the industry.
- **Threat of substitutes**: what alternative products and services may customers choose? Many people choose to receive their news online rather than in print, seriously threatening print newspapers, which need to build strategies for survival.
- **Power of buyers**: if they have strong bargaining power they force down prices and reduce profitability. Small food companies are attracted by the prospect of doing business with large retailers, but are wary of the power of the retailers to dictate prices.
- **Power of suppliers**: if suppliers have few competitors they can raise prices at the expense of customers. Companies that have few alternative sources of energy or raw materials are exposed when stocks are low.
- **Competitive rivalry**: the four forces combine to affect the intensity of rivalry between an organisation and its rivals. Factors such as industry growth or the ease with which companies can leave it also affect this.

The model remains popular, and Porter published a revised version in 2008, mainly by adding current examples: the five forces remain the same. They help strategists to understand the fundamental conditions of their industry, and to work out how to make their company less vulnerable and more profitable.

Source: Porter (1980a, 2008).

At the macro-level of the general environment, the PESTEL framework helps to identify the major drivers of change affecting their strategy. These may conflict: an aging population might seem like good news for businesses such as Southern Cross or Care UK, but budget problems in local authorities, which buy most of the places in care homes, mean that they prefer, whenever they can, to provide care in an elderly person's home, rather than admitting him/her to a residential home. A company may also, like Motorola, miss signals about changes in the outside world (see the following Management in Practice).

Management in practice   Motorola misreads the market www.motorola.com

In 2009 Greg Brown, Motorola's joint chief executive, explained the dramatic decline in the company's mobile phone business. He said that the company did not spot quickly enough how mobiles were evolving from simple devices for making phone calls into sophisticated handsets for surfing the internet and sending email. Smartphones have thrived with the arrival of third-generation mobile technology, and Motorola has been weak in that area. As Brown says:

> Motorola didn't see the trends coming in smartphone and 3G with the kind of foresight and customer attention it should have.

He went on to describe Motorola's failure to anticipate the growing importance of mobile software rather than handset design – accepting that most of the challenges the company faces were their own doing.

The company was the world's largest mobile maker in the 1990s until Nokia stole that mantle in 1998. It then followed a strategy of selling cheap handsets in developing countries, but abandoned that as it was unprofitable. In the fourth quarter of 2006 the company's market share of mobile sales was 23.3 per cent – in the same quarter of 2008 it was 6.6 per cent.

Source: *Financial Times*, 2 March 2009.

Case questions 8.3

Referring to the analytical frameworks in Chapter 3:

- What are the main external factors affecting the HMV Group at present?
- How do these differ between the HMV and Waterstone's businesses?

Kay (1996) defined strategy as the match between the organisation's external relationships and its internal capabilities, describing 'how it responds to its suppliers, its customers, its competitors, and the social and economic environment within which it operates'. Before establishing a direction, managers need an internal analysis to show how well they can cope with external changes.

Activity 8.4   Using Porter's five forces to analyse a competitive environment

- Identify an industry which features in one of the cases in this book, such as airlines or retailing.
- Gather specific evidence and examples of each of the five forces, and of how it affecting competition.
- Try to identify how one company in the industry has changed their strategy to take account of this change in one or more of the five forces.

Internal analysis: resources, capabilities and dynamic capabilities

Managers analyse the internal environment to identify the organisation's strengths and weaknesses. This means identifying what the organisation does well, where it might do better and whether it has the resources and competences to deliver a preferred strategy. Those that are considered essential to outperforming the competition constitute critical success factors.

Chapter 1 introduced the idea of strategic capability as the ability to perform at the level required to survive and prosper, and showed how this depends on the resources available to the organisation, and its competence in using them. Tangible resources are the physical assets such as buildings, equipment, people or finance, while intangible resources include reputation, knowledge or information. **Unique resources** are those which others cannot obtain: a powerful brand, access to raw material or a distinctive culture.

Organisations also need to develop *competences* – activities and processes which enable it to deploy resources effectively. Joe Morris, operations director at TJ Morris, a Liverpool-based chain of discount stores (in 2010 the second largest independent grocer in the UK) claims that its IT system (which his brother Ed designed) gives them a competitive advantage:

> It is our own bespoke product. It is extremely reliable and simple. We can do what we want to do very quickly.

While the amount and quality of these resources matter, how people use them matters more. If managers encourage staff to develop higher skills, co-operate with each other, be innovative and creative, the company is likely to perform better than one where managers treat staff indifferently.

Understanding competitive advantage requires a further distinction:

- **Threshold capabilities** (resources and competences) – an organisation must have these to be in a market (adequate IT systems, for example).
- **Core capabilities** (resources and competencies) – an organisation can deploy these to gain a competitive advantage, because others cannot imitate them.

Ryanair has prospered not because it has resources (a fleet of modern, standard aircraft) – other airlines have similar resources but are unprofitable. The difference is that Ryanair has developed competencies, such as quick turnrounds which enable it to use aircraft more efficiently. GlaxoSmithKline has a strategy to acquire half of its new drugs from other organisations: for this to work, it will need to develop a **core competence** of identifying and working with suitable partners.

Management's task in internal analysis is to identify those capabilities (resources and competencies) that distinguish it to the customer. At the *corporate level*, this could be the overall balance of activities that it undertakes – the product or service portfolio. Does it have sufficient capabilities in growing rather than declining markets? Does it have too many new products (which drain resources) relative to established ones? Are there useful synergies between the different lines of business? At the *divisional or strategic business unit level*, performance depends on having adequate resources (physical, human, financial and so on) and competences (such as design, production or marketing).

In highly uncertain business conditions the factors which once enabled an organisation to prosper may no longer be enough. It may need to create new capabilities which enable it to remain competitive in the new conditions, such as the ability to bring new products to the market more rapidly than competitors, or to develop skills of developing alliances with other businesses. These are called **dynamic capabilities**, which enable it to renew and recreate its strategic capabilities to meet the needs of a changing environment. These capabilities may be relatively formal, such as systems for developing new products or procedures for acquiring firms with valuable skills or products. They may also be informal, such as the ability to reach decisions quickly when required, or the ability of staff to work well in multi-professional teams.

Value chain analysis

The concept of the **value chain**, introduced by Porter (1985), is derived from an accounting practice that calculates the value added at each stage of a manufacturing or service process.

Unique resources are resources that are vital to competitive advantage and which others cannot obtain.

Core competences are the activities and processes through which resources are deployed to achieve competitive advantage in ways that others cannot imitate or obtain.

Dynamic capabilities are an organisation's abilities to renew and recreate its strategic capabilities to meet the needs of a changing environment.

A **value chain** 'divides a firm into the discrete activities it performs in designing, producing, marketing and distributing its product. It is the basic tool for diagnosing competitive advantage and finding ways to enhance it' (Porter, 1985).

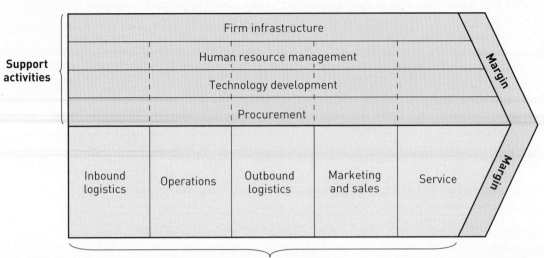

Figure 8.5 The value chain

Porter applied this idea to the activities of the whole organisation, as an analysis of each activity could identify sources of competitive advantage.

Figure 8.5 shows primary and support activities. *Primary* activities transform inputs into outputs and deliver them to the customer:

- **inbound logistics**: receiving, storing and distributing the inputs to the product or service; also material handling and stock control, etc.;
- **operations**: transforming inputs into the final product or service, by machining, mixing and packing;
- **outbound logistics**: moving the product to the buyer – collecting, storing and distributing; in some services (a sports event) these activities will include bringing the customers to the venue;
- **marketing and sales**: activities to make consumers aware of the product;
- **service**: enhancing or maintaining the product – installation, training, repairs.

These depend on four *support* activities:

- **firm infrastructure**: organisational structure, together with planning, financial and quality systems;
- **human resource management**: recruitment, training, rewards, etc.;
- **technology development**: relate to inputs, operational processes or outputs;
- **procurement**: acquiring materials and other resources.

Case questions 8.4

As part of the recovery plan, HMV is widening the range of products it stocks, and changing the ways it receives these and delivers them to customers. Use the value chain to analyse these changes, doing it separately for HMV and Waterstone's when necessary.

- How do these changes fit into the value chain?
- What new challenges may they have raised for the linkages between stages in the chain?

Value chain analysis enables managers to consider which activities benefit customers and which are more troublesome – perhaps destroying value rather than creating it. The business might, say, be good at marketing, outbound logistics and technology development, but poor at operations and human resource management. That awareness may lead managers to consider which activities it should do, and which it should outsource to other firms. Each activity in the chain:

> can contribute to a firm's relative cost position and create a basis for differentiation. (Porter, 1985)

the two main sources of competitive advantage. Analysing the value chain helps management to consider:

- Which activities have most effect on reducing cost or adding value? If customers value quality more than costs, then that implies a focus on ensuring quality of suppliers.
- What linkages do most to reduce cost, enhance value or discourage imitation?
- How do these linkages relate to the cost and value drivers?

SWOT analysis

Strategy follows a 'fit' between internal capabilities and external changes – managers try to identify key issues from each and draw out the strategic implications. A SWOT analysis (see Chapter 6) summarises the internal and external issues and helps identify potentially useful developments, which are shown schematically in Figure 8.6.

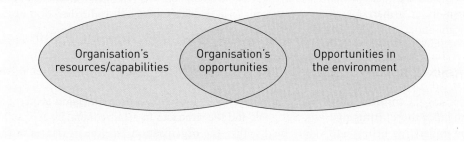

Figure 8.6
Identifying the organisation's opportunities

Hodgkinson *et al.* (2006) found that managers often use the technique in strategy workshops, although like any technique the value depends on how thoroughly people use it; for example by taking time to gather evidence about the relative significance of factors identified, rather than simply making a long list of items without challenge.

Case questions 8.5

Drawing on your answers to previous questions:

- Make a summary SWOT analysis for the two businesses in the HMV Group.
- Consult the HMV Group's website to read recent statements from the CEO and other information.

If the SWOT analysis is done thoroughly, managers can use the output to develop and evaluate strategic alternatives, aiming to select those that make the most of internal strengths and external opportunities. Managers in large enterprises develop strategies at corporate, business and functional levels, although in smaller organisations there will be less complexity. Figure 8.7 shows this.

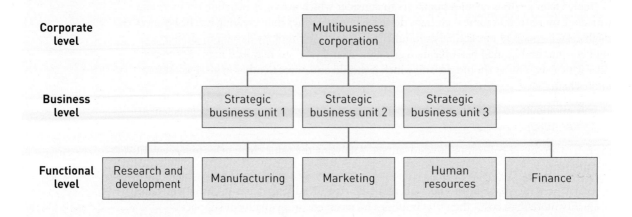

Figure 8.7 Levels of strategy

8.6   Making choices – deciding strategy at corporate level

At corporate level the strategy reflects the overall direction of the organisation, and the part which the respective business units will play in that. What is the overall mission and purpose? Should it focus on a small range of activities or diversify? Should it remain a local or national business, or seek to operate internationally? These decisions establish the direction of the organisation.

The corporate mission

A **mission statement** is a broad statement of an organisation's scope and purpose, aiming to distinguish it from similar organisations.

Defining the mission is intended to provide a focus for work. A broad **mission statement** can guide those setting more specific goals and the strategies to achieve them, by expressing the underlying beliefs and values held within the organisation (see the examples in the following Management in Practice).

Management in practice   Examples of missions and visions

Ikea (www.ikea.com)
A better everyday life.
Google (www.google.com)
To organize the world's information.
Royal Society for the Protection of Birds (www.rspb.org.uk)
To secure a healthy environment for birds and wildlife, helping to create a better world for us all.
Cancer Research UK (www.cancerresearchuk.org)
Together we will beat cancer
Nokia (www.nokia.com)
To connect people in new and better ways.

Mission statements may be idealistic aspirations rather than guides to action. Employees only believe, and act upon, the mission statement if they see managers doing so. The mission needs to be cascaded through the structure to ensure it guides day-to-day actions.

Setting a strategic direction

Strategies can aim for growth, stability or renewal. Growth strategies try to expand the number of products offered or markets served. Stability is when the organisation offers the same products and services to much the same group of customers. Renewal often follows a period of trouble and involves significant changes to the business to secure the required turnaround.

Management in practice   A new strategy at ABB   www.abb.com

ABB is a Swiss-Swedish electrical engineering group, which in 2009 surprised observers by appointing a new chief executive, Joe Hogan, who had spent over 20 years at the US giant, General Electric. He had taken a low-key approach to managing the business in his early months in the job, preferring to move carefully. A few months into the job he had made three big strategic adjustments:

Boosting services. ABB is already active in areas such as facilities management and energy conservation, but he wants to increase services revenue from 16 per cent of total sales to 25 per cent: 'the great thing about services is that it also gets you much closer to your customer, helping you understand their needs'.

A sharper sales culture. 'I want to see more of an external focus. Like many engineering companies ABB has tended to be inward looking.' It must become more sensitive to market signals and immediate customer needs.

Plugging geographic weaknesses. ABB is admired for having moved early into China and India. Mr Hogan believes the group can deepen its activities in existing markets and grow where it is weak. 'We need to improve our global footprint. ABB has always been heavily focused on Europe.'

Source: *Financial Times*, 8 June 2009.

Managers can decide how to achieve their chosen option by using the product/market matrix, shown in Figure 8.8. They can achieve growth by focusing on one or more of the

	Existing products/services	**New products/services**
Existing markets	Market penetration Consolidation Withdrawal	Product/service development
New markets	Market development: • new territories • new segments • new uses	Diversification: • horizontal • vertical • unrelated

Figure 8.8
Strategy development directions – the product/market matrix

Source: As adapted in Johnson *et al.* (2008) from Chapter 6 of H. Ansoff, *Corporate Strategy* published by Penguin 1988.

quadrants: stability by remaining with existing products and services; and renewal by leaving some markets followed by entry into others.

Existing markets, existing product/service

Choice within this segment depends on whether the market is growing, mature or in decline, or has reached maturity. Each box shows several possibilities:

- A market penetration strategy aims to increase market share, which will be easier in a growing than in a mature market. It could be achieved by reducing price, increasing advertising or improving distribution.
- Consolidation aims to protect the company's share in existing markets. In growing or mature markets this could mean improving efficiency and/or service to retain custom. In declining markets management might consolidate by acquisition of other companies.
- Withdrawal is a wise option when, for instance, competition is intense and the organisation is unable to match its rivals; staying in that line of business would destroy value, not create it. In the public sector, changing priorities lead to the redeployment of resources. Health boards have withdrawn accident and emergency services from some hospitals to make better use of limited resources.

Existing markets, new products/services

A strategy of product or service development allows a company to retain the relative security of its present markets while altering products or developing new ones. In retail sectors such as fashion, consumer electronics and financial services, companies continually change products to meet perceived changes in consumer preferences. Car manufacturers compete by adding features and extending their model range. Some new products, such as 'stakeholder pensions' in the UK, arise out of changes in government policy. Many new ideas fail commercially, so that product development is risky and costly.

New markets, existing products/services

Market development aims to find new outlets by:

- extending geographically (from local to national or international);
- targeting new market segments (groups of customers, by age, income or lifestyle); or
- finding new uses for a product (a lightweight material developed for use in spacecraft is also used in the manufacture of golf clubs).

Management in practice   P&G targets poorer customers www.pg.com

Procter & Gamble, the world's largest consumer goods company, has built its success on selling detergent, toothpaste and beauty products to the world's wealthiest 1 billion consumers. When chief executive A.G. Lafley arrived in 2002 and said

> We're going to serve the world's consumers'

he surprised the company's staff. One recalled:

> We realised that we didn't have the product strategy or the cost structure to be effective in serving lower income consumers. What's happened in the last five years has been one of the most dramatic transformations I've seen in my career. We now have all of our functions focused on meeting the needs of poorer consumers.

By 2005 it was devoting 30 per cent of the annual research and development budget to low-income markets, a 50 per cent increase on five years earlier. Developing markets are expected to grow twice as fast as developed markets over the next five years. The transformation has been evident in three areas:

- how the company finds out what customers want;
- how this affects R&D; and
- manufacturing facilities.

Sources: Published sources; company website.

New markets, new products/services

Often described as diversification, this can take three forms:

- **Horizontal integration** Developing related or complementary activities, such as when mortgage lenders extend into the insurance business, using their knowledge of, and contact with, existing customers to offer them an additional service. The advantages include the ability to expand by using existing resources and skills, such as Kwik-Fit's use of its database of depot customers to create a motor insurance business.
- **Vertical integration** Moving either backwards or forwards into activities related to the organisation's products and services. A manufacturer might decide to make its own components rather than buy them from elsewhere. Equally, it could develop forward, for instance into distribution.
- **Unrelated diversification** Developing into new markets outside the present industry. Virgin has used its strong brand to create complementary activities in sectors as diverse as airlines, trains, insurance and soft drinks. The extension by some retailers into financial services is another example. It is a way to spread risk where demand patterns fluctuate at different stages of the economic cycle, and to maintain growth when existing markets become saturated.

Alternative development directions are not mutually exclusive: companies can follow several at the same time. Apple Inc. has a clear strategy to move away from being a computer manufacturer and into areas which would give their products a very wide appeal. One observer predicted, at the time of the iPad launch in 2010:

> Get on any train in five years' time, and people will be reading the newspaper (downloaded at home or automatically when they walk through Waterloo Station on the way home), books, watching TV, playing games (quite possibly with fellow passengers!) on their iPads.

Case study   HMV – the case continues   www.hmv.com

In late 2009 the company expanded its already small presence in the live music market by buying venue owner Mama Group for £46 million. Mama runs 11 concert venues in the UK including the Hammersmith Apollo, and has other interests including an artist management business. HMV chief executive said he was delighted with the deal as the two companies were already partners in the Mean Fiddler joint venture, which runs venues in London, Birmingham, Edinburgh and Aberdeen. Mr Fox believed the deal would enable HMV to accelerate the growth into live music.

In early 2010 the company reported that it expected the total live music market to be around a third larger than recorded music by 2012. The group is able to benefit from this channel change through its acquisition of Mama Group which, apart from its venues, is also a leading operator of live music festivals. It expects this new division to grow organically through driving utilisation, occupancy and related sales at the existing venues, and adding new venues at the rate of two to three per year.

In the festival market, new events will be added to the range. It also believes a significant opportunity exists in the market for tickets, and aims to sell 3 million tickets for Mama and third-party venues in 2012/13.

Sources: Company website.

> ### Case questions 8.6
>
> - Use the product/market matrix to classify the elements of HMV's current strategy.
> - How has the company chosen to deliver the next stage of the strategy?

> | 8.7 | **Making choices – deciding strategy at business unit level** |

At the business unit level, firms face a choice about how to compete. Porter (1980b, 1985) identified two types of competitive advantage: low cost or differentiation. From this he developed the idea that there are three generic strategies a firm can use to develop and maintain competitive advantage: cost leadership, differentiation and focus. Figure 8.9 shows these strategies. The horizontal axis shows the two bases of competitive advantage. Competitive scope, on the vertical axis, shows whether company's target market is broad or narrow in scope.

A **cost leadership strategy** is one in which a firm uses low price as the main competitive weapon.

Economies of scale are achieved when producing something in large quantities reduces the cost of each unit.

Cost leadership

Cost leadership is when a firm aims to compete on price rather than, say, advanced features or excellent customer service. They will typically sell a standard no-frills product and try to minimize costs. This requires **economies of scale** in production and close attention to efficiency and operating costs, although other sources of cost advantage, such as preferential access to raw materials, also help. However, a low cost base will not in itself bring competitive

Figure 8.9
Generic competitive strategies

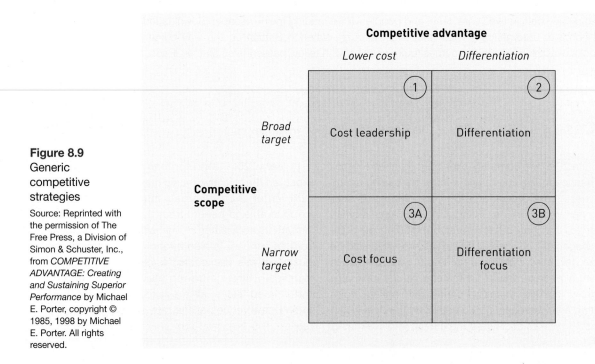

advantage – consumers must see that the product represents value for money. Retailers that have used this strategy include Wal-Mart (Asda in the UK), Argos and Superdrug; Dell Computers is another example, as is Ryanair (Chapter 1 case).

Key ideas   **The experience curve**

An important feature of cost leadership is the effect of the experience curve, in which the unit cost of manufacturing a product or delivering a service falls as experience increases. In the same way that a person learning to knit or play the piano improves with practice, so 'the unit cost of value added to a standard product declines by a constant percentage (typically 20–30 per cent) each time cumulative output doubles' (Grant, 2003). This allows firms to set initial low selling prices in the knowledge that margins will increase as output grows and costs fall. The rate of travel down the cost experience curve is a crucial aspect of staying ahead of the competition in an undifferentiated market and underlines the importance of market share – if high volumes are not sold, the cost advantage is lost. Examples of products where costs have fallen as volumes have risen are semiconductors, watches, cars and online reservations.

Differentiation

A **differentiation strategy** is seen when a company offers a service that is distinct from its competitors, and which customers value. It is 'something unique beyond simply offering a low price' (Porter, 1985) that allows firms to charge a high price or retain customer loyalty. Chatterjee (2005) shows the strategic benefits of identifying very clearly the outcomes that customers value, and Sharp and Dawes (2001) contrast companies' methods of differentiation:

> **Differentiation strategy** consists of offering a product or service that is perceived as unique or distinctive on a basis other than price.

- Nokia achieves differentiation through the individual design of its product;
- Sony achieves it by offering superior reliability, service and technology;
- BMW differentiates by stressing a distinctive product/service image;
- Coca-Cola differentiates by building a widely recognised brand.

The form of differentiation varies. In construction equipment durability, spare parts availability and service will feature in a differentiation strategy, while in cosmetics differentiation is based on images of sophistication, exclusivity and eternal youth. Cities compete by stressing differentiation in areas such as cultural facilities, available land or good transport links.

Focus

A **focus strategy** involves targeting a narrow market segment, either by consumer group (teenagers, over-60s, doctors) or geography. The two variants – cost focus and differentiation focus – are simply narrow applications of the broad strategies. Examples include:

> A **focus strategy** is when a company competes by targeting very specific segments of the market.

- Saga offers travel and insurance for those over 50;
- Rolls-Royce offers luxury transport to the wealthy;
- NFU Mutual offers insurance for farmers, Female Direct offers insurance for women;
- Cooperative Financial Services appeals to consumers with social concerns.

Management in Practice   **Strategic focus at Maersk** www.maersk.com

I think because of the size of our organisation now, our strategy is really targeted to focus on certain segments. One of the things we did this year was start a brand new service from Costa Rica to the UK, specifically bringing in bananas. That was a new service for us and provided a

different service for the customer, whereas before they've always been shipped in bulk vessels, and now we've containerised them. So we try and be very specific about the marketing. Once the customer is on board, then we have small teams of customer service people looking after specific customers, both here and elsewhere in the world.

Once we've locked them into the customer experience, what we want to do then is build a long term relationship with the customer, get to know the business, get to know where we can improve them. Not just on the service but also from a cost point of view, because obviously cost is very important in this market. So we like to go into partnerships. Some of the biggest retailers in the UK for instance we have long-term relationships with, one of those being Tesco, where we've been able to take a lot of costs out of their supply chain by giving them a personalised service by actually knowing their business.

Source: Interview with Brian Godsafe, Customer Services Manager.

Activity 8.5   Critical reflection on strategy

- Select two companies you are familiar with and, in each case, gather evidence to help you decide which generic strategy they are following.
- Then consider what features you would expect to see if the company decided to follow the opposite strategy.

Porter initially suggested that firms had to choose between cost leadership and differentiation. Many disagreed, observing how companies often appeared to follow both strategies simultaneously. By controlling costs better than competitors, companies can reinvest the savings in features that differentiate them. Porter (1994) later clarified his view:

> Every strategy must consider both relative cost and relative differentiation . . . a company cannot completely ignore quality and differentiation in the pursuit of cost advantage, and vice versa . . . Progress can be made against both types of advantage simultaneously. (p. 271)

However, he notes there are trade-offs between the two and that companies should 'maintain a clear commitment to superiority in one of them'.

Functional-level strategy

Business-level strategies need the support of suitable functional level strategies - Chapters 9, 11 and 12 give examples.

8.8   Making things happen – deciding how to deliver strategy

---

Organisations deliver their strategies internal development, acquisition, or alliance – or a combination of these.

Internal development

The organisation delivers the strategy by expanding or redeploying relevant resources that it has or can employ. This enables managers to retain control of all aspects of the development of new products or services, especially where the product has technologically advanced features. Microsoft develops its Windows operating system in-house.

Public sector organisations typically favour internal development, traditionally providing services through staff whom they employ directly. Changes in the wider political agenda have meant that these are often required to compete with external providers, while some, such as France Telecom, Deutsche Post or the UK Stationery Office, have been partially or wholly sold to private investors.

Merger and acquisition

One firm merging with, or acquiring, another allows rapid entry into new product or market areas and is a quick way to build market share. It is also used where the acquiring company can use the other company's products to offer new services or enter new markets. Companies such as Microsoft and Cisco Systems frequently buy small, entrepreneurial companies and incorporate their products within the acquiring company's range. A company might be taken over for its expertise in research or its knowledge of a local market. Financial motives are often strong, particularly where the merger leads to cost-cutting. When The Royal Bank of Scotland acquired NatWest it achieved major economies by merging the two companies' computer systems. Other mergers extend the range of activities. Vodafone made several large acquisitions in its quest to become the world's largest mobile phone company.

Mergers and acquisitions frequently fail, destroying rather than adding value. When Sir Roy Gardner took over as chairman of Compass (a UK catering company) at which profits and the share price had fallen rapidly, he was critical of the previous management:

> (They) concentrated far too much on growing the business through acquisition. They should have stopped and made sure (that) what they had acquired delivered the expected results. Compass was being run by its divisional mangers, which resulted in a total lack of consistency. (*Financial Times*, 19 January 2007, p. 19)

Joint developments and alliances

Organisations sometimes turn to partners to co-operate in developing products or services. Arrangements vary from highly formal contractual relationships to looser forms of co-operation, but there are usually advantages to be gained by both parties. One attraction of this method is that it limits risk. UK construction firm John Laing has a joint venture with the Commonwealth Bank of Australia to invest in UK hospital and European road projects: rather than borrow funds for a project, Laing shares the risk (and the reward) with the bank. HMV acquired a 50 per cent equity stake in 7digital in September 2009, as this will enable it to use that company's technological expertise to enhance its own digital offers in entertainment and e-books.

| Management in practice | GSK's drug development strategy www.gsk.com |

Half of the new drug discovery projects at GlaxoSmithKline may be undertaken by external partners by the turn of the decade as part of a radical overhaul designed to improve the pipeline of new drugs at the group. The research and development will be co-ordinated by GSK's Centre of Excellence for External Drug Discovery (CEEDD) which the company created in 2005 to boost innovation. The company's research director estimated that between one-quarter to one-third of GSK's existing research pipeline of new drugs already involved work conducted with external partners and a growing role would be played by the CEEDD, managing a 'virtual' portfolio of research run by such companies:

In the future we are going to have many more external projects.

Source: *Financial Times*, 31 May 2006, p. 22.

A second reason for JVs is to learn about new technologies or markets. Alliances also arise where governments want to keep sensitive sectors, such as aerospace, defence and aviation, under national control. Airbus, which competes with Boeing in aircraft manufacture, was originally a JV between French, German, British and Spanish manufacturers. Alliances, such as the Star Alliance led by United Airlines of the United States and Lufthansa of Germany, are also common in the airline industry, where companies share revenues and costs over certain routes. As governments often prevent foreign ownership, such alliances avoid that barrier.

Other forms of joint development include franchising (common in many retailing activities – Ikea uses this method), licensing and long-term collaboration between manufacturers and their suppliers.

Alliances and partnership working have also become commonplace in the public sector. In many cities alliances or partnerships have been created between major public bodies, business and community interests. Their main purpose is to foster a coherent approach to planning and delivering services. Public bodies often act as service commissioners rather than as direct providers, developing partnerships with organisations to deliver services on their behalf.

Activity 8.6   Critical reflection on delivering strategy

- Select two companies you are familiar with, and in each case gather evidence to help you decide which of the available options (or a combination) they have chosen to deliver their strategy.
- What are the advantages of the route they have chosen compared to the alternatives?
- Compare your evidence with other students on your course and identify any common themes.

8.9   Making revisions – implementing and evaluating

Implementation turns strategy into action, moving from corporate to operational levels. Many strategies fail to be implemented, or fail to achieve as much as management expected. A common mistake is to assume that formulating a strategy will lead to painless implementation. Sometimes there is an 'implementation deficit', when strategies are not implemented at all, or are only partially successful. A common reason for this is that while formulating strategy may appear to be a rational process, it is often a political one. Those who were content with the earlier strategy may oppose the new one if it affects their status, power or career prospects. Chapter 13 shows how implementing change is a complex, often conflicting process.

Evaluate results

Managers, shareholders (current and potential) and financial analysts routinely compare a company's performance with its published plans. Only by tracking results can these and other interested parties decide if performance is in line with expectations or if the company needs to take some corrective action. Many targets focus on financial and other quantitative aspects of performance, such as sales, operating costs and profit.

Although monitoring is shown as the last stage in the strategy model, it is not the end of the process. This is continuous as organisations adjust to changes in their business environment. Regular monitoring alerts management to the possibility that targets might not be achieved and that operational adjustments are needed. Equally, and in conjunction with continuous scanning of the external environment, performance monitoring can prompt wider changes to the organisation's corporate and competitive strategies.

Donald Sull (2007) advises that in any discussions to revise strategy, people should treat actions as experiments:

> they should analyse what's happened and use the results to revise their assumptions, priorities and promises. As such, the appropriate time to have such conversations is after the team has reached a significant milestone in making things happen . . . Managers must acknowledge that that their mental models are merely simplified maps of complex terrain based on provisional knowledge that is subject to revision in the light of new information (pp. 36–37)

8.10   Integrating themes

Sustainable performance

If managers are to enhance the sustainability of their activities, they will need to ensure that it becomes part of their strategic discussions. Chapter 5 contrasted the 'Friedmanite' and 'stakeholder' perspectives: the former arguing that the business leaders should focus on the financial interests of shareholders, while the latter believe that managers have responsibilities to a wider constituency. Claims for and against the idea that corporations should act responsibly often reflect deeply-held moral and ethical principles, and this makes it a challenge to relate them to a company's strategic decisions.

A perspective that can help to clarify the issue was suggested by Vogel (2005), who concludes that while advocates of corporate responsibility (in this context, sustainability) are genuinely motivated by a commitment to social goals, it is only sustainable if 'virtue pays off'. Responsible action is both made possible and constrained by market forces.

Virtuous behaviour can make business sense for some firms in some areas in some circumstances, but does not in itself ensure commercial success. Companies that base their strategy on acting responsibly may be commercially successful, but equally they may fail – responsible behaviour carries the same risks as any other kind of business behaviour. While some consumers or investors will give their business to companies that appear to be acting responsibly, others will not. Some customers place a higher priority on price, appearance or any other feature than they do on whether goods are produced and delivered in a sustainable way. As Vogel (2005) observes:

> There *is* a place in the market economy for responsible firms. But there is also a large place for their less responsible competitors. (p. 3)

While some companies can benefit from a strategy based on acting responsibly, market forces alone cannot prevent others from having a less responsible strategy, and profiting from doing so. Hawken *et al.* (1999) and Senge *et al.* (2008) provide abundant evidence that sustainable performance can be both good for the planet and good for profits.

Governance and control

Pye (2002) sees a close link between what she terms the process of governing and strategising. Having conducted long-term research with the boards of several large companies she notes:

i. in 1987–89, no one talked of corporate governance, whereas now most contributors raise this subject of their own volition, implying greater awareness of and sensitivity to such issues; and

ii. relationships with major shareholders have changed considerably across the decade and directors now see accounting for their *strategic direction* as crucial in this context. (p. 154, emphasis added)

She distinguished between governance and governing:

> Corporate governance is often identified through indicators such as board composition, committee structure, executive compensation schemes, and risk assessment procedures etc, which offer a snapshot view of governance practice, rather than the dynamic process of governing. To explore governing, i.e. how governance is enacted, means unraveling the complex network of relationships amongst [the board] *as well as* relationships with 'outsiders' who observe [the board's] governance. (p. 156)

She refers to strategising as the process by which directors go about deciding the strategic direction of the organisation, although this is primarily shaped by the executive directors. She found that almost all directors agreed that what is crucial is not so much the words on paper as the process of dialogue and debate by which those words are created – the strategising process is more important than the final document.

Internationalisation

As the business world becomes ever more international, companies inevitably face difficult strategic choices about the extent to which they develop an international presence, and the way in which they develop their international strategy. The nature of the challenge is shown by the fact that, while many companies have done very well from international expansions, many overseas ventures fail, destroying value rather than creating it.

Chapter 4 outlines the nature of the challenges faced as companies respond to what they perceive to be international opportunities. They need, for example, to deal with complex structural and logistical issues when products are made and sold in several countries, ensure that there are adequate links between research, marketing and production to speed the introduction of new products, and facilitate the rapid transfer of knowledge and ideas between the national components of the business. These are complex enough issues in themselves, but the extra dimension is that solutions that work in one national context may not work as well in another. Differences in national culture mean that people will respond in perhaps unexpected ways to strategies and plans, especially if these are perceived in some way to be inconsistent with the local culture (as the examples cited in Chapter 4 testify).

The content of an international strategy will be shaped by the process of its production, and the extent to which different players in the global enterprise take part in it.

Summary

1 **Explain the significance of managing strategy and show how the issues vary between sectors**

   - Strategy is about the survival of the enterprise; the strategy process sets an overall direction with information about the external environment and internal capabilities. Defining the purposes of the organisation helps to guide the choice and implementation of strategy.

2 **Compare planning, learning and political perspectives on the strategy process**

   - The planning approach is appropriate in stable and predictable environments; while the emergent approach more accurately describes the process in volatile environments, since strategy rarely unfolds as intended in complex, changing and ambiguous situations. A political perspective may be a more accurate way of representing the process when it involves the interests of powerful stakeholders. It is rarely an objectively rational activity, implying that strategy models are not prescriptive but rather frameworks to guide managers.

3 Summarise evidence on how managers develop strategies

- The evidence is accumulating that companies in turbulent environments follow a strategy process that is relatively informal, with shorter planning meetings, and greater responsibility placed on line managers to develop strategy rather than on specialist planners.
- Formulating strategy and designing the organisation appear to be done as closely linked practical activities.
- Sull uses the 'strategy loop' to describe how managers continually develop and renew their strategy.

4 Explain the tools for external and internal analysis during work on strategy

- External analysis can use Porter's five forces model and the PESTEL framework to identify relevant factors.
- Internally, managers can use the value chain to analyse their current organisation.
- The two sets of information can be combined in a SWOT diagram.

5 Use the product/market matrix to compare corporate level strategies

- Strategy can focus on existing or new products, and existing or new markets. This gives four broad directions, with options in each, such as market penetration, product development, market development or diversification.

6 Use the concept of generic strategies to compare business level strategies

- Key strategic choices are those of cost leader, differentiation or a focus on a narrow segment of the market.

7 Give examples of alternative methods of delivering a strategy

- Strategy can be delivered by internal (sometimes called organic) development by rearranging the way resources are deployed. Alternatives include acquiring or merging with another company, or by forming alliances and joint ventures.

8 Show how ideas from the chapter add to your understanding of the integrating themes

- Sustainable performance in the environmental sense will only be sustainable in the economic sense if it is part of the organisation's strategy: i.e., that it makes business sense as well as environmental sense. The sources cited provide many examples of company's which have done this.
- Pye (2002) found that directors were more likely to be taking responsibility for strategic direction of the business as well as for their narrower governance responsibilities – emphasising the benefits of the process as much as of the final outcomes.
- International expansion and diversification strategies often fail, probably when managers underestimate the complexity of overseas operations.

Review questions

1 Why do managers develop strategies for their organisation?

2 How does the planning view of strategy differ from the learning and political views respectively?

3 Describe the main features of the ways in which recent research suggests managers develop strategy.

4 Draw Sull's strategy loop and explain each of the elements.

5 Discuss with a manager from an organisation how his/her organisation developed its present strategy. Compare this practice with the ideas in this chapter. What conclusions do you draw?

6 What are the main steps to take in analysing the organisation's environment? Why is it necessary to do this?

7   Describe each stage in value chain analysis and illustrate each one with an example. Why is the model useful to management?

8   The chapter describes three generic strategies that organisations can follow. Give examples of three companies each following one of these strategies.

9   Give examples of company strategies corresponding to each box in the product/market matrix.

10 What are the main ways of delivering strategy?

11 Summarise an idea from the chapter that adds to your understanding of the integrating themes.

Concluding critical reflection

Think about the way your company, or one with which you are familiar, approaches issues of strategy. Review the material in the chapter, and perhaps visit some of the websites identified. Then make notes on the following questions:

- What examples of the issues discussed in this chapter are currently relevant to your company – such as whether to follow a differentiation or focus strategy, or the balance between planning and learning?

- In responding to these issues, what **assumptions** about the strategy process appear to have guided what people have done? To what extent do these seem to fit the environmental forces as you see them? Do they appear to stress the planning or the learning perspectives on strategy?

- What factors such as the history or current **context** of the company appear to have influenced the prevailing view? Is the history of the company constraining attempts to move in new directions? How well are stakeholders served by the present strategy? How would they benefit from a significantly different one?

- Have people put forward **alternative** strategies, or alternative ways of developing strategy, based on evidence about other companies? If you could find such evidence, how may it affect company practice?

- What limitations can you see in any of the ideas presented here? For example, does Porter's value chain adequately capture the variable most relevant in your business, or are there other features you would include? What limitations are there in the way strategy is formed in an organisation with which you are familiar?

Further reading

Cummings, S. and Angwin, D. (2004), 'The future shape of strategy: Lemmings or chimera?' Academy of Management Executive, vol. 18, no. 2, pp. 21–36.

> Based on research among executives in Europe and Australasia, this article develops an approach to strategy formulation that takes account of the current need to manage multiple customer groups in complex environments.

Greenley, G.E. (1986), 'Does strategic planning improve company performance?', *Long Range Planning*, vol. 19, no. 2, pp. 101–109.

> This shows the benefits of a sceptical view towards claims about the planning–performance link, and is also a good example of a systematic literature analysis.

Mintzberg, H., Ahlstrand, B. and Lampel J. (1998), *Strategy Safari*, Prentice Hall Europe, Hemel Hempstead.

> Excellent discussion of the process of strategy making from various academic and practical perspectives.

Moore, J.I. (2001), *Writers on Strategy and Strategic Management* (2nd edn), Penguin, London.

> Summarises the work of the major contributors to the fields of strategy and strategic management – Part 1 contains a useful overview of the work of the 'movers and shakers', including Ansoff, Porter and Mintzberg.

Weblinks

These websites have appeared in the chapter:

www.hmv.com
www.MySpace.com
www.unilever.com
www.pg.com
www.nestle.com
www.ikea.com
www.motorola.com
www.google.com
www.rspb.org.uk
www.cancerresearch.org
www.nokia.com
www.abb.com

Visit two of the business sites in the list, or any other company that interests you, and navigate to the pages dealing with news or investor relations.

- What are the main strategic issues they seem to be facing?
- What information can you find about their policies?

 **www** For video case studies, audio summaries, flashcards, exercises and annotated weblinks related to this chapter, visit **www.pearsoned.co.uk/mymanagementlab**

CHAPTER 9
MANAGING MARKETING

Aims

To explain how marketing can add value to resources, and to introduce some marketing techniques.

Objectives

By the end of your work on this chapter you should be able to outline the concepts below in your own terms and:

1 Define marketing and the role it plays in managing organisations of all kinds

2 Explain the importance of understanding customers and markets, and the sources of marketing information

3 Illustrate the practices of segmenting markets and targeting customer groups

4 Explain the meaning and significance of customer relationship management

5 Compare a marketing orientation with other orientations and explain its significance

6 Describe the components of the marketing mix

7 Explain the stages of the product life cycle

8 Show how ideas from the chapter add to your understanding of the integrating themes

Key terms

This chapter introduces the following ideas:

marketing	target market
customers	market offering
customer satisfaction	exchange
needs	transaction
wants	customer relationship
demands	management (CRM)
marketing information system	marketing orientation
marketing intelligence	customer-centred organisation
marketing environment	marketing mix
market segmentation	product lifecycle

Each is a term defined within the text, as well as in the Glossary at the end of the book.

Case study   Manchester United FC www.manutd.com

With over 50 million fans across the globe, Manchester United Football Club (MU) is one of the best-known soccer clubs. Founded in 1878, it rose to prominence in the early 1950s. Since then, the club has never been out of the sports headlines, hiring a series of almost legendary managers (including Sir Matt Busby and, since 1986, Sir Alex Ferguson) and buying or developing world-recognised players (including David Beckham, Ruud van Nistelrooy and Wayne Rooney).

In May 2005 the club was taken over in a £790 million pound bid by American sports tycoon Malcolm Glazer in a deal that was heavily financed by debt. *Forbes* magazine ranked it in 2009 as the world's wealthiest club, valuing it $1,870 million, well ahead of nearest rivals Real Madrid and Arsenal. In early 2010 it issued bonds worth £500 (paying interest at 9 per cent), mainly to repay loans from international banks.

The 2009 operating income was £516 million, generated from a wide range of football-related businesses (gate and TV revenues, sports clothes, etc.) and brand-related activities (MUTV, mobiles, travel and finance). MU is only a part of the worldwide operations. The holding company (Manchester United plc) owns MU, Manchester United Catering (Agency Company) and Manchester United Interactive. MUTV, the club's official channel, is a joint venture between Manchester United plc, Granada, and BSkyB.

The Club's ambition is to be the most successful team in football. Its business strategy is to do this by having the football and commercial operations work hand-in-hand, both in current and new domestic markets, and in the potential markets represented by the Club's global fan base, especially Asia. The marketing strategy is built on maintaining success on the field and leveraging global brand awareness through new products and partnered services designed to appeal to MU's worldwide fans. A substantial partner is Nike, whose development and marketing channels are used to generate new value from the MU trademarks (for example, replica kits) by supplying the millions of MU fans in the UK and Asia.

PA Photos:Kin Cheung/AP.

MU attempts to control and develop its own routes to market for media rights (for example, MUTV), thereby exploiting the Club's own performance and reputation rather than relying on the collective appeal of competition football. The management believes this enhances the ability to deliver branded services to customers anywhere in the world. They rely strongly on IT-based CRM (customer relationship management) technology to convert fans to customers.

Sources: Based on material from Butterworth Heinemann Case 0181, *Manchester United and British Soccer: Beautiful game, brutal industry;* 'Can football be saved?'; other published material.

Case questions 9.1

● Consider the marketing implications of MU's activities. What is MU offering to customers?

● What groups would MU see as competitors? Are they simply other successful football clubs?

● What distinctive challenges do you think may arise in marketing a football club?

9.1 Introduction

Manchester United (MU) depends on good marketing to ensure the continued loyalty and support of its customers – who all seek different things. An MU football fan might buy a season ticket to fulfil a psychological need to be part of a group with a common purpose: someone with no interest in football might use an MU mobile phone because he/she trusts the product, based on the MU reputation. Someone who buys a replica MU jersey is making a statement about his/her personality, and is not sensitive to price: he/she pays up to £40 for something that costs less than £2 to supply.

How should MU management manage the brand in these often unrelated markets? How best to understand the needs of different customers, so as to offer them profitable goods and services? How to manage relationships with customers to encourage long-term loyalty – even if the club does badly on the field? What can it do in the way it presents its goods and services to make as much revenue from them as it can?

All organisations face the challenge of understanding what customers want, and ensuring that they can meet those expectations. Managers of successful firms often attribute their success to placing marketing at the heart of their strategy. Ikea, the Swedish furniture retailer,

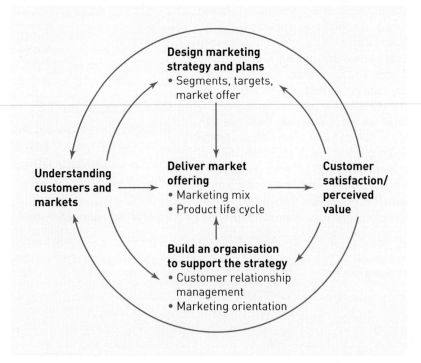

Figure 9.1
The marketing management process

has found and refined a formula that appeals to its target market, growing in 40 years from a single store to a business with over 300 stores in 38 countries. Virgin has also grown from a single store to become a global brand – by offering a wide range of products and services. Successful not-for-profit organisations such as the Eden Project demonstrate the benefits of understanding and communicating with a market. All need to give value for money, by understanding and meeting supporters' needs.

This chapter clarifies 'marketing' and shows how it can add value to resources. It explains how marketers try to understand customers' needs, in order to decide which segments of a market to target. Doing so effectively depends on developing close customer relations, building a marketing orientation and using specific marketing capabilities – known as the 'marketing mix'. Figure 9.1 gives an overview of the tasks of managing marketing.

9.2 What is marketing?

We are all familiar with the techniques of advertising and selling, when companies:

- distribute brochures;
- offer promotional prices;
- sponsor television programmes;
- persuade celebrities to endorse their products or services; or
- send advertisements to mobiles.

These selling techniques are only the most visible part of a wider **marketing** process, through which organisations aim to identify and satisfy customer needs in a way that brings value to both parties. This depends on skills in researching customers, designing products, setting prices, communicating with potential customers, ensuring delivery and evaluating customer reaction. These diverse activities bring marketing staff into contact with most parts of their organisation.

> **Marketing** is the process by which organisations create value for customers in order to receive value from them in return.

The underlying idea is that if managers understand what current and potential **customers** value, they find it easier to develop products that ensure **customer satisfaction**. In commercial businesses this means that customers are willing to pay a price that earns the company a profit. In public or not-for-profit organisations it means they are willing to make donations, use the service or otherwise support it. Managers can then secure the resources they need to maintain and grow the enterprise. Those who neglect marketing will not understand their customers, will not satisfy them and will have trouble securing resources. Organisations fail when staff do what they prefer, not what customers or service-users expect. Kotler *et al.* (2008) describe marketing as:

> **Customers** are individuals, households, organisations, institutions, resellers and governments that purchase products from other organisations.

> **Customer satisfaction** is the extent a customer perceives that a product matches their expectations.

> the homework which managers undertake to assess needs, measure their extent and intensity and determine whether a profitable opportunity exits. Marketing continues throughout the product's life, trying to find new customers and keep current customers by improving product appeal and performance, learning from product sales results and managing repeat performance. (pp. 6–7)

Peter Drucker (1999) places the activity even more firmly at the centre of business:

> Because the purpose of business is to create and keep customers, it has only two central functions – marketing and innovation. The basic function of marketing is to attract and retain customers at a profit.

While many organisations have a designated 'Marketing Department', people throughout the enterprise can contribute by, for example, telling marketing staff what customers think of the product, or what competitors are doing. The more that employees understand what customers want, and the more the organisation's systems and processes help staff to meet those expectations, the more they will satisfy them. As David Packard, co-founder of Hewlett-Packard, said:

> Marketing is too important to be left to the marketing department, i.e. the entire organisation should be marketing the company, from the company receptionist as 'Director of First Impressions' to the chief executive as 'Director of Shareholder Interests'.

Key ideas   **Consumer marketing and organisational (B2B) marketing**

There are two categories of marketing: (a) consumer marketing, which concerns creating and delivering products to satisfy consumers; and (b) industrial or business-to-business (B2B) marketing, which aims to satisfy the needs of other businesses and organisations, including national and local government. Companies such as Rio Tinto Zinc (mining), Maersk (freight shipping) or PricewaterhouseCoopers (consultancy services) are solely engaged in B2B marketing. The underlying concepts are similar, but the buying behaviour of professional purchasing staff is quite different from the individual consumer – and so requires a different marketing approach.

This chapter is mainly concerned with consumer marketing.

Managers in all types of organisations can use marketing to increase the value they offer. Local authority services such as libraries, museums or concert halls routinely survey samples of actual and potential users to evaluate their satisfaction with existing services. They also assess likely demand for new ones, before they incur the expense of providing them.

Management in practice   **Marketing in the voluntary sector**

Many staff and volunteers in charities are uncomfortable with the idea that they are in marketing – preferring to see themselves as helpers or carers. Yet

> – donors, local authorities, opinion formers, the media, all have the choice of whether or not to support a charity . . . They make up the markets within which the charity operates. Without knowledge and understanding of those markets, the charity . . . will fail . . . By knowing themselves and their mission, and by knowing the markets they . . . serve or work in, charities can match their activities to external needs and make sure that they achieve as much as possible for their beneficiaries. (Keaveney and Kaufmann, 2001, p. 2)

Source: Keaveney and Kaufmann (2001).

9.3   Understanding customers and markets

Marketing begins with trying to understand customers and what influence them.

Needs, wants and demands

Needs are states of felt deprivation, reflecting biological and social influences.

Psychologists have developed theories of human **needs** – states of felt deprivation – that people try to satisfy. Chapter 15 presents several such theories (Maslow, 1970; McClelland, 1961) which identify needs ranging from basic necessities to those that are intangible: knowledge, achievement or public image. They also show that their strength varies between people – some are content to satisfy basic needs, while some find that once they have satisfied their

Figure 9.2
Influences on buyer behaviour

basic needs they seek opportunities to satisfy other needs – such as physical or intellectual challenge.

Wants are the form which human needs take, as they are shaped by someone's personality and the culture in which they live (Hofstede and Hofstede, 2005). Everyone needs food, but satisfy that need in many ways – which they express by describing objects or experiences that will satisfy their need.

People have limited resources, so needs and wants only become relevant to a supplier when the person can pay – when a want becomes a **demand**. Given their needs, wants and re-sources, people demand products and services they believe will satisfy them. The more effort an enterprise makes to understand these, the better it will satisfy them. This involves investing in research and development to create an attractive market offering.

Internal and external factors influence consumers' willingness to pay the expected price for a product – which Figure 9.2 illustrates and Table 9.1 summarises. Social factors clearly

Wants are the form which human needs take as they are shaped by local culture and individual personality.

Demands are human wants backed by the ability to buy.

Table 9.1 Influences on buying behaviour

Influence	Description	How marketers use this influence
Internal influences **Perception**	How people collect and interpret information	Design promotional material so that the images, colours and words attract the attention of intended consumers
Motivation	Internal forces that shape purchasing decisions to satisfy need	Design products to meet needs. Insurers remind people of dangers against which a policy will protect
Attitudes	Opinions and points of view that people have of other people and institutions	Design products to conform. Increasing stress on environmental benefits of products and services
Learning	How people learn affects what they know about a product, and hence their purchasing decisions	Associate product with unique colours or images (Coca-Cola with red and white)
External influences **Reference groups**	Other people with whom the consumer identifies	Marketers establish the reference groups of their consumers, and allude to them in promotions, e.g. sponsoring athletes in return for product endorsement
Culture	The culture to which a consumer belongs affects their values and behaviour	Subcultures associated with music or cars influence buying behaviour – which marketers use in positioning products for those markets
Social class	People identify with a class based on income, education or locality.	Purchase decisions reaffirm class affinities or aspirations. Marketers design promotional material to suit

shape demand for mobile phones – teenagers display them as a sign of social standing, so the appearance and functions of the device become status symbols – which marketers try to satisfy. To track how factors in the table affect attitudes to their products, marketers use marketing information systems.

Activity 9.2	**What influenced you to buy?**

Identify a significant purchase you have made: either a physical product or a service.

- Which, if any, of the factors in Table 9.1 affected your decision? Write down what you find.
- Can you identify any factors which influenced your decision that are not in the list?
- Compare your lists with other students, and try to identify which factors appear most frequently as influences on your purchases. Do they vary between goods and services?

Marketing information systems

A **marketing information system** is the systematic process for the collection, analysis and distribution of marketing information.

Marketing managers need a **marketing information system** – clear processes to collect and analyse information about the marketing environment – and to distribute it through the organisation. Figure 9.3 details the typical components. A marketing information system contains internal and external sources of data, and mechanisms to analyse and interpret the data so that marketing staff can use the information. It includes information about customers and the market as a whole, for example its size, rate of growth and the main competitors.

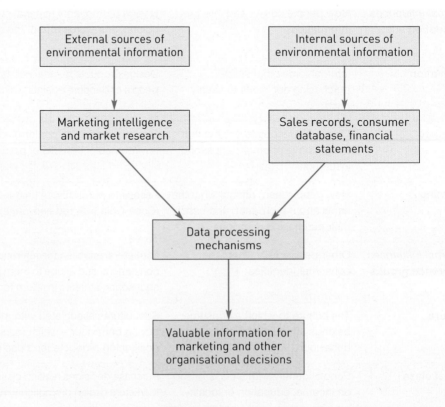

Figure 9.3
A marketing information system

Table 9.2 Sources of marketing information

Source	Description and examples
Internal records	Records of sales, costs, customer transactions, demographics, buyer behaviour, customer satisfaction, quality trends, reports from the sales force
Marketing intelligence	Data on micro- and macro-environments. For example, who are the main competitors, potential new entrants and substitute products? What economic and social changes are likely to affect demand; what political or legislative changes that may affect the market? Data is usually based on secondary sources – websites, newspapers, trade associations and industry reports. Informal sources – staff or customers – are valuable guides to competitors or market trends
Market research	Involves five stages: 1 Defining the problem and research objectives (how many people with X income, living in place Y are aware of product Z?) 2 Developing hypotheses (is awareness higher or lower in area B where the product has been advertised than in C?) 3 Developing the research plan to collect data to refute or confirm hypotheses 4 Implementing the research plan – collecting and analysing the data 5 Interpreting and reporting the findings

Management in practice   Market information from the Tesco Clubcard
www.tesco.com

The Tesco Clubcard scheme (Part 6 Case) has over 11 million active holders. Shoppers join the scheme by completing a simple form with some personal information about their age and where they live. Their purchases earn vouchers based on the amount they spend. Every purchase they make at Tesco is electronically recorded, and the data analysed to identify their shopping preferences. This is then used to design a package of special offers which are most likely to appeal to that customer, based on an analysis of what they have bought. These offers are mailed to customers with their quarterly vouchers, and each mailing brings a large increase in business.

The company also analyses the data to identify the kind of people the Clubcard holders are – whether they have a new baby, young children, whether they like cooking, and so on. Each product is also ascribed a set of attributes – expensive or cheap? An ethnic recipe or a traditional dish? Tesco own-label or an upmarket brand? The information on customers, shopping habits and product attributes is used to support all aspects of the business – identifying possible gaps in the product range, assessing the effect of promotional offers, noting variations in taste in different parts of the country.

Source: Part 6 case.

Figure 9.4 shows the steps in completing a market research project.

As well as gathering data about a specific product or service, marketers also gather **marketing intelligence** about competitors and other developments in the wider marketing environment.

Marketing intelligence is information about developments in the marketing environment.

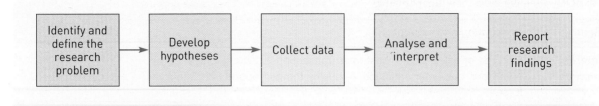

Figure 9.4 Market research process

Identifying trends in the marketing environment

The **marketing environment** consists of the actors and forces outside marketing that affect the marketing manager's ability to develop and maintain successful relationships with its target consumers.

In order to take these decisions, managers need information about consumer demands, competitor strategies and changes in the **marketing environment** that are likely to impact upon consumer demands. This part of the organisation's environment presented in Chapter 3, Figure 3.1, partially repeated as Figure 9.5, shows the micro- and macro-environments. The competitive (micro-) environment is that part of an organisation's marketing environment within which it operates. Each organisation has a unique micro-environment, including suppliers, distributors, customers and competitors. All organisations have some influence over their competitive environment and the likely impact this will have upon their marketing activities. Marketers have been quick to see that young people are big users of mobiles, which offer a possible way of advertising to young consumers who are hard to reach by traditional means such as TV or direct mail.

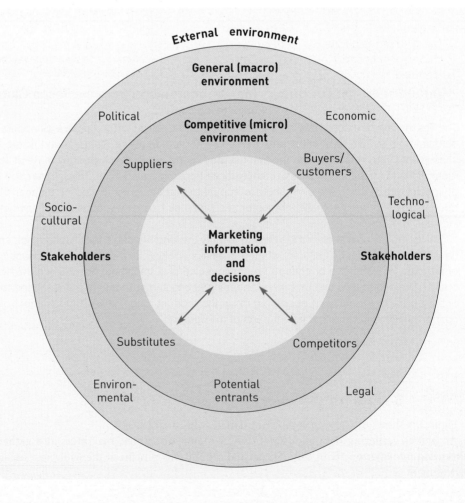

Figure 9.5
The marketing environment

The general, or macro component of an organisation's marketing environment is more remote and will be similar for all those in the same industry. Organisations have little direct influence over their macro-environment, which consists of the PESTEL factors shown in Figure 9.5

Activity 9.3 Identifying the marketing environment

- Use Figure 9.5 to identify, for each of these organisations, those parts of their micro- and macro-environments that have most impact upon their marketing activities: Ryanair, the BBC, Innocent Drinks.
- How have they responded to these environmental influences?

Such frameworks can help managers identify opportunities and threats for the organisation from external changes – for an example of a company that missed a trend, see the Management Practice featuring Motorola in Chapter 8 (page 236).

Case study Manchester United – the case continues – what makes people buy?

A football game is not a tangible product. A regular and significant intangible purchase by a Manchester United football fan is the £27–£49 ticket to see a home game at Old Trafford or £10 on a pay-per-view TV basis. There is no guarantee of satisfaction and no exchange or refund. No promotional advertising is needed and the ticket demand is relatively 'inelastic', i.e. prices can increase without sales volumes necessarily falling.

An important question for a marketing manager is 'how does a fan reach the decision to buy this experience and how is value measured?'. The buyer behaviour framework described above can help: domestic UK fans are typically lifelong, acquiring perceptions of and loyalty to the Club at school or in the home. Influencers would include peers and older pupils. Although football was formerly male-dominated, young females are an increasing part of the market. Most fans travel in groups of two or more, so this is a segment attribute that can be managed in raising awareness and favourability. Publicity photos can depict fans celebrating or commiserating together and the whole emphasis of attending a football match can be positioned away from 'did we win?' to 'did we have a good time?'. This approach is one of MU's declared marketing strategies.

Case questions 9.2

- What customer demands were MU seeking to satisfy at the time of the case study?
- What other demands does the business have to satisfy?
- What marketing tools are mentioned in the case?

Table 9.1 shows the factors that influence individual purchasing decisions: to the extent that several individuals share these influences, marketers identify distinct segments within a population, rather than seeing a market as homogenous.

9.4 Segments, targets and the market offer

Organisations use **market segmentation** to satisfy the needs of different people within a market. Airlines offer first, business, economy or budget flights: while the basic service attribute (transport from A to B) is the same for all, the total offering is not: those in

Market segmentation is the process of dividing markets comprising the heterogeneous needs of many consumers into segments comprising the homogeneous needs of smaller groups.

first will receive superior service at all stages of their journey. Universities offer degrees by full-time, part-time and distance learning study. Athletic shoe companies offer shoes specifically for running, aerobics, tennis and squash, as well as 'cross' trainers for the needs of all these sports.

Customers are more likely to respond positively to offerings that appeal to the needs of their particular segment of the market, from product design through to promotion and advertising. The personal computer market consists of all those who need a PC, but contains distinct segments of people with similar needs: travellers needing a laptop; parents wanting a cheap machine for their children; or corporate customers requiring a large number of standard machines.

Key ideas   **Young consumers keep spending**

Advertising agency JWT asked 18- to 29-year-olds in several countries which items they would never cut back on, no matter how bad their finances. Brits ranked 'buying new clothes' as fourth on the list – higher than any other country in the poll. Above that, they prioritised the internet, mobile phones and satellite television. While young people in the US also said they could not do without home entertainment, they ranked alcohol consumption as the fifth most cherished area of spending. Brits put boozing at only 16 on their list. Half of the Brazilians said paying for college was their most important outgoing.

A separate survey conducted by a retailer in May 2009 found that 70 per cent of customers between 18 and 35 said they were spending the same amount or more on clothes and eating out, despite the recession:

Slaves to fashion and free of financial commitments, young people have kept spending during the economic downturn, while others have cut back. As a result, retailers geared towards the youth market – particularly clothing chains – have been basking in their good fortune. (p. 14)

Source: *Financial Times*, 9 July 2009.

Segmenting depends on identifying variables that distinguish consumers with similar needs:

- **Demography** The easiest way to segment a consumer market is by using demographic variables such as age, gender and education level. Magazine companies use gender and age to ensure that within their portfolio they have titles suitable for females, males and those of different ages. Local authorities use information on age and family structures to help decide the distribution of facilities in their area.
- **Geography** This segment markets by country or region, enabling multinational companies to 'think global but act local'. While maintaining uniform global standards of service and a common promotional theme, they vary the product to suit local tastes.
- **Socioeconomic** This segments markets by variables such as income, social class and lifestyle. Lifestyle segmentation means identifying groups of consumers that share similar values about the ways in which they wish to live.

When segmenting consumer markets, marketers typically use a mix of these variables to provide an accurate profile of distinct groups. *Marie Claire* uses age, gender, education, lifestyle and social class to attract a readership of educated, independently minded women between the ages of 25 and 35, in income brackets ABC1. Pubs aim for particular segments: sophisticated city centre, food-led, urban community, country – each aiming to meet the needs of different people.

Management in practice   **The target market for Hiscox** www.hiscox.com

The company provides insurance services to wealthy individuals and small professional service businesses. The Director of Marketing explained their strategy:

The strategy is to offer a high quality of product and service, and ultimately an ethos that we promise to pay and honour the intent of an insurance policy rather than the letter of the law. So we don't seek to use the small clauses on page 33, 3a to wiggle out of paying claims.

The critical thing is to understand our target markets. We are absolutely focused on 10 per cent of the UK audience; understanding their needs and delivering products and service tailored to them. So we're not trying to be generalists. That really reflects in the product offering and the service level is really tailored to high net worth individuals and we do believe that they are prepared to pay more for products and services that reflect their needs, and that increased premium will reflect in acceptable returns for our business and the shareholder while still offering the consumer good value.

Source: Extracts from an interview with Glen Caton, Marketing Director.

Having segmented a market using these variables, marketers have to decide which to select as their **target market**, usually based on the criteria that it:

- contains demands they can satisfy;
- is large enough to provide a financial return;
- is likely to grow.

> A **target market** is the segment of the market selected by the organisation as the focus of its activities.

The market offer – products, services and experiences

Information about customers' wants and demands helps companies to develop a **market offering:** a combination of products, services and experiences that they hope will satisfy their customers. While the features of a physical product are part of the value for the customer, service and experience also affect this: how staff treat the customer, their ability to answer questions and the quality of after-sales service. The experience of using the product also matters – both the thing itself (good to use?), and how others react (does it boost your image?). Effective marketers look beyond the basic attributes of their products, aiming to create brands that mean something significant for their customers. They are then willing to pay a higher price.

> A **market offering** is the combination of products, services, information or experiences that an enterprise offers to a market to satisfy a need or want.

9.5   Customer relationship management

People aim to satisfy needs and wants through **exchange** – the act of obtaining a desired object from someone by offering something in return – a process that is at the core of many human activities, including marketing. It only happens if both parties can offer something of value to the other, and if they can communicate this. If both agree, this leads to a **transaction** in which they exchange things of value at a specified time and place. Countless transactions take place without further contact between buyer and seller – such as buying a newspaper or petrol during a journey. Some marketers are content if they achieve a satisfactory number of transactions, if this achieves their financial or other targets.

> **Exchange** is the act of obtaining a desired object from someone by offering something in return.

> A **transaction** occurs when two parties exchange things of value to each at a specified time and place.

Others choose to focus on what is called **customer relationship management (CRM)** – they aim to develop long-term profitable relationships with customers in the hope that this will add more value to both parties. By increasing customer satisfaction they hope to build their loyalty to the product or service, so that they continue to make purchases over many years. This of course depends on understanding what features of the service will not only attract current purchases, but also encourage return visits, which are quite different things.

> **Customer relationship management (CRM)** is a process of creating and maintaining long-term relationships with customers.

A narrow interpretation of CRM is to gather data on individual customers, and use that to build customer loyalty. Many hotels, airlines and retailers use loyalty schemes whereby every purchase earns points, which customers exchange for other benefits (see Smith and Sparks (2009) for a study of how these work, and of the different ways in which consumers redeem their points).

Others use CRM technologies that enable sales staff to build relationships with customers as they complete transactions. These are typically portable devices which sales staff use to share market information with colleagues, manage their customer contacts, create sales presentations, prepare quotations during a sales call and submit call reports.

Management in practice How banks assess customers

Banks are becoming more skilful in identifying people to whom it may be unwise to lend money. According to the British Bankers' Association (BBA), banks now collect four kinds of data to assess client risk: 'negative' data, such as court fines and convictions; 'positive' data on commitments; income data; and reports on spending. The banks acquire this data from three sources – the electoral roll; their own systems which link to payment organisations such as Visa; and credit-checking agencies. A spokesman for the BBAs said:

> People are creatures of habit. You put your salary into your account once a month and may go to the supermarket weekly. From that analysis, you see the ability of someone to repay. Banks all look at the same data.

Source: *Financial Times*, 3 October 2007.

CRM also has a broader meaning that includes all aspects of building and maintaining close relations with customers by understanding their needs, and delivering superior value to them. Simple techniques are listed below – the following Key Ideas feature illustrates a more substantial approach, with greater implications for the organisational changes needed to support it:

- involving customers in product review and development;
- sponsoring consumer clubs and especially online communities;
- inviting customers to corporate sporting or cultural events;
- inviting online comments;
- sending promotional offers to a customers' mobiles.

More significant approaches to CRM involve a substantial commitment to organisational change (see Key Ideas).

Key ideas Elements of CRM

After reviewing of the spread of customer relationship management, Plakoyiannaki *et al.* (2008) say that in essence its aim is to add value by creating and maintaining relationships with customers. While the approach promises many benefits, it depends on the critical role of employees in delivering enhanced value, and so on policies which encourage that contribution. They find that CRM consists of four sub-processes:

- **Strategic planning sub-system** – provides the direction for CRM, and cultivates a strategic orientation around the organisation that sees CRM as a priority.
- **Information sub-system** – to acquire, disseminate and use information from customer contacts to understand their preferences and to improve the dialogue with customers across the organisation.

- **Value creation sub-system** – design and delivery of products and services that enhance value to the customer, thus ensuring they experience positive benefits throughout the interaction.
- **Performance measurement sub-system** – monitoring, evaluating and continuously improving the whole CRM experience, to ensure it has met the goals.

Their study of a CRM programme in an automotive repair company showed that the benefits depended heavily on managing employees in ways that encouraged them to develop an appropriate attitude to customers. It also depended on ensuring that the four sub-systems were in place and working satisfactorily.

Source: Plakoyiannaki *et al.* (2008).

The intention behind these diverse activities is to build the sponsoring company's knowledge of the customer's current and emerging needs, so that they can try to meet those needs profitably. As always, managers continually seek for evidence about the effectiveness of such expenditure, and what aspects are most effective in building close relationships (see the following Key Ideas).

Key ideas   What makes an online community effective?

Porter and Donthu (2008) noted that while many companies have launched virtual communities for their customers, many received little benefit. They therefore conducted a study to help managers understand how sponsoring virtual communities could add more value. Trust is essential for successful online marketing, so their central premise was that a community's value to the sponsoring firm depends on the sponsor's ability to cultivate trust with the community's members. They predicted that three factors would most affect a community's trust in a site:

- providing quality content (e.g. relevant content, frequently updated);
- fostering member embeddedness (e.g. seek opinions about community policies);
- fostering member interaction (e.g. encourage members to share information);

and that trust in turn would increase members' willingness to:

- share personal information;
- co-operate in new product development; and
- express loyalty intentions.

Their empirical study (based on 663 responses from users of online communities) concluded that fostering member embeddedness in the community had more effect on trust than the other two factors. It also led the authors to stress the importance of using technology to build relationships with customers, rather than only to generate transactions – especially as many customers use the internet for activities other than shopping.

Source: Porter and Donthu (2008).

While there are evidently potential benefits from developing long-term relationships with customers, this is not the case in all markets. Zolkiewski (2004) shows that relationship marketing is not suitable for all organisations, and that not all relationships are beneficial or necessary.

Case questions 9.3

- Use the frameworks in this section to identify segments in the MU market.
- Visit the website to find specific examples of products the company offers to each segment.
- List your segments and examples, and exchange what you have found with other students.
- Can you identify any segments which may represent new target markets for the company?

Activity 9.4   Examples of customer relationship management

Select an organisation in which you have an interest, ideally as a customer, which tries to build relationships with its customers.

- Which of the tools mentioned above (using customer data; CRM technologies; sponsored online communities; or those mentioned in the Key Ideas feature) does it use?
- How have they affected your attitude and behaviour towards the company?
- If it sponsors an online community, which of the three practices suggested in the Key Ideas feature does it use?
- Is there any evidence about their effects?

9.6   A marketing orientation

Chapter 3 outlines the idea of organisational culture, and how it influences where people focus their efforts and attention. Four such cultures (or 'orientations') relevant in marketing are: product, production, sales and marketing.

Four orientations

- **Product.** In units with a product orientation people focus on the design and perhaps the perfection of the product itself. This could mean focusing on developing highly sophisticated products using the latest scientific developments; or it could mean continuing to deliver a familiar product in a familiar way. This can work well in small or protected markets which others find hard to enter, but risk missing external changes in what people want to buy. Burgers *et al.* (2008) show how Polaroid (whose successful business sold cameras cheaply, and made money from selling film) used their *technical* skills to develop digital cameras. Unfortunately they lacked the *market* skills to generate revenues from the new (film-free) cameras, and failed to establish a position in this business.
- **Production.** Here the aim is to produce large quantities of a limited range of products efficiently and economically. This works well in situations where few goods and services are available, as customers have little choice. Companies with a production focus may suffer if conditions change towards greater competition and wide choice. A focus on volume production may make it hard to meet the needs of customers who expect variety and change.
- **Sales.** Units with this orientation aim to turn available products into cash, often using aggressive sales techniques. This may be the only way to sell products (sometimes called 'distress purchases') which people do not enjoy buying, such as tyres or insurance, or

where a concert has unsold seats a few days before the show. Companies also use this approach when they must raise cash urgently to meet pressing financial commitments.

- **Marketing.** Here the focus is on understanding and satisfying customer needs and demands. This approach is likely to be especially useful when the supply of goods exceeds demand, so that competition is intense. Many believe this is the situation most commonly facing modern organisations, and advocate that managers develop this approach in preference to the others. The next sub-section outlines the features of the approach, while Table 9.3 summarises the alternatives.

Marketing orientation

Most commercial organisations have a marketing function – a group of people who work on market research, competitor analysis and product strategy or promotion. A **marketing orientation** means much more than this, in that it refers to a situation where the significance of marketing is deeply embedded throughout the organisation. This means, among other things, that staff who are not in direct contact with customers nevertheless understand their needs, and give time and effort to satisfy them. While all the orientations in Table 9.3 work in some business conditions, many commentators believe that a marketing orientation is best suited to modern competitive environments (see, for example, Kirca *et al.*, 2005; Morgan *et al.*, 2009).

Marketing orientation refers to an organisational culture that encourages people to behave in ways that offer high-value goods and services to customers.

Levitt pointed out many years ago the danger of focusing on the features of the product, at the expense of its ability to satisfy needs and wants. A marketing orientation is hard to achieve, as it depends on developing a culture that encourages appropriate behaviour in relation to:

- customers – understanding and anticipating their needs and demands;
- competitors – identifying and anticipating their marketing plans;
- co-ordination – ensuring that all the separate functions within the organisation work together to meet customer needs in a way that adds value to both parties.

It seems plausible that companies which pay attention to these factors will perform well, and this seems, on balance, to be supported by evidence of staff being in such organisations being willing to support the marketing focus. Kirca *et al.* (2005) reviewed 114 quantitative studies of the relationship between firms claiming to have a marketing orientation and their performance. They found that, especially in manufacturing firms, there was a positive and significant link between marketing orientation and innovativeness, and customer loyalty and quality: this in turn enhanced business performance.

Table 9.3 Alternative organisational orientations

Organisational orientations	Focus	Benefits	Risks
Product	Technological skills and product features	High-quality, innovative products	Does not meet customer needs, so sales are poor
Production	Efficient, high volume, low-cost production	Low price may build sales	Competition from lower cost producers. Inflexible
Sales	Seller's need to convert product into cash	May work for 'unsought goods' (insurance) and in cash-flow crises	Sales techniques may damage future sales prospects
Marketing	Understanding and meeting consumers' needs	Satisfying consumer needs improves firm performance	High costs of building and maintaining a marketing orientation

Key ideas   **Theodore Levitt and marketing myopia**

Levitt (1960) sets out with great clarity the case for a customer orientation. Beginning with the example of great industries which had suffered dramatic declines in demand, he claimed this was not because their market was saturated, but because their senior managers suffered from 'marketing myopia'. That is, they defined their businesses too narrowly: railway businesses saw themselves as providing railways, not transportation; Hollywood film companies saw themselves as producing films, not providing entertainment. In each case this prevented them from quickly seizing opportunities to enter new markets – road and air transport, or TV production, respectively.

Levitt gives examples of companies that were indeed product focused, yet that prospered: not because of their product focus, but because they *also* had a strong customer-orientation. They constantly looked for opportunities to apply their acknowledged technical expertise to satisfy new customers. He concludes by proposing that managers must view the entire corporation as a customer-satisfying organism – not as producing products, but as providing customer satisfaction:

It must put this into every nook and cranny of the organisation, continuously, and with the flair that excites and stimulates the people in it. (p. 56)

Source: Levitt (1960).

Morgan *et al.* (2009) developed this line of research by showing the specific processes by which firms deploy a marketing orientation to improve performance. Their marketing orientation means they are skilled at generating, disseminating and responding to market information, and are then able to put this information to good use through their marketing capabilities – a set of 'marketing mix' practices (see Section 9.7) such as product management, pricing, communication and distribution.

A **customer-centred organisation** is focused upon, and structured around, identifying and satisfying the demands of its consumers.

Concentrating on the market and being a **customer-centred organisation** enables managers to discover what consumers want. They can then decide how best to use the strengths of the organisation to *return* to the market with a product for which a demand exists. They use information about demand and the price that consumers will pay to decide how much to produce and at what cost. While the sales orientation focuses on shifting products, the marketing orientation focuses on satisfying consumers and building mutually satisfying relationships – they anticipate changing demands and develop new products to meet them. For a study of two fashion retailers with different approaches, see Newman and Patel (2004), and for some further insight consider the views of Tim Smit of the Eden Project (Chapter 15 Case), who says:

Of course we have to give people a good day out, a cup of tea they enjoy, and all that. But I think we have actually struck a vein which has got deeper and more important to us as a society, which is people are not just looking for leisure: what many are looking for is a purpose in their lives, and I think the combination of a great day out, with something meaningful, learning about your environment, learning about your relationship with nature, was a killer proposition. That's why I think we get the numbers we do.

Key ideas   **Customer-oriented activities in manufacturing**

Bowen *et al.* (1989) found that two sets of customer-oriented activities enhanced competitiveness:

Augmenting products by:

- designing products that have characteristics that enhance customer satisfaction;
- delivering products safely and reliably;
- providing responsive and friendly after-sales service.

Incorporating customer focus into strategy by:

- understanding customer needs and using that to develop innovative products;
- increasing customer involvement early in design;
- tracking and communicating customer satisfaction and loyalty metrics across the organisation.

All of these activities require that employees throughout the business embrace the idea of customer orientation, and use it to guide their day-to-day activities.

Source: Bowen *et al.* (1989).

Management in practice   Unilever reconnects with customers www.unilever.com

After several years of performing less well than other consumer goods companies such as Nestlé and Procter & Gamble, Unilever appointed a new chief executive in 2009. Commenting on his task, Paul Polman said:

> We need to move increasingly from an efficiency-driven, manufacturing-driven supply chain. At the end what counts is to get the right product, at the right place, at the right price.

To help achieve that, he is creating 'customer innovation centres' in the US, Europe and Asia as hubs for testing new products and conducting consumer research. Most exciting, potentially, is the new product pipeline. Mr Polman wants Unilever to develop fewer products but to commercialise them faster.

Underpinning the whole cultural reinvention of Unilever, Mr Polman is trying to create a more performance-based culture among staff, with six-monthly, instead of annual, evaluations and bonus targets linked to volume growth and operating margins.

Source: *Financial Times*, 7 May 2009.

Activity 9.5   Gathering examples

Select an organisation (or unit) with which you are familiar, or about which you can find out.

- Which of the four cultural types in Table 9.3 most closely describes it?
- Describe briefly the features which best describes the way it works.
- If it has a marketing orientation, what examples can you give of the way people throughout the organisation work?
- Compare what you have found with other students, and identify any common themes.

Developing a marketing orientation

While a marketing orientation is a desirable goal for companies in volatile markets, such cultural change is hard to achieve. Staff at all levels and in all functions need to share a common commitment to work together in the interests of customers. It requires consistent and sustained effort by senior managers to clarify and implement the direction, sometimes replacing staff who are unable or unwilling to work in new ways (see Gebhardt *et al.* (2007) for a comprehensive empirical analysis of the scale of the task required). Chapter 13 contains ideas about implementing large organisational changes, of which developing a marketing orientation is an example.

| 9.7 | Using the marketing mix |

The **marketing mix** is the set of marketing tools – product, price, promotion and place – that an organisation uses to satisfy consumers' needs.

Marketing managers select the tools to satisfy the customers in their target market – everything they can do to influence demand. There are many of these, depending on the product or service being delivered. A convenient way to group the factors in the **marketing mix** is known as the 'four Ps' – product, price, promotion and place – which Figure 9.6 illustrates by showing some components in each

Key ideas   Marketing mix – strengths and limitations

The marketing mix comprises four levers which marketing managers can control. The mix *positions* products in the market in a way that makes them attractive to the target consumers. A product's position reflects what consumers think of it, in comparisons with competitors – classy and desirable, cheap and affordable, pricey but reliable and so on. Marketers aim to position their products *within the minds of their target consumers* as better able to satisfy their needs than competing products. To position products effectively, the marketing manager develops a co-ordinated, coherent marketing mix.

The 'four Ps' are of course an over-simplification, and it is not hard to add other dimensions. However, the aim should not be to seek an (unattainable) precision about the list of factors, but to have a reasonably simple framework about the factors to manage in trying to meet customer needs.

Product

Product refers to the range of goods and services which the company offers the target market. Some are physical products, others intangible services and most are a mixture of the two since the full experience of a product includes services such as delivery, customer advice and after-sales service. Figure 9.6 shows that it also includes items such as packaging, maintenance and insurance.

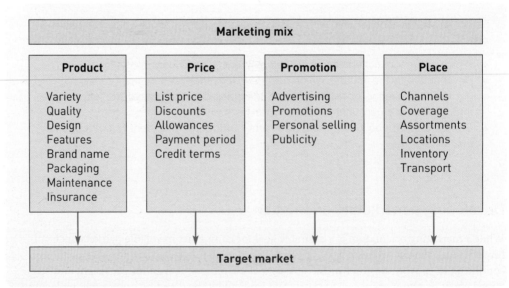

Figure 9.6 The four Ps in the marketing mix

Source: KOTLER, PHILIP; ARMSTRONG, GARY, *PRINCIPLES OF MARKETING*, 13th ed. © 2010, p. 52. Reprinted by permission of Pearson Education, Inc., Upper Saddle River, NJ.

Management in practice   **Swatch** www.swatch.com

The development and introduction of Swatch is a classic example of marketing techniques being used by a traditional industry to launch a new product. Faced with competition from low-cost producers SMH, an established Swiss watchmaker (whose brands include Longines and Omega), urgently needed a new product line. Its engineers developed a radically new product – the Swatch – which combined high quality with an affordable price. The company worked closely with advertising agencies in the US on product positioning and advertising strategy. In addition to the name 'Swatch', a snappy contraction of 'Swiss' and 'watch', this research generated the idea of downplaying the product's practical benefits and positioning it as a 'fashion accessory that happens to tell the time'. Swatch would be a second or third watch used to adapt to different situations without replacing the traditional 'status symbol' watch.

Swatch is now the world's largest watch company and continues to reposition itself through new products (such as Snowpass). It has been appointed official timekeeper of the Olympic Games until 2020.

Sources: Based on 'Swatch', Case No. 589-005-1, INSEAD-Cedep, Fontainebleau; and company website.

The extent to which offerings are tangible or intangible affects how marketing staff deal with them. Services present marketing with particular challenges because they are perishable and intangible, heterogeneous and inseparable.

Perishable

Perishable services cannot be held in stock for even the shortest amount of time. Empty seats on a flight, unoccupied rooms in a hotel or unsold newspapers are permanently lost sales.

Intangible

Intangible services are those that cannot usually be viewed, touched or tried before their purchase, so it is difficult for the customers to know what they are getting before their purchase – holidays, concerts, health clubs would be examples. Consumers have difficulty assessing whether the product will meet their needs, so many providers of such services build customer groups where users can share experiences with others, and encourage current members to invite friends and family with trial memberships.

Heterogeneous and inseparable

Services rely on the skills, competences and experiences of the people who provide them, and this creates particular marketing challenges. Services are *heterogeneous* in that their personal nature means the customer may experience a slightly different product each time, even though it is essentially the same meal or dental treatment that is being provided. Services are *inseparable* in that the customer interacts with the producer during delivery: it is consumed as it is produced, as in a medical appointment. Providers and consumers have personalities, opinions and values that make them unique, so the service delivered is always unique.

Organisations operating through branch systems such as banks or fast-food restaurants have to overcome these hazards to ensure that staff deliver consistent standards, otherwise customers will be dissatisfied. Organisations such as Pizza Hut and UCI cinemas try to minimise differences by providing staff with company uniforms, decorating premises in a similar way and setting firm guidelines for the way staff deliver the service.

Consumer products (both goods and services) can be classified as convenience, shopping, speciality or unsought products. Each poses a different marketing challenge, which Table 9.4 summarises.

Price

Price is the value placed upon the goods, services and ideas exchanged between organisations and consumers. The money price is the commonest measure, although this part of the mix also

Table 9.4 Market challenges by type of product, using the marketing mix

Type of product	Examples	Marketing challenge
Convenience	Regular purchases, low price – bread, milk, magazines	Widely available and easy to switch brands. Managers counter this by heavy advertising or distinct packaging of the brand
Shopping	Relatively expensive, infrequent purchase – washing machines, televisions, clothes	Brand name, product features, design and price are important, and managers will spend time searching for the best mix. Managers spend heavily on advertising and on training sales staff
Speciality	Less frequent, often luxury purchases – cars, jewellery, perfumes	Consumers need much information. Sales staff vital to a sale – management invest heavily in them, and in protecting the image of a product by restricting outlets. Also focused advertising and distinctive packaging
Unsought	Consumers need to buy – but don't get much pleasure from – insurance, a car exhaust	Managers need to make customers aware that they supply a product that meets this need

includes discounts, trade-in allowances payment period and credit terms. Airlines often levy charges for elements of the service, which they formerly offered as part of an inclusive fare.

In selecting the price that will position a product competitively within consumers' minds, the marketing manager must be aware of the image that consumers have of the product. Consumers have expected price ranges for certain types of product. For children's products and those associated with their health or self-image, consumers have a *minimum* price they expect to pay. A price below this will discourage a purchase, as customers will associate that with poor quality or low value.

Dynamic pricing was initially used by hotels and airlines, which face the problem that since their services are provided at a specified time, they have no value if they are not used by then. Companies try to raise revenue in this situation by varying prices in response to demand for a particular day. Airlines usually start with low prices, rising as the date of travel approaches: sometimes falling sharply if there is spare capacity just before the date of travel. They hope in this way to reallocate demand across time (those who can be flexible will learn to avoid peak times) and so make better use of a limited supply. Some suppliers of clothing, mobile phones and consumer electronics now use the practice, partly to dispose of stocks whose value depreciates as newer versions become available (Sahay, 2007).

Promotion

Properly referred to as marketing communications, this element of the marketing mix involves informing customers about the merits of the product, and persuading them to buy. Technological developments are increasing the number of ways in which organisations can communicate with their target markets. Packaging can provide information, a company logo may transmit a particular message, and sponsoring a football team or concert indicates an organisation's values and attitudes. Common ways to encourage consumers to buy are advertising, sales promotions, personal selling and publicity.

- *Advertising* is used to transmit a message to a large audience. It is impersonal, as it does not involve direct communication between an organisation and a potential consumer. Advertising is effective in creating awareness of the offering but is less effective in persuading consumers to buy.

Table 9.5 Top five companies in the Bowen Craggs Index of corporate websites, 2010

Company	Construction	Message	Contact	Serving society	Serving investors	Serving media	Serving job seekers	Serving customers	Total
Maximum score	60	38	12	32	28	32	32	32	280
Royal Dutch Shell	44	38	9	27	28	21	24	22	213
BP	43	35	10	25	27	21	24	25	210
Siemens	43	42	10	26	20	27	20	22	210
Roche	42	40	8	24	22	27	23	23	209
Rio Tinto	42	35	7	25	24	20	25	23	201

Source: FT Bowen Craggs & Co Index of Corporate Website Effectiveness 2010.

- *Sales promotions* encourage consumers who are considering a product to take the next step and buy it. They also use promotions to encourage repeat purchases and to try new products.
- *Personal selling* provides consumers with first-hand information before they buy. It is most useful for infrequently purchased products such as DVD players and cars. Personal selling is a direct transfer of product information to potential consumers: it is able to respond to questions that consumers might have and to explain complicated or technical product features.
- *Publicity* or public relations (PR) aims to build a positive image of the organisation. It depends on good working relationships with the media to ensure that positive events such as launching a new product are fully reported, and that negative ones do as little damage as possible.
- *Websites* have rapidly become the first place that many users go to check products, prices and availability, and are probably the most-read publication a company produces. The FT Bowen Craggs & Co Index of corporate website effectiveness evaluates the websites of the world's largest companies against eight criteria (such as 'serving customers' and 'serving the media'). The scores of the top five companies in the 2010 index are shown in Table 9.5.
- *Online communities* enable users of a product to share experiences. These are often formed independently, but others are sponsored by the company as a way to build relationships.

Management in practice   Online retailing – the benefits of user-generated content

Many people enjoy telling others about their shopping experiences, whether good or bad, which has helped to increase the popularity of online shopping communities. If people find they cannot air their views on a retailer's website, they will soon do so elsewhere on the internet.

Companies can eavesdrop on these conversations to gain valuable marketing information, and some now host these conversations by opening their websites to what is called 'user-generated content'. The most common type of content is when users provide product reviews. Negative comments may indicate genuine problems with a product that the company needs to deal with: good ones may be a signal to increase stocks to be ready for higher demand.

There is also evidence that shoppers are more likely to buy on a site that contains user-generated content, and that they have more trust in brands that offer product reviews.

Place

This refers to how products can best be distributed to the final consumer, either directly or through intermediaries. Some, especially those in luxury goods or fashion markets, take great care to ensure that products are only available through carefully controlled distributors, to help ensure consistent quality or promote their market image. One company developed an e-book service which can sell full 'e-books', highlights or chapters to users – probably onto their laptops, mobiles or iPads. It decided to sell the device through publishers, rather than to individual consumers. Many companies debate whether how to combine online distribution with traditional channels – partly influenced by their understanding of why people buy the product. As one publisher observed:

> Music is only there to be listened to, but books are also shared, given as presents, used as furniture. (*Financial Times*, 13 April 2009, p. 17)

In developing a marketing mix that will place products competitively within the minds of consumers, marketing managers aim for coherence. In positioning a supermarket chain as, for example, value for money, they ensure that each part of the mix supports and reinforces this image. This means familiar products features, relatively low prices and promotion messages that stress the value for money. The stores should be simple, to avoid sending a message that the costs of creating a smart place will raise prices. An effective marketing mix is one where there is coherence among the elements, giving the customer a consistent positive experience.

Management in practice   **Using the marketing mix in the pub business**

The UK pub business has experienced significant changes, with legislation on drink-driving and smoking, together with competition from supermarkets selling cheap alcoholic drinks, thus reducing revenues. Many have responded by changing the product, offering food and a wide range of entertainment, especially live big-screen sport. They have also segmented the market, with pubs being developed in ways that appeal to different groups of drinkers.

Source: Pratten and Scoffield (2007).

Case questions 9.4

- Use the frameworks in this section to identify how MU uses the marketing mix.
- Visit the website and identify two significant target markets for the company.
- For each market, analyse how the company has used the market mix to construct its market offering.
- List your markets and examples of the 'four Ps', and exchange what you have found with other students. Can you identify any significant aspects of the offering that are not covered by one the '4 Ps'?

 9.8   **The product lifecycle**

The **product lifecycle** suggests that products pass through the stages of introduction, growth, maturity and decline.

In managing the organisation's product decisions, marketing managers use a concept called the **product lifecycle** (Figure 9.7). The central assumption is that all products have a limited life, varying from months to decades. Depending on the stage reached in its lifecycle, a known set of competitive conditions exists that can guide the marketing activities for that stage.

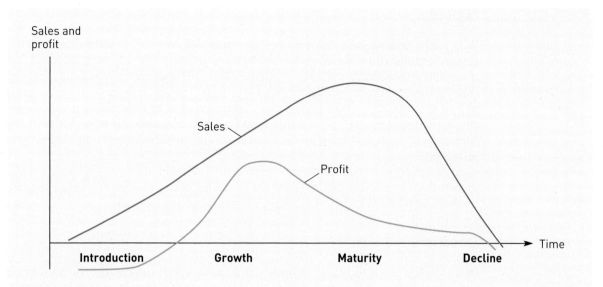

Figure 9.7 The product lifecycle

Mapping the sales and profit generated, the product lifecycle suggests that products pass through five stages – development, introduction, growth, maturity and decline.

Development

In many commercial markets, companies only survive if they can show a steady stream of new products, a small proportion of which will be profitable. Sometimes they acquire already developed products from other companies, as a way of quickly filling a perceived gap in their product range. Alternatively, they depend on their own research and development department to develop new products – whether these are completely new devices or modifications and improvements to an earlier design. This is an expensive process, during which the company is spending large sums with no immediate return.

Introduction

This is the stage at which products enter the marketplace. Profits are still negative because sales from the early adopters have not reached the level needed to pay back investment in R&D. Few consumers are aware of – and therefore interested in – buying the product and few organisations are involved in producing and distributing it. The aim of the marketing manager at this stage is to invest in marketing communication and make as many potential consumers as possible aware of the product's entry into the marketplace.

Growth

At this stage consumers have become aware of and started buying the product. Sales rise quickly and profits peak. As people buy the product, more consumers become aware of it and the high profit levels attract new competitors into the industry. The aim of the marketing manager at this stage is to fight off existing competitors and new entrants. This can be done by (a) encouraging consumer loyalty, (b) distributing the product as widely as is demanded by consumers, and (c) cutting selling prices: production costs fall as the total units increase, due to the learning curve effect. Competitors arriving later have not had time to cut costs, so may baulk at entering the market.

Maturity

With profits peaking during the growth stage, profit and sales start to plateau and then decline towards the end of this stage. By this stage in a product's lifecycle, many consumers are aware of and have bought the product and there are many organisations competing for a decreasing amount of consumer demand for the product. The aim of the marketing manager is to fight competition by reducing the price of the product or by differentiating it by, for example, altering its packaging and design. Swatch continues to add value to its product in the later stages of its product lifecycle with items such as the Infinity Concept watch launched in early 2007.

At this stage product differentiation can successfully reposition products to an earlier stage in their lifecycle. It is also important that the marketing manager begins to consider ideas for replacement products and to select ideas for research and development.

Decline

In the decline phase, there is little consumer demand and all competing organisations are considering removing the product from the marketplace. It is important that, by this stage, the marketing manager has a new product ready to enter the marketplace and replace the product that is being removed. Certain rarity products can still generate profits in the decline phase, e.g. spare parts for old cars.

An awareness of the stage which a product is at in its lifecycle can assist the marketing manager in deciding upon a course of action. Aware that a product is in maturity, the marketing manager might decide to reposition the product by changing the packaging or image created by the branding of the product. Lucozade was traditionally marketed as a health drink for older people, but product changes, new packaging and celebrity endorsement have repositioned it as a youth sports drink (**www.lucozade.com**).

Activity 9.6 Using the product lifecycle

- State the stage that you believe each of the following products to be in and comment on how long, in years, you believe their lifecycle to be: drawing pins, iPods, umbrellas, hand soap.

Some products appear not have a limited lifespan and others have been repositioned to an earlier stage. Despite these criticisms, the product lifecycle offers the marketing manager a useful aid to many product decisions.

Case study Manchester United – the case continues

One of the challenges facing Manchester United is the best organisational marketing structure to design and the internal culture to induce in managing its huge operation. At corporate level, the Glazer family owns football-related and non-football-related businesses, and is involved with various joint ventures in TV, financial services and mobile phones. At business and product levels, management have to deal directly with their target segments. Promotional campaigns for individual products have to be sensitive to the image of sister MU products. Hoarding adverts of a noisy football crowd having a good time will be exciting to other potential fans but could be off-putting for someone who has to produce their MU credit card at local stores.

Preserving the perceived value of the brand is also important: the replica jersey product manager will not want stores such as Tesco to sell them at a discount. This raises important questions of channel management and relationship with companies whose strategy might be more cost focused than differentiated. In 2009 MU signed a deal worth £80 million over four years with Aon, an American financial services group, to be its principal sponsor: this was the largest-ever football sponsorship deal. They also signed a three-year deal with Turkish Airlines to be their official carrier.

9.9   Integrating themes

Sustainable performance

Marketing is both part of the problem and part of the solution to sustainability. Companies in many areas of the economy have used the skills of marketing to promote the greater consumption of goods and services that have contributed to the current situation. Some are now using those same skills to identify segments of their markets in which there are customers willing to switch to products that use more sustainable methods of production, and to that extent have less environmental impact. As Chapter 5 shows, such responsible practices are limited by market circumstances, and are themselves only sustainable if they are commercially viable in the face of competition from other suppliers who may feel less constrained to meet these demands.

Key ideas   Naomi Klein's No Logo: Taking aim at the brand bullies

Klein (2000) presents a powerful argument against the growing dominance of some global brands in consumer markets, and how many use advertising to exploit impressionable teenagers. She argues that companies such as Microsoft, Gap and Starbucks now present themselves as purveyors of lifestyles, images and dreams rather than products. In doing so they harm both the cultures in which they operate and the workers they employ. She also reports a growing backlash by ethical shareholders, human rights activists and McUnion organisers demanding a citizen-centred alternative to the rule of the brands.

However, not everyone agrees that Klein is correct. She is accused of overstating her case, and brand advocates point out the many positives that brands have for consumers, manufacturers and retailers. What is not in dispute, however, is that companies are now facing up to social and ethical responsibility as never before.

Source: Klein (2000).

The discipline of marketing could also be part of the solution of achieving a sustainable economic system, since any set of proposals about the changes needed in the way people live and work will only work if they are widely accepted by members of the public. Surveys regularly show that even among the (minority) who accept the problem, many are unwilling to commit to the personal changes required. Marketing skills in the area of understanding attitudes and interests, and in developing policies intended to change behaviour, have been applied to many areas of policy, such as public health, alcohol abuse and domestic violence. The same skills may be relevant in promoting widespread acceptance of more sustainable lifestyles.

Governance and control

One aspect of governance is that of assessing risks – indeed it is one of the requirements of The Combined Code (2006) that Boards appoint a risk assessment committee. While this would normally focus on the financial or perhaps technological risks potentially embodied in a strategy, reputational risk will sometimes also be worth evaluating as new products or services are developed. This is where a company acts in a way that many believe to be unethical, leading to long-term damage to its reputation. A clear example of this would be the way in which companies in financial services, in the years before the 2008 financial crisis, encouraged people to support their lifestyles on debt which they could not afford.

While governance has traditionally been concerned primarily with the immediate financial arrangements of a company, some now suggest that part of the governance process should include an assessment of the risks to which the company is exposed through the way it conducts the business. In some lines of business, especially financial services, governance and control could arguably include the role of marketing in shaping the risks to which the company is exposed.

Internationalisation

The majority of the top 100 most valuable brands are global, which derive their value from making strong emotional connections with customers across countries and cultures. With some exceptions, such as Google and Amazon which have achieved global status very quickly, most did so by following three principles:

- Adapt to local needs and culture – spend time finding out which features of the product can remain constant, and which will need to be adapted.
- Seek to tap a universal truth – strong brands are founded on a promise that resonates with consumers, so identify some essential aspect of human nature with which to associate the brand.
- align the organisation around the global strategy – people at all levels need to be clear about how their work supports the brand, and how it could equally be how inconsistent actions would undermine it.

Activity 9.7   Revising your definition

- Having completed this chapter, how would you define marketing?

- Compare this definition with the one that you were asked to make in Activity 9.1 and comment on any changes.

Summary

1 **Define marketing and the role it plays in managing organisations of all kinds**
   - Marketing is the activity of creating value for customers to receive value (resources) from them in return. All organisations depend on being able to attract inputs from the outside world and need resources to do that.

2 **Explain the importance of understanding customers and markets, and the sources of information marketers can use**
   - Understanding customers' needs, wants and demands is the foundation of marketing, as only then can suppliers know how to satisfy them. They also aim to understand what influences buying behaviour.
   - A marketing information system uses internal and external data, and also conducts marketing research to learn more about actual and potential customers.

3 **Illustrate the practices of segmenting markets and targeting customer groups**

- Greater consumer understanding enables a company to segment the market according to groups of customers with different needs.
- Targeting is when the company decides which of the distinct segments of the market it will aim to serve to meet their distinctive needs.

4 **Explain the meaning and significance of customer relationship management**

- The practice of building close long-term relationships with significant customers.
- A narrow interpretation of the term is when companies use information technology to manage data about customers, and perhaps use that to target special offers.
- A wider interpretation extends the idea to practices such as involving customers closely in product design and development, or creating online communities for customers.

5 **Compare a marketing orientation with other orientations and explain its significance**

- This is contrasted with product, production and sales orientations, which are suitable in certain circumstances.
- A marketing orientation implies that the organisation focuses all activities on meeting consumer needs and is organised with that in mind. It is especially useful in very competitive markets, where customers have a wide choice of suppliers.
- Adopting a marketing orientation makes the customer the centre of attention and is different from product, production and sales philosophies. It becomes a guiding orientation for the whole organisation.

6 **Describe the components of the marketing mix**

- Product, price, promotion and place. There are many other formulations, but a simple one such as this serves as a useful reminder of the tasks involved in shaping an offering.

7 **What are the stages of the product lifecycle**

- Birth, growth, maturity, decline.

8 **Show how ideas from the chapter add to your understanding of the integrating themes**

- While many see marketing as part of the sustainability problem, others see it as part of the solution: customers as well as organisations need to change the way they behave in order to achieve a sustainable economy, and a marketing orientation can help to do that.
- Innovative marketing practices, especially, but not solely, in financial services have exposed some companies to risks that threatened their existence. In sectors with this scale of risk, marketing practices could legitimately be part of an effective governance regime.
- Successful international brands have become so by identifying universal consumer needs, adapting products to fit local cultures, and aligning the organisation to support the international business.

Review questions

1 Why do charities and local authorities need to devote resources to marketing?

2 Explain why understanding what customers want is a valuable investment.

3 Outline sources of marketing information and illustrate each with an example.

4 In what way is an organisation's micro-environment different from its macro-environment? How do these environments affect marketing activities?

5 What are the main stages in conducting a market research project?

6 What are the advantages of market segmentation and what variables do marketers typically use to segment consumer markets?

7 What are the two broad approaches to customer relationship management?

8 Does the marketing orientation have advantages over product, production or sales philosophies?

9 Illustrate each element in the marketing mix with an original example.

10 Use a product of your choice to illustrate all or part of the product lifecycle.

11 Summarise an idea from the chapter that adds to your understanding of the integrating themes.

Concluding critical reflection

Think about the ways in which your company, or one with which you are familiar, manages marketing. Review the material in the chapter and visit some of the websites identified. Then make notes on the following questions:

- What examples of the marketing issues discussed in this chapter struck you as being relevant to practice in your company?

- Considering the people you normally work with, what **assumptions** about the nature of the business and its customers appear to guide their approach – a production, sales or marketing orientation? How does this affect the way the business operates?

- What factors such as the history or current **context** of the company appear to influence this? Does the current approach appear to be right for the company in its context – or would a different view of the context lead to a different approach? What would the implications for people in the company be of a distinctive marketing orientation?

- Has there been any pressure to adopt a more customer-focused approach, perhaps based on evidence about similar organisations? If you could find evidence about such **alternatives**, how may it affect company practice? What would be the obstacles to a greater emphasis on marketing?

- The chapter has stressed the benefits of a marketing orientation, and of understanding customer needs in ever greater detail. What **limitations** can you identify in this philosophy, to others within the chapter? Are people only to be valued in their roles as consumers? How valid might ideas on marketing be in other cultures? What, if any, limitations can you now identify in the way an organisation with which you are familiar approaches marketing?

Further reading

Andreasen, A. and Kotler, P. (2002), *Strategic Marketing for Non-profit Organisations*, (6th edn), Prentice Hall, Harlow.

Outlines a conceptual and practical foundation for marketing in non-profit organisations.

Gronroos, C. (2007), *Service Management and Marketing: A customer relationship management approach* (3rd edn), Wiley, Chichester.

Highly recommended for students wishing to read more about services marketing from one of Europe's leading writers on marketing.

Newman, A.J. and Patel, D. (2004), 'The marketing directions of two fashion retailers', *European Journal of Marketing*, vol. 38, no. 7, pp. 770–789.

Compares the performance of Topshop and Gap, relating the variation to their success (or not) in developing a marketing orientation throughout the respective businesses.

Plakoyiannaki, E., Tzokas, N., Dimitratos, P. and Saren, M. (2008), 'How critical is employee orientation for customer relationship management? Insights from a case study', *Journal of Management Studies*, vol. 45, no. 2, pp. 268–293.

Qualitative study of a UK company, showing the links between customer relationship marketing and staff motivation.

Schor, J.B. (2004), *Born to buy: The commercialized child and the new consumer culture*, Schribner, New York.

A revealing account of the ploys which some marketers use to sell products to children – turning them, she argues, into miniature consumption machines.

Weblinks

These websites have appeared in the chapter:

www.manutd.com
www.tesco.com
www.hiscox.com
www.unilever.com
www.swatch.com
www.lucozade.com

Visit two of the sites in the above list (or that of another organisation in which you have an interest).

- What markets are they in? How have they segmented the market?

- What information can you find about their position in their respective markets, and what marketing challenges they face?

- Gather information from media websites (such as **www.FT.com**) which relate to the orgnanisations you have chosen. What stories can you find that relate to the marketing decisions they have made and what the outcomes have been?

 For video case studies, audio summaries, flashcards, exercises and annotated weblinks related to this chapter, visit **www.pearsoned.co.uk/mymanagementlab**

PART 3 CASE
THE VIRGIN GROUP
www.virgin.com

Virgin is a branded venture capital organisation, known all over the world and seen as standing for value for money, quality, innovation and fun. Founded by Richard Branson, it has created over 200 companies worldwide, employing about 50,000 people in 30 countries.

The first record shop was opened in 1971 and the record label launched in 1973. Virgin Atlantic Airways began operating in 1984, quickly followed by Virgin Holidays. In 1995 the company entered a joint venture offering financial services. By 1997 it was an established global corporation with airline, retailing and travel operations. In 2010 its main activities are grouped into Travel, Lifestyle, Media and Mobile, Music, Money, and People and Planet.

The original record business was launched shortly after the UK government had abolished retail price maintenance, a practice that had limited competition and kept prices high. Richard Branson saw the opportunity and began a mail order business offering popular records at prices about 15 per cent below those charged by shops.

The business prospered until there was a postal strike. Branson's response was to open a retail outlet, which was an immediate success, and the start of Virgin Retail. These retail interests were later consolidated around the Megastore concept in a joint venture with a major retailer. At prestige locations in major cities, Megastores began to sell home entertainment products – music, videos and books – on a large scale. The success of the Megastore concept was exported to major cities throughout the world, frequently through joint ventures.

In the early 1980s Branson was approached by Randolph Fields, who was seeking additional finance for his cut-price airline. The airline business then was tightly regulated, with routes, landing rights, prices and service levels established and maintained by inter-governmental arrangements. These regulations were mainly used to protect inefficient, often state-owned, national 'flag carriers', keeping fares high. After three months of intense activity, Branson and Fields had gained permission to fly, arranged to lease an aircraft and recruited staff. The first flight was in June 1984. To grow, Branson needed more landing rights, and would need to persuade government ministers to secure them at both ends of each route. Those ministers would also

Visual Media

be lobbied by the established airlines, to persuade them not to approve the low fares that Branson was proposing. Alternatively, they could undercut his fares and subsidise the losses from profits on other routes.

Virgin Atlantic grew successfully and by 1990, although still a relatively small player, it competed with the major carriers on the main routes from London, winning awards for innovation and service. The airline was now the focus of Branson's interests and was becoming a serious threat to the established airlines. It now serves 30 destinations around the world. Virgin America (created in 2007) is based in California and offers high-quality, innovative services. The company is also involved in the low-cost airline business through Virgin Blue (founded 1997) in Australia.

The Virgin brand

Research on the Virgin brand name demonstrated the impact over time of quirky advertising and publicity stunts. The brand was recognised by 96 per cent of UK consumers, and Richard Branson was correctly identified by 95 per cent as the company's founder. The Virgin name was associated by respondents with words such as fun, innovation, success and trust, and identified with a range of businesses, confirming what Branson and others had believed: in principle there were no product or service boundaries limiting a brand name, provided it was associated with a quality offering.

Encouraged by the research, Virgin began entering new sectors outside its core activities of travel and retail. Virgin businesses as diverse as radio broadcasting, book publishing and computer games found a home in the same stable, as well as hotels, railways, personal computers, cola drinks, cinemas and financial services. Branson continued to work at the centre, supported by a small business development group, a press office, and advisers on strategy and finance. The early Virgin style of informality and openness remains – ties are rarely worn, denim jeans are common and everybody is on first-name terms.

The Virgin organisation

Having a centre did not mean a centralised operation. Each operating unit was expected to stand alone, having little interaction with either head office or other units. Unit managers networked informally (usually at parties or similar events), but were not obliged to follow prescriptive corporate policies; these were 'understood' rather than codified. For example, there was no common human resource policy. Managers knew that employees must be treated 'fairly' since 'that is what Richard would want', and they complied in their own way. Similarly there was no group information technology strategist or central purchasing function, because Branson believed that those roles would constitute interference and discourage managerial creativity. Nor was there any systematic seeking out of synergy, either at the centre or by unit managers.

At the centre is Virgin Management Ltd (VML), providing advisory and management support to all of the Virgin companies and to specialist Sector teams around the world. In conjunction with the Sector teams (such as those for Travel or Finance) VML manages Virgin's assets around the world. While finance, marketing and human resource management policies are guided by the centre, the businesses have a high degree of autonomy in how they work. The company describes the style as a collaborative and supportive relationship between the centre and the businesses.

Criteria for investing in new ventures

When they start a new venture they base it on hard research and analysis. Typically they review the industry from the perspective of the customer, and try to see what they could do to improve the experience. They ask questions such as:

- Is this an opportunity for restructuring the market and creating competitive advantage?
- What are competitors doing?
- Is the customer confused or badly served?
- Is this an opportunity for the Virgin brand?
- Can we add value?
- Will it interact with our other business?

New ventures are often steered by managers seconded from other parts of the business, who bring with them the distinctive management style, skills and experience. The company frequently works by creating partnerships to combine industry specific skills with the Virgin style. Managers in the companies are empowered to run the businesses without VML interfering, but are also expected to help one another to overcome problems.

The Virgin Charter is an agreement between VML (in effect the holding company) and the subsidiaries. It defines the role of the centre in relation to the subsidiaries in such matters as taxation, legal affairs, intellectual property and real estate. It also outlines closer links in areas previously left to individual units: IT, people, purchasing. Thus the Charter sets out ways for the many Virgin companies to tackle common activities with a common approach. Nearly all are private and owned entirely by the Virgin Group or Branson's family trusts. Business should be 'shaped around people', Branson believes, citing his experience of subdividing the record company as it grew. Each new record label was given to up-and-coming managers, creating in-house entrepreneurs who were highly motivated to build a business with which they identified.

He believes that expanding by creating discrete legal entities gives people a sense of involvement with, and loyalty to, the small unit to which they belong. He gives substantial autonomy to those running the subsidiaries and offers them share options – Virgin has produced many millionaires. Branson does not want his best people to leave the company to start a venture outside; he prefers to make millionaires within. He has created a structure of numerous small companies around the world, each operated quasi-independently. Both systems embody the maxims 'small is beautiful' and 'people matter'.

Virgin.com

During one significant management meeting participants realised that, more by chance than planning, Virgin was in businesses 'that were ideally suited to e-commerce and in which growth is expected to occur – travel, financial services, publishing, music, entertainment'. To exploit this potential the participants decided to streamline their online services with a single Virgin web address: Virgin.com.

Branson believes that the Virgin name, known for its consumer-friendly image and good service, would translate well across a range of businesses – 'Virgin isn't a company, it's a brand', commented one senior manager in the company. This is attractive to partners, who provide the expertise and capital for a joint venture in their area of business (such as insurance or share trading), while Virgin provides the brand image. By putting all Virgin's business on one easily accessible site, Branson hopes to cross-promote a wide range of offerings. The site groups these under headings such as online shopping, finance and money, media and telecommunications, leisure and pleasure, travel and tourism, and health. Throughout the group, the company claims that it aims to deliver a quality service by empowering employees, and by facilitating and monitoring customer feedback to continually improve the customer's experience though innovation.

In October 2006 Richard Branson, at a meeting of the Clinton Global Initiative, announced that he would invest all future profits of the Virgin Group's transportation businesses – mainly airlines and trains – into renewable energy initiatives. These would be within the Virgin transportation companies and in new biofuel research and development projects.

In 2010 Virgin Galactica announced that the first commercial manned spaceship, VSS Enterprise, had made its first test flight. The craft is intended to carry six fare-paying passengers on sub-orbital space flights: the company has already taken $45 million in deposits from 330 people who want to share the experience. Virgin Media, the UK's dominant cable television operator, claimed to be the only company able to exploit the market for superfast broadband, although it faced intense competition from BT.

Sources: Based on material from INSEAD Case 400-002-1, *The House that Branson Built: Virgin's entry into the new millennium; Financial Times,* 15 December 2008; company website.

Part case questions

- What examples does the case give of links between Branson's strategy for Virgin and the environment in which it operates?
- Which of these are similar to, and which are different from, those facing HMV?
- Are the decisions mentioned in the case programmed or non-programmed? How do you sense, from the information in the case, that the company ensures the quality of those decisions?
- What common themes link the different businesses in the group?
- Which generic strategy has Virgin followed at different periods in its history?
- On balance, does the Virgin story support the planned or the emergent view of strategy?
- Why does Branson use joint ventures with other companies to realise the Virgin strategy? Are there any disadvantages in this method of working?
- To what extent has Virgin implemented a marketing orientation?
- Visit Virgin's website and comment on how it has used this to support its marketing activities.
- Where do Richard Branson's publicity stunts fit into the company's marketing strategy?

PART 3
SKILLS DEVELOPMENT

To help you develop your skills, as well as knowledge, this section includes tasks that relate the key themes covered in the Part to your daily life. Working through these will help you to deepen your understanding of the topic, and develop skills and insights which you can use in many situations.

Task 3.1	Clarifying objectives for a task

Chapter 6 pointed out that a difficulty in planning is being clear about the longer-term objectives of the project or task. A useful skill to help reconcile apparently conflicting objectives is to try to relate them to a wider set of purposes by developing a 'why/how network'. This can make it easier to relate immediate, tangible and possibly conflicting objectives to a wider, and perhaps less conflicting, set of purposes for the activity.

Select a project from your work, or perhaps concerned with your career plans. Write the name of the project at the bottom of a large sheet of paper, and then ask 'why?'. Answer by one or more sentences beginning with the phrase 'in order to . . .', and write these answers above the project task. For each of these answers, repeat the process of asking 'why?', and answering with 'in order to . . .', writing your answers on the sheet. Repeat this several times, until it makes sense to stop – by which time you will probably have some broad, long-term purposes which the project can serve.

Figure 1 illustrates the method, and you will need to work over the chart several times to ensure it is clear.

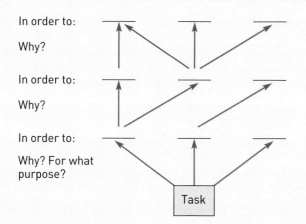

Figure 1 A method for clarifying objectives

Task 3.2   Developing an outline plan for a task

Suppose that the flight tests for VSS *Enterprise* have gone well, and the company expects the first commercial flight will happen about 12 months from now. Use Figure 6.5 to outline (one page only) the main issues that the Virgin managers responsible should have on their agenda for managing that event successfully.

Then use Figure 6.6 to sketch a programme overview chart to show how the different projects within the programme might fit together. Check the company website to see if you can find any information about the progress of the investment.

Task 3.3   How to reach a decision

This activity invites you to use Vroom and Yetton's model of the different ways in which managers can involve staff in reaching a decision. Review that section of Chapter 7. Then read the following four cases and decide which of Vroom and Yetton's decision-making methods would generate the most effective decision. Note your choice and your reasons. You could then work through the decision tree and discuss your answers with other students.

Case 1

You are the manager of a small television, radio and electronics business. For some time you have had complaints from your sales staff about the need to redecorate the large shop in which they work. You recently agreed to this and you have received three tenders from reliable and well-known local contractors. They are all able to do the work to the required standard and there is little difference in the quoted costs or times for the job.

You recently asked your employees for their suggestions on suitable colour schemes and there was considerable difference of opinion. You now have to decide which tender to accept, and to tell the contractor the colour scheme.

Which decision method would you use and why?

Case 2

You are an engineer in charge of commissioning a chemical plant. You need to estimate the rate of progress of the stages of the work to schedule the materials and equipment. You are familiar with the work and you possess all the information you need to estimate when materials and equipment will be required at the various commissioning stages. It is very important that your estimates are accurate, since if materials are not available at the right time, work will be held up. Equally, if materials and equipment arrive too soon they will be lying around idle. Your team are all committed to the plant being commissioned on time.

Which decision method would you use and why?

Case 3

You are a training manager employed by a firm of consultants. You have to select three of your eight training advisers to work on an assignment abroad. The assignment involves a training needs analysis, preparation of training programmes and training local instructors.

The assignment is expected to last about six months. It is in a remote part of the Middle East with poor facilities and a ban on the consumption of alcohol. Your advisers are all experienced personnel and each of them is capable of performing the task satisfactorily.

Which decision method would you use and why?

Case 4

You are a project leader and you need to decide which operators to transfer to a new plant, Line 2. Your objective is to commission this on time without adversely affecting production on the existing plant, Line 1. Most of the operatives working on Line 1 want to transfer to Line 2 because working conditions will be better and the rates of pay higher. Senior operatives working on Line 1 expect to be given preference over less senior ones, and all those on Line 1 expect to be given preference over operatives working in other departments.

You, however, want to transfer only the best operatives from Line 1 to Line 2 and make up the balance with operatives from other departments. Your reason for wanting to do this is that Line 2 will work much faster than Line 1. This means that operatives working on Line 2 will need to be much more skilled at fault rectification than those working on Line 1. The ability to react quickly to control panel and video display unit (VDU) cues is essential.

Which decision method would you use and why?

Task 3.4	Growth through mergers

Chapter 8 shows that one popular way of implementing strategy is through a merger or acquisition. Use the internet (such as by accessing the online versions of the *Financial Times* (www.ft.com) or *The Economist* (www.economist.com)) to identify mergers and acquisitions announced within the past month. For a selection of these, list the companies involved, the industries in which the companies worked, and how the acquiring company relates the acquisition to its broader strategy. Which of the strategic directions shown in Figure 8.8 is best represented by the stated strategy in this case? Follow the story over the coming months.

PART 4
ORGANISING

Introduction

Part 4 examines how management creates the structure within which people work. Alongside planning the direction of the business, managers need to consider how they will achieve the direction chosen. A fundamental component of that is the form of the organisation. This is a highly uncertain area of management as there are conflicting views about the kind of structure to have and how much influence structure has on performance.

Chapter 10 describes the main elements of organisation structure and the contrasting forms they take. Chapter 11 deals with one aspect of organisation structure, namely its human resource management policies. These are intended to ensure that employees work towards organisational objectives.

Chapter 12 focuses on information technology and e-business, showing how information technologies have deep implications for organisations and their management. Chapter 13 looks at some of the issues that arise in implementing organisational change and in stimulating innovation.

The Part case is The Royal Bank of Scotland, which has gone from being a highly regarded and innovative bank, to one that came close to failure. Now majority owned by the UK government, it is trying to rebuild its reputation.

CHAPTER 10
ORGANISATION STRUCTURE

Aim

To introduce terms and practices that show the choices managers face in shaping organisational structures.

Objectives

By the end of your work on this chapter you should be able to outline the concepts below in your terms and:

1 Outline the links between strategy, structure and performance

2 Give examples of how managers divide and co-ordinate work, with their likely advantages and disadvantages

3 Compare the features of mechanistic and organic structures

4 Summarise the work of Woodward, Burns and Stalker, Lawrence and Lorsch and John Child, showing how they contributed to this area of management

5 Use the 'contingencies' believed to influence choice of structure to evaluate the structure unit

6 Explain and illustrate the features of a learning organisation

7 Show how ideas from the chapter add to your understanding of the integrating themes

Key terms

This chapter introduces the following ideas:

organisation structure
organisation chart
formal structure
informal structure
vertical specialisation
horizontal specialisation
formal authority
responsibility
delegation
span of control
centralisation
decentralisation
formalisation
functional structure

divisional structure
matrix structure
network structure
mechanistic structure
organic structure
contingencies
technology
differentiation
integration
contingency approaches
determinism
structural choice
learning organisation

Each is a term defined within the text, as well as in the Glossary at the end of the book.

Case study   Oticon www.oticon.com

Oticon is a small Danish company which competes successfully with larger firms – in part because of its unusual organisation structure. It employs about 1,200 staff in Denmark in its research and production facilities, which supply high-tech devices to the rapidly growing number of people with hearing difficulties. Competition intensified during the 1980s and the company began to lose market share to larger rivals such as Siemens. Lars Kolind was appointed chief executive in 1988. In 1990 he concluded that a new approach was needed to counter the threats from larger competitors that were becoming stronger. Oticon's only hope for survival was to be radical in all aspects of the business. Kolind intended the changes to turn Oticon from an *industrial* organisation into a *service* organisation with a physical product.

He organised product development around projects. The project leader was appointed by the management team and recruited staff from within the firm to do the work: they chose whether or not to join – and could only do so if their current project leader agreed. Previously most people had a single skill; they were now required to be active in at least three specialties – one based on professional qualification and two others unrelated to the first. A chip designer could develop skills in customer support and advertising, for example. These arrangements allowed the company to respond quickly to unexpected events and use skills fully.

Previously Oticon had a conventional hierarchical structure, and a horizontal structure of separate functional departments. The only remnant of the hierarchy is the ten-person management team, each member of which acts as an 'owner' to the many projects through which work is done. Kolind refers to this as 'managed chaos'. The company tries to overcome the dangers of this by developing a strong and clear mission – 'to help people with X problem to live better with X'; and a common set of written values. Examples include: 'an assumption that we only employ adults (who can be expected to act responsibly)', and 'an assumption that staff want to know what and why they are doing it', so all information is available to everyone (with a few legally excepted areas).

There are no titles – people do whatever they think is right at the time. The potential for chaos is averted

Oticon

by building the flexible organisation on a foundation of clearly defined business processes, setting out essential tasks:

The better your processes are defined, the more flexible you can be.

The absence of departments avoids people protecting local interests and makes it easier to cope with fluctuations in workload.

Oticon was one of the earliest companies to redesign the workplace to maximise disturbance. This was most visible in the 'mobile office', in which each workstation was a desk without drawers (nowhere to file paper). There were no installed telephones, although everyone had a mobile. The workstations were equipped with powerful PCs through which people worked (staff had a small personal trolley for personal belongings which they wheeled to wherever they were working that day). Although common today, this arrangement was revolutionary at the time

Sources: Based on Bjorn-Andersen and Turner (1994); Rivard *et al.* (2004): and company website.

Case questions 10.1

- What factors persuaded management to change the structure at Oticon?
- How would you expect staff to react to these changes?

10.1   Introduction

Managers at Oticon had to adapt its structure to survive new competition. This required not only lower costs, but also an ability to respond more quickly to the needs of individual customers and to broader changes in technology and the market. The move to a project-based team approach allows staff to work on a wide range of tasks – which also bring them into close contact with customers. Each new product is designed in conjunction with members of a test-user panel who take part in analysis, design and testing phases of the work. This allows the company to maintain a rapid pace of innovation, and is one of the top three suppliers in the industry.

Senior managers of other companies whose performance has been below expectations often respond by announcing structural changes. Motorola's mobile devices have been losing market share for several years, and in 2009 the Board responded by dividing the company in two: one unit to focus exclusively on the handset market, the other on home and business communication networks. Others follow a policy of frequent small changes. The chairman of L'Oreal, the world's biggest beauty company refers to its

culture of permanent mini-restructuring. I don't think there has ever been a major restructuring in the whole of L'Oreal's corporate history . . . but there have been hundreds of little ones. What we do is try to live a life of permanent small change to avoid the major disasters. (*Financial Times*, 3 March 2008)

When an owner-manager is running a small business he/she decides what tasks to do and co-ordinates them. If the enterprise grows the entrepreneur usually passes some of the work to newly recruited staff, although the division will probably be flexible and informal. Owner and staff can easily communicate directly with each other, so co-ordination is easy. If the business continues to grow, some find that informality causes problems – so begin to introduce more structure. This often means clarifying tasks to ensure that people know where to focus their effort, and finding ways to ensure they communicate with others.

There are many elements in a structure, and some work better than others in different circumstances. This chapter will outline some of the choices available for dividing and co-ordinating work, and give examples of how managers have used them. It will contrast 'mechanistic' and 'organic' forms, and present a theory which predicts when each is likely to be most suitable. The chapter concludes with some ideas on learning organisations. Figure 10.1 shows these themes.

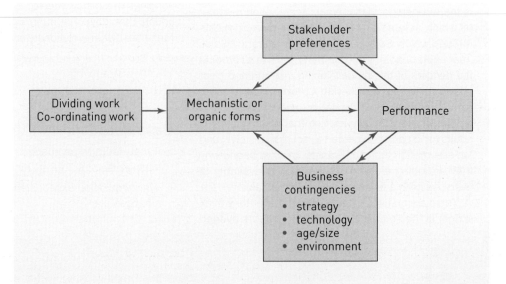

Figure 10.1
Alternative structures and performance

> ## 10.2   Perspectives on strategy, structure and performance

Alfred Chandler (1962) traced the evolution of America's largest industrial firms, showing how their strategies of growth and diversification placed too many demands on the centralised structures they had created. As the diversity of products and geographies grew, issues arose which those at the (increasingly remote) centre could not handle, as they lacked the knowledge of local circumstances. Chandler's historical analysis of du Pont, General Motors, Standard Oil and Sears, Roebuck shows how they responded by creating decentralised, divisional structures – a significant organisational innovation which many companies use today. It allowed managers at corporate headquarters to provide overall guidance and control, leaving the detailed running of each division to local managers (strategy shaped structure).

Chandler also shows that structure could influence strategy. A new legal requirement to break Standard Oil into small regional companies encouraged one of these – Standard Oil (New Jersey) – to expand into foreign markets as a way of increasing profits (structure shaped strategy). Chandler's aim was to study the interaction of strategy and structure in a changing business environment. In successive cases he traces how strategies to launch new products or enter new regions strained current structures, and how managers responded by gradually, through trial and error, developing new variants of the decentralised divisional form.

That research tradition continues in, for example, Grant's (2003) study of strategy in major oil companies – see Chapter 8. Eli Lilly (**www.lilly.com**), a pharmaceutical company, provides further evidence. The company faced commercial disaster when, quite unexpectedly, it lost patent protection of Prozac: at the time its most profitable drug. Colville and Murphy (2006) show how recovery involved intense debate about a new strategy and a new structure, followed by rapid implementation. This was so successful that the group began launching new drugs at an unprecedented rate, rapidly returning to profit. Whittington *et al.* (2006) also found that managers frequently re-think strategies and structures, and Table 10.1 gives examples of visible, corporate changes.

Table 10.1 Examples of strategic and organisational decisions

Example	Strategic issue	Structural issue
Royal Dutch Shell, 2009. **www.shell.com**	Shell's new CEO decided the present structure was too complex and costly. Aim of change was to cut costs and speed up large projects	Combined two largest divisions into one; some common functions (such as IT) moved from divisions to a central service.
Reed Elsevier, 2008 **www. reed-elsevier.com**	Long-serving CEO accelerates move to profitable online information services, and out of businesses with fluctuating revenue	Sells print-based educational publishing business, and uses funds to buy online risk assessment firm. Integrating this will reduce costs
Multi-show Events (see p. 297)	How to control growing business to ensure continued success.	Divided staff into departments to improve focus and skill; created distinct management roles
Sony Ericsson joint venture 2009 **www. sonyericsson.com**	Had not yet developed a smartphone, and lacked a plan to sell cheap mobiles in emerging markets. Development groups competing	New CEO cut 30 per cent of staff; centralised decision making to end internal rivalry; will use other companies' technology in first smartphone

While senior managers discuss these prominent changes, those at other levels work on fundamentally similar issues within their respective units, such as:

- Should we divide a job into three parts and give each to a separate employee, or have them work as a team with joint responsibility for the whole task?

- Should Team A do this task, or Team B?
- Should that employee report to supervisor A or supervisor B?

Whether the issue is at a multi-national business such as Motorola or a small company such as Multi-show Events, the fundamental structural task is the same – how to enhance performance by clarifying and co-ordinating peoples' roles and responsibilities.

The next section introduces the main tools that people can use to shape the structure of an organisation or of a unit within it.

10.3	**Designing a structure**

Organisation structure
'The structure of an organisation [is] the sum total of the ways in which it divides its labour into distinct tasks and then achieves co-ordination among them' (Mintzberg, 1979).

Organisation structure describes how managers divide, supervise and co-ordinate work. It gives someone accepting a job a reasonably clear idea of what they should do – the marketing assistant should deal with marketing, not finance. The topic is closely related to culture (Chapter 3) and to human resource management (Chapter 11), since managers intend recruitment, appraisal and reward systems to support the basic structure by encouraging people to act consistently with it.

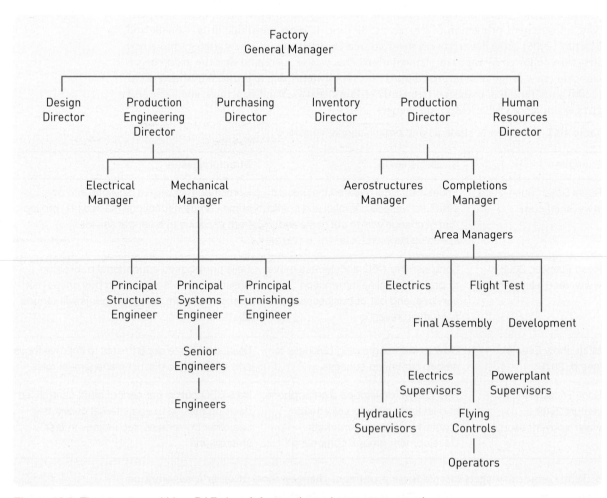

Figure 10.2 The structure within a BAE aircraft factory (**www.baesystems.com**)

The organisation chart

The **organisation chart** shows the main departments and job titles, with lines linking senior executives to the departments or people for whose work they are responsible. It shows who people report to, and clarifies four features of the **formal structure**:

* tasks – the major tasks or activities of the organisation;
* subdivisions – how they are divided;
* levels – the position of each post within the hierarchy;
* lines of authority – these link the boxes to show who people report to.

Organisation charts give a convenient (although transient) summary of tasks and who is responsible for them. Figure 10.2 shows that for an aircraft factory which was then part of BAE Systems, a UK defence contractor. There are six departments; design, production engineering, purchasing, inventory, production and human resources. It also shows the chain of command within the plant and the tasks of the respective departments (only some of which are shown). In this case the chart includes direct staff such as operators and engineers, and shows the lines of authority throughout the factory. It does *not* show the **informal structure** – the many patterns of work and communication that are part of organisational life.

Work specialisation

Within the formal structure managers divide work into smaller tasks, in which people or departments specialise. They become more expert in one task than they could be in several and are more likely to come up with improved ideas or methods. Taken too far it leads to the negative effects on motivation described in Chapter 15.

> An **organisation chart** shows the main departments and senior positions in an organisation and the reporting relations between them.
>
> **Formal structure** consists of guidelines, documents or procedures setting out how the organisation's activities are divided and co-ordinated.
>
> **Informal structure** is the undocumented relationships between members of the organisation that emerge as people adapt systems to new conditions, and satisfy personal and group needs.

Management in practice   Multi-show Events

Multi-show Events employs 11 people providing a variety of entertainment and promotional services to large businesses. When Brian Simpson created the business there were two staff – so there was no formal structure. He reflected on the process of growth and structure:

> While the company was small, thinking about a structure never occurred to me. It became a consideration as sales grew and the complexity of what we offered increased. There were also more people around and I believed that I should introduce a structure so that clear divisions of responsibility would be visible. It seemed natural to split sales and marketing from the actual delivery and production of events as these were two distinct areas. I felt that by creating 'specialised' departments we could give a better service to clients as each area of the company could focus more on their own roles. [Figure 10.3 shows the structure.]
>
> We had to redesign the office layout and introduce a more formalised communication process to ensure all relevant information is being passed on – and on the whole I think this structure will see us through the next stage of business growth and development.

Source: Private communication.

Figure 10.2 shows specialisation in the BAE factory: at the top it is between design, production, purchasing and so on. It shows a **vertical specialisation** in that people at each level deal with distinct activities, and a **horizontal specialisation.** Within production engineering some specialise in electrical problems and others in mechanical: within the latter, people focus on structures, systems or furnishings. Although Multi-show Events is still a small company, it also has begun to create a structure showing who is responsible for which tasks.

> **Vertical specialisation** refers to the extent to which responsibilities at different levels are defined.
>
> **Horizontal specialisation** is the degree to which tasks are divided among separate people or departments.

Chain of command

The lines of authority show the links between people – who they report to and who reports to them. It shows who they can ask to do work, who they can ask for help – and who will be expecting results from them. In Figure 10.2 the Production Director can give instructions to the Aerostructures Manager, but not to the Electrical Manager in production engineering. Figure 10.3 shows the lines of authority in Multi-show Events. In both, people have countless informal contacts which make the system live, and help people to cope with unplanned events.

In drawing the lines of authority, managers decide where to allocate **formal authority** – giving people the right to make decisions, allocate resources or give instructions. It is based on the position, not the person. The Production Engineering Director at BAE has formal authority over a defined range of matters – and anyone else taking over the job would have the same formal authority.

Subordinates comply with instructions because they accept the person has the formal (sometimes called legitimate) authority to make them. An operator in the hydraulics area of final assembly would accept an instruction from the hydraulics foreman, but probably not from the powerplant foreman (they may help as a personal favour, but that is different from accepting formal authority). If managers give instructions beyond their area of formal authority, they meet resistance.

Responsibility is a person's duty to meet the expectations associated with a task. The Production Director and the Hydraulics Foreman are responsible for the tasks that go with those positions. To fulfil those responsibilities they require formal authority to manage relevant resources.

Formal authority is the right that a person in a specified role has to make decisions, allocate resources or give instructions.

Responsibility refers to a person's duty to meet the expectations others have of him/her in his/her role.

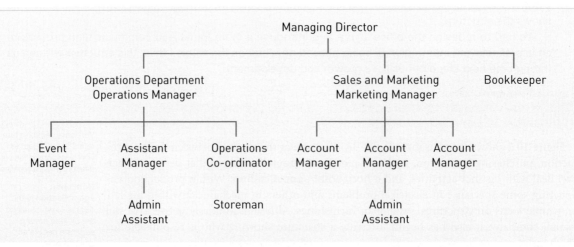

Figure 10.3 The organisation structure at Multi-show Events

Accountability means that people with formal authority over an area are required to report on their work to those above them in the chain of command. The Principal Systems Engineer is accountable to the Mechanical Manager for the way he/she has used resources: have they achieved what was expected as measured by the cost, quantity, quality or timeliness of the work?

Case study   Oticon – the case continues – hierarchy and rank

Before the change, the company had six distinct hierarchical levels, with privileges based on rank:

> Not only was there a specific company car assigned to each management level, but other material signs existed . . . prestige and reward were very apparent: in the length of the curtains, the type of carpet . . . the size of people's desks. It all gave status. And that was what people strove for. (Rivard *et al.*, 2004, p. 181)

Horizontal boundaries were also strong, as the two main divisions – Electronics (product development) and International (sales) communicated poorly. Within these divisions work was organised round specific departments and tasks.

> People were locked into specific roles and responsibilities and were rewarded only for those – nobody took initiatives (Rivard *et al.*, 2004, p. 180)

Sources: Based on Bjorn-Andersen and Turner (1994); Rivard *et al.* (2004).

Delegation is the process by which people transfer responsibility and authority for part of their work to people below them in the hierarchy. While the Production Director is responsible and accountable for all the work in that area, he/she can only do this by delegating. He/she must account for the results, but pass responsibility and necessary authority to subordinates – and this continues down the hierarchy. If managers delegate to their subordinates this enables quicker decisions and more rapid responses, although some managers are reluctant to delegate in case it reduces their power (Chapter 14).

> **Delegation** occurs when one person gives another the authority to undertake specific activities or decisions.

The span of control

The **span of control** is the number of subordinates reporting to a supervisor. If managers supervise staff closely there is a narrow span of control – as shown in the top half of Figure 10.4. If they allow staff to have more autonomy and responsibility that means less supervision, so more can report to the same manager: the span of control becomes wider, and the structure flatter – the lower half of Figure 10.4.

> A **span of control** is the number of subordinates reporting directly to the person above them in the hierarchy.

Key ideas   Joan Woodward's research

Joan Woodward's study of 100 firms in Essex found great variety between them in the number of subordinates managers supervised (Woodward, 1965). The number of people reporting directly to the chief executive ranged from 2 to 18, with the median span of control being 6. The average span of control of the first line supervisors varied from 10 to 90, with a median of 37. Woodward explained the variation by the technological system used (more in Section 10.7).

Centralisation and decentralisation

As an organisation grows, managers divide work vertically, delegating decisions to those below them – and so begin to create a hierarchy as in Figure 10.4. As the business grows, the

(a) A tall structure, with narrow spans of supervision

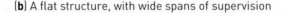

(b) A flat structure, with wide spans of supervision

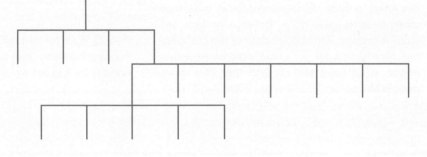

Figure 10.4
Tall and flat
organisation
structures

hierarchy becomes more complex, but it is usually possible to see three levels – corporate, divisional and operating – such as at The Royal Bank of Scotland (RBS) (**www.rbs.com**).

● **Corporate** The most senior group: the Board of RBS has overall responsibility for leading and controlling the company. It approves strategy across the group, monitors performance at major units, and maintains links with significant external institutions such as regulators and political bodies.

● **Divisional** Responsible for implementing policy, and allocating budgets and other resources. RBS is organised partly by customer (UK Personal and UK Corporate); partly by product (RBS Insurance); and partly geographically (Europe and Middle East Retail and Commercial Banking). Division managers are responsible for meeting the targets which the Board sets for them. They also represent the division's interests to the Board and monitor the performance of the division's operating units.

● **Operating** Responsible for the technical work of the organisation – making products, catching thieves, caring for patients or delivering services. Within UK Personal at RBS there are teams responsible for ensuring that, for example, branches and cash machines work smoothly.

The vertical hierarchy establishes what decisions people at each level can make. The theme is especially relevant in large multinational companies, which experience constant tension between calls for global integration and local responsiveness – see Section 10.10 (Internationalisation).

Centralisation is when those at the top make most decisions, with managers at divisional level ensuring those at operating level follow the policy.

Decentralisation is when a relatively large number of decisions are taken in the divisions or operating units. Branch managers in ATMays, a chain of retail travel agents (now part of Going Places) had considerable freedom over pricing and promotional activities, but were required to follow very tight financial reporting routines.

Centralisation is when a relatively large number of decisions are taken by management at the top of the organisation.

Decentralisation is when a relatively large number of decisions are taken lower down the organisation in the operating units.

> ## Management in practice   A decentralised structure at Roche   www.roche.com
>
> Roche, based in Switzerland, is one of the world's most successful and profitable pharmaceutical companies. The board appointed a new chief executive in 2010 – Severin Schwan (a graduate in business and law) who, at the age of 40, has spent his career in the company. The group has a decentralised structure and a hands-off relationship with subsidiaries which analysts believe has been a major factor in its success. The federal structure fosters focused research, with each company concentrating on specific diseases, but supple enough to collaborate on marketing. Mr Schwan says teamwork is essential in this knowledge-based business:
>
> > When I toured our labs, I grasped the potential and the enthusiasm of our people. We have to capitalise on that. If you tell your people all the time what to do, don't be surprised if they don't come up with new ideas. Innovative people need air to breathe. Our culture of working together at Roche is based on mutual trust and teamwork. An informal friendly manner supports this: at the same time this must not lead to negligence or shoddy compromises – goals must be achieved and, at times, tough decisions have to be implemented.
>
> Source: *Financial Times*, 4 August 2008.

Many organisations display a mix of both. Network Rail (responsible for all the railway track and signals) has highly standardised processes and highly centralised control systems, but local managers have high autonomy in deciding how to organise their resources. They can co-ordinate track improvements and engineering schedules to meet the needs of local train operating companies (*Financial Times*, 23 July 2007).

This tension between centralising and decentralising is common, with the balance at any time reflecting managers' relative power and their views on the advantages of one direction or the other (see Table 10.2).

Table 10.2 Advantages and disadvantages of centralisation

Factor	Advantages	Disadvantages
Response to change	Thorough debate of issues	Slower response to local conditions
Use of expertise	Concentration of expertise at the centre makes it easier to develop new services and promote best practice methods	Less likely to take account of local knowledge or innovative people
Cost	Economies of scale in purchasing Efficient administration by using common systems	Local suppliers may be better value than corporate suppliers
Policy implications	Less risk of local managers breaching legal requirements	More risk of local managers breaching legal requirements
Staff commitment	Backing of centre ensures wide support	Staff motivated by greater local responsibility
Consistency	Provides consistent image to the public – less variation in service standards	Local staff discouraged from taking responsibility – can blame centre

Formalisation

Formalisation is the practice of using written or electronic documents to direct and control employees.

Formalisation is when managers use written or electronic documents to direct and control employees. These include rule books, procedures, instruction manuals, job descriptions – anything that shows what people must do. Operators in most call centres use scripts to guide their conversation with a customer: managers create these to bring consistency and predictability to the work.

There is always tension between formality and informality. If people want to respond to individual needs or local conditions, they favour informal arrangements with few rules, as this seems the best way to meet those needs. Industry regulators or consumer legislation may specify detailed procedures that companies must follow: these are meant to protect customers against unsuitable selling methods, or to protect staff against unfounded complaints. This leads to more formal systems and recording procedures.

Activity 10.2 Critical reflection on structures

Select an organisation with which you are familiar, or which you can find out about. Gather information about aspects of the structure, such as:

- Does the organisation chart look tall or flat?
- What evidence is there of high or low levels of formality?
- Which decisions are centralised and which are decentralised?
- Share your information with colleagues on your course, to increase your awareness of the range of ways in which people have designed structures.

10.4 Grouping jobs into functions and divisions

While work specialisation divides tasks into smaller jobs for individuals, an opposite process groups them together in functional, divisional or matrix forms. Two other forms use teams and networks as the basis of structure. Figure 10.5 shows these alternatives.

Specialisation by function

A **functional structure** is when tasks are grouped into departments based on similar skills and expertise.

In a **functional structure**, managers group staff according to their profession or function, such as production or finance. The BAE chart shows design, production engineering, purchasing, inventory, production and human resources functions. Figure 10.6 shows a hospital chart, with a functional structure at senior level.

The functional approach can be efficient as people with common expertise work together to provide a service, and follow a professional career path. It can lead to conflict if functions have different perceptions of organisational goals (Nauta and Sanders, 2001) or priorities. Le Meunier-FitzHugh and Piercy (2008) show how staff in sales and marketing experience this – the former stressing immediate sales, the latter long-term customer relations. Functional staff face conflicts when product managers compete for access to functional resources such as information technology.

Specialisation by divisions

A **divisional structure** is when tasks are grouped in relation to their outputs, such as products or the needs of different types of customer.

Managers create a **divisional structure** when they arrange the organisation around products, services or customers, giving those in charge of each unit the authority to design, produce and deliver the product or service. Functions within the division are likely to co-operate as they depend on satisfying the same set of customers.

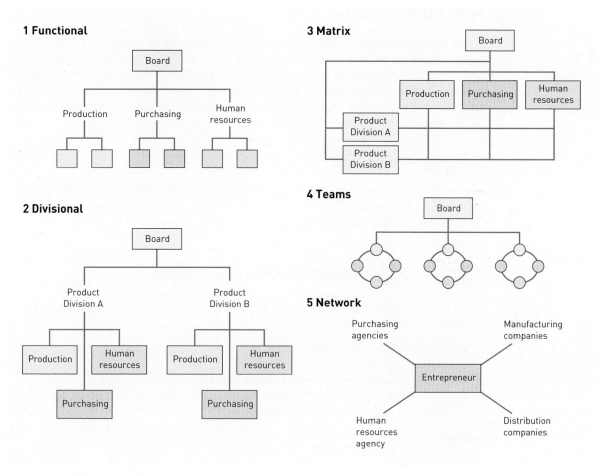

Figure 10.5 Five types of structure

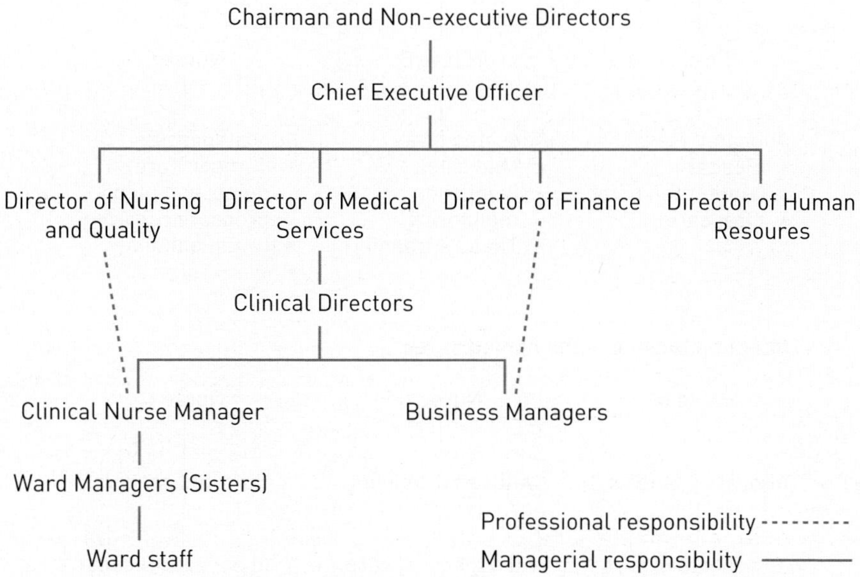

Figure 10.6 Partial organisation structure in a hospital

Product or customer

Divisional structures enable staff to focus on a distinct group of customers – HMV Group (**www.hmv.co.uk**) has two divisions – the HMV stores, and Waterstone's bookshops. Hospitals can use the 'named-nurse' system, in which one nurse is responsible for several identified patients. That nurse is the patient's point of contact with the system, managing the delivery of services to the patient from other (functional) departments. Figure 10.7 contrasts 'task' and 'named-nurse' approaches.

Geographic divisions

Here managers in companies with many service outlets – such as Tesco or Wetherspoon's – group them by geography. This allows front-line staff to identify local needs, and makes it easier for divisional managers to control local performance (see Table 10.3).

Activity 10.3   Choosing between approaches

Go to the website of a company that interests you and gather information about the structure of the company.

- Decide whether it has a functional or a divisional structure – and, if the latter, is that based on products or geography?
- If it has international operations, how are they shown in the structure?
- Compare your research with colleagues on your course, and prepare a short presentation summarising your conclusions

---

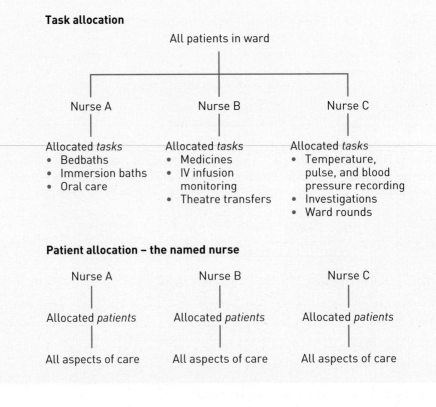

Figure 10.7
Task and named-
nurse structures

Table 10.3 Advantages and disadvantages of functional and divisional structures

Structure	Advantages	Disadvantages
Functional	Clear career paths and professional development	Isolation from wider interests damages promotion prospects
	Specialisation leads to high standards and efficiency	Conflict over priorities
	Common professional interests support good internal relations	Lack of wider awareness damages external relations
Divisional	Functional staff focus on product and customer needs	Isolation from wider professional and technical developments
	Dedicated facilities meet customer needs quickly	Costs of duplicate resources
	Common customer focus enables good internal relations	Potential conflict with other divisions over priorities
		Focus on local, not corporate, needs

10.5   Grouping jobs in matrices, teams and networks

Matrix structure

A matrix structure combines functional and divisional structures: function on one axis of the matrix and products or projects on the other. Functional staff work on one or more projects, moving between them as required. They report to two bosses – a functional head and the head of the current project.

A **matrix structure** is when those doing a task report both to a functional and a project or divisional boss.

Teams

In their search for more flexibility, lower costs and faster response some companies organise work into teams – especially those that depend on a steady flow of new products, such as Nokia or EMI Music. Management delegates significant responsibility and authority to an identifiable team, which is then accountable for results (Chapter 17).

Management in practice   **Team launches new albums at EMI**   www.emi.com

New music albums often fail when managers are unable to manage the launch effectively. There is often tension between marketing staff who have a short-term outlook, being expected to satisfy current consumers by exploiting existing resources, and creative staff who take a medium-term view. The latter do so as they are expected to find new artists to change the repertoire – and who therefore need longer to become credible.

Ordanini *et al.* (2008) show how EMI Music adopted a team approach to launching new albums. They appointed a single team to be responsible for all aspects of the launch of an album by an unknown and possibly controversial artist. The team included marketing and creative staff, and enabled them to work together in this way for the first time. In this case the launch was successful on several dimensions, and appeared to vindicate the choice of a team approach.

Source: Ordanini *et al.* (2008).

Networks

A **network structure** is when tasks required by one company are performed by other companies with expertise in those areas.

Network structures refer to situations in which organisations remain independent but agree to work together to deliver products or services. Sometimes this happens when managers arrange for other companies to undertake certain non-core activities on their behalf. The remaining organisation concentrates on setting strategy direction and managing the core units. Electronic companies often do this: Dell's products are made under contract by companies that specialise in such work. The arrangement is becoming common in personal services – such as when Care UK runs schools for disturbed children for local government, and in Community Health Partnerships (see the following Management in Practice).

Management in practice — Community Health Partnerships (CHP)
www.communityhealthpartnerships.co.uk

Many social and health problems are caused by a range of conditions which have traditionally been the responsibility of distinct public bodies – health, social work, education, housing and police. Many practitioners believe that effective solutions depend on these independent agencies working together to offer a more comprehensive service than any agency could do alone.

A prominent example is Community Health Partnerships (CHP), an independent company, wholly owned by the UK Department of Health. It aims to deliver innovative ways to improve health and local authority services through the Local Improvement Finance Trust (LIFT) Initiative which provides modern premises for health and local authority services in England.

It has established 48 LIFT partnerships, covering two-thirds of England's population, and is responsible for more than 250 buildings that are either open or under construction. More recently, CHP has developed new models of public–private partnership, such as Community Ventures and Social Enterprises, to improve health and social care.

The different backgrounds, priorities and cultures of the organisations taking part make such ventures challenging to manage.

Sources: Company website; other published sources.

Mixed forms

Large organisations typically combine functional, product and geographical structures within the same company – see for example BP (Part 2 Case) or RBS (Part 4 Case).

The counterpart of dividing work is to co-ordinate it, or there will be confusion and poor performance.

Activity 10.4 — Comparing structures

Think of an organisation you have worked in or about which you can gather information.

- Which of the five structural forms did it correspond to most closely?
- What were the benefits and disadvantages of that approach?
- Compare your conclusions with colleagues on your course, and use your experience to prepare a list of the advantages and disadvantages of each type of structure.

10.6   Co-ordinating work

There are five common ways to co-ordinate work.

Direct supervision

This is where a manager ensures co-ordination by directly supervising his/her staff to ensure they work as expected. The number of people whom a manager can effectively supervise directly reflects the idea of the span of control – that beyond some (variable) point direct supervision is no longer sufficient.

Hierarchy

If disputes or problems arise between staff or departments, they can put the arguments to their common boss in the hierarchy, making it the boss's responsibility to reach a solution. At BAE (Figure 10.2), if the engineer responsible for structures has a disagreement with the Systems Engineer, they can ask the Mechanical Manager to adjudicate. If that fails they can escalate the problem to the Production Engineering Director – but this takes time. In rapidly changing circumstances the hierarchy cannot cope with the many issues requiring attention and so delays decisions.

Standardising inputs and outputs

If the buyer of a component specifies exactly what is required, and the supplier meets that specification, co-ordination between any users will be easy. If staff meet the specifications, that helps them to co-ordinate with the next stage. If they receive the same training they will need less direct supervision, as their manager can be confident they will work consistently. All new staff at Pret A Manger must complete a very precise training course before they begin work, which is then constantly reinforced once they are in a post.

Rules and procedures

Another method is to prepare rules or procedures, like those in the following Management in Practice. As another example, organisations have procedures for approving capital expenditure. To compare proposals accurately they set strict guidelines on the questions a bid should answer, how people should prepare a case and to whom they should submit it. Software developers face the challenge of co-ordinating the work of the designers working on different parts of a project, so they use strict change control procedures to ensure that the sub-projects fit together.

Management in practice   Safety procedures in a power station

The following instructions govern the steps that staff must follow when they inspect control equipment in a nuclear power station:

1 Before commencing work you must read and understand the relevant Permit-to-Work and/or other safety documents as appropriate.
2 Obtain keys for relevant cubicles.
3 Visually inspect the interior of each bay for dirt, water and evidence of condensation.
4 Visually inspect the cabling, glands, terminal blocks and components for damage.
5 Visually check for loose connections at all terminals.
6 Lock all cubicles and return the keys.
7 Clear the safety document and return it to the Supervisor/Senior Authorised person.

Information systems

Information systems help to ensure that people who need to work in a consistent way have common information, so that they can co-ordinate their activities. Computer systems and internet applications enable different parts of an organisation, as well as suppliers and customers, to work from common information, making co-ordination much easier (see Chapter 12).

Key ideas   **Co-ordinating sales and marketing**

Large organisations typically create separate sales and marketing departments, which must then co-ordinate their work to ensure co-operation, customer satisfaction and profitability. Homberg *et al.* (2008) concluded (from a survey of German firms in financial services, consumer goods and chemicals) that the best performance was in firms where managers had:

- developed strong structural links between the two functions, especially by using teams, and requiring staff to plan projects jointly; and
- ensured that staff in both functions had high market knowledge, by rotating them between other functions in the firm to develop knowledge about customers and competitors, which then helped the two functions to work effectively together.

Source: Homburg *et al.* (2008).

Most companies purchase goods and services electronically, ensuring that orders and payments to suppliers flow automatically to match current demand. This co-ordinates a laborious task where mistakes were common.

Direct personal contact

The most human form of co-ordination is when people talk to each other. Mintzberg (1979) found that people use this method in both the simplest and the most complex situations. There is so much uncertainty in the latter that information systems cannot cope – only direct contact can do this, by enabling people to making personal commitments across business units (Sull and Spinosa, 2005) (see the above Key Ideas and the following Management in Practice).

Management in practice   **Co-ordination in a social service**

The organisation cares for the elderly in a large city. Someone who had worked there for several years reflected on co-ordination:

Within the centre there was a manager, two deputies, an assistant manager, five senior care officers (SCOs) and 30 officers. Each SCO is responsible for six care officers, allowing daily contact between the supervisor and the subordinates. While this defines job roles quite tightly, it allows a good communication structure to exist. Feedback is common as there are frequent meetings of the separate groups, and individual appraisals of the care officers by the SCOs. Staff value this opportunity for praise and comments on how they are doing.

Contact at all levels is common between supervisor and care officers during meetings to assess the needs of clients, for whom the care officers have direct responsibility. Frequent social gatherings and functions within the department also enhance relations and satisfy social needs. Controls placed on the behaviour of the care officers come from senior management, often derived from legislation such as the Social Work Acts or the Health and Safety Executive.

Source: Private communication.

Activity 10.5   Comparing co-ordination

Think of an organisation you have worked in or about which you can gather information

- Which forms of co-ordination did it use?
- What were the benefits and disadvantages of that approach?
- Compare your conclusions with colleagues on your course, and use your experience to prepare a list of the advantages and disadvantages of each method of co-ordination.

Managers make a succession of decisions on any or all of these ways to divide and co-ordinate work: as they do so they build a structure which in varying degrees correspond to a mechanistic or organic form.

10.7   Mechanistic and organic structures

The purpose of structure is to encourage people to act in a way that supports strategy. Some structures emphasise the vertical hierarchy by defining responsibilities clearly, taking decisions at the centre, delegating tightly defined tasks and requiring frequent reports. This enables those at the centre to know what is happening and whether staff are working correctly. The organisation presents a uniform image and ensures that customers receive consistent treatment. Communication is mainly vertical, as the centre passes instructions down and staff pass queries up. Burns and Stalker (1961) called this a **mechanistic structure**.

Others develop a structure with broadly defined, flexible tasks, many cross-functional teams, and base authority on expertise rather than position. Management accepts that the centre depend on those nearest the action to find the best solution. Communication is mainly horizontal among those familiar with the task. There may not be an organisation chart, as the division of work is so fluid. Burns and Stalker (1961) called this an **organic structure**. Table 10.4 compares mechanistic and organic forms.

A **mechanistic structure** means there is a high degree of task specialisation, people's responsibility and authority are closely defined and decision making is centralised.

An **organic structure** is one where people are expected to work together and use their initiative to solve problems; job descriptions and rules are few and imprecise.

Management in practice   An organic structure at Pixar   www.pixar.com

The company's string of successful movies depends not only on the creative people that it employs, but on how it manages that talent. Ed Catmull (co-founder of Pixar and president of Pixar and Disney Animation Studios) has written about what he calls the 'collective creativity' of the process, and how the senior team fosters this. Something that he believes sets Pixar apart from other studios is the way that people at all levels support each other. An example of how they do this is the process of daily reviews. He writes:

> The practice of working together as peers is core to our culture, and it's not limited to our directors and producers. One example is our daily reviews, or 'dailies' a process for giving and getting constant feedback in a positive way . . . People show work in an incomplete state to the whole animation crew, and although the director makes decisions, everyone is encouraged to comment. There are several benefits. First, once people get over the embarrassment of showing work still in progress, they become more creative. Second, director or creative leads . . . can communicate important points to the entire crew at the same time. Third, people learn from and inspire each other: a highly creative piece of animation will spark others to raise their game. Finally, there are no surprises at the end: when you're done, you're done. People's overwhelming desire to make sure their work is 'good' before they show it to others increases the possibility that their finished version won't be what the director wants. The dailies process avoids such wasted efforts.

Source: Catmull (2008), p. 70.

Table 10.4 Characteristics of mechanistic and organic systems

Mechanistic	Organic
Specialised tasks	Contribute experience to common tasks
Hierarchical structure of control	Network structure of contacts
Knowledge located at top of hierarchy	Knowledge widely spread
Vertical communication	Horizontal communication
Loyalty and obedience stressed	Commitment to goals more important

Source: Based on Burns and Stalker (1961).

Within a large organisation some units will correspond to a mechanistic form and others to an organic. A company may have a centralised information system and tightly controlled policies on capital expenditure – while also allowing business units autonomy on research or advertising budgets.

Case questions 10.2

- What was the role of strategy and technology in encouraging the change at Oticon?
- What features of the present form correspond to the organic model?
- How does management hope that the new structure will support their strategy?

Contingencies are factors such as uncertainty, interdependence and size that reflect the situation of the organisation.

Why do managers favour one form of structure rather than another? One (though disputed) view is that it depends on how they interpret **contingencies**:

> the essence of the contingency paradigm is that organizational effectiveness results from fitting characteristics of the organization, such as its structure, to contingencies that reflect the situation of the organization. (Donaldson, 2001, p. 1)

Successful organisations appear to be those in which managers maintain a good fit between contingent factors and the structure within which people work. Figure 10.1 illustrates four contingent factors – strategy, technology, age/size and environment.

Strategy

Chapter 8 outlines Porter's view that firms adopt one of three generic strategies: cost leadership, differentiation or focus. With a cost leadership strategy managers try to increase efficiency to keep costs low. A mechanistic structure is likely to support this strategy, with closely defined tasks in an efficient functional structure. A hierarchical chain of command ensures that people work to plan and vertical communication keeps the centre informed. Powergen, an electricity utility, initially had a cost-leadership strategy, supporting this with a functional structure with detailed rules and performance measures.

A differentiation strategy focuses on innovation – developing new products rapidly and imaginatively. An organic structure is most likely to support this, by enabling ideas to flow easily between people able to contribute, regardless of their function. Hill and Pickering (1986) showed that companies which allowed business units more decision-making authority were more successful than those which limited this. The Part 5 Case shows how, like Pixar in animation, W.L. Gore uses an organic form in its high-tech businesses. Oticon adopted a team-based structure, as has Monsanto (see the following Management in Practice).

Management in practice   **Changing Monsanto**   www.monsanto.com

Although many see Monsanto as a predatory chemical company pressing genetically modified seeds on the world, its chief executive (Mr Grant) sees it as a vibrant biotechnology company with all the dynamism of a Silicon Valley start-up:

> In some companies the scientists are in the back room, separate from the business people. The culture here is much closer to a software company, where there are developers that invent cool stuff and there is a very intimate link between the scientists and the business people.

This is reflected, Mr Grant says, in the company's day-to-day operations.

> If we're making decisions, there's usually five or six people at the table. That makes for a culture that is extraordinarily team-based – not in the sense of group hugs and the fluff factor, but because most decisions we make are multi-disciplinary and if you want to make a decision once, you had better have those people at the table.
>
> It's an environment where people need to have an equal voice . . . Quite often you will have a business person, a regulatory person, a breeding person, a production person and a couple of others. That has created a culture where people come together, form teams, make decisions, break up and move on to the next thing. It's more amorphous than the hierarchical corporate structure, and that makes it feel more like a modern company than an old world company.

Source: *Financial Times*, 15 June 2009.

Figure 10.8 expresses the idea that different strategies require different structures. The more the strategy corresponds to cost leadership, the more likely it is that managers will support it with a functional structure. If the balance is towards differentiation, the more likely there will be a divisional, team or network structure.

Technology

Technology refers to the knowledge, tools and techniques used to transform inputs into outputs. It includes buildings, machines, computer systems, and the knowledge and procedures associated with them.

Joan Woodward (1965) gathered information from 100 British firms to establish whether structural features such as the span of control or the number of levels in the hierarchy varied between them, and whether this affected performance. The researchers saw no pattern until they analysed companies by their manufacturing process, grouping these into three types according to their technical complexity. This showed a relationship between technical complexity and company structure.

> **Technology** is the knowledge, equipment and activities used to transform inputs into outputs.

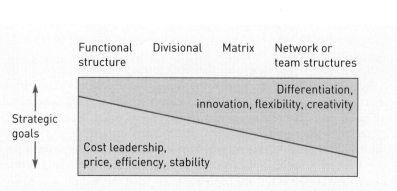

Figure 10.8
Relationship between strategies and structural types

- **Unit and small batch production** Firms make unique goods to a customer's order. It is similar to craft work, as people and their skills are deeply involved in the process – custom-built cycles, designer furniture, luxury yachts.
- **Large batch and mass production** Large quantities of standard products move along an assembly line, with people complementing the machinery – mobile phones, Ford cars or Electrolux washing machines.
- **Continuous process** Material flows through complex technology which makes the product as operators monitor it, fixing faults and generally overseeing the process – a Guinness Brewery, BP refinery or Mittal steel plant.

Woodward concluded that the different technologies impose different demands on people. Unit production requires close supervision to ensure each staff meet each customer's unique requirements. Supervisors can communicate directly with those working on different parts of the task and so manage the uncertainties involved in producing 'one-off' items. On an assembly line the work is routine and predictable, so a supervisor can monitor more staff: there is a wide span of control. Commercially successful firms were those where managers had created a structure providing the right support to staff using the technology.

Technology also delivers services, and managers create structures to shape the way staff interact with customers. Bank staff used to handle many cash transactions, and sat behind secure glass screens which made them remote. Technology means that bank branches now handle very little cash, so banks re-designed them to bring staff and customers closer together. The Part 4 Case – The Royal Bank of Scotland – traces structural changes in that service business, including the centralised Manufacturing Division which has a mechanistic structure. When Steve Jobs was at Pixar, like Lars Kolind at Oticon, he designed the building:

> to maximize inadvertent encounters. At the centre is a large atrium which contains the cafeteria, meeting rooms, bathrooms, and mailboxes. As a result, everyone has strong reasons to go there repeatedly during the course of the workday. It's hard to describe just how valuable the resulting chance encounters are. (Catmull, 2008, p. 71)

Environment

Chapter 3 shows how environments vary in terms of their complexity and dynamism: does this mean that firms need a structure that suits the nature of their environment? Burns and Stalker (1961) compared the structure of a long-established rayon plant in Manchester with the structures of several new electronics companies then being created in the east of Scotland. Both types of organisation were successful – but they had different structures.

The rayon plant had clearly set-out rules, tight job descriptions, clear procedures and coordination was primarily through the hierarchy. There was a high degree of specialisation, with tasks divided into small parts. Managers had defined responsibilities clearly and discouraged people from acting outside of their remit. They had centralised decisions, with information flowing up the hierarchy and instructions flowing down.

The small companies in the newly created electronics industry had few job descriptions, while procedures were ambiguous and imprecise. Staff were expected to use their initiative to decide priorities and to work together to solve problems. Communication was horizontal, rather than vertical (see Table 10.4).

Burns and Stalker (1961) concluded that both forms were appropriate for their circumstances. The rayon plant had a stable environment, as its purpose was to supply a steady flow of rayon to the company's spinning factories. Delivery schedules rarely changed and the technology of rayon manufacture was well known. In contrast, the electronics companies were in direct contact with their customers, mainly the Ministry of Defence. The demand for commercial and military products was volatile, with frequent changes in requirements. The technology was new, often applying the results of recent research. Contracts were often taken, in which neither the customer nor the company knew what the end product would be: it was likely to change during the course of the work.

Case study   Oticon – the case continues – communication and technology

Lars Kolind knew that the dramatic change in structure he proposed would not be achieved without pain: he was attacking the established culture, privileges tied to seniority and titles, and wasteful work processes. In moving to an organisation in which there would be only project members, project leaders and project owners, many would not easily accept losing the power they derived from controlling information. He used his power to drive the change, announcing:

> I am 100 per cent sure that we will try this. There's enough time so that you can make a choice – whether you are going to try it with us or whether . . . you find another job. (Quoted in Rivard *et al.*, 2004, p. 174)

While the company used advanced IS for many functions, Kolind believed that dialogue is better than email, and designed the building to support face-to-face dialogue between staff. The problem owner will usually use email or personal contact to bring two or three people together and have a stand-up meeting. Decisions are noted on the computer (accessible by everyone).

By 1994 the company had halved product development time and more than doubled sales. It employed half as many administrative staff as in 1990, but double the number on product development. Financial performance improved dramatically in the years following the change.

> Hardware companies have organisations that look like machines: a company that produces knowledge needs an organisation that looks like a brain, i.e. which looks chaotic and is unhierarchical. (Lars Kolind)

Sources: Based on Bjorn-Andersen and Turner (1994); Rivard *et al.* (2004).

Case questions 10.3

● Oticon has had both mechanistic and organic structures: what prompted the change?

● Why has the new structure improved business performance?

Burns and Stalker (1961) concluded that stable, predictable environments were likely to encourage a mechanistic structure. Volatile, unpredictable environments were likely to encourage an organic structure. This recognition that environmental conditions place different demands upon organisations was a major step in understanding why companies adopt contrasting structures – an idea which Figure 10.9 illustrates.

	Structure	
	Mechanistic	*Organic*
Uncertain (unstable)	**Incorrect fit:** Mechanistic structure in uncertain environment Structure too tight	**Correct fit:** Organic structure in uncertain environment
Certain (stable)	**Correct fit:** Mechanistic structure in certain environment	**Incorrect fit:** Organic structure in certain environment Structure too loose

Environment

Figure 10.9 Relationship between environment and structure

Activity 10.6 Comparing mechanistic and organic forms

Think of a department you have worked in or about which you can gather information.

- Was it broadly mechanistic or organic?
- Why has that form evolved and is it suitable?
- How does it compare with other departments in the organisation?

Management in practice   Organic problem solving in a mechanistic structure

The organisation I work for has just come through a short-term cash-flow crisis. The problem arose because, while expenditures on contracts are relatively predictable and even the income flow was disrupted by a series of contractual disputes.

The role culture permeates the head office, and at first the problem was pushed ever upwards. But faced with this crisis all departments were asked for ideas on how to improve performance. Some have been turned into new methods of working, and others are still being considered by the 'ideas team', drawn from all grades of personnel and departments. This was a totally new perspective, of a task culture operating within a role culture – that is, we developed an organic approach. What could be more simple than asking people who do the job how they could be more efficient?

To maintain the change in the long run is difficult, and some parts have now started to drift back to the role culture.

Source: Private communication.

Differentiation The state of segmentation of the organisation into subsystems, each of which tends to develop particular attributes in response to the particular demands posed by its relevant external environment.

Integration is the process of achieving unity of effort among the various subsystems in the accomplishment of the organisation's task.

Organisations do not face a single environment. People in each department try to meet the expectations of players in the wider environment, and gradually develop structures which help them to do that. A payroll section has to meet legal requirements on, among other things, salary entitlements, taxation and pensions records. Staff must follow strict rules, with little scope to use their initiative: they work in a mechanistic structure. Staff in product development face different requirements – and will expect to work in a structure that encourages creativity and innovation: they expect to work in an organic structure.

An implication of this is that co-ordination between such departments will be difficult, as they will work in different ways. Paul Lawrence and Jay Lorsch explored this issue, and their contribution is in the following Key Ideas.

Key ideas   Lawrence and Lorsch: differentiation and integration

Two American scholars, Paul Lawrence and Jay Lorsch, developed Burns and Stalker's work. They observed that departments doing different tasks face a separate segment of the environment – some relatively stable, others unstable. Lawrence and Lorsch predicted that to cope with these varying conditions departments will develop different structures and ways of working. Those in stable environments would move towards mechanistic forms, those in unstable environments would move towards organic.

Empirical research in six organisations enabled Lawrence and Lorsch to show that departments did indeed differ from each other, and in ways they had predicted. Those facing unstable environments (research and development) had less formal structures than those facing stable ones (production). The greater the **differentiation** between departments the more effort was needed to integrate their work. Successful firms achieved more **integration** between units by using a variety of integrating devices such as task forces and project managers with the required interpersonal skills. The less effective companies in the uncertain environment used rules and procedures.

Source: Lawrence and Lorsch (1967).

Age and size

Small organisations tend to be informal – people work on several tasks and co-ordinate with each other by face-to-face contact or direct supervision. Weber (1947) noted that larger organisations had formal, bureaucratic structures: research by Blau (1970) and Pugh and Hickson (1976) confirmed that as organisations grow they develop formal structures, hierarchies and specialised units. Like the head of Multi-show Events, as managers divide a growing business into separate units they need more controls such as job descriptions and reporting relationships.

Management in practice   Growth and structure in a housing association

A manager in a housing association, which was created to provide affordable housing for those on low incomes, describes how its structure changed as it grew.

> Housing associations have to give tenants and their representatives the opportunity to influence policy. In the early days it had few staff, no clear division of labour and few rules and procedures. It was successful in providing housing, which attracted more government funds, and the association grew. Managing more houses required a more formal structure to support the work. The association no longer served a single community, but several geographical areas. Staff numbers grew significantly and worked in specialised departments. The changes led to concerns among both staff and committee that the organisation was no longer responsive to community needs and that it had become distant and bureaucratic.

Source: Private communication from the manager.

This implies that organisations go through stages in their lifecycle, with structures adapting to suit. The entrepreneur creates the business alone, or with a few partners or employees. They operate informally with little division of labour – tasks overlap (for a discussion of the unique structural issues facing entrepreneurs in high technology industries, see Alvarez and Barney (2005)). There are few rules or systems for planning and co-ordination. The owner makes the decisions, so they have a centralised structure. If the business succeeds it will need to raise more capital to finance growth. The owner no longer has sole control, but shares decisions with members of the growing management team. Tasks become divided by function or product, creating separate departments and more formal controls to ensure co-ordination. Many small companies fail when they expand rapidly, but fail to impose controls and systems for managing risks – as an executive of a publishing company which got into difficulties recalled:

> We were editors and designers running a large show, and we were completely overstretched. Our systems were simply not up to speed with our creative ambitions.

This observation is consistent with a study by Sine *et al.* (2006), which shows how successful internet companies were those which balanced their essential creativity with a degree of formalisation, specialisation and administrative intensity. They survived, while those which lacked even the most rudimentary structures failed.

If a business continues to grow, it becomes more bureaucratic with more division of responsibilities, and more rules and systems to ensure co-ordination. Mature, established firms tend to become mechanistic, with a strong vertical system and well-developed controls. More decisions are made at the centre – bringing the danger of slower responses to change and, in some industries, a less competitive position than newer rivals. The managing director of Iris, an advertising agency, said:

> Iris London is our oldest and our most mature office – about 300 people. When an agency grows to that sort of size there are things about it that start to become dysfunctional. You start to have to invent admin systems, processes, bureaucracy, and that's countercultural and it stops you being any good, it stops you getting closer to clients and being creative. So in London we've reorganised around clients [with five groups] of between 30 and 60 people: the creative, the planning, the commercial guys are all sat together, all around dedicated clusters of client type. And that we think will make us more efficient, more effective, more instinctive as an agency.

Case study   Oticon – the case continues – limiting risks

While the changes at Oticon had spurred creativity, the Board of the firm also became concerned about profitability in the early years, as the new structure was creating so many initiatives and new products that it was difficult to manage them all effectively. They therefore appointed Neils Jacobsen as co-chief executive in 1992, to place more emphasis on financial discipline and performance. Jacobsen took over from Kolind as chief executive in 1998.

In 1996 more controls were introduced, to balance some of the risks of the new form. A Competence Centre was established which took over some of the rights previously held by project managers. It alone now had the right to initiate projects and appoint project managers – thus restraining the earlier principle that anyone could start a project. It also took over the task of negotiating salaries which had initially been delegated to project managers.

These changes were intended to overcome some of the costs associated with the radical structure. When there was no limit to the number of projects, nor to the number of projects on which a person could work, it had become hard to ensure completion: the most capable staff were spread over too many projects. There was also some concern that staff and teams were not always sharing knowledge as fully as expected. Despite these adjustments, the company remains a radically different form of organisation.

Source: Based on Foss (2003).

Contingencies or managerial choice?

Contingency approaches propose that that the performance of an organisation depends on having a structure that is appropriate to its environment.

Contingency approaches propose that the most effective structure will depend (be contingent) upon the situation in which the organisation is operating:

> The organization is seen as existing in an environment that shapes its strategy, technology, size and innovation rate. These contingent factors in turn determine the required structure; that is, the structure that the organization needs to adopt if it is to operate effectively. (Donaldson, 1996, p. 2)

Determinism is the view that the business environment determines an organisation's structure.

Effective management involves formulating an appropriate strategy and developing a structure which supports that strategy by encouraging appropriate behaviour. The emphasis is **determinist** (the form is determined by the environment) and functionalist (the form is intended to serve organisational effectiveness) (Donaldson, 1995). Management's role is to make suitable adjustments to the structure to improve performance as conditions change – such as by increasing formality as the company grows.

John Child (1972, 1984) disagrees, suggesting that contingency theorists ignore the degree of **structural choice** that managers have. The process of organisational design is not a solely rational matter but one also shaped by political processes. The values and interests of powerful groups are able to influence the structure that emerges even if this reduces performance to some degree. The standards used to assess performance are in any case not always rigorous, and people may tolerate some under-performance caused by an inappropriate structure. There is other evidence that managers have choice over the structure they design without necessarily damaging performance (see the following Management in Practice).

Structural choice emphasises the scope which management has to decide the form of structure, irrespective of environmental conditions.

Management in practice   Retailers' response to the internet

The internet enables online grocery shopping, initially allowing customers to order online and receive home delivery. Sainsbury's responded by creating a new division to handle this business, with a separate management structure, warehouses and distribution system. Tesco chose to integrate the online business with existing stores – staff pick the customer's order from the shelves of a conventional store. Other chains offer the choice of doing the whole transaction in-store, ordering online and collecting from the store, or ordering online for home delivery. The underlying internet technology is the same for all, but managers have chosen to use it in different ways.

Activity 10.7   Critical reflection – contingency or choice?

- Recall some significant changes in the structure of your organisation. Try to establish the reasons for them, and whether they had the intended effects. Do those reasons tend to support the contingency or management choice perspectives?

Case questions 10.3

- Does the Oticon example support contingency or management choice approaches?
- Does the role of management in the company support either of these approaches?

Another consideration is that the direction of causality is not necessarily from strategy to structure. It is also possible that an organisation with a given structure finds that that makes it easier to embark on a particular strategy.

10.8   Learning organisations

Innovation is the main reason why many advocate the development of 'learning organisations', since organisations which operate in complex and dynamic environments can only be successful innovators if they develop the capacity learn and respond quickly to changing circumstances. The term **learning organisation** is used to describe an organisation that has developed the capacity to continuously learn, adapt and change. In a learning organisation the focus is on acquiring, sharing and using knowledge to encourage innovation.

A **learning organisation** is one that has developed the capacity to continuously learn, adapt and change.

According to Nonaka and Takeuchi (1995) the ability to create knowledge and solve problems has become a core competence in many businesses. In their view, everyone is a knowledge worker – someone dealing with customers, for example, quickly finds out about their likes and dislikes, and their view of the service. Because they are typically in low-paid jobs far from corporate headquarters, this valuable intelligence is often overlooked.

Table 10.5 (based on Pedler *et al.*, 1997) presents a view of the features of an ideal learning organisation – features to which managers can aspire. These features cluster under five headings as shown in Figure 10.10.

In a learning organisation members share information and collaborate on work activities wherever required – including across functional and hierarchical boundaries. Boundaries between units are either eliminated (as at Oticon) or are made as porous as possible to ensure that they do not block the flow of ideas and information. Learning organisations tend to emphasise team working, and employees operate with a high degree of autonomy to work as they think will best enhance performance. Rather than directing and controlling, managers act as facilitators, supporters and advocates – enabling their staff to work and learn to the greatest degree possible.

Learning depends on information, so there is an emphasis on sharing information among employees in a timely and open manner. This too depends on managers creating a structure which encourages people to pass information in this way. Leadership is also important in the

Table 10.5 Features of a learning organisation

Feature	Explanation
A learning approach to strategy	The use of trials and experiments to improve understanding and generate improvements, and to modify strategic direction
Participative policy making	All members are involved in strategy formation, influencing decisions and values and addressing conflict
Informative	Information technology is used to make information available to everyone and to enable front-line staff to use their initiative
Formative accounting and control	Accounting, budgeting and reporting systems are designed to help people understand the operations of organisational finance
Internal exchange	Sections and departments think of themselves as customers and suppliers in an internal 'supply chain', learning from each other
Reward flexibility	A flexible and creative reward policy, with financial and non-financial rewards to meet individual needs and performance
Enabling structures	Organisation charts, structures and procedures are seen as temporary, and can be changed to meet task requirements
Boundary workers as environmental scanners	Everyone who has contact with customers, suppliers, clients and business partners is treated as a valuable information source
Inter-company learning	The organisation learns from other organisations through joint ventures, alliances and other information exchanges
A learning climate	The manager's primary task is to facilitate experimentation and learning in others, through questioning, feedback and support
Self-development opportunities for all	People are expected to take responsibility for their own learning, and facilities are made available, especially to 'front-line' staff

Source: Based on Pedler *et al.* (1997).

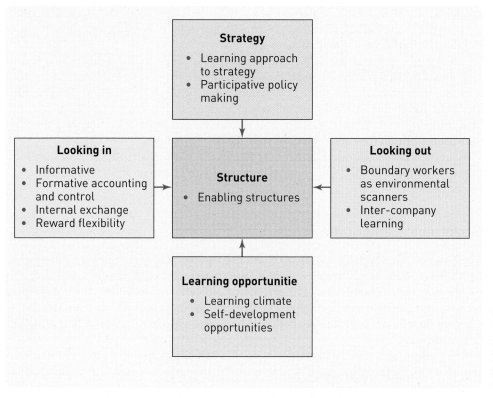

Figure 10.10
Clusters of learning organisation features.

Source: Pedler *et al.* (1997).

sense that one of their primary roles is to facilitate the creation of a shared vision for the business, and ensuring employees are enabled to work continually towards that. Finally, the culture is one in which all agree on a shared vision and understands how all aspects of the organisation – its processes, activities and environment – are related to each other. There is a strong sense of community and mutual trust. People feel free to share ideas and communicate, share and experiment – able to learn without fear of criticism or punishment.

Argyris (1999) distinguished between single-loop and double-loop learning. The classic example of single-loop learning is the domestic thermostat which, by detecting temperature variations, takes action to correct deviations from a predetermined level. In single-loop learning, the system maintains performance at the set level, but is unable to learn that the temperature is set too high or too low. Learning how to learn involves double-loop learning – challenging assumptions, beliefs and norms, rather than accepting them and working within their limitations. In single-loop learning, the question is 'how can we better achieve that standard of performance?' In double-loop learning the question becomes: 'is that an appropriate target in the first place?' In the context of developing the skills to cope more effectively with change, the aim is to enhance the ability of members to engage in double-loop learning.

10.9 Integrating themes

Sustainable performance

Changes in the business environment are encouraging managers to experiment with new forms of organisation, many favouring decentralisation which allows local business units greater autonomy over many decisions. They believe this encourages flexibility and innovation.

The dilemma is that decentralised structures expose the organisation to the risk that decisions by managers in the autonomous units may damage the reputation of the business as a whole. BP (Part 2 Case) suffered when staff at the US subsidiary were careless about safety, as did Union Carbide after the disaster at Bhopal in India. In both cases, the companies had decentralised decisions to local managers.

The same dangers arise in relation to sustainability: while the parent company may seek to meet and exceed international standards on emissions, a policy to give local managers autonomy over their practices, and those of suppliers, may impede corporate efforts. That in turn may harm its reputation. Critics are unlikely to be impressed by the arguments in favour of local autonomy, and will claim that this does not absolve the organisation from responsibility for what happens in their subsidiaries or suppliers.

Conversely decentralising authority over sustainability may have better results, since local managers are more familiar with the operations, and how best to improve their environmental performance.

Governance and control

The financial crises which began in 2008 showed that many bankers had been taking great risks with the bank funds by investing in loans that were not only very risky, but were also packaged in such a complex way that others had difficulty understanding them. Few complaints were raised when things appeared to be going well but, as confidence fell and investors asked for their money back, the extent to which managers had been acting without sufficient control became clear.

The bankers' behaviour had been encouraged in part by a culture in their banks which encouraged them to take risks, and by an incentive structure which rewarded them handsomely for their profits, even if these were short lived. This was not intentional fraud, but a sign of the negligence which failed to pay enough attention to banks' systems of accounting and risk management, and of their governance structures.

The Combined Code (2006) gives clear guidance to companies on how to structure their Boards to ensure adequate governance and control. This is a voluntary Code of Best Practice, with which the Boards of all companies listed on the London Stock Exchange are expected to comply – or to explain why they have not done so. It includes guidance on matters such as:

- **The Board** Every company should be headed by an effective Board, which is collectively responsible for the success of the company.
- **Chairman and chief executive** There should be a clear division of responsibilities . . . between the running of the board and the executive responsible [for running the business]. No one individual should have unfettered powers of decision.
- **Board balance** The Board should include a balance of executive and [independent] non-executive directors so that no individual or small group can dominate the Board's decision taking.
- **Board appointments** There should be a formal, rigorous and transparent procedure for appointing new directors to the Board.

Paradoxically, while this Code is widely seen as a valuable aid to corporate governance, it did not prevent the financial crisis: all the banks which had to be rescued by the government had complied with the Code.

Internationalisation

The growth of multinationals – based in one country but with significant production and sales in many others – continues as managers see new opportunities beyond their home territory. At the same time they have to defend their position against new entrants from other countries. A perennial topic in multinationals is the balance between global integration and local responsiveness. Bartlett and Ghoshal (2002) show how managers at some firms – such as the Japanese Kao and Matsushita – sought to integrate worldwide operations to achieve global efficiency through economies of scale. Others, including Philips and Unilever, were more sensitive to local differences, permitting national subsidiaries high levels of autonomy to respond to local conditions.

They go on to suggest that as global pressures increase, companies needed to develop a more complex range of capabilities:

> To compete effectively, a company had to develop global competitiveness, multinational flexibility, and worldwide learning capability simultaneously. Building these [capabilities] was primarily an organizational challenge, which required organizations to break away from their traditional management modes and adopt a new organizational model. This model we call the transnational. (Bartlett and Ghoshal, 2002, p. 18)

They also observe that successful transnational companies have:

> recognized that formal structure is a powerful but blunt weapon for effecting strategic change . . . a company must go beyond structure . . . and re-shape the core decision-making systems, and in doing so, the management processes of the company – the administrative systems, communication channels and interpersonal relationships, often provided tools for managing such change that were more subtle but also more effective than formal structure. (p. 37)

Bartlett and Ghoshal go on to elaborate the evidence and research on the organisational challenges that companies face if they wish to perform effectively in the international economy.

Summary

1 **Outline the links between strategy, structure and performance**

- The structure signals what people are expected to do within the organisation, and is intended to support actions that are in line with strategy, and so enhance performance. Equally, a structure may enable a new strategy to emerge which a different structure would have hindered.

2 **Give examples of management choices about dividing and co-ordinating work, with their likely advantages and disadvantages**

- Managers divide work to enable individuals and groups to specialise on a limited aspect of the whole, and then combine the work into related areas of activity. Task division needs to be accompanied by suitable methods of co-ordination.
- Centralisation brings consistency and efficiency, but also the danger of being slow and out of touch with local conditions. People in decentralised units can respond quickly to local conditions but risk acting inconsistently.
- Functional forms allow people to specialise and develop expertise and are efficient, but they may be inward looking and prone to conflicting demands.
- Divisional forms allow focus on particular markets of customer groups, but can duplicate facilities thus adding to cost.
- Matrix forms try to balance the benefits of functional and divisional forms, but can again lead to conflicting priorities over resources.
- Networks of organisations enable companies to draw upon a wide range of expertise, but may involve additional management and co-ordination costs.

3 **Compare the features of mechanistic and organic structures**

- Mechanistic – people perform specialised tasks, hierarchical structure of control, knowledge located at top of hierarchy, vertical communication, loyalty and obedience valued.

- Organic – people contribute experience to common tasks, network structure of contacts, knowledge widely spread, horizontal communication, commitment to task goals more important than to superiors.

4 **Summarise the work of Woodward, Burns and Stalker, Lawrence and Lorsch, and John Child, showing how they contributed to this area of management**

- Woodward: appropriate structure depends on the type of production system ('technology') – unit, small batch, process.
- Burns and Stalker: appropriate structure depends on uncertainty of the organisation's environment – mechanistic in stable, organic in unstable.
- Lawrence and Lorsch: units within an organisation face different environmental demands, which implies that there will be both mechanistic and organic forms within the same organisation, raising new problems of co-ordination.
- John Child: contingency theory implies too great a degree of determinism – managers have a greater degree of choice over structure than contingency theories implied.

5 **Use the 'contingencies' believed to influence choice of structure to evaluate the suitability of a form for a given unit**

- Strategy, environment, technology, age/size and political contingencies (Child) are believed to indicate the most suitable form, and the manager's role is to interpret these in relation to their circumstances.

6 **Explain and illustrate the features of a learning organisation**

- Learning organisations are those which have developed the capacity to continuously learn, adapt and change. This depends, according to Pedler *et al*. (1997), on evolving learning-friendly processes for looking in, looking out, learning opportunities, strategy and structure.

7 **Show how ideas from the chapter add to your understanding of the integrating**

- The drive for sustainable is another example of the dilemma between central and local control. Decentralisation may harm the company if local managers ignore corporate policy, or may lead to more sustainable performance if local managers use their knowledge to find better solutions.
- The financial crisis led many to call for tighter systems of governance and control – but many troubled banks already appeared to have such systems in place, which were not used.
- Bartlett and Ghoshal (2002) trace the many dilemmas companies face in creating a structure for their international operations.

Review questions

1 What did Chandler conclude about the relationship between strategy, structure and performance?

2 Draw the organisation chart of a company or department that you know. Compare it with the structures shown in Figure 10.5, writing down points of similarity and difference.

3 List the advantages and disadvantages of centralising organisational functions?

4 Several forms of co-ordination are described. Select two that you have seen in operation and describe in detail how they work – and how well they work.

5 Explain the difference between a mechanistic and an organic form of organisation.

6 Explain the term 'contingency approach' and give an example of each of the factors that influence the choice between mechanistic and organic structures.

7   If contingency approaches stress the influence of external factors on organisational structures, what is the role of management in designing organisational structures?

8   What is the main criticism of the contingency approaches to organisation structure?

9   What examples can you find of organisational activities that correspond to some of the features of a learning organisation identified by Pedler *et al.* (1997)?

10 Summarise an idea from the chapter that adds to your understanding of the integrating themes.

Concluding critical reflection

Think about the structure and culture of your company or one with which you are familiar. Review the material in the chapter, and perhaps visit some of the websites identified. Then make notes on the following questions:

●   What examples of the themes discussed in this chapter are currently relevant to your company? What type of structure do you have – centralised or decentralised; functional or divisional, etc? Which of the methods of co-ordination identified do you typically use? Which form of culture best describes the one in which you work? What structural or cultural issues arise that are not mentioned here?

●   In responding to issues of structure, what **assumptions** about the nature of organisations appear to guide your approach? If the business seems too centralised or too formal, why do managers take that approach? What are their assumptions, and are they correct?

●   What factors in the **context** of the company appear to shape your approach to organising – what kind of environment are you working in, for example? To what extent does your structure involve networking with people from other organisations, and why is that?

●   Have you seriously considered whether the present structure is right for the business? Do you regularly compare your structure with that in other companies to look for **alternatives**? How do you do it?

●   What **limitations** can you identify in any of the ideas and theories presented here? For example, how helpful is contingency theory to someone deciding whether to make the organisation more or less mechanistic?

Further reading

Burns, T. and Stalker, G.M. (1961), *The Management of Innovation*, Tavistock, London.

Lawrence, P. and Lorsch, J.W. (1967), *Organization and Environment*, Harvard Business School Press, Boston, MA.

Woodward, J. (1965), *Industrial Organization: Theory and practice*, Oxford University Press, Oxford. Second edition 1980.

These influential books give accessible accounts of the research process, and it would add to your understanding to read at least one of them in the original. The second edition of Woodward's book (1980) is even more useful, as it includes a commentary on her work by two later scholars.

Bartlett, C.A. and Ghoshal, S. (2002), *Managing Across Borders: The transnational solution* (2nd edn) Harvard Business School Press, Boston, MA.

Applies ideas on organisations and their structure to international management.

Catmull, E. (2008), 'How Pixar fosters collective creativity', *Harvard Business Review*, vol. 86, no. 9, pp. 64–72.

> The cofounder explains how it works.

Homburg, C., Jensen, O. and Krohmer, H. (2008), 'Configurations of marketing and sales: A taxonomy', *Journal of Marketing,* vol. 72, no. 2, pp. 133–154.

> An account of research into one of the continuing questions in organisation structure, of particular interest to students with an interest in marketing.

Ordanini, A., Rubera, G. and Sala, M. (2008), 'Integrating functional knowledge and embedding learning in new product launches: How project forms helped EMI Music', *Long Range Planning*, vol. 41, no. 1, pp. 17–32.

> How a team approach helped to launch an unknown artist.

Weblinks

These websites have appeared in the chapter:

> www.oticon.com
> www.lilly.com
> www.shell.com
> www.reed-elsevier.com
> www.sonyericsson.com
> www.baesystems.com
> www.rbs.com
> www.roche.com
> www.hmv.com
> www.emi.com
> www.communityhealthpartnerships.co.uk
> www.pixar.com
> www.monsanto.com

Visit two of the business sites in the list, and navigate to the pages dealing with corporate news, investor relations or 'our company'.

● What organisational structure issues can you identify that managers in the company are likely to be dealing with? Can you find any information about their likely culture from the website?

● What kind of environment are they likely to be working in, and how may that affect their structure and culture?

For video case studies, audio summaries, flashcards, exercises and annotated weblinks related to this chapter, visit **www.pearsoned.co.uk/mymanagementlab**

CHAPTER 11

HUMAN RESOURCE MANAGEMENT

Aim

To introduce the topic of human resource management and to examine some of the major practices.

Objectives

By the end of your work on this chapter you should be able to outline the concepts below in your own terms and:

1 Understand the contribution of HRM to organisational performance
2 Understand the potential links between strategy and HRM
3 Describe the HRM practices concerned with the flow of people into and through the organisation
4 Describe the HRM practices concerned with reward management
5 Understand how HRM aims to manage workforce diversity
6 Recognise the issues you will face as a potential job seeker
7 Show how ideas from the chapter add to your understanding of the integrating themes

Key terms

This chapter introduces the following ideas:

human resource management	validity
external fit	personality test
internal fit	assessment centres
job analysis	performance-related pay
competencies	

BMW www.bmwgroup.com

BMW, whose headquarters are in Munich, was established in 1916, and by 2010 was the world's leading premium automobile company, employing about 96,000 people on the BMW, Mini and Rolls-Royce brands. It has 24 production facilities in 13 countries, with a global sales network in more than 140 countries. Management has chosen to focus on three premium segments of the international car market, with each of its brands being the market leader in its segment. The BWM corporate Strategy Number ONE expresses the vision to be the leading provider of premium products and premium services for individual mobility.

In 2009 it delivered 1,286,000 automobiles to customers, about 10 per cent fewer than in the previous year, which it believed was due to the world recession. Western Europe is its major market, accounting for about 60 per cent of all BMW cars sold (although China is an increasingly important market for luxury Rolls-Royce vehicles). BMW also manufactures motorcycles and has a joint venture with Rolls-Royce to produce aircraft jet engines. It concentrates on the top end of the car market, which commands high prices, and has also invested in overseas manufacturing plants – in 2009 it opened a second plant in China.

BMW's business strategy includes providing purchasers with a wide variety of choices in terms of how their car is equipped. The variety of possible combinations is so great that exactly the same car is produced only about once every nine months. The company also emphasises the quality of the product. This combination of variety and quality is a challenge to achieve in a product as complex as the modern car. It requires both advanced technology in manufacturing, and employees who are highly skilled and flexible. Recognising this, the company places great stress on only recruiting the highest-quality workers, with technical and team working skills. The strategy is supported by its approach to HRM, which derives from, and is highly consistent with, the company's 'six inner values': communication, ethical behaviour to its staff, achievement and remuneration, independence, self-fulfilment and the pursuit of new goals.

© BMW Group

This underlying philosophy guides the design of new BMW plants ('an open design' that makes all operations easy to see, and so helps communication) and the process of introducing new or reformed HRM practices. The company consults widely about these, sharing information on proposals and trying to ensure that successive changes are consistent with each other and build on established policies.

The company provides virtually unprecedented job security. And that is part of the reason why, for many Germans, getting a job at BMW is the ultimate accomplishment. The company's human resource department receives more than two hundred thousand applicants annually. (Lawler, 2008, p. 18)

Sources: Lawler (2008); company website.

Case questions 11.1

- What issues concerning the management of people are likely to be raised in a group such as BMW that has rapidly expanded its production and distribution facilities?

- How have these issues been affected by domestic developments in Germany?

- How is increased overseas production likely to affect HRM policies?

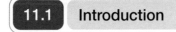

Activity 11.1   Defining HRM

Before reading on, note down how you would define human resource management. What topics and issues do you think it deals with, and how does it relate to management as a whole? Keep your notes by you and compare them with the topics covered in the chapter as you work through it.

11.1   Introduction

BMW is a large and successful business in a growing area of the world economy – automobile production. Yet it faces competitive problems, stemming in part from high employment costs in its German operations and competition from new sources. Management is attempting to retain the company's position by diversifying the product range and the number of countries in which it manufactures. The company believes that HRM strategy and practices must support the wider business strategy, by providing a better-trained and more flexible workforce suited to the new conditions.

Such activities are part of a broader change taking place in many Western companies, as managers try to align the way they deal with people with their broader company strategies. Management influences other people through both personal and institutionalised practices. It seeks to be less reactive, and less focused on grievances and the routine aspects of personnel administration. Instead it wants to be more proactive in developing a labour force at all levels that will support the organisation's strategy. It also seeks greater coherence between the main aspects of HRM – especially in the areas of selection, development, appraisal and rewards.

Human resource management refers to all those activities associated with the management of work and people in organisations.

This chapter focuses on some policies and practices intended to influence employee attitudes and behaviour. These practices are commonly referred to as **human resource management** (HRM), which covers four main areas (Beer *et al.*, 1984):

- employee influence (employee involvement in decision making);
- work systems (work design, supervisory style);
- human resource flow (recruitment, selection, training, development and deployment);
- reward management (pay and other benefits).

Employee influence and work systems are discussed in Chapters 14 and 15. Consequently this chapter focuses on human resource flow and reward management. Human resource flow is concerned with the flow of individuals into and through the organisation – human resource planning, job analysis, employee recruitment and selection. Management designs these practices to help ensure that the organisation has the right people available to help it achieve its larger strategic objectives. Reward management aims to attract, retain and acknowledge employees.

The chapter begins by discussing the basic purpose and objectives of HRM, and the reasons for its prominence in management discussions. It then presents current practices in the areas of human resource flow and reward management. HRM is more than a sum of policies and it is important to see how these fit together within a company's broad approach to HRM.

11.2   Perspectives on HRM

HRM refers to all aspects of managing people in the workplace: this section outlines why the function is an essential component in organisational success.

From personnel management to HRM

The term 'human resource management' is relatively new, gaining prominence in US companies and business schools in the early 1980s (Brewster, 1994). Traditionally, managers institutionalised the way they managed staff by creating personnel departments. Partly influenced by the human relations model (Chapter 2), they believed they could ensure a committed staff by dealing with grievances and looking after their welfare. Growing trade union power also led management to create departments to negotiate with them over pay and working conditions.

Such personnel management departments had limited power, and found it difficult to show that they enhanced organisational performance (Legge, 1978). Senior management saw them as reactive, self-contained and obsessed with procedures, employee grievances, discipline and trade unions. Their aim was to minimise costs and avoid disruption – and they had little influence on strategy.

Changes in the business world led some observers to propose that issues concerned with managing people should have a higher profile, and especially that line managers should take a larger role (Fombrun *et al.*, 1984). Guest (1987) attributes this change to:

- The emergence of more globally integrated markets in which competition is more extensive and severe. Product lifecycles are shorter, with innovation, flexibility and quality often replacing price as the basis of competitive advantage.
- The economic success during the 1980s of countries that had given employee management a relatively high priority, such as Japan and (West) Germany.
- The highly publicised 'companies of excellence' literature (Peters and Waterman, 1982) which suggested that high performance organisations were characterised by a strong commitment to HRM.
- Changes in the composition of the workforce, particularly the growth of a more educated staff.
- Declining trade union membership and collective bargaining in many economies.

Early advocates of HRM proposed that key themes would be integration, planning, a long-run orientation, proactive and strategic – believing that managing people more effectively would improve organisational performance. This reflected the resource based view of strategy which emphasises the importance of firm-specific resources and competences which are difficult to imitate (see Chapters 1 and 8).

Models of HRM

Beer *et al.* (1984) developed an influential model of HRM, describing it as a 'map of the territory' – see Figure 11.1. It places HRM within the wider environment of the business (Chapter 3) both by indicating the interests of stakeholders and by the situational factors that shape HRM policy choices.

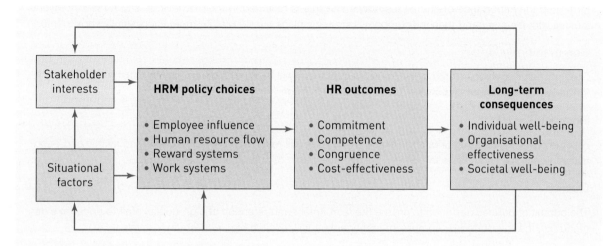

Figure 11.1 Map of the HRM territory

Source: Beer *et al.* (1984). Reproduced with permission from Professor Michael Beer.

Table 11.1 Policies for supporting HRM and organisational outcomes

Policies	Human resource outcomes	Organisational outcomes
Organisational and job design		High job performance
Managing change	Strategic planning and integration	High problem solving
Recruitment, selection and socialising	Commitment	Successful change
Appraisal, training and development	Flexibility/adaptability	Low turnover
Manpower flows through the organisation		Low absence
Reward systems	Quality	Low grievance level

Source: Guest (1987), p. 503.

Building on this model Guest (1987) developed a framework for an empirically grounded theory of HRM. He proposed four human resource outcomes, and showed how HRM policies could support those goals, and in turn enhance organisational outcomes (see Table 11.1). Guest stresses that the effect of these policies will depend on:

- the extent to which other policies support them, so creating an adequate degree of internal fit; and
- the extent to which the wider context was suitable for an HRM approach (so creating an external fit). He suggested that some sectors of the economy would provide more suitable conditions in which to introduce HRM practices than others. Large bureaucracies or those prone to conflict would probably not find HRM helpful.

Finally, Guest (1987) suggested propositions for each of the human resource outcomes as the first step in developing an empirically based theory of the links between HRM policies and organisational outcomes (see Key Ideas).

Key ideas — David Guest – four propositions in a theory of HRM

Integration

If human resources can be integrated into strategic plans, if strategic plans cohere, if line managers have internalised the importance of human resources and this is reflected in their behaviour, and if the employees identify with the company, then the company's strategic plans are likely to be more successfully implemented.

Commitment

Organisational and job-related behavioural commitment will result in high employee satisfaction, high performance, longer tenure and a willingness to accept change.

Flexibility

Flexible organisation structures and flexible employees will result in a capacity to respond swiftly and effectively to changes and ensure the continuing high utilisation of human and other resources.

Quality

The pursuit of policies designed to ensure the recruitment and retention of high-quality staff to undertake demanding jobs, supported by competent management will result in high performance levels.

Source: Guest (1987).

Case questions 11.2

- What HRM policies (as listed in Table 11.1) would you expect BMW to use to support the company's 'six inner values' listed in the case?

Activity 11.2   Assessing the changes needed

Senior managers in an organisation have decided to pursue a strategy which includes enhancing the quality of its products. It will do this partly by introducing team working to production areas that have traditionally been focused on individual work. Use Table 11.1 to note down three areas of HRM policy which may need to be revised to support this strategy, and why.

The philosophy of HRM

Those advocating HRM believe that it would contribute to organisational performance by managing staff effectively. They aim for a 'win-win' situation for both employer and employee, since the organisation benefits from greater profitability and employees gain from work that is both financially rewarding and intrinsically satisfying. This assumes that employees and employer share the same goal – the long-term success of the organisation. This is an example of the unitary perspective, introduced in Chapter 2, alongside the pluralist perspective which recognises the legitimacy of different views – between trade unions, between managerial functions, and between managers and trade unions.

HRM and performance

A distinction within HRM itself is between 'hard' and 'soft' approaches (Legge, 2005). The former takes a business-led perspective, while the latter sees people as valuable assets whose motivation, involvement and development should have priority. Those advocating a business-led view point to studies showing a positive relationship between HRM practices and organisational performance, such as that by Huselid (1995). This survey of around 1,000 firms in the US reported a strong relationship between a set of HRM practices and measures of performance such as employee turnover, productivity and financial performance. Similarly, West *et al.* (2006) found that greater use of a complementary set of HRM practices had a positive effect on the quality of care in hospitals.

Others take a more sceptical view, seeing the quantity and quality of evidence positive relationship between HRM and organisational performance as weak and ambiguous (Legge, 1995; Zheng *et al.*, 2006).

A common theme in all reviews is that organisations can only obtain strategically important benefits if they take a strategic orientation towards HRM, in the sense of ensuring a high degree of external and internal fit.

External fit

Fombrun *et al.* (1984) see an organisation's structure (Chapter 10) as the main mechanism through which to deliver its strategy; and also that HRM practices (such as those in Table 11.1) provide a complementary set of tools for this purpose. Figure 11.2 shows this relationship, in which there is a close external fit between a firm's strategy, structure and HRM strategy.

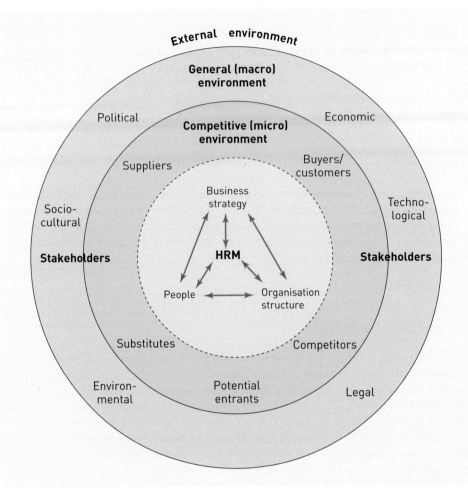

Figure 11.2
Fit between HRM,
strategy, structure
and environment

External fit is when
there is a close and
consistent relationship
between an
organisation's
competitive strategy
and its HRM strategy.

In aiming for **external fit** managers try to establish a close and consistent link between HRM and strategy, and with the wider environment. For example, Chapter 8 distinguished low-cost and differentiation strategies, which will require different employee attitudes and behaviours. Do the firm's HRM policies encourage the behaviours required to support the strategy? Extensive training, team working and shop-floor problem-solving arrangements are likely to be needed to support a differentiation strategy based on, say, flexible response to customer needs. A low-cost strategy may be best served by paying low wages to a casual labour force. A review by Greer (2001) suggests that HRM practices have a greater performance impact when they match strategy, although it also found that some HRM practices (thorough selection and training processes) increase performance in almost any setting.

Case questions 11.3

- What is your image of BMW cars? What words would you use to describe them?
- In order to meet the image you expect, what kind of behaviour would you expect of employees?
- What HRM practices will encourage/discourage that behaviour?

> **Activity 11.3**   Comparing HRM policies
>
> List the major differences in HRM policies that you would expect to observe between two organisations, one pursuing a low-cost strategy and the other a quality enhancement strategy. (Use the Key Ideas on page 330 to assist you.)

Internal fit

Organisations also benefit if their HRM policies are internally consistent, in the sense that individual practices complement and reinforce each other by sending consistent signals to the workforce. An organisation that encourages team working can support this through a payment system that recognises and rewards contributions to the team. Managers will weaken team working if they use a payment system that rewards individual performance as this will discourage co-operation.

Few organisations achieve the degree of **internal fit** required to gain the most from HRM policies. In the UK, the *2004 Workplace Employee Relations Survey* (Kersley *et al.*, 2006) investigated the use of practices often cited as indicators of a sophisticated approach to HRM, such as team working or multi-skilling. There was no marked change in the use of these practices since the previous survey in 1998, leading to the conclusion that the 'diffusion of so-called "high involvement management" practices has been rather muted in recent years' (p. 107).

> **Internal fit** is when the various components of the HRM strategy support each other and consistently encourage certain attitudes and behaviour.

11.3   What do HR managers do?

Identifying HR roles

Given the range of HR tasks, who does them and how? This depends on how general managers balance their responsibilities and those of the HR specialists (see the following Key Ideas).

> **Key ideas**   Michael Beer on the general manager's perspective
>
> Michael Beer and his colleagues (1984) set out the roles of general managers and HR specialists, pointing out that many decisions taken by general managers are HRM decisions, even if they do not realise it:
>
> > HRM involves all management decisions and actions that affect the nature of the relationship between the organization and its employees – its human resources. General managers make important decisions daily that affect this relationship, but that are not immediately thought of as HRM decisions: introducing new technology into the office place in a particular way, or approving a new plant with a certain arrangement of production operations, each involves important HRM decisions. In the long run both the decisions themselves and the manner in which those decisions are implemented have a profound impact on employees: how involved they will be in their work, how much they trust management, and how much they will grow and develop new competencies on the job. (pp. 1–2)
>
> They then advocate their view of the respective roles:
>
> > First, the general manager accepts more responsibility for ensuring the alignment of competitive strategy, personnel policies, and other policies impacting on people. Second, the personnel staff has the mission of [ensuring that] personnel activities are developed and implemented in ways that make them more mutually reinforcing. That is what we mean by the general manager's perspective. (pp. 2–3).
>
> Source: Beer *et al.* (1984).

To identify how personnel and HR managers have interpreted their role, Storey (1992) studied 15 'mainstream' UK companies, from which he developed a typology of four roles, as

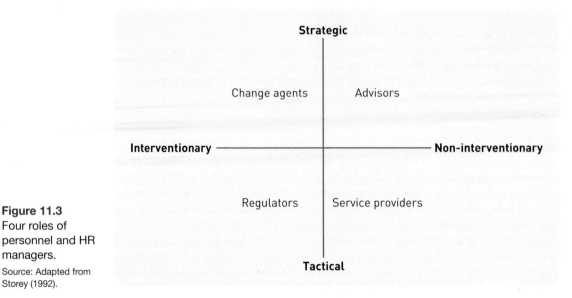

Figure 11.3
Four roles of
personnel and HR
managers.

Source: Adapted from
Storey (1992).

shown in Figure 11.3. He identified two dimensions – intervention or non-intervention on the horizontal axis, and strategic or tactical on the other.

This gives four roles (slightly re-named as suggested by Caldwell, 2003):

- **Advisors** – a facilitating role, acting as internal consultants offering expertise and advice to senior managers and line managers.
- **Service providers** – called in by line managers to provide specific HR assistance and support as required. Also provide administrative services to support HR policies such as recruitment, selection and training.
- **Regulators** – formulating, disseminating and monitoring the observance of personnel or HR policy and practice, including trade union agreements where relevant.
- **Change agents** – actively promoting proposals for cultural or organisational change, including those related to the strategic agenda and business performance.

Caldwell (2003) found that in the 98 organisations he studied, the most common main role was that of advisor, followed by that of change agents. He also found that most respondents had identified one of these as their main role, with the others present in varying degrees. He also found that HR managers experienced high levels of role ambiguity and role conflict – they were unclear what others expected of them.

While this indicates what HR managers do, it does not show how they do it. Truss and Gill (2009) provide insight into how HR managers build the resources they need to do their job – namely by combining structural arrangements with good working relationships. Structural arrangements include:

- providing opportunities to meet with colleagues;
- holding regular meetings of the whole department to discuss policy;
- agreeing personal targets that link staff and departmental objectives;
- seconding staff to line departments;
- taking account of line managers' objectives in deploying HR resources; and
- creating communication mechanisms to link with line managers.

They had used these techniques to build good working relationships:

- sharing positive experiences with line managers;
- ensuring line managers could communicate easily with informed HR practitioners; and
- ensuring HR staff understand organisational needs.

Truss and Gill conclude that in organisations where HR staff had invested time and effort in building these relationships, line managers perceived HR to be making an effective contribution to organisational performance. That contribution is made in part through their work on human resource planning.

Activity 11.4   What do HR managers do?

Arrange to talk to someone who works in HRM about their work.

- Use the categories in Figure 11.3 to help analyse what they do, and which of the four categories they spend most time on.
- Use the research by Truss and Gill to analyse how they manage their working relationships with line managers.
- Compare what you have found with others on your course, and summarise your results.

11.4   Human resource planning

Human resource planning is the process through which employers anticipate and meet their needs for staff. It requires estimating the number and type of staff the business requires over successive periods, and then deciding how to ensure they are available, partly through recruitment and selection.

Forecasting

Large organisations may use complex forecasting techniques to identify their staff requirements – and governments do the same to estimate the likely demand for professional staff who require long training, such as teachers or doctors – Bechet and Maki (1987) describe the methods. Planners use models which typically start with the organisational strategy or with demographic changes that affect demand for services. They forecast the number of staff required to meet those demands and their likely availability – staff in post at the start, together with likely inflows, outflows and internal movements during the planning period. The Management in Practice feature shows how McDonald's forecasts short-term demand for staff in the restaurants.

Management in practice   Forecasting staff at McDonald's www.mcdonalds.co.uk

McDonald's has suffered from the perception that it only offers 'McJobs' – unstimulating jobs with low prospects – and since 2006 has embarked on a campaign to improve its reputation as an employer. It claims to have less labour turnover than its competitors, and that when it needs to recruit entry level 'crew member' positions in the restaurants it can usually select from a large number of unsolicited applicants. Its policy is to promote from within, and claims that more than half the Executive team started in the restaurants.

There are seasonal peaks in the demand for labour, and the company has implemented a sophisticated human resource planning software system that enables restaurant managers – who are responsible for recruitment – to plan their staff needs with precision. The software uses data such as past and projected sales figures and labour turnover statistics to forecast the required level of recruitment.

Source: *IRS Employment Review* 853, 18 August 2006, pp. 42–44.

A limitation of long-term forecasting is the uncertainty of the social and economic environment. For example, attempts to forecast the future demand for nurses (and so for nursing education) cannot take account of long-term changes in:

- population demographics;
- how that changing population uses healthcare; and
- how the hospitals providing care use nurses.

Since policy-makers cannot rely on long-term forecasts of demand, they may be wiser to increase flexibility of supply, so that it is easier to adapt to changes when they happen.

11.5 Job analysis

Job analysis is the process of determining the characteristics of an area of work according to a prescribed set of dimensions.

Job analysis identifies the main constituents of a role, including skills and level of responsibility. It typically leads to a written job description that guides selection, training and performance appraisal. Issues to consider in job analysis include:

- How is the data collected? Possibilities include interviewing the job incumbent, observing people doing the job, and distributing questionnaires.
- Who should collect this data? Should it be the job incumbent, the supervisor or an internal or external specialist?
- How should the job information be structured and laid out?

The process aims to describe the purpose of a job, its major duties and activities, the conditions under which it is performed and the necessary knowledge, skills and abilities. Jobs are broken into *elements* which can then be rated on dimensions such as extent of use, importance, amount of time involved and frequency. Job analysis is made difficult by the volume and complexity of data (McEntire *et al.*, 2006) and web-based job analysis programs have been created to solve this (Reiter-Palmon *et al.*, 2006).

The result of the analysis is a job description, which will usually include the following headings in some form:

- job title;
- job purpose;
- job dimensions (e.g. responsibilities for managing budgets or staff);
- organisation chart (who reports to you and who you report to);
- role of department;
- key result areas;
- assignment and review (who allocates and monitors work);
- communication and working relationships (internal and external);
- most challenging part of the job.

Competencies

Competencies (in HRM) refer to knowledge, skills, ability and other personal characteristics required to perform a job well.

Rather than thinking about jobs as a set of tasks, HRM practitioners now aim to identify and develop the **competencies** an individual requires to meet the job requirements (Kalb *et al.*, 2006). This reflects the need for organisations to be flexible and responsive, from which it follows that they often require employees with broad competences rather than narrow skills for prescribed tasks. The following Management in Practice gives an example.

Essex County Council uses a competency approach www.workingforessex.com

Essex County Council employs about 39,000 people and its competency framework applies to about 15,000 of these. It reflects the behaviours, skills and abilities needed to deliver council services, and is directly related to the requirements of jobs with the council.

There are 11 generic competences in the framework, which applies to all employees, but not all of them are required in an individual job: the manager responsible for drawing up the profile of a job decides which of them need to be demonstrated by someone in that job. As an example, the competence 'self-awareness and control' has these sub-themes, each of which is measured as shown:

- **Self-awareness** Demonstrates awareness of own personal strengths and development needs, understands the impact of these on others, and takes action to modify own behaviours accordingly.
- **Self-discipline and organisation** Manages time and prioritises work in an effective and productive way.
- **Self-control** Manages own stress, remains objective and stable in stressful situations, and accepting constructive criticism.
- **Integrity** Maintains high ethical standards both personally and professionally; shows integrity and is reliable and trustworthy.

The competencies feature throughout the recruitment and selection process – job profiles and specifications are built around them, and candidates are expected to give practical evidence of how they meet the competency requirements in their application. The interviews and assessment centres probe for specific evidence of the extent to which the candidate possesses the required set of competencies.

Source: *IRS Employment Review* 853, 18 August 2006, p. 46.

Team working and job analysis

Moves towards team working also have implications for job analysis, as the work done by each person within a team may be fluid, especially if managers encourage members to develop a wide range of skill which they can contribute to the task. As teams work together and their members develop wider skills, the jobs between them change, so an analysis of an individual job would probably soon be out-of-date. The BMW case illustrates team working.

Case study   **BMW – the case continues – teams and flexibility www.bmw.com**

Most production staff work in self-managing groups of between eight and 15 members with a high degree of autonomy and clearly defined tasks. Members of the group decide upon each individual's responsibility and how they will move between jobs, as well as making suggestions and decisions about product improvement. Applicants for jobs are screened for their ability to work in a team environment and co-operate with others. Those who are interviewed go through elaborate tests designed to screen out individuals who can't work in a team environment.

Each group elects a spokesperson to co-ordinate activities and to represent them, although they have no power to give orders or take disciplinary action. Supervisors remain as the group's immediate superior in technical and disciplinary matters, but play more of an advisory/facilitating role. The supervisor is responsible for proposing and agreeing objectives, presenting progress figures, helping to progress continuous improvements and ensuring that group members improve their qualifications. The company has to ensure that adequate training is available, goals are agreed upon and results circulated. Improved product quality and job satisfaction are the aims, leading in turn to greater productivity.

Staff are also expected be flexible in terms of time, place and assignment. They can save or overdraw up to 300 hours a year, which enables the company to reduce or increase the labour supply by that amount (for each employee), to cope with temporary changes in demand. They offer those nearing retirement the chance to gradually reduce working hours, which can vary, by mutual consent, with economic conditions. Staff are also expected to show local flexibility and mobility, moving between plants in BMW's facilities as requirements change.

Sources: Lawler (2008); company website.

Case questions 11.4

- How would the introduction of teamworking have helped to improve the external fit between HRM and broader strategy?
- To achieve internal fit, what other changes would BMW have needed to make to support teamworking and flexibility?

Job analysis aims to produce a comprehensive and accurate job description, to inform recruitment and selection.

Activity 11.5 Collect examples of job descriptions or competences

Go to the website of an organisation that interests you, and navigate to the pages on careers or current vacancies.

- Try to find examples of job descriptions – compare them with the headings in the text. What factors do they omit and what do they add?
- Try to find a job description that includes a statement of competences required. What does that tell you about the requirements of the job?
- Compare what you find with others on your course, and summarise your results.

11.6   Recruitment and selection

The goal of recruitment is to produce a good pool of applicants for work, while that of selection is to choose from among those the ones most likely to be suitable. Managers hope to choose methods that give best value for time and money spent.

Recruitment

Options for attracting applicants include word of mouth, careers fairs, advertisements and employment agencies. Some companies use social networking sites such as Facebook to identify potential recruits based on their interests and personal profiles. Online recruitment is growing rapidly through websites such as **www.monster.com** and through organisations using their own websites to advertise vacancies. Cober *et al.* (2004) provide a model predicting how factors in the website such as its aesthetics, features and perceived usability shape a job-seeker's opinion of the organisation, and whether they intend to apply for a position. Parry and Tyson (2008) find that to benefit from online recruitment managers need to use additional online functions to manage the large number of applicants by automatically acknowledging applications, doing some initial screening to exclude clearly unsuitable candidates, and forwarding them to recruitment managers.

Selection

This aims to choose the most promising candidates from those which the recruitment phase generates. Managers use methods they hope will minimise:

- *false positive errors*, where the selection process predicts success in the job for an applicant, who is therefore hired, but who fails; and
- *false negative errors*, where an applicant who would have succeeded in the job is rejected because the process predicted failure.

As the costs of the latter are not directly experienced by the organisation, managers are more concerned about the former. Selecting the wrong person can cost the organisation dearly and create serious long-term problems (Geerlings and van Veen, 2006).

Most studies of selection focus on the **validity** of the process, in the sense of its ability to predict future performance. The three most commonly used techniques are interviews, personality tests and assessment centres. Figure 11.4 shows estimates of the relative accuracy of selection methods, based on the relation between predicted and actual job performance (with zero for chance prediction and 1.0 for perfect prediction).

Validity occurs when there is a statistically significant relationship between a predictor (such as a selection test score) and measures of on-the-job performance.

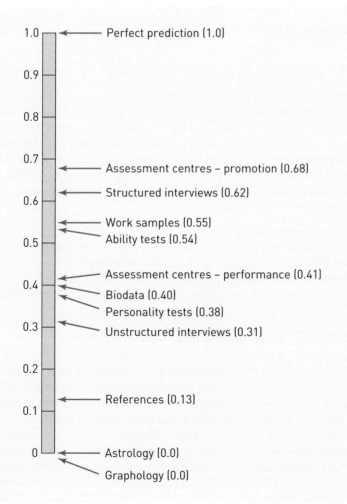

Figure 11.4
The predictive accuracy of selection methods.

Source: Adapted from Anderson and Shackleton (1993), cited in Beardwell and Claydon (2007), p. 212.

Management in practice   Selection for training at RMA Sandhurst

James Greaves, an officer seconded to Sandhurst explained the selection process:

The Royal Military Academy Sandhurst takes people from all aspects of British life, and once they meet the minimum educational entrance requirements they enter a two-part selection process. The first lasts a day and a half and consists of psychometric and physical tests to identify individuals who have talents in four domains:

- physical;
- character and personality;
- intellectual; and
- practical ability.

We try to identify these as early as we can for selection for training. The critical one, and probably the most difficult to actually analyse is the character and personality issue.

We assess them physically, and they have an assault course to go over, you have to run about 600 metres, and during the classroom we look for the ability to perform under pressure, so in a very time-short environment we would look for written assessment and also the ability to stand and think quickly on your feet in front of not only your own peer group (those you're being assessed against) but also a member of the directing staff: he or she sits at the back and asks the questions to see if the individual has what it takes to be trained to become an army officer.

Source: Interview with James Greaves.

Interviews

Management traditionally relies on application forms, references and interviews for selecting employees. The interview remains popular as it has low direct costs and can be used for most jobs, despite research showing it has low validity (Robertson, 1996; Newell and Tansley, 2001), especially in group interviews (Tran and Blackman, 2006). Interviewer ratings correlate poorly with measures of subsequent performance of the candidates hired (i.e. they generate too many false positive errors). Many interviewers are not good at seeking, receiving and processing the amount and quality of information needed for an informed decision. Problems with the interview as a selection device are:

- decisions are made too quickly;
- information obtained early in the interview has a disproportionate influence;
- interviewers compare applicants with an idealised stereotype;
- appearance and non-verbal behaviour strongly shape decisions;
- interviewers are poorly prepared and ask too many questions of limited value.

Activity 11.6   Interviewing interviewees

Arrange to talk to some friends or colleagues who have recently been interviewed for jobs. Ask them to describe the overall process and to identify any features or aspects of the experience that they particularly liked or disliked. Ideally you should talk to at least one person who was offered the job and to one who was not.

As background work for this exercise, compile a checklist of the key features of 'good practice' interviews that should help inform the way you ask questions. A useful reference here is Rebecca Corfield's (2009) *Successful Interview Skills*. As well as practising your interviewing skills you should compare the experience of the interviewees with best practice techniques.

Aware of these difficulties, organisations can spend more on training staff in interview techniques, and/or use structured interview schedules for all applicants (see the following Management in Practice).

Management in practice   A structured interview to assess competencies

This is a short extract from the structured interview which Essex County Council uses to assess competencies in applicants.

To assess the competence 'customer/client orientation' the interviewer will say:

What sort of service standards have you had to work towards?
Why were they important?
What difficulties did you encounter maintaining them?
How did you ensure that others also complied with these standards?

To assess the competence 'managing and developing people' the interviewer will say:

Give an example of when you have had to delegate responsibility?
Why did you need to do this?
How did you go about this?

Source: *IRS Employment Review* 853 18 August 2006, p. 47.

Personality tests

The weaknesses of the interview method and the changing nature of jobs has encouraged managers to use more formal methods – especially **personality tests**. These can provide a relatively objective measure of the dimensions of someone's personality, and most can now be administered online, making them a more affordable selection method.

Some organisational psychologists are cautious about their value on the grounds that:

A **personality test** is a sample of attributes obtained under standardised conditions that applies specific scoring rules to obtain quantitative information for those attributes that the test is designed to measure.

- they should only be used and interpreted by qualified and approved experts;
- candidates can give the answers they think the tester is looking for;
- an individual's personality may vary with circumstances;
- good performers in the same job may have different personalities.

They will still probably be more accurate than a manager's subjective perception of an applicant's personality, and many see them as one, but only one, component in the selection process. Wolf and Jenkins (2006) found that a common reason for using tests is that they can help to justify a selection decision if someone challenges it.

Assessment centres

Assessment centres use many systematic tests and several assessors to create a comprehensive picture of a candidate's abilities and potential (Melancon and Williams, 2006; Newell, 2006). They appear to have higher validity than interviews, since using many tests and several assessors simulates more closely the work to be done. The snag is their cost, so they are used mainly by public sector and large private organisations.

Assessment centres are multi-exercise processes designed to identify the recruitment and promotion potential of personnel.

Do individuals fit the organisation?

This essentially narrow, technical task of achieving an 'individual employee/individual job fit' has been questioned by some who stress the strategic nature of HRM. For instance, some studies of culture change programmes have emphasised the need to select employees who fit the larger direction of change in the organisation. In uncertain business conditions some organisations build a culture that relies on self-motivated, committed people – and try to ensure they select people with suitable personality attributes rather than specific skills for a current job. The Chapter 15 Case on the Eden Project is an example (**www.edenproject.com**) also see the Management in Practice feature.

Management in practice   **Hiring for Hiscox** www.hiscox.co.uk

Kevin Kerridge, Head of Direct and Partnerships at Hiscox (a very successful insurance business) talks about ensuring recruits fit the company:

When people want to work for Hiscox they have to go through a very rigorous recruitment process and that starts with the HR team doing initial interviews, sifting CVs and doing aptitude tests. If they pass that then the managers who are recruiting for the positions get involved: candidates have at least one, probably two or three interviews with the teams and the managers they'll be working with.

I like to really put people on the spot when they come and work for me so the most important thing is about that energy and drive and that willingness to make a difference. Not just a job but somewhere you live and breathe the culture of what you're trying to achieve. So I meet them, assess the energy and also set them a task, maybe a presentation on a challenge that I've got. I see the ideas and things that people come up with around those challenges. I think that's a good way of actually testing whether people fit here or not.

Source: Interview with Kevin Kerridge.

11.7 Reward management

Table 11.2 summarises some common methods of reward management.

Changes in reward management aim to align employer and employee objectives by encouraging action in line with organisational goals (Daniels *et al.*, 2006). There has also been a shift towards flexible and variable reward systems, driven by the search for greater flexibility. Trends include:

- a shift from collectively bargained pay towards more individual performance or skills-driven systems;

Table 11.2 Reward management systems

Type of system	Explanation
Time rate	Reward is related to the number of hours worked
Payment by results	Reward is related to the quantity of output
Skill-based pay	Reward is based on the knowledge and skills of the employee
Performance-related pay	Reward is based upon individual performance in relation to agreed objectives
Flexible benefits packages	Reward is based upon selection of benefits (for example, healthcare or company car) to suit individual's preferences and lifestyles

- linking pay systems more directly to business strategy and organisational goals;
- emphasising non-pay items, such as life assurance and childcare vouchers;
- flexible pay components and individualised reward packages.

Developments in pay policies are also linked to changes in work organisation, and the BMW case illustrates both.

Case study   BMW – the case continues – changes to reward structures

The company states that it depends on motivated staff – high performers for whom the commitment to their work and the willingness to perform are a matter of course. The design of the pay system is based on fairly rewarding an individual's performance and the performance of the entire team. BMW implements this philosophy of performance and reward consistently across all markets and all hierarchical levels. The performance-based element in pay increases with a person's level in the hierarchy. The components of salary are:

- **Fixed salary** Each employee receives a fixed pay of 12 monthly salaries, with no difference between male and female employees. This is assessed and adapted once a year.
- **Company bonus** The company supplements the fixed pay with a share in company profit – in 2008,

for example, this meant that the total pay of most employees amounted to 15 monthly salaries.
- **Individual bonus** The company also rewards individual performance, the amount depending on an evaluation by their immediate boss.

Source: Company website.

Case questions 11.5

- What external factors may have prompted this review of the payment system at BMW?
- How would it affect the management of the appraisal system?
- What demands would it make on the management information system (see Chapter 12)?

Performance-related pay

Performance-related pay aims to link a human resource flow activity (performance appraisal) with reward, which brings the risk of expecting the appraisal process to achieve too many objectives. Some organisations have used such arrangements for many years and report positive effects on both individual and organisational performance. At others, the results of performance-related pay have been less impressive. Either there has been little positive impact on organisational performance or the arrangements have been counter-productive for other reasons (Beer and Cannon, 2004). Research by Lawson (2000) noted:

> the amount of work being undertaken in organisations to modify, change and improve individual performance pay schemes indicates a trend of unhappiness with them. In short, the record of performance-related pay arrangements has been highly variable. (p. 315)

Possible reasons include:

- introducing the new pay arrangements without adequate discussion, consultation and explanation;
- performance-related pay fits the circumstances of some organisations better than others: it is unlikely to work where employees and managers do not trust each other;
- performance-related pay has multiple goals, not all of which can be achieved by one set of arrangements. It may demonstrate to staff that performance affects pay, but inhibit co-operation between them.

Performance-related pay involves the explicit link of financial reward to performance and contributions to the achievement of organisational objectives.

Management in practice   **Performance-related pay: avoiding conflict**

In this voluntary organisation the annual appraisal system was used to set a performance-related payment which could be quite substantial. In practice, managers were overwhelmingly concerned not to risk de-motivating staff or disrupting working relationships. The appraisal scores therefore always tended to be 'on the overly generous side', which resulted in a substantial increase in salary costs for the organisation – with no obvious improvements to employee motivation, effort or organisational performance.

Source: Interview with manager.

Flexible reward systems

More flexible mechanisms for calculating pay have become popular, under labels such as cafeteria benefits, flexible benefits and package compensation. Essentially, remuneration is calculated within an overall compensation package that may include life insurance, medical care or a company car.

Benefits for the employer include aligning reward strategy with both HRM and business strategies; ensuring benefits match the requirements of an increasingly diverse workforce; value for money; and the creation of an employer brand. This individualistic approach to remuneration can, however, be costly and complicated (Benders *et al.*, 2006). For the employee a choice of benefits means they can balance work–life issues more successfully.

11.8   Managing diversity

The workforce in advanced industrialised economies is diverse, and the management challenge is to match that diversity within their organisation. This is both for legal compliance and to gain possible business advantage from this environmental change – there is indeed a 'business case' for diversity.

Gender and ethnic origin are but two dimensions of diversity. Anti-discrimination legislation has largely concentrated on demographic or visible diversity spreading beyond the early locus of gender and race to increasingly embrace other dimensions such as disability, age and sexual orientation.

Key ideas   **An argument for diversity**

Diversity is a reality in labour markets and customer markets today. To be successful in working with and gaining value from this diversity requires a sustained, systematic approach and long-term commitment. Success is facilitated by a perspective that considers diversity to be an opportunity for everyone in an organisation to learn from each other how better to accomplish their work and an occasion that requires a supportive and co-operative organisational culture, as well as group leadership and process skills that can facilitate effective group functioning. Organisations that invest their resources are taking advantage of the opportunities that diversity offers and should outperform those that fail to make such investments.

Source: Kochan *et al.* (2003), p. 18.

Gendered segregation

Although the number of women in the workforce has increased, they still do not have equal access to all occupations. Many tasks are still predominantly male or female occupations. For example, women are much more likely than men to work as teachers, nurses or librarians than as doctors, judges or chartered accountants. They often do routine office work and shop work, but rarely do what is defined as skilled manual work. The reverse is true for men.

Gender segregation is both horizontal and vertical. Horizontal segregation occurs where men and women are associated with different types of jobs. In the UK Labour Force Survey, statistics relating gender and occupation show that women provided 79 per cent of staff in health and social work, and 73 per cent of staff in education: but only 24 per cent in transport and 10 per cent in construction (Equal Opportunities Commission, 2006). Women in management roles also tend to be concentrated in certain areas – principally in HRM and other staff functions, rather than in line functions. In 2005 women in full-time work earned about 17 per cent less than men.

If women are confined to lower occupational positions and to less responsible work they will have fewer opportunities for professional growth and promotion. This in turn distances them from positions of power and the exercise of formal authority. This results in vertical segregation – men in the higher ranks of an organisation and women in the lower. A study of the proportion of women in senior management positions in large UK companies showed that of the 1,048 directors of the 100 largest UK companies by market value, only 58, less than 7 per cent, were women (Linstead *et al.*, 2004, p. 59). Alvesson and Billing (2000) concluded that in Sweden gender division of labour was as pronounced as in most Western countries: 'in most high-level jobs male over-representation is very strong. Only about 10–15 per cent of higher middle and senior managers and seven per cent of all professors are women' (p. 4).

Gender in management

Another question is whether men and women differ in the way they interpret and perform the management role. Researchers have focused on identifying distinctive characteristics of 'masculine' and 'feminine' management styles. Rosener (1997) found that male managers tended to adopt what she termed a transactional style. This uses the principle of exchange as the dominant way of managing – giving rewards for things done well and punishing failure. Male respondents tended to rely mainly on their positional authority – the status conferred on them by their formal role to influence others. Women tended to use a relational style, motivating staff by persuasion, encouragement and using personal qualities rather than position: they generally try to make staff feel good about themselves. She believes that this female model of leadership is more suited to modern, turbulent conditions than the command and control styles typical of the male managers in her research.

Other studies have found similar differences in the styles of women; Helgesen (1995), for example, suggested that women are better at developing cooperation, creativity and intuition than men. She also found that women prefer to manage through relationships rather than by their place in the hierarchy, and claims that they listen and empathise more than men. However, those in a position to make promotion decisions may see it differently, and use the supposedly masculine nature of organisational work to prevent women reaching senior positions. Managers who emphasise the value of hard analytical skills above soft interpersonal skills support, perhaps unwittingly, the progression of men and discourage that of women. Stressing competitiveness, tension and long unsocial working hours has a similar effect. It drives some women away from senior positions owing to domestic responsibilities that continue to be primarily theirs.

The business case for a diverse workforce

The increasing scope of anti-discrimination legislation may have reduced discrimination, but alongside that is a more proactive stance, which stresses the business case for diversity, that the business will gain from promoting diversity by:

- gaining access to a wider range of individual strength, experiences and perspectives;
- a greater understanding of the diverse groups of potential and existing customers represented within a workforce;
- better communication with these diverse groups of potential and existing customers.

Case study   BMW the case continues – 'today for tomorrow'   www.bmw.com

The BMW group is aware of demographic changes in the workforce where the birth rate in many Western countries has consistently been lower than the number of deaths, while life expectancy has continued to rise. This aging workforce affects nations' social security systems and businesses. BMW has formed a project called 'today for tomorrow' to help the group adapt to changing demographics, through five areas:

- design of the working environment: ergonomically designed work stations in offices and manufacturing to help avoid physical strain;
- health management and preventive healthcare: gyms and fitness courses are available at all plant locations;
- needs-based retirement models: flexible retirement packages that allow individuals to retire early or continue after the age of 65;

- qualifications and skills: the increasing importance of life-long learning
- communications: increase awareness of social and corporate changes among managers and associates.

Source: Company website.

Case questions 11.6

- What benefits might BMW gain from a higher proportion of older workers?
- What do you think are the problems associated with an older workforce?
- How might human resource practices change as a result of an older workforce?

11.9   Integrating themes

Sustainable performance

Winstanley and Woodall (2000) point out that

> until very recently, the field of business ethics was not preoccupied with issues relating to the ethical management of employees . . . The main debates in business ethics have centred round the social responsibility of business in relations with clients and the environment. (p. 5)

They state that Beer *et al.*, (1984) suggested that HRM should aim to enhance individual as well as business well-being. They claim that most HRM research and practice has focused on the business case, and largely ignored the implications for the ethical treatment of employees, even though several dimensions are clearly relevant. Flexibility in pay systems and employment contracts, together with high performance work practices, raise ethical questions through their effect on employee working hours, stress and work–life balance. Such considerations can also be part of an assessment of the sustainability of an organisation's performance.

Governance and control

Corporate governance systems aim to regulate the ownership and control of organisations, in the hope of securing the commitment of stakeholders to the organisation, by regulating their conflicting interests. This is also the aim of modern HRM practices, which have generally replaced the tight control of workers implied by scientific management with attempts to involve workers more fully in planning, organising and conducting production.

Konzelmann *et al.* (2006) note that there has not been a comparable development in arrangements of corporate governance, which still give primacy to financial stakeholders. The dilemma is that these stakeholders are perceived to give priority to short-term interests, rather than to the long-term interests of the enterprises in which they invest. These long-term interests may be best served by developing modern HRM practices which integrate the interests of the organisation and the employees, but may conflict with short-term interests of shareholders. It is also likely that financial interests who are represented in governance arrangements will have little interest or knowledge of HRM practices, and will not see it as their role to comment on these essentially detailed management issues.

Corporate governance arrangements are thus likely to do little, if anything, to support the development of modern HRM practices.

Internationalisation

An international strategy needs to be supported by HRM practices that take account of the international dimensions of employee influence, work systems, human resource flows and reward management.

Companies operating internationally face the dilemma between standardising the HRM practices of overseas subsidiaries towards HQ practices. In contrast, localisation refers to the adoption by overseas subsidiaries of those management practices commonly employed by domestic companies in their respective host countries. Managers are likely to adopt a mixed approach – just as they do in marketing where promotion and distribution practices are usually localised, even if advertising is standardised across all countries. They need to integrate different approaches into a coherent international HRM strategy, balancing a desire for closer regional or global integration of HRM practices, with the need to make these responsive to probably contradictory local demands. Their workforce will include different national cultures, working physically distant from each other. They will also be working in different management systems, which, as Chapter 4 shows, have implications not only for the overall structure and management of business enterprises, but for the rights and responsibilities of employees.

Sparrow *et al.* (2004) identify three areas of uncertainty:

- the structures adopted by international companies;
- how multinationals staff and manage their subsidiaries; and
- factors that influence the choice between consistency of HRM practice and adapting it to suit local conditions.

Summary

1 **Understand the contribution of HRM to organisational performance**

- The rise of HRM can be explained by issues such as more globally integrated markets, highly publicised 'companies of excellence', changing composition of the workforce and the decline of trade unions.

2 **Understand the potential importance for organisational performance of HRM**

- The importance of achieving external fit by linking the wider business strategy and HRM strategy.
- Internal coherence among HRM policies is crucial.

3 **Describe the HRM practices concerned with the flow of people into and through the organisation**

- In recent years, due to the need for flexibility, there has been a move away from viewing jobs as a set of tasks to thinking about the set of competencies a person requires to accomplish a job successfully.

4 **Describe some HRM practices concerned with reward management**

- In the search for more flexibility, employers have introduced more individually determined pay systems and linked pay more closely to organisational goals.

5 **Understand how HRM aims to manage workforce diversity**

- Gender segregation has led to men and women being associated with certain types of job, with women often being confined to work with fewer opportunities for promotion.

- Many HRM professionals stress the business case for a more diverse workforce, which can bring access to a wider range of skills and better access to a wider range of customers.

6   **Show how ideas from the chapter add to your understanding of the integrating themes**
- An organisation's HRM practices affect many aspects of employee well-being through their effects on matters such as working hours, stress and work–life balance. Such considerations could be included in a assessments of the sustainability of its performance.
- Corporate governance arrangements and modern HRM practices are both intended to support the long-term interests of stakeholders. Few of those involved in current governance procedures are familiar with HRM (being mainly from financial backgrounds), so these are unlikely to support the development of modern HRM practices.
- Companies operating internationally face the dilemma between standardising the HRM practices of overseas subsidiaries towards HQ practices, or favouring localisation, whereby overseas subsidiaries adopt management practices commonly used in that host country.

Review questions

1   What are the arguments put forward in favour of an organisation adopting a deliberate HRM strategy?

2   What do the terms internal and external fit mean in an HRM context?

3   Summarise the criticism of HRM that it is based on a unitary perspective (see Chapter 2) of organisations.

4   There is little evidence that HRM has achieved the business objectives claimed for it. What evidence would you look for, and how would you show the link between cause and effect?

5   How can the concept of organisational analysis support the recruitment process?

6   What are the main criticisms of personality testing?

7   What are the advantages and disadvantages of performance-related pay?

8   What lessons can you draw from the way BMW has used the payment system to support other aspects of the HRM policy? More generally, summarise the lessons you would draw from the BMW case.

9   Summarise an idea from the chapter that adds to your understanding of the integrating themes.

Concluding critical reflection

Think about the way your company, or one with which you are familiar, deals with HRM. Review the material in the chapter and make notes on the following questions:

- Which of the issues discussed in this chapter are most relevant to your approach to HRM? Is there a clear and conscious attempt to link HRM with wider strategy? Can you give examples of issues where the two support, or do not support, each other? How did those arise, and what have been the effects?
- What **assumptions** do people make in your business about the role of HRM? Is it, for example, seen as mainly a topic for the specialist, or as part of every manager's responsibility? Does the workforce as a whole buy in enthusiastically to the policies adopted, or do they perceive a gap between the rhetoric and the reality?
- What is the dominant view about how changes in the business **context** will affect staff commitment, and the need for new HRM policies to cope with this? Why do they think that? Do people have different interpretations?

- Can you compare your organisation's approach to HRM with that of colleagues on your course, especially those in similar industries, to see what **alternatives** others use?
- If there are differences in approach, can you establish the likely reasons, and does this suggest any possible **limitations** in the present approach? How open is your organisation to innovation in this area?

Further reading

Bechet, T.P. and Maki, W.R. (1987), 'Modelling and forecasting focusing on people as a strategic resource', *Human Resource Planning*, vol. 10, no. 4, pp. 209–217.

A detailed but clear explanation of personnel forecasting methods.

Beer, M., Spector, B., Lawrence, P.R., Quinn Mills, D. and Walton, R.E. (1984), *Managing Human Assets*, Macmillan, New York.

A short and very clear text which influenced the popularity of HRM ideas.

Lawler, E. (2008), *Talent*, Jossey Bass, San Francisco, CA.

A very useful analysis of how some managers ensure that policies and practices through-out the organisations help to make good use of their employees, including a chapter on the role of HRM.

Legge, K. (2005), *Human Resource Management: Rhetorics and realities*, (anniversary edn), Macmillan, London.

A critical examination of HRM, emphasising the gap between the ideal and the practice.

Scullion, H. and Lineham, M. (2005), *International Human Resource Management: A critical text*, Palgrave Macmillan, London.

An international perspective on the topic.

Weblinks

Visit the websites of companies that interest you, perhaps as possible places to work. Or you could choose some of those featured in this chapter such as:

www.bmw.com
www.mcdonalds.co.uk
www.workingforessex.com
www.hiscox.co.uk
www.monster.com

Navigate to the pages dealing with 'about the company' or 'careers':

- What do they tell you about working there?
- What do they say about the recruitment and selection process?
- What clues do they give about their appraisal and rewards policy?

 For video case studies, audio summaries, flashcards, exercises and annotated weblinks related to this chapter, visit **www.pearsoned.co.uk/mymanagementlab**

CHAPTER 12

INFORMATION SYSTEMS AND E-BUSINESS

Aim

To show how converging information systems can transform organisations if people manage them intelligently.

Objectives

By the end of your work on this chapter you should be able to outline the concepts below in your own terms and:

1 Explain how converging technologies change the ways in which people add value to resources

2 Recognise that, to use these opportunities, managers change both technology and organisation

3 Distinguish between operations information systems and management information systems

4 Illustrate how organisations use the internet to add value by using three types of information system (IS) – enterprise, knowledge management and customer relations

5 Understand the relationship between IS, organisation and strategy

6 Show how ideas from the chapter add to your understanding of the integrating themes

Key terms

This chapter introduces the following ideas:

internet
intranet
extranet
blogs
social networking sites
user generated content (UGC)
wikinomics
co-creation
Metcalfe's law
information systems management
data
information
transaction processing system (TPS)

process control system
office automation system
management information system
decision support systems
executive information system
e-commerce
e-business
disintermediation
reintermediation
enterprise resource planning (ERP)
knowledge
knowledge management (KM)

Each is a term defined within the text, as well as in the Glossary at the end of the book.

Case study   Google www.google.com

Sergey Brin and Larry Page founded Google in 1999 and by 2010 it was the world's largest search engine, with the mission: 'to organise the world's information and make it universally accessible and useful'. The need for search services arose as the world wide web expanded, making it progressively more difficult for users to find relevant information. The company's initial success was built on the founders' new approach to online searching: their PageRank algorithm (with 500 million variables and 3 billion terms) identifies material relevant to a search by favouring pages that have been linked to other pages. These links were called 'votes', because they signalled that another page's webmaster had decided that the focal page deserved attention. The importance of the focal page is determined by counting the number of votes it has received.

As a business Google generates revenue by providing advertisers with the opportunity to deliver online advertising that is relevant to the search results on a page. The advertisements are displayed as sponsored links, with the message appearing alongside search results for appropriate keywords. They are priced on a cost-per-impression basis, whereby advertisers pay a fixed amount each time their ad is viewed. The charge depends on what the advertiser has bid for the keywords, and the more they bid the nearer the top of the page their advertisement will be.

A feature of Google is the speed with which it returns search results – usually within a second. From the start its focus has been on developing 'the perfect search engine', defined by Larry Page as something that 'understands what you mean and gives you back what you want'. Rather than use a small number of large servers that tend to run slowly at peak times, Google invested in thousands of linked PCs that quickly find the answer to each query.

The software behind the search technology conducts a series of simultaneous equations in a fraction of a second. It uses PageRank to determine which web pages are most important, and then analyses their content to decide which are relevant to the

Photo courtesy Google UK

current search. By combining overall importance and query-specific relevance, Google claims to be able to put the most relevant results first. That enhances its value to advertisers who have bid for the relevant keywords. One estimate is that in October 2008 it took 30 per cent of US online advertising revenue.

When the company offered shares to the public in 2004, Page warned potential investors that Google was not a conventional company and did not intend to become one. In the interests of long-term stability the share ownership structure was such that the founders owned roughly one-third of the shares, but controlled over 80 per cent of the votes. The company had also, in its short existence, developed a distinctive culture.

Sources: Based on Harvard Business School case 9-806-105, *Google Inc.*, prepared by Thomas R. Eisenmann and Kerry Herman; company website.

Case questions 12.1

- What are the inputs and the outputs of the Google business?
- What are the distinctive features of the Google story set out here?
- How would you expect it to have organised the business to secure such a rapid and profitable growth?

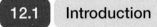

12.1 Introduction

Google is an organisation founded on data – it gathers, processes and disseminates it from and to millions of people in a way that gives them valuable information. All have different requirements and work in different ways, yet Google has developed a search engine that works at astonishing speed to meet their needs. Since the search is free, Google survives on income from advertisements – which depends on the quality of the search systems.

Google (like eBay, Facebook or YouTube) is an example of a company created to use the internet – it is a pure 'e-business' company, whose managers built it around computer-based information systems (IS). In that sense it differs from companies founded long before the internet but which now depend on it to support the business. Their managers began by implementing relatively simple information systems which they progressively built, through trial and error, into the complex ones used today. Traditional businesses such as British Airways, Ford or Sainsbury's depend on information about each stage of the value-adding process:

- inputs – cost and availability of materials, staff and equipment;
- transformation – delivery schedules, capacity utilisation, efficiency, quality and costs;
- outputs – prices, market share and customer satisfaction.

Their information systems gather data about inputs, transformation processes and outputs, and feed the information to those working at different levels of the organisation. Figure 12.1 shows how information systems support these fundamental management processes.

Computer-based information systems can make operations more efficient, change the way people work together, and offer new strategic possibilities and threats. Used well, they help managers to add value to resources. Used badly, they destroy wealth – such as when managers decide to implement an expensive IS project which does not deliver what they expected, and is abandoned or replaced. The UK National Health Service Programme for Information Technology (NPfIT) (**www.connectingforhealth.nhs.uk**) contains examples of both – some parts (the Picture Archiving and Communication System) work well; while many observers (in early 2010) see the Electronic Patient Record System as a controversial failure.

Progressively more managers face this kind of responsibility, as information systems move rapidly from background activities (such as accounting and stock control) into foreground activities (online banking or sponsored websites) which directly involve customers, and then into activities which members of the public manage themselves (social networks or music downloads). No organisation is immune: if dissatisfied customers use a popular social networking

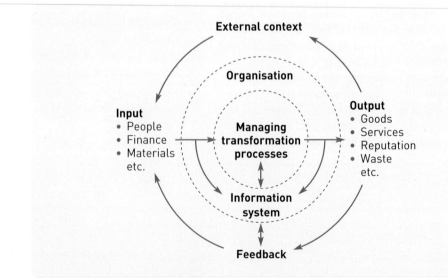

Figure 12.1
The role of information systems in organisations
Source: Boddy *et al.* (2005)

site to spread bad news about a business, managers need to respond – even if they have never heard of the site.

This chapter will show you how IS can transform organisations. It shows how traditional businesses progressively widened the role of computer-based systems in managing data about their operations, and how technical developments have led to the convergence of data, voice and vision systems. This led to the new phenomenon of co-creation of value, in which users not only view content on a site but also create it. In either case, adding value depends on managing both technological and organisational issues – which the chapter will illustrate with accounts of three widely used systems.

Activity 12.1   **Applying the open systems model**

Apply the open systems model in Figure 12.1 to an organisation that you know.

- What are the inputs and outputs?
- Describe the transformation process.
- List examples of information systems that provide information about inputs, outputs and transformations.

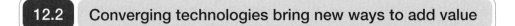

12.2   Converging technologies bring new ways to add value

Using IS to add value to data

Since the 1950s, organisations that make and deliver products or services have progressively extended the tasks which computer-based information systems (IS) undertake, beginning with routine accounting and stock control systems, extending to manufacturing and transport, and now covering almost every aspect of the organisation:

- Allied Bakeries use engineering maintenance systems to monitor equipment and plan maintenance to reduce lost production time.
- The UK Vehicle Licensing Agency encourages drivers to pay their road tax online.
- BP maintains all human resource information on a single database, allowing staff to access their records and company policies online, so that all work to common information.
- Many firms link internal processes electronically with suppliers and customers, to receive orders, arrange supplies and pay invoices electronically.

Such systems are embedded throughout the organisation and still raise management issues as requirements change or new systems become available: managers then begin costly (and often unsuccessful) projects to change or enhance their systems.

Using convergence to add value to data, sound and vision

The information systems just described are all computer-based. The revolutionary changes now taking place – blogging, social networking and downloading music – follow from the convergence of three technologies – computer, telephone and television. Engineers developed these devices quite independently, so they have always worked in different ways and as isolated systems. As the cost of computing power fell, the digital technology at the heart of computing was used to re-design how telephones transmit voice signals, and then how television transmits images. Engineers could then combine the three technologies in a single device – such as your mobile phone. The common language and set of rules specifying the format in which to send data between devices enabled them to communicate electronically, creating the **internet** (Berners-Lee, 1999). Another relevant term is an **intranet**, a private computer network operating within

The **internet** is a web of hundreds of thousands of computer networks linked together by telephone lines and satellite links through which data can be carried.

An **intranet** is a version of the internet that only specified people within an organisation can use.

An **extranet** is a version of the internet that is restricted to specified people in specified companies – usually customers or suppliers.

an organisation by using internet standards and protocols. The opposite is an **extranet**, a network that uses the internet to link organisations with specified suppliers, customers or trading partners, who gain access to it through a password system.

Linking mobile phones to the internet led to the explosive growth of the 'wireless internet', which liberates the computer from the desktop, enabling people to send and/or receive text, voice and visual data wherever they are.

Countless organisations in all sectors of the economy use these technical advances to change traditional enterprises and to create new ones. Many now only accept orders online, and use the internet to manage all aspects of their businesses; established media companies offer online as well as paper copies of their publications; national and local governments increasingly expect to interact with their citizens online. The BBC claims that the iPlayer is changing the way people watch television, with over a million programmes being viewed over the online video site each day (**www.bbc.co.uk**). But the most dramatic shift currently observable is that of co-creation.

Producers and consumers co-create value

A **blog** is a weblog that allows individuals to post opinions and ideas.

Social networking sites use internet technologies which enable people to interact within an online community to share information and ideas.

Individuals using blogs and social network sites are now driving the growth of internet traffic. Convergence enables people to communicate over the internet in many ways – using blogs and social networking sites to send emails, share music files, and search websites for social and business information. **Blogs** attract individuals with an interest in the topic to ask questions or express their views in a discussion group. **Social networking sites** developed from blogs, by providing a communication channel for people who want to share their interests with other members of the online community.

Management in practice **SelectMinds – social networks for professionals**
www.selectminds.com

The company helps organisations to build connections between groups of employees, former employees, and other constituencies to increase knowledge sharing and productivity. It offers secure, online social networking solutions that organisations use to recruit and retain scarce knowledge workers, and increase the speed of information and knowledge flow.

It pioneered an early form of corporate social networking in 2000 when it began delivering online networks to connect former employees of organisations with each other and their former employer. Employees of professional services firms often leave to work for customers, so are able to refer business to their former employer. Seeding this population with information about their previous company (new services, client successes) helps them to become better brand ambassadors, speaking knowledgeably about it. The site enables companies to benefit from customer and employee relationships as well as to build new relationships based on continued personal connections among current and ex-employees.

Products now include systems to link organisations with customers, retirees, potential new staff and among current employees.

Source: Company website.

User generated content (UGC) is text, visual or audio material which users create and place on a site for others to view.

Wikinomics describes a business culture in which customers are no longer only consumers but also co-creators and co-producers of the service.

This digital culture erodes boundaries between producers and consumers. Wikipedia, written by volunteers, quickly became the world's largest encyclopaedia. YouTube claims to hold the world's largest collection of videos, including a large collection of professional work. Amazon encourages visitors to the site to review books, which others can read before they buy. Media groups encourage readers to write stories for publication. All are examples of **user generated content (UGC)** – content which users create and place on a site for other to view.

Tapscott and Williams (2006) refer to this as **wikinomics**, a business culture that sees customers not as consumers but as co-creators and co-producers. Amazon and Google encourage **co-creation**. Amazon uses customer reviews to exchange information among readers and

(a) Traditional pattern of production and delivery of product
   or service, followed by payment by a customer.

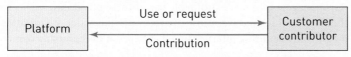

(b) New pattern of consumption by customers, who also
   contribute to a platform, such as Wikipedia, Google or Linux.

Figure 12.2
Traditional delivery
and customer
participation

uses buying patterns of customers to suggest books to others with similar interests. Google analyses search requests to develop profiles and make advertisements available to searchers with certain profiles. In both cases, customers create the content, and the more people view the content, the more valuable the network becomes.

This follows from **Metcalfe's law** 'the value of a network increases with the square of the number of users connected to the network'. In other words, the more people who have phones, the more valuable a phone becomes to the next adopter. This 'network effect' encourages more people to use an existing website, and creates barriers for new entrants who at first have few users to attract others.

In a traditional economic system producers create products which consumers order, receive and pay for (Figure 12.2a). The alternative is when companies such as Google, Facebook and many more provide a platform that customers use to offer and view information. They add value to the platform as they provide more information and so enhance the perceived quality of the platform. Consumption does not reduce value but increases it (Figure 12.2b) (see Management in Practice).

Co-creation is product or service development that makes intensive use of the contributions of customers.

Metcalfe's law states that the value of a network increases with the square of the number of users connected to the network.

Management in practice   An online forum in healthcare

A physician dealing with fertility treatment at the University Hospital Nijmegen, the Netherlands, spent a lot of time informing couples on the pros and cons of the treatments, and in providing emotional support. As an experiment he started an online forum in which his clients (exclusively) share information and anxieties. It also provides relevant medical information. From time to time the doctor and other staff join the sessions. The 'electronic fertility platform' saves a lot of the time the doctor used to spend advising and supporting clients. Clients contribute anonymously to the platform and so help each other.

Source: Boddy *et al.* (2009a), p. 62.

Activity 12.2   Reflect on your use of social networking sites

Have you used a social network or similar site to interact with, or make comments about, an organisation?

● What were the circumstances?
● Did it change your view of the company?
● What evidence was there of staff from the company being aware of the site?
● What could management have done to benefit from the exchanges?

12.3 Managing the new opportunities to add value

Adding value in traditional delivery systems

The internet is evidently challenging established ways of doing business. Combined with political changes, this is creating a wider, often global, market for many goods and services. The challenge for managers is to make profitable use of these possibilities. This includes looking beyond technology – which receives most attention – to the wider organisation. A manager who played a major role in guiding internet-based changes at his company commented:

> The internet is not a technology challenge. It's a people challenge – all about getting structures, attitudes and skills aligned.

The significance of the internet for everyone who works in organisations cannot be overstated. It affects all aspects of organisational activity, enabling new forms of organisation and new ways of doing business. Established organisations typically go through successive stages in the way they use the internet, which Figure 12.3 illustrates.

The simplest internet applications provide information, enabling customers to view product or other information on a company website; conversely suppliers use their website to show customers what they can offer. The next stage is to use the internet for interaction. Customers enter information and questions about, for example, offers and prices. The system then uses the customer information, such as preferred dates and times of travel, to show availability and costs. Conversely, a supplier who sees a purchasing requirement from a business (perhaps expressed as a purchase order on the website) can agree electronically to meet the order. A third use is for transactions, when customers buy goods and services through a supplier's website. The whole transaction, from accessing information through ordering, delivery and payment, can take place electronically.

A company achieves integration when it links its internal system to the website, so that when a customer orders a product online, it automatically passes to the internal operating systems. These then begin all the processes (including the links with suppliers' systems) required to manufacture and/or deliver the product. Transformation refers to the situation where it is not only linking internal–external systems, but where it is within the participation culture, in which customers are actively involved in the design and consumption of the products, and where the company is actively engaging with online communities of customers and others.

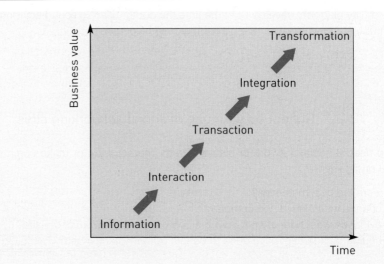

Figure 12.3
Stages in using
the internet

Case study
Google – the case continues: customers and product development
www.google.com

Beyond its core search and advertising capabilities, the company has embarked on ventures involving online productivity, blogging, radio and television advertising, online payments, social networks, mobile phone operating systems, and many more information domains. What information management tools the company hasn't developed it has acquired: Picasa for photo management; YouTube for online videos; DoubleClick for web ads; Keyhole for satellite photos (now Google Earth); Urchin for web analytics (now Google Analytics).

Google engineers prototype new applications on the platform; if any of these begin to get users' attention, developers can launch beta [test] versions to see whether the company's vast captive customer base responds enthusiastically. If one of the applications becomes a hit, Google's enormous 'cloud' of computing capability can make room for it. In the development process, Google simultaneously tests and markets them to the user community. In fact, testing and marketing are virtually indistinguishable from one another. This creates a unique relationship with consumers, who become an essential part of the development team as new products take shape and grow. Google does more than just alpha and beta test applications – it can host them on its infrastructure. Google's customers then transition seamlessly from testing to using products as they would any other commercial offering.

The company allows independent developers to share access and create new applications that incorporate elements of the Google system. They can easily test and launch applications and have them hosted in the Google world, where there is an enormous target audience – 132 million customers globally – and a practically unlimited capacity for customer interactions.

Source: Iyer and Davenport (2008).

Case questions 12.2
- What benefits do you expect Google will gain from this close involvement with developers?
- What do the developers gain?
- What may be the risks to either Google or the developers?

Adding value through co-creation

Many managers are working out how to use social networking sites to their advantage, for instance by creating their own customer platforms or by contributing actively to others. While people use these applications to interact socially with friends or with people who share a common interest, the trend gives managers a potentially useful opportunity. While initially uneasy, many now actively encourage the practice. Some create and host customer communities, to move closer to their customers, and to learn how best to improve a product or service more quickly than by using conventional market research techniques. They host discussions about their products: if people are being critical, managers want to know this so that they can deal with the problem. A blog discussion among users might identify possible new uses for a product, or hint at features which the company could add. Some companies offer a service to businesses, monitoring what people are saying about the company, and giving advice on how best to add to the discussion in ways that build a positive image, or at least prevent a negative one (see Key Ideas).

Key ideas
Managers learn to use the social web

Bernoff and Li (2008) note that:

Companies are used to being in control. They typically design products, services and marketing messages based on their . . . view of what people want . . . Now, though, many customers are no longer cooperating. Empowered by online social technologies . . . customers are connecting with, and drawing power from, each other. They're defining their own perspectives on companies and brands, a view that's often at odds with the image a company wants to project. This groundswell of people using technologies to get the things they need from one another, rather than from companies, is now tilting the balance of power from company to customer. (p. 36)

The authors then advise managers how they can best respond to these changing conditions, by 'working with the groundswell' – developing a clear view of how they can put social applications on an equal footing with other business projects to achieve their business goals. Among their examples:

- **'Listening'** A software development company uses an application that allows customers to suggest new product features and then vote on them: this gives valuable information when the company has to decide which of the (thousands of) suggestions to develop.
- **'Talking'** A car company wanted to increase students' awareness of a new model. They created a stunt in which students lived in the car for a week: from there they wrote blogs, posted YouTube videos and contacted thousands of friends through Facebook and MySpace, greatly increasing awareness of the brand, at a fraction of the cost of traditional publicity methods.
- **'Energising'** An old and respected company wanted to build enthusiasm among current and new customers for the brand. It hired four enthusiastic customers to act as 'lead ambassadors', whose job was to build an online community of users to exchange ideas and experiences with the product. The size of this community quickly exceeded expectations, and has generated a substantial increase in sales.

Source: Bernoff and Li (2008).

Whether a business is in a traditional delivery or co-creation mode, it will only add value if managers look beyond the technology, however sophisticated, to see that they also need to manage some organisational issues.

Adding value depends on managing technology AND organisation

Whether the company is an internet-based start-up or a century-old business, it requires deliberate management action to create the IS infrastructure to engage with the internet. Building and maintaining Google's network of an estimated 1 million PCs requires a vast management effort – with established businesses also requiring to devote significant resources to their information systems. **Information systems management** is the term used to describe the activities of planning, acquiring, developing and using IS such as this (the following Management in Practice gives the views of one IS manager).

> **Information systems management** is the planning, acquisition, development and use of these systems.

| **Management in practice** | Jean-Pierre Corniou – Renault's CIO www.renault.com |

Frankly my job (as Chief Information Officer) consists of being a bilingual guy: I speak both the language of business and the language of technology. Renault, like other companies, started investing in information technology (IT) in the middle 1960s. It was pioneering work – there were just a few people in IT, working on large systems of great complexity. People inside still have that pioneering attitude, of an era when IT was seen as secret, and complex . . . but we need to open up, to build transparency, to build the confidence and trust of all stakeholders in the company.

We have invested a lot of money in [advanced applications] and websites, and when we analysed the level of utilization of these products and tools, we were very surprised to see how much money had been spent on products that people were not using.

I spend a lot of time in plants, in discussions with foremen in the field, trying to understand how they use technology to increase their efficiency. I spend lots of time in commercial departments too, to understand the key business processes. Bringing IT to the business community means the CIO has to be embedded in the day to day life of the organization, and of course to have a seat on the board. I consider myself more a business guy than an IT guy.

Source: *Financial Times*, 17 September 2003.

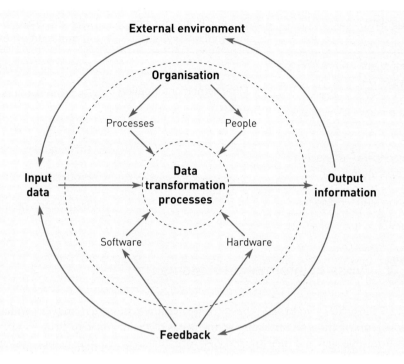

Figure 12.4
The elements of a
computer-based IS

Source: Boddy *et al.*
(2009a)

As M. Corniou's comments clearly show, any information system (internet-based or other-wise) includes people and processes as well as hardware and software, as shown in Figure 12.4.

A computer-based student record system illustrates this. The hardware consists of computers and peripherals such as printers, monitors and keyboards. This runs the record system, using software to manipulate the data and to either print the results for each student or send them electronically – which they see as information. The system also requires people (course administrators) to enter data (name and other information about students and their results) following certain processes – such as that one person reads from a list of grades while another keys the data into the right field on the student's record. Managers of a department might use the output to compare the pass rate of each course, so the record system is now part of the university's management information. Staff will use their knowledge (based on learning and experience) to interpret trends and evaluate their significance.

Figure 12.4 also shows that the hardware and software is part of a wider organisational context, which includes people, working processes, structures and cultures. An information system includes identifiable elements of this context, which affect the outcomes of an IS project, for better or worse, just as much as the design of the technological elements of hardware and software.

Activity 12.3   Using the model

Use Figure 12.4 to analyse an IS that you know or about which you can gather information.

- Who promoted the system and what were their objectives?
- Describe the system they implemented, especially the hardware and software.
- What changes did the system lead to for people and procedures?
- What changes for other aspects of the organisation such as its culture and structure?
- What were the outcomes and how did they compare with the objectives?
- What can you learn from the evidence of this case?

Management levels	Generic Categories of Information system	Specific types of information system
Top managers – managing the business	Management information system	Executive information
Middle managers – managing managers		Decision support
		Information reporting
Line managers – managing direct operators	Operations information system	Office automation
		Process control
Operating staff – doing the direct work		Transaction processing

Figure 12.5
Types of
information system

12.4   Types of information systems

Figure 12.5 illustrates two broad types of information system that are very widely used. Operational information systems support the needs of the day-to-day business operations, and how front-line staff and their supervisors work. Management information systems typically guide the decisions of middle and senior managers.

Data and information

Data are raw, unanalysed facts, figures and events.

Information comes from data that have been processed so that they have meaning for the person receiving it.

Both types of system turn 'data' into 'information'. **Data** refers to recorded descriptions of things, events, activities and transactions – their size, colour, cost, weight, date and so on. It may be a number, a piece of text, a drawing or photograph, or a sound. In itself it may or may not convey information to a person. **Information** is a subset of data that means something to the people receiving them, which they judge to be useful, significant or urgent. It comes from data that have been processed (by people or with the aid of technology) so that it has meaning and value, by linking it to other pieces of data to show a comparison, sequence of events or trend. The output is subjective since what one person sees as valuable information, another may see as insignificant data – their interpretation reflects diverse backgrounds and interests.

Operations information systems

Operations systems support the information processing needs to keep current work moving efficiently. They include technologies that help people perform standalone tasks more efficiently, such as word processors and spreadsheets. Most professional people use these technologies routinely – for instance, research and development (R&D) engineers can use a computer-aided design (CAD) program to improve the way they work, as the system includes software that performs routine tasks automatically, so that the engineer can focus on design issues.

A **transaction processing system (TPS)** records and processes data from routine transactions such as payroll, sales or purchases.

A **process control system** monitors and controls variables describing the state of a physical process.

An **office automation system** uses several systems to create, process, store and distribute information.

    Transaction processing systems (TPS) record and process data from customer and supplier transactions, salary and other systems affecting employees, as well as those with banks and tax authorities. A TPS collects data as transactions occur and stores this in a central database, which is then the source of other reports such as customer statements or supplier payments. Such systems help managers to keep track of recent transactions, especially their financial implications.

    They also need systems to monitor and control physical processes. So breweries, bakeries, refineries and similar operations use **process control systems** to monitor defined variables such as temperature, pressure or flow, compare them with the required state, and adjust as necessary. Staff monitor the systems to check if they need to take further action.

    Office automation systems bring together email, word processing, spreadsheet and many other systems to create, process, store and distribute information. They can also link to TPS or process control systems to make structured decisions. Banks analyse the pattern of a customer's transactions to decide whether to grant a request for credit. Office automation systems stream-line the administrative processes of a business, and can provide an input into other systems.

Management information systems (MIS)

A **management information system (MIS)** is a computer-based system that provides managers with the information they need for effective decision making. The MIS is supported by the oper-ations information systems, as well as other sources of internal and external information. It typi-cally includes systems for information reporting, decision support and executive information, each of which is described below. An important management choice is how many people throughout the organisation can access and use information from these systems, with many advo-cating their widespread use as a way of supporting decentralised and responsive decision making.

> A **management information system** provides information and support for managerial decision making.

Managers in charge of production or service facilities constantly face choices about, for ex-ample, whether to engage more or fewer staff, arrange schedules or accept a reservation. To increase the chances that their decisions add value, they need information about, for ex-ample, existing capacity, current orders or available materials. Good information increases their confidence, and information reporting systems help to achieve this, by providing accu-rate and up-to-date information on the current operation.

Decision support systems (DSS), sometimes called expert or knowledge systems, help managers to calculate the likely consequences of alternative actions. A DSS incorporates a model of the process or situation, and will often draw data from operational systems. Some examples include:

> **Decision support systems** help people to calculate the consequences of alternatives before they decide which to choose.

- businesses use DSS to calculate the financial consequences of investments;
- banks use knowledge systems to analyse proposed loans. These incorporate years of lend-ing experience and enable less experienced staff to make decisions;
- NHS Direct in the UK uses an expert system to enable nurses in a call centre to deal with calls from patients who would otherwise visit their doctor. The system proposes the questions to ask, interprets the answers and recommends the advice the nurse should give to the caller.

Executive information systems are essentially management information systems aimed at the most senior people in the business. Rather than great detail, they aim to provide easy access to data that have been derived from many sources, and processed in a way that meets top management requirements.

> An **executive information system** provides those at the top of the organisation with easy access to timely and relevant information.

Activity 12.4   Collecting examples of applications

Collect new examples of one operational and one management information system, from someone working in an organisation.

- What information do they deal with?
- How do they help people who use them in their work?
- What issues about the design of these systems should managers be considering, in view of the growth of social networking and similar technologies?
- Have they begun to think about these in the organisations you have studied?

12.5   The internet and e-business

> **e-commerce** refers to the activity of selling goods or service over the internet.

The internet is clearly transforming the way many organisations work, and creating new re-lationships between them and their customers, suppliers and business partners. Two com-monly used terms are **e-commerce** and **e-business**.

> **e-business** refers to the integration, through the internet, of all an organisation's processes from its suppliers through to its customers.

e-commerce and e-business

Many businesses use the internet to support their distribution, by offering goods and services through a website – which is defined here as e-commerce. A more radical way to use the internet is for what is here called e-business, when companies use a website to manage information about sales, capacity, inventory, payment and so on – and exchange that information with their suppliers or business customers. This enables them to use the internet to connect all the links in their supply chain, so creating an integrated process to meet customer needs (see the following Management in Practice).

Management in practice   **Using the internet at Siemens**   www.siemens.com

Siemens' plans to do much of their business over the internet includes:

1 Knowledge management – using a company-wide system to capture and share knowledge about scientific and technical developments throughout the business.
2 Online purchasing (or e-procurement). Large savings are expected from pooling the demands of buying departments through a company-wide system called click2procure.
3 Online sales. Most of Siemens' customers are other companies who can click on 'buy from Siemens' on the website and place orders for most Siemens products.
4 Internal administrative processes – such as by handling 30,000 job applications a year online, or expecting employees to book their business travel arrangements over the internet.

The chief executive at the time said:

If you want to transform a company to an e-business company, the problem is not so much e-procurement and the face to the customer. All this can be done rather fast. What is truly difficult is to reorganise all the internal processes. That is what we see as our main task and where the main positive results will come from.

Sources: Boddy *et al.* (2009a); company website.

Disintermediation
Removing intermediaries such as distributors or brokers that formerly linked a company to its customers.

The relationship between a company and its channel partners can be changed by the internet because electronic networks can bypass channel partners, also called **disintermediation**. Figure 12.6 shows how a manufacturer and a wholesaler can bypass other partners and reach customers directly.

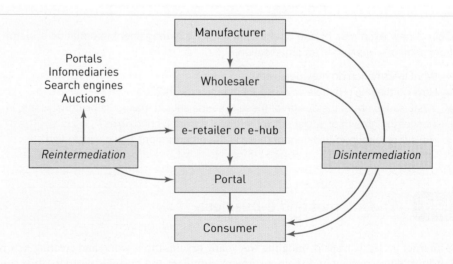

Figure 12.6
Reinventing the supply chain

The benefits of disintermediation are that transaction costs are reduced and that it enables direct contact with customers. This also makes it possible to increase the reach of companies, e.g. from a local presence to a national or international presence. **Reintermediation** is the creation of new intermediaries between customers and suppliers by providing (new) service such as supplier search and product evaluation. Examples are portals such as **www.Yahoo.com**, **www.amazon.com** and **www.moneyfacts.co.uk** which help customers to compare offers and link them to suppliers.

Reintermediation
Creating intermediaries between customers and suppliers, providing services such as supplier search and product evaluation.

A major concern of companies moving towards e-commerce or e-business has been to ensure that they can handle the associated physical processes. These include handling orders, arranging shipment, receiving payment and dealing with after-sales service. This gives an advantage to traditional retailers who can support their website with existing fulfilment processes.

Kanter (2001) found that the move to e-business for established companies involves a deep change. She found that top management absence, shortsighted marketing staff and other internal barriers were common obstacles. Based on interviews with more than 80 companies on their move to e-business, her research provides 'deadly mistakes' as well as some lessons, including:

- create experiments and act simply and quickly to convert the sceptics;
- create dedicated teams, and give them resources and autonomy;
- recognise that e-business requires systemic changes in many ways of working.

Three widely used internet applications are known as customer relationship management, enterprise resource planning and knowledge management systems.

Customer relationship management (CRM)

Chapter 9 (Section 9.5) introduces the idea of customer relationship management, a process by which companies aim to build long-term, profitable relationships with their customers. This involves many changes in the way the organisation works, and information systems play a major role in supporting this. CRM software tries to align business processes with customer strategies to recruit, satisfy and retain profitable customers (Ryals, 2005; Kumar *et al.*, 2006). Figure 12.7 shows three approaches. The first treats all customers in the same way by sending impersonal messages in one direction. The second sends one-sided, but different messages to customers, depending on their profile. The third personalises the messages which may lead to real interaction, in the hope of increasing customer loyalty.

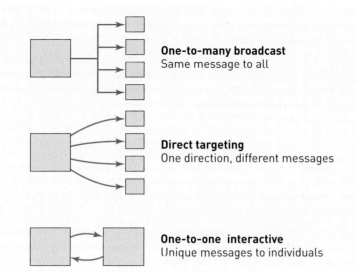

One-to-many broadcast
Same message to all

Direct targeting
One direction, different messages

One-to-one interactive
Unique messages to individuals

Figure 12.7
Communications methods and message

In many businesses the key to increasing profitability is to focus on recruiting and retaining high lifetime value customers. So the promise of CRM is to:

- gather customer data swiftly;
- identify and capture valuable customers while discouraging less valuable ones;
- increase customer loyalty and retention by providing customised products;
- reduce costs of serving customers;
- make it easier to acquire similar customers.

Some CRM systems consolidate customer data from many sources to answer questions such as:

- Who are our most loyal customers?
- Who are our most profitable customers?
- What do these profitable customers want to buy?

The Tesco Clubcard described in the Part 6 Case (**www.tesco.com**) is an excellent example of this, which has played a major role in the success of the company: the system processes the information about what each customer purchases, and uses this to identify promotional vouchers that are most likely to be useful to that customer. Suitable vouchers encourage them to return to the store to make further purchases. Ahearne *et al.* (2008) analysed the effectiveness of a CRM system designed to automate the collection, processing and distribution of customer data to sales staff. The company hoped this would enable them to share market intelligence more widely, help staff manage customer contacts, make better presentations and deal more efficiently with post-visit reports. Studying the impact of the system in a pharmaceutical company showed that it did indeed improve sales-force performance, mainly through enabling them to provide better customer service, and through being more adaptable to customer needs (see also Management in Practice).

Management in practice   Iris and 'The Source'   www.irisnation.com

Iris is a rapidly growing advertising agency, with close relationships with international customers. As an example of the services it offers, Ian Millner, Managing Director describes 'The Source':

A key part of our global relationship with Sony Ericsson is a digital asset management system, that has now been branded The Source. The role of that system is to collect all marketing assets of value, most of which will have been originated by Iris, have it all in one place so that if you're Sony Ericsson in Brazil or in Indonesia or in China, instantly you're able to access marketing materials that have value and relevance for you to use really, really quickly in your marketplace.

So this idea of real time sharing is a key part of working with clients in dynamic and competitive markets, and I think the other bit that comes with that is not only value but also speed to market. It's so important now to be able to do things quickly, so that is a massive asset in our sort of overall strategic relationship with that client but also our anticipation is that there'll be more and more clients now who want that type of agency partner globally.

Source: Interview with Ian Millner.

Massey *et al.* (2001) shows how implementing successful CRM depends more on strategy than on technology, and that even when a customer strategy is established, other dimensions such as business processes, (other) systems, structure and people need to change to support it. If a company wants to develop better relationships with its customers it needs first to rethink the key business processes that relate to customers, from customer service to order fulfilment. If consumers have a choice of channels – such as email, web or telephone – marketing, sales and service can no longer be treated separately. A customer may place an order by phone, use the web page to check the status of the order and send a complaint by mail. Multi-channel interactions pose considerable challenge if the company is to maintain a single comprehensive and up-to-date view of each customer.

For companies focused on products or services, this means realigning around the customer – which can be a radical change in a company's culture. All employees, but especially those in marketing, sales, service and any other customer contact functions, have to think in a customer oriented way. Much time and financial resource of CRM projects has to be spent on organisational issues. Successful CRM depends on co-ordinated actions by all departments within a company rather than being driven by a single department (Boulding *et al.*, 2005).

Enterprise resource planning (ERP) systems

Fulfilling a customer order requires that people in sales, accounting, production, purchasing and so on co-operate with each other to exchange information. However the IS on which they depend were often designed to meet the needs of a single function. They were built independently and cannot automatically exchange information. Manufacturing will not automatically know the number and types of product to make because their systems are not linked to the systems that process orders. A common solution is to use **enterprise resource planning (ERP)** systems, which aim to co-ordinate activities and decisions across many functions by creating an integrated platform which integrates them into company-wide business processes. Information flows between the functions and levels, as shown in Figure 12.8.

At the heart of an enterprise system is a central database that draws data from and feeds data into a series of applications throughout the company. Using a single database streamlines the flow of information. Table 12.1 shows examples of business processes and functions

Enterprise resource planning (ERP) An integrated process of planning and managing all resources and their use in the enterprise. It includes contacts with business partners.

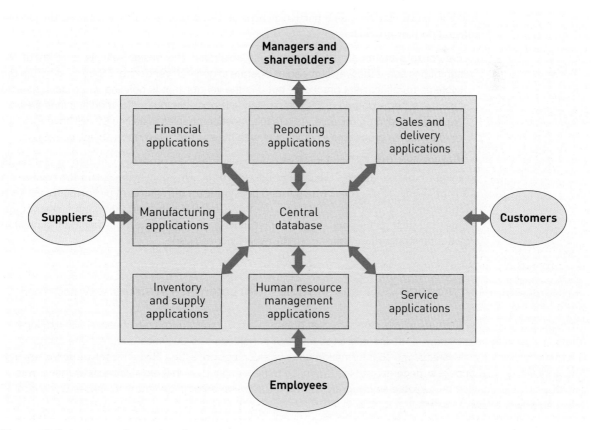

Figure 12.8 Anatomy of an enterprise system.

Table 12.1 Examples of business processes supported by enterprise systems

Financial	Accounts receivable and payable, cash management and forecasting, management information, cost accounting, profitability analysis, profit-centre accounting, financial reporting
Human resources	Payroll, personnel planning, travel expenses, benefits accounting, applicant tracking
Operations and logistics	Inventory management, maintenance, production planning, purchasing, quality management, vendor evaluation, shipping
Sales and marketing	Order management, pricing, sales management, sales planning, billing

which enterprise systems support. These 'modules' can be implemented separately, but promise much greater benefits when they are linked to exchange information continuously through the central database.

ERP systems give management direct access to current operating information and so enable companies to, among other things:

- integrate customer and financial information;
- standardise manufacturing processes and reduce inventory;
- improve information for management decisions across sites;
- enable online connections with systems of suppliers and customers with the internal information processing.

There is controversy about whether adopting an ERP system gives a competitive advantage (McKeen and Smith, 2003). ERP systems promote centralised co-ordination and decision making, which may not suit a particular firm, and some companies do not need the level of integration they provide:

> Enterprise systems are basically generic solutions. The design reflects a series of assumptions about the way companies operate in general. Vendors of ES try to structure the systems to reflect best practices, but it is the vendor that is defining what 'best' means. Of course, some degree of ES customisation is possible, but major modifications are very expensive and impracticable. As a result, most companies installing ES will have to adapt or rework their processes to reach a fit with the system. (Davenport, 1998, p. 125)

Some believe that ERP systems lock companies into rigid processes which make it difficult to adapt to market changes (Hagel and Brown, 2001). This may help explain the results of a study by Wieder *et al.* (2006) which found no significant differences in performance between adopters and non-adopters of ERP systems. Bozarth (2006) illustrates the complexities of implementing such systems and contrasts alternative approaches. The following Management in Practice illustrates these issues from the experience of Nestlé.

Management in practice   Nestlé struggles with enterprise systems www.nestle.com

Nestlé is a food and pharmaceuticals company that operates all over the world. Traditionally it allowed local units to operate as they saw fit, taking into account local conditions and business cultures. The company had many purchasing systems and no information on how much business they did with each supplier: each factory made independent arrangements. Nestlé's management concluded that these local differences were inefficient and costly. They wanted to integrate the systems to act as a single entity, using its worldwide buying power to lower prices.

Managers therefore started a program to standardise and co-ordinate its processes and information systems. The project team decided to install SAP's financial, purchasing, sales and distribution modules throughout every Nestlé USA division. The new system would standardise and co-ordinate the company's information systems and processes.

A year after the project started, a stock market analyst in London doubted its success: 'it touches the corporate culture, which is decentralised and tries to centralise it. That's risky. It's always a risk when you touch the corporate culture'. Jeri Dunn from Nestlé later agreed: at an American plant most of the key stakeholders failed to realise how much the project would change their business processes. Dunn said: 'they still thought it was just software'. A rebellion had taken place when the plant moved to install the manufacturing modules. The lower-level workers did not understand how to use the new system and did not understand the changes. Their only hope was to call the project help desk, which received 300 calls a day. Turnover increased and no one seemed motivated to learn and use the system.

The project team stopped the project and removed the project leader. This person had put too much pressure on the project and the technology. By doing so the team had lost sight of the bigger picture.

Sources: Laudon and Laudon (2004); 'Nestlé's ERP Odyssey', *CIO-magazine*, 15 May; Konicki (2000), 'Nestlé Taps SAP for e-business', *Information Week*, 26 June 2000.

Knowledge management (KM) systems

'**Knowledge** builds on information that is extracted from data' (Boisot, 1998, p. 12). While data are a property of things (size, price, etc.) knowledge is a property of people, which predisposes them to act in a particular way. It embodies prior understanding, experience and learning, and is either confirmed or modified as people receive new information. The significance of the distinction is that knowledge enables people to add more value to resources, since they can react more intelligently to information and data than those without that experience and learning. Someone with good knowledge of a market will use it to interpret information about current sales. They can identify significant patterns or trends, and so attach a different meaning to the information than someone without that knowledge.

> **Knowledge** builds on information and embodies a person's prior understanding, experience and learning.

Managers (especially those employing many skilled professionals) have long wanted to make better use of their employees' knowledge, believing it to be vital to innovation and the primary source of wealth in modern economies. People in large organisations often believe that the knowledge they need to improve performance is available within the business – but that they cannot find it. **Knowledge management (KM)** refers to attempts to improve the way organisations create, acquire, capture, store, share and use knowledge. This will usually relate to customers, markets, products, services and internal processes, but may also refer to knowledge about relevant external developments.

> **Knowledge management systems** are a type of IS intended to support people as they create, store, transfer and apply knowledge.

Managing knowledge is not new – the Industrial Revolution occurred when people applied new knowledge to manufacturing processes. What is new is the degree to which developments in IS make it easier for people to share data, information and knowledge irrespective of physical distance. This growing technological capacity has encouraged many to believe that implementing KM or similar systems to make better use of knowledge assets will enhance performance – and some studies, such as that by Feng *et al.* (2004), support that view. Three common purposes of KM systems are to:

- code and share best practices;
- create corporate knowledge directories;
- create knowledge networks.

Echikson (2001) outlined how the oil company BP uses advanced information systems to enable staff in the huge global business (including those in recently acquired companies) to share and use information and knowledge. These include a web-based employee directory (an intranet) called 'Connect', which contains a home page for almost every BP employee. Clicking on someone's name brings up a picture, contact details, interests (useful for breaking the ice between people who have not met) and areas of expertise. When a manager in a BP business needed to translate his safety video into French, he used Connect to identify French-speaking employees who could do the work, rather than an external translation service. At the core of the business, decisions on where to drill are now informed by an internet system which brings geological data to one of several high-tech facilities. Engineers view the images and make decisions in hours, which used to take weeks – and help reduce the danger of expensive drilling mistakes.

Management in practice   Buckman Labs – successful KM   www.buckman.com

Buckman Labs is a science-based company, operating around the world. The founder realised that the company needed to become more effective in managing the knowledge of its 1,300 scientific staff. The company has steadily developed systems which connect codified databases around the world – containing information on current global best-practice methods, ideas and problems. This enables scientists throughout the company to keep in touch with each other and to share knowledge electronically among themselves and with customers. 'This single knowledge network aims to encompass all of the company's knowledge and experience, empowering Buckman representatives to focus all of their company's capabilities on customer challenges' (Pan, 1999, p. 77).

A notable feature of the company's approach has been the extent to which it has supported technological innovation with organisational change. Initial attempts at knowledge sharing were unsuccessful, with little activity on the system. Managers then instituted a series of changes to encourage greater use. These included producing weekly statistics showing which staff had used the system. Non-users were penalised, frequent contributors rewarded. Processes were also changed to ensure the immediate capture of information during projects.

Source: Pan (1999).

Recall the distinction between data, information and knowledge. Many systems that people refer to as 'knowledge' management systems appear on closer examination to deal with data and information, rather than knowledge. While computer-based systems are effective at dealing with (structured) data and information, they are much less effective at dealing with (unstructured) knowledge. As Hinds and Pfeffer (2003) observe:

> systems (to facilitate the sharing of expertise) generally capture *information or data*, rather than *knowledge or expertise*. Information and information systems are extremely useful but do not replace expertise or the learning that takes place through interpersonal contact. (p. 21)

This point was developed by Scarbrough and Swan (1999) who propose that while technological systems deal well with explicit data and information, they are much less use when dealing with tacit knowledge, which develops among people as they learn to work together. Tacit knowledge reflects the shared understanding and meaning that is unique to a situation. While a 'cognitive' model of KM is an appropriate way to deal with explicit knowledge, a 'community' model is more suitable for tacit knowledge. Table 12.2 contrasts these views.

Presenting the community model alongside the cognitive model helps to identify the issues in the success or failure of knowledge management projects:

> whilst it might be relatively easy to share knowledge across a group that is homogenous, it is extremely difficult to share knowledge where the group is heterogeneous. Yet it is precisely the sharing of knowledge across functional or organisational boundaries . . . that is seen as the key to the effective exploitation of knowledge. (Scarbrough and Swan, 1999, p. 11)

Systems with a technical, cognitive perspective do not take account of structures and cultures, which represent peoples' beliefs and values about what to do and how to reward it. These contexts may inhibit people from sharing knowledge in the way intended.

Table 12.2 Two views of the knowledge management process

Cognitive model	Community model
Knowledge is objectively defined concepts and facts	Knowledge is socially constructed and based on experience
Knowledge is transferred through text, and information systems have a crucial role	Knowledge is transferred through participation in social networks including occupational groups and teams
Gains from KM include recycling knowledge and standardising systems	Gains from KM include greater awareness of internal and external sources of knowledge
The primary function of KM is to codify and capture knowledge	The primary function of KM is to encourage individuals and groups to share knowledge
The dominant metaphor is human memory	The dominant metaphor is human community
The critical success factor is technology	The critical success factor is trust

Source: *Case studies in knowledge management*, CIPD (Scarborough, H. and Swan, J. 1999) with the permission of the publisher, the Chartered Institute of Personnel and Development, London (www.cipd.co.uk).

Case study   **Google – the case continues: a culture built to build**
www.google.com

Google has a technocratic culture, in that individuals prosper based on the quality of their ideas and their technological acumen. Engineers are expected to spend 20 per cent of their time working on their own creative projects. The company provides plenty of intellectual stimulation which, for a company founded on technology, can be the opportunity to learn from the best and brightest technologists.

There are regular talks by distinguished researchers from around the world. Google's founders and executives have thought-through many aspects of the knowledge work environment, including the design and occupancy of offices (jam-packed for better communication); the frequency of all-hands meetings (every Friday); and the approach to interviewing and hiring new employees (rigorous, with many interviews). None of these principles is rocket science, but in combination they suggest an unusually high level of recognition for the human dimensions of innovation. Brin and Page have taken ideas from other organisations – such as the software firm SAS Institute – that are celebrated for how they treat their knowledge workers.

Source: Iyer and Davenport (2008).

Case questions 12.3

- What are the likely advantages to Google, and to its staff, of these practices?
- Read the cases studies of Oticon (Chapter 10 Case), W.L. Gore (Part 5 Case) and Pixar (pages 309 and 403), and note any similarities and differences between their practices and those of Google.

Emerging technical possibilities provide an infrastructure that enables global access to data, information and knowledge. KM tools can exploit explicit knowledge about previous projects, technical discoveries or useful techniques. But re-using existing knowledge may do less for business performance than using it to create new knowledge that suits the situation. This creative process depends more on human interaction than on technology. Since most managers receive too much information it does not follow that pushing more information across such boundaries will improve performance. That depends not only on knowledge, but also on insight and judgement. Gupta and Govindarajan (2000) observed:

> effective knowledge management depends not merely on information-technology plat-forms but . . . on the social ecology of an organisation – the social system in which people operate [made up of] culture, structure, information systems, reward systems, processes, people and leadership. (p. 72)

People are more likely to use a KM system if the culture recognises and rewards knowledge sharing – lively communities of practice will be more effective than technology (Thompson and Walsham, 2004).

Activity 12.5 What knowledge do you need for a task?

- Identify for an employee (perhaps yourself) what knowledge he/she creates, acquires, captures, shares and uses while doing a specified task.
- Identify examples of explicit and tacit knowledge in this example.
- Discuss to what extent could a computerised knowledge system be useful in managing that knowledge.
- Also discuss whether such a system would be in your interests or those of the organisation?

12.6 IS, strategy and organisation – the big picture

Computer-based IS can contribute to an organisation's strategy, in the same way as any other capability – human resources, finance or marketing. They are all resources which managers can incorporate into their strategic planning. Equally, to use these resources to add value to them, managers need to ensure that they align with each other, so that they complement each other, rather than pull in opposite directions. The following sections illustrate this by show-ing how managers can take a strategic perspective on IS, and on the major organisational changes this requires.

Case study Google – the case continues www.google.com

The company has rapidly extended the range of ser-vices it offers, while remaining rigorously focused on search. Although the headquarters are in California, their mission is to facilitate access to information across the world – more than half of their searches are delivered to users living outside the US, in more than 35 languages. The company offers volunteers the opportunity to help in translating the site into ad-ditional languages.

While a principle within the company has been that it did not interfere with the results of a search (not favouring one advertiser over another, once they had bid for keywords) it faced criticism when it agreed to place certain restrictions on the site in China.

The company acquired YouTube, the video-sharing site, in 2006, as a further extension of its services. In 2007 Viacom, a major entertainment pro-ducer, sued YouTube and Google, contending that 160,000 unauthorised clips of Viacom programmes were available on YouTube, and that this infringed the company's copyrights over the material.

Such acquisitions can be seen as a way of grow-ing the business in a way that stays focused on Google's distinctive competence, (developing superior search solutions) and earning revenue from these through targeted advertising. One alternative direction would be to aggregate the content into thematic channels, similar to Yahoo! Another could be to extend its service beyond the search process (which helps buyers to identify suitable sellers) and into the transaction process – by developing systems (such as eBay) that would facilitate the actual transactions.

Sources: Company website; other published sources.

IS and strategy

Chapter 8 shows that strategy sets the overall direction of the business, and suggests that a Porter's five forces model is a useful tool for identifying the competitive forces affecting a business. Figure 12.9 shows that IS can become a source of competitive advantage that can use technology to strengthen one or more of the forces, and Table 12.3 gives some examples.

This helps managers to identify ways of using their IS as a source of competitive advantage (or to identify potential threats from others).

Managers also use IS to support their chosen strategy, such as a differentiation or cost leadership. They can use IS to achieve a cost leadership strategy by, for example, using:

- computer-aided manufacturing (CAM) to replace manual labour;
- stock control systems to cut expensive inventory; or
- online order entry to cut order processing costs.

They can support a differentiation strategy by using:

- computer-aided manufacturing to offer flexible delivery;

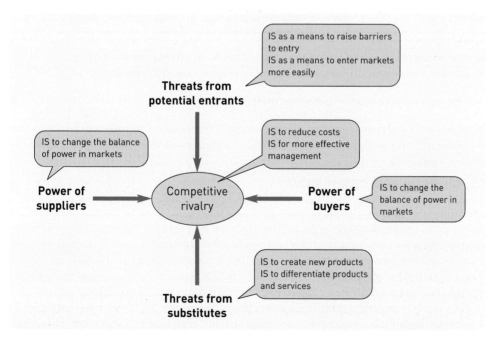

Figure 12.9 How information systems can change competitive forces: Porter's model

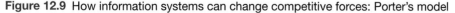

Source: Adapted and reprinted by permission of Harvard Business Review. Exhibit adapted from Strategy and the Internet, *Harvard Business Review,* vol. 79, no. 3, pp. 63–78 by M. E. Porter, Copyright © 2001 by Harvard Business School Publishing Corporation; all rights reserved.

Table 12.3 Using information systems to affect the five forces

Porter's five forces		Examples of information systems support
Threat of potential entrants	Raise entry barriers	Electronic links with customers make it more costly for them to move to competitors. Supermarkets use electronic links to banks and suppliers, and so gain a cost advantage over small retailers
	Entering markets more easily	Bertelsmann, a German media group, entered book retailing by setting up an online store. Virgin offers financial services by using online systems
Threat of substitutes	Creating new products	Online banking has only been possible with modern information systems
	Differentiating their products	Using database technology and CRM systems to identify precise customer needs and then create unique offers and incentives
Bargaining power of suppliers	Increasing power of suppliers	Airlines use yield management systems to track actual reservations against capacity on each flight, and then adjust prices for the remaining seats to maximise revenue
	Decreasing power of suppliers	Online recruitment through a website reduces the need to advertise vacancies in newspapers, reducing their power to earn advertising revenue
Bargaining power of buyers		Buyers can use the internet to access more suppliers and compare prices for standard commodities
Intensity of rivalry	Using IS to reduce costs	Enterprise resource planning systems make it possible to make radical changes in manufacturing systems, leading to greater consistency in planning and lower costs
	More effective management	Information systems provide more detailed information on trading patterns, enabling management to make more informed decisions

- stock control systems to extend the range of goods on offer at any time; or
- using online systems to remember customer preferences, and suggest purchases.

They can support a focus strategy by using:

- computer-aided manufacturing to meet unique, non-standard requirements;
- online ordering to allow customers to create a unique product by selecting its features.

IS, strategy and organisation

Managers who wish to use one or more of these applications of IS to support their strategy also need to ensure that their organisation structure supports the strategy, as there is abundant evidence that having a structure and culture that complements, or is aligned with, the strategy will produce better results than one that is not (Sabherwal *et al.*, 2001; Boddy and Paton, 2005). Whittington *et al.* (2006) showed that in a world of accelerating change strategising and organising are best conducted as tightly linked practical activities.

One aspect of organisation that illustrates this is that of how the IS function is organised – especially whether it is centralised or decentralised. In a centralised arrangement, a corporate IS unit is responsible for all computing activities. When a user department requires a new or enhanced system, it applies for it through the IS department. The IS department sets priorities using guidelines agreed with senior management, and then delivers and supports the services. This approach can be very efficient, allowing tight integration of all systems, and the benefits of expertise being concentrated in one unit. A disadvantage is that the dominant, centralised department can be inflexible and remote from the business and may appear technologically arrogant to users. Departments have different information needs, so a system that gives a common service to all will find it hard to satisfy everyone. The centralised model fits best with organisations that make other decisions centrally, that work in a stable environment and where there is little communication between units.

The opposite approach is to decentralise IS delivery, so that managers of each major unit are responsible for their own system – including development, acquisition, operations and maintenance. This is only possible when the units are independent, with little communication between them. Kahay *et al.* (2003) discussed with more than 100 IS executives their plans to decentralise IS. The researchers concluded that while most believed that IS should be decentralised in the interests of responsiveness, they also advocated that a central unit should be responsible for security, standards and IS governance. If managers see the advantages of decentralisation but also the disadvantages of full independence, they may choose a mixed model, in which business units decide their requirements and manage their systems, but the centre retains control over tasks such as data standards and hardware compatibility. A centralised department can determine information strategy for the organisation and administer the corporate system and database. The decentralised departments can develop and manage local IS within those corporate guidelines. This model fits best in organisations with a high interdependence, a high need to share data and a turbulent environment.

The theme, however, is to ensure that managers are conscious of the benefits of maintaining alignment between strategy, organisation and information systems.

12.7 Integrating themes

Sustainable performance

Developments in information technology have had, and will continue to have, both negative and positive effects on sustainability. The electronics industry itself adds massively to the emission of greenhouse gases by:

- Manufacturing and distribution – the products themselves are produced in worldwide manufacturing supply chains, usually linked by air-freight; frequent updates mean that many machines are discarded after a few years, most of which are still dumped in landfill sites.
- Use – the energy consumption of millions of users, together with the energy used by websites. Greenpeace has called on technology giants such as Apple, Microsoft and Google to power their data centres with renewable energy sources. At present their electricity comes from utility companies which generate power from burning coal, leading to a growing carbon footprint. The launch of portable online devices such as smartphones, netbooks and the iPad means more data are stored remotely so that it can be accessed from wherever the user has an internet connection. So firms are building massive data centres to cope with the demand (*BBC News*, 30 March 2010).

Conversely (Hawken *et al.*, 1999) show that the clever use of IT can significantly reduce the use of energy and raw materials by applications such as:

- online meeting facilities such as video-conferencing or social networking sites, which can reduce the need for people to travel to meetings;
- energy management systems to monitor and control energy use in buildings and other physical facilities;
- manufacturing planning systems which enhance the design and manufacture of products to minimise the use of energy and raw materials;
- transport systems which monitor and control engine efficiency to save fuel.

Governance and control

Advances in information systems technology offer senior managers the promise of greatly improved performance: but many IS projects fail to deliver, and destroy a great deal of wealth. Weill and Ross (2005) believe that the waste of resources this represents could be avoided by better IS governance systems, since:

> without them individual managers resolve isolated issues as they arise, and those individual actions may be at odds with each other. Our study of almost 300 companies around the world suggests that IT governance is a mystery to key decision makers in most companies . . . [yet] when senior managers take time to design, implement and communicate IT governance processes, companies get more value from IT. (p. 26)

They believe that the key issue for managers is to be clear about how they are going to control decisions about investments in IS. This is a multi-stage process in which players at various levels and in many functional areas exercise their power to influence IS decisions. To ensure that these decisions align information systems' wider organisational objectives, IS governance is the practice of allocating decision rights, and establishing an accountability framework for IS decisions. These decisions arise in five domains:

- principles – high level choices about the strategic role of IS in the organisation;
- architecture – an integrated set of technical choices to satisfy business needs;
- infrastructure – the shared resources that are the foundation of the enterprise's IS capability;
- business applications – what the business needs from IS; and
- investment priorities – how much and where to invest.

Each of these areas can be addressed at corporate, business unit or functional levels, or a combination of them all. So, they suggest, the first step in designing IS governance is to decide who should make, and be held accountable for, each decision area, and whether this should be a centralised or decentralised approach, or something in between.

Finally they suggest that senior managers design a set of governance mechanisms that clarify:

- decision-making structures – the organisational committees and roles that specify and locate decision making responsibilities;
- alignment processes – management techniques for securing wide involvement in governance decisions and their implementation according, for example to the degree of centralisation;
- formal communications – ensuring that all players are aware of, and understand, the governance processes through which IS decisions are made.

Internationalisation

New technologies are enabling the processes of international business, since firms can disperse their operations around the globe, and manage them economically from a distance. The technology enables managers to keep in close touch with dispersed operations and to transfer knowledge between them. Paik and Choi (2005) showed the difficulties in applying technology across national boundaries, in their study of one of the leading global management consultancies, with over 75,000 consultants in over 40 countries. Like most such firms, it considers the knowledge of its staff to be a core capability for achieving competitive advantage. To ensure that this knowledge is widely shared, it has spent large sums on KM systems, especially knowledge exchange (KX) – a repository of internally generated knowledge about clients, topics, best practices and so on – to which consultants were expected to contribute ideas as they completed projects for clients.

However, the authors found that few East Asian consultants contributed to the database and identified three reasons:

- a perception among East Asian consultants that others did not appreciate their regional knowledge;

- a requirement to provide ideas in English; East Asian consultants were conversant in English, but found it difficult and time-consuming to translate documents into English before submitting them;
- cultural differences; in some countries staff were not motivated to contribute if there was no direct personal incentive – which the global reward system did not take into account.

They conclude that their study shows that global companies seeking a common approach to knowledge management need to make allowances for local cultural differences, as shown in Chapter 4.

Summary

1 **Explain how converging technologies change the way people add value to resources**

- Continuing advances in information systems for processing data have been enhanced by the convergence of systems so that they now integrate data, sound and visual systems.
- The radical result is that this enables producers and customers to co-create value.

2 **Recognise that, to use these opportunities, managers change both technology and orginisation**

- Established organisations use IS to make radical changes in the services they offer and how they work.
- They also, as do new internet-based organisations, find ways to benefit from the possibilities of co-creation with customers.
- Both depend on managing both technical and organisational issues.

3 **Distinguish between operations information systems and management information systems**

- Operations information systems – such as transaction processing and office automation systems – support processes that keep current work running smoothly.
- Management information systems – for information reporting, decision support and executive systems provide managers with information to support decision making.

4 **Illustrate how organisations use the internet to add value by using three types of information system – customer relations, enterprise and knowledge**

- Internet-based (e-business) are systems which operate across organisational boundaries, enabling new relations with business partners and customers.
- Enterprise systems use a central database to integrate data about many aspects of the business as an aid to planning.
- Knowledge management systems attempt to improve the ability of an organisation to use the information which it possesses.
- Customer relations systems aim to capture and process information about each customer, so that products and services can be tailored more closely to individual needs.

5 **Understand the relation between IS, strategy and organisation**

- Computer-based IS can support strategy: each of Porter's five forces are potentially affected by IS, leading to either threats or opportunities.
- Similarly managers can use IS to support a low cost, differentiation or niche strategy.
- Whatever strategy they follow it will be more successful if they ensure that complementary organisational changes – such as ensuring the alignment of strategy and structure, and the appropriate governance structures for the IS function – to ensure, for example, the right balance between central and local provision.

6 **Show how ideas from the chapter add to your understanding of the integrating themes**

- The rapid spread in the use of information systems is both one cause of the unsustainable use of resources, and also part of the solution, by enabling managers to re-design and monitor their processes to minimise resource use.
- Organisations waste huge amounts of money on information systems projects that fail to deliver what was expected, partly because senior managers have not paid sufficient attention to their systems for the governance and control of the IS function.
- While information systems enable managers to monitor and control international operations, to be effective they need to take account of national cultural differences (see Chapter 4), and of how people in different countries interpret and use information.

Review questions

1 Explain the significance of information systems to the management of organisations? How do they relate to the core task of managing?

2 Give some original examples of companies using information systems to add value.

3 Identify examples of co-creation or 'wikinomics', and explain the benefits to company and customer.

4 For what purposes are commercial companies using social networking sites?

5 Draw a sketch to illustrate why computer-based information systems require more than the management of technology.

6 Give examples of how an information system can affect at least two of the forces in Porter's model and so affect the competitiveness of a business.

7 Outline the stages through which organisations go in using the internet, giving an original example of each.

8 Use the Nestlé case (Management in Practice feature) to identify some possible difficulties in using ERP systems.

9 What is the difference between a cognitive and a communal view of knowledge?

10 Describe how the five forces model can show the likely effects of information systems on strategy.

11 Summarise an idea from the chapter that adds to your understanding of the integrating themes.

Concluding critical reflection

Think about the main computer-based information systems that you use in your company, or that feature in one with which you are familiar. Review the material in the chapter and perhaps visit some of the websites identified. Then make notes on these questions:

- What examples of the themes discussed in this chapter are currently relevant to your company? How have information systems helped or hindered managers' performance? How well have the social as well as the technological aspects of new systems been managed? How, if at all, have they altered the tasks and roles of managers, staff or professionals? What stage have you reached in using the internet?
- If the business seems to pay too much attention to the technical aspects of IS projects, and not enough to the social and organisational aspects, why is that? What **assumptions** appear to have shaped the managers' approach?
- How have changes in the business **context** shaped the applications being implemented? Do they seem well-suited to their organisational (structural, cultural, etc. factors) and external contexts? Have managers considered any **alternatives** to the way IS projects are managed differently to improve their return on investment, for example by greater user involvement in the projects?
- Do they regularly and systematically review IS projects after implementation to identify any **limitations** in their approaches? Do the presentations on ERP and CRM systems match experience in your organisation with such systems?

Further reading

Bernoff, J. and Li, C. (2008), 'Harnessing the power of the oh-so-social web', *MIT Sloan Management Review*, vol. 49, no. 3, pp. 36–42.

Boulding, W., Staelin, R. and Ehret, M. (2005), 'A customer relationship management roadmap: What is known, potential pitfalls, and where to go', *Journal of Marketing*, vol. 69, no. 4, pp. 155–166.

Bozarth, C. (2006), 'ERP implementation efforts at three firms', *International Journal of Operations & Production Management*, vol. 26, no. 11, pp. 1223–1239.

Three recent empirical studies of the organisational aspects of managing information systems.

Iyer, B. and Davenport, T. H. (2008), 'Reverse engineering Google's innovation machine', *Harvard Business Review*, vol. 86, no. 4, pp. 58–68.

Many insights into the company.

Laudon, K.C. and Laudon, J.P. (2004), *Management Information Systems: Organization and technology in the networked enterprise*, Prentice Hall, Harlow.

This text, written from a management perspective, focuses on the opportunities and pitfalls of information systems.

Phillips, P. (2003), *E-Business Strategy: Text and cases*, McGraw-Hill, Maidenhead.

A comprehensive European perspective on internet developments relevant to business and strategy.

Tapscott, E. and Williams, A.D. (2006), *Wikinomics: How mass collaboration changes everything*, Viking Penguin, New York.

Best-selling account of the rise of co-creation.

Weblinks

These websites are those that have appeared in the chapter:

www.google.com
www.connectingforhealth.nhs.uk
www.bbc.co.uk
www.selectminds.com
www.renault.com
www.siemens.com
www.Yahoo.com
www.amazon.com
www.moneyfacts.co.uk
www.tesco.com
www.irisnation.com
www.nestle.com
www.buckman.com

Visit two of the business sites in the list, or any others that interest you, and answer the following questions:

- If you were a potential employee, how well does it present information about the company and the career opportunities available? Could you apply for a job online?

- Evaluate the sites on these criteria, which are based on those used in an annual survey of corporate websites:
  - Does it give the current share price on the front page?
  - How many languages is it available in?
  - Is it possible to email key people or functions from the site?
  - Does it give a diagram of the main structural units in the business?
  - Does it set out the main mission or business idea of the company?
  - Are there any other positive or negative features?

 **www** For video case studies, audio summaries, flashcards, exercises and annotated weblinks related to this chapter, visit **www.pearsoned.co.uk/mymanagementlab**

CHAPTER 13
MANAGING CHANGE AND INNOVATION

Aim

To outline theories of change and innovation, and show how these can guide practice.

Objectives

By the end of your work on this chapter you should be able to outline the concepts below in your own terms and:

1 Explain the meaning of organisational change and give examples
2 Explain what the links between change and context imply for those managing a change
3 Compare lifecycle, emergent, participative and political theories of change
4 Evaluate systematically the possible sources of resistance to change
5 Explain how innovations benefit organisations
6 Illustrate the organisational factors believed to support innovation
7 Show how ideas from the chapter add to your understanding of the integrating themes.

Key terms

This chapter introduces the following ideas:

perceived performance gap
performance imperatives
organisational change
interaction model
receptive contexts
non-receptive contexts
lifecycle

emergent models
participative model
political model
creativity
incremental innovations
radical innovations

Each is a term defined within the text, as well as in the Glossary at the end of the book.

Case study

Vodafone/Ericsson www.vodafone.com
www.ericsson.com

In 2010 Vodafone offered mobile services to sub-scribers in 31 countries and was the world's largest mobile network operator, with about one-quarter of the market. Ericsson was the world's largest supplier of mobile network infrastructure, and Vodafone its largest customer. Vodafone has achieved its strong market position partly by internal growth and by ac-quiring other operators, such as AirTouch (USA) in 1998 and Mannesmann (Germany) in 2000. Many of these acquisitions also had shareholdings in other mobile operators, meaning that in some countries Vodafone operates through partially rather than wholly owned subsidiaries.

As demand for mobile services grew, Vodafone extended the network on a country-by-country basis, with local management teams running the business. It usually ordered network equipment from Ericsson, negotiating terms with Ericsson staff in their country. Although Vodafone's in-country man-agers communicated with their counterparts in other countries, Vodafone did not attempt to co-ordinate the way they operated. Ericsson operated in a more centralised fashion, although with some scope for local managers to establish terms of business that reflected their market or competitive environment. This had the following consequences:

- Terms and conditions for purchasing network equipment varied between countries.
- Communication between the two companies in each country was direct, through meetings, tele-phones, letters, fax and email.
- Communication about Ericsson products be-tween Vodafone operators in different countries was *ad hoc*.
- Sharing of product information between Ericsson and Vodafone was in-country, mainly through written documents.
- Ordering and order tracking was done by local systems in each country.
- Configuration of network equipment varied be-tween countries, as did service and support arrangements.

Before the merger with AirTouch, Vodafone man-agement had begun to assess what synergies it could gain from the merger, especially in the supply of network equipment. The company expected to make big savings if it could aggregate its worldwide

© Vodafone 2007

requirements for network equipment, and source this from common global suppliers. The acquisition of Mannesmann increased the scope for synergy – and claims about the potential savings in this area were made to shareholders and the financial markets.

Vodafone therefore began a project with Ericsson to develop new ways of managing the relationship. The intention was to find ways of aggregating Vodafone's global requirements so that the com-panies would manage their relationship in a unified way. They realised that managing a change of this scale would raise difficult issues about the:

- degree of planning to undertake;
- scale and value of the synergies from a new global relationship;
- attitudes of those managing Vodafone operations in the various countries;
- resources that would be needed to manage the change.

Source: Based on Ibbott and O'Keefe (2004).

Case questions 13.1

- How may the structure of Vodafone's in-country operations affect the project?
- Will a new global relationship mean a more centralised or a more decentralised company?
- Should the two companies put significant re-sources into planning the change in advance?

13.1   Introduction

The manager whom Vodafone appointed to lead this change faces a familiar problem that is familiar to many managers. The chief executive has put him in charge of implementing a major change that will affect many people, some of whom will be uneasy about how it will affect them. Changing from a country to a global structure will have implications for the way they run the business in their country, and change their relationship with their main equipment supplier.

Managers initiate or experience change so regularly that in many organisations change is the normal state of affairs, interrupted by occasional periods of relative stability. In the most innovative areas of the economy senior managers see their primary task as being to challenge current practices, fostering a climate of exploration and innovation. They want people to see change as the norm: one intervention in a continuing flow, rather than as something from which stability will follow. At BP, for example, the challenge to successive senior managers has been to continue transforming the business from a relatively small (for that industry), diversified business into one of the world's largest oil companies. Mergers, such as that between Chrysler (USA) and Daimler (Germany), are usually followed by internal changes as the companies integrate.

The external environment described in Chapter 3 is the main source of change. The evolving PESTEL factors change what people expect of a business: which may encourage managers to alter their strategy or operations. Anecdotal evidence is that while most managers accept the need for change, many are critical of the way their organisations introduce it. Managers still experience great difficulty in implementing major organisational changes.

This chapter presents theories about the nature of change in organisations. It begins by explaining current external pressures for change, and how these prompt internal change to one or more elements of the organisation. The chapter then outlines a model that shows how change depends on the interaction between the external and internal environments of the organisation. It then presents four complementary perspectives on how people try to manage that interaction. It finishes by investigating how innovation can be managed to bring change to organisations, products and markets.

Activity 13.1   Recording a major change

From discussion with colleagues or managers, identify a major attempt at change in an organisation. Make notes on the following questions and use them as a point of reference throughout the chapter.

- What was the change?
- Why did management introduce it?
- What were the objectives?
- How did management plan and implement it?
- How well did it meet the objectives?
- What lessons have those involved taken from the experience?

13.2   Initiating change

Chapter 1 introduced the idea that managers work within a context that shapes what they do, which they may also change. This chapter explains the interactive nature of that process, and Figure 13.1 illustrates the themes it will cover. A particular episode of change begins when enough people perceive a gap between desired and actual performance – usually because the internal context of the organisation is unable to meet the external demands upon it. Using

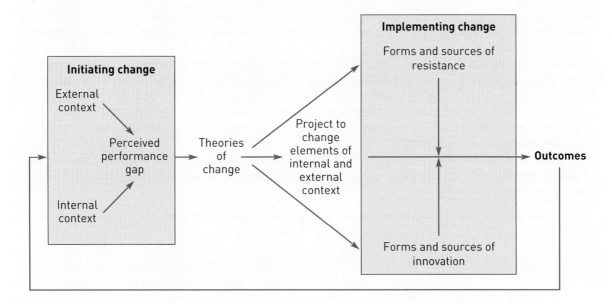

Figure 13.1 A model of the change process

their implicit or explicit theory of change, they initiate a project to change one or more aspects of the internal context in the hope of closing the performance gap. The outcomes of the change effort will be affected by practical issues of design and implementation – but whatever the outcomes they will in turn affect the subsequent shape of the external and internal contexts, providing the starting point for future changes.

The external context

Chapter 3 describes the external environment (or context) of business, and successive chapters have illustrated the changes taking place, such as internationalisation, information technology and expectations about sustainable performance. Together with deregulation and the privatisation of former state businesses, these are transforming the competitive landscape and threatening the survival of established players. Managers at British Airways and KLM have had to respond to the pressure of new competition from low-cost airlines such as Ryanair and easyJet. Established banks face competition from new entrants such as retailers (Sainsbury's) or conglomerates (Virgin) offering financial services. The growth of the internet has enabled companies offering high-value/low-weight products to open new distribution channels and invade previously protected markets.

Management in practice   Successful change at GKN www.gknplc.com

GKN is a leading global supplier to automotive, aerospace and off-highway manufacturers, employing 40,000 people in GKN companies and joint ventures. It was created by a series of mergers at the start of the twentieth century, creating Guest, Keen and Nettlefolds – then one of the largest manufacturing businesses in the world. It was involved in iron and coal mining, steel production and finished products such as nuts, bolts and fasteners.

Its present form reflects a small number of successful decisions made in the 1980s. The first was to abandon any thought of re-entering the steel industry (its interests there had been nationalised in the 1960s), and to focus instead on seeking growth in the motor components business. This decision was shaped by a piece

▶

of luck, in that in 1966 it had bought a UK engineering company and in doing so acquired a share in a German business which had worldwide patents for a unique constant velocity joint system for powering front-wheel drive cars.

A second decision was to cut back sharply on non-vehicle activities, into which the group had diversified in the 1970s. At that time unrelated diversification was a popular management strategy, but it soon became clear that unrelated businesses were best run independently: GKN soon disposed of most of that portfolio.

The third decision was to purchase Westland Helicopters – mainly because it gave GKN entry into the rapidly growing business of manufacturing aerospace components, which complemented the automotive business (Westland was sold in 2004).

In his book *Change Without, Pain* Abrahamson (2004) identifies GKN as one of the most successful companies at managing significant strategic changes – not by disposing of skills but by recombining them in ways that create even greater value.

Sources: *Financial Times*, 6 January 2004, 28 February 2007; *Independent*, 15 March 2007; company website.

These forces have collectively meant a shift of economic power from producers to consumers, many of whom now enjoy greater quality, choice and value. Managers wishing to retain customers continually need to seek new ways of adding value to resources if they are to retain their market position. Unless they do so they will experience a widening performance gap.

Perceived performance gap

A **perceived performance gap** arises when people believe that the actual performance of a unit or business is out of line with the level they desire. If those responsible for transforming resources into outputs do so in a way that does not meet customer expectations, there is a performance gap. Cumulatively this will lead to other performance gaps emerging – such as revenue from sales being below the level needed to secure further resources. If uncorrected this will eventually cause the business to fail.

In the current business climate, two aspects of performance dominate discussion – what Prastacos *et al.* (2002) call '**performance imperatives**': the need for flexibility and the need for innovation. In a very uncertain business world the scope for long-term planning is seriously limited. Successful businesses are likely to be those that develop a high degree of strategic and organisational flexibility, while also maintaining efficient and stable processes. This apparent paradox reflects the fact that while companies need to respond rapidly they also need to respond efficiently. This usually depends on having developed a degree of stability and predictability in the way they transform resources into goods and services.

The other imperative identified by Prastacos *et al.* (2002) is innovation:

> to generate a variety of successful new products or services (embedding technological innovation), and to continuously innovate in all aspects of the business. (p. 58)

In many areas of business, customers expect a constant flow of new products, embodying the latest scientific and technological developments: companies that fail to meet these expectations will experience a performance gap. Nokia selling an advanced mobile phone profitably depends not only on the quality of the applied research which goes into a better screen display, but also on turning that research into a desirable product *and* delivering the devices at a price that customers will pay. This depends on organisation – the internal context of management.

The internal context

Chapter 1 introduces the internal context (Figure 1.3, repeated here as Figure 13.2) as the set of elements within an organisation that shape behaviour. Change begins to happen when

---

A **perceived performance gap** arises when people believe that the actual performance of a unit or business is out of line with the level they desire.

Performance imperatives are aspects of performance that are especially important for an organisation to do well, such as flexibility and innovation.

Figure 13.2
Elements of the internal context of management

sufficient influential people believe, say, that outdated technology or a confusing structure is causing a performance gap, by inhibiting flexibility or innovation. They notice external or internal events and interpret them as threatening the performance that influential stakeholders expect. This interpretation, and their (implicit) theory of change, encourages them to propose changing one or more aspects of the organisation shown in Figure 13.2.

They then have to persuade enough other people that the matter is serious enough to earn a place on the management agenda. People in some organisations are open to proposals for change, others tend to ignore them – BP faced new competitive pressures throughout the 1980s, but it was only around 1990 that sufficient senior people took the threats seriously enough to initiate a period of rapid change.

People initiate organisational change for reasons other than a conscious awareness of a performance gap – fashion, empire building or a powerful player's personal whim can all play a part. Employees or trade unions can propose changes in the way things are done to improve working conditions. The need for change is subjective – what some see as urgent others will leave until later. People can affect that process by managing external information – magnifying customer complaints to make the case for change, or minimising them if they wish to avoid change.

Whatever the underlying motivations, **organisational change** is an attempt to change one or more of the elements shown in Figure 13.2. Table 13.1 illustrates specific types of change that people initiate under each element, including some that appear elsewhere in this book.

Change in any of these areas will have implications for others – and these interconnections make life difficult. When Tesco introduced its online shopping service alongside its established retail business, the company needed to create a website (technology). Managers also needed to decide issues of structure and people (would it be part of the existing stores or a separate unit with its own premises and staff?) and about business processes (how would an order on the website be converted to a box of groceries delivered to the customer's door?). They had to manage these ripples initiated by the main decision. Managers who ignore these consequential changes achieve less than they expect.

Organisational change is a deliberate attempt to improve organisational performance by changing one or more aspects of the organisation, such as its technology, structure or business processes.

Table 13.1 Examples of change in each element of the organisation

Element	Example of change to this element
Objectives	Developing a new product or service Changing the overall mission or direction Oticon's new strategic objectives as a service business (Chapter 18 Case)
Technology	Building a new factory Creating an online community Building Terminal 5 at Heathrow
Business processes	Improving the way maintenance and repair services are delivered Redesigning systems to handle the flow of cash and funds Zara's new system for passing goods to retailers (Chapter 18 Case)
Financial resources	A set of changes, such as closing a facility, to reduce costs New financial reporting requirements to ensure consistency The Royal Bank of Scotland reducing costs after the NatWest merger (Part 4 Case)
Structure	Reallocating functions and responsibilities between departments Redesigning work to increase empowerment Vodafone/Ericsson moving to a global structure (Chapter 13 Case)
People	Designing a training programme to enhance skills Changing the tasks of staff to offer a new service
Culture	Unifying the culture between two or more merged businesses Encouraging greater emphasis on quality and reliability
Power	An empowerment programme giving greater authority to junior staff Centralising decisions to increase the control of HQ over subsidiaries

---

Case questions 13.2

Identify the possible ripple effects that may need to be managed in the Vodafone/Ericsson change, using the elements in Figure 13.2 as a guide.

- How may the move to a global relationship affect the structure area?
- What implications may that change have for other elements?
- Which of these are likely to cause most difficulty?

These begin to form the management agenda for this project. If possible compare your answers with others on the course, to see how many alternative possibilities you have identified.

The **interaction model** is a theory of change that stresses the continuing interaction between the internal and external contexts of an organisation, making the outcomes of change hard to predict.

13.3   The interaction of context and change

How managers implement change depends on their theory about its nature. This section presents an **interaction model**, a theory of how change and context interact. The following section outlines four complementary perspectives on managing that interaction.

People introduce change to alter the context

Management attempts to change elements of its context to encourage behaviours that close the performance gap. Vodafone wanted to change the context within which it worked with Ericsson. By moving from country relationships with Ericsson to a more unified global structure, management hoped to create a structure that enabled people in both companies to reduce the cost of expanding the network. When Tesco introduced online shopping, management needed (at least) to change technology, structure, people and business processes to enable staff to deliver the new service. When people plan and implement a change they are creating new 'rules' (Walsham, 1993) that they hope will guide the behaviour of people involved in the activity.

People do not necessarily accept the new arrangements without question, or without adapting them in some way: in doing so they make further changes to the context. As people begin to work in new circumstances – with a new technology or new structure – they make small adjustments to the original plan. As they use a new information system or website they decide which aspects to ignore, use or adapt.

As people become used to working with the new system their behaviours become routine and taken for granted. They become part of the context that staff have created informally. These new elements add to, or replace, the context that those formally responsible for planning the change created, and may or may not support the original intentions of the project. People and context continue to interact.

The context affects the ability to change

While people managing a project aim to change the context, the context within which they work will itself help or hinder them. All of the elements of Figure 13.2 will be present as the project begins, and some of these will influence how people react. Managers who occupy influential positions will review a proposal from their personal career perspective, as well as that of the organisation. At Tesco the existing technology (stores, distribution systems and information systems) and business processes would influence managers' decisions about how to implement the internet shopping strategy.

The prevailing culture (Chapter 3) – shared values, ideals and beliefs – influences how people view change. Members are likely to welcome a project that they believe fits their culture or subculture, and resist one that threatens it.

Management in practice   Culture and change at a European bank

While teaching a course to managers at a European bank, the author invited members to identify which of the four cultural types identified in Chapter 2 best described their unit within the bank. They were then asked to describe the reaction of these units to an internet banking venture that the company was introducing.

Course members observed that colleagues in a unit that had an internal process culture (routine back-office data processing) were hostile to the internet venture. They appeared to be 'stuck with their own systems', which were so large and interlinked that any change was threatening. Staff in new business areas of the company (open systems) were much more positive, seeing the internet as a way towards new business opportunities.

Source: Data collected by the author.

Culture is a powerful influence on the success or failure of innovation (see Jones *et al.*, 2005, for evidence of how it affected the acceptance of a new computer system). Some cultures support change: a manager in Sun Microsystems commented on that fast-moving business:

A very dynamic organisation, it's incredibly fast and the change thing is just a constant that you live with. They really promote flexibility and adaptability in their employees.

Change is just a constant, there's change happening all of the time and people have become very acclimatised to that, it's part of the job. The attitude to change, certainly within the organisation, is very positive at the moment.

At companies such as Google or Facebook the culture encourages change, while elsewhere it encourages caution. Cultural beliefs are hard to change, yet shape how people respond:

Managers learn to be guided by these beliefs because they have worked successfully in the past. (Lorsch, 1986, p. 97)

Key ideas	Receptive and non-receptive contexts

Pettigrew *et al.* (1992) sought to explain why managers in some organisations were able to introduce change successfully, while others in the same sector (the UK National Health Service) found it very hard to move away from established practices. Their comparative research programme identified the influence of context on ability to change: **receptive contexts** are those where features of the context 'seem to be favourably associated with forward movement. On the other hand, in **non-receptive contexts** there is a configuration of features that may be associated with blocks on change' (p. 268).

Their research identified seven such contextual factors, which provide a linked set of conditions that are likely to provide the energy around change. These are:

1 quality and coherence of policy;
2 availability of key people leading change;
3 long-term environmental pressure – intensity and scale;
4 a supportive organisational culture;
5 effective managerial–clinical relations;
6 co-operative interorganisational networks;
7 the fit between the district's change agenda and its locale.

While some of these factors are specific to the health sector, they can easily be adapted to other settings. Together these factors give a widely applicable model of how the context affects ability to change.

Source: Pettigrew *et al.* (1992).

Receptive contexts are those where features of the organisation (such as culture or technology) appear likely to help change.

The distribution of power also affects receptiveness to change. Change threatens the status quo, and is likely to be resisted by stakeholders who benefit from the prevailing arrangements. Innovation depends on those behind the change developing political will and expertise that they can only attempt within the prevailing pattern of power.

Non-receptive contexts are those where the combined effects of features of the organisation (such as culture or technology) appear likely to hinder change.

The context has a history and several levels

The present context is the result of past decisions and events: Balogun *et al.* (2005) show how internal change agents adapted practice to suit aspects of their context, such as the degree of local autonomy, senior management preferences, rewards systems and financial reporting systems. Management implements change against a background of previous events that shaped the context. The promoter of a major project in a multinational experienced this in his colleagues' attitudes:

They were a little sceptical and wary of whether it was actually going to enhance our processes. Major pan-European redesign work had been attempted in the past and had failed miserably. The solutions had not been appropriate and had not been accepted by the divisions. Europe-wide programmes therefore had a bad name. (Boddy, 2002, p. 38)

Beliefs about the future also affect how people react. Optimists are more open to change than those who feel threatened and vulnerable.

Case study
Vodafone/Ericsson – the case continues www.vodafone.com www.ericsson.com

Vodafone conducted business in each country in partnership with other operators, with Vodafone sometimes having a minority shareholding in the company. For example, in the UK it owned 100 per cent of the equity, in Germany 99 per cent and in Australia 91 per cent. In the Netherlands, Portugal and Spain this fell to 70, 50 and 22 per cent respectively.

This meant that considerable political skill and discussion were required to handle the attitudes of the various operating companies with regard to Ericsson's local in-country operations. Some countries had acquired very favourable terms and conditions that would not necessarily be matched by the global agreements, while others had key skills that would now be 'given up' to the global effort.

Source: Ibbott and O'Keefe (2004), p. 226.

The context represented by Figure 13.2 occurs at, say, operating, divisional and corporate levels. People at any of these levels will be acting to change their context – which may help or hinder those managing change elsewhere. A project at one level may depend on decisions at another about resources, as the manager leading an oil refinery project discovered:

> One of the main drawbacks was that commissioning staff could have been supplemented by skilled professionals from within the company, but this was denied to me as project manager. This threw a heavy strain and responsibility on myself and my assistant. It put me in a position of high stress, as I knew that the future of the company rested upon the successful outcome of this project. One disappointment (and, I believe, a significant factor in the project) was that just before commissioning, the manager of the pilot plant development team was transferred to another job. He had been promised to me at the project inception, and I had designed him into the working operation. (Boddy, 2002, pp. 38–39)

Acting to change an element at one level will have effects at this and other levels, and elements may change independently. The manager's job is to create a coherent context that encourages desired behaviour, by using his/her preferred model of change.

Case questions 13.3

- How may the existing context of Vodafone and Ericsson affect how in-country managers react to the proposed change?
- How may that affect the way the project leader manages the change?

13.4 Four models of change

There are four complementary models of change, each with different implications for managers: lifecycle, emergent, participative and political.

Lifecycle

Much advice given to those responsible for managing projects uses the idea of the project **lifecycle**. Projects go through successive stages, and results depend on managing each one in an orderly and controlled way. The labels vary, but common themes are:

1 Define objectives.
2 Allocate responsibilities.
3 Fix deadlines and milestones.

Lifecycle models of change are those that view change as an activity which follows a logical, orderly sequence of activities that can be planned in advance.

Task	Week ending																	
	January			February				March					April				May		
	11	18	25	1	8	15	22	1	8	15	22	29	5	12	19	26	3	10	17
Find site	███	███	███	███	███	███	███	███	███	███									
Acquire site											███	███	███						
Gain planning permission															███	███			
Begin construction																	███		

Figure 13.3 A simple bar chart

4 Set budgets.
5 Monitor and control.

This approach (sometimes called a 'rational–linear' approach) reflects the idea that people can identify smaller tasks within a change and plan the (overlapping) order in which to do them. It predicts that people can make reasonably accurate estimates of the time required to complete each task and when it will be feasible to start work on later ones. People can use tools such as bar charts (sometimes called Gantt charts after the American industrial engineer Henry Gantt, who worked with Frederick Taylor), to show all the tasks required for a project, and their likely duration. These help to visualise the work required and to plan the likely sequence of events, which Figure 13.3 illustrates.

In the lifecycle model, successfully managing change depends on specifying these elements at the start and then monitoring them to ensure the project stays on target. Ineffective implementation is due to managers failing to do this. Figure 13.4 shows the stages in the lifecycle of

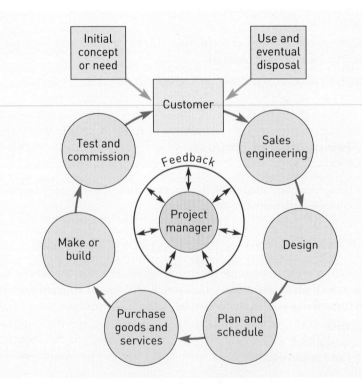

Figure 13.4
A project lifecycle
Source: Lock (2007) p. 8.

a small project (Lock, 2007). It is cyclical because the stages begin and end with the customer. Lock emphasises this is an oversimplification of a complex, iterative reality, but that it helps identify where decisions arise:

> Travelling clockwise round the cycle reveals a number of steps or *phases*, each of which is represented by a circle in the diagram. The boundaries between these phases are usually blurred in practice, because the phases tend to overlap. (Lock, 2007, pp. 8–9)

Many books on project management, such as Lock (2007), present advice on tools for each stage of the lifecycle. Those advising on IS changes usually take a similar approach, recommending a variety of 'system development lifecycle' approaches (Chaffey, 2003). For some changes the lifecycle gives valuable guidance. It is not necessarily sufficient in itself, since people may not be able at the start to specify the end point of the change – or the tasks which will lead to that. In uncertain conditions it may make little sense to plan the outcomes in too much detail. It may be wiser to set the general direction, and adapt the target to suit new conditions that develop during the change. Those managing such change need an additional theory to cope with emergent change.

Activity 13.2   Critical reflection on the project lifecycle

You may be able to gain some insight into the project lifecycle by using it on a practical task. For example:

- If you have a piece of work to do that is connected with your studies, such as an assignment or project, sketch out the steps to be followed by adapting Figure 13.4; alternatively do the same for some domestic, social or management project.
- If you work in an organisation, try to find examples of projects that use this approach, and ask those involved when the method is most useful, and when least useful.
- Make notes summarising how the lifecycle approach helps, and when it is most likely to be useful.

Emergent

In Chapter 8 (Section 8.6) Barthélemy (2006) offers an insight into the strategy process at Ikea (Chapter 7 Case), showing how many of its strategies have emerged from chance events or external conditions, rather than from a formal planning process. Evidence such as this led Quinn (1980) and Mintzberg (1994a, 1994b) to see strategy as an *emergent* or adaptive process. These ideas apply to change projects as much as they do to strategy. Projects are the means through which organisations deliver strategy. They take place in the same volatile, uncertain environment in which the organisation operates. People with different interests and priorities influence the means and ends of a project. So while the planning techniques associated with the lifecycle approach can help, their value will be limited if the change is closer to the **emergent model**.

Emergent models of change emphasise that in uncertain conditions a project will be affected by unknown factors, and that planning has little effect on the outcome.

Case study   Vodafone/Ericsson – the case continues www.vodafone.com
www.ericsson.com

The globalisation strategy was developed and implemented through the Global Supply Chain Management (GSCM) forum that first met in 1999. Initially it was attended by representatives from both companies in those countries where Vodafone had a majority shareholding in the local operating company, although membership gradually expanded to include most countries in which Vodafone operated. The initial meeting resolved that all joint activities should be conducted in an open and transparent way: 'It would be a process of learning through experience; there would be no requirement to produce plans that formed a rigid basis of change control' (Ibbott and O'Keefe, 2004, p. 224).

The members believed that a planned project approach would not have worked, as it was important to be able to cope with rapid change:

> **Both the end point and direction were uncertain, and fundamental process changes had to be agreed within and between companies. The acquisition of Mannesmann of Germany, unplanned at the start of the transformation, provided an opportunity for further benefits.** (Ibbott and O'Keefe, 2004, p. 229)

The forum also recognised that the two sides would benefit in different ways, but there was no attempt to plan how to share the benefits – either party would retain whatever benefits they secured. Vodafone's equity-based structure in the different countries meant that those leading the project had to sell the concept of the global endeavour to the management teams of each entity. Ericsson's more unified structure of wholly owned subsidiaries gave it less scope for resisting proposals.

GSCM meetings set up several work streams that would move the relationship towards global collaboration. The leadership of each work stream was assigned to one or other of the participating countries. The teams leading them had to secure resources for the project from within their country operations, working as they saw fit. Examples of work streams were:

- creating a global price book for all products bought from Ericsson (UK team);
- agreeing a standard base station design (UK team);
- agreeing a common procedure for software design and testing (Australia);
- developing a computer-based information system linking the parties for information sharing – initially called groupware (the Netherlands).

While the groupware project was at first intended to support communications between the teams working on the globalisation project, it later evolved into a system through which both parties conducted routine transactions – such as ordering products. The simple communication system emerged, without any formal plan, into a system for handling all orders from Vodafone to Ericsson that had a global price.

Source: Ibbott and O'Keefe (2004).

Boddy *et al.* (2000) show how this emergent process occurred when Sun Microsystems began working with a new supplier of the bulky plastic enclosures that contain their products, while the supplier wished to widen its customer base. There were few discussions about a long-term plan. As Sun became more confident in the supplier's ability, it gave them more complex work. Both gained from this emerging relationship. A sales co-ordinator commented:

> It's something we've learnt by being with Sun – we didn't imagine that at the time. Also at the time we wouldn't have imagined we would be dealing with America the way we do now – it was far beyond our thoughts. (Boddy *et al.*, 2000, p. 1010)

Mintzberg's point is that managers should not expect rigid adherence to a plan. Some departure is inevitable as circumstances change, so a wise approach to change recognises that:

> the real world inevitably involves some thinking ahead of time as well as some adaptation en route. (Mintzberg, 1994a, p. 24)

Case questions 13.4

- Were those leading the change taking a lifecycle or an emergent view?
- Which of those views does the evidence of later events seem to support?

Participative

The **participative model** is the belief that if people are able to take part in planning a change they will be more willing to accept and implement the change.

Those advocating **participative models** stress the benefits of personal involvement in, and contribution to, events and outcomes. The underlying belief is that if people can say 'I helped to build this', they will be more willing to live and work with it, whatever it is. It is also *possible* that since participation allows more people to express their views, the outcome will be better. Ketokivi and Castañer (2004) found that when employees participated in planning strategic change, they were more likely to view the issues from the perspective of the organisation, rather than their own position or function. Participation can be good for the organisation, as well as the individual.

While participation is consistent with democratic values, it takes time and effort, and may raise unrealistic expectations. It may be inappropriate when:

- the scope for change is limited, because of decisions made elsewhere;
- participants know little about the topic;
- decisions must be made quickly;
- management has decided what to do and will do so whatever views people express;
- there are fundamental disagreements and/or inflexible opposition to the proposed change.

Participative approaches assume that a sensitive approach by reasonable people will result in the willing acceptance and implementation of change. Some situations contain conflicts that participation alone cannot solve.

Activity 13.3   Critical reflection on participation

Have you been involved in, or affected by, a change in your work or studies?
If so:

- What evidence was there that those managing the change agreed with the participative approach?
- In what way, if any, were you able to participate?
- How did that affect your reaction to the change?

If not:

- Identify three advantages and three disadvantages for the project manager in adopting a participative approach.
- Suggest how managers should decide when to use the approach.

Political models

Change often involves people from several levels and functions pulling in different directions:

> Strategic processes of change are . . . widely accepted as multi-level activities and not just as the province of a . . . single general manager. Outcomes of decisions are no longer assumed to be a product of rational . . . debates but are also shaped by the interests and commitments of individuals and groups, forces of bureaucratic momentum, and the manipulation of the structural context around decisions and changes. (Whipp *et al.*, 1988, p. 51)

Several analyses of organisational change emphasise a **political model** (Pettigrew, 1985, 1987; Pfeffer, 1992a; Pinto, 1998; Buchanan and Badham, 1999). Pettigrew (1985) was an early advocate of the view that change requires political as well as rational (lifecycle) skills. Successful change managers create a climate in which people accept the change as legitimate – often by manipulating apparently rational information to build support for their ideas.

Political models reflect the view that organisations are made up from groups with separate interests, goals and values, and that these affect how they respond to change.

Key ideas   Tom Burns on politics and language

Tom Burns (1961) observed that political behaviour in the organisation is invariably concealed or made acceptable by subtle shifts in the language that people use:

> Normally, either side in any conflict called political by observers claims to speak in the interests of the corporation as a whole. In fact, the only recognised, indeed feasible, way of advancing political interests

is to present them in terms of improved welfare or efficiency, as contributing to the organisation's capacity to meet its task and to prosper. In managerial and academic, as in other legislatures, both sides to any debate claim to speak in the interests of the community as a whole; this is the only permissible mode of expression. (Burns, 1961, p. 260)

Pfeffer (1992a) also believes that power is essential to get things done, since decisions in themselves change nothing – people only see a difference when someone implements them. He proposes that projects frequently threaten the status quo: people who have done well are likely to resist the change. Innovators need to ensure the project is put onto the senior management agenda, and that influential people support and resource it. Innovators need to develop a political will, and build and use their power. Buchanan and Badham (1999) conclude that the roots of political behaviour:

lie in personal ambition, in organisation structures that create roles and departments which compete with each other, and in major decisions that cannot be resolved by reason and logic alone but which rely on the values and preferences of the key actors. Power politics and change are inextricably linked. Change creates uncertainty and ambiguity. People wonder how their jobs will change, how their work will be affected, how their relationships with colleagues will be damaged or enhanced. (p. 11)

Reasonable people may disagree about means and ends, and fight for the action they prefer. This implies that successful project managers understand that their job requires more than technical competence, and are able and willing to engage in political actions.

Key ideas — Henry Kissinger on politics in politics

In another work Pfeffer (1992b) quotes Henry Kissinger:

Before I served as a consultant to Kennedy, I had believed, like most academics, that the process of decision-making was largely intellectual and all one had to do was to walk into the President's office and convince him of the correctness of one's view. This perspective I soon realised is as dangerously immature as it is widely held. (p. 31)

Source: Pfeffer (1992b).

The political perspective recognises the messy realities of organisational life. Major changes will be technically complex and challenge established interests. These will pull in different directions and pursue personal as well as organisational goals. To manage these tensions managers need political skills as well as those implied by life cycle, emergent and participative perspectives.

Management in practice — Political action in hospital re-engineering

Managers in a hospital responded to a persistent performance gap (especially unacceptably long waiting times) by 're-engineering' the way patients moved through and between the different clinical areas. This included creating multi-functional teams responsible for all aspects of the flow of the patient through a clinic, rather than dealing with narrow functional tasks. The programme was successful, but it was also controversial. One of those leading the change recalled:

I don't like to use the word manipulate, but . . . you do need to manipulate people. It's about playing the game. I remember being accosted by a very cross consultant who had heard something about one of the changes and he really wasn't very happy with it. And it was about how am I going to deal with this now? And it is about being able to think quickly. So I put it over to him in a way that he then accepted, and he was quite happy with. And it wasn't a lie and it wasn't totally the truth. But he was happy with it and it has gone on.

Source: Buchanan (2001), p. 13.

These perspectives (lifecycle, emergent, participative, political) are complementary in that successful large-scale change, such as that at Vodafone/Ericsson, is likely to require elements of each. Table 13.2 illustrates how each perspective links to management practice.

Table 13.2 Perspectives on change and examples of management practice

Perspective	Themes	Example of management practices
Lifecycle	Rational, linear, single agreed aim, technical focus	Measurable objectives; planning and control devices such as Gantt charts and critical path analysis
Emergent	Objectives change as learning occurs during the project and new possibilities appear	Open to new ideas about scope and direction, and willing to add new resources if needed
Participative	Ownership, commitment, shared goals, people focus	Inviting ideas and comments on proposals, ensuring agreement before action, seeking consensus
Political	Oppositional, influence, conflicting goals, power focus	Building allies and coalitions, securing support from powerful players, managing information

13.5   Forms and sources of resistance to change

Most managers are expected to implement change by using their power to influence others to act in a particular way. People at all levels will sometimes resist, either because they see change as a threat to their interests or because they believe it will damage the organisation. Many change programmes fade from view – unless someone is able to make the change stick by creating a favourable context.

Forms of resistance

Overt and public resistance is often unnecessary. There are many other ways in which those opposed to a change can delay it, including:

- making no effort to learn;
- not attending meetings to discuss the project;
- excessive fault finding and criticism;
- saying it has been tried before and did not work then;
- protracted discussion and requests for more information;
- linking the issue with pay or other industrial relations matters;
- not releasing staff for training.

These delaying tactics come from anywhere in the organisation – they are as likely to come from managers who see a change as a threat to their interests as they are to come from more junior staff.

> ## Activity 13.4   Critical reflection on resistance
>
> Discuss with someone who has tried to introduce change in an organisation what evidence there was of resistance. Then consider the following questions:
>
> - Have you ever resisted a proposed change?
> - What form did your resistance take?

Sources of resistance

Kotter and Schlesinger (1979) identified that sources of resistance included self-interest, misunderstanding and lack of trust: 'people also resist change when they do not understand its implications and perceive that it might cost them much more than they will gain' (p. 108). Employees assess the situation differently from their managers and may see more costs than benefits for both themselves and the company. Change requires learning and exposure to uncertainty, insecurity and new social interactions, yet communication about the changes is often poor. Additional factors identified as causing resistance are reward systems that do not reward the desired behaviour and a poor fit between the change and the culture.

> ## Key ideas   Lewin's driving and restraining forces
>
> Lewin (1947) observed that any social system is in a state of temporary equilibrium. Driving forces try to change the situation in directions they favour. Restraining forces push the other way to prevent change. This equilibrium 'can be changed either by adding forces in the desired direction, or by diminishing the opposing forces' (p. 26). Figure 13.5 illustrates the idea.
>
> Driving forces encourage change from the present position. They encourage people and groups to give up past practice and to act in ways that support the change. They take many forms, such as a newly available technology or the support of a powerful player. Mr Yun Jong-yon, chief executive of Samsung Electronics, transformed the company into one of the world's best-performing and most respected IT companies. He explained part of his approach:
>
> > I'm the chaos-maker. I have tried to encourage a sense of crisis to drive change. We instilled in management a sense that we could go bankrupt any day. (*Financial Times*, 13 March 2003, p. 15)
>
> Restraining forces include the already-installed technology, shortage of finance, or the company culture, or the perceived complexity of implementing the change.
>
> Source: Lewin (1947).

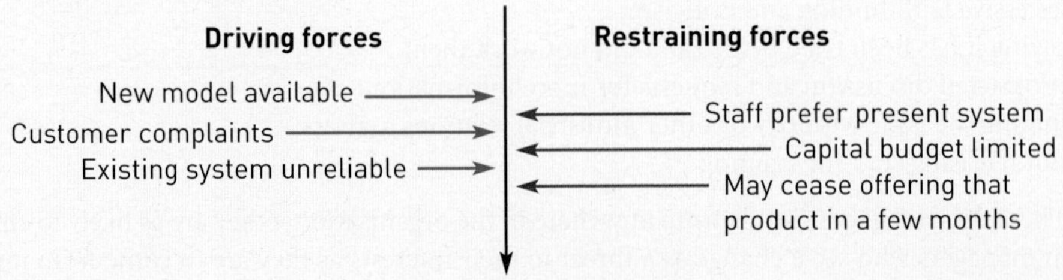

Driving forces

New model available ⟶
Customer complaints ⟶
Existing system unreliable ⟶

Restraining forces

⟵ Staff prefer present system
⟵ Capital budget limited
⟵ May cease offering that product in a few months

Figure 13.5
Driving and restraining forces

Table 13.3 Sources of resistance to change

Element	Source of resistance
Objectives	Lack of clarity or understanding of objectives, or disagreement with those proposed
People	Change may threaten important values, preferences, skills, needs and interests
Technology	May be poorly designed, hard to use, incompatible with existing equipment, or require more work than is worthwhile
Business processes	As for technology, and may require unwelcome changes to the way people deal with colleagues and customers
Financial resources	Scepticism about whether the change will be financially worthwhile, or less so than other competing changes; lack of money
Structure	New reporting relationships or means of control may disrupt working relationships and patterns of authority
Culture	People likely to resist a change that challenges core values and beliefs, especially if they have worked well before
Power	If change affects ownership of and access to information, those who see they will lose autonomy will resist

These views can be enlarged by using the elements of the organisation shown in Figure 13.2. People can base their resistance on any of these contextual elements, as shown in Table 13.3.

13.6 Forms and sources of innovation

Creativity and innovation

Creativity refers to the ability to combine ideas in a new way or to make unusual associations between ideas. This helps people and organisations to generate imaginative ideas or ways of working, but that in itself does not ensure added value.

> **Creativity** is the ability to combine ideas in a unique way or to make unusual associations between ideas.

The systems model introduced in Chapter 1 helps to understand how organisations can become more innovative. Figure 13.6 shows that getting the desired outputs (more innovative products or work methods) depends on both the inputs and the transformation of those inputs.

Inputs include having creative people and groups who are able to generate novel ideas and methods, but they only flourish in a favourable context. Managers need to create a context which encourages both creative people and then the application of those creative ideas into goods and services that people want to buy. So in the business context it is useful to think of innovation as the process through which new ideas, objects, behaviours and practices are created, developed and implemented into a product or service.

Degrees of innovation – radical and incremental

Some innovations – such as the aerofoil that allows heavier than air flight and the transistor that is the basis of all modern electronics – have fundamentally changed society. Others such as Velcro or the ball-point pen are useful, but have more modest effects on life as we know it.

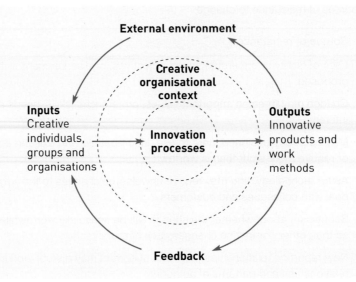

Figure 13.6
Systems view of
innovation

The effects of an innovation depend on how they are used, what they are replacing and who is evaluating them. Using hydrogen-fuelled engines instead of fossil-fuelled ones is a very useful technological innovation, but will have little effect on how people drive cars: so from the driver's perspective it is an **incremental innovation**. However it will have a very large environmental effect – so from the point of view of someone who cares about the environment it will be a **radical innovation**.

Organisational impact of innovations

Managers have to decide whether to invest possibly large sums to develop an innovation – when they cannot know whether it will succeed in the market. They can gain some sense of the likely cost to the organisation of using the innovation by relating it to their resources and competencies (Chapters 1 and 8). An incremental innovation will use existing skills, processes, equipment and infrastructure – such as one that involves resetting machinery or re-arranging a production line. It requires few internal changes, so will be low cost and low risk. A radical innovation requires significant revision to skills, processes and equipment, such as a metal working company developing a product that uses carbon fibre. It requires major internal changes, so will be high cost and high risk.

Most (although by no means all) innovations are incremental. The motor car has evolved from early radical innovations (internal combustion engine, inflatable tyres and plastics technology) to a situation in which new models incorporate incremental improvements to the suspension or electrics. Similarly in services, most innovations involve doing something a little differently and a little better.

Incremental innovations are small changes in a current product or process which brings a minor improvement.

Radical innovations are large game changing developments that alter the competitive landscape.

Activity 13.5 **Everyday Innovation**

- We are surrounded by so-called innovative products. Consider everyday items such as the iPod or the mobile phone. Try to identify the radical innovations that made the technology possible and the incremental innovations that matured the product to its current level of sophistication.

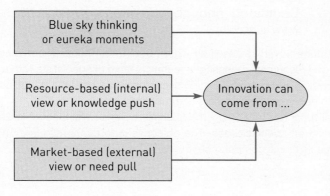

Figure 13.7
Sources of innovation

The sources of innovation

Figure 13.7 illustrates the main sources of innovation.

Eureka moments

The word 'eureka' is associated with the experience of having an idea. A common example of a 'eureka' moment was when Art Fry used a recently invented 'sticky but not too sticky' adhesive to keep his bookmark in place. This gave him the idea for the Post-it note which, after a process of design and development, became the familiar product range. The Management in Practice describes a recent example.

Management in practice   **Plugging a 'mole' in the market** www.magnamole.co.uk

Sharon Wright had her eureka moment while having a phone-line installed in her home. Under pressure for time, she offered to help the engineer thread the cable through the wall of her house. To Sharon's surprise the engineer produced a makeshift tool made from a wire coat-hanger. As well as being difficult to use, Sharon's experience in health and safety management told her this device was unsuitable and hazardous. Market research showed there were no alternative tools available for cable threading.

Within hours she had sketched the design of the Magnamole tool, a plastic rod with a magnet at one end and an accompanying metallic cap for attaching to the wire to be threaded through the wall. She soon had a prototype, and orders followed from large customers around the world.

What is remarkable about Sharon is that she had little knowledge or experience of this area of business, but that did not stop her from taking advantage of an obvious gap in the market.

Source: Company website.

Knowledge push

Most innovation now comes from the research and development laboratories of large companies – GlaxoSmithKline, DuPont, Apple and many more. They have a strong commitment to innovation, reflected in the systematic organisation of scientific staff, equipment and facilities to solve specific problems. To produce consistent innovation, specialising in one area is critical, as only by developing a depth of expertise will understanding be created.

Need pull

No matter how innovative a new product might be, it will not make money unless there is a market for it. Before investing significant resources in developing a new product, managers need a sense of the likely need. This may not be as straightforward as it seems: before lightweight digital music players and headphones became available, sportsmen and women trained without equipment to combat boredom. However, this technology is now an essential part of a runner's or cyclist's training kit, and versions are now available for swimmers.

Many products, especially in the area of consumer electronics, were inconceivable a few years ago. While it is logical that the typewriter could pave the way for a product such as Microsoft Word it is less conceivable that it would lead to PowerPoint. While the link between the home phone and the mobile phone is clear, the jump from the basic mobile phone to the functionality embodied in the iPhone would have been difficult to envisage. Another way to think of need pull is that it results in more niches being carved in a market as product differentiation becomes more subtle.

It is important to be aware of the driving forces in the external environment that may yield an opportunity. While scanning the market by analysing what competitor products may be useful, there are other more specific external areas that may yield opportunity for an innovative product or service.

Regulation changes

The makers of the Segway encountered regulatory problems in relation to safety and traffic laws, and regulations often hinder innovation. Others trigger it by requiring change – of which those on environmental pollution are a current example, in that they have encouraged the search for renewable sources of energy. On a smaller scale, regulations intended to improve road safety have led to the development of speed cameras and air bags. Potential innovators ensure that they are aware of impending changes in relevant regulations.

Management in practice   **Innovating on health** www.rjrt.com
www.philipmorristobacco.com

Legislative change can also have indirect effects on innovation. Restrictions on advertising and other actions to curb smoking have encouraged tobacco companies to invest heavily in alternatives to tobacco aiming for a new 'safe' cigarette such as the Philip Morris Accord and the RJR Eclipse.

Sources: Company websites.

Accidents and the unexpected

Many innovations have been accidental – from Fleming's discovery of Penicillin to the Post-it note. Indeed, the innovative gyro which makes the Segway possible was developed in BAE Systems' defence laboratories. Terrorist attacks have led to innovations in safety and security products, such as the biometric scanning device. One of the largest service industries in the world – personal insurance – developed from the need to guard against unplanned events, and is highly innovative in the risks against which it will offer cover to those prepared to pay – including Bruce Springsteen's voice for $6 million. Hedge funds are an innovative form of insuring against negative movements in the investment markets.

Users as innovators

Users are sometimes the source of ideas for innovation, three categories being particularly important:

- Lead users – people who not only use the product but also help in its development. Ivor Tiefenbrun, the founder of hi-fi maker Linn Products, developed his model when he became dissatisfied with products then available.
- User communities – groups of users who congregate around a product or product platform, such as early personal computer users, and find new and innovative ways to use the systems.
- Extreme users – push products to their limit, creating a need for improved performance. The bicycle is an example, with the relentless drive for more durable and higher performing machines.

Case study   **Vodafone/Ericsson – the case continues** www.vodafone.com
www.ericsson.com

Today, Vodafone is a global telecommunications company and as such sees innovation in products and services as critical to its strategy. As part of this they have set up the Joint Innovation Lab (JIL) with Verizon Wireless, China Mobile and Softbank Mobile. Together, these operators have access to over 1.1 billion customers around the world.

The four companies will use the JIL as a platform to develop mobile services and drive innovation. The purpose of the JIL is to launch projects based on emerging technologies and market demand and will focus on the rapidly growing areas of mobile internet services.

JIL's first project is to develop a widget (interactive virtual tool) ecosystem that will allow developers to benefit from access to the combined customer base of the four JIL operators. Consumers will get access to the innovation and creativity of a global developer community and operators benefit by providing great content to their customers.

This is an example of a mechanism to help users become part of the innovation process by, in effect, combining technology 'push' and need 'pull'.

Sources: *Vodafone Annual Report 2009*; company website.

13.7 The process of innovation

Organisations which depend on innovation implement deliberate systems to ensure an adequate flow. Figure 13.8 shows a model of the innovation process, portraying it as a filter through which ideas are gathered, channelled and focused before selecting those believed to have most potential. Generating the initial idea is necessarily random – but thereafter firms try to create order from this randomness as quickly as possible. They apply resources and effort to these promising ideas to develop them into something that can be implemented. The steps in this system are sequential but their duration and complexity will vary – some may require a significant research and development, others merely a change in the focus of the sales effort.

The 4 P's of innovation

Innovations become manifest in one or more of four areas; the product itself, the process of delivery or manufacture, positioning in the market and in the overall paradigm of the business.

Product innovations

An innovation here could be a change in the function or feature of a product such as the incorporation of a music player within a mobile phone or, in relation to a service, the incorporation of the facility to carry out personal banking on the internet. These innovations are intended to enhance the utility of the offering to make sales more likely.

Process innovations

An innovation here could be the addition of a self-service checkout at a supermarket where customers can scan their purchases using a barcode reader, or an online banking system to allow customers to manage their finances. Examples in manufacturing would be using robots for assembly to give higher quality and more efficiently produced products.

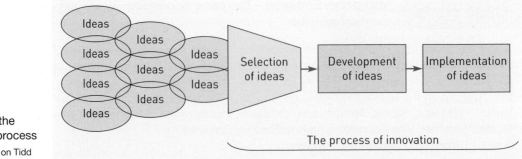

Figure 13.8
A model of the innovation process

Source: Based on Tidd and Bessant (2009).

Position innovations

These are changes in the target market or customers base for a product or service. Lucozade is a familiar example – once aimed at people recovering from illness, it is now for healthy people engaged in sport. Another example is the four-wheel drive: originally used for off-road work, but now sold as a fashionable family car to carry large loads.

Paradigm innovations

These are changes in how companies frame what they do; for example the reframing of a supermarket such as Sainsbury's from a simple seller of food products to a provider of many more of a family's needs such as petrol, clothing and financial products. Here the reframing has provided synergies where shoppers can buy all that they require, and pay for it all with their Sainsbury's bank card.

Organisational factors in managing innovation

One of the most notable innovative companies is Pixar, with a unique record of technological and artistic advances (see the following Management in Practice).

Management in practice — Behind Pixar's magic www.pixar.com

Ed Catmull (co-founder of Pixar, and president of Pixar and Disney Animation Studios) has written about the 'collective creativity' at the company: many of its methods are relevant to other organisations. He emphasises the uncertainty of the innovative process – the idea that starts the process may not work – by definition it is new, and the innovator cannot know at the start if it will lead to a worthwhile result:

> at the start of making [Ratatouille] we simply didn't know if [it] would work. However, since we're supposed to offer something that isn't obvious, we bought into somebody's initial vision and took a chance. (p. 66)

'Taking chances' that consistently succeed is not due to luck, but to the principles and practices that Pixar uses to support the people who turn the idea into a useful product. These include:

Getting talented people to work effectively with each other . . . [by constructing] an environment that nurtures trusting relationships and unleashes everyone's creativity. If we get that right, the result is a vibrant community where talented people are loyal to one another and their collective work. (p. 66)

Everyone must be free to communicate with anyone . . . the most efficient way to deal with numerous problems is to trust people to work out the difficulties directly with each other without having to check for permission. (p. 71)

We must stay close to innovations happening in the academic community. We strongly encourage our technical artists to publish their research and participate in industry conferences. Publication may give away ideas . . . but the connection is worth far more than any ideas we may have revealed: it helps us attract exceptional talent and reinforces the belief throughout the company that people are more important than ideas. (p. 71)

[Measure progress]. Because we're a creative organization, people [think that what we do can't be measured]. That's wrong. Most of our processes involve activities and deliverables that can be quantified. We keep track of the rates at which things happen, how often something had to be reworked, whether a piece of work was completely finished or not when it was sent to another department . . . Data can show things in a neutral way, which can stimulate discussion. (p. 72).

See Chapter 10 (p. 309) for more on Pixar.

Source: Catmull (2008).

Organisations that depend on innovation aim to create an environment which encourages all staff (not just those with specific R&D responsibilities) to help create and implement a strong flow of successful new things. Smith *et al.* (2008) developed a prescriptive model of the organisational features shaping the effectiveness of its innovation process – the 4 S's of innovation: strategy, structure, style and support.

- *Strategy* The organisational strategy must communicate a shared vision and goals (Jager *et al.*, 2004), indicating that innovation is central to its competitive advantage.
- *Style* The strategy must be enacted by the management style of the senior team to reinforce the strategic intention. A 'facilitate and empower' style is more likely to foster innovation than a 'command and control' style (Muthusamy *et al.*, 2005). But, in addition, employees are likely to require resources and time for ideas to emerge.
- *Structure* A highly specialised division of tasks is detrimental to innovation, while enriched jobs (Chapter 15) and easy horizontal communication will support it. While lone employees can be innovative, teams of employees working together are more likely to succeed.
- *Support* Technology can facilitate the transfer of knowledge by creating a knowledge repository (Jantunen, 2005), enabling staff to access information easily.

Staff as innovators

Lastly it is worth returning to the people aspects of innovation. Designing an organisational structure that emphasises communication and flexibility supported by an empowering management style and the appropriate information technology is the beginning of this journey and must be supplemented by other mechanisms. Recently much has been made of employee participation. This initially emerged with the 'quality miracle' of the Japanese manufacturers which was enabled by the system of *Kaizen* or 'continuous improvement' (Imai, 1986), where employees were encouraged to question work processes and look for incremental improvements in all that they did, leading to a better production process and therefore better product quality and organisational efficiency.

While suggestion schemes are not new, the more systematic and proactive approach of the Japanese was a key factor in the success of *Kaizen*. It has been joined by other systems such as total quality management (George and Weimerskirch, 1998) and lean manufacturing (Womack and Jones, 1996). While differing slightly in emphasis, the key to them all is in getting employees involved in the thinking behind the product and process, and encouraging them to generate ideas that lead to improvements that ultimately benefits overall revenue and profit.

As a framework it is useful to think of areas where employees can contribute ideas. Tonnessen (2005) has identified places that staff can be encouraged to become involved in innovation. These are within their immediate work area and activity, within the overall process that they are involved in, within their group or department and in relation to the overall company operation and strategy.

13.8 Integrating themes

Sustainable performance

Across the world, governments and international agencies are setting targets with the aim of reducing greenhouse gas emissions: an example is that by the EU to aim for a 20 per cent reduction by 2020. This is a significant opportunity for innovative businesses in developing new technologies that reduce CO_2 emissions. As well as the existing hydro-electric power infrastructure, currently there are 254 operational wind-farms in the UK, generating 5,100 MW, with another 28 under construction. In addition significant investment is now being made in marine forms of generation such as wave, tidal and current.

Innovation opportunities are not limited to the generation of power but also arise in infrastructure and especially transport. Hydrogen fuel cells for use in personal vehicles are maturing as a technology and solar powered vehicles for public transport are being developed. An example is the Solar-shuttle project which is developing solar powered boats for passenger transport on the Thames during the 2012 Olympic Games (**www.solarshuttle.co.uk**).

Governance and control

Thomas Midgely, although unknown to most people, has possibly done more damage to the environment that any other individual. A prolific innovator, among other things he put the lead in petrol and the CFCs in aerosols – doing great damage to the ozone layer. Midgely's is a cautionary tale, showing how lack of governance and control of innovation in product design can have disastrous and unforeseen consequences.

The financial crisis in 2008 is a contemporary example of innovation out of control. Its origins lay in some banks selling mortgages to (sub-prime) customers who could not afford the repayments. The innovation was the way in which the companies making the loans 'packaged' these loans and sold them to other players in the financial supply chain. Innovative bankers converted the original (very dubious) loans into financial products called mortgage-backed securities. These were sold on to hedge funds and investment banks which saw them as high return investments. When borrowers started to default on their loans, the value of the investments fell, leading to huge losses. Investors then became nervous about buying any investment linked to mortgages, no matter how high their quality, so that lenders found it increasingly difficult to borrow money in the capital markets – with the familiar results.

Much of the blame was placed on the lack of governance within the banking industry that allowed innovative ideas to be implemented without regard to the risks they posed or their longer-term consequences. The Management in Practice feature gives an example of a bank with very tight governance and control systems.

Management in practice	Governance and control at Banco Santander
	www.santander.com

In a speech to the first Santander Conference on International Banking, Emilio Botin, the chairman said:

> Banks must focus on customers, focus on recurring business based on long-term relationships and be cautious in managing risk. You do not need to be innovative to do this well. You do not need to invent anything. You need to dedicate time and attention at the highest level.
>
> Many are surprised to learn that the Banco Santander board's risk committee meets for half a day twice a week and that the board's 10-person executive committee meets every Monday for at least four hours, devoting a large portion of that time to reviewing risks and approving transactions. Not many banks do this. It consumes a lot of our directors' time. But we find it essential and it is never too much.

Source: *Financial Times*, 16 October 2008.

Internationalisation

The growing internationalisation of business has implications for the way international or global firms manage change and innovation. The issue here reflects one of the central themes within Chapter 4, namely the balance between a unified, global approach seeking to establish a common identity across all operations, or an approach that adapts the way the company operates to local conditions. Managers of local business units will have local priorities, and are likely to be unreceptive to change that the centre, or even another unit, appears to be imposing. This balancing act faces all companies operating internationally.

The same dilemma arises in relation to innovation: companies often want to allow research teams considerable autonomy, yet to do so could lead to expensive duplication of scientific resources and potentially harmful competition between national units. As an example an associate at W.L. Gore (see Part 5 Case) commented:

> One challenge is to retain the team-working ethos while working globally. There is a danger of duplication if the interests of separate teams in different parts of the world evolve in such a way that they are working on similar products. Yet at the same time we don't want to create structures or processes that stifle creativity. We don't want to say that people should focus on specific areas of research. We need to find ways of sharing expertise globally. (Part 5 Case, p. 540)

Summary

1 **Explain the meaning of organisational change and give examples**
   - Organisational change refers to deliberate attempts to change one or more elements of the internal environment, such as technology or structure. Change in one element usually stimulates change in other areas.

2 **Explain what the links between change and context imply for those managing a change**
   - A change programme is an attempt to change one or more aspects of the internal context, which then provides the context of future actions. The prevailing context can itself help or hinder change efforts.

3 **Compare lifecycle, emergent, participative and political theories of change**
   - Lifecycle: change projects can be planned, monitored and controlled towards achieving their objectives.
   - Emergent: reflecting the uncertainties of the environment, change is hard to plan in detail but emerges incrementally from events and actions.
   - Participative: successful change depends on human commitment, which is best obtained by involving participants in planning and implementation.
   - Political: change threatens some of those affected, who will use their power to block progress, or to direct the change in ways that suit local objectives.

4 **Evaluate systematically the possible sources of resistance to change**
   - Reasons can be assessed using the internal context model, as each element (objectives, people, power, etc.) is a potential source of resistance. Analysing these indicates potential ways of overcoming resistance.
   - The force field analysis model allows players to identify the forces driving and restraining a change, and implies that reducing the restraining forces will help change more than increasing the driving forces.

5 **Explain how innovations can be used to benefit companies**
   - Product innovation – changes what the organisation offers for sale.
   - Process innovation – changes how it creates the product.
   - Position innovation – changes how the product is offered or targeted.
   - Paradigm innovation – changes how a company frames what it does.

6 **Illustrate the organisational factors believed to support innovation**
   - Strategy – innovation is explicitly called for in the corporate strategy.
   - Structure – roles and jobs are defined to aid in innovative behaviour.
   - Style – management empowers the workforce to behave innovatively.
   - Support – IT systems are available to support innovative behaviour.

7 **Show how ideas from the chapter add to your understanding of the integrating themes**

- The search for sustainable performance offers significant opportunities to innovators who can find ways of reducing the use of energy throughout the value-adding chain.
- The 2008 financial crisis showed the negative side of innovation, when it is not balanced by effective governance and control systems – such as those at banks like Santander whose managers take risk seriously.
- International companies often wish to encourage local units to be innovative but, as the W.L. Gore case shows, they also need to avoid wasteful duplication if several sites work on similar projects.

Review questions

1 What does the term 'performance gap' mean, and what is its significance for change?

2 What are the implications for management of the systemic nature of major change?

3 Can managers alter the receptiveness of an organisation to change? Would doing so be an example of an interaction approach?

4 Outline the lifecycle perspective on change and explain when it is most likely to be useful.

5 How does it differ from the 'emergent' perspective?

6 What are the distinctive characteristics of a participative approach, and when is it likely to be least successful?

7 What skills are used by those employing a political model?

8 Is resistance to change necessarily something to be overcome? How would you advise someone to resist a change to which he/she was opposed?

9 In a technology product such as the Segway do you think further technological innovation or marketing innovation will be the key to its continued success?

10 Think of products and services that are currently successful, determine the innovations that created that success and categorise them using the 4Ps model.

11 Summarise an idea from the chapter that adds to your understanding of the integrating themes.

Concluding critical reflection

Think about the way people handle major change in your company, or one with which you are familiar. Review the material in the chapter, and perhaps visit some of the websites identified. Then make notes on these questions:

- What examples of the themes discussed in this chapter are currently relevant to your company? What performance imperatives are dominant, and to what extent do people see a performance gap? What perspective do people have on the change process – life cycle, emergent, participative or political?
- In implementing change, what **assumptions** about the nature of change in organisations appear to guide the approach? Is one perspective dominant, or do people typically use several methods in combination?
- What factors in the **context** of the company appear to shape your approach to managing change – is your organisation seen as being receptive or non-receptive to change, for example, and what lies behind that?
- Has there been any serious attempt to find **alternative** ways to manage major change in your organisation – for example by comparing your methods systematically with those of other companies, or with the theories set out here?
- Does the approach typically used generally work? If not, do managers recognise the **limitations** of their approach, and question their assumptions?

Further reading

Balogun, J., Gleadle, P., Hailey, V.H. and Willmott, H. (2005), 'Managing change across boundaries: boundary-shaking practices', *British Journal of Management,* vol. 16, no. 4, pp. 261–278.

An empirical study of the practices that change agents used to introduce major boundary-shaking changes in large companies, and how the context shaped their use.

Catmull, E. (2008), 'How Pixar fosters collective creativity', *Harvard Business Review*, vol. 86, no. 9, pp. 64–72.

The co-founder explains how it works.

Pettigrew, A., Ferlie, E. and McKee, L. (1992), *Shaping Strategic Change*, Sage, London.

Pettigrew, A.M. and Whipp, R. (1991), *Managing Change for Competitive Success*, Blackwell, Oxford.

Both of these books provide detailed, long-term analyses of major changes – the first in four commercial businesses and the second in several units within the UK National Health Service. Although the cases are old, they still provide useful empirical insights into the task of managing change.

Roberto, M.A. and Levesque, L.C. (2005), 'The art of making change initiatives stick', *MIT Sloan Management Review*, vol. 46, no. 4, pp. 53–60.

Another empirical study, this time in a single organisation, of how the context affected the willingness of people to change, and how senior managers needed to create a supportive context.

Tidd, J. and Bessant, J. (2009), *Managing Innovation: Integrating technological, market and organisational change*, Chichester, Wiley.

An easy to read text combining a comprehensive account of innovation theories with many contemporary examples.

Weblinks

These websites have appeared in this chapter:

www.vodafone.com
www.ericsson.com
www.gknplc.com
www.magnamole.co.uk
www.dupont.com
www.audi.com
www.segway.com
www.rjrt.com
www.philipmorristobacco.com
www.pixar.com
www.solarshuttle.co.uk
www.santander.com

Visit two of the business sites in the list, and navigate to the pages dealing with corporate news, investor relations or 'our company'.

- What signs of major changes taking place in the organisation can you find?
- Does the site give you a sense of an organisation that is receptive or non-receptive to change?
- What kind of environment are they likely to be working in, and how may that affect their approach to change?

 **WWW** For video case studies, audio summaries, flashcards, exercises and annotated weblinks, related to this chapter, visit **www.pearsoned.co.uk/mymanagementlab**

PART 4 CASE

THE ROYAL BANK OF SCOTLAND

www.rbs.co.uk

In 2007 many saw the Royal Bank of Scotland (RBS) as one of the most innovative and best-performing banks in the United Kingdom. By 2008 it was on the point of collapse, and only survived because the UK government invested £45.5 billion in the bank (at about 50 pence a share), in return for an 84 per cent stake in the business. In 2010 it was beginning to recover, and was developing a plan to buy back the government stake, so that it would return to private ownership.

What happened to bring about this change? Before 2007 management made many internal changes followed by some successful acquisitions. The internal changes took place between 1992 and 1997 during what was called Project Columbus. This made radical changes throughout the retail division, including:

- segmenting customers into three new streams – retail, commercial and corporate;
- creating new management roles and organisation structures;
- new human resource policies to base appointment and promotion on achievement and ability.

This transformed the bank's business, and provided the base for growth and acquisitions.

An evolving structure

Over the years the bank had become more centralised, as developments in IT during the 1960s enabled it to centralise administrative functions. Control brings more centralised decisions over products, margins and risk management. Against that, the customer relationship managers press for more local flexibility to override the system to meet the needs of a valuable customer.

The Manufacturing Division, which deals with routine functions such as clearing cheques, account opening and various other paper processes, is a very mechanistic structure. The bank created the division in 1999 by transferring most administrative tasks from the branches to a central location. To select staff for the

© The Royal Bank of Scotland Group plc

new division they used personality tests to identify those more comfortable with processes and systems. Those who were more interested in people remained in the branches.

With many brands, RBS uses different sales and marketing channels to reach its customers. However, it aims to make the underlying processes of banking as uniform as possible, whether for customers of NatWest, the retail bank, or a corporate client.

The branches themselves had been mechanistic, with staff working on strictly defined tasks. Now the branches are more organic, with staff trying to interest customers in other products within a more open physical layout. The bank tries to be organic at the customer-facing areas, with customer relationship managers trying to improve service quality.

The bank was quick to exploit the opportunities that new technology offers. It was an early innovator when it launched Direct Line as one of the first examples of delivering financial services by telephone, and now one of the UK's largest private motor insurers. An online bank complements the services offered by the bank branches.

The formal structure in early 2010 was that it had six 'customer-facing' divisions:

- UK Personal (retail and wealth management);
- UK Corporate (larger UK companies);
- RBS Insurance;
- US Retail and Commercial;
- Europe and Middle East Retail and Commercial;
- Global Banking and Markets.

These were supported by seven Group divisions – Restructuring and Risk, Finance, Manufacturing, Legal, Strategy, Communications and Human Resources.

A culture of acquisition

RBS had developed a reputation for acquiring other financial institutions and integrating them profitably. Most notable was the acquisition of NatWest Bank in 2000, not least because NatWest was three times the size of RBS at the time. To win the bank, RBS had to demonstrate its ability to extract major cost savings from the combined operations, and drive greater income from the combination of brands, customers, products and skills. The RBS bid promised to deliver a 'new force in banking' with the scale and strength to exploit new opportunities in the UK, Europe and the USA. Some industry analysts doubted the ability of RBS to deliver on its bid promises, so the company was under pressure to complete the integration process on time and meet the cost savings and income benefits quoted during the bid.

The Integration Programme was quickly established following the takeover, dividing the task into 154 integration initiatives to be completed in three years. These were expected to yield £1.1 billion in annual cost savings and reduce staff by 18,000. Programme Management teams were established in each affected business and technology area, and control and reporting procedures were set up. The key elements of the integration strategy were agreed and widely communicated:

- To use RBS information systems as the single platform for operations across the merged bank.
- To migrate customer-facing systems such as credit cards, ATMs and internet screens to RBS systems.
- To transfer the NatWest customer and accounting data to the RBS systems in a single weekend.

This last was the largest of the integration tasks, involving the migration of 18 million customer accounts worth £158 billion and with huge daily transaction volumes. Planning for this took over two years, and paid off when all the accounts were transferred over one weekend in October 2002.

The Integration Programme was completed in early 2003, and was widely seen as a successful strategic move by Fred Goodwin and his team (Kennedy *et al.*, 2006). Having made 23 acquisitions since 2000, and although not ruling out further ones if the opportunity arose, the group claimed to be focusing on growing 'organically', by building up existing businesses.

However, Fred Goodwin, the chief executive who had led the bank's ambitious acquisition programme, completed a deal (in partnership with Fortis, a Belgo-Dutch lender, and Santander of Spain) another deal in late 2008 – which was to prove disastrous. In the biggest deal in banking history the consortium acquired ABN AMRO, a Dutch bank. Many had doubted the wisdom of the deal, since RBS would need to raise more capital to complete the purchase. At first Goodwin denied this would be necessary, but his reputation suffered when he asked shareholders to contribute £12 billion in a rights issue. Many believe that RBS picked the wrong time and paid the wrong price for the ABN AMRO business.

A failure of governance?

Worse was to come as, when the 2008 financial crisis developed, the bank found that it was unable to fund its operations. In October 2008 the UK government unveiled an historic bail-out – including a capital injection of state money that amounts to partial nationalisation. This led shareholders to press for management changes, and especially for the dismissal of Sir Fred Goodwin. Despite having had to seek a government bail-out, and to the fury of public and politicians alike, Sir Fred insisted that he was entitled to his full pension of over £700,000 a year, due at once, although he is only 50. The bank's remuneration committee agreed to Sir Fred's massive payoff as part of the negotiations to get rid of him, and the government did not try to reduce it when it rescued the bank. Sir Fred had a contract.

Others pointed out that bankers' pay during the bubble was too high, but that it would be a mistake for the state to impose pay limits. Finance relies on individuals, and employers compete for their skills. If taxpayers were to get their money back, RBS would need to become profitable, and it was unlikely to do so if it could not attract good staff by paying competitive salaries. This view appeared to prevail, as in early 2010 the bank (with government acquiescence) approved what appeared to many to be a generous bonus package for its staff – although some senior managers declined to take a salary increase.

A related issue was to reconsider the structure of bank pay, such as awarding more bonuses in shares rather than cash, and paying them over longer periods – so that those which had been earned by taking excessive risks could be clawed back. Rewards should be more tightly dependent on exceptional performance, not the rising tide of the markets. But whether such policies worked would depend on how they were applied.

This is a matter of governance. Shareholders suffered in the crash, but they had not tried to restrain their Boards during the good times. RBS had all of the formal mechanisms of corporate governance in place – independent non-executive directors, audit and risk committees, and a remuneration committee. None of the people on these boards and committees appears to have been able and willing to stand up to the chief executive as he created a culture which encouraged bankers to take great risks (such as investing in the troubled US housing market, and in many new and complex financial instruments) with shareholders money. Whatever misgivings they may have had in private, they continued to support the management team in public – 90 per cent of shareholders approved the ABN AMRO deal.

Where next?

Stephen Hester replaced Goodwin as chief executive, and has been trying to rebuild the bank. He aims to focus on its traditional strengths such as UK retail banking, wealth management, and global payments and insurance. The investment banking business will be halved in size. It will try to dispose of other parts of the business, such as other foreign retail assets, and weak parts of the investment bank.

In 2009 Mr Hester reached a new pay deal, which was agreed by UK Financial Investments, which manages the state's shareholding in RBS. While the headline figure of £9.6 million attracted wide criticism, defenders pointed out that most of it depended on the share price rising from 35p to 70p – which would bring big benefits to the taxpayer. Others pointed out that it was such short-term incentives that caused many of the problems at the bank in the first place.

It is also targeting the world's wealthiest people through the Coutts subsidiary. These are mainly entrepreneurs, media and entertainment stars. It has a joint venture with Bank of China which offers services to the rapidly growing number of Chinese people with more than $1 million to invest.

Sources: Kennedy *et al.* (2006); *Economist*, 14 February 2009, *Financial Times,* 6 May 2009, 23 June 2009; company website.

Part case questions

- Is RBS becoming more centralised or more decentralised?
- What form(s) of structure has the bank used to divide the business? Since it is also necessarily a geographically dispersed organisation, what methods of co-ordination is it likely to use?
- Does RBS have a mechanistic or an organic structure?
- What are the main issues of an HRM nature that are likely to be topical within RBS?
- The issue of bank bonuses was still highly topical and contentious in early 2010. Explain the dilemma that Stephen Hester faces, and comment on any recent developments in this area.
- Refer to Chapter 7, Sections 7.6 and 7.7. Use them to analyse possible explanations for the troubles at RBS.
- Why do you think the Board was unable to influence Fred Goodwin and the senior team? What sources of power did (a) Goodwin and (b) the board, possess? (See Chapter 14.)

PART 4
SKILLS DEVELOPMENT

To help you develop your skills, as well as knowledge, this section includes tasks that relate the key themes covered in the Part to your daily life. Working through these will help you to deepen your understanding of the topic, and develop skills and insights which you can use in many situations.

| Task 4.1 | Analysing a department or organisation |

While every organisation is unique, all are made up of the elements shown in Figure 1.3. These form the internal context within which managers operate, and shape the demands which the manager faces. A useful skill is that of being able to use this model to identify and analyse significant features of an organisation or business unit. This exercise invites you to analyse just four of the elements – select more if they seem relevant to the situation.

Analyse a department or organisation with which you are familiar, by making a few notes in response to these questions:

- What is the main objective or mission of the department or organisation?
- What is the structure?
- What are the main characteristics of the people?
- What technologies (and in what layout) do people use to meet the objectives? This includes all kinds of physical facilities, including computer systems.

Consider a recent large change. What were the direct and indirect effects on each of these components? What difficulties, if any, had to be managed?

Compare your answers with those prepared by another student, to further increase your skills of analysis, and of identifying key organisational features.

| Task 4.2 | Distinguishing mechanistic from organic structures |

Chapter 10 distinguished between mechanistic and organic forms. Since these greatly affect how people work, a manager needs to be able to identify each type, and the practices which can, whether intended or not, lead an organisation towards one or the other.

Analyse a department or organisation with which you are familiar by making a few notes in response to the following questions:

- Identify a department that is mainly mechanistic, and indicate the features or practices that illustrate it.
- Identify a department that is mainly organic, and indicate the features or practices that illustrate that.
- Why do you think each takes the form they do?

- Is that form the appropriate one for the work being done?
- If not, what specific features or practices would you recommend that management change to move towards the form you think most suitable?
- Are there any examples of problems in the working relationships between units which may be attributed to their having mechanistic and organic characteristics?

Task 4.3   Analysing information systems

Choose an organisation of which you have some direct knowledge – one you work in or in which you are studying. Write a short report analysing the organisation's main information systems using themes from Chapter 12, and from other relevant chapters in the book, such as:

- What types of IS do different people in the organisation use – perhaps locating them on the grid provided in Figure 12.6?
- Do the information systems provide users with information which meets the usual criteria of high-quality information? If not, is the problem mainly technical or mainly organisational?
- How do the information systems affect the ability of the organisation to compete in terms of innovation, quality, delivery or cost?
- Use Figures 12.4 and 12.5 to analyse the organisation's stage of development in using IS.
- Review Sections 12.6 to 12.8. Has the organization used one or more of these systems, and what have been the effects?
- To what extent are managers using the internet to help manage the business?

Task 4.4   Analysing stakeholders

A valuable skill in managing any kind of organisational change (such as in strategy, structure or technology) is that of managing those with a stake in the project, and who can affect its success. This exercise enables you to practice using a tool which helps to understand and manage stakeholders constructively.

Select a major organisational change project with which you are familiar, or which you can ask someone about. Write the name of the project in a circle at the centre of a sheet of paper. Draw other circles around the sheet, each identifying an individual or group with a stake in the project. Place the most significant nearer the centre, and others around the edge.

Use a scale such as that shown below to assess the 'present' (X) and 'hoped for' (Y) level of commitment of each stakeholder to the project.

Key Stakeholder	Vigorous opposition	Some opposition	Indifferent towards it	Will let it happen	Will help it happen	Will make it happen
				X		Y
				X	Y	
			X		Y	
				X		Y
	X				Y	

Rate each of the stakeholders on whether their power to affect the project is high or low.

Use a grid such as that shown below to note your answers to these questions for the main (powerful) stakeholders.

Stakeholder	Their goals	Current relationship	What is expected of them?	Positive or negative to them?	Likely reaction?	Ideas for action

- What are their priorities, goals and interests?
- What is the general tone of our present relationship with them?
- What specific behaviour is expected of them, in relation to this project?
- Are they likely to see this as positive or negative for them?
- What is their likely action to defend their interests?
- What actions can we consider to influence them?

Compare your answers with those prepared by another student for his/her project, to further increase your skills of analysis, and of identifying ideas for managing stakeholders.

PART 5
LEADING

Introduction

Generating the effort and commitment to work towards objectives is central to managing any human activity. One person working alone, be it in private life or in business, has only him- or herself to motivate. As an organisation grows, management activities become, in varying degrees, separated from the core work activities. The problem of generating effort changes, as now one person or one occupational group, has to secure the willing co-operation of other people and their commitment to the task. Those other people may be subordinates, peers or superiors whose support, and perhaps approval, needs to be generated and maintained.

The quality of that commitment is as important as whether or not it is secured. Staff are often in direct contact with customers. They are aware of their unique and changing requirements, and have an immense effect on the view the customer forms of the organisation. Others are in creative roles, with a direct impact on the quality of the service delivered to the final customer, whether they are contributing to a core R&D project or a TV show. Others must work reliably and flexibly to meet changing external or internal customer needs. Unwilling or grudging commitment damages the service offered and eventually the business itself.

How does management secure the motivation it needs from others? Part 5 offers perspectives on the dilemma. Chapter 14 examines ideas on influencing others, while Chapter 15 presents a range of theories about what those others may want from work. Communication is central to most management functions and activities, and Chapter 16 examines this topic. Finally, teams are an increasingly prominent aspect of organisations, and the motivation and commitment generated within them is often central to performance: Chapter 17 introduces ideas on teams.

The Part case is W.L. Gore & Associates, an organisation renowned for its use of teams.

CHAPTER 14
INFLUENCE AND POWER

Aim

To examine how people influence others by using personal skills and/or power.

Objectives

By the end of your work on this chapter you should be able to outline the concepts below in your own terms and:

1 Distinguish leading from managing and explain why each is essential to performance

2 Explain why leading and managing both depend on being able to influence others

3 Compare trait, behavioural and contingency perspectives on influencing

4 Outline theories that focus on power (both personal and organisational) as the source of influence

5 Contrast the style and power perspectives, and explain why sharing power may increase it

6 Outline a model of the tactics that people use to influence others, including the use of cooperative networks

7 Show how ideas from the chapter add to your understanding of the integrating themes.

Key terms

This chapter introduces the following ideas:

influence	**initiating structure**
leadership	**consideration**
traits	**situational (contingency) models**
big five	**power**
transactional leader	**political behaviour**
transformational leader	**delegating**
behaviour	

Each is a term defined within the text, as well as in the Glossary at the end of the book.

Case study   Apple Inc.   www.apple.com

When Apple launched the iPad in 2010 it added a further product to a range that already included Mac computers, iPods, iPhones and the Apple stores. Some saw it as a bold attempt by Apple to merge the netbook, phone and mobile entertainment sectors, with the iPad bridging the gap between laptops and smartphones. The full-colour touch-screen enables users to watch movies, surf the internet, listen to music, view photos, and read digital versions of books and newspapers.

The company had signed deals with several major publishers, including Penguin and HarperCollins, and hoped other publishers would make their content available on the platform. As an example, a *New York Times* application allows readers to view videos embedded within online articles, which look and feel like the print edition. Applications and games available in the App Store can be used on the iPad, and developers will be encouraged to build software specifically for the larger-screen device.

With successive products Apple's influence has grown – the iPod represents more than 70 per cent of the mp3 market, and the device has helped to reshape the music publishing industry. The similar success of the iPhone meant that every manufacturer has followed Apple's lead, and now offers a touch-screen smartphone. Apple has the power to reshape markets and influence competitors.

The company has a tradition of innovation, going back to the first Apple computers in 1976, followed by the Macintosh in 1984 – the first commercially successful PC that allowed users to point and click with a mouse. Steve Jobs (the company's co-founder) had spotted the technology in another company, seen its potential and developed it into a successful product.

Mr Jobs' success with the Macintosh was soon followed by a major difficulty. He was chairman of the business he had founded with Steve Wozniak in 1976, and the chief executive (Mike Markkula) wished to leave. The Board (including Jobs) decided to appoint John Sculley, from Pepsi-Cola, to the post. Jobs and Sculley frequently disagreed and in 1987 Sculley persuaded the Board to dismiss Jobs (then aged 30).

Jobs then entered what he regards as one of the most creative periods of his life – typified by his purchase of Pixar in 1986. The company struggled until Mr Jobs struck a deal with Walt Disney in the 1990s. Using Pixar's creative flair and Disney's marketing and distribution power, Mr Jobs oversaw an uninter-

© KIMBERLY WHITE/Reuters/Corbis

rupted string of blockbusters, starting with *Toy Story* in 1995. He also started a new computer company, NeXT, which was intended to make computers for large companies – taking him out of his natural milieu. Instead of trying to satisfy millions of individual customers he was in a market where committees made decisions. Products were delayed, cash was limited and the company was in difficulty.

Jobs returned to Apple in 1997 since when the company has continued to grow. His management style is distinctive – but he and the company are keen to stress that he has built a strong executive team to ensure the continuity of the business.

Sources: Moritz (2009); *Economist*, 1 October 2009; and other published material.

Case questions 14.1

- What examples are there of managers influencing others?
- What clues can you see about how Apple has been able to exert so much power in the market?
- How much of that influence and power depends on one person?

> ### 14.1 Introduction

When Steve Jobs and Steve Wozniak founded Apple they faced more than technical challenges. They also had to persuade staff to leave good jobs to work for an unknown company, investors to risk their money, suppliers to deliver components – and above all the public to buy the new machines. Clearly they did all of this – but not by accident: they did it by successfully influencing other people to support the business and ensure it survived, while many others failed.

That pattern has continued, though with interruptions – notably when other senior managers opposed what Jobs was doing, and persuaded the Board to dismiss him in 1986. Events took another turn, and Jobs returned to the company in 1997, since when it has had many successes – due to the way Jobs and others have influenced staff, competitors, customers and suppliers.

All managers have to influence others – as Willie Walsh, chief executive at British Airways tried, in 2010, to influence staff to accept new working practices designed to make the company more competitive. Crossrail managers (Chapter 6) successfully influenced many interest groups – including local and national politicians, business leaders, financial institutions, Network Rail – to secure approval for the project in 2009. As construction began the following year they continued to exert influence – now focused on contractors, financiers and residents affected by construction work – to deliver the new line.

Management in practice   **Terri Kelly, chief executive at W.L. Gore** www.gore.com

Terry Kelly has worked for the company since graduating as an engineer in 1983, and was elected as chief executive in 2005. This appointment was a group decision, with the opinions of dozens of staff being sought – typical of decision-making processes in the company (see Part case). She says of her role:

> It's not a title where you've got assumed authority or control, you really have to earn that every day. It's still very much the same leadership model that all of our successful leaders subscribe to, which is that you have to sell your ideas, even if you're the chief executive. You have to explain the rationale behind your decision, and do a lot of internal selling.

Source: *Financial Times*, 2 December 2008. See also Part case.

Influence is the process by which one party attempts to modify the behaviour of others by mobilising power resources.

Whatever their role, people add value to resources by influencing others. The tasks of planning, organising, leading and controlling depend on other people agreeing to co-operate within a web of mutual **influence**. Senior managers influence big investors to retain their support, sales staff influence customers, someone designing a new product influences others to back it. Everyone's performance depends on how well they do this, and the targets of their influence are often in more senior positions.

In that sense the work of the manager is not that of the careful analyst, working out the ideal solution. It is closer to that of an entrepreneur who is determined to get things done in a hostile or indifferent setting. Managers typically operate across functional or departmental boundaries, working with people who have other priorities and interests.

This chapter explores the topics shown in Figure 14.1. It begins by clarifying what influence means in the context of managing and then presents three perspectives – traits, behavioural and contingency. It examines theories on how people use power to influence others, power which has both personal and organisational sources. Finally it presents a model of the influencing tactics people use, including networking. The figure also shows that the outcomes of an influence attempt depend not only on the method but on the circumstances – the context. Those outcomes then affect the influencer's power: a successful result will increase it, a failure will reduce it. The chapters on motivation, communication and teams are closely linked to influence and power.

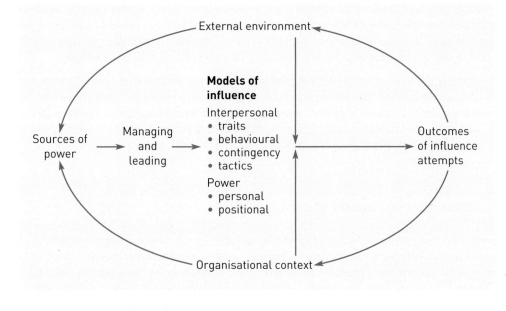

Figure 14.1
A model of the influencing process

14.2   Purposes, targets and responses

Managing and leading

Research and commentary on influencing use the terms 'manager' and 'leader' (and their derivatives) interchangeably, as there is no definitive distinction. It is worth briefly clarifying the meanings that some attach to them.

Chapter 1 defined a manager as someone who gets things done with the support of others. Most commentators view an 'effective manager' as one who 'gets things done' to ensure order and continuity. They maintain the steady state – keeping established systems in good shape and making incremental improvements. People generally use the term 'effective leader' to denote someone who brings innovation, moves an activity out of trouble into success or makes a worthwhile difference. They (like Julian Metcalf at Pret A Manger – see Management in Practice) see opportunities to do new things, take initiatives, inspire people.

Management in practice   Julian Metcalf, founder of Pret A Manger   www.pret.com

 Commenting on the leadership of Julian Metcalf, who founded Pret A Manger in 1986 (it now has about 225 shops) one of his directors said:

> Pret has always been very innovative because our founder, Julian Metcalf, is a true entrepreneur: he is here most days and he is really the spirit for all things entrepreneurial here and that is fantastic. The benefit of that is that we don't spend months and months and months developing new products, we're very quick to turn things around and it's very fast paced here. We have lots of new products and upgrades to our ingredients going on month in month out. And people comment when they come here, in terms of the pace of change, sometimes it can be hard to keep up with, but it's exciting, and makes us feel like a small organisation when in fact we're not.

Source: Interview with the director.

Leadership refers to the process of influencing the activities of others towards high levels of goal setting and achievement.

Peter Drucker (1999) writes of the leader's ability to generate unusual or exceptional commitment to a vision, and of **leadership** being 'the lifting of people's vision to a higher sight, the raising of their performance to a higher standard, the building of their personality beyond its normal limitations'. And Anita Roddick (founder of The Body Shop) wrote:

> [People] are looking for leadership that has vision . . . You have to look at leadership through the eyes of the followers and you have to live the message. What I have learned is that people become motivated when you guide them to the source of their own power and when you make heroes out of employees who best personify what you want to see in the organization. (Roddick, 1991, p. 223)

Key ideas   John Kotter on leading and managing

Kotter (1990) distinguishes between the terms leadership and management – while stressing that organisations need both – and that one person will often provide both. He regards good management as bringing order and consistency to an activity – through the tasks of planning, organising and controlling. He observed that modern management developed to support the large companies which developed from the middle of the nineteenth century. These complex enterprises tended to become chaotic, unless they developed good management practices to bring order and consistency. The pioneers of management (such as Robert Owen, Chapter 1 Case) created the discipline:

> **to help keep a complex organization on time and on budget. That has been, and still is, its primary function. Leadership is very different. It does not produce consistency and order . . . it produces movement.** (p. 4)

Individuals whom people recognise as leaders have created change – whether for the better or not. Good leadership is that which

> **moves people to a place in which they and those who depend on them are genuinely better off, and when it does so without trampling on the rights of others.** (p. 5)

Leaders succeed by establishing direction and strategy, communicating it to those whose co-operation is needed, and motivating and inspiring people. Managing and leading are closely related, but differ in their primary functions – the one to create order, the other to create change. Organisations need both if they are to prosper.

Source: Kotter (1990).

People work to create change and to create order in varying degrees, so there is no value in a sharp distinction between managing and leading: John Adair (1997) quotes a Chinese proverb:

> What does it matter if the cat is black or white, as long as it catches mice. (p. 2)

Managing and leading both depend on influencing others to put effort and commitment into the task – whether to create order or to create change.

Targets of influence

People at all levels who want to get something done need to influence others. The effectiveness of senior managers in influencing others has the most visible effect on performance: shaping the overall direction of the business or changing the way it operates. Yet they depend on people lower down the organisation also being able and willing to exercise influence – whether to bring stability or to initiate change in their area of responsibility.

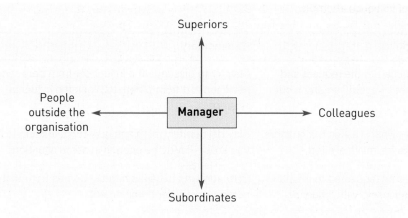

Figure 14.2
Influencing in four
directions

Managers (and leaders) often influence people who are equally powerful – as the first woman to take the top management job at a leading City of London legal practice observed:

> The hardest things in management . . . are complicated people issues. Sometimes you realise you can't solve everything. Our assets are the brains and personalities of some highly intelligent people, so there are a huge number of relationship issues. Most of these 250 people are very driven. If you get it right, the commitment is already sorted out. But you've got to take a lot of people with you a lot of the time. (*Financial Times*, 15 February 2001, p. 17)

So managing and leading require people to influence colleagues on the same organisational level, those formally above them in the hierarchy and people outside the organisation. Figure 14.2 illustrates this.

How do managers and leaders try to ensure that others do what they want them to do? The sections which follow present answers to that question, beginning with trait theories.

Responses to influence

To increase the chances of a successful outcome, someone attempting to influence another can also consider possible outcomes and plan accordingly. Kelman (1961) identified three outcomes – compliance, identification, and internalisation – to which this section adds a fourth: resistance. Table 14.1 summarises these.

- **Resistant** staff will have no commitment to the work. They will either refuse to do what is asked, or do what is required grudgingly and without enthusiasm.
- **Compliance** occurs when 'an individual accepts influence from another person or [group because they hope] to achieve a favorable reaction from the other. . . '. They do what is asked of them, not because they believe in it, or agree with it, but because in that way they will avoid further trouble and interference – 'I'll do it to keep the peace.'
- **Identification** occurs when someone acts in the way requested because the person feels that by doing so he/she is identifying with the person making the request. It is a way of maintaining a desired relationship with the influencer. They do what they are asked, but not because they find it intrinsically satisfying or worthwhile. Identification differs from compliance, as here the individual believes in his/her actions – but only when they are conscious of their relationship with the person making the request: 'I'll do it – but only because it's you who's asking.'
- **Internalisation** occurs when a person accepts influence – does what they are asked to do – because it is consistent with their values and beliefs. They accept the request because they fundamentally agree that it is the right thing to do – they see that it will solve the problem, be a congenial thing to do, or bring other valuable rewards: 'sure, that should work' could be a typical response indicating that a person has internalised the request.

Table 14.1 Four outcomes of influence attempts

Outcome	Description	Commentary
Resistance	Target opposed to the request and actively tries to avoid carrying it out	May try to dissuade the influencer from persisting. May seek support from others to block the influence attempt
Compliance	Target does what is asked but no more. No enthusiasm, minimal effort	May deliberately let things go wrong, leading to 'I told you so . . .'. May be enough in some situations
Identification	Target does as requested to maintain valued relationship with influencer	Only agreeing because request comes from that person – no wider commitment
Internalisation	Target internally agrees with a request and commits effort to make it work	The most successful outcome for the influencer, especially when task requires high levels of commitment

Resistance or grudging compliance show there may be trouble ahead. Complex work processes require people to work with imagination and flexibility: in service industries customers immediately see that staff are merely complying rather than working with care and enthusiasm. An influencer can repeat a request more forcefully, but this will often bring little improvement. Alternatively (and more wisely) they can pause to consider why people reacted this way. That may give useful information about either what was asked for, or how it was done: either way, it should enable them to use another approach next time.

14.3 Traits models

Many people have tried to identify the personal characteristics associated with effective leaders. They observed the personalities of prominent figures, and distinguished what they believed were enduring aspects of their personality, which they displayed in a variety of settings, and which appeared to influence them to behave in a particular way. Early work on personality and leadership identified numerous such **traits** – and this in itself hindered the development of a practically useful theory, as the lists of potentially valuable traits grew longer.

A **trait** is a relatively stable aspect of an individual's personality that influences behaviour in a particular direction.

The big five

A major advance in this area of study came when researchers noted that they could group the many observed traits into five clusters (McCrae and John, 1992). These are known as the **big five**: the left-hand column in Table 14.2 shows the label for each cluster, and the other columns show adjectives describing their extreme positions.

McCrae and John (1992) show that each cluster contains six traits. Using these in personality assessments enables researchers to identify the pattern of traits an individual displays, and predict how this pattern will affect performance. Colbert and Witt (2009) note that conscientiousness is the most consistent predictor of work outcomes, probably because such people tend to be dutiful, take care, deal with tasks accurately and persist to overcome difficulties. They also found that supervisors could influence such workers to perform well by emphasising the value of achieving goals, and helping them to do so. Anderson *et al.* (2008) show that people had more influence when certain big five personality traits 'fit' the work situation. Extroverts had more influence in a team-oriented consulting firm, while conscientious individuals had more influence in a telecommunications support unit, where they typically worked alone to solve technical problems.

The **big five** refers to trait clusters that appear consistently to capture main personality traits: openness, conscientiousness, extraversion, agreeableness and neuroticism.

Table 14.2 The big five trait clusters

Openness	Explorer (O+): creative, open-minded, intellectual	Preserver (O−): unimaginative, disinterested, narrow-minded
Conscientiousness	Focused (C+): dutiful, achievement-oriented, self-disciplined	Flexible (C−): frivolous, irresponsible, disorganised
Extraversion	Extravert (E+): gregarious, warm, positive	Introvert (E−): quiet, reserved, shy
Agreeableness	Adapter (A+): straightforward, compliant, sympathetic	Challenger (A−): quarrelsome, oppositional, unfeeling
Neuroticism	Reactive (N+): anxious, depressed, self-conscious	Resilient (N−): calm, contented, self-assured

James Burns: transactional and transformational leaders

James Burns (1978) distinguished between a **transactional leader** and **transformational leader**. Transactional leaders influence subordinates' behaviour through a bargain. The leader enables followers to reach their goals, while at the same time contributing to the goals of the organisation. If subordinates behave in the way desired by the leader they receive rewards – transactional leaders tend to support the *status quo* by rewarding subordinates' efforts and commitment.

> A **transactional leader** is one who treats leadership as an exchange, giving followers what they want if they do what the leader desires.

Burns contrasted this approach with that of transformational (sometimes called charismatic) leaders. They are thought to change the *status quo* by infusing work with a meaning which encourages subordinates to change their goals, needs and aspirations. Transformational leaders raise the consciousness of followers by appealing to higher ideals and moral values. They energise people by, for example, articulating an attractive vision for the organisation, reinforcing the values in that vision, and empowering subordinates to come up with new and creative ideas. They also articulate

> A **transformational leader** is a leader who treats leadership as a matter of motivation and commitment, inspiring followers by appealing to higher ideals and moral values.

> transcendent goals, demonstration of self-confidence and confidence in others, setting a personal example for followers, showing high expectations of followers' performance, and the ability to communicate one's faith in one's goals. (Fiedler and House, 1994, p. 112)

Key ideas   How do charismatic leaders gain support?

Conger and Kanungo (1994) note that people often use the terms 'charismatic' and 'transformational' leadership interchangeably, but suggest that the first term directs attention to leader behaviours, while the second focuses on the effects on followers:

> In essence the two formulations of charismatic and transformational are highly complementary, and study the same phenomenon only from different vantage points. (p. 442)

They developed behavioural scales to measure charismatic leadership, with 25 items in six groups:

- vision and articulation, e.g. 'consistently generates new ideas';
- environmental sensitivity, e.g. 'recognises barriers that may hinder progress';
- unconventional behaviour, e.g. 'uses non-traditional methods';

- personal risk, e.g. 'takes high personal risk for the sake of the organisation';
- sensitivity to member needs, e.g. 'shows sensitivity to needs and feelings of others';
- not maintaining the *status quo*, e.g. 'advocates unusual actions to achieve goals'.

The full scales have been validated and used widely in research on charismatic (or transformational) leadership (see, for example, Groves, 2005).

While many claim that transformational leadership styles generate higher performance than transactional styles, Garcia-Morales *et al.* (2008) find that few studies 'trace the causal path of the effects of transformational leadership on performance' (p. 299). They propose that since knowledge and innovation are vital to performance in modern economies, perhaps transformational leaders use their charisma and inspiration to encourage practices in these areas – which then lead to enhanced business performance. Their study in over 400 Spanish companies confirmed this. Identifiable practices associated with transformational leadership (such as allocating resources to develop knowledge, and to build the skills to use it) helped to build organisational knowledge, and to ensure people absorbed it and used it. This in turn led to innovation, which managers believed had enhanced their performance relative to competitors.

A limitation of the traits model is that a trait that is valuable in one situation is not necessarily valuable in another. Whatever traits Fred Goodwin had during his early (successful) years as chief executive at The Royal Bank of Scotland were still there when he resigned from the almost bankrupt company in 2009. Certain traits are probably necessary for effective leadership, but will not be sufficient for all conditions – which may explain the inconclusive

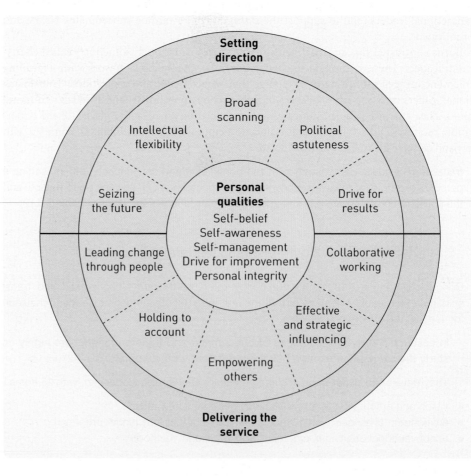

Figure 14.3
NHS leadership qualities framework

Source: NHS Institute for Innovation and Improvement (2005), *NHS Leadership Qualities Framework*, www. nhsleadershipqualities. nhs.uk/

results of research into whether traits influence performance (Bono and Judge, 2004). Their effect depends on the situation: De Hoogh *et al.* (2005) found that while four of 'the big five' had a positive effect on both transactional and charismatic leadership in a stable environment, in a dynamic environment they only had a positive effect on transformational leadership. Different conditions seem to need different traits.

Despite these limitations the traits model may explain why some people get to positions of great influence and others do not. Baum and Locke (2004) note a revival of interest in the personal characteristics of potential leaders, such as entrepreneurs creating new ventures. When people specify desirable traits or personal qualities as part of a selection process they are implicitly assuming that they enhance performance. Figure 14.3 is an example developed for the UK National Health Service.

As two of the foremost scholars of leadership concluded:

> There is no one ideal leader personality. However, effective leaders tend to have a high need to influence others, to achieve; and they tend to be bright, competent and socially adept, rather than stupid, incompetent and social disasters. (Fiedler and House, 1994, p. 111)

Case study   Apple Inc. – the case continues www.apple.com

Apple is credited with putting Silicon Valley on the map, and creating Silicon Valley's hard-working yet corporate-casual environment. Even as the company grew, Jobs worked hard to maintain Apple's rebel spirit.

Apple's corporate culture is characterised by its intense work ethic and casual dress code. Staff surveys regularly refer to a 'relaxed', 'casual', 'collegial' environment with 'long hours, weekends included' and 'no end to challenges and cool projects'. When Jobs returned in 1997 he was known for walking around the Apple campus barefoot in cutoff shorts and a black shirt. Jobs' commitment to casual wear is so thorough, he reportedly showed up barefoot to meetings with Microsoft executives.

Many trend-watchers credit Jobs and Apple with spawning the corporate casual philosophy that has affected the business culture of Silicon Valley, and greater American corporate culture in general. The *LA Times* quotes employment specialists John Challenger and Miriam Wardak, saying, when Gen X and Y workers see 'T-shirt-and-jeans donning Steve Jobs, chief executive of Apple Computer Inc.', they realise they can 'doff their suits and still get rich'.

Michael Moritz, who has observed Jobs for many years notes:

> Steve is a founder of the company [and the best founders] are unstoppable, irrepressible forces of nature . . . Steve has always possessed the soul of the questioning poet – someone a little removed from the rest of us who, from an early age, beat his own path. [He has a sharp] sense of the aesthetic – that influence is still apparent in all Apple products and advertising. Jobs's critics will say he can be wilfull, obdurate, irascible, temperamental and stubborn [which is true, but he is also a perfectionist]. There is also . . . an insistent, persuasive and mesmerizing salesman.

Source: Moritz (2009).

Case questions 14.2

- What features of the transactional and transformational leader does Jobs display?
- How well do you think they fit the type of staff which the company employs, and the tasks they do?

Activity 14.1   Which traits do employers seek?

- Collect some job advertisements and recruitment brochures. Make a list of the traits that the companies say they are looking for in those they recruit.

| 14.4 | Behavioural models |

Another set of theories sought to identify the behavioural styles of effective managers. What did they do to influence subordinates that less effective managers did not? Scholars at the Universities of Ohio State and Michigan respectively identified two categories of **behaviour**: one concerned with interpersonal relations, the other with accomplishing tasks.

Behaviour is something a person does that can be directly observed.

Ohio State University model

Researchers at Ohio State University (Fleishman, 1953) developed questionnaires that subordinates used to describe the behaviour of their supervisor, and identified two dimensions – 'initiating structure' and 'consideration'.

Initiating structure refers to the degree to which a leader defines peoples' roles, focuses on goal attainment and establishes clear channels of communication. Those using this approach focused on getting the work done – they expected subordinates to follow the rules and made sure they were working to full capacity. Typical behaviours included:

Initiating structure is a pattern of leadership behaviour that emphasises the performance of the work in hand and the achievement of production or service goals.

- Allocating subordinates to specific tasks.
- Establishing standards of job performance.
- Informing subordinates of the requirements of the job.
- Scheduling work to be done by subordinates.
- Encouraging the use of uniform procedures.

Consideration refers to the degree to which a leader shows concern and respect for followers, looks after them and expresses appreciation (Judge *et al.*, 2004). Such leaders assume that subordinates want to work well and try to make it easier for them to do so. They place little reliance on formal position, typical behaviours including:

Consideration is a pattern of leadership behaviour that demonstrates sensitivity to relationships and to the social needs of employees.

- Expressing appreciation for a job well done.
- Not expecting more from subordinates than they can reasonably do.
- Helping subordinates with personal problems.
- Being approachable and available for help.
- Rewarding high performance.

Surveys showed that supervisors displayed distinctive patterns: some scored high on initiating structure and low on consideration, while others were high on consideration and low on initiating structure. Some were high on both, others low on both. Research into the effects on performance were often inconclusive, but a recent review of over 130 such studies (Judge *et al.*, 2004) concluded that there was evidence that consideration tended to be more strongly related to follower satisfaction, while initiating structure was slightly more related to measures of leader performance.

University of Michigan model

Researchers at the University of Michigan (Likert, 1961) conducted similar studies and found that two types of behaviour distinguished effective from ineffective managers: job-centred and employee-centred behaviour.

- **Job-centred supervisors** ensured that they worked on different tasks from their subordinates, concentrating especially on planning, co-ordinating and supplying a range of support activities. These correspond to the initiating structure measures at Ohio.
- **Employee-centred supervisors** combined the task-oriented behaviour with human values. They were considerate, helpful and friendly to subordinates, and engaged in broad supervision rather than detailed observation. These behaviours were similar to what the Ohio group referred to as considerate.

From numerous studies, Likert (1961) concluded that:

Supervisors with the best records of performance focus their primary attention on the human aspects of their subordinates' problems and on endeavouring to build effective work groups with high performance goals. (p. 7)

Managerial grid model

Blake and Mouton (1979) developed the managerial grid model to extend and apply the Ohio State research. Figure 14.4 shows various combinations of concern for production (initiating structure) and concern for people (consideration).

The horizontal scale relates to concern for production, which ranges from 1 (low concern) to 9 (high concern). The vertical scale relates to concern for people, also ranging from 1 (low concern) to 9 (high concern). At the lower left-hand corner (1,1) is the impoverished style: low concern for both production and people. The primary objective of such managers is to stay out of trouble. They merely pass instructions to subordinates, follow the established system, and make sure that no one can blame them if something goes wrong. They do only as much as is consistent with keeping their job.

At the upper left-hand corner (1,9) is the country club style: managers who use this style try to create a secure and comfortable family atmosphere. They assume that their subordinates will respond productively. Thoughtful attention to the need for satisfying relationships leads to a friendly atmosphere and work tempo.

High concern for production and low concern for people is found in the lower right-hand corner (9,1) – the 'produce or perish' style. These managers do not consider subordinates' needs – only the perceived needs of the organisation. They use their formal authority to pressure subordinates into meeting production quotas, believing that efficiency comes from arranging the work so that employees who follow instructions will complete it satisfactorily.

In the centre (5,5) is the middle-of-the-road style. These managers obtain adequate performance by balancing the need to get the work done with reasonable attention to the interests of employees. In the upper right-hand corner (9,9) is the team style which, according to Blake and Mouton (1979), is the most effective approach, aiming for both high performance and high job satisfaction. The manager fosters performance by building relationships of trust and respect.

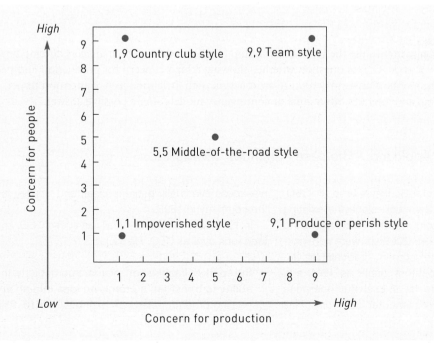

Figure 14.4
The managerial grid

> ### Activity 14.2   Critical reflection on the managerial grid
>
> - Reflect on two managers you have worked with, one effective and one ineffective from your point of view.
> - Which of the positions in the Blake and Mouton (1979) grid most closely describe their style? Note some of their typical behaviours.
> - What were they like to work for? Does your reflection support or contradict the model? If the latter, what may explain that?

Management in practice   Two leaders' styles

Jeroen Van der Veer, CEO of Shell

'Good leadership . . . means being clear about what is weak and what is strong, and where you want to go in the longer term, and having the ability to put it into clear words. The best way for a leader to take a company forward is to have some very simple words about how you would like to change it and the culture of the company'

Source: *Financial Times*, 2 February 2007, p. 19.

Kwon Young-Soo, chief executive of LG Philips LCD

The company is the world's second largest flat panel maker, and Mr Young-Soo believes it will thrive on argument:

The era for authoritarian management is gone. When I make a proposal, I want my staff to say 'no' when it does not make sense.

Although the company is a joint venture, its culture, like that of many Korean companies, was based on strict hierarchical structures, reflecting Confucian values. While rising through the ranks of the company he became acutely aware of the importance of internal communication, and since taking over as CEO has encouraged more open exchange of ideas.

Source: *Financial Times*, 10 September 2007.

Many trainers use the Blake and Mouton (1979) model to help managers develop towards the '9,9' style. Others question whether showing a high concern for production and people always works: a crisis may require swift action with little time to pay attention to personal feelings and interests. Situational or contingency models offer a possible answer.

Case study   Apple Inc. – the case continues   www.apple.com

In the early years of John Sculley's time as CEO, Apple appeared to perform well, since the existing products were being sold into the rapidly growing personal computer market. But there were no significant innovations and the company gradually fell victim to stronger competitors such as IBM and Microsoft, which made its successful operating system available to any computer company. This weakness eventually became clear, and Sculley left the company in 1993.

In 1997 Jobs re-joined, initially as acting CEO, and then took over as CEO. He found:

the spark of imagination, or, more particularly, the ability to transform a promising idea into an appealing product, had been extinguished. (p. 331)

The Apple he inherited in 1997 had lost its creative zest and leadership position in the technology industry, was almost out of cash, was unable to recruit bright young engineers, was drowning in inventory of unsold computers, and had nothing imaginative in the works. (p. 35)

An early advertising campaign ('think different') was an expression of the artistic, sensuous, romantic, mystical, inquisitive, seductive, austere and theatrical side of Jobs . . . attributes that eventually came to be expressed in Apple's products, which Jobs turned into objects of desire . . . It also said that the company needed to forge its own path.

He forced the company to act differently, cutting costs, making many staff redundant, and scrapping product lines he deemed worthless or undistinguished. He brought in new senior managers whom he had worked with, and replaced the increasingly dysfunctional board – which Sculley and his successors had built – with practical members whom he could trust.

Source: extracts from Moritz (2009), pp. 331–336.

Case questions 14.3

- The traits which are part of Steve Jobs personality are becoming clear in the case. If they work in Apple, will they work elsewhere?
- We know nothing directly about Sculley's traits – but whatever they were, did they work better for him at Pepsi-Cola than at Apple?

14.5 | Situational (or contingency) models

Situational (contingency) models present the idea that managers influence others by adapting their style to the circumstances. Three such models are set out below (a fourth, developed by Vroom and Yetton (1973) featured in Chapter 7).

> **Situational (contingency) models** of leadership attempt to identify the contextual factors that affect when one style will be more effective than another.

Tannenbaum and Schmidt's continuum of leader behaviour

Unlike the 'one best way' model implied by the behavioural models, Robert Tannenbaum and Warren Schmidt (1973) saw that leaders worked in different ways, which they presented as a continuum of styles, ranging from autocratic to democratic. Figure 14.5 illustrates these extremes and the positions in between. Which of these the leader uses should reflect three forces:

- **Forces in the manager:** personality, values, preferences, beliefs about participation and confidence in subordinates.
- **Forces in subordinates:** need for independence, tolerance of ambiguity, knowledge of the problem, expectations of involvement.
- **Forces in the situation:** organisational norms, size and location of work groups, effectiveness of team working, nature of the problem.

House's path–goal model

House (House and Mitchell, 1974; House, 1996) believed that effective leaders clarify subordinates' paths towards achieving rewards which they value – by, for example, helping them identify and learn behaviours that will assist them to perform well, and so secure the rewards. House identifies four styles of leader behaviour:

- **Directive:** letting subordinates know what the leader expects; giving specific guidance; asking subordinates to follow rules and procedures; scheduling and co ordinating their work.

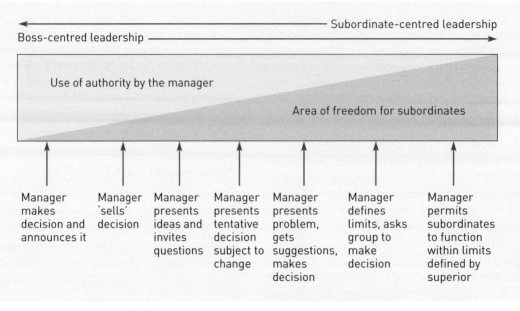

Figure 14.5 The Tannenbaum–Schmidt continuum of leadership behaviour

- **Supportive:** treating them as equals; showing concern for their needs and welfare; creating a friendly climate in the work unit.
- **Achievement oriented:** setting challenging goals and targets; seeking performance improvements; emphasising excellence in performance; expecting subordinates to succeed.
- **Participative:** consulting subordinates; taking their opinions into account.

House suggested that the appropriate style would depend on the situation; the characteristics of the subordinate and the work environment. For example, if a subordinate has little confidence or skill then the leader needs to provide coaching and other support. If the subordinate likes clear direction he/she will respond best to a leader who gives it. Most skilled professionals expect to use their initiative and resent a directive style: they will respond best to a participative or achievement-oriented leader. The work environment includes the degree of task structure (routine or non-routine), the formal authority system (extent of rules and procedures) and the work group characteristics (quality of teamwork).

Figure 14.6 summarises the model which predicts, for example, that:

- a directive style works best when the task is ambiguous and the subordinates lack flexibility – the leader absorbs the uncertainty and shows them how to do the task;
- a supportive style works best in repetitive, frustrating or physically unpleasant tasks – subordinates respect the leader who joins in and helps;
- an achievement-oriented style works best when the group faces non-repetitive ambiguous tasks, which will challenge their ability – they need encouragement and pressure to raise their ambitions;
- a participative approach works best when the task is non-repetitive and the subordinate(s) are confident that they can do the work.

Contingency models indicate that participative leadership is not always effective and that, as Table 14.3 shows, a directive style is sometimes appropriate.

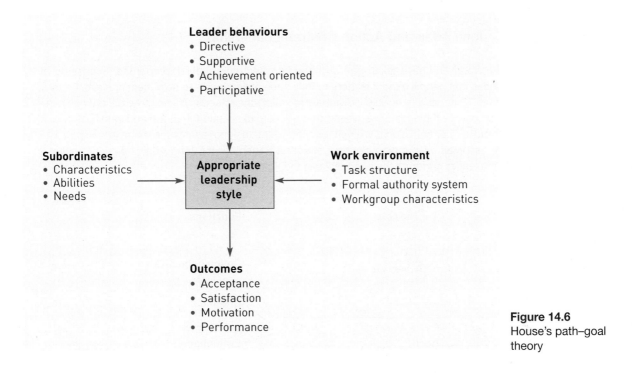

Leader behaviours
- Directive
- Supportive
- Achievement oriented
- Participative

Subordinates
- Characteristics
- Abilities
- Needs

Appropriate leadership style

Work environment
- Task structure
- Formal authority system
- Workgroup characteristics

Outcomes
- Acceptance
- Satisfaction
- Motivation
- Performance

Figure 14.6
House's path–goal theory

Table 14.3 Conditions favouring participative or directive styles

Participative style most likely to work when:	Directive style most likely to work when:
Subordinates' acceptance of the decision is important	Subordinates do not share the manager's objectives
The manager lacks information	Time is short
The problem is unclear	Subordinates accept top-down decisions

Management in practice   Helmut Panke, chief executive of BMW   www.bmw.com

Helmut Panke became CEO of Bavarian Motor Works (BMW) in 2002, since when he has overseen a rapid expansion of the model range. Sales, and the company's share price, have risen strongly in the two years since he took charge of the company. Panke demands top performance from staff, and from himself. He first demonstrated his skills at building BMW's global business as head of North American operations in the mid-1990s, during which time the US became BMW's largest market.

Panke's management style could be called Socratic. He loves to pose questions and lead debates with groups of managers – a practice that reflects his academic training (he has a doctorate in nuclear physics) and gets results . . . By encouraging debate, Panke has forged a performance-driven culture that isn't afraid to send tough questions up the ranks. 'Panke takes a huge amount of time to discuss with people, then he lets them manage on their own. That way he gets 120% from everyone', says a manager who has seen Panke rise up the ranks over 20 years . . . 'My biggest challenge is saying "no" to projects that are exciting but don't fit BMW's strategy', comments Panke. (p. 48)

Source: *Business Week*, 7 June 2004.

John Adair and Action Centred Leadership

Over 2 million people worldwide have taken part in the Action Centred Leadership approach pioneered by John Adair. He proposes that people expect leaders to fulfil three obligations – to help them achieve the task, to build and maintain the team and to enable individuals to satisfy their needs. These three obligations over-lap and influence each other – if the task is achieved that will help to sustain the group and satisfy individual needs. If the group lacks skill or cohesion it will neither achieve the task nor satisfy the members. Figure 14.7 represents the three needs as overlapping circles – almost a trademark for John Adair's work. To achieve these expectations the leader performs the eight tasks in the figure.

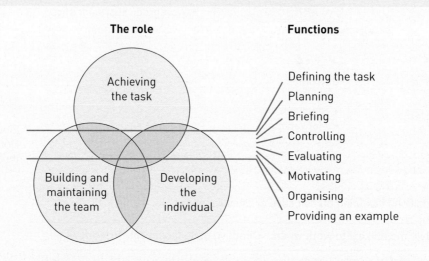

Figure 14.7 Adair's model of leadership functions

Source: *Leadership skills*, CIPD (Adair, J. 1997, p. 21) with the permission of the publisher, the Chartered Institute of Personnel and Development, London (www.cipd.co.uk).

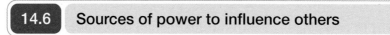

14.6 Sources of power to influence others

Power is 'the capacity of individuals to exert their will over others' (Buchanan and Badham, 1999).

Earlier sections have shown that people use personal skills to influence others, including their ability to adapt their methods to the situation. Another perspective is that people use **power** to influence others.

Sources of power

What are the bases of one person's power over another? French and Raven's (1959) widely quoted classification identifies five sources:

- **Legitimate power** flows from the person's formal position in the organisation. The job they hold gives them the power, for example, to make capital expenditures, offer overtime, choose a supplier or recruit staff.
- **Reward power** is the ability to reward another if they comply with a request or instruction. The reward can take many forms – pay, time off or interesting work.
- **Coercive power** is the ability to obtain compliance through fear of punishment or harm. It includes reprimands, demotions, threats, bullying language or a powerful physical presence.

Table 14.4 Personal and positional sources of power

Power resource	Personal	Positional
Coercive	Forcefulness, insistence, determination	Authority to give instructions, with the threat of sanctions or punishment available
Reward	Credit for previous or future favours in daily exchanges	Authority to use organisational resources, including the support of senior people
Expertise		
Administrative	Experience of the business, whom to contact, how to get things done	Authority to use or create organisational policies or rules
Technical	Skill or expertise relevant to the task	Authority to access expertise, information and ideas across the business
Referent	Individual beliefs, values, ideas, personal qualities	Authority to invoke norms and values of the organisational culture

Source: Based on Hales (2001).

- **Referent power**, also called *charismatic* power, is when some characteristics in a person are attractive to others: they identify with them, which gives the charismatic person power.
- **Expertise power** is when people acknowledge someone's knowledge and are therefore willing to follow his/her suggestions. This knowledge or skill may be *administrative* (how an organisation operates) or *technical* (how to do a task).

Table 14.4 develops the French and Raven list, by showing that each type of power can have both a personal and a positional source. The most significant change to the French and Raven model is to show that referent (charismatic) power is not just personal but can also have a positional source (Hales, 2001). Chapter 3 shows how organisations develop distinctive cultures and sub-cultures. When people refer to the prevailing culture in an attempt to influence behaviour ('what I'm asking fits the culture') they are drawing on a positional form of referent power.

Someone who has little access to these sources of power will have less influence than someone with much access. People continually defend their power sources and try to gain new ones.

Perceptions of power

Power is only effective if the target of an influence attempt recognises the power source as legitimate and acceptable. If they dispute the knowledge base of a manager, or challenge his/her positional authority over a matter, the influence attempt is likely to fail. A project manager in an IT company reported how in one project she was leading a team of 40 change agents, who worked for about one day a week on her project, and for their line manager for the rest of the time. Some line managers did not agree with their staff being used on this project, and influenced some of them by using coercive and reward power to keep them full-time on their line job. The project manager retaliated by using her influencing skills to persuade senior managers to alter the pay system slightly, so that the annual review for each employee now included an item related to the contribution they had made to the change project. This reduced the reward power of line managers, who caused less trouble (private communication). Managers who are successful influencers (like this project manager) ensure that they sustain their power sources and take every opportunity to enhance them (see the following Management in Practice).

In a questionnaire study of 250 managers, David Buchanan (2008) found that most believed it was ethical and necessary to engage in political behaviour at work. They worked at (mainly) middle and senior levels in public and private organisations. Respondents saw five frequent behaviours:

- building a network of useful contacts;
- using 'key players' to support initiatives;
- making friends with power brokers;
- bending the rules to fit the situation; and
- self-promotion.

They were also asked if they saw politics as a useful tool to improve organisational effectiveness:

- 60 per cent agreed that 'politics becomes more important as organisational change becomes more complex';
- 79 per cent agreed that 'politics can be used to initiate and drive useful change initiatives'; and
- 81 per cent agreed that 'political tactics can be effective in dealing with resistance to change'.

They believed that political skills helped careers:

- 90 per cent agreed that 'managers who play organisation politics well can improve their career prospects'.

Management in practice   Marketing brand Me

People should manage their reputation like a brand. The most effective candidates [for promotion] do not leave their image to chance. They work at it, and massage its growth. They know that the best publicists they can have are their immediate staff. They are aware that team members talk about them more than anyone else. So they provide evidence to feed that grapevine – Staff need stories about their leader.

Another way to manage your reputation is to manage your boss . . . People keen to manage their reputation should find out what motivates the boss and try to satisfy those goals. If your boss likes punctuality and conscientiousness, turn up on time and work hard. If he or she needs reassurance, give it. If it is power, respond as someone who is less powerful. Why irritate a person who can influence your career path?

Source: John Hunt, 'Marketing brand Me', *Financial Times*, 22 December 2000.

Activity 14.3   Critical reflection on sources of power

- Try to identify at least one example of each of the personal and positional power sources. Examples could come from observing a manager in action (including people in your university or college) or from your reading of current business affairs.
- Can you identify what the person concerned has done to develop his/her power?
- Have other events helped to build or undermine his/her power?

Case questions 14.4

- Which of the sources of power in Table 14.5 has Steve Jobs used?
- What has he done to increase his power in the eyes of those he is trying to influence?
- What other forms of authority has he acquired?
- Which of the sources of power in Table 14.5 could staff use?

14.7   Using positional power to influence others

Those who want to be effective influencers can increase their chances of doing so by building up those sources of power that come from their position within the organisation. Kanter (1979) observed that people are more likely to be influenced by strong and powerful managers than by weak and isolated ones. She identified many ways in which a manager's position in the organisation affects his/her power, such as:

- Approvals needed for non-routine decisions (fewer approvals mean more power).
- Relation of job to current organisational priorities (central relation means more power).
- External contact (more opportunities for this mean more power).
- Senior contact (more opportunities for this mean more power).

The nature of the job and the pattern of contacts that come with it give the manager access to three 'lines of power':

- **Supply**: money and other resources that can be used to bestow status or rewards on others in return for their support.
- **Information**: being in the know, aware of what is happening, familiar with plans and opportunities that are in the making.
- **Support**: able to get senior or external backing for what he/she wants to do.

The more of these lines of power the manager has, the more will subordinates co-operate. They do so because they believe that the manager has the power to engage in **political behaviour** and make things happen: they have 'clout' – weight or political influence in the organisation. A person's position in the organisation gives them access to the sources of power shown in Table 14.5.

> **Political behaviour** is 'the practical domain of power in action, worked out through the use of techniques of influence and other (more or less extreme) tactics' (Buchanan and Badham, 1999).

Coercive

This is the ability to give instructions or threaten penalties, derived from a person's formal position in the hierarchy. Kramer (2006) observed how 'Great Intimidators' work – often achieving great success, at other times failing badly. Their tactics included:

- getting up close and personal – being directly confrontational, often using aggressive behaviour and language;
- being angry – often using a calculated loss of temper to strike fear into their opponent;
- keeping them guessing – revealing as little as possible about their plans, to increase opponents' anxiety;
- know it all – extensive preparation to be able to dominate any discussion. This includes being aware of weaknesses in the opponent's history or character.

Reward

This is the ability that position gives to use the financial and other resources of the organisation in return for support. Managers with large budgets and valuable networks of contacts use these resources, or the promise of them, to exert influence. Managers who choose to be remote and isolated in back-room work will not have that power – and so will have little influence on people or events.

Expertise

Administrative expertise

This is the power that the holder of a position has to create formal policies which support their influence attempts. They can create rules, procedures or positions that sustain their power – especially if they can also appoint loyal supporters, or those in their debt, to those positions. In this way they encourage others to act in the way they prefer.

> **Key ideas** **Sir John Harvey-Jones's leadership at ICI**
>
> In a classic study of ICI under Sir John Harvey-Jones, Pettigrew traced the link between the leadership of the company and the change process. Sir John implemented fundamental changes in what was then a very large company, but Pettigrew shows he did not achieve this by a few dramatic acts or decisions. Rather it depended on actions he took over many years to change the structure of the organisation so that managers had more access to sources of power with which to influence others to make radical change. For example, greater power was given to divisional directors to reward staff according to their performance.
>
> Pettigrew concluded that studies of leadership should not focus only on the actions of individuals, important though they are. Rather they should view leadership within a context. The leader exerts influence by shaping that context and providing others with positional power to initiate change.
>
> Source: Pettigrew (1985, 1987).

> **Management in practice** **Too much internal focus**
>
> A department of a local authority consisted of a director, two senior officers, three officers and 14 staff. The director's style was to involve himself in operational matters, and he rarely worked with other senior managers. He normally met only the senior officers in his department and rarely involved others, believing that officers should not be involved in policy. He saw himself as the only competent person in the department and was comfortable in this operational role.
>
> Staff consider themselves to be capable and professional. They expect to be involved more fully and are used to taking initiatives. The director's involvement in operational detail annoyed staff as it showed that he did not trust their abilities. They were even more annoyed at the low status of their department, due to the director not being active externally and so lacking influence outside the department.
>
> Source: Private communication to the author.

Technical expertise

This is the power a person gains from holding a position that gives them access to information, of being in the know, aware of what is happening and of opportunities that are emerging. They can use their position, and the contacts that go with it, to build their image as a competent person. This credibility adds to their power to influence others. It is a contentious area, since people compete for access to information, and the power that goes with it – as the 'flowering of feudalism' feature indicates.

Referent

This is where managers use their position to influence others by showing that what they propose is consistent with the accepted values and culture of the organisation. They invoke wider values in support of their proposal. The effectiveness of the influence attempt depends on the other people having a similar view of the culture.

The more of these sources of power the manager has, the more others will co-operate. They do so because they believe that the manager has the power to make things happen. Such a manager has weight or political influence, which encourages others to co-operate.

Delegation occurs when one person gives another the authority to undertake specific activities or decisions.

'To increase power, share it'

Kanter (1979) also proposed that managers can increase their power by, paradoxically, **delegating** some of it to subordinates. As subordinates carry out tasks previously done by the manager, he/she has more time to build the external and senior contacts – which further boost power. By delegating not only tasks but also lines of supply (giving subordinates a generous budget), lines of information (inviting them to high-level meetings) and lines of support (giving visible encouragement), managers develop subordinates' confidence, and at the same time enhance their own power. They can spend more time on external matters, making contacts, keeping in touch with what is happening, and so building their visibility and reputation. A manager who fails to delegate, and who looks inward rather than outward, becomes increasingly isolated.

Case study Apple Inc. – the case continues www.apple.com

By 2001 Apple was still in trouble, and losing money: the technology bubble of the 1990s had burst, and the world economy was in recession. Apple had to fend for itself to survive – and the first example of this determination was the iPod – which went from conception to being on the shelves in eight months.

In the same year Apple opened its first retail store – an unusual move as there were few examples of manufacturer's becoming successful retailers. Both the iPod and the stores were popular – and the company's management saw that their bold gambles were likely to pay off. They increased the pace at which they released iPod variants, and pushed forward with opening more stores, so that they reached $1 billion in sales faster than any other company.

The iPhone began with a few people trying to design a product they would want to use and be proud to own. This involved analysing the weaknesses of other products and adapting ideas from them to create another distinctive Apple product. Moritz (2009) writes:

> Jobs achievement . . . was to ensure that technology company employing tens of thousands of people could make and sell millions of immensely complicated yet exquisite products that were powerful and reliable, while also containing a lightness of being . . . [the achievement] is to steer, coax, nudge, prod, cajole, inspire, berate, organise and praise, – on weekdays and at weekends – the thousands of people all around

the world required to produce something that drops into pockets and handbags or . . . rests on a lap or sits on a desk. (pp. 339–340)

Apple is vertically integrated, designing its own operating system, software and hardware, and selling products through Apple stores. It invests heavily in research and development, and in marketing and advertising, to extend market position.

It has also been effective in identifying other companies whose products it can use, and either buying them or creating joint ventures. An example was its purchase of PA Semi in April 2008, which meant that it can closely control the way a processor chip is built. Its designers, led by the Briton, Jonathan Ive, are known for their fastidious approach and their secrecy.

The company has tight control over the retailing end of the business – the Apple network of dealers and its own Apple Stores ensure that the image of the brand is closely dovetailed with the products themselves.

Source: Moritz (2009).

Case question 14.5

- What sources of power have people used in the case and how have they helped the company?

14.8   Choosing tactics to influence others

Another approach to the study of influence has been to identify directly how managers try to influence others. An early example of this was work by Kipnis *et al.* (1980), who identified a set of influencing tactics that managers used in dealing with subordinates, bosses and co-workers. Yukl and Falbe (1990) replicated this work in a wider empirical study, and refined the categories (shown in Table 14.5).

Table 14.5 Influence tactics and definitions

Tactic	Definition
Rational persuasion	The person uses logical arguments and factual evidence to persuade you that a proposal or request is viable and likely to result in the attainment of task objectives
Inspirational appeal	The person makes a request or proposal that arouses enthusiasm by appealing to your values, ideals and aspirations or by increasing your confidence that you can do it
Consultation	The person seeks your participation in planning a strategy, activity or change for which your support and assistance are desired, or the person is willing to modify a proposal to deal with your concerns and suggestions
Ingratiation	The person seeks to get you in a good mood or to think favourably of him/her before asking you to do something
Exchange	The person offers an exchange of favours, indicates a willingness to reciprocate at a later time, or promises you a share of the benefits if you help accomplish the task
Personal appeal	The person appeals to your feelings of loyalty and friendship towards him/her before asking you to do something
Coalition	The person seeks the aid of others to persuade you to do something, or uses the support of others as a reason for you to agree also
Legitimating	The person seeks to establish the legitimacy of a request by claiming the authority or right to make it or by verifying that it is consistent with organisational policies, rules, practices or traditions
Pressure	The person uses demands, threats or persistent reminders to influence you to do what he or she wants

Source: Based on Yukl and Falbe (1990).

The nine tactics cover a variety of behaviours that people can use as they try to influence others – whether subordinates, bosses or colleagues.

Management in practice	Power balances in a charity

I worked for a charity providing advice to small companies in the Middle East. I was newly appointed, and wanted to run some of our courses through two of the business organisations in the region, as this was both fair and would give better results. One of my team members went behind my back, and told one of the organisations that we would only run the courses through them. She also persuaded our chief executive (CEO) that this was the best thing to do: I had no choice but to adhere to the decision.

Being new, almost the only influence tactic I could use with the CEO was *rational persuasion*. The other person had worked there for several years, and had developed close relations with the CEO, and was able to combine *exchange, personal appeal* and perhaps *pressure* to get her way.

Thinking back, and having read Yukl and Falbe's ideas, I realise I could have tried other tactics, such as *coalition* (persuading other team members of the benefits of my view) and *pressure* (threatening not to run the project: this could have worked, because I was the only person there who spoke the local language).

Source: Private communication from the project manager.

Yukl and Tracey (1992) extended the work by examining which tactics managers used most frequently with different target groups. They concluded that managers were most likely to use:

- rational persuasion when trying to influence their boss;
- inspirational appeal and pressure when trying to influence subordinates;
- exchange, personal appeal and legitimating tactics when influencing colleagues.

14.9 Influencing through networks

An important way to influence others is the ability to draw on a network of informal relationships. Networking refers to 'individuals' attempts to develop and maintain relationships with others [who] have the potential to assist them in their work or career' (Huczynski, 2004, p. 305). Table 14.6 shows several types of network.

The ability to influence can be greatly enhanced by being connected to many such networks, giving access to contacts and information. They help people to know what is happening in their business and to extend their range of contacts in other organisations. Strong anecdotal evidence that networking influences career progression was supported by Luthans' (1988) research described in Chapter 1, which showed that people who spent a relatively large amount of time networking received more rapid promotion than those who did not. As Thomas (2003) observed: 'in management what you know and what you have achieved will seldom be sufficient for getting ahead. Knowing and being known in the networks of influence, both for what you have achieved and for who you are may be essential'.

Key ideas   Art Kleiner and Core Groups

Kleiner suggests that organisations, despite the rhetoric about customers and stakeholders, exist to serve the interests of what he calls their Core Group – 'the people who really matter'. The nature of the Core Group varies from place to place – sometimes concentrated among senior managers, at others widely dispersed – but every organisation is continually acting to fulfil the perceived needs and priorities of its Core Group – the organisation goes wherever people 'perceive the core group needs and wants to go' (p. 8). 'If we are going to act effectively in a society of organizations, we need a theory to help us see organizations clearly, as they are' (p. 6).

Source: Kleiner (2003).

Table 14.6 Types of network

Practitioners	Joined by people with a common training or professional interest, and may be formal or informal
Privileged power	Joined by people in powerful positions (usually by invitation only)
Ideological	Consisting of people keen to promote political objectives or values
People-oriented	Formed around shared feelings of personal warmth and familiarity – friendship groups which people join on the basis of identity with existing participants
Strategic	Often built to help develop links with people in other organisations

Kotter (1982) observed that general managers rely heavily on informal networks of contacts to get things done. This is especially necessary to influence those in other organisations – to make a sale, to gain access to a country's market or to set up a joint venture – although as Anand and Conger (2007) found, few people have the abilities required to be fully effective networkers. Hillman (2005) showed how senior managers increase their influence over the business environment by appointing ex-politicians to their Boards of Directors. Government policy and regulations are a major source of uncertainty in some industries, and one way to reduce that is to build close links with politicians and others with access to or influence over the government process. She found that firms in heavily regulated industries did indeed have more directors with political experience, and that firms with politicians on their Board were associated with better financial performance, especially in the heavily regulated industries.

Management in practice   Influence in China and Taiwan

Star TV (a subsidiary of Rupert Murdoch's News Corporation) developed close links with the Chinese authorities, in the hope of expanding the delivery of its entertainment channel on Chinese TV. This paid off in 2003, when it became the first foreign-owned company to receive permission for a limited nationwide service.

'Everything in China is about relationships and mutual benefit', said Jamie Davis, head of Star TV in China. 'I think Rupert Murdoch has a very good relationship with the Chinese Government . . . and we work hard at it.'

Source: *Financial Times*, 9 January 2003.

The sudden elevation of Ho-chen Tan to the top job at Chunghwa Telecom last month was demonstration of the value of having friends in high places. He was in charge of transport in Taipei in the mid-1990s, when the Taiwanese President, Chen Shui-bian, was mayor of the city. Mr Ho-chen says his contacts in the administration will help Chunghwa to win a voice in how the government handles the company's privatization: 'I hope our company can win the right to make suggestions. Perhaps my network in the current government and the faith put in me will help the company to get more opportunities.'

Source: *Financial Times*, 21 February 2003.

Most people in organisations need to use other forms of influence, and Sparrowe and Liden (2005) note that informal networks are probably becoming more important as a means of influencing others:

As traditional hierarchical structures have given way to flatter and more flexible forms, informal networks have become even more important in gaining access to valuable information, resources, and opportunities. The structure and composition of an individual's network allows him or her to identify strategic opportunities, marshal resources, assemble teams and win support for innovative projects . . . Individuals who hold central positions in informal advice networks enjoy greater influence than those in peripheral positions . . . and receive more favorable performance ratings (Sparrowe *et al.*; 2001). (p. 505)

Whichever methods are used, the outcome of an influence attempt will depend not only on the tactics used but on how well the influencer is able to meet the needs of the person they are influencing (see Chapter 15).

14.10 Integrating themes

Sustainable performance

Managers wishing to encourage more sustainable performance within their organisation will be engaging on a process of influence – and to achieve their aims they will need to use both interpersonal and structural techniques ways of influencing others. They will need to gain the support of those above them in the organisation, as well as of other possibly significant stakeholders over whom they have no formal authority – customers, suppliers, bankers and so on. They are likely to meet opposition or indifference from some, as well as enthusiastic support from others – and it is unlikely that, in terms of the Yukl and Falbe (2002) model, they will win the case by rational arguments alone.

They are likely to need to use a range of interpersonal and political strategies, articulated through a suitable combination of tactics. The methods used at the Eden Project may be instructive (see the following Management in Practice).

Management in practice   How people at Eden try to influence www.edenproject.com

The Eden Project (Chapter 15 Case) aims to help people to re-connect with the natural environment, and Tim Smit (co-founder and chief executive) explains their approach:

We're facing the most incredible challenges over the next 30 years, and I think that's why Eden is so important because to persuade people to change you can't do that with that waggy finger of sanctimony. The only way do to it is to write a story in which people see a better future coming up if we act in a different way: that's been a big weakness of the environment movement in that they get into arguments between themselves about arcane things, and they just leave the general public behind. So I think this storytelling side is vital and that's what we do best. The very creation of Eden is a story. I think we stand for something that makes other people believe in themselves and do stuff – that would be the greatest tribute you could ever pay us if that's what we could achieve.

Source: Interview with Tim Smit.

Governance and control

Corporate governance has become more prominent in response to recent financial scandals, which have shown that investors take a risk when they entrust their wealth to professional managers, since the latter may manage the business in their personal interest, rather than those of the shareholders.

Mechanisms of corporate governance are the balance against this (Chapter 3, Section 3.7), whereby investors can try to ensure that managers act in the interests of investors. The theory is that institutional investors (especially) can use their power (either in their votes at shareholder meetings, or by influencing the media) to force companies to reform their governance arrangements. This might advocate changes to the structure and composition of Boards to make them more independent of management, or to the way executive pay is decided.

Westphal and Bednar (2008) show that CEOs are not passive in the face of these potentially threatening moves by shareholders. Their survey of some 400 companies shows that CEOs actively used persuasion and ingratiation tactics to deter representatives of institutional investors from using their power to obstruct CEOs' interests. These attempts at influence were generally effective. They note that although institutional investors have the power to impose governance changes, such changes have been adopted slowly. They claim that part of the reason for that is because CEOs have been able, by using some of the Yukl and Falbe (1990) influence tactics, to deter shareholders from using their power to influence governance systems.

Internationalisation

The ability to manage internationally depends on being able to influence others in culturally mixed circumstances, where influence tactics that work in one place may be ineffective in another. Cross-cultural studies have found that cultural values (Chapter 4) affect the preferred influence tactics. For example, Fu and Yukl (2000) found that Chinese managers rated coalition formation, giving gifts and favours, and personal appeals as more effective, and rational persuasion, consultation, and exchange, as less effective, than American managers. The authors noted that these preferences for influencing tactics were consistent with their respective cultural values: for the Chinese with their values of collectivism, feminism and a long-term orientation, and for the Americans with their values of equality, direct confrontation and pragmatism.

There is also evidence that styles of leadership vary between countries. Shao and Webber (2006) found that certain of 'the big five' personality traits associated with transformational leadership behaviour in North America are not evident in China. They attributed this to differences in the prevailing cultures:

> The Chinese culture, characterized as high power distance, high uncertainty avoidance and collectivism, fundamentally reinforces the hierarchical and conformist attributes of the top-down command structure. This structure emphasizes a centralized authority and leadership, stability and predictability, which create barriers for the emergence of transformational leaders, who tend to challenge the status quo and raise performance expectations. (p. 943)

Summary

1 **Distinguish leading from managing, and explain why each is essential to performance**
   - Although both are essential and the difference can be overstated, leading is usually seen as referring to activities that bring change, whereas managing brings stability and order. Many people both lead and manage in the course of their work.

2 **Explain why leading and managing both depend on being able to influence others**
   - Achieving objectives usually depends on the willing commitment of other people. How management seeks to influence others affects people's reaction to being managed. Dominant use of power may ensure compliance, but such an approach is unlikely to produce the commitment required to meet innovative objectives.

3 **Compare trait, behavioural and contingency perspectives on styles of influence**
   - Trait theories seek to identify the personal characteristics associated with effective influencing.
   - Behavioural theories distinguish managers' behaviours on two dimensions, such as initiating structure and consideration.
   - Contingency perspectives argue that the traits or behaviours required for effective influence depend on factors in the situation, such as the characteristics of the employee, the boss and the task.

4 **Outline theories that focus on power (both personal and organisational) as the source of influence**
   - The more power a person has, the more he/she will be able to influence others. Table 14.5 identifies sources of power as coercion, reward, expertise (administrative

and technical) and referent – all of which can have both personal and organisational dimensions.

5 **Contrast the style and power perspectives, and explain why sharing power may increase them**

- Sharing power with subordinates may not only enable them to have more satisfying and rewarding work but, by enabling the manager to have more time to develop senior and external contacts, he/she can then enhance his/her power more than if he/she focused on internal matters.

6 **Outline a model of the tactics that people use to influence others, including the use of co-operative networks**

- Yukl and Falbe have identified these tactics in attempts to influence others: rational persuasion, inspirational appeal, consultation, ingratiation, exchange, personal appeal, coalition, legitimating and pressure. They have also found that effective influencers vary their tactics depending on the person they are trying to influence. A further line of research identifies the value of building collaborative networks as part of effective influencing.

7 **Show how ideas from the chapter add to your understanding of the integrating themes**

- Proposals to achieve more sustainable performance depend on managers being able to influence others – over whom they will usually have no formal authority. Like any organisational change, sustainability projects will sometimes meet opposition: so managers or others promoting change will need to use a variety of influencing tactics to achieve their objectives (including methods used in marketing).
- Governance and control systems are intended to influence the behaviour of chief executives and senior managers to act in the interests of shareholders. As with most interactions between managers and their context, chief executives do not passively accept such constraints, and the section included evidence of chief executives actively lobbying to obstruct proposals which the chief executives thought were against their interests.
- There is accumulating evidence that cultural values affect the influencing tactics used in different countries, and that leadership styles vary between countries.

Review questions

1 Why is the ability to influence others so central to the management role?

2 What evidence is there that traits theories continue to influence management practice?

3 What are the strengths and weaknesses of the behavioural approaches to leadership?

4 What is meant by the phrase a '9,9 manager'?

5 Discuss with someone how he/she tries to influence people (or reflect on your own practice). Compare this evidence with one of the contingency theory approaches.

6 Evaluate that theory in the light of the evidence acquired in review question 5 and other considerations.

7 Explain in your own words the main sources of power available to managers. Give examples of both personal and institutional forms of each.

8 List the lines of power that Kanter identifies and give an example of each.

9 What does the network perspective imply for someone wishing to be a successful influencer?

10 Summarise an idea from the chapter that adds to your understanding of the integrating themes.

Concluding critical reflection

Think about the ways in which you typically seek to influence others, and about how others in your company try to exert influence. Review the material in the chapter, and then make notes on the following questions:

- What examples of the issues discussed in this chapter struck you as being relevant to practice in your company?

- Thinking of the people you typically work with, who are effective and who are less effective influencers? What do the effective people do that enables them to get their way? What interpersonal skills do they use? What sources of power, or what networks, do they use? Do the prevailing **assumptions** fit with Kanter's view that 'to increase power, share it'? On balance, do their assumptions accurately reflect the reality you see?

- What factors in the **context** – including the history of the company or your personal experience – have shaped the way you manage your attempts at influencing? Does your current approach appear to be right for your present position and company – or would you use a different approach in other circumstances? (Perhaps refer to some of the Management in Practices for how different managers exert influence.)

- Have people put forward **alternative** approaches to influencing, based on evidence about other companies? If you could find such evidence, how may it affect company practice?

- How do you and your colleagues react to Steve Jobs' approach to influencing others, which appears to have helped create a successful, profitable business? What **limitations** can you see in it?

Further reading

Buchanan, D. and Badham, R. (1999), *Power, Politics and Organizational Change: Winning the turf game*, Sage, London.

> A modern approach to politics in organisations, offering a theoretical and practical guide, based on extensive primary research.

Huczynski, A.A. (2004), *Influencing Within Organizations* (2nd edn), Routledge, London.

> Draws on a wide range of academic research to provide a practical guide to influencing – from how to conduct yourself at a job interview to coping with organisational politics.

Kleiner, A. (2003), *Who Really Matters: The core group theory of power, privilege and success*, Doubleday, New York.

> Absorbing perspective of the realities of corporate power, with many practical implications for career planning.

Pedler, M., Burgoyne, J. and Boydell, T. (2004), *A Manager's Guide to Leadership*, McGraw-Hill, Maidenhead.

> A highly practical book, based on the philosophy that leadership is defined by what people do when faced with challenging situations. The authors use their well-established self-development approach to encourage readers to act on situations requiring leadership, and then to reflect and learn from the experience.

Yukl, G.A. (2004), *Leadership in Organizations* (6th edn), Prentice Hall, Upper Saddle River, NJ.

> Combines a comprehensive review of academic research on all aspects of organisational leadership with clear guidance on the implications for practitioners.

Weblinks

Visit these websites (or others of similar companies of which you learn):

www.oticon.com
www.gore.com
www.apple.com
www.bmw.com
www.edenproject.com

Each of these organisations has tried to develop new approaches to managing and influencing staff, and have, despite some difficult circumstances, survived and prospered. They are still quite rare, as relatively few entrepreneurs have successfully followed their example.

- Use the House model to analyse what conditions may explain their success.

- Why do you think so few others have adopted the same approach?

 For video case studies, audio summaries, flashcards, exercises and annotated weblinks related to this chapter, visit **www.pearsoned.co.uk/mymanagementlab**

CHAPTER 15
MOTIVATION

Aim

To examine theories of behaviour at work and to connect them with management practice.

Objectives

By the end of your work on this chapter you should be able to outline the concepts below in your own terms and:

1 Explain why managers need to understand and use theories of motivation

2 Give examples showing how the context, including the psychological contract, affects motivation

3 Compare behaviour modification, content and process theories

4 Use expectancy theory and work design theories to diagnose motivational problems and recommend actions

5 Show how ideas on motivation link to those on strategy

6 Show how ideas from the chapter add to your understanding of the integrating themes.

Key terms

This chapter introduces the following ideas:

motivation	subjective probability
psychological contract	instrumentality
perception	valence
behaviour modification	equity theory
existence needs	goal-setting theory
relatedness needs	self-efficacy
growth needs	intrinsic rewards
motivator factors	extrinsic rewards
hygiene factors	job characteristics theory
expectancy theory	

Each is a term defined within the text, as well as in the Glossary at the end of the book.

The Eden Project is one of the most visited attractions in Europe: over 10 million people have visited it since it opened in 2001. Tim Smit (who had earlier been responsible for re-opening the Lost Gardens of Heligan to the public, which have become the most visited gardens in Britain) co-founded the project, which developed from his Heligan experience. This had convinced him that people (even those who did not initially like gardens) could be attracted by anecdotes – accessible stories about what they were looking at. He also noticed that people felt very positive about being in well-made, abundant gardens.

This led him to develop the idea of creating a place that looked good, was technically sophisticated, and which was dedicated to explaining how all life on Earth depends on plants. More than that, it could become:

> a place where you started to think about your connection with nature, and whether you might want to get closer to nature again and whether some lessons of life might not be buried in there.

From this initial vision, Eden has, within only nine years, become one of the 50 most recognised brands, alongside established businesses such as Nokia and Pepsi-Cola; has generated over £90 million in revenues for other businesses in Cornwall; and employs some 500 staff.

The first task in turning the idea into reality was to persuade people to invest in the project – which was to cost about £76 million to build. Smit approached one of the leading architects of the time, who, after consulting with his colleagues, agreed to work on the project: Smit says:

> So for the next 18 months we had possibly the best design team in the world working for us for nothing. I think the reason Eden came into being was that we formed an enormous gang. There was a bunch of people that were really interested in the idea and we would meet in motorway service stations and in pubs and in people's houses and this just grew as people heard about it. People started leaving their jobs because

Eden Project

they became so obsessed with it. And it suddenly had an inevitability, when we realised we were saying 'when' not 'if' . . . and the dice rolled unbelievably well for us.

The environment became a big thing, plants are good, people can imagine the Crystal Palace and this is bigger than the Crystal Palace. We said we wanted the biggest in the world, to contain a full-size rainforest, we don't just want some namby-pamby greenhouse. I said we wanted to build a global must-see like the Guggenheim. The tourism people thought we might get 500,000 visitors in the first year: we actually had 1.8 million.

And in the middle of all that there was a huge fund-raising effort to raise the money for what we called the eighth wonder of the world.

Source: Interview with Tim Smit; Eden Project website.

Case questions 15.1

Creating Eden has depended on motivating people.

- Which groups of people have featured in the case so far?
- What has Tim Smit wanted these people to do for the Eden Project?
- What clues are there about what motivates them to give their support?

15.1 Introduction

The Eden Project has captured the public's imagination, rapidly becoming one of Europe's most successful visitor attractions, with a thriving educational charity running alongside. Tim Smit and his colleagues secured the help of talented architects, the support of local agencies and significant funding bodies – and that of staff, visitors and many partner institutions. In good times as well as in bad, charities must raise income and recruit staff to survive: like any business, Eden's management have been thinking up new ways to **motivate** people to continue to support the project as enthusiastically as they have done so far.

All businesses need enthusiastic and committed employees who work in a way that supports organisational goals. This is clearest in service organisations like Eden where customers are in direct contact with staff – Culbertson (2009) shows how employee satisfaction affects service quality – but matters just as much in manufacturing or administrative operations. Microsoft and Apple depend on their engineers being motivated to develop a constant flow of innovative products. Hospitals depend on medical and nursing staff being willing to work in a way that provides good patient care.

Managers want people to work well and occasionally to 'go the extra mile' – doing more than usual to fix a problem or help a colleague. The problem is how to achieve this: surveys regularly show that while some staff are fully engaged with their work, many are not. The manager's task is to create a context in which people engage with their work, and willingly add value. Yet motivation arises within people – so managers need to ensure that people can satisfy their needs through work. People have different motivations, so a reward that is attractive to one may not matter to another.

Motivation refers to the forces within or beyond a person that arouse and sustain their commitment to a course of action.

Key ideas **Douglas McGregor – Theory X and Theory Y**

Douglas McGregor (1960) set out two views of motivation, Theory X and Theory Y, which he believed represented managers' views about people. To find out which you agree with, complete this questionnaire. Read each pair of statements, and circle the number that best represents your view:

The average person inherently dislikes work	1 2 3 4 5	Work is as natural as rest to people
People must be directed at work	1 2 3 4 5	People will exercise self-discretion and self-control
People wish to avoid responsibility	1 2 3 4 5	People enjoy real responsibility
People feel that achievement at work is irrelevant	1 2 3 4 5	People value achievement highly
Most people are dull and uncreative	1 2 3 4 5	Most people have imagination and creativity
Money is the only real reason for working	1 2 3 4 5	Money is only one benefit from work
People lack the desire to improve their quality of life	1 2 3 4 5	People have needs to improve the quality of their life
Having an objective is a form of imprisonment	1 2 3 4 5	People welcome objectives as an aid to effectiveness

Add the numbers you circled to give you a score between 8 and 40. If you scored 16 or less, then you subscribe to Theory X. If you scored 32 or more, then you subscribe to Theory Y. So what? Managers often wonder how they can motivate staff to higher performance – and use their theory of motivation to decide how to do it. Someone who believes in Theory X will take a different approach from someone who believes in Theory Y. McGregor's ideas are a vivid way of illustrating different views on the topic.

Source: Based on Huczynski and Buchanan (2007), p. 239

Money is evidently a major motivator for many people, especially for many on low incomes. Others find deep satisfaction in the work itself – like Theresa Marshall, who is a classroom assistant in a city primary school:

I've found my niche and couldn't be happier – it's no exaggeration to say that I absolutely love my job. My favourite part is helping the children with their reading skills and seeing the pleasure that they can get out of books.

Some enjoy working with physical things or the challenge of designing an innovative product – while others enjoy working directly with people in sales or customer service jobs.

With people having such diverse needs and interests, how can managers motivate them to work in ways that meet the manager's priorities? In small organisations the relationship between an owner-manager and a few employees is close and direct. Each can develop a good idea of what the other expects and adjust the pattern of work and the pattern of rewards to meet changing requirements. As the organisation grows the links become less personal. Motivation increasingly depends on more formal approaches, based on managers' theories of motivation – what they believe will influence employees. They make working assumptions about how staff would respond to new policies. Staff evaluate what is on offer and respond according to how well it meets their needs.

This chapter outlines and illustrates the main theories of human needs, as shown in Figure 15.1. How managers interpret the wider context shapes what they expect from people – who also have needs and expectations of the organisation. The next section examines the psychological contract that expresses these mutual expectations. The following sections then present three groups of theories about motivation at work – content, process and work design. Content theories help explain why people work, by identifying human needs that work may satisfy. Process theories help explain how people decide which of several possible actions will best satisfy their needs. Work design theories connect the content and process approaches to workplace practice.

| 15.2 | **Perspectives on motivation – and the psychological contract** |

Much behaviour is routine, based on habit, precedent and unconscious scripts. This chapter is concerned with the larger, precedent-setting choices people make about behaviour at work. For some people, work is an occasion for hard, enthusiastic and imaginative activity, a source of rich satisfaction. They are motivated, in the sense that they put effort (arousal) into their work (direction and persistence). For others it is something they do grudgingly – work does not arouse their enthusiasm, or merely passes the time until they find something more interesting. Managers try to understand why such differences occur, and seek to encourage the former rather than the latter. Theories of motivation, which try to identify and explain the factors that energise, channel and sustain behaviour, can inform that consideration.

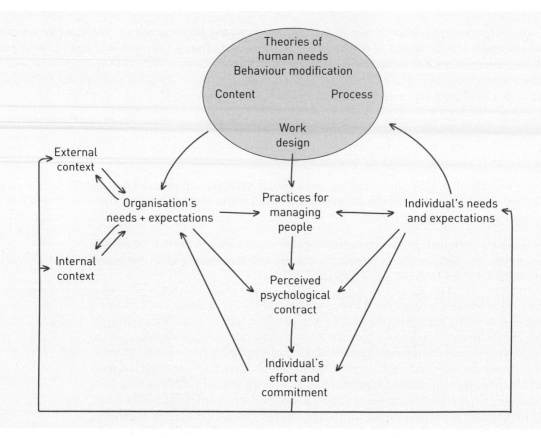

Figure 15.1 A model of motivation at work

Targets of attempts to motivate

Who are managers trying to motivate? Theories of motivation originally concentrated on how managers motivate subordinates, but they need to influence many other people: colleagues, their own senior managers, people in other organisations. They also try to influence consumers – marketers also use theories of human motivation. In all of these cases people try to understand human needs in the belief that doing so accurately makes it easier to influence what they do.

Case study   Eden – the case continues   www.edenproject.com

Gaynor Coley is managing director at the Eden Project, and her financial background was crucial in raising the money which the project needed.

I left a safe, pensionable university job to join Eden in early 1997, having met this crew who had no money in the bank, but who were going to build the eighth wonder of the world in a derelict Cornish clay pit. I spent the next three years raising the money: a really exciting period, using all those skills you learn in the City about

having a robust business plan, together with skills you may use in fringe theatre, which are about how to get something off the ground when nothing exists. The art of persuasion was putting Tim in front of the right people so he could really get them behind the purpose, but then following that up with the real mechanics of what the business needs which is a robust plan and a bank and a set of stakeholders who are prepared to come with you.

One thing that's really important about this project is teamwork – we had a horticultural director who was superb, we had an education director who could persuade anybody that education really is the route to a better world.

To get the finance we had to identify people with a similar purpose to us. So the Millennium Commission wanted to put really landmark architecture into the landscape and it was obvious that there was nothing else in the south west that would meet this brief. The South West Regional Development Agency was there to generate economic activity, well-paid jobs, and a reason for people to come to the south west. So they had a different agenda, and part of our task there was also to say, 'well, we will fulfil that agenda'. So it was research around what agendas a portfolio of stakeholders had, understanding them and actually making a pitch relevant to that particular stakeholder.

Source: Interview with Gaynor Coley.

Case questions 15.2

- What motivational skills has the managing director demonstrated in raising the funds that Eden required?

- How transferable do you think they would be to other management situations?

Those with a more critical perspective believe that 'workers need to be influenced to cooperate because of their essential alienation from the productive process' (Thompson and McHugh, 2002, p. 306): employers try to maintain their power over employees, which the latter accept in the absence of realistic alternatives. Staff may even express satisfaction with a new arrangement as a way of coming to terms with the inherent stability of the power structure. As always in management, people see the topic from different perspectives: motivation is not a neutral or value-free subject.

Key ideas   Generation Y

'Generation Y' (also known as the 'iPod Generation') is commonly defined as people born between the late 1970s and 2000. Managers and marketers are keenly interested in their attitudes as future workers and consumers. Two studies (the US and UK respectively) suggest that the attitudes of Generation Ys who are in the workplace are not as different from those of other generations as some people believe. While craving excitement and challenge, nearly 90 per cent describe themselves as loyal to their employer, and two-thirds prefer face-to-face communication at work, rather than emails and texts. They are also highly adaptable and realistic about the need to move on if they are not promoted or not gaining new experiences.

The UK study, based on in-depth interviews with 42 young professionals, showed that they want to shape their careers and have autonomy over their work lives, but they also crave feedback; that they seek work–life balance but also challenges; and that they want to improve themselves, learn fast and dislike rigid rules.

Two factors do set the generation apart – the unprecedented pace of technological change, which affects how they expect to work; and the disappearance of the secure job for life. The UK study's author said:

A flexible approach is the core strength of this generation. They adapt incredibly quickly to a changing environment.

Source: From an article by Alison Maitland, *Financial Times*, 18 June 2009.

Figure 15.2 illustrates a simple model of human motivation. We all have needs for food, social contact or a sense of achievement, which motivate behaviour to satisfy that need. If the action leads to a satisfactory outcome we experience a sense of reward. The feedback loop shows that we then decide whether the behaviour was appropriate and worth repeating.

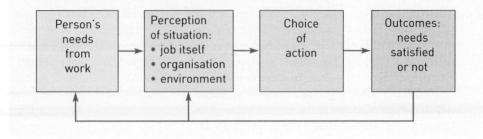

Figure 15.2
Human needs
in context – the
situational
perspective

The figure also shows that individuals do not act in isolation, but within a context that includes both immediate and wider elements:

● the job itself – e.g. how interesting, varied or responsible it is;
● the organisation – e.g. supervision, career and promotion prospects, pay systems;
● the environment – e.g. career threats and opportunities.

These contextual factors affect how people see their job. When jobs are hard to get in a recession, many will lower their expectations of work, and be content with an acceptable job that pays the mortgage. In more affluent times, they can afford to be more choosey. In considering this model, remember that:

● we can only infer, or make reasonable assumptions about, the needs that matter to someone;
● needs change with age, experience and responsibilities;
● we face choices, when we can only satisfy one at the expense of another; and
● the effect of satisfying a need on the future strength of that need is uncertain.

The psychological contract

A **psychological contract** is the set of understandings people have regarding the commitments made between themselves and their organisation.

The **psychological contract** expresses the idea that each side to an employment relationship has expectations of the other – of what they will give and what they will receive in return. Employers (or their agents, their managers) offer rewards in the expectation of receiving some level of performance. Employees contribute a level of performance in the expectation that they will receive rewards in return. The parties modify these expectations (usually informally) as the relationship develops, reflecting the influence of changing organisational contexts or individual circumstances. There is a constant risk that a contract which satisfied both parties at one time may, perhaps inadvertently, cease do so – which will have consequences for attitudes and behaviour.

Rousseau and Schalk (2000) refer to psychological contracts as:

> the belief systems of individual workers and their employers regarding their mutual obligations. (p. 1)

Some elements in the contract are written but most are implicit, or at least not written down. A consequence of this is that both parties may have different understanding of what obligations have been promised and whether they have been delivered. If both parties are content with the current balance this is likely to lead to a positive relationship: if either side believes the other has breached the contract, the relationship is likely to suffer.

Perception is the active psychological process in which stimuli are selected and organised into meaningful patterns.

Guest (2004) proposed the model shown in Figure 15.3 to assist analysis and research into aspects of this evolving relationship. One line of research has been into the effects on employee behaviour of perceived breaches in the contract. In times of rapid economic change researchers have studied employees' **perceptions** of the state of the psychological contract with their employer, since competitive business conditions may lead employers to make changes which employees see as breaking the contract. If they do, what are the effects?

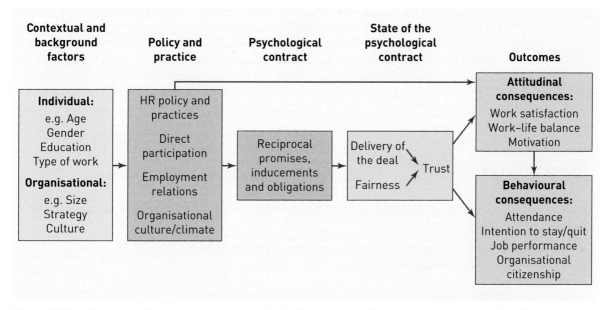

Figure 15.3 A framework for applying the psychological contract to the employment relationship
Source: Based on Guest (2004).

Deery *et al.* (2006) studied employees in a call centre who perceived their employer had breached the contract in that managers had:

- failed to implement a pay-for-performance system;
- did not respect staff knowledge and skills; and
- did not ask for their opinions.

These breaches of the psychological contract led employees to have lower trust in management, to experience less co-operative employment relations, and to have higher rates of absence.

Restubog *et al.* (2007) measured the effects of perceived contract breaches on sales staff in the pharmaceutical industry. Relating their work to Guest's model, they assessed the state of the psychological contract by the responses staff gave (on a five-point scale) to statements such as:

- I have not received everything promised to me in exchange for my contributions.
- Almost all the promises made by my employer during recruitment have been kept thus far.

This gave the researchers a measure of the extent to which employees believed the contract had been breached. They assessed the effects of this on two of Guest's outcomes (Figure 15.3) – 'job performance' and 'organisational citizenship behaviour' (OCB). These were assessed by supervisors' ratings of the employee on statements such as:

Job performance:

- adequately completes assigned duties;
- fulfils responsibilities specified in the job description; and
- performs tasks that are expected of him/her.

Organisation citizenship (which benefits colleagues):

- helps others who have been absent;
- takes time to listen to co-workers' problems and worries; and
- passes along information to co-workers.

Organisation citizenship (which benefits company):

- attendance at work is above the norm;
- gives advance notice when unable to come to work; and
- adheres to informal rules devised to maintain order.

They found that, as expected, those who believe that the contact has been breached were less likely to perform well on the job, and less likely to behave in ways that would help colleagues and/or the company. They also found individuals differed in how they reacted to a breach, with some being more tolerant of this than others. While this study was of one industry in one country it adds to the accumulating evidence that how people feel about their psychological contract affects the contribution they are willing to make. As Kolb *et al.* (1991) remarked:

> a company staffed by cheated individuals who expect far more than they get is headed for trouble. (p. 6)

Management in practice   'Employees leave managers, not companies'

From the employee's point of view, there is clear evidence that good management rests squarely on four foundations:

- Having a manager who shows care, interest and concern for each of them.
- Knowing what is expected of them.
- Having a role that fits their abilities.
- Receiving positive feedback and recognition regularly for work well done.

In a Gallup study of performance at unit level, covering more than 200,000 employees across many industries, teams that rated managers highly on these four factors were more productive and more profitable. They also had lower staff turnover and higher customer satisfaction ratings.

Source: *People Management*, 17 February 2000, p. 45.

At a time of great change in the business world, previously stable psychological contracts are easily broken. Technological changes and increased competition lead senior management to change employment policies and working conditions, or put staff under great pressure to meet demanding performance targets.

Management in practice   What Ikea expects and offers   www.ikea.com

On its website Ikea explains that working for the company is a matter of give and take:

> 'Ikea co-workers enjoy many advantages and opportunities from working in such a free and open environment – but all freedoms are counter-balanced with expectations. For example, the expectation that each co-worker is able to assume responsibility for his/her actions.

> **What do we expect from you?**

- You have the ambition to do a good job and the desire to take on responsibility and to take the consequences that this entails.
- You do your best on the basis of your abilities and experience.
- You are service-oriented and have the customers' best interests at heart.
- You are not status minded, but rather open in your approach to others.

> **What do we offer you?**

- The chance to work in a growing company with a viable business idea.
- The opportunity to further develop your professional skills.
- The opportunity to choose between many different jobs in the company.
- A job with fair and reasonable conditions.
- The chance to assume responsibility following recognised good results, regardless of age.'

Source: Company website.

> ### Activity 15.1   Mutual expectations
>
> Identify a time when you were working in an organisation, or think of your work as a student.
>
> - Describe what the organisation expected of you.
> - What policies or practices did the organisation use to encourage these?
> - What did you expect of the organisation?
> - How well did the organisation meet your expectations?
> - How did the 'balance' between the two sets of expectations have on your behaviour?

The next section outlines an early theory of motivation which some companies use to influence the actions of staff.

15.3   Behaviour modification

Behaviour modification refers to a range of techniques developed to treat psychological conditions such as eating disorders and heavy smoking: managers have used them to deal with issues such as lateness and absenteeism. The techniques developed from Skinner's (1971) theory that people learn to see relationships between actions and their consequences, and that this learning guides behaviour. If we receive a reward for doing something, we tend to do it again: if the consequences are unpleasant, we do not.

Behaviour modification techniques focus on specific observable behaviours rather than on attitudes and feelings.

> In promoting safety . . . we did not dwell on accident-prone workers or probe for personality or demographic factors, none of which can be changed. Instead we focused on the organization and what it can do to rearrange the work environment. (Komaki, 2003, p. 96)

This includes specifying what people should do, measuring actual behaviour and identifying the consequences that people experience. If the influencer sees the behaviour as undesirable, he/she tries to influence the person by changing the consequences – rewarding or punishing them.

Komaki (2003) explains how she and her colleagues used the method in a bakery to encourage safe working practices. They worked with management to design these steps:

- *Specify desired behaviour.* This included defining very precisely the safe working practices that were required – such as walking around conveyor belts, how to sharpen knives, and using precise terms when giving instructions.
- *Measure desired performance.* Trained observers visited the site and recorded whether workers were performing safely by following the specified behaviours.
- *Provide frequent, contingent, positive consequences.* In this case, the positive consequence was feedback, in the form of charts showing current accident figures, which were much lower than previous levels.
- *Evaluate effectiveness.* Collecting data on accident levels and comparing these with earlier data. In this case people were now working more safely, and the number of injuries had fallen from 53 a year to 10.

Practitioners emphasise that several principles must be used for the method to be effective (Komaki *et al.*, 2000):

- payoffs (benefits) must be given only when the desired behaviour occurs;
- payoffs must be given as soon as possible after the behaviour, to strengthen the link between behaviour and reward;

Behaviour modification is a general label for attempts to change behaviour by using appropriate and timely reinforcement.

- desirable behaviour is likely to be repeated if reinforced by rewards;
- reinforcement is more effective than punishment, as punishment only temporarily suppresses behaviour;
- repeated reinforcement can lead to permanent change in behaviour in the desired direction.

Management in practice　Behaviour modification in a call centre

In our call centre staff are rewarded when behaviour delivers results in line with business requirements. Each month staff performance is reviewed against a number of objectives such as average call length, sales of each product and attention to detail. This is known as Effective Level Review and agents can move through levels of effectiveness ranging from 1 to 4, and gain an increase in salary after six months of successful reviews. Moving through effective levels means that they have performed well and can mean being given other tasks instead of answering the phone. The role can become mundane and repetitive so the opportunity to do other tasks is seen as a reward for good performance. Thus it reinforces acceptable behaviour.

Conversely staff who display behaviour that is not desirable cannot move through these levels and repeated failure to do so can lead to disciplinary action. This can be seen as punishment rather than behaviour modification. People can become resentful at having their performance graded every month, particularly in those areas where it is their line manager's perception of whether or not they have achieved the desired results.

Source: Private communication from the call centre manager.

Above all, advocates stress the need to *reward* desirable behaviours rather than treat them with indifference. These rewards can result from individual action (a word of praise or thanks) or from organisational practices (shopping vouchers for consistently good timekeeping). Supporters believe the approach encourages management to look directly at what makes a particular person act in a desirable way, and to ensure those rewards are available. It depends on identifying rewards the person will value (or punishments they will try to avoid). Theories that attempt to understand these are known as content theories of motivation.

15.4　Content theories of motivation

Most writers on this topic have tried to identify human needs so that they can use this knowledge to influence their actions. Frederick Taylor (Chapter 2) believed that people worked for money and that they would follow strict working methods if management rewarded them financially. Chapter 2 also shows how Mary Parker Follett and Elton Mayo identified other human needs, such as being accepted by a group: if people value this more than the financial incentive, they will conform with what the group expects. Maslow developed a theory which incorporates these and other needs.

Activity 15.2　Was Taylor wrong?

Many managers believe that money is a powerful incentive.

- Find someone who works for an organisation where incentives or commissions make up a significant part of that person's pay and ask how that affects his/her behaviour.
- Are there are any negative effects?

Abraham Maslow – a hierarchy of needs

Maslow was a clinical psychologist who developed a theory of human motivation to help him understand the needs of his patients. He stressed the clinical sources of the theory and that it lacked experimental verification, although he was aware that Douglas McGregor (see p. 450) had used the theory to interpret his observations of people at work.

Maslow proposed that individuals experience a range of needs, and will be motivated to fulfil whichever need is most powerful at the time (Maslow, 1970). What he termed the lower-order needs are dominant until they are at least partially satisfied. Normal individuals would then turn their attention to satisfying needs at the next level, so that higher-order needs would gradually become dominant. He suggested these needs formed a hierarchy: the middle column of Table 15.1 shows this, while the others indicate how they can be satisfied at work and away from it.

Physiological needs are those that must be satisfied to survive – food and water particularly. Maslow proposed that if all the needs in the hierarchy are unsatisfied then the physiological needs will dominate. People will concentrate on obtaining the necessities of life, and ignore higher needs.

Once the physiological needs were sufficiently gratified a new set of needs would emerge, which he termed *safety needs* – the search for

security; stability; dependency; protection; freedom from fear, anxiety and chaos; need for structure, order, law, limits . . . and so on.' (Maslow, 1970, p. 39)

People then concentrate on satisfying these to the exclusion of others. If this need is dominant they can satisfy it by seeking a stable, regular job with secure working conditions and access to insurance for ill-health and retirement. They resent sudden or random changes in job prospects.

Belongingness needs would follow the satisfaction of safety needs:

[If] both the physiological and the safety needs are fairly well gratified, there will emerge the love and affection and belongingness needs . . . now the person will feel keenly the absence of friends . . . and will hunger for affectionate relations with people in general. (p. 43)

These needs include a place in the group or family, and at work they would include wanting to be part of a congenial team. People object when management changes work patterns or locations if this disrupts established working relationships. They welcome change that brings them closer to people they know and like.

Maslow observed that most people have *esteem needs* – self-respect and the respect of others. Self-respect is the need for a sense of achievement, competence, adequacy and confidence. People also seek the respect of others, what he called a desire for reputation in the eyes

Table 15.1 How Maslow's needs can be satisfied on and off the job

Ways to satisfy on the job	Hierarchy of needs	Ways to satisfy off the job
Opportunities for personal growth, wider challenges	**Self-actualisation**	Education, hobbies, community activities
Recognition, thanks, more responsibilities	**Esteem**	Approval of family, friends and community
Relations with fellow workers, customers, supervisors	**Belongingness**	Acceptance by family, friends, social groups
Safe work, well-designed facilities, job security	**Safety**	Freedom from violence, disturbance, pollution
Basic salary, warmth	**Physiological**	Food, oxygen, water

of other people: prestige, status, recognition and attention. They can satisfy this by taking on challenging or difficult tasks to show they are good at their job and can accomplish something worthwhile. If others recognise this, they earn status and respect.

Key ideas **Research on organisation-based self-esteem**

Pierce and Gardner (2004) reviewed research on organisation-based self-esteem (OBSE) – that esteem which was influenced by a person's experience at their place of work. Earlier research had found that system-imposed controls through a division of labour, rigid hierarchy, centralisation, standardisation and formalisation carry with them assumptions about the inability of individuals to self-regulate and self-control. Conversely, systems that allowed higher levels of self-expression and personal control were likely to enhance OBSE. They reviewed over 50 studies and concluded that they:

> **support the claim that an individual's self-esteem, formed around work and organizational experiences, may well play a significant role in shaping employee intrinsic motivation, attitudes . . . and behaviors. (P. 613)**

Structures that provide opportunities for the exercise of self-direction and self-control promote OBSE, as do signals to employees that they 'make a difference around here'. They also noted that

> **adverse role conditions (such as role ambiguity), anticipated organizational change, job insecurity, discrimination and harassment . . . undermine experiences of self-worth. (p. 613)**

Source: Pierce and Gardner (2004).

Lastly, Maslow used the term *self-actualisation* needs to refer to the desire for self-fulfilment and for realising potential:

> At this level, individual differences are greatest. The clear emergence of these needs usually rests upon some prior satisfaction of the physiological, safety, love, and esteem needs. (pp. 46–47)

People seeking self-actualisation look for personal relevance in their work, doing things that matter deeply to them, or which help them discover new talents.

Management in practice **A new manager at a nursing home**

Jean Parker was appointed manager of a nursing home for the elderly. Recent reports by the Health Authority and Environmental Health inspectors had been so critical that they threatened to close the home. Jean recalls what she did in the first eight months:

> My task was to make sweeping changes, stabilise the workforce and improve the reputation of the home. I had no influence on pay, and low pay was one of the problems. To motivate staff I had to use other methods. Staff facilities were appalling – the dining areas were filthy, showers and some toilets were not working, there were no changing rooms and petty theft was rife. Given the lack of care and respect shown to staff, it is little wonder that care given to residents was poor, and staff were demotivated. They turned up to work, carried out tasks and went home. There had been little communication between management and staff. My approach was to work alongside the staff, listen to their grievances, gain their trust and set out an action plan.
>
> The first steps were easy. The staff room was cleaned and decorated, changing rooms and working showers and toilets were provided. Refreshments were provided at meal breaks. Police advice was sought to combat petty theft and lockers were installed in each area. The effect of these changes on

staff commitment was astounding. They felt somebody cared for them and listened. In turn, quality of care improved and staff started to take pride in the home, and bring in ornaments and plants to brighten it.

I then started to hold monthly meetings to give management and staff an opportunity to discuss expectations. Policies and procedures were explained. Noticeboards displaying 'news and views' were put up. A monthly newsletter to residents and relations was issued. Staff took part enthusiastically in fund-raising activities to pay for outings and entertainment. This gave them the chance to get to know residents in a social setting, and was a break from routine. A training programme was introduced.

Some staff did not respond and tried to undermine my intentions. Persistent unreported absence was quickly followed by disciplinary action. By the end of the year absenteesim was at a more acceptable level, many working problems were alleviated and the business started to recover.

Source: Private communication and discussions with the manager.

Maslow did *not* claim that the hierarchy was a fixed or rigid scheme. His clinical experience suggested that most people had these needs in about this order, but he had seen exceptions – people for whom self-esteem was more important than love. For others, creativity took precedence, in that they did not seek self-actualisation *after* satisfying basic needs, but did so even when they were *not* being satisfied. Others had such low aspirations that they experienced life at a very basic level.

Nor did he claim that as people satisfy one need completely, another emerges. Rather he proposed that most normal people are partially satisfied and partially unsatisfied in their needs. A more accurate description of the hierarchy would be in terms of decreasing percentages of satisfaction at successive levels. So a person could think of themselves as being, say, 85 per cent satisfied at the physiological level and 70 per cent at the safety level (the percentages are meaningless). A higher-level need does not emerge suddenly – a person gradually becomes aware that he/she could now attain a higher need.

In summary, Maslow believed that people are motivated to satisfy needs that are important to them at that point in their life, and offered a description of those needs. The strength of a particular need would depend on the extent to which lower needs had been met. He believed that most people would seek to satisfy physiological needs first, before the others became operative. Self-actualisation was fulfilled last and least often, although he had observed exceptions.

How does Maslow's approach compare with Skinner's? Skinner believed that by providing positive reinforcement (or punishment) people would be motivated to act in a particular way. The rewards they obtained would satisfy their needs. Maslow took the slightly different position that people would seek to satisfy their needs by acting in a particular way. Both believed that to change behaviour it would be necessary to change the situation. Skinner emphasised that this would take the form of positive reinforcement to satisfy needs after an activity. Maslow implied that influencers should provide conditions that enable people to satisfy their needs from the activity.

Activity 15.3   Critical reflection on the theory

- Which of the needs identified by Maslow did Jean Parker's changes at the nursing home help staff to satisfy?
- Do your studies and related activities on your course satisfy needs identified by Maslow?
- What evidence can you gather from your colleagues on the relative importance to them of these needs?

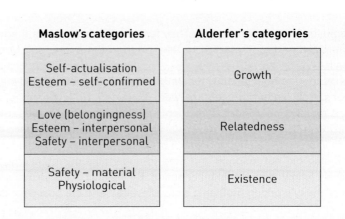

Maslow's categories

Alderfer's categories

Maslow's categories	Alderfer's categories
Self-actualisation Esteem – self-confirmed	Growth
Love (belongingness) Esteem – interpersonal Safety – interpersonal	Relatedness
Safety – material Physiological	Existence

Figure 15.4
Comparison of the Maslow and Alderfer categories of needs

Clayton Alderfer – ERG theory

Doubting the empirical support for the hierarchy of motives proposed by Maslow, Alderfer developed another approach (Alderfer, 1972). He developed and tested his theory by questionnaires and interviews in five organisations – a manufacturing firm, a bank, two colleges and a school. He identified three primary needs, towards which a person can feel satisfied or frustrated.

Existence needs reflect a person's requirement for material and energy.

Existence needs include all the physiological and material desires – hunger and thirst represent deficiencies in existence needs; pay and benefits represent ways of satisfying material requirements.

Relatedness needs involve a desire for relationships with significant other people.

Relatedness needs involve relationships with significant other people – family members, colleagues, bosses, subordinates, team members or regular customers. People satisfy relatedness needs by sharing thoughts and feelings. Acceptance, confirmation and understanding help to satisfy relatedness needs.

Growth needs are those that impel people to be creative or to produce an effect on themselves or their environment.

Growth needs impel a person to be creative or to have an effect on themselves and their surroundings. People satisfy them by engaging with problems that use their skills or require them to develop new ones: being able to exercise talents fully brings a greater sense of completeness.

Figure 15.4 compares Alderfer's formulation of needs with Maslow's. Alderfer proposed that his three categories are active in everyone, although in varying degrees of strength. Unlike Maslow, he found no evidence of a hierarchy of needs, although he did find that if higher needs are frustrated, lower needs become prominent again, even if they have already been satisfied.

Both theories are hard to test empirically as it is difficult to establish whether a person has satisfied a need. One of the very few empirical tests (Arnolds and Boshoff, 2002) concluded that top managers were primarily motivated by growth needs, while front-line staff were primarily motivated by existence and relatedness needs. There was also some evidence that satisfying growth needs could also increase the motivation of front-line staff, by enhancing their self-esteem.

Case study   Eden – the case continues www.edenproject.com

Tim Smit on the reasons for Eden:

Of course we have to give people a good day out, a cup of tea they enjoy and all that. But I think we have actually struck a vein which has got deeper and more important to us as a society, which is

people are not just looking for leisure: what many are looking for is a purpose in their lives, and I think the combination of a great day out, with something meaningful, learning about your environment, learning about your relationship with nature, was a killer proposition. That's why I think we get the numbers we do.

The mission of Eden has changed and developed over the years, but I think there's a seed of an idea that's never gone away and that is about how important it is for us as human beings to understand our relationship with nature. We aren't independent of it: we are dependent on it and part of it. So we give visitors a narrative which is about 'let's protect the habitat of the plants we rely on: coffee, tea, sugar, the things we use in out everyday life'. It's about understanding humans' place in nature, understanding that human ingenuity is going to be the thing that provides really good solutions to challenges as well as to some of the poor behaviour.

We think about how we operate, how we do business, and we believe that what you do is really, really important. So the authenticity of the welcome that you get when you come here, the authenticity of how we treat our suppliers, is what I think lies behind the strength of the Eden brand.

Source: Interview with Tim Smit.

Case questions 15.3

- What human needs is Eden seeking to satisfy?
- How attractive do you think you would find Eden if you worked there, and for what reasons?

David McClelland

McClelland (1961) and his colleagues examined how people think and react in a wide range of situations. This work led them to identify three categories of human need, which individuals possess in different amounts:

- Need for affiliation – to develop and maintain interpersonal relationships.
- Need for power – to have control over one's environment.
- Need for achievement – to set and meet standards of excellence.

McClelland believed that, rather than being arranged in a hierarchy, individuals possess each of these possibly conflicting needs, which motivate their behaviour when activated. McClelland used the Thematic Apperception Test to assess how significant these categories were to people. The research team showed people pictures with a neutral subject and asked them to write a story about it. The researchers coded the stories and claimed these indicated the relative importance to the person of the affiliation, power and achievement motives.

You can assess your scores on these motives by completing Activity 15.4.

Activity 15.4   Assessing your needs

- From each of the four sets of statements below choose the one that is most like you.

    1 (a) I set myself difficult goals, which I attempt to reach.
       (b) I am happiest when I am with a group of people who enjoy life.
       (c) I like to organise the activities of a group or team.
    2 (a) I only completely enjoy relaxation after the successful completion of exacting pieces of work.
       (b) I become attached to my friends.
       (c) I argue zealously against others for my point of view.
    3 (a) I work hard until I am completely satisfied with the result I achieve.
       (b) I like to mix with a group of congenial people, talking about any subject that comes up.
       (c) I tend to influence others more than they influence me.

> 4 (a) I enjoy working as much as I enjoy my leisure.
>   (b) I go out of my way to be with my friends.
>   (c) I am able to dominate a social situation.
>
> - Now add your responses as follows:
>   The number of (a) responses ( ) Achievement
>   The number of (b) responses ( ) Affiliation
>   The number of (c) responses ( ) Power
>
> This exercise will give you an insight into McClelland's three types of motive and into your preference – indicated by the area with the largest score.
>
> Compare your answers with others whom you know in your class. Discuss whether the results are in line with what you would have expected, given what you already know of each other.

Frederick Herzberg – two-factor theory

While Maslow and McClelland focused on individual differences in motivation, Herzberg (1959) related motivation to the nature of a person's work. He developed his theory following interviews with 200 engineers and accountants about their experience of work. The researchers first asked them to recall a time when they had felt exceptionally good about their job, and then asked about the events that had preceded those feelings. The research team then asked respondents to recall a time when they had felt particularly bad about their work, and the background to that. Analysis showed that when respondents recalled good times they frequently mentioned one or more of these factors:

- achievement;
- recognition;
- work itself;
- responsibility;
- advancement.

They mentioned these much less frequently when describing the bad times. When talking about the bad times they most frequently recalled these factors:

- company policy and administration;
- supervision;
- salary;
- interpersonal relations;
- working conditions.

Motivator factors are those aspects of the work itself that Herzberg found influenced people to superior performance and effort.

They mentioned these much less frequently when describing the good times.

Herzberg concluded that factors associated with satisfaction describe people's relationship to what they were doing – the nature of the task, the responsibility or recognition received. He named these '**motivator factors**', as they seemed to influence people to superior performance and effort. The factors associated with dissatisfaction described conditions surrounding the work – such as supervision or company policy. He named these '**hygiene**' or ('**maintenance**') **factors** as they served mainly to prevent dissatisfaction, not to encourage high performance. Figure 15.5 illustrates the results.

Hygiene (or **maintenance**) **factors** are those aspects surrounding the task which can prevent discontent and dissatisfaction but will not in themselves contribute to psychological growth and hence motivation.

Herzberg concluded that satisfaction can only come from within, through the satisfaction of doing a task which provides a sense of achievement, recognition or of other motivator factors in Figure 15.5. Managers cannot require motivation, although they can certainly destroy it by some thoughtless act. In his *Harvard Business Review* article (Herzberg, 1968) he wrote about what he termed 'Kick in the Ass' management:

> If I kick my dog . . . he will move. And when I want him to move again what must I do? I must kick him again. Similarly, I can change a person's battery, and then recharge it, and

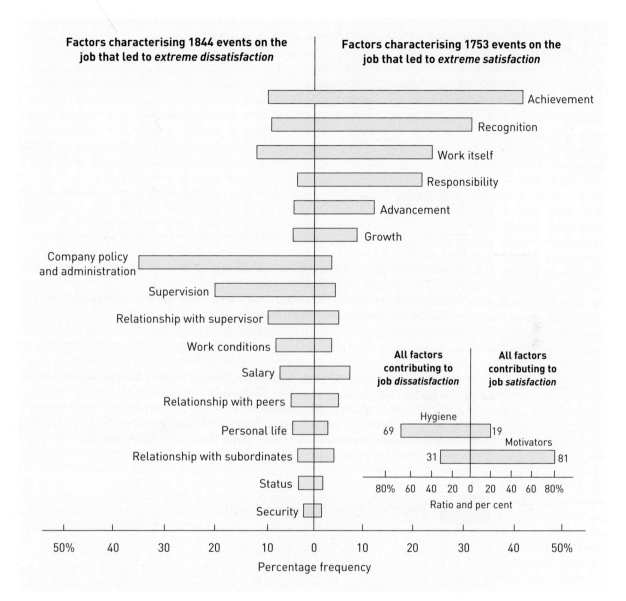

Figure 15.5 Herzberg's comparison of job satisfaction and job dissatisfaction scores

Source: Reprinted by permission of Harvard Business Review. Figure from One more time: How do you motivate employees?, *Harvard Business Review*, vol. 65, no. 5, pp. 109–120 by F. Herzberg, Copyright © 1987 Harvard Business School Publishing Corporation, all rights reserved.

recharge it again. But it is only when one has a generator of one's own that we can talk about motivation. One then needs no outside stimulation. One wants to do it. (p. 55)

Management in practice   Gamma Chemical (part 1) – a focus on hygiene factors

Gamma Chemical purchased another chemical company that had recently failed, and re-employed 30 of the 40 employees. While there was no overt dissatisfaction, management found it hard to motivate staff. They showed no initiative or creativity, and no commitment to the new company or its goals. Yet the company had:
● increased the salaries of the re-employed staff;
● improved working conditions and provided better equipment;
● placed people in positions of equal status to their previous jobs;
● operated an 'Open Door' policy, with supervisors easily approachable;

- offered security of employment and a no-redundancy policy.
  Other aspects of practice included:
- no structured training or development programmes;
- the small unit restricted opportunities for career advancement;
- people had little responsibility as management made decisions;
- there was no clear connection between individual work and company performance.

Source: Private communication and discussions with the manager.

Activity 15.5   Critical reflection on Herzberg's theory

- Comment on Gamma Chemical's assumptions about motivating the re-engaged staff.
- Evaluate the empirical base of Herzberg's research. What reservations do you have about the wider applicability of the theory?
- Gather other evidence of changes in working practice, and decide whether it supports or contradicts Herzberg's theory.

Herzberg believed that motivation depends on whether a job is intrinsically challenging and provides opportunities for recognition. He linked thinking about motivation with ideas about job design, and especially the motivational effects of job enrichment. There are many examples where management has redesigned people's jobs with positive effects. Few if any of these experiments were the result of knowing about Herzberg's theory, but their effects are often consistent with its predictions. Section 15.6 has more on this.

15.5   Process theories of motivation

Process theories try to explain why people choose one course of action towards satisfying a need rather than another. A person who needs a higher income could satisfy it by, say, moving to another company, applying for promotion or investing in training. What factors will influence their choice?

Expectancy theory

Expectancy theory argues that motivation depends on a person's belief in the probability that effort will lead to good performance, and that good performance will lead to them receiving an outcome they value (valence).

Vroom (1964) developed one attempt to answer that question with what he termed the **expectancy theory** of motivation. It focuses on the thinking processes people use to achieve rewards. Stuart Roberts is studying a degree course in Chemistry and has to submit a last assignment. He wants an A for the course, and so far has an average of B+. His motivation to put effort into the assignment will be affected by (a) his expectation that hard work will produce a good piece of work, and (b) his expectation that it will receive a grade of at least an A. If he believes he cannot do a good job, or that the grading system is unclear, then his motivation will be low.

The theory assumes that individuals:

- have different needs and so value outcomes differently;
- make conscious choices about which course of action to follow;
- choose between alternative actions based on the likelihood of an action resulting in an outcome they value.

There are, then, three main components in expectancy theory. First, the person's expectation (or **subjective probability**) that effort (E) will result in some level of performance (P):

$$(E \rightarrow P)$$

This will be affected by how clear they are about their roles, the training available, whether the necessary support will be provided and similar factors. If Stuart Roberts understands what the assignment requires and is confident in his ability to do a good job, his $(E \rightarrow P)$ expectancy will be high.

The second component is the person's expectation that performance will be **instrumental** in leading to a particular outcome (O):

$$(P \rightarrow O)$$

This will be affected by how confident the person is that achieving a target will produce a reward. This reflects factors such as the clarity of the organisation's appraisal and payment systems and previous experience of them. A clear grading system, which Stuart understands and knows that staff apply consistently, will mean he has a high $(P \rightarrow O)$ expectancy. If he has found the system unpredictable this expectancy would be lower.

The third component is the **valence** that the individual attaches to a particular outcome:

$$(V)$$

This term is best understood as the power of the outcome to motivate that individual – how keen Roberts is to get a good degree. It introduces the belief that people differ in the value they place on different kinds of reward. So the value of V varies between individuals, reflecting their unique pattern of motivational needs (as suggested by the content theories). Someone who values money and achievement would place a high valence on an outcome that was a promotion to a distant head office. He/she would try to work in a way which led to that. Such an outcome would be much less welcome (have a much lower valence) to a manager who values an established pattern of relationships or quality of life in the present location.

In summary:

$$F = (E \rightarrow P) \times (P \rightarrow Q) \times V$$

in which F represents the force exerted, or degree of motivation a person has towards an activity. Two beliefs will influence that motivation, namely the expectation that:

- making the effort will lead to performance $(E \rightarrow P)$
- that level of performance will lead to an outcome they value $(P \rightarrow O)$.

Adjusting these beliefs for valence – how desirable the outcome is to the person – gives a measure of his/her motivation. The beliefs that people hold reflect their personality and their experience of organisational practices, as shown in Figure 15.6.

Using the multiplication sign in the equation signifies that both beliefs influence motivation. If a person believes that however hard he/she tries he/she will be unable to perform well, he/she will not be motivated to do so (so $E \rightarrow P = 0$). The same applies for $(P \rightarrow O)$. A low score in either of these two parts of the equation, or in V, will lead to low effort, regardless of beliefs about the other part.

A criticism of the theory is that it implies a high level of rational calculation, as people weigh the probabilities of various courses of action. It also implies that managers estimate what each employee values, and try to ensure that motivational practices meet them. Neither calculation is likely to be made that rationally, which may diminish the model's practical value.

However, it is useful in recognising that people vary in their beliefs (or probabilities) about the components in the equation. It shows that managers can affect these beliefs by redesigning the factors in Figure 15.6. If people are unclear about their role, or receive weak feedback, the theory predicts that this will reduce their motivation.

Subjective probability (in expectancy theory) is a person's estimate of the likelihood that a certain level of effort (E) will produce a level of performance (P) which will then lead to an expected outcome (O).

Instrumentality is the perceived probability that good performance will lead to valued rewards, measured on a scale from 0 (no chance) to 1 (certainty).

Valence is the perceived value or preference that an individual has for a particular outcome.

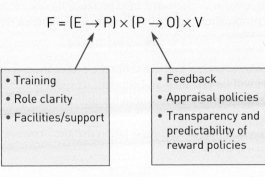

$$F = (E \rightarrow P) \times (P \rightarrow O) \times V$$

- Training
- Role clarity
- Facilities/support

- Feedback
- Appraisal policies
- Transparency and predictability of reward policies

Figure 15.6
Organisational practices affecting subjective probabilities

Management in practice   **Employee ownership at Child Base Nurseries**
www.childbase.com

Mike Thompson established Child Base Nurseries in 1989, and the company now operates (in early 2010) 38 nurseries in the South of England. Being a network helps staff development, as the nursery nurses can move up a career change – the company's operations director began as a nursery worker. The company is privately owned by the employees, who can buy shares from the Thompson family holding – which is now down to about 28 per cent. The family can only sell its shares to the Employee Benefit Trust which administers the share scheme. The company's legal rules make it clear that Child Base is established for the benefit of employees – past, present and future.

Mr Thompson believes strongly in the principle of employee ownership – he could have made more money by selling his shares in the business to external investors. He says:

> You get where you are in business because of other people. Why not put the business back in the hands of the people who helped build it?

Source: *Financial Times*, 22 April 2009.

The theory predicts that managers can influence motivation by practical actions such as:

- Establishing the rewards people value.
- Identifying and communicating performance requirements.
- Ensuring that reasonable effort can meet those requirements.
- Providing facilities to support the person's effort.
- Ensuring a clear link between performance and reward.
- Providing feedback to staff on how well they are meeting performance requirements.

The theory links insights from the content theories of motivation with organisational practice.

J. Stacey Adams – equity theory

Equity theory argues that perception of unfairness leads to tension, which then motivates the individual to resolve that unfairness.

Equity theory is usually associated with J. Stacy Adams (a behavioural scientist working at the General Electric Company) who put forward the first systematic account (Adams, 1963) of the idea that fairness in comparison with others influences motivation. People like to be treated fairly and compare what they put into a job (effort, skill, knowledge, etc.) with the rewards they receive (pay, recognition, satisfaction, etc.). They express this as a ratio of their input to their reward. They also compare their ratio with the input-to-reward ratio of others whom they consider their equals. They expect management to reward others in the same way, so expect the ratios to be roughly equal. The formula below sums up the comparison:

$$\frac{\text{Input (A)}}{\text{Reward (A)}} : \frac{\text{Input (B)}}{\text{Reward (B)}}$$

Person A compares the ratio of her input to her reward to that of B. If the ratios are similar she will be satisfied with the treatment received. If she believes the ratio is lower than that of other people she will feel inequitably treated and be dissatisfied.

The theory predicts that if people feel unfairly treated they will experience tension and dissatisfaction. They will try to reduce this by one or more of these means:

- Reducing their inputs, by putting in less effort or withholding good ideas and suggestions
- Attempting to increase their outcomes, by pressing for increased pay or other benefits
- Attempting to decrease other people's outcomes by generating conflict or withholding information and help
- Changing the basis of their comparison, by making it against someone else where the inequity is less pronounced
- Increasing their evaluation of the other person's output so the ratios are in balance.

As individuals differ, so will their way of reducing inequity. Some will try to rationalise the situation, suggesting that their efforts were greater or lesser than they originally thought them to be, or that the rewards are reasonable. For example, a person denied a promotion may decide that the previously desired job would not have been so advantageous after all. Members may put pressure on other members of the team whom they feel are not pulling their weight. Some may choose to do less, so bringing their ratio into line with that of other staff.

Case study Eden – the case continues www.edenproject.com

Tim Smit on work at Eden:

> To work at Eden you've got to be interested in a lot of stuff. You've got to be prepared to catch people when they fall, because people are trying stuff all the time, and you've got to be prepared for the unexpected because part of the way we work is almost deliberately create chaos by doing more stuff than we've possibly got time to do, which means more junior members have more chance to become leaders because the senior ones can't do it all.
>
> One of the things I think is very special about Eden is that the letters after your name don't make any difference. It's what you can do . . . Sure the Finance Director's got to be an accountant and all that sort of stuff, but in the wider scheme of things, to be an Eden person you've got to be optimistic and smiley and damned hard working.

Gayle Conley adds:

> We try not to be prescriptive about defining talent and we try to encourage people to take individual responsibility for their own career path here as much as we can help them to a career path

Jess Ratty speaks about her work:

> I began at Eden as a waitress when I was 16 years old with no qualifications: I'm now 24 and the Press Officer. So I've worked in about eight departments and worked my way up through the company. I think Eden's been a fantastic opportunity for me – the ethos and the way you don't have to have a degree – you know they'll give people a chance . . . after working as a waitress I moved to the Stewards team where I learnt a lot about dealing with people. I worked

in plant sales, learning a lot about different plants, which was great to learn at 18. Then I worked in retail, the product side of things, and was then picked up by the design team . . . . and after a few more jobs one of the managers said 'do you want to go for the job of communications assistant?' And I thought, 'people actually believe in me, they want me to do a job they think I'll be good at'!

Sources: Interviews with staff members.

Case questions 15.4

- Consider how the company has helped to generate positive attitudes with this member of staff.

- Analyse these accounts using Herzberg's theory – which of his 'motivating factors' do staff refer to?

Clearly the focus and the components of the comparisons are highly subjective, although the theory has an intuitive appeal. The subjective nature of the comparison makes it difficult to test empirically, and there has been little formal research on the theory in recent years (though see Mowday and Colwell, 2003). There is, however, abundant anecdotal evidence that people compare their effort/reward ratio with that of other people or groups.

Edwin A. Locke – goal-setting theory

Goal-setting theory argues that motivation is influenced by goal difficulty, goal specificity and knowledge of results.

Goal-setting theory refers to a series of propositions designed to help explain and predict work behaviour. Its best-known advocate is Edwin Locke (Locke, 1968; Locke and Latham, 1990, 2002; Latham and Locke, 2006) and the theory has four main propositions:

1 *Challenging goals* lead to higher levels of performance than a vague goal, such as 'do your best'. Difficult goals are sometimes called 'stretch' goals because they encourage us to try harder, to stretch ourselves. However, beyond a point this effect fades – if people see a goal as being impossible, their motivation declines.

2 *Specific goals* lead to higher levels of performance than vague goals (such as 'do your best'). We find it easier to adjust behaviour when we know exactly what the objective is, and what is expected of us.

3 *Participation* in goal setting can improve commitment to those goals, since people have a sense of ownership and are motivated to achieve the goals. However, if management explains and justifies the goals, without inviting participation, that can also increase motivation.

4 *Knowledge of results* of past performance – receiving feedback – is necessary to motivation. It is motivational in itself, and contains information that may help people attain the goals.

The main attraction of goal theory is the directness of the practical implications, including:

- *Goal difficulty:* set goals that are hard enough to stretch employees, but not so difficult as to be impossible to achieve.
- *Goal specificity:* set goals in clear, precise and if possible quantifiable terms.
- *Participation:* allow employees to take part in setting goals, to increase ownership and commitment.
- *Acceptance:* if goals are set by management, ensure they are adequately explained and justified, so that people understand and accept them.
- *Feedback:* provide information on past performance to allow employees to use it in adjusting their performance.

While goal theory has many implications for appraisal schemes and other performance management techniques, several variables have been shown to moderate the relationship between goal difficulty and performance – such as ability, task complexity and situational constraints. Another major question is whether personality traits also moderate the relationship – someone with a high need for achievement may be more likely to respond positively to a challenging goal than someone to with a lower need for achievement. Equally, someone with a high level of self-confidence in his/her abilities will respond to challenging goals in a different way from someone with little self-confidence.

The context may affect the motivational quality of challenging goals. In some careers entry to, or advancement within, the high-status aspects of the job depends on spending months or years, on less challenging assignments. People may be willing to work diligently at less challenging tasks, if they see them as a stepping stone to a future with more challenging work. A person's career stage will also affect the motivational effect of challenging – in late career they may be less-inclined to seek challenge than they were when young.

15.6   Designing work to be motivating

People value both **extrinsic** and **intrinsic rewards**. Extrinsic rewards are those that are separate from the task, such as pay, security and promotion. Intrinsic rewards are those that people receive as they do the task itself – using skills, sensing achievement, doing satisfying work. Recall that a central element in scientific management was the careful design of the 'one best way' of doing a piece of manual work. Experts analysed how people did the job and identified the most efficient method, usually breaking the job into many small parts. Such work provided few if any intrinsic rewards – and Taylor's system concentrated on providing clear extrinsic rewards.

Working on a small element of a task is boring to many people, making them dissatisfied, careless and frequently absent. As these limitations became clear, managers looked for ways to make jobs more intrinsically rewarding – so that the work itself brought a reward of interest or challenge. The ideas from Maslow, Herzberg and McGregor prompted attempts to increase the opportunity for people to satisfy higher-level needs at work. The assumption was that staff would work more productively if management offered intrinsic rewards (motivators in Herzberg's terms) as well as extrinsic ones (Herzberg's hygiene factors), leading to ideas about job enrichment.

Extrinsic rewards are valued outcomes or benefits provided by others, such as promotion, a pay increase or a bigger car.

Intrinsic rewards are valued outcomes or benefits that come from the individual, such as feelings of satisfaction, achievement and competence.

Job characteristics theory

Hackman and Oldham (1980) built on these ideas to develop and test empirically an approach to the design of work which focused on the objective characteristics of employees jobs. Their basic idea was to build into those jobs the attributes which are likely to offer intrinsic motivation to staff, and so encouraging them to perform well. Their **job characteristics theory** predicts that the design of a job will affect internal motivation and work outcomes, with the effects being mediated by individual and contextual factors. Figure 15.7 shows the model, with the addition of implementing concepts in the left-hand column. The model provides guidance in how to design enriched jobs which satisfy more of employees' higher-level needs.

The model identifies three *psychological states* that must be present to achieve high motivation. If any are low, motivation will be low. The three states are:

Job characteristics theory predicts that the design of a job will affect internal motivation and work outcomes, with the effects being mediated by individual and contextual factors.

- **Experienced meaningfulness** The degree to which employees perceive their work as valuable and worthwhile. If workers regard a job as trivial and pointless, their motivation will be low.
- **Experienced responsibility** How responsible people feel for the quantity and quality of work performed.
- **Knowledge of results** The amount of feedback employees receive about how well they are doing. Those who do not receive feedback will care less about the quality of their performance.

> **Management in practice**   **Enriching the work of a software engineer**
>
> A skilled software engineer found that others were expecting him to help them out on too many routine tasks, and this was preventing him from developing new skills – so he became disengaged from the work he enjoyed. He discussed the problem with his manager, who responded effectively in that he:
>
> - made the engineer responsible for two junior engineers who could share the load;
> - assigned him to visit customers (previously done by a customer engineer);
> - authorised him to plan how to meet customers needs.
>
> The engineer said:
>
> After these changes, I experienced total fulfillment. I was aware of the customers' problems. And by contacting them directly I knew what they needed. I also saw directly how our solutions helped them;
>
> - Natural work groups to share loading,
> - Customer relations – significant outcomes,
> - Vertical loading training engineers,
> - Feedback channel.
>
> Source: Private communication with the engineer.

These psychological states are influenced by five *job characteristics* that contribute to experienced meaningfulness of work:

- **Skill variety** The extent to which a job makes use of a range of skills and experience. A routine administrative job is low in variety, whereas that of a marketing analyst may require a wide variety of statistical and interpersonal skills.
- **Task identity** Whether a job involves a complete operation, with a recognisable beginning and end. A nurse who organises and oversees all the treatments for a hospital patient will have more task identity than one who provides a single treatment to many different patients.
- **Task significance** How much the job matters to others in the organisation or to the wider society. People who can see that their job contributes directly to performance, or that it is a major help to others, will feel they have a significant task.
- **Autonomy** How much freedom and independence a person has in deciding how to go about doing the work. A sales agent in a call centre following a tightly scripted (and recorded) conversation has less autonomy than a sales agent talking face to face with a customer.
- **Feedback** The extent to which a person receives feedback on relevant dimensions of performance. Modern manufacturing systems can provide operators with very rapid information on quality, scrap, material use and costs. Operators can then receive a high level of feedback on the results of their work.

The extent to which a job contains these elements can be calculated using a tested instrument, and then using the scores to calculate the *motivating potential* score for the job. Figure 15.7 presents the model schematically.

The model also shows how to increase the motivating potential of a job, by using one or more of five 'implementing concepts':

- **Combine tasks** Rather than divide the work into small pieces, as Taylor recommended, staff can combine them so they use more skills and complete more of the whole task. An order clerk could receive orders from a customer and arrange transport and invoicing instead of having these done by different people.

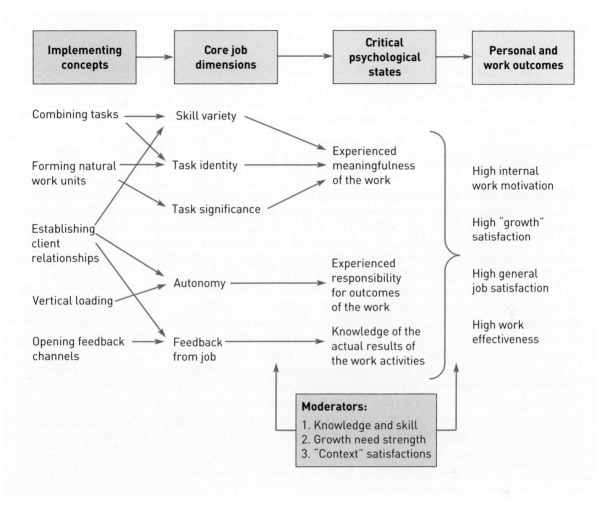

Figure 15.7 The job characteristics model
Source: Adapted from Hackman and Oldham (1980).

- **Form natural workgroups** In order to give more responsibility and enable sharing of skills, groups could be created that carry out a complete operation. Instead of a product passing down an assembly line, with each worker performing one operation, a group may assemble the whole product, sharing out the tasks among themselves.
- **Establish customer relations** This would bring home to employees the expectations of the people to whom their work goes, whether inside or outside the organisation, enabling them to see how their job fits into the larger picture. Instead of people doing part of the job for all customers, they can look after all the requirements of some customers. They establish closer relationships and gain a better understanding of their customers' needs.
- **Vertical loading** This involves workers taking on some responsibilities of supervisors to solve problems and develop workable solutions, thus adding to their autonomy. Operators may be given responsibility for checking the quantity and quality of incoming materials and reporting any problems. They may use more discretion over the order in which they arrange a week's work.
- **Open feedback channels** This would ensure that people receive feedback on their performance from internal or external customers. Operators can attend meetings at which customers give their views on the service provided as a basis for improving performance and building client relationships.

The last feature of the Hackman–Oldham model is the specification of three moderating influences:

- knowledge and skill – a person's ability to do the work;
- growth need strength – the extent to which an individual desires personal challenges, accomplishment and learning on the job – which clearly varies; and
- 'context' satisfaction – pay and other conditions surrounding the job.

Key ideas   **Meaningful work leads to positive outcomes**

Many research teams have used the work design model to test empirically the effects of the variables on work outcomes. Most have confirmed the positive relationships predicted by Hackman and Oldham (1980), in the sense that jobs which were assessed to be relatively high on the motivational factors tended to enhance job satisfaction and performance, and to be negatively associated with absenteeism. Humphrey *et al.* (2007) conducted a meta-analysis of 259 such studies, doing so in a way that enabled them both to test the general validity of the original model, and to extend it in two significant ways.

They found that the five motivational characteristics shown in Figure 15.7 were indeed positively related to job satisfaction, growth satisfaction, internal work motivation and positive job performance; and were negatively related to absenteeism. They also found that experienced meaningfulness was a particularly significant mediating factor – in other words, it confirmed that the reason why motivating factors lead to positive work outcomes is that they enable people to see meaning in their work.

The team also extended the original model by including measures of two aspects of the wider context in which people were performing their work. They assessed two aspects – social characteristics (such as social support and opportunities for interaction outside the organisation) and work context characteristics (such as physical demands and working conditions). Their analysis showed that these contextual factors also affect work outcomes: how people design them has a positive or negative effect on work outcomes.

Source: Humphrey *et al.* (2007).

Many managers, such as those at Gamma Chemical (see the following Management in Practice), have changed the kind of work they expect employees to do. This has not usually been to provide more interesting jobs, but as a response to business conditions. Nevertheless, the results of such changes often support what the theory predicts. Using ideas from this section to enhance staff motivation can enable staff to work in ways that add more value to resources, and so support wider strategy.

Management in practice   **Gamma Chemical (part 2) – a focus on motivating factors**

After taking control, Gamma Chemical made the following changes to working arrangements:

- introduced a cross-training programme to improve job diversity and individual growth;
- created problem-solving teams from natural work units to give operators a sense of ownership and achievement;
- expected operators to make more decisions, increasing individual authority and accountability;
- introduced an appraisal system that shows operators how their function affects company performance.

Management believed these changes had resulted in 20 per cent more output and 50 per cent less wastage.

Source: Private communication and discussions with the manager.

15.7   Interaction of motivation and strategy

Jeffrey Pfeffer (2005) drew upon his extensive experience to outline ways of achieving a high-performance organisation by working with people, not by replacing them or limiting the scope of their activities. He regards the workforce as a source of strategic advantage, not as a cost to be minimised or avoided. Mot successful companies owe their sustained (*not* temporary) success to the collection of practices through which they managed people. This becomes a strategic capability (Chapter 8) that cannot easily be copied, because the practices fitted together, and reinforced each other. They include:

- Employment security – which signals a long-term commitment to its work force.
- Selective recruiting – offering security implies careful selection, and makes those appointed feel part of an elite.
- High wages – attracts good applicants, and signals the organisation values people.
- Employee ownership – aligns the interests of employees and shareholders.
- Sharing information about performance and plans – shows trust.
- Participation and empowerment – motivating for able staff.
- Self-managed teams – a further route to flexible and profitable performance.
- Training and skill development – indicates the need for continued growth.
- Symbolic egalitarianism – scrapping status symbols that only serve to divide.

Pfeffer stresses that paying attention to these human aspects cannot guarantee survival and success – financial downturn, a misguided strategy or bad luck can destroy the healthiest of organisations. But the examples of Innocent Drinks (Part 1), BMW (Chapter 11 Case) or W.L. Gore and Associates (Part 5 Case) show what is possible – as does the following Management in Practice example.

Management in practice   Empowering nurses at Western General Hospital

A nurse manager at the Western General Hospital in a large city commented on the empowerment of nurses at the hospital:

> The service has been trying to be more responsive to the needs of patients by delegating power and responsibility to local level. Nurses have recognised the benefits to patients if nurses carry out their work by patient allocation rather than by task allocation. This has developed into the 'named nurse' concept, which intriguingly incorporates four of the five core dimensions of the job characteristics model. The nurse assesses needs, plans, implements and evaluates the care of his or her patients, so having skill variety, task identity, task significance and autonomy.
>
> Perhaps even the feedback element is provided from the evaluation stage of each patient's care. The empowerment approach fits with the organisation's unpredictable environment, the individualised service relationship and staff needs and characteristics. The recently appointed nurse managers are enthusiastic, and this has filtered down to staff. They are gradually becoming aware of the move from Theory X to Theory Y style of management. They appreciate that at last their skills and experience are being recognised and used.
>
> Information flows more freely and openly. Decisions are made only after discussion with the staff who will be affected by the outcome. Nurses in the wards are aware of their allocated budgets and what they are spending. Recruitment of staff is now done by existing staff on the ward, where previously managers decided whom to appoint.

Source: Private communication from a senior nurse in the hospital.

Lawler (2008) shows how organisations can gain sustainable competitive advantage by the way they organise and manage their employees (their 'human capital'). Organisations that put people at the centre of their activities follow a coherent set of management practices and, above all, aim to align their features towards creating a working relationship that attracts talented individuals and enables them to work together in an effective manner. He identifies the main features of such 'human capital-centric' (HC-centric) organisation as:

Business strategy is determined by talent considerations, which in turn drives human capital management practices. Senior managers consider issues of strategy and people together, and care is taken to ensure that employees understand and support the strategy.

Every aspect of the organisation is obsessed with human capital and its management. HC-centric organisations take great care to recruit, assess and develop employees to ensure they fit the skills the organisation needs.

Performance management is one of the most important activities. A systematic process establishes strategy-driven goals, assesses performance against goals and provides feedback on performance.

The information system gives as much time to measures of employee costs, performance and condition as it does to other assets such as finance and materials. HC-centric organisations have systems that report rigorously on performance and how well it is using these human resources.

The HR department is the most important staff group. It is staffed with the best HR staff available, and other executives see it as a valuable source of ideas on managing people.

The corporate board has the expertise it needs to advise on human capital issues. It receives regular information about the effectiveness with which the organisation is using talent and the commitment of people to the organisation.

Leadership is shared, and managers are highly skilled in managing people. Managers in HC-centric organisations understand and use sound principles when making decisions about motivation, organisational change, organisation structure and performance management. (Lawler, 2008, pp. 9–12)

Lawler's book illustrates these propositions with examples from many organisations – including BMW and W.L. Gore.

15.8 Integrating themes

Sustainable performance

Organisations in many sectors of the economy now include measures of sustainable performance as part of their strategy, and depend on their staff to achieve them. To what extent are staff motivated to do so?

Lawler (2008) believes that a characteristic of high-performing HC-centred organisations is that they ensure their strategy is practical by involving people from all parts of the business in the process of formulating it. This enables them to take account of many perspectives and sources of information, not only about the external environment and the customers, but also about the ability of the organisation to deliver the strategy. Equally, the reward system in HC-centred organisations will align personal rewards with the strategy by, for example, rewarding people for their contribution to sustainability; the following Management in Practice feature gives an example.

> ### Management in practice   Bonuses depend on sustainability www.dsm.com
>
> The Dutch life sciences company DSM has begun linking top management pay to targets such as the reduction of greenhouse gas emissions, energy use and the introduction of environmentally friendly products. Feike Sijbesma, the chief executive, said DSM would focus on the triple bottom line – people, profits and planet:
>
> **Sustainability is the key driver of our whole strategy. Pay is the ultimate expression of your values.**
>
> Half of DSM's short-term bonus will be determined by the number of environmentally friendly products it introduces and whether it reduces energy consumption. The other half will be determined by financial targets such as sales and cash flow.
>
> Source: *Financial Times*, 24 February 2010.

Governance and control

One controversial theme in the corporate governance debate is that of executive pay – where large salaries and bonuses paid to executives, even those in failing firms, has been the target of public and political criticism. Shareholders also have been active in some high-profile cases, trying to reduce or eliminate what they see as excessive payments to senior managers.

Boards face the need to attract and retain qualified and experienced staff, yet need to find ways to structure incentives so that they discourage short-term or risky behaviour by senior managers, and instead support long-term returns to shareholders. These moves may also forestall public pressure for stricter legislation limiting base pay, bonuses and other executive benefits.

Setting realistic goals for performance-based plans is difficult in uncertain economic times, making it harder to set profitability and growth targets in business plans, which are the basis of compensation plans. Compensation committees are being asked to approve a wider range of targets, which are moving from traditional measures such as revenue growth and earnings per share to ones based on the growth of working capital and cash flow. These changes aim to align variable pay with business strategy, and especially to encourage participants to take a long-term perspective.

Internationalisation

The growing significance of managing internationally sits uncomfortably with the fact that the theories outlined were developed in the US. Do they apply to people working in other countries? Hofstede (1989) articulated the 'unspoken cultural assumptions' present in both Theory X and Theory Y (p. 450). He writes:

> . . . in a comparative study of US values versus those dominant in ASEAN countries, I found the following common assumptions on the US side and underlying both X and Y:
>
> 1 Work is good for people.
> 2 People's capacities should be maximally utilised.
> 3 There are 'organisational objectives' that exist apart from people.
> 4 People in organisations behave as unattached individuals.
>
> These assumptions reflect value positions in McGregor's US society; most would be accepted in other Western countries. None of them, however, applies in ASEAN countries. Southeast Asian assumptions would be:
>
> 1 Work is a necessity but not a goal in itself.
> 2 People should find their rightful place in peace and harmony with their environment.

3 Absolute objectives exist only with God. In the world, persons in authority positions represent God so their objectives should be followed.

4 People behave as members of a family and/or group. Those who do not are rejected by society.

Because of these different culturally determined assumptions, McGregor's Theory X and Theory Y distinction becomes irrelevant in Southeast Asia. (p. 5)

Hofstede's work in Chapter 4 showed marked differences in national cultures. These are likely to influence the relative importance that people in those countries attach to the various motivational factors. People in Anglo-Saxon countries tend to display a relatively high need for achievement, strong masculinity scores and low uncertainty avoidance. This is not the norm in other cultures.

Summary

1 **Explain why managers need to understand and use theories of motivation**
- People depend on others within and beyond the organisation to act in a particular way, and understanding what motivates them is critical to this. Motivation includes understanding the goals which people pursue (content), the choices they make to secure them (process) and how this knowledge can be applied to influence others (including through work design).

2 **Show how the context, including the psychological contract, affects motivation**
- Social changes affect the people managers try to motivate, so they may need to adapt their approach to suit.
- The relationship between employer and employee is expressed in the psychological contract, which needs to be in acceptable balance for effective performance.

3 **Understand behaviour modification, content and process theories of motivation**
- Behaviour modification theories attempt to explain that people can influence the behaviour of others by using appropriate and timely reinforcement.
- Content theories seek to understand the needs which human beings may seek to satisfy at work and include the work of Maslow, Alderfer and Herzberg as well as of earlier observers such as Taylor and Mayo.
- Expectancy theory explains motivation in terms of valued outcomes and the subjective probability of achieving those outcomes.
- Equity theory explains motivation in terms of perceptions of fairness by comparison with others.
- Goal-setting theory believes that motivation depends on the degree of difficulty and specificity of goals.

4 **Use work design theories to diagnose motivational problems and recommend actions**
- Most of the models can be used to analyse the likely effects of organisational practices on motivation, and to indicate areas for possible management action.
- People are only motivated if the job meets a need which they value – providing appropriate content factors leads to satisfaction and performance.
- Herzberg suggests that motivation depends on paying attention to motivating as well as hygiene factors.
- Jobs can be enriched by increasing skill variety, task identity, task significance, autonomy and feedback.

5 Show how ideas on motivation link to those on strategy

- Pfeffer (2005) shows how the workforce can be a source of strategic advantage, and that successful companies attribute this to a collection of practices they use to manage people.
- Changing competitive conditions mean that critical performance indicators for many organisations stress responsiveness, creativity and innovation – which can only be encouraged by motivational policies that encourage these behaviours. Economic and predictable performance also remain important for many organisational functions, which raises possible dilemmas for organisation-wide motivational policies.

6 Show how ideas from the chapter add to your understanding of the integrating themes

- Like any strategy, that of building a more environmentally sustainable performance depends on people working with commitment to achieve it. Whether they do so will depend on aligning their motivation with that of the sustainability goal – the section includes examples of how some organisations try to achieve this.
- Using spectacular levels of pay and bonus to motivate skilled (and highly mobile) professional staff has attracted criticism from many outside the industries concerned. Managers in companies in those industries point out that in the context of an international, market economy they need to pay the market rate.
- Hofstede has pointed out that discussion about McGregor's Theory X and Theory Y is based on observations in Western societies – which are different in many ways from the new economic powers in the East.

Review questions

1 Outline the basic assumptions of McGregor's Theory X and Theory Y.
2 Describe the psychological contract. What are you expecting: (a) from an employer in your career; and (b) from an employer who provides you with part-time work while you are studying?
3 Which three things are pinpointed when using behaviour modification?
4 How does Maslow's theory of human needs relate to the ideas of Frederick Taylor?
5 How does Alderfer's theory differ from Maslow's? What research lay behind the two theories?
6 How did you score on the McClelland test? How did your scores compare with those of others?
7 Explain the difference between Herzberg's hygiene and motivating factors.
8 Explain the difference between E → P and P → O in expectancy theory.
9 What are the five job design elements that may affect a person's satisfaction with their work?
10 Give an example of an implementing concept associated with each element.
11 Summarise an idea from the chapter that adds to your understanding of the integrating themes.

Concluding critical reflection

Think about the ways in which you typically seek to motivate other people (staff, colleagues or those in other organisations) and about your company's approach to motivation. Review the material in the chapter, and then make notes on the following questions:

- What examples of the issues discussed in this chapter struck you as being relevant to motivational practice in your company?

- Thinking of the people you typically work with, who are effective and who are less effective motivators? What do the effective people do that enables them to motivate others? Do they seem to take a mainly Theory X or mainly Theory Y approach? Do their **assumptions** seem to be broadly correct or not? To what extent does the work people do have a high Motivational Potential Score (see p. 472)?

- What factors in the **context**, such as the history of the company or your experience have shaped the way you motivate others, and your organisation's approach to motivation? Do these approaches appear to be right for your present position and company – or would you use a different approach in another context? (Perhaps refer to some of the Management in Practice features for how different managers motivate others.)

- Have people put forward **alternative** approaches to motivating, based on evidence about other companies? If you could find such evidence, how may it affect company practice?

- What **limitations** can you identify in any of these motivational theories? For example, you could consider their usefulness in hi-tech working environments, or how well they apply in non-Western economies.

Further reading

Maslow, A. (1970), *Motivation and Personality* (2nd edn.), Harper & Row, New York.

McGregor, D. (1960), *The Human Side of Enterprise*, McGraw-Hill, New York.

Herzberg, F. (1959), *The Motivation to Work*, Wiley, New York.

Roethlisberger, F.J. and Dickson, W.J. (1939), *Management and the Worker*, Harvard University Press, Cambridge, MA.

   The original accounts of these influential works are unusually readable books showing organisations and research in action. Roethlisberger and Dickson's account of the Hawthorne experiments is long, but the others are short and accessible.

Culbertson, S.S. (2009), 'Do satisfied employees mean satisfied customers?', *Academy of Management Perspectives*, vol. 23, no. 1, pp. 76–77.

   Shows the link between employee satisfaction and customer responses – also relevant to marketing.

Deery, S., Iverson, R.D. and Walsh, J.T. (2006), 'Towards a better understanding of psychological contract breach: A study of customers service employees', *Journal of Applied Psychology*, vol. 91, no. 1, pp. 166–175.

   Empirical study of the consequences of not meeting staff expectations.

Lawler, E. (2008), *Talent*, Jossey Bass, San Francisco, CA.

   A very useful analysis of how some managers ensure that policies and practices throughout the organisations help to make good use of their employees.

Locke, E.A. and Latham, G.P. (2002), 'Building a practically useful theory of goal setting and task motivation – A 35-year odyssey', *American Psychologist*, vol. 57, no. 9, pp. 705–717.

   Review by the founders of goal-setting theory, including the results of many empirical studies.

Weblinks

Visit the websites of companies that interest you, perhaps as possible places to work.

www.childbase.co.uk
www.edenproject.com
www.dsm.com
www.gore.com
www.greatplacetowork.co.uk
www.ikea.com
www.irisnation.com
www.timpson.co.uk

Navigate to the pages dealing with 'about the company' or 'careers'.

● What do they tell you about working there? What seem to be the most prominent features?

● What needs do they seem to be aiming to meet? Would they meet your needs?

For video case studies, audio summaries, flashcards, exercises and annotated weblinks related to this chapter, visit **www.pearsoned.co.uk/mymanagementlab**

CHAPTER 16

COMMUNICATION

Aims

To describe and illustrate the main aspects of communication in organisations, and how these can help or hinder performance.

Objectives

By the end of your work on this chapter you should be able to outline the concepts below in your own terms and:

1 Explain the role of communication in managing

2 Identify and illustrate the elements and stages in the communication process

3 Use the concept of information richness to select a communication channel

4 Compare the benefits of different communication networks

5 Outline some essential interpersonal communication skills

6 Consider how communication interacts with strategy and the wider context

7 Show how ideas from the chapter add to your understanding of the integrating themes

Key terms

This chapter introduces the following ideas:

communication	non-verbal communication
message	selective attention
coding	stereotyping
decoding	channel
noise	information richness
feedback	information overload

Each is a term defined within the text, as well as in the Glossary at the end of the book.

In early 2010 Facebook was the world's largest on-line social network with over 350 million users, who post over 55 million updates a day and share more than 3.5 billion pieces of content every week. It has expanded far beyond its American roots, with 70 per cent of users being outside the US. Early that year it reported that more than 100 million people were actively using the site from their mobile devices – up from 65 million only six months previously.

Mark Zuckerburg founded the site which allows users to create a profile page and make links with friends and acquaintances. Other students at Harvard claim the original idea, and that they hired Zuckerburg to write the programs: lawyers are on the case.

About 800 employees work at the main Facebook campus at Palo Alto, California, but in May 2007 it introduced Facebook Platform, which allows independent software developers to create applications for Facebook. Over 1 million now do so, creating an online directory with over 500,000 apps (games, music, photo-sharing tools and many more), which serve to attract further users to the site. That leaves the company's developers free to concentrate on innovations that encourage even more sharing.

Like other social network sites Facebook has benefited from a continuing fall in the cost of hardware needed to store and process data. It has also been able to use free, open-source software to build systems that scale quickly and easily. And it has built some unique solutions to cope with rapid growth. The firm's software engineers built a system called MultiFeed that searches databases near-instantly for relevant news from a person's friends. This has allowed the network to add many millions of new users without damaging its ability to provide a constant stream of up-to-date news to people's pages.

Paying attention to the quality of the site's technology is believed to be one of the reasons why Facebook had, by 2010, become the dominant global social network (available in 70 languages, and also as Facebook Lite, a stripped-down version that is popular in countries without fast broadband connections).

Mr Zuckerberg's goal is to connect as much of the world's population as possible via the network and then to persuade them to use it as their main way into the internet. He is so keen to realise his vision

© Kim Komenich/San Francisco Chronicle/Corbis

that he is said to have turned down offers to buy the company which would have made him an instant billionaire.

In May 2009 a Russian investment firm, Digital Sky Technologies invested $200 million in return for a 1.96 per cent shareholding in the business. Microsoft had earlier bought a 1.6 per cent stake. Facebook had, by mid-2009, raised $600 million from investors.

Sources: *New York Times,* 27 May 2009, 25 December 2009; *The Economist*, 30 January 2010.

Case questions 16.1

- What examples are there here of people communicating to (directly or indirectly) build Facebook?

- If you use Facebook (or similar), what changes, if any, has it made to the way you communicate?

16.1 Introduction

Facebook (and similar sites) have become widely accepted tools for mass communication, representing a dramatic and permanent upgrade in people's ability to communicate with others. The sites make people's personal relationships more visible and quantifiable than ever before. They have also become useful vehicles for news and channels of influence. Some companies doubt the benefits of online social networking in the office and try to block access – concerned about security and staff wasting time. Others see many potential benefits in these new communication tools, enhancing connections, and spreading ideas and innovations around the world faster than ever before.

Managers at Facebook themselves face communication challenges: they need (among other things) to communicate the attractions of working at the company to potential staff, ensure rapid and accurate communication among their software developers and between them and other functions, and to understand what people want and expect from Facebook. They also watch for information on developments at Twitter and MySpace – two competitors.

Most managers experience similar communication issues, though in less challenging circumstances. The success of the pharmaceutical company, GSK, depends on intense communication between research teams, clinical trial staff, regulators and marketers as they develop new drugs. Those in service organisations such as HMV want staff to communicate ideas and suggestions – and understand company policy. Professionals providing care for the sick and vulnerable need to communicate accurate and timely information, often in stressful conditions; spectacular failures are often found traced back to poor communication.

Even with the technologies now available, people continue to experience ineffective communication. Computer-based systems provide useful tools, but they do not replace the need for human communication. Company-wide information systems make it easy for geographically separated people to exchange messages – but how they interpret those messages depends on their relationship:

> Technology won't make messages more useful unless we build personal relationships first. The message will get through more easily if the recipient has some pre-existing relationship with the sender. (Rosen, 1998)

Until people meet they cannot develop the mutual trust and shared knowledge essential for true communication.

Some managers underestimate the communication problems. Someone who works with a major utility business recently wrote to the author:

> The majority of managers within [the business] consider themselves to be effective communicators. Staff have a different perspective, and a recent staff survey rated communications as being very poor, with information being top down, no form of two-way communications and managers only hearing what they want to hear.

This chapter begins by showing how communication is essential to managing. People send and receive messages through one or more distinct channels (or media), passing along formal and informal organisational networks. While technology can help, communication remains a human activity that depends on developing identifiable skills. People exercise these within an organisational context, which affects the choice of communication methods and whether communication leads to mutual understanding. Figure 16.1 provides an overview.

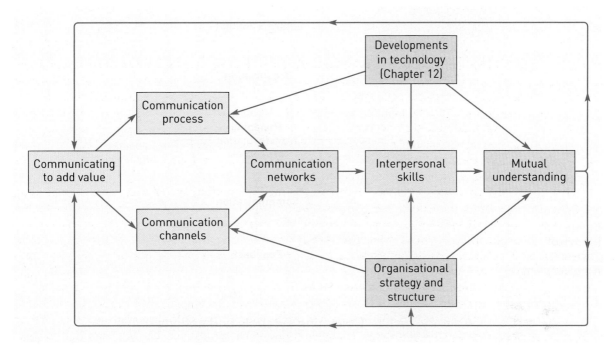

Figure 16.1 An overview of communication in organisations

| 16.2 | **Communicating to add value** |

We base our understanding of the world on information and feelings that we receive and send. People at all levels of an organisation need to communicate with others about:

- inputs – e.g. the availability of materials or equipment;
- transformation – e.g. about capacity or quality; and
- outputs – e.g. customer complaints or advertising policy.

Information about an order needs to flow accurately to all the departments that will help to satisfy it – and then between departments as the task progresses. People communicate information up and down the vertical hierarchy, and horizontally between functions, departments and other organisations. Figure 16.2 shows how communication supports these value-adding processes.

Stewart (1967) and Mintzberg (1973) showed that both formal and informal communication was central to the management job. This is most evident in the informational role – but equally managers can only perform their interpersonal and decisional roles by communicating with other people. Computer-based information systems are clearly part of the communication system – but only part. They deal very efficiently with structured, explicit data and information – but much less so with the unstructured, tacit information and knowledge.

What is communication?

Communication happens when people share information to reach a common understanding. Managing depends on conveying and interpreting messages clearly so that people can work together. Speaking and writing are easy: achieving a common understanding is not. Background and personal needs affect our ability to absorb messages from those with different histories, but until people reach a common understanding, communication has not taken place.

Communication is the exchange of information through written or spoken words, symbols and actions to reach a common understanding.

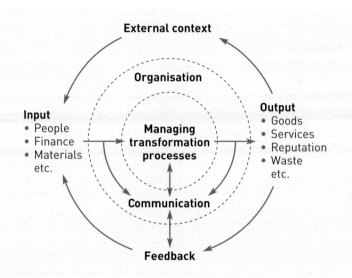

Figure 16.2
The role of communication in organisations

How communicating adds value

Communication features in some way in every chapter – influencing others, working in teams, giving marketing information to senior management, interpreting financial data or posting a job vacancy on the company website. It is through communication that people add value through innovation, quality, delivery and cost. *Innovation* depends on good information about customer needs and relevant discoveries, which comes from communication with the scientific community. Embodying ideas in usable products requires communication within cross-functional project teams and with suppliers and customers. Efforts to enhance *quality* depend on everyone involved understanding what quality means to the customer. Without communication there is no quality.

Management in practice   Communication failure in a small Dutch company

The company was founded in 1881 and the present owner is one of the fourth generation of the family. The company trades and manufactures packaging machines and employs 16 people. Someone who has recently joined the company said:

Last year was difficult. Five people left the company and took with them much knowledge and experience. The company really consists of one person – the owner. He does not delegate much and there is little communication between him and the rest of the organisation. The only part of the company that interests him is the game of selling machines. He describes the rest of his tasks as annoying. The result is that, for example:

1 When we sell a machine, Operations do not know exactly what Sales has promised a customer. The customer expects the machine they specified, but do not always get it.
2 There is lack of internal communication: people in the company do not know their precise responsibilities or who is responsible for which tasks.
3 There is no time planning for ordered machines. No one knows the delivery date that we have promised a customer.
4 There is no budget system for a machine project. When we sell a machine we do not know if we will make a profit or a loss.

All together, the company faces serious problems because of a lack of policy, management, information and communication.

Source: Private communication from the manager.

Another measure of performance is *delivery* – supplying the customer with what they expect, when they expect it. That is only possible if people communicate accurate, reliable and timely information up and down the supply chain. Competition adds to pressure to continually reduce the *cost* of goods and services – so people need information about current performance and ways of removing waste.

Management in practice   Twitter and Facebook as marketing tools

Social networking sites offer small businesses a quick and free way to promote their wares to a large audience. Two sisters who opened a bakery in 2008 use Twitter and Facebook as a marketing tool: one said:

Together they work like a virtual focus group, a bulletin board, and a marketing campaign rolled into one.

As well as posting details of new flavours, specials and events, they use the social networking sites to promote their new nationwide delivery service together with a new store.

Many small business owners find traditional advertising channels such as television, radio and newspapers too expensive. For others, the web is a medium more in tune with their potential customers. Someone who runs a pizza business in a university town said:

They're not a good fit for everyone, but if you're a small business with a customer base who uses social media, you can't afford not to use them. It's a great way to interact one on one and build a relationship with our customers.

She recently asked her Twitter and Facebook followers to vote on which company she should use to supply soft drinks.

Facebook offers businesses special pages, and the option to show advertisements to users who like similar companies.

Source: *BBC News*, 15 October 2009.

Chapter 12 shows how modern information and communication technologies transform how people receive, use and distribute information, (including through sites such as Facebook). It also shows that when managers implement such systems they also need to ensure that the context (structure, culture and so on) and the system are compatible. Technically sophisticated systems only add value if the people responsible for them manage familiar human issues. A similar lesson applies to the communication process itself. Modern technology only improves communication if those using it pay attention to familiar issues in the communication process: most human barriers to communication endanger hi-tech interactions just as much as they do low-tech ones.

16.3   Communication processes

The **message** is what the sender communicates.

We communicate whenever we send a **message** to someone and as we think about what he/she says in return. This is a subtle and complex process, through which people easily send and receive the wrong message. Whenever someone says: 'That's not what I meant' or 'I explained it clearly, and they still got it wrong' there has been a communication failure. We waste time when we misunderstand directions, or cause offence by saying something that the listener misinterprets.

We infer meaning from words and gestures and then from people's reply to our message. We continually interpret their messages and create our own. As colleagues have a conversation, each listens to the other's words, sees their gestures, reads the relevant documents or looks over the equipment to understand what the other means. When they achieve a mutual understanding about what to do, they have communicated effectively. Figure 16.3 shows a model of the process (Berlo, 1960) which enables someone to analyse the sources of communication success or failure.

Communication requires at least two people: a sender and a receiver. The *senders* initiate the communication when they try to transfer ideas, facts or feelings to the *receivers*: the people to whom they send the message. The sender **encodes** the idea they wish to convey into a message by using symbols such as words, actions or expressions. Deciding how to encode the message is an important choice and depends in part on the purpose:

Encoding is translating information into symbols for communication.

- Is it to convey specific and unambiguous information?
- Is it to raise an open and unfamiliar problem and a request for creative ideas?
- Is it to pass on routine data or to inspire people?

The message is the tangible expression of the sender's idea. The sender chooses one or more channels (the communication medium) – such as an email, a face-to-face meeting or a

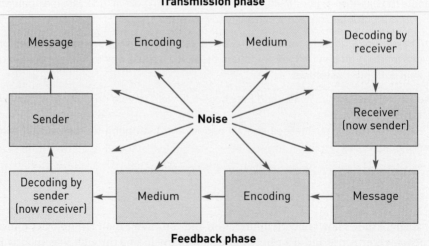

Figure 16.3
The communication process

Key ideas   Accurate encoding

The following five principles help to encode a message accurately:

- **Relevancy** Make the message meaningful and significant, carefully selecting the words, symbols or gestures to be used.
- **Simplicity** Put the message in the simplest possible terms, reducing the number of words, symbols or gestures used.
- **Organisation** Organise the message as a series of points to facilitate understanding. Complete each point in the message before proceeding to the next.
- **Repetition** Restate key points of the message at least twice. Repetition is particularly important in spoken communication because words may not be clearly heard or fully understood the first time.
- **Focus** Concentrate on the essential aspects of the message. Make the message clear and avoid unnecessary detail.

---

letter – to transmit the coded message. The receiver **decodes** the symbols contained in the message, and tries to reconstruct the sender's original thought. Coding and decoding are sources of communication failure, as the sender and receiver have different knowledge, experience and interests. Receivers also evaluate a message by their knowledge of the sender, which affects whether they regard the information received to be valuable. These 'filters' interfere with the conversion of meaning to symbols and *vice versa* and, along with other distractions and interruptions, are referred to as **noise**. Dimbleby and Burton (2006) identify three types of filter – arising within individuals (psychological filters), within the message (semantic filters) and within the context (mechanical filters).

> **Decoding** is the interpretation of a message into a form with meaning.

> **Noise** is anything that confuses, diminishes or interferes with communication.

The final stage in the episode is when the receiver responds to the message by giving **feedback** to the sender. This turns one-way communication into two-way. Without feedback the sender cannot know whether the receivers have the message or whether they have interpreted it as the sender intended. The flow of information between parties is continuous and reciprocal, each responding by giving feedback to the other, and is only completed when the sender knows that the receiver has received and understood the message as intended.

> **Feedback** (in communication) occurs as the receiver expresses his or her reaction to the sender's message.

Effective communicators understand it is a two-way process, and positively check for feedback. They do not rely only on making their message as clear as possible, but also encourage the receiver to provide feedback. Without some response – a nod, a question that implies understanding, a quick email acknowledgement – the sender has not communicated successfully.

Assume that communication is going to fail, and put time and effort into preventing that.

Key ideas   Quality of information

The quality of information depends on four criteria:

1. **Reliability (accuracy)** People expect information to reflect accurately the situation it describes – that a sales report is an accurate account of sales or that a report of a conversation is true.
2. **Timeliness** Information is only useful if it is available in time. A manager who needs to keep expenditure within a budget requires cost information frequently enough to be able to act on unfavourable trends.
3. **Quantity** Most managers receive more information than they can interpret and use, suggesting that some available technologies may damage performance unless they think carefully about how they use them.
4. **Relevance** This depends on a person's tasks and responsibilities and again requires managers to evaluate critically which of the information they receive is essential.

Non-verbal communication

Non-verbal communication is the process of coding meaning through behaviours such as facial expression, gestures and body postures.

Interpersonal communication includes **non-verbal communication**, sometimes called body language, which can have more impact on the receiver than the words in the message. Signals include the tone of voice, facial expression, posture and appearance, and provide most of the impact in face-to-face communication (Knapp and Hall, 2002; Beall, 2004).

Small changes in eye contact, raising eyebrows or a directed glance while making a statement, add to the meaning that the sender conveys. A stifled yawn, an eager nod, a thoughtful flicker of anxiety gives the sender a signal about the receiver's reaction. Gestures and body position give strong signals: leaning forward attentively, moving about in the chair, hands moving nervously, gathering papers or looking at the clock – all send a message. A skilful manager will use non-verbal cues to detect that something is worrying an employee even if he/she is hesitant to speak out.

Positive non-verbal feedback helps to build relations within a team. A smile or wave to someone at least acknowledges that they exist. Related to a task, it indicates approval in an informal, rapid way that sustains confidence. Negative feedback can be correspondingly damaging. A boss who looks irritated by what the staff member sees as a reasonable enquiry is giving a negative signal, as is one who looks bored during a presentation.

Management in practice   Virtual teams at Cisco www.cisco.com

Cisco Systems supplies much of the physical equipment which supports the Internet, and most design teams contain staff working in facilities across the world. One team member said:

> It means you have to be a bit more careful when it comes to communication. Most of the time you have to use email and instant messaging to discuss issues, which means there can be misunderstandings if you're not careful. When you interact in person you use things like facial expression and hand gestures – none of these are available when emailing so you have to state your arguments more clearly.

Source: Private communication.

As with any interpersonal skill, some people are better at interpreting non-verbal behaviour than others. The sender of a spoken message can benefit by noting the non-verbal responses to what they say. If they do not seem appropriate (raised eyebrows or an anxious look), the speaker should pause and check that the receiver has received the message that the sender intended.

Perception

Selective attention is the ability, often unconscious, to choose from the stream of signals in the environment, concentrating on some and ignoring others.

Perception is the process by which individuals make sense of their environment by selecting and interpreting information. We receive a stream of information beyond our capacity to absorb, and **selective attention** keeps us sane. We actively notice and attend to only a small fraction of the available information, filtering out what we do not need, based in part on the strength of the signal and our evaluation of the sender.

When people observe information they interpret it, and react to it, uniquely. This 'perceptual organisation' arranges incoming signals into patterns that give meaning to data – relating it to our interest, the status of the sender or the benefits of attending to it. Experience, social class and education affect the meanings people attach to information.

Activity 16.2   Understanding communication practices

- Think of an example where communication between two or more people failed. Note down why you think that happened, using the model in Figure 16.3.
- Use Figure 16.3 to analyse the communication process of someone using Facebook. Note how it differs from face-to-face communication.
- Email is widely used in business: list the advantages and disadvantages of that medium compared with face-to-face communication.

A common form of perceptual organisation is **stereotyping**. 'They always complain' or 'You would expect people from marketing to say that' are signs that someone is judging a message not by its content but by the group to which the sender belongs. It leads us to misinterpret a message because we are making inaccurate assumptions about the sender. Perceptual differences are natural but interfere with communication. Our unique personalities and perceptual styles affect how we interpret a message, so senders cannot assume that receivers attach the same meaning to a message as they intended.

> **Stereotyping** is the practice of consigning a person to a category or personality type on the basis of his/her membership of some known group.

Case questions 16.2

- As Mark Zuckerberg began to build Facebook, he would have needed to secure support from powerful players for his new venture.
- Review the model of the communication process and identify how each of the steps could have been a source of difficulty in building that support.

16.4   Selecting communication channels

The model of communication in Figure 16.3 shows the steps that people take to communicate effectively. The process fails if either the sender or receiver does not encode or decode the symbols of the message in the same way. Selecting the wrong communication **channel** also lead to difficulty: sending a message that requires subtle interpretation as a written instruction with no chance for feedback is not good practice.

Lengel and Daft (1988) developed the idea of **information richness** to compare the capacity of channels to promote common understanding between sender and receiver (see Figure 16.4).

The richness of a medium (or channel) depends on its ability to:

- handle many cues at the same time;
- support rapid two-way feedback; and
- establish a personal focus for the communication.

> A **channel** is the medium of communication between a sender and a receiver.

> **Information richness** refers to the amount of information that a communication channel can carry, and the extent to which it enables sender and receiver to achieve common understanding.

Face-to-face communication

Face-to-face discussion is the richest medium, as both parties can pick up many information cues (concentration, eye contact, body movements or facial expression) in addition to the

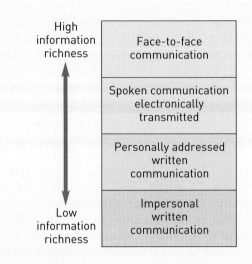

Figure 16.4
The Lengel–Daft media richness hierarchy

Source: Lengel and Daft (1988).

spoken words. This enables them to gain a deep understanding of the nuances of meaning. Someone who had recently started a business said:

> I find the best way to communicate with people is very simply to talk to them and to be upfront and honest and forthright with as much information as you possibly can.

Managers spend most of their time in face-to-face contact with others. Oral communication is quick, spontaneous and enriched by non-verbal signals. It takes place in one-to-one conversation (face-to-face), through meetings of several people or when someone addresses an audience at a conference. Management by wandering around is a widely used and effective communication technique. Rather than having formal meetings, managers go into the work areas and talk to employees about the issues that concern them. They gain insights into what is happening, which reports from supervisors may filter.

Management in practice   Carlos Ghosn, CEO of Renault-Nissan

Carlos Ghosn became one of the motor industry's most prominent figures when he saved the failing Nissan company from the collapse which many thought was inevitable. He is a charismatic figure, mobbed for autographs during plant tours, and generally heaped with national adulation for saving a car company once given up for dead. At auto shows from Paris to Beijing, his cosmopolitan air and impressive track record make him a star attraction.

He reaches deep into the organisation by constant – and often unannounced – visits to dealerships, test tracks, assembly plants and parts suppliers. On a visit to Nissan's Iwaki engine plant, 180 km north of Tokyo, he was mobbed by eager factory hands. He doubtless enjoyed the attention but, at each stop it was evident he was looking for nuggets that would help him squeeze yet another ounce of productivity from the plant. He worked the floor, chatting to assembly workers, drilling foremen, all to get that extra fact which would edge the company forward. The visit clearly paid off for Ghosn, who knows he is nothing without an inspired workforce. He advises:

> The only power that a CEO has is to motivate. Be transparent and explain yourself in clear, lucid terms. Do as you say you are going to do. Listen first: then think.

Sources: *Business Week*, 4 October 2004; *Fortune*, 30 November 2006.

Despite the benefits of face-to-face communication, few managers rely on it entirely. It takes time and becomes less practical as managers and staff become geographically dispersed. There is also no written record, so some prefer to combine it with a written communication confirming what was agreed. Advances in technology are helping in this area. Videoconferencing allows people to communicate face to face (and so see each others' facial expressions and gestures) without the time and cost of travel.

Management in practice   Videoconferencing at Cisco Systems

When Cisco Systems held its annual summit in May 2009 for its top 3,100 executives, no-one flew to the group's headquarters in California. Instead staff in China, India and the UK gathered in front of high definition screens in conference rooms, and communicated via instant messaging.

The company saved millions of dollars that had been spent on previous events – and found that interaction improved. Managers and directors responded live to some of the more than 10,000 questions posed electronically, with many more being archived for follow-up sessions.

Cisco is not alone, as many more companies with far-flung operations are using similar communication technologies. Nokia, Siemens, IBM, and Procter and Gamble have all made savings on travel costs.

Source: *Financial Times*, 26 May 2009.

Spoken communication electronically transmitted

This is the second highest form of communication in terms of media richness. Although when we use a telephone or mobile we cannot see the non-verbal expressions or body language, we can pick up the tone of voice, the sense of urgency or the general manner of the message, as well as the words themselves. Feedback is quick so both parties can check for understanding.

Voicemail systems and answering machines can supplement telephone systems, by allowing people to record messages by both the sender and the intended receiver. Many companies use message recording systems to pass customers to the right department, by offering options to which they respond by pressing the buttons on their keypads. These systems reduce costs but often annoy customers, especially when they want to speak to a human being.

Personally addressed written communication

Personally addressed written communication has the advantage of face-to-face communication in that, being addressed personally to the recipient, it tends to demand his/her attention. It also enables the sender to phrase the message in a way that best suits the reader. If both parties express their meanings accurately and seek and offer feedback, a high level of mutual understanding can be reached, which is also recorded. Even if people reach their understanding by communicating face to face, they will often follow it up with a written email, fax or letter.

Email and more recently social networking (more messages are now sent through social networking sites than by email) have grown rapidly to communicate within and between organisations, and between individuals. They have the 'permanent record' advantage of the letter, while instant delivery allows people to complete an exchange in minutes that could have taken days. Sending them from mobiles enables people to stay in touch from wherever they are. The disadvantages are:

- lack of body language;
- adding many recipients to the 'copy' box, leading to email overload; and
- using the technology to send unsolicited messages.

Friedman and Currall (2003) propose that using emails can make it more likely that conflicts escalate. Anecdotal reports of this happening led them to analyse the structural features of email that may make this more or less likely. Features include the lack of visual and verbal cues common in face-to-face transactions, although this might be balanced by being able with email to revise a possibly inflammatory comment before sending it. Byron (2008) finds that people sending emails (intentionally or not) communicate emotions, and the nature of email makes misunderstanding of these expressions more likely.

Activity 16.3   Critical reflection on communication methods

- Think of a task you have done with a small group of people, either at work or during your studies. How did you communicate with each other? List all the methods used, and their advantages and disadvantages.

Impersonal written communication

This is the least information-rich medium, but it is suitable for sending a message to many people. Newsletters and routine computer reports are lean media because they provide a single cue, are impersonal and do not encourage response.

Managers use them to send a simple message about the company and developments in it to widely dispersed employees and customers. They also use them to disseminate rules, procedures, product information and news about the company, such as new appointments. The medium also ensures that instructions are communicated in a standard form to people in different places, and that a record of the message is available. Electronic means such as emails and company websites supplement paper as a way of transmitting impersonal information. The ease with which electronic messages can be sent to large numbers of people leads to **information overload**, when people receive more information than they can read, let alone deal with adequately.

Information overload arises when the amount of information a person has to deal with exceeds his/her capacity to process it.

Each channel has advantages and disadvantages. If the message is to go to many people and there is a significant possibility of misunderstanding, some relatively structured written or electronic medium is likely to work best. If it is an unusual problem which needs the opinion of several other people, then a face-to-face discussion will be more effective.

In a study of 95 executives in a petrochemical company, Lengel and Daft (1988) found that the preferred medium depended on how routine the topic was:

> Managers used face-to-face [communication] 88 per cent of the time for non-routine communication. The reverse was true for written media. When they considered the topics [were] routine and well understood, 68 per cent of the managers preferred . . . written modes. (p. 227)

Management in practice   Communication during a merger

When two insurance companies merged, management used a variety of channels for different kinds of communication. As soon as the merger was agreed they wanted all staff to receive the same message very quickly. They told all branch managers to be in their office by 7a.m. on the day of the announcement to receive a fax, which branch managers used to brief their staff (personal static media).

When the company sought the views of staff on the kind of organisation that the company should create to meet customer needs, they arranged large gatherings of staff to debate these issues in small groups for several days (physical presence).

Source: Based on an article in *People Management*, 2 September 1999.

Case study   Facebook – the case continues www.facebook.com/facebook

Facebook developers pay much more attention to the 'plumbing' that connects people with each other than to the content that flows through it. Matt Cohler, a former employee, explains:

> The people at Facebook are essentially utilitarians. They want to give people the very best technology for sharing and then get out of their way.

That technology is so good that people are willing to stay loyal to the site as it grows, rather than abandoning it for something edgier. The firm has what some have called a hacker-type culture that has produced the innovations that have made the service so addictive. Mike Schroepfer, Facebook's head of engineering, says that one of its mottos is 'move fast and break stuff'. What matters is getting fresh products out to users quickly, even if they do not always work as intended. To help generate new ideas it gives staff plenty of freedom to try out their ideas on Facebook's site.

The company competes fiercely with Google for talented staff (it employs many former 'Googlers') and offering free food encourages employees to work long hours. Many are in their early 20s, fresh from college where they were often up all night. Facebook continues this tradition with its 'hackathons', where employees are invited to work all night on programs and other tasks that are not part of their normal assignments. The kitchen staff participate by creating new dishes that are available throughout the night.

Food is a lubricant that keeps the innovation machine running. A Facebook spokeswoman said:

> The thinking for us is, what can we do to make our employees' lives easier so they can focus on the job? They come into work and don't have to worry about packing lunch.

Sources: *New York Times,* 27 May 2009, 25 December 2009; *The Economist,* 30 January 2010.

Case questions 16.3

- What evidence is there in the case about the communication channels that Facebook developers use?
- How does the company encourage this?

Activity 16.4   Assessing university communications

List the communications channels that your university or college uses to send you information about the following aspects of your course:

- changes to rooms, timetables, or dates;
- reading lists and other study materials;
- ideas and information intended to stimulate your thinking and encourage discussion and debate;
- your performance so far and advice on what courses to take.

Were the methods appropriate or not? What general lessons can you draw?

Blogs and social network sites

A blog is a frequently updated, interactive website through which people can communicate (by blogging) with anyone who has access to the medium. Dearstyne (2005) distinguished five types:

- individual/personal – set up by individuals to share personal and family news and ideas;
- news/commentary – report, comment and interpret current events;
- advertising/promotional/customer service – communicate with potential customers;

- business/professional – insight and commentary on business and professional issues, including company practices;
- internal/knowledge management – used within companies to share information about products and projects.

Managers in many companies are actively considering how best to engage with social network sites. They represent a shift from vertical to horizontal communication on the web. Where, until now, most organisational communication has been transmitted downward from sender to receiver, the receivers – individual web users – now have a mass of tools they can use to talk to each other. These consumer-focused devices hold threats and opportunities for business. Technical concerns centre on employees' use of the sites, since this can mean a loss of time and network capacity. There have also been concerns about employees posting inappropriate comments about customers, or the company, on the website, which in extreme cases have led to further bad publicity. The biggest danger, however, is that managers ignore the trend, as it will not go away.

Companies that want to make use of the medium take several paths. Some feature positive stories which it hopes will be picked up by other sites: if they are, this makes the site more visible. Others (Dell – **www.dell.com** – is one) ask customers for ideas upon which they can then vote: Dell receives some free market research and some good publicity. Innocent Drinks (**www.innocentdrinks.com**) encourages staff and customers to share information and ideas about current projects or marketing ideas, as well as to chat socially. They can also highlight articles or other information, enabling instant access across the company. Other companies use social network sites for recruitment, identifying suitable candidates, and keeping in touch with former employees. News services such as the BBC and political candidates now use them to reach new audiences, to interact with present audiences and try to gather and form opinion.

While some companies are cautious about blogging, others have established a blog on an internal website (their intranet). Most large companies featured in this book, and most newspapers, now have company blogs which the public can join. As with any technology, using blogs effectively depends on dealing with organisational issues (Chapter 12).

16.5   Communication networks

The grapevine

The grapevine is the spontaneous, informal system through which people pass information and gossip. It happens throughout the organisation and across all hierarchical levels as people meet in the corridor, by the photocopier, at lunch or on the way home. The information that passes along the grapevine is usually well ahead of the information in the formal system. It is about who said what at a meeting, who has applied for another job, who has been summoned to explain their poor results to the directors or what orders the company has won.

The grapevine does not replace the formal system but passes a different kind of information around – qualitative rather than quantitative, current ideas and proposals rather than agreed policies. As it is uncensored and reflects the views of people as a whole rather than of those in charge of the formal communications media, it probably gives a truer picture of the diversity of opinions within the company than the formal policies will. Nevertheless, the rumours and information on the grapevine might be wrong or incomplete. Those passing gossip and good stories of spectacular disasters in department X may also have their own interests and agendas, such as promoting the interests of department Y. The grapevine is as likely to be a vehicle for political intrigue as any of the formal systems.

The grapevine can be a source of early information about what is happening elsewhere in the organisation. This allows those affected but not yet formally consulted to begin preparing their position. Put the other way round, someone preparing proposals or plans can be quite sure that information about them will be travelling round the grapevine sooner than they expect. Sometimes it is useful to deliberately let the matter slip out and begin circulating information to be able to gauge reaction before going too far with a plan.

Communicating in groups and teams

To understand how people in a group communicate members need to have some tools to analyse the patterns of interaction. Shaw (1978) conducted a laboratory experiment to identify which communication processes groups used, and how they affected task performance (see Figure 16.5). Autocratic leadership was associated with the wheel, and a democratic style with the all channel structure. Shaw noted that in centralised networks (chain, wheel and 'Y') groups had to go through someone at the centre of the network to communicate with others, which led to unequal access. In the decentralised networks (circle and all channel) information flowed freely and equally between members.

Different tasks require different communication and Figure 16.6 illustrates two patterns. In a centralised network, information flows to and from the person at the centre, while in the decentralised pattern more of the messages pass between those in the network. If the task is simple, the centralised pattern will work adequately. An example would be to prepare next year's staff budget for the library when there are to be no major changes. The person at the centre can give and receive familiar, structured information from section heads.

If the task is uncertain the centralised structure will obstruct performance. Imagine that a team is developing a new product rapidly in conjunction with suppliers and customers. Because of the novelty of the task, unfamiliar questions will arise, and the group members can only deal with these by exchanging information rapidly. If all information has to pass through a person at the centre they will not cope with the volume of queries, leading to delays.

As organisations grow, they supplement informal methods with more formal ones to communicate downwards, upwards and horizontally (see Figure 16.7).

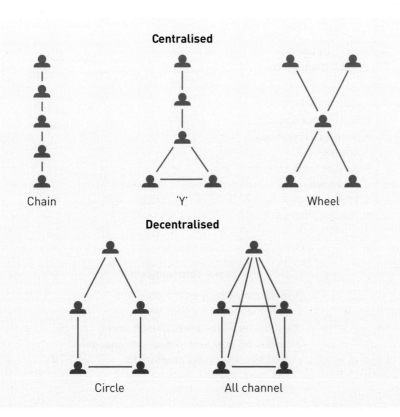

Figure 16.5
Centralised and decentralised communication networks in groups
Source: Shaw (1978).

Simple tasks
Centralised networks
Information flows to central person
Central person can perform task alone
Good performance
Centralised networks are superior on simple tasks
Decentralised networks
Information flows all around the network
No one person has all the required information
Poor performance
Complex tasks
Centralised networks
Information flows to central person
Central person becomes saturated
Poor performance
Decentralised networks
Information flows all around the network
No one person becomes saturated
Good performance
Decentralised networks are superior on complex tasks

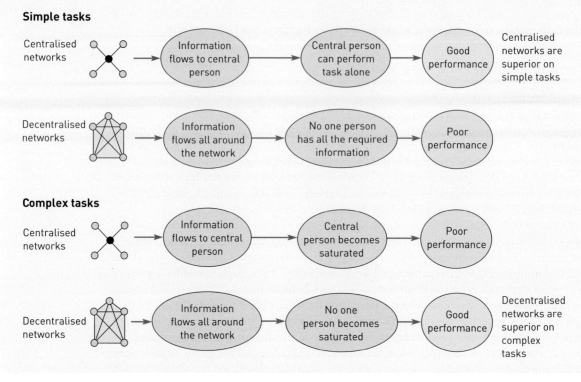

Figure 16.6 Communication structure and type of task

Source: Based on Baron and Greenberg (1997).

Upward communication
• Requests for additional budgets
• Customer complaints
• Progress reports on projects
• Scheduled reports on sales, enquiries, performance
• Regular financial reports
Downward communication
• New policies and procedures
• Budget limits
• Sales/performance targets
• Merger announcements
Horizontal communication
• Exchanging task-based ideas and information
• Adjusting plans to suit mutual needs
• Exploring how best to deal with changes that affect several departments

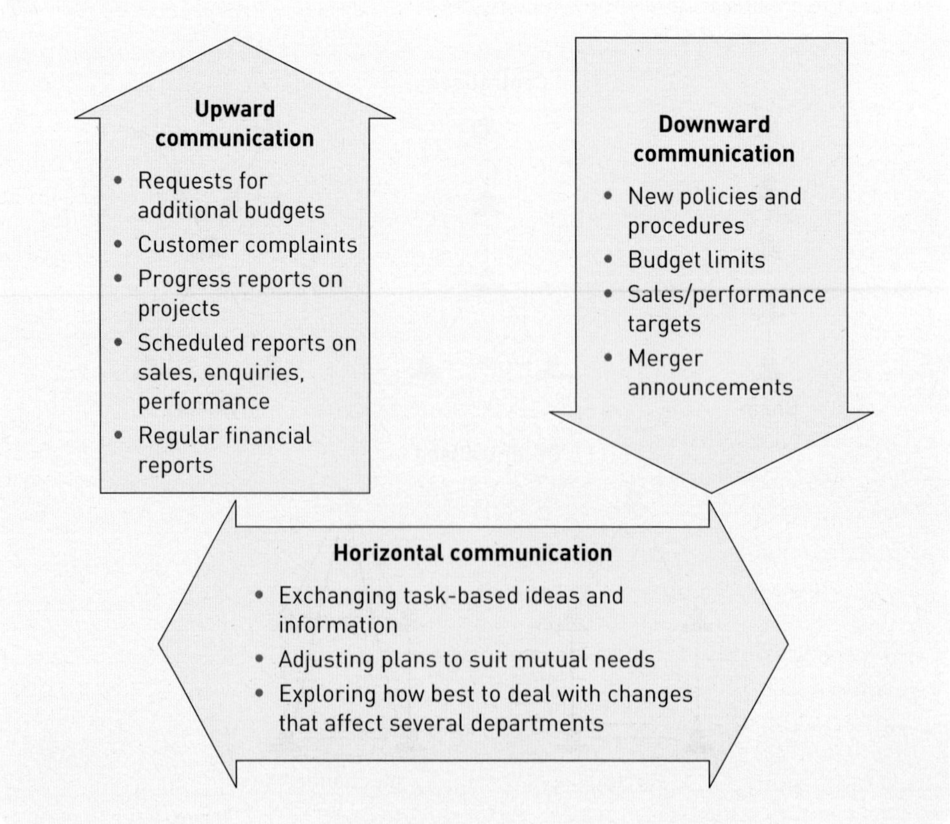

Figure 16.7 Directions of formal communications in organisations

Communicating downwards

Managers communicate downwards when they try to co-ordinate activities of separate units. They may issue instructions or procedures about, for example:

- new policies, products or services;
- budget changes or any changes in financial reporting and control systems;
- new systems and procedures;
- new appointments and reorganisations;
- changes to roles or job descriptions.

If the downward communication inhibits comments or responses, the sender will be unclear how receivers reacted to the message. If it is unclear, people will interpret it in ways that suit them, perhaps making things worse. Managers can avoid this by checking a draft with one or two colleagues, to ensure that what it says is what they mean.

Team briefings

Team briefings are a popular way of passing information rapidly and consistently throughout the organisation – Blakstad and Cooper (1995) quote the results of a survey of 915 companies in which 57 per cent of respondents rated team briefings as the most common method of communicating with employees. Under this method senior management provides a standard message and format, and briefs the next level in the hierarchy. Those managers then brief their subordinates following the same format, and this continues down the organisation. Addressing small groups with a common structure enables managers to:

- deliver a consistent message;
- involve line managers personally in delivering the message;
- deliver the message to many people quickly;
- reduce the possible distortions by 'the grapevine';
- enable staff to ask questions.

Communicating upwards

Companies can install systems that encourage employees to pass on views and ideas to managers. In small organisations this is usually fairly easy as the owner-manager is likely to be close to the action and so aware of employees' ideas. As the business grows, the layers of the hierarchy can easily break the flow. Unless they create mechanisms to allow information to move upwards, their Boards may be acting on the wrong information.

> ### Key ideas   Why businesses ignore vital information
>
> Sidney Finkelstein (2003) has studied the causes of corporate failure – one of which is when managers fail to recognise and act on vital information. He found that this was not usually due to incompetence or idleness, but to a combination of circumstances that made them unreceptive to information that mattered. These included:
>
> - **Undirected information** when staff are slow to recognise the importance of new information, because they have not been shown that they need to take the implied danger seriously. It may also be that there is no one who is able to act on the information.
> - **Missing communication channels** when companies cannot act on vital information because there are no communication channels between people receiving the information and those who need to act on it. This also happens if channels are blocked – a subordinate reports a problem to a boss but cannot pass it elsewhere if the boss takes no action.

- **Missing motives** when employees are reluctant to share vital information because there is no incentive, such as fearing ridicule or displeasure if they bring bad news. If the payment system encourages competition between divisions, there will be no incentive to share information between them.
- **Missing oversight** when senior managers assume that the information they receive is correct, without checking that this is the case. It is easy to accept good news unquestioningly, but that carries the danger that someone may be deliberately hiding news of severe problems.

Source: Finkelstein (2003).

Management in practice   **Communication failures at BP** www.bp.com

In March 2005 an explosion at BP's Texas City refinery killed 15 and injured 500 people. A US Chemical Safety Board report showed that the oil group was so intent on improving the big picture on safety – its statistics – that it missed the pointers to deeper problems. The company focused on improving compliance with procedures and reducing occupational injury rates, while leaving 'unsafe and antiquated equipment designs and unacceptable deficiencies in preventive maintenance'. Supervisors knew that key instruments did not work or were unreliable.

Yet Don Holmstrom, the CSB investigator leading the investigation, said the poor state of the refinery was hidden in the statistics. Indeed, in 2004 the refinery had the lowest injury rate in its history, but that did not take account of catastrophic hazards or distinguish between injuries and fatalities. 'When personal safety statistics improved, the refinery leadership thought it had turned the corner', he said. 'However, existing process safety metrics and the results of a safety culture survey indicated continuing problems with safety systems and concerns about another major accident.'

Source: *Financial Times*, 31 October 2006. See also Part 2 Case.

Employee opinion surveys

Some companies conduct regular surveys among their employees to gauge their attitudes and feelings towards company policy and practice. They may also seek views on current issues, or about possible changes in policy or practice. The surveys can be valuable both as a general indicator of attitudes and as a way to identify issues that need attention. Many specialists offer to conduct such surveys for companies, usually through an online, web-based system (see, for example, *Personnel Today* – **www.personneltoday.com**).

Suggestion schemes

These are devices by which companies encourage employees to suggest improvements to their job or other aspects of the organisation. Employees usually receive a cash reward if management accepts their idea.

Activity 16.5   **Researching opinion surveys**

Gather some evidence from a company about its experience of using employee opinion surveys or suggestion schemes. What are their purposes? Who designs them and interprets the results? What have the benefits been?

Formal grievance procedures

These set out the steps to be followed when an individual or group is in dispute with the company. For example, an employee who has been penalised by a supervisor for poor timekeeping may disagree with the facts as presented or with the penalty imposed. The grievance procedure states how the employee should set about pursuing a claim for a review of the case. Similar procedures now exist in colleges and universities, setting out how a student with a grievance about his/her assessment can appeal against his/her results to successively higher levels of the institution.

Horizontal communication

Horizontal communication crosses departmental or functional boundaries, usually connecting people at broadly similar levels within the organisation. Computer-based information systems have greatly increased the speed and accuracy with which routine information can pass between departments. As a customer places an order, modern systems can quickly pass the relevant information to all the departments that will play a part in meeting it, making production a much smoother and predictable process.

Management in practice   An online tyre service www.blackcircles.com

Michael Welch founded Blackcircles when he was 22. Customers order their tyres online or by phone, then drive to a garage where the tyres will have been delivered ready for fitting. He claims to sell tyres for about 40 per cent less than high street retailers – being able, among other things, to stock a greater range of tyres ready for delivery than would be possible for any single garage. He has also cut his cost of acquiring a new customer from £12 in 2006 to about 12p now – mainly through alliances with bigger brands such as Tesco, the AA and Barclaycard:

> Two years ago we communicated with 400,000 potential customers through partnerships. Last year it was 4 million and this year it will be 22 million . . . the more communication with potential customers, the more sales we make, and the lower our cost of acquisition is – and therefore we can invest that back in the price.

Sources: *Financial Times*, 8 April 2009; company website.

Much horizontal communication is about less routine, less structured problems: when different parts of the organisation co-operate on projects to introduce new products or systems, people communicate frequently. They need to pass information to each other on the current state of affairs so that each distinct unit can be ready to contribute to the project as required.

This also includes communication with other organisations – especially suppliers, customers or partners in collaborative projects. Modern technology makes it technically much easier to pass information between people irrespective of where they are – and this can be used to improve the quality of service. Organisational factors are sometimes a barrier to implementing such systems, especially functional, structural and professional boundaries.

16.6 Interpersonal communication skills

If communication was perfect the receiver would always understand the message as the sender intended. That rarely happens, as people interpret information from their perspectives, and their words fail to express feelings or emotions adequately. Power games affect how people send and receive information, so we can never be sure that the message sent is the message received. Breakdowns and barriers can disrupt any communication chain.

Communication skills for senders

The ideas presented in this section suggest some practices which are likely to help improve anyone's interpersonal communication skill.

Send clear and complete messages

The subject, and how the sender views it, is as much part of the communication process as the message itself. The sender needs to compose a message that will be clear to the receiver, and complete enough to enable both to reach a mutual understanding. This implies anticipating how others will interpret the message, and eliminating potential sources of confusion.

Encode messages in symbols the receiver understands

Senders need to compose messages in terms that the receiver will understand – such as avoiding the specialised language (or jargon) of a professional group when writing to an outsider. Similarly, something that may be read by someone whose native language is different should be written in commonplace language, and avoid the clichés or local sayings that mean nothing to a non-native speaker.

Select a medium appropriate for the message

The sender should consider how much information richness a message requires, and then choose the most appropriate of the alternatives (such as face to face, telephone, individual letter or newsletter), taking into account any time constraints. The main factor in making that choice is the nature of the message, such as how personal it is or how likely it is to be misunderstood.

Select a medium that the receiver monitors

The medium we use greatly affects what we convey. Receivers prefer certain media and pay more attention to messages that come by a preferred route. Some dislike over-formal language, while others dislike using casual terms in written documents. Putting a message in writing may help understanding, but others may see it as a sign of distrust. Some communicate readily by email, others are reluctant to switch on their system.

Avoid noise

Noise refers to anything that interferes with the intended flow of communication, which includes multiple – sometimes conflicting – messages being sent and received at the same time. If non-verbal signals are inconsistent with the words, the receiver may see a different meaning in your message from what was intended. Noise also refers to the inclusion in a message of distracting or minor information that diverts attention from the main business. Communication suffers from interruptions that distract both parties and prevent the concentration essential to mutual understanding.

Communication skills for receivers

Pay attention

Busy people are often overloaded and have to think about several things at once. Thinking about their next meting or a forthcoming visit from a customer, they become distracted and do not attend to messages they receive. In face-to-face communication the sender will probably notice this, and that in turn will affect further actions.

Be a good listener

Communication experts stress the importance of listening. While the person sending the message is responsible for expressing the ideas they want to convey as accurately as they can, the receiver also has responsibilities for the success of the exchange. Listening involves the active skill of attending to what is said, and gaining as accurate a picture as possible of the meaning the sender wished to convey.

Many people are poor listeners. They concentrate not on what the speaker is saying but on what they will say as soon as there is a pause.

Key ideas	Six practices for effective listening

- **Stop talking,** especially that internal, mental, silent chatter. Let the speaker finish. Hear him/her out. It is tempting in a familiar situation to complete the speaker's sentence and work out a reply. This assumes you know what they are going to say: you should instead listen to what he/she is actually saying.
- **Put the speaker at ease** by showing that you are listening. The good listener does not look over someone's shoulder or write while the speaker is talking. If you must take notes, explain what you are doing. Take care, because the speaker will be put off if you look away or concentrate on your notes instead of nodding reassuringly.
- Remember that your **aim is to understand** what the speaker is saying, not to win an argument.
- Be aware of your **personal prejudices** and make a conscious effort to stop them influencing your judgement.
- Be alert to **what the speaker is not saying** as well as what is being said. Very often what is missing is more important than what is there.
- **Ask questions.** This shows that you have been listening and encourages the speaker to develop the points you have raised. It is an active process, never more important than when you are meeting someone for the first time – when your objective should be to say as little and learn as much as possible in the shortest time.

Be empathetic

Receivers are empathetic when they try to understand how the sender feels, and try to interpret the message from the sender's perspective, rather from their own position. A junior member of staff may raise a problem with a more senior colleague, which perhaps reflects his/her inexperience. The senior could be dismissive of the request, indicating that the subordinate ought to know how to deal with the situation. An empathetic response would take account of the inexperience and treat the request with greater understanding.

Supportive communication

Whetten and Cameron (2002) argue that ineffective communication leads people to dislike each other, and to become defensive, mistrustful and suspicious. That in turn leads to a further decline in the quality of communication, and a further decline in relationships: a cycle that harms personal satisfaction and organisational performance. To break out of this cycle they advocate the use of supportive communication – communication that seeks to preserve a positive relationship between the communicators while still dealing with the business issues. There are eight principles in the model, illustrated in the following Key Ideas.

Key ideas Whetten and Cameron – supportive communication

- **Problem oriented not person oriented**
  A focus on problems and issues that can be changed rather than people and their characteristics.

  | Example: | 'How can we solve this problem?' | Not: | 'Because of you there is a problem.' |

- **Congruent not incongruent**
  A focus on honest messages in which verbal messages match thoughts and feelings.

  | Example: | 'Your behaviour really upsets me.' | Not: | 'Do I seem upset? No, everything's fine.' |

- **Descriptive not evaluative**
  A focus on describing an objective occurrence, your reaction to it, and offering an alternative.

  | Example: | 'Here is what happened, here is my reaction, here is a suggestion that would be more acceptable.' | Not: | 'You are wrong for doing what you did.' |

- **Validating not invalidating**
  A focus on statements that communicate respect, flexibility and areas of agreement.

  | Example: | 'I have some ideas, but do you have any suggestions?' | Not: | 'You wouldn't understand, so we'll do it my way.' |

- **Specific not global**
  A focus on specific events or behaviours, avoiding general, extreme or vague statements.

  | Example: | 'You interrupted me three times during the meeting.' | Not: | 'You're always trying to get my attention.' |

- **Conjunctive not disjunctive**
  A focus on statements that flow from what has been said and facilitating interaction.

  | Example: | 'Relating to what you've just said, I suggest . . .' | Not: | 'I want to say something (regardless of what you have just said).' |

- **Owned not disowned**
  A focus on taking responsibility for your statements by using personal ('I') words.

  | Example: | 'I have decided to turn down your request because . . .' | Not: | 'Your suggestion is good, but it wouldn't get approved.' |

- **Supportive listening, not one-way listening**
  A focus on using a variety of responses, with a bias towards reflective responses.

  | Example: | 'What do you think are the obstacles standing in the way of improvement?' | Not: | 'As I said before, you make too many mistakes: you're just not performing.' |

Source: WHETTEN, DAVID A.; CAMERON, KIM S., *DEVELOPING MANAGEMENT SKILLS*, 6th Edition © 2002, 2005, p. 216. Reprinted by permission of Pearson Education, Inc., Upper Saddle River, NJ.

They argue that following these principles ensures greater clarity and understanding of messages, while at the same time making the other person feel accepted and valued. As such they can be effective tools for achieving the mutual understanding, as well as the accuracy, of whatever is being communicated.

16.7   Communication and strategy – the wider context

Strategy

Argenti *et al.* (2005) show how managers can apply the themes of this chapter to strategic performance. They suggest that while there are adequate models for developing strategies, less attention has been paid to communicating. Citing examples of corporate disasters which show the damage that poor communication of strategy can do to a company's reputation, they propose that managers ensure a close link between communication practices and strategy, quoting Michael Dell:

> I communicate to customers, groups of employees and others, while working on strategy. A key part of strategy is communicating it. Communication is key to operations and an integral part of the process. (2005, p. 84)

Argenti *et al.*'s (2005) research enabled them to develop a framework for strategic communication shown in Figure 16.8, comprising a variety of iterative loops between elements of a strategy and the constituencies likely to be affected.

They claim that putting the approach into practice requires an integrated, multilevel approach, linking communication functions with relevant stakeholder groups and the channels most likely to be suitable for each topic and group. They stress that while the approaches shown in Table 16.1 can be tailored to each stakeholder group, the messages need to be consistent with each other and with the intended strategy.

Structure

Organisations are typically divided into separate units, focusing on their particular part of the total task. In hierarchical, mechanistic structures (see Chapter 10) most information passes vertically between managers and subordinates. This sometimes creates a 'silo' mentality, in which people are focusing too much on their interests and priorities and not enough on other players. They forget that others will have an interest in what they are doing, or will be affected by it – and fail to communicate information that would be relevant to both parties. Finkelstein (2003) quotes the example of Nissan's US operation:

> Nissan, for example, operated for years with a rigid bureaucratic culture that required its sales, manufacturing and R&D divisions in the US to report separately to Japan, and not interact with each other. In effect all the corporate communication channels led only to Tokyo. To make matters worse, there was no direct interaction between regional managers in America and top corporate executives in Japan. This meant that if the Nissan sales people discovered customers were rejecting an automobile because of a small but irritating design feature, the design department was unlikely ever to hear about it. (p. 197)

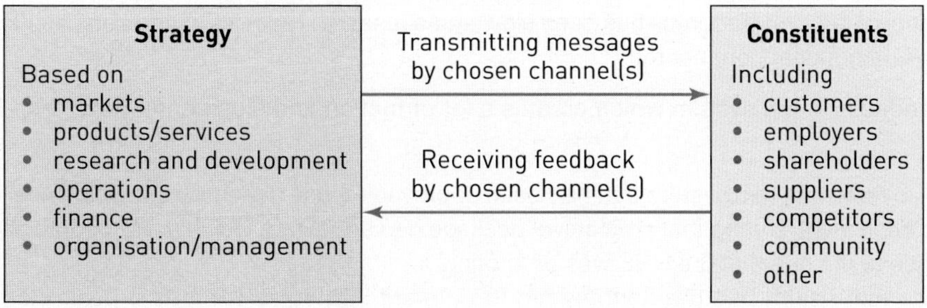

Figure 16.8
The framework for strategic communication

Source: The strategic communication imperative, *MIT Sloan Management Review*, vol. 46, no. 3, pp. 83–89 (Argenti, P. A., Howell, R. A. and Beck, K. A. 2005) © 2010 from MIT Sloan Management Review/Massachusetts Institute of Technology. All rights reserved. Distributed by Tribune Media Services.

Strategy	Transmitting messages by chosen channel(s)	**Constituents**
Based on		Including
• markets		• customers
• products/services		• employers
• research and development	Receiving feedback by chosen channel(s)	• shareholders
• operations		• suppliers
• finance		• competitors
• organisation/management		• community
		• other

Table 16.1 Elements of a strategic approach to communications.

Communication functions	Objectives	Constituencies Primary	Secondary	Channels
Media relations	Public relations, crisis management	All constituents	Media	Press releases, interviews
Employee communications	Internal consensus building	Employees	Customers, families	Public meetings, memos, newsletters
Financial communications	Transparency, meeting financial expectations	Investors	Analysts, media	Conference calls, CEO, CFO
Community relations	Image building	Communities	NGOs media	Events, speeches, philanthropy
Government relations	Regulatory compliance, meeting social expectations	Regulators	Media customers	Lobbying efforts, one-to-one meetings
Marketing communications	Driving sales, building image	Customers	All key constituencies	Advertising, promotions

Source: Based on Argenti *et al.* (2005).

Conversely, people in an organic structure which encourages and rewards co-operation and teamwork (such as those at Oticon or W.L. Gore) will experience freer communication.

Structural factors also affect the ability of staff to use technology to support information flow between organisations or between professional groups. The units within a care system are separated by boundaries that distinguish and protect them from others. Functional boundaries are particularly apparent between health and social care, but there are also structural and professional divisions within each discipline. At whatever level of analysis, boundaries demarcate a unit from its environment, defending it from others (e.g. by helping to protect its budget) and providing an interface for interactions with others (e.g. by exchanging resources). The following Management in Practice gives some evidence on how these boundaries can impede the use of new communication technologies.

Management in practice   Communication barriers in healthcare

Boddy *et al.* (2009b) report on a study into the limited progress in implementing electronic systems in healthcare ('e-health'). Many available systems permit information to pass between professional staff irrespective of their physical or organisational location. Progress has been slow and a research team sought to establish the nature of the barriers. One respondent commented:

> There's some disjointedness in the system which creates a lot of friction and slower progress [than is desirable].

Another illustrated this by referring to a system that had been approved for use nationally but which health boards had been slow to implement. During that time a rival package had appeared, which many people had started to use in preference to the one that the NHS was promoting.

A common theme was that health board autonomy led to different strategies towards e-health, and to incompatible local systems. This was partly due to different technologies, but also because people adapt working practices to fit the technology: both forces inhibit acceptance of national systems. One said:

> We've sorted out [a national solution], but then our lab system won't feed the correct data. A lot of it's to do with the fact that the UK has multiple systems for doing exactly the same thing, which is ludicrous. Some boards have put money into e-health and others haven't.

Source: Boddy *et al.* (2009b).

Power

Information has great value. Those who possess it have something others do not have and may need or want. Sole ownership of information can also be used to boost or protect a person's status or the significance of his/her role. Chapter 14 shows that access to information and the means of communicating it to others is a source of power. People may hoard it rather than share it, and use it at the most opportune moment. Those with access to inside information have both prestige and power.

Management in practice   **PricewaterhouseCoopers and groupware**

The company installed a sophisticated electronic system to support communication between the separate units of the business, but not all were at first keen to co-operate. A manager closely involved in the project made the comment below, illustrating that information is 'currency'.

> We had to overcome a number of issues to encourage (groupware) use because some of the consultant managers think they're competing with each other. The competition still exists in practice units. So we've 'incentivised' them to share. If they're not meeting the culture, not sharing, that's not going to help them. We have a peer recognition system and an upward appraisal system. So if a consultant thinks a manager is not applying the culture, that will show up. And the peer recognition system allows people who have been sharing and helping others to be acknowledged and rewarded. We apply peer recognition throughout the business. It also needs certain disciplines – people must see it as part of their job to maintain information and record details of their projects. It's part of how they manage a client.

Source: Private communication from a manager in the company.

16.8 Integrating themes

Sustainable performance

Moving towards a more sustainable economy depends on communicating information about both the problem and the solutions being proposed. Being controversial, issues of structure and power are bound to influence the communication process, which those wishing to promote sustainable performance need to take into account.

They could use the Argenti *et al.* (2005) model to help ensure that they exchange information with relevant constituencies, and so come up with a sustainability strategy which is both environmentally worthwhile and commercially viable.

Equally, they could check their communications practices against the communications model to ensure that they pay adequate attention to all the elements of the communication process. People vary in their understanding of the topic, and practice should reflect this.

Governance and control

High-profile scandals, mistakes and quality failures place an organisation's reputation at risk – possibly destroying in weeks what managers have taken years to build. Governance arrangements could include a regular review of how senior managers handle communications in the face of bad publicity. How customers and members of the public view an event is substantially influenced by how managers handle communications about it. Toyota experienced this in early 2010, when a series of faults led the company to recall millions of vehicles in many countries. The company was widely perceived to have handled the episode badly, causing more damage to the reputation of the brand than was necessary – especially when the media have become interested in the topic. Mattila (2009) shows the importance of anticipating (inevitable) damaging publicity from unintentional events by having comprehensive and tested communications strategies in place.

Governance and control arrangements, however robust they appear, depend on people exchanging information – both sending and paying attention to it. The communication models in this chapter highlight the barriers to the effective transmission of information about, for example, risky business being done. Structural and political factors, as well as interpersonal ones, often prevent information reaching those who require it – and/or prevent them from acting on it. Groupthink (Chapter 7) also impedes communication.

Internationalisation

Many managers who develop their companies into international operations find that communicating across cultures makes the process even more hazardous than communicating within a single culture. Insights into the obstacles to such communication, and into a way of resolving them, are provided by this further insight from Carlos Ghosn in the Management in Practice feature.

Management in practice   Carlos Ghosn of Renault-Nissan

Carlos Ghosn, the high-profile chief executive of Renault-Nissan, has created many cross-company teams to study urgent problems such as product planning, vehicle engineering, power trains and purchasing – even when two companies with such different values have to work together. Asked about his experience of managing Nissan's largely Japanese workforce, he said:

It's interesting to see how human beings handle difference. People have always had problems with what is different from them. Different religion, race, sex, age, training – human beings have always had a challenge confronting what is different.

You feel more comfortable, more secure, with somebody who is like you. You feel insecure with someone who is different from you – younger, or a foreigner. But I recognise that even if someone is different, I'm going to learn a lot. We have a tendency to reject what is different – and yet we need what is different. Because what is different is the only way we can grow by confronting ourselves.

I have no doubt that cultural influences can affect the outcomes of discussions among multi-cultural teams, contributing much richer solutions than those teams' members would have developed on their own.

Generally speaking, my impression is that Japanese people are naturally process-oriented thinkers. French people are conceptual, ingenious and innovative. Americans are direct, get-to-the-point, bottom-line driven. The mix of those traits can be a tremendous asset during problem-solving or brainstorming sessions.

Source: *Business Week*, 4 October 2004.

Summary

1   **Explain the role of communication in managing**

*   People at all levels of an organisation need to add value to the resources they use, and to do that they need to communicate with others – about inputs, the transformation process and the outputs. It enables the tasks of planning, organising, leading and controlling.
*   It also enables managers to perform their informational, decisional and interpersonal roles.

2   **Identify and illustrate the elements and stages in the communication process**

*   Sender, message, encoding, medium, decoding receiver and noise.

3   **Use the concept of information richness to select a communication channel:**

*   In descending order of information richness, the channels are:
    *   face-to-face communication;
    *   spoken communication electronically transmitted;
    *   personally addressed written communication;
    *   impersonal written communication.

4   **Compare the benefits of different communication networks**

*   Centralised networks work well on structured, simple tasks, but are less suitable for complex tasks as the centre becomes overloaded.
*   Decentralised networks work well on complex tasks, as information flows between those best able to contribute. On simple tasks this is likely to cause confusion.

5   **Outline some essential interpersonal communication skills**

*   Send clear and complete messages.
*   Encode messages in symbols that the receiver understands.
*   Select a medium appropriate for the message.
*   Include a feedback mechanism in the message.
*   Pay attention.
*   Be a good listener.

6   **Show how communication interacts with strategy and the wider context**

*   Argenti *et al.* (2005) have advocated that managers develop coherent arrangements for communicating with key constituencies in formulating strategy, identifying the functions, objectives and channels to use.
*   An organisation's structure has a significant effect on the flow of communication between units, and the same applies to the exchange of information between organisations. While technology enables easier communication, structures can impede the flow in practice.

7   **Show how ideas from the chapter add to your understanding of the integrating themes**

*   Proposals for sustainable performance depend on effective communication with many constituencies, which have varying interests towards the topic. Those promoting such projects could use the Argenti *et al.* (2005) model to guide them.
*   Governance and control systems also depend on accurate information not only being sent, but received and attended to be those who could act on it. The ideas in this chapter show how structural and political factors, as well as interpersonal ones, can block the flow of information through a governance system – as can the phenomenon of groupthink.

- Communication between those conducting business internationally is an opportunity for enriching the range of ideas and contributions available, provided those conducting the dialogue have the ability to overcome the common human anxiety about differences.

Review questions

1 Explain why communication is central to managing.

2 Draw a diagram of the communication process, showing each of the stages and elements. Then illustrate it with a communication episode you have experienced.

3 How does feedback help or hinder communication?

4 What is non-verbal communication, and why is it important to effective communication?

5 What do you understand by the term 'information richness', and how does it affect the choice of communication method?

6 What is team briefing?

7 Name three practices that can improve interpersonal communication skills.

8 Outline Argenti's model of strategic communications.

9 Give examples of the way in which the structure of an organisation can affect communication.

10 Summarise an idea from the chapter that adds to your understanding of the integrating themes.

Concluding critical reflection

Think about the ways in which you typically communicate with others, and about communication in your company. Review the material in the chapter, and then make notes on the following questions:

- What examples of the issues discussed in this chapter struck you as being relevant to practice in your company?

- Thinking of the people you typically work with, who are effective and who are less effective communicators? What do the effective communicators do? What interpersonal communication skills do they use? How have modern communications systems supported communication in your company? On balance, have **assumptions** about their value been supported? Can you see examples of structural, cultural and political factors affecting the degree of mutual understanding?

- What factors such as the history of the company or your personal experience have shaped communication practices? Does your current approach appear to be right for your present **context** – or would you use a different approach in other circumstances? (Perhaps refer to some of the Management in Practice features for how different managers communicate.)

- Have people put forward **alternative** approaches to communicating, based on evidence about other companies? If you could find such evidence, how may it affect company practice?

- What **limitations** can you identify in any of these communication theories? For example, do you find the Lengel–Daft model (Section 16.4) a helpful way of choosing a channel?

Further reading

Beall, A.E. (2004), 'Body language speaks: Reading and responding more effectively to hidden communication', *Communication World*, vol. 21, no. 2, pp. 18–20.

A well-illustrated article about body language, which also lists some further resources.

Dimbleby, R. and Burton, G. (2006), *More Than Words: An introduction to communication* (4th edn), Routledge, London.

Accessible introduction to all aspects of communication.

Finkelstein, S. (2003), *Why Smart Executives Fail: And what you can learn from their mistakes*, Penguin, New York.

Fascinating account of the sources of communication failure in public and private organisations.

Goffman, E. (1959), *The Presentation of Self in Everyday Life*, Doubleday, New York.

A classic (and short) work that gives many insights into interpersonal communications.

Whetten, D.A. and Cameron, K.S. (2002), *Developing Management Skills*, Prentice Hall International, Upper Saddle River, NJ.

Extended discussion of interpersonal communication skills, with useful exercises.

Weblinks

These websites have appeared in the chapter:

www.facebook.com/facebook
www.cisco.com
www.grace.com
www.dell.com
www.innocentdrinks.com
www.bp.com
www.blackcircles.com
www.personneltoday.com

Visit two of the sites, or others which interest you, and navigate to the pages dealing with recent news, press or investor relations.

● In what ways is the company using the website to communicate information about inputs, outputs and transformation processes?

● Is it providing a one-way or a two-way communication process?

For video case studies, audio summaries, flashcards, exercises and annotated weblinks related to this chapter, visit **www.pearsoned.co.uk/mymanagementlab**

CHAPTER 17
TEAMS

Aim

To outline the significance of teams and how they develop.

Objectives

By the end of your work on this chapter you should be able to outline the concepts below in your own terms and:

1   Distinguish the types of teams used by organisations
2   Use a model to analyse the composition of a team
3   Identify the stages of team development and explain how they move between them
4   Identify specific team processes and explain how they affect performance
5   Evaluate the outcomes of a team for the members and the organisation
6   Outline contextual factors that influence team performance.
7   Show how ideas from the chapter add to your understanding of the integrating themes

Key terms

This chapter introduces the following ideas:

formal team	team
informal group	preferred team roles
self-managing team	team-based rewards
virtual teams	observation
structure	content
working group	concertive control

Each is a term defined within the text, as well as in the Glossary at the end of the book.

Case study   Cisco Systems   www.cisco.com

Cisco Systems is a company at the heart of the internet. It is a leading developer and supplier of the physical equipment and software that allow digital data to travel around the world over the internet, and also provides support services that enable companies to improve their use of the network. It was founded in 1984 by a group of scientists from Stanford University, and its engineers have focused on developing Internet Protocol (IP)-based networking technologies. The core areas of the business remain the supply of routing and switching equipment, but it is also working in areas such as home networking, network security and storage networking.

Courtesy of Cisco Systems, Inc. Unauthorised use not permitted

The company employs 34,000 staff working from 70 offices around the world, developing new systems and working with customers to implement and enhance their network infrastructure. Most projects are implemented by staff from several sites working as virtual teams, in the sense that they are responsible for a collective product but work in physically separate places.

The company created a team to co-ordinate the testing and release of a new version of Cisco's Element Management Framework (EMF), a highly complex piece of software that monitors the performance of large numbers of elements in a network. When the product was released a few months later, the members of the team were free to work on other projects. The team had eight members, drawn from four sites and three countries:

Name	Location	Role
Steve	Raleigh, North Carolina	Project co-ordinator
Richard	Cumbernauld, Scotland	Development manager
Graham	Cumbernauld, Scotland	Development engineer
Eddie	Cumbernauld, Scotland	Development engineer
Rai	Austin, Texas	Test engineer
Silvio	Austin, Texas	Test engineer
Jim	Raleigh, North Carolina	Network architect
Gunzal	Bangalore, India	Release support engineer

The role of the co-ordinator was to ensure the smooth operation of the team and to monitor actual progress against the challenging delivery schedule. The software was developed in Cumbernauld, by engineers writing the code and revising it as necessary after testing by the test engineers. They were responsible for rigorously testing all software and reporting all problems concisely and accurately to the development engineers.

The network architect has extensive knowledge of the network hardware that the software would manage, and supervised the development and testing of the software to ensure that it worked as efficiently as possible with the hardware. The release support engineer dealt with the logistics of software release, such as defining each version and ensuring that deliverables are available to the manufacturing departments at the appropriate times.

Each member worked full-time on the project, although they never met physically during its lifetime. All members took part in a weekly conference call, and also a daily call attended by the co-ordinator, development manager and a member of the test team. Communication throughout the team was mainly by electronic mail, together with instant messaging.

Source: Communication from members of the project team.

Case questions 17.1

- What challenges would you expect a team that never meets will face during its work?
- In what ways may it need to work differently from a conventional team?

17.1 Introduction

Managers at Cisco use teams extensively to deliver products and services to customers. The people with the skills it needs for a particular project are widely dispersed around the organisation but need to work together to meet customer needs. Teams bring them together for the duration of a project – they then disperse and re-form in different combinations to work on other projects. The company also uses teams for internal development projects, where staff from a variety of functions and geographical areas work together on a part-time basis to deal with a pressing management problem, such as improving a financial or marketing system.

People at work have always developed loyalties among small groups of fellow workers and there are well-documented examples of industries where work was formally organised in small, self-managing teams (Trist and Bamforth, 1951). This is now happening much more widely, with teams rather than individuals becoming the basic building block of many organisations. This is most evident in research-based organisations such as Microsoft (Cusumano, 1997), W.L. Gore and Associates or GlaxoSmithKline (GSK), where scientists or engineers from different disciplines come together to work on a common project and then disband when the work is complete. There are many cross-organisational teams – such as when BAA created many integrated teams from suppliers, consultants, contractors and their own staff during the construction of Terminal 5 at London's Heathrow Airport. Teams bring together people with different ideas and perspectives to solve difficult problems. Most economic and social problems require the contribution of several disciplines or organisations. Creating a team draws people from these areas together to work on the problem.

Forming a team does not mean it will work well. Some, such as that at Cisco, work to very high standards and levels of achievement while others fail to add value, wasting time and other resources. Despite their popularity with managers and with team members, the evidence about teams and performance is mixed – perhaps because the diversity of backgrounds that makes a team worthwhile also makes it harder for the team to work. Figure 17.1 helps to explain this variation, by showing teams as an open system. The inputs are mainly the team members – so one factor in performance is its composition. Members then need to learn to work together

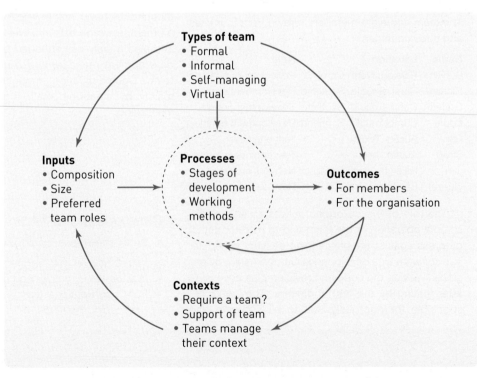

Figure 17.1
A model of team performance

collaboratively to deliver their task: the processes they use will help or hinder them in that. They also work within a context made up from organisational and external factors – which also help or hinder performance. And finally we need to be aware of the different kinds of outcomes which teams may deliver.

The chapter begins by outlining the types of team you may encounter (including 'virtual' teams), which leads to a definition. You will then learn about the composition of teams, their stages of development and internal processes, and how context affects performance. A final section examines the outcomes of teams.

Activity 17.1   Gathering information on teams

Gather some original information on how an organisation uses teams to get work done. Use the questions below as a starting point for your enquiry. What you collect may be useful in one of your tutorials, as well as adding to your knowledge of teams.

- What is the main task of the organisation or department?
- How are staff grouped into teams?
- What type of team are they? (Use the ideas in Section 17.2 as a guide.)
- Use the definition of a team to describe the main features of one of the teams.
- What do management and team members see as the benefits of team working?

17.2   Types of team

Teams have many functions and are of many types, which have different implications for those who work in them, or who depend on them.

Functions of teams

Hackman (1990) identified seven team functions, and Table 17.1 summarises the risks and opportunities associated with each.

Case questions 17.2

- What kinds of team does Cisco use in Hackman's typology?
- What other kinds of team from the list have you experienced?

Formal teams

Managers often create **formal teams** as they shape the organisation's basic structure, and allocate specific tasks to them. Vertical 'teams' consist of a manager and his/her subordinates within a single department or function. The manager and staff in the treasury department of a bank, or the senior nurse, nursing staff and support staff in a unit of the Western General Hospital, are formally constituted into (possibly several) vertical teams. So is a team leader and his/her staff in a BT call centre. In each case senior managers created them to support their goals.

Horizontal teams consist of staff from roughly the same level, but from different functions. The Cisco EMF team is an example, being brought together to release the new software. In Hackman's typology, taskforces would be an example: often called cross-functional teams,

A formal team is one that management has deliberately created to perform specific tasks to help meet organisational goals.

Table 17.1 Hackman's classification of team types and their associated risks and opportunities

Type	Risks	Opportunities
Top management teams – to set organisational directions	Underbounded; absence of organisational context	Self-designing; influence over key organisational conditions
Task forces – for a single unique project	Team and work both new	Clear purpose and deadline
Professional support groups – providing expert assistance	Dependency on others for work	Using and honing professional expertise
Performing groups – playing to audiences	Skimpy organisational supports	Play that is fuelled by competition and/or audiences
Human service teams – taking care of people	Emotional drain; struggle for control	Inherent significance of helping people
Customer service teams – selling products and services	Loss of involvement with parent organisation	Bridging between parent organisation and customers
Production teams – turning out the product	Retreat into technology; insulation from end users	Continuity of work; able to hone team design and product

Source: Hackman (1990), p. 489.

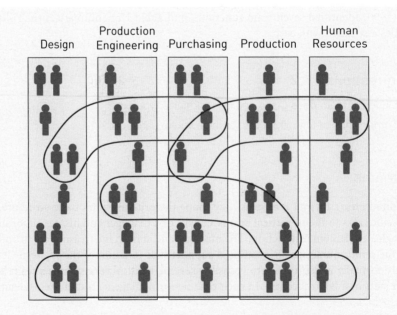

Figure 17.2
Horizontal and vertical teams in an engineering company

these deal with non-routine problems that require several types of professional knowledge, such as how to develop new products or processes illustrated in Figure 17.2.

Informal groups

Informal groups are a powerful feature of organisational life. They develop as day-to-day activities bring people into contact with each other – who then discover common sporting or social interests. Work-related informal groups arise when people in different formal groups exchange information and ideas: staff using a software package may begin to pass around problems or tips. Staff in separate departments dealing with a customer may start passing information to each other to avoid misunderstandings, even though this is not part of the specified job. Sometimes people use their initiative and volunteer to work on an organisational problem which they believe is affecting performance – and then suggest their proposed solution to managers.

> An **informal group** is one that emerges when people come together and interact regularly.

Informal groups sometimes develop in opposition to management – as when people believe they are being unfairly treated, and come together from across groups to express a common dissatisfaction with current policy.

Self-managing teams

Self-managing teams are responsible for a complete area of work and operate without close supervision. Members are responsible for getting the work done but have a high degree of autonomy in how they do it: they manage themselves, including planning and scheduling tasks, and assigning tasks among the members. They are also likely to establish the pace of work, make operating decisions, work out how to overcome problems and manage quality. They usually have a considerable influence over selecting new employees.

> A **self-managing team** operates without an internal manager and is responsible for a complete area of work.

Key ideas   Informal networks: the company behind the chart

According to Krackhardt and Hanson (1993):

> If the formal organization is the skeleton of the company, the informal is the central nervous system. This drives the collective thought processes, actions and reactions of the business units. Designed to facilitate standard modes of production, management create the formal organization to handle easily anticipated problems. When unexpected problems arise, the informal organization becomes active. Its complex web of social ties form every time colleagues communicate and solidifies over time into surprisingly stable networks. Highly adaptive, informal networks move diagonally and elliptically, skipping entire functions to get work done.

> The authors argue that these informal networks can either foster or disrupt communication processes. They recommend that managers try to understand them in order to make use of their strengths, or even adjust aspects of the formal organisation to complement the informal.

Source: Krackhardt and Hanson (1993), p. 104.

Virtual teams

Modern communications technologies enable and encourage people to create teams in which the members are physically distant for most of the time, even though they are expected to deliver high-quality collective outcomes. Many of the teams in Cisco are like this. The growing internationalisation of management means that people frequently work in **virtual teams** drawn from different nations and cultures, as well as working remotely, raising new teamwork challenges (Govindarajan and Gupta, 2001; Robey *et al.*, 2003).

> **Virtual teams** are those in which the members are physically separated, using communications technologies to collaborate across space and time to accomplish their common task.

Virtual teams use computer technology to link members together, communicating by email, videoconferencing and online discussion through a website. They can perform all the functions of a team that is located in the same place, but lack the face-to-face interaction and discussion which helps to smooth working relationships. While virtual teams can sometimes use the fact that they are in different time zones to their advantage, Saunders *et al.* (2004) examine some of the challenges. At a superficial level, differences of time zone create problems of managing different working hours, lunch breaks and holiday cycles. More fundamental difficulties arise from contrasting visions of time between cultures and nations – such as whether it is an objective or subjective notion, or differences in the meaning of words such as 'soon' or 'urgent'.

While virtual teams bring expertise together without the expense of travel, they require careful management to ensure that the benefits of team working are retained. Practices include ensuring that some regular (or at least initial) face-to-face contact occurs, and that members resolve issues of roles, working methods and conflict management.

Activity 17.2   Reflect on an experience of team working

Recall times when you have been part of a team.

- Which of the seven types listed by Hackman have you experienced? Do you agree with his comments on the risks and opportunities of those types? If not, what were they?
- Which of the other types have you experienced? Make a note of the circumstances, as you will be able to use this experience during the chapter.
- If possible compare your notes with other members of your course

17.3   Crowds, groups and teams

The types of team described in the previous section were not just random collections of people. A crowd in the street is not usually a team: they are there by chance, and will have little if any further contact. What about the staff in a supermarket or in the same section of a factory? They are not a crowd: they have some things in common, and people may refer to them as a team. Compare them with five people designing some software for a bank, each of whom brings distinct professional skills to their collective discussions of the most suitable design, or with seven students working together on a group assignment. They have a **structure** to handle the whole process, work largely on their initiative, and move easily between all the tasks, helping each other as needed.

Structure is the regularity in the way a unit or group is organised, such as the roles that are specified.

Activity 17.3   Crowds, groups and teams

Note down a few words that express the differences between the examples given. Do some sound more like a group or a team than others?

Consider a Davis Cup tennis or Ryder Cup golf team, in which most of the action takes place between individual participants from either side. No significant co-ordination occurs between the members during a match.

- In what ways would such teams meet the above definition?
- Can you think of other examples of people who work largely on their own but are commonly referred to as a team?

In normal conversation, people typically use the words 'group' and 'team' as if they mean the same thing, and this book follows that usage. However, some people do distinguish between the two, and it is useful to be aware of this to avoid confusion. Katzenbach and Smith's (1993) definition of a team illustrates this: 'A small number of people with complementary skills who are committed to a common purpose, performance goals, and working approach for which they hold themselves mutually accountable' (p. 45). A few people working together may do so very amiably and productively, but may be quite loosely associated with each other – they may not think of themselves as having a shared purpose, may not use a common method of working, and may not see themselves as mutually accountable. They may exchange normal social courtesies and perhaps exchange task advice and information. But they are accountable for their work as individuals. In many situations such '**working groups**' meet the required performance standards, provided that individuals do their job competently. **Teams** use collective discussion, debate and decision to deliver 'collective work products' – something more than the sum of individual efforts.

The essential point is that whether we use the term 'group' or 'team', they differ in their outcomes: some will perform well, and others will fail. The practical task is not to debate what to call them, but to understand the causes and consequences of differences in performance. As long as people are aware of this distinction, they should use whichever term seems suitable. It is what groups and teams *do* that matter, not what they are called. Katzenbach and Smith's (1993) definition suggests some criteria against which to evaluate features of a team.

A **working group** is a collection of individuals who work mainly on their own but interact socially and share information and best practices.

A **team** is 'a small number of people with complementary skills who are committed to a common purpose, performance goals, and approach for which they hold themselves mutually accountable' (Katzenbach and Smith, 1993).

Small number

Groups of more than about 12 people find it hard to operate as a coherent team. It becomes harder to agree on a common purpose and the practicalities of where and when to meet become tricky. Most teams have between two and ten people – with between four and eight probably being the most common range. Larger groups usually divide into subgroups.

Complementary skills

Teams benefit from having members who, between them, share *technical*, *functional* or *professional skills* relevant to the work. A team implementing a networked computer system will require at least some members with appropriate technical skills, while one developing a new strategy for a retailer will contain people with strategic or marketing skills.

Second, a team needs people with *problem-solving* and *decision-making skills*. These enable members to approach a task systematically, using appropriate techniques such as SWOT or five forces analysis. Finally, a team needs people with *interpersonal skills* to hold it together. Members' attitudes and feelings towards each other and to the task change as work continues. This may generate irritation and conflict, so someone needs the skill to manage these disagreements constructively.

Common purpose

Teams cannot work to a common purpose unless members spend time and effort to clarify and understand it. They need to express it in clear performance goals upon which members can focus their time and energy. A common purpose helps members to communicate, since they can interpret and understand their contributions more easily.

Common approach

Teams need to decide how they will work together to accomplish their purpose. This includes deciding who does what, how the group should make and modify decisions and how to deal with conflict. The common approach includes integrating new members into the team, and generally working to promote mutual trust necessary to team success.

Mutual accountability

A team cannot work as one until its members willingly hold themselves to be collectively and mutually accountable for the results of the work. As members do real work together towards a common objective, commitment and trust usually follow. If one or more members are unwilling to accept this collective responsibility, the team will not become fully effective.

Activity 17.4   Using the definition to analyse a team

Recall a team of which you have been a member. Alternatively, arrange to gather information for this activity from someone who has experience of team working in an organisation.

- To what extent do you feel the team was effective?
- To what extent did it meet the five criteria listed in the definition?
- Can you identify how, if at all, meeting these criteria, or not doing so, affected performance?
- If possible, compare your evidence with other members of your course.

17.4   Team composition

Figure 17.1 shows that teams depend first on inputs – especially their composition. In a mechanical sense, team composition includes size and membership. Is there an acceptable balance of part-time and full-time members? Are the relevant functions represented? Equally important is whether members have the right skills and ways of working to form an effective team. Uhl-Bien and Graen (1998) warn:

> Although cross-functional teams may be highly effective if implemented correctly (for instance, staffed with strong team players), if implemented incorrectly (staffed with independently focused self-managing professionals) they may . . . harm organizational functioning. (p. 348)

As people work in a team they behave in ways that reflect diverse perspectives, skills and interests, which lead them to take on distinctive roles. A group needs a balance of these, so a task for the team leader is to do what he/she can to shape its composition. Two useful ideas are the distinction between task and maintenance roles, and Belbin's research on team roles.

Task and maintenance roles

Some people focus on the task, on getting the job done and on meeting deadlines. Others put their energy into keeping the peace and holding the group together. Table 17.2 summarises the two.

Teams need both roles, and skilful project managers try to ensure this happens.

Meredith Belbin – team roles

Meredith Belbin and his colleagues systematically observed several hundred small groups while they performed a task, and concluded that each person in a group tends to behave in a way that corresponds to one of nine distinct roles. The balance of these roles in a group affects how well or badly it performs.

Table 17.2 Summary of task and maintenance roles

Emphasis on task	Emphasis on maintenance
Initiator	Encourager
Information seeker	Compromiser
Diagnoser	Peacekeeper
Opinion seeker	Clarifier
Evaluator	Summariser
Decision manager	Standard setter

Key ideas   Belbin's research method

Henley School of Management based much of its training on inviting managers to work in teams of up to ten on exercises or business simulations. The organisers had long observed that some teams achieved better financial results than others – irrespective of the abilities of the individual members as measured by standard personality and mental tests. The reasons for this were unclear. Why did some teams of individually able people perform less well than teams that appeared to contain less able people?

Belbin conducted a study in which observers, drawn from course members, used a standard procedure to record the types of contribution that members made. Team members voluntarily took psychometric tests, and team performance led to a quantifiable result. The researchers formed teams of members with above-average mental abilities, and compared their performance with the other teams. The 'intelligent' teams usually performed less well. Of 25 such teams only three were winners, and the most common position was sixth in a league of eight. The explanation lay in the way they behaved, typically spending time in debate, arguing for their point of view to the exclusion of others. These highly intelligent people were good at spotting flaws in others' arguments, and became so engrossed in these that they neglected other tasks. Failure led to recrimination. The lesson was that behaviour (rather than measured intelligence) affected group performance.

Source: Belbin (1981).

The researchers identified different preferred team roles. Some people were creative, full of ideas and suggestions. Others were concerned with detail, ensuring that the team dealt with all aspects and that quality was right. Others spent their time keeping the group together. Table 17.3 lists the nine roles identified in Belbin (1993). Belbin observed that winning teams had members who fulfilled a balance of roles that was different from the less successful ones.

Winning teams have an appropriate balance, such as:

- a capable co-ordinator;
- a strong plant – a creative and clever source of ideas;
- at least one other clever person to act as a stimulus to the plant;
- a monitor–evaluator – someone to find flaws in proposals before it is too late.

Ineffective teams usually have a severe imbalance, such as:

- a co-ordinator with two dominant shapers – since the co-ordinator will almost certainly not be allowed to take that role;
- two resource investigators and two plants – since no one listens or turns ideas into action;
- a completer with monitor–evaluators and implementers – probably slow to progress, and stuck in detail.

Table 17.3 Belbin's team roles

Role	Typical features
Implementer	Disciplined, reliable, conservative and efficient. Turns ideas into practical actions
Co-ordinator	Mature, confident, a good chairperson. Clarifies goals, promotes decision making, delegates well
Shaper	Challenging, dynamic, thrives on pressure. Has the drive and courage to overcome obstacles – likes to win
Plant	Creative, imaginative, unorthodox – the 'ideas' person who solves difficult problems
Resource investigator	Extrovert, enthusiastic, communicative – explores opportunities, develops contacts, a natural networker
Monitor–evaluator	Sober, strategic and discerning. Sees all options, judges accurately – the inspector
Teamworker	Co-operative, mild, perceptive and diplomatic. Listens, builds, averts friction, calms things – sensitive to people and situations
Completer	Painstaking, conscientious, anxious. Searches out errors and omissions. Delivers on time
Specialist	Single-minded, self-starting, dedicated. Provides scarce knowledge and skill

Source: Based on Belbin (1993).

Preferred team roles are the types of behaviour that people display relatively frequently when they are part of a team.

Belbin did *not* suggest that all teams should have nine people, each with a different **preferred team role**. His point was that team composition should reflect the task:

> The useful people to have in a team are those who possess strengths or characteristics that serve a need without duplicating those that are already there. Teams are a question of balance; what is needed is not well-balanced individuals but individuals who balance well with one another. In that way human frailties can be underpinned and strengths used to full advantage. (Belbin, 1981, p. 77)

Trainers use the model widely to enable members to evaluate their preferred roles. They also consider how the balance of roles within a team affects performance. Some managers use it when filling vacancies. A personnel director joined a new organisation and concluded that it employed few 'completer–finishers'. Management started initiatives and programmes but left them unfinished as they switched to something else. She resolved that in recruiting new staff she would try to bring at least one more 'completer–finisher' to the senior team.

Management in practice   Using Belbin's roles in film-making teams

Hollywood had experienced a shift from long-term jobs to short-term project teams. With their highly skilled freelance staff who come together for a brief period to carry out specific tasks and then disband, film making offers a model for the future of work in the wider world. Angus Strachan has been using Belbin's model to help film directors manage expensive production teams more effectively:

> Managing film teams requires a mature coordinator who can handle creative people with delicate egos and strong opinions – a good unit production manager is a strong monitor–evaluator, someone who can carefully analyse the overall situation and make the big calls. The second assistant director needs

to be a strong completer–finisher, passing on accurate information that enables the unit production manager to keep abreast of the situation . . . A successful assistant director also needs to be a good communicator and organizer who has the flexibility to adjust schedules – in Belbin's terms to take on the resource investigator role.

Source: Angus Strachan, 'Lights, camera, action', *Personnel Management*, 16 September 2004, pp. 44–46.

However, there is little evidence that companies deliberately use the model when forming teams from existing staff. Managers typically form teams on criteria of technical expertise, departmental representation or who is available. How the team processes will work is a secondary consideration. This is understandable, but in doing so managers make the implicit assumption that people will be able and willing to cover roles if one seems to be lacking. Whether managers use the theory or not, it implies that anyone responsible for a team may find the work goes better if he/she puts effort into securing the most suitable mix of members.

The performance of a team is affected by how well it moves through distinct stages of development, and by the team processes the members establish.

Case study   Cisco – the case continues   www.cisco.com

Recalling the roles within the team, Steve, a member of the project team, said:

My job was mainly to ensure that everything in the virtual team runs smoothly – often just a matter of arranging and co-ordinating meetings, but also encouraging some kind of creative spark that'll help discussion along. Gunzal takes his time to make decisions, but when he does, he's usually correct. Eddie is very systematic in his work, and very hard working.

Another member commented:

I'd say Graham is often the one who comes up with original ideas, while Jim has an incredible range of contacts within the company, and can usually find the right person to go to. Rai is very precise in everything he does and it's very important that he receives the correct information from the engineers. If they don't explain something properly he's good at going back to ask for more information.

Source: Communication from members of the project team.

Case questions 17.3
- Which of the Belbin roles can you identify among the members of the team?
- Are any of the roles missing, and how may that have affected team performance?

Activity 17.5   Critical reflection on team composition

Evaluate a team you have worked with using Belbin's team roles:

- Which roles are well represented and which are missing?
- Has that affected the way the team has worked?
- Which of the roles most closely matches your own preferred role?
- What are the strengths and weaknesses of Belbin's model to the manager?
- Have you any evidence of managers using it to help them manage teams? If so, in what way was it used and with what effect?

17.5 Stages of team development

Putting people into a team does not mean that they perform well immediately, as teams need to go through stages of growth. Some never perform well. Tuckman and Jensen (1977) developed a theory that groups can potentially pass through five fairly clearly defined stages of development. Figure 17.3 shows these.

Teams need to have the chance to grow up and to develop trust among the members. As the work makes progress people learn about each other, and how they can work well together. The closer they get, the easier it becomes to develop mutual trust.

Forming

Forming is the stage at which members choose, or are told, to join a team. Managers may select them for their functional and technical expertise or for some other skill. They come together and begin to find out who the other members are, exchanging fairly superficial information about themselves, and beginning to offer ideas about what the group should do. People are trying to make an impression on the group and to establish their identity with the other members.

Storming

Conflicts may occur at the storming stage, so it can be an uncomfortable time for the group. As the group begins the actual work members begin to express differences of interest that they withheld, or did not recognise, at the forming stage. People realise that others want different things from the group, have other priorities and, perhaps, have hidden agendas.

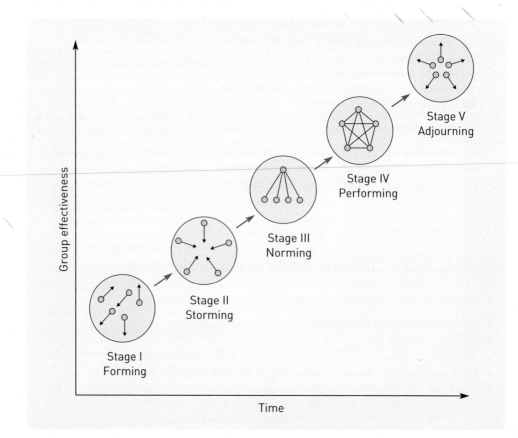

Figure 17.3
Stages of team development

Different personalities emerge, with contrasting attitudes towards the group and how it should work. Some experience conflicts between the time they are spending with the group and other duties. Differences in values and norms emerge.

Some groups never pass this stage. There may be little open conflict and members may believe the group is performing well – but may be deluding themselves. If the group does not confront disagreements it will remain at the forming or storming stage, and will do no significant work. Performance depends on someone doing or saying something to move the group to the next stage.

Norming

Here the members are beginning to accommodate differences constructively and to establish adequate ways of working together. They develop a set of shared norms – expected ways of behaving – about how they should interact with each other, how they should approach the task, how they should deal with differences. People create or accept roles so that responsibilities are clear. The leader may set those roles formally or members may accept them implicitly during early meetings. Members may establish a common language to guide the group and allow members to work together effectively.

Performing

Here the group is working well, gets on with the job to the required standard and achieves its objectives. Not all groups get this far.

Adjourning

The team completes its task and disbands. Members may reflect on how the group performed and identify lessons for future tasks. Some groups disband because they are clearly not able to do the job and agree to stop meeting.

Key ideas   **Managing the virtual team lifecycle**

Furst *et al.* (2004) noted the benefits of virtual teams in eliminating boundaries of time and space, but also found that they more often fail than succeed. To explain this they tracked the evolution of six virtual teams in a company, using the Tuckman and Jensen model. They found that virtual teams faced additional problems at each stage of the model, compared with those working in the same place.

- **Forming** is more difficult, and takes longer, as there is less frequent communication, especially the informal chat between workers who meet regularly. This reduces the speed at which people make friendships and increases the risk of forming false impressions or stereotypes about other team members.
- **Storming** can also be more fraught, as the absence of frequent non-verbal clues increases the risks of misunderstanding. Disagreements can be exacerbated or prolonged if people do not respond quickly to electronic communication – even if caused by differences in working times or poor technology.
- **Norming** in virtual teams needs to clarify how to co-ordinate work, how to communicate and how quickly to respond to requests. The process of norming itself is made more complex with electronic communication, as it is harder to try out ideas tentatively and to gauge reactions.
- **Performing** depends on sharing information, integrating ideas and seeking creative solutions. The challenges of virtual working at this stage include competing pressure from local assignments, losing focus, and the fear of a failure that would damage a career.

Furst *et al.* use their analysis to suggest what those managing a virtual team could do at each stage to increase the chances of virtual teams reliably adding value.

Source: Furst *et al.* (2004).

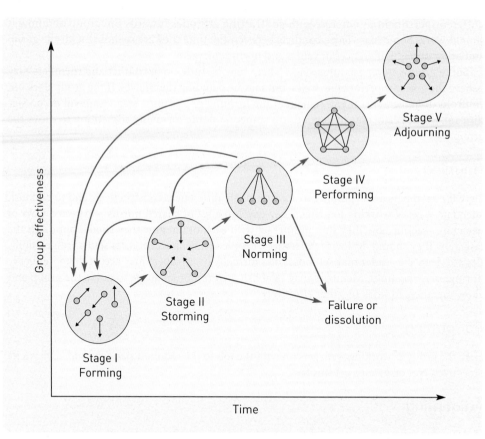

Figure 17.4
Modified model of
the stages of team
development

A team that survives will go through these stages many times. As new members join, as others leave, as circumstances or the task change, new tensions arise that take the group back to an earlier stage. A new member implies that the team needs to revisit, however briefly, the forming and norming stages. This ensures the new members are brought psychologically into the team and understand how they are expected to behave. A change in task or a conflict over priorities can take a team back to the storming stage, from which it needs to work forward again. The process will be more like Figure 17.4 than the linear progression implied by the original theory.

Members of the project team commented on the way the team developed. A common issue was the problem of scheduling meetings:

> I've always found in virtual teams that when the team is first formed it isn't really getting any serious work done (unless we're under severe time pressure), it's about getting everyone together so they at least have some knowledge of the others in the team. (Steve)

Another member said:

> It was strange when we first started working together, because we didn't push on and get any testing or fixing done straight away. Steve was really pushing for us all to spend a few hours in conference calls getting to know each other and how we were all going to work together. We took our time to get into the actual work that was required. (Graham)

Other reflections included:

I had a few discussions with Steve . . . he wanted us to spend most of our time in conference meetings with the rest of the team, while my engineers already had a good understanding of the work that was needed and just wanted to get on with it. But Steve is the team lead so we had to go along with his approach. (Richard)

It's weird having to form such a close relationship with someone [when] you don't even know what they look like. But as we're using IM [Instant Messenger] just about every day you get used to it. I think you sometimes have to make an extra effort to talk directly to people, just to keep the relationship going. Sometimes it'd be easier for me to email Rai, but I phone him, just so we can have a bit of a chat. (Eddie)

It means you have to be a bit more careful when it comes to communication. Most of the time you have to use email and IM to discuss issues, which means there can be misunderstandings if you're not careful. When you interact in person you use things like facial expression and hand gestures – none of these are available when emailing so you have to state your arguments more clearly. (Jim)

Source: Communication from members of the project team.

Case questions 17.4

- Relate these accounts to the stages of team development.
- What examples of forming, storming and norming does it contain?

17.6 Team processes

Effective teams, often with the help of skilled team coaches (Hackman and Wageman, 2005), develop working methods, or team processes, that help them to accomplish their tasks. These include developing a common approach, understanding categories of communication and observing team practices.

Common approach

A primary outcome of an effective 'norming' stage is that members agree both the administrative and social aspects of working together. This includes deciding who does which jobs, what skills members need to develop, and how the group should make and modify decisions. In other words the group needs to agree the work required and how it will fit together. It needs to decide how to integrate the skills of the group and use them co-operatively to advance performance.

The common approach includes supporting and integrating new members into the team. It also includes practices of remembering and summarising agreements. Working together on these tasks helps to promote the mutual trust and constructive conflict necessary to team success. Groups need to spend as much time on developing a common approach as they do on developing a shared purpose.

Team members need to control their meetings effectively – whether face to face or at a distance. That involves ensuring they are conducted in a way that suits the purpose of the task, without participants feeling that they are being manipulated. Table 17.4 is an example of the advice widely available to managers about effective and ineffective meetings.

Categories of communication

Group members depend on information and ideas from others to help them perform the group task; a useful skill is to be able to identify the kind of contribution that people make

Table 17.4 Five tips for effective meetings

Meetings are likely to succeed if:	Meetings are likely to fail if:
• they are scheduled well in advance	• they are fixed at short notice (absentees)
• they have an agenda, with relevant papers distributed in advance and invite additions at the start	• they have no agenda or papers (no preparation, lack of focus, discussion longer)
• they have a starting and finishing time and follow prearranged time limits on each item	• they are of indefinite length (discussion drifts), time is lost and important items are not dealt with (delay, and require a further meeting)
• decisions and responsibilities for action are recorded and circulated within 24 hours	• decisions lack clarity (misunderstanding what was agreed, delay, reopening issues)
• they keep subgroups or members of related teams informed of progress	• the team is not aware of work going on in other teams that is relevant to its work

(Chapter 16 illustrated patterns of group communication), and whether this helps the group to manage the task. To study and learn how people behave in groups we need a precise and reliable way to describe events. There are many such models, each suited to a purpose: Table 17.5 illustrates one such list of behaviours. The significance of this is the evidence that how a group uses its time between these categories of communication will affect performance. A group that devotes most of its time to proposing ideas and disagreeing with them will not progress far. A more effective group will spend more time proposing and building, which of course implies developing better listening skills.

Observing the team

Observation is the activity of concentrating on how a team works rather than taking part in the activity itself.

Content is the specific substantive task that the group is undertaking.

Members can develop the skill of assessing how well a team is performing a task. There are many guides to help them do this, and anyone can develop their ability to **observe** groups by concentrating on this aspect rather than on the **content** of the immediate task. They work

Table 17.5 Categories of communication within a group

Category	Explanation
Proposing	Putting forward a suggestion, idea or course of action
Supporting	Declaring agreement or support for an individual or their idea
Building	Developing or extending an idea or suggestion from someone else
Disagreeing	Criticising another person's statement
Giving information	Giving or clarifying facts, ideas or opinions
Seeking information	Seeking facts, ideas or opinions from others

slightly apart from the team for a short time and keep a careful record of what members say or do. They also note how other members react, and how that affects the performance of the team. At the very least, members can reflect on these questions at the end of a task:

- What did people do or say that helped or hindered the group's performance?
- What went well during that task, which we should try to repeat?
- What did not go well, which we could improve?

With practice, skilled members of a team are able to observe what is happening as they work on the task. They can do this more easily and powerfully if they focus their observations on certain behaviour categories – such as those shown in Table 17.8 – but only those suited to the purpose of the observation.

Teams have outcomes that can benefit the members, the organisation – and perhaps both.

17.7   Outcomes of teams – for the members

The Hawthorne studies described in Chapter 2 show that a supportive work group had more influence on performance than physical conditions. People have social needs that they seek to satisfy by being acknowledged and accepted by other people. This can be done person to person (mutual acknowledgement or courteous small-talk on the train), but most people are also members of several relatively permanent co-operative groups. These provide an opportunity to express and receive ideas and to reshape one's views by interacting with others. Acceptance by a group meets a widely held human need.

Mary Parker Follett observed the social nature of people and the benefits of co-operative action. She saw the group as an intermediate institution between the solitary individual and the abstract society, and believed that it was through the group that people organised co-operative action:

> Early psychology was based on the study of the individual; early sociology was based on the study of society. But there is no such thing as the 'individual', there is no such thing as 'society'; there is only the group and the group-unit – the social individual. Social psychology must begin with an intensive study of the group, of the selective processes which go on within it, the differentiated reactions, the likenesses and the unlikenesses, and the spiritual energy which unites them. (Quoted in Graham, 1995, p. 230)

Likert (1961) developed this theme of organising work in groups. He observed that effective managers encouraged participation by group members in all aspects of the job, including setting goals and budgets, controlling costs and organising work. Individuals became members of a team who were loyal to each other and who had high levels of team-working skills. Likert maintained that these groups were effective because of the *principle of supportive relationships*. He agreed with Maslow that people value a positive response from others, which helps to build and maintain their self-esteem. Social relationships at work serve the same purpose, especially when people spend much of their time in a group. Managers in effective organisations had deliberately linked such groups to ensure that people had overlapping membership of more than one group: 'each person . . . is a member of one or more functioning workgroups that have a high degree of group loyalty, effective skills of interaction and high performance goals' (Likert, 1961, p. 104). Figure 17.5 shows the principle.

These ideas continue to influence practice. Katzenbach and Smith (1993) observed that members of a team who surmount problems together build trust and confidence in each other. They benefit from the buzz of being in a team, and of 'being part of something bigger than myself'.

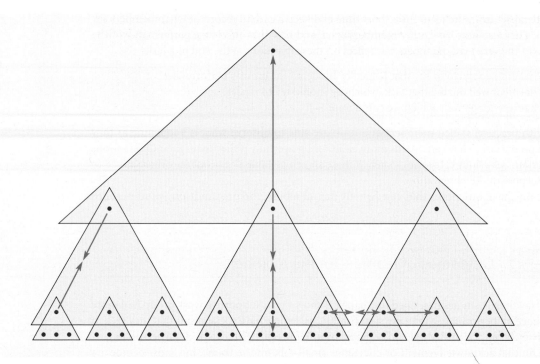

Figure 17.5 Likert's principle of supporting relationships

Note: The arrows indicate the linking-pin functions, both vertical and horizontal – as in cross-functional teams.

Source: Adapted from Likert (1967), p. 50.

Key ideas	Mary Parker Follett and Japanese management

According to Tokihiko Enomoto, Professor of Business Administration at Tokai University, Japan:

> Follett's work has become part of our teaching on management, and is well known to quite a number of . . . managers in our government institutions and business organisations. Much of what Follett says about individuals and groups reflects to a substantial extent our Japanese view of the place of individuals in groups, and by extension their place in society . . . She sees individuals not as independent selves going their separate ways, but as interdependent, interactive and interconnecting members of the groups to which they belong. This is something close to the Japanese ethos. We can fully agree with Follett when she writes that 'the vital relation of the individual to the world is through his groups'.

Source: Quoted in Graham (1995), pp. 242–243.

Concertive control is when workers reach a negotiated consensus on how to shape their behaviour according to a set of core values.

On the other side, some teams subject their members to what Barker (1993) refers to as a system of **concertive control**, which arise as workers negotiate a consensus among themselves.

Barker studied an electronic components company whose founders decided to organise the 90 manufacturing staff (two-thirds of them women) into self-managing teams, each being responsible for part of the product range and able to decide how they would work together. An example of concertive control occurred when the late delivery of components meant that a team would miss a delivery target. To recover the position the team agreed to work late and also to accommodate the external commitments of some members. This set a precedent for the way members would behave:

> I work my best at trying to help our team to get stuff out the door. If it requires overtime, coming in at five o'clock and spending your weekend here, that's what I do. (Barker, 1993, p. 422)

Members rewarded those who conformed by making them feel part of the team. They punished those who had 'bad' attitudes. The norms evolved from a loose system that workers 'knew' to a tighter system of objective rules. One explained:

> Well we had some disciplinary thing. We had a few certain people who didn't show up on time and made a habit of coming in late. So the team got together and kind of set some guidelines and we told them, you know, 'If you come in late the third time and you don't do anything to correct it, you're gone.' That was a team decision that this was a guideline that we follow. (p. 426)

Barker concludes that creating autonomous or self-managed teams does not free workers from the obligation to follow rules. Instead:

> The iron cage becomes stronger. The powerful combination of peer pressure and rational rules in the concertive system creates a new iron cage whose bars are almost invisible to the workers it incarcerates. They must invest a part of themselves in the team: they must identify strongly with their team's values and goals, its norms and rules. (pp. 435–436)

17.8 Outcomes of teams – for the organisation

Teams can bring together professional and technical skills beyond those of any individual. In health and social care there is a growing interest in team working to deliver care, since patients' frequently have conditions that require inputs from several professions – health, social work and housing, for example. More generally, the ability to deal with customer requirements requires the exchange of ideas among those from different professions, which is made easier if they are part of a recognised team:

> When representatives from all of the relevant areas of expertise are brought together, team decisions and actions are more likely to encompass the full range of perspectives and issues that might affect the success of a collective venture. Multidisciplinary teams are therefore an attractive option when individuals possess different information, knowledge, and expertise that bear on a complex problem. (Van Der Vegt and Bunderson, 2005, p. 532)

Management in practice   Teamwork pays off at Louis Vuitton www.vuitton.com

The French company Louis Vuitton is the world's most profitable luxury brand. The success of the company is attributed to a relentless focus on quality, a rigidly controlled distribution system and ever-increasing productivity in design and manufacture. Eleven of the 13 Vuitton factories are in France: although they could move to cheaper locations, management feels more confident about quality control in France.

Employees in all Vuitton factories work in teams of between 20 and 30 people. Each team, such as the ones at the Ducey plant in Normandy, works on one product, and members are encouraged to suggest improvements in manufacturing. They are also briefed on the product, such as its retail price and how well it is selling, says Stephane Fallon, who runs the Ducey factory. 'Our goal is to make everyone as multi-skilled and autonomous as possible', says team leader Thierry Nogues.

The teamwork pays off. When the Boulogne Multicolour (a new shoulder bag) prototype arrived at Ducey, workers who were asked to make a production run discovered that the decorative metal studs caused the zipper to bunch up, adding time and effort to assembly. The team alerted factory managers, and technicians quickly moved the studs a few millimetres away from the zipper. Problem solved.

Source: *Business Week*, 22 March 2004.

Teams can bring both high efficiency and high-quality jobs by:

- providing a structure within which people work together;
- providing a forum in which issues can be raised and dealt with – rather than being ignored;
- enabling people to extend their roles, perhaps increasing responsiveness and reducing costs;
- encourage acceptance and understanding by staff of a problem and the solution proposed; and
- promote wider learning by encouraging reflection, and spreading lessons widely

Key ideas   The romance of teams?

Allen and Hecht (2004) note that the empirical evidence about the benefits of teams to the organisation is variable: some showing they have added value, others not. Part of the problem is that when managers introduce team working, they often do so as part of a package of other changes, so it is hard to isolate the effects of teams from those of, say, a change in payment systems.

This led them to consider possible reasons for the gap between evidence and enthusiasm towards teams, concluding that the main reason is that teams provide people with social benefits (as set out above) and with competence-related benefits. The latter include the benefit someone gains (in terms of self-confidence and pride) from being part of a successful team, and from being able to distance themselves from failure in an unsuccessful one ('I said they should do X, but they didn't listen').

Source: Allen and Hecht (2004).

Teams can also obstruct performance. The discussion which generates new perspectives takes longer than it would for an individual to make a decision. If a team strays onto unrelated issues or repeats a debate, it loses time. Opponents of a decision can prolong discussion to block progress. Some teams allow one member to dominate, such as the formal leader in a hierarchical organisation, where people do not challenge those in authority. It may also be a technical expert who takes over, when others hesitate to show their lack of knowledge or to ask for explanations. In either case the group will probably be a dissatisfying and unproductive experience. It may produce a worse result, and be more costly, than if one person had dealt with the issue.

Some research has assessed the effects of teams on organisational-level variables such as output or profitability. As an example of the latter, Walton (1977) found that productivity improved at a manufacturing plant after managers re-designed the working processes to incorporate self-managed work teams. Wall and Clegg (1981) found that performance improved when employees' tasks were re-designed to incorporate team work, but in contrast Wall *et al.* (1986) found no differences in productivity between a traditionally organised plant and one using team working. Glassop (2002) found that companies with self-managing work groups and quality circles (another form of team work) reported higher productivity and lower labour turnover than those with no team structures.

Others, such as Hackman (1990), have focused on the analysis of performance of the team itself, proposing three ways of evaluating their effectiveness, summarised in Table 17.6.

Research with 27 teams of different types led Hackman to propose that to perform well a group must surmount three hurdles. Members must:

- be willing to exert sufficient effort to accomplish the task to an acceptable level;
- bring adequate knowledge and skill to the task;
- use group processes that are appropriate to the work and the setting.

Table 17.6 Criteria for evaluating team effectiveness

Criteria	Description
Has it met performance expectations?	Is the group completing the task managers gave to it – not only the project performance criteria, but also measures of cost and timeliness?
Have members experienced an effective team?	Is it enhancing their ability to work together as a group? Have they created such a winning team that it represents a valuable resource for future projects?
Have members developed transferable teamwork skills	Are members developing teamwork skills that they will take to future projects?

Source: Based on Hackman (1990).

Table 17.7 Points of leverage for enhancing group performance

Requirements for effectiveness	Internal conditions	Organisational context
Effort (see Chapter 15)	Motivational structure of task	Remedying co-ordination problems and rewarding team commitment
Knowledge and skill	Team composition	Available education and training, including coaching and guidance
Group processes	Working processes that foster review and learning	Information system to support task and provide feedback on progress

Source: Based on Hackman (1990), p. 13.

To overcome them, Hackman suggested that a team needs both internal and external support, as the manager cannot rely only on internal team practices or personal enthusiasm. He/she should also attend to wider organisational conditions such as the availability of **team-based rewards**. If both are in place it is more likely that the group will put in the effort, have the skill and use good team processes. Table 17.7 summarises these points.

Hackman's work is especially valuable as it makes specific reference to the context within which teams work, and to the way these contextual factors affect team performance.

Team-based rewards are payments or non-financial incentives, provided to members of a formally established team, that are linked to the performance of the group.

17.9	**Teams in context**

Does the task require a team approach?

Despite their potential benefits, teams are not always worth the cost, since they may represent an expensive solution to a simple problem. The usefulness of teams depends on the task:

- **simple puzzles of a technical nature** can be done effectively by competent staff working independently;

- **familiar tasks with moderate degrees of uncertainty** need some sharing of information and ideas, but the main requirement is reasonable co-operation and co-ordination between people;
- **a high degree of uncertainty and relatively unknown problems** requires high levels of information sharing and deep interpersonal skills to cope with the 'shared uncertainty'.

If the task requires people to work together to create joint work products beyond what an individual could do, then the cost of creating a team will be worthwhile.

Does the context support the team?

There are many situations in which an effective team would add value to the members and to the organisation – but is unable to do so because of factors in the external context. Table 17.7 notes specific organisational factors that affect the performance of teams – such as the availability of training and support: Chapter 11 shows how BMW had ensured that the payment system was designed to support team working, rather than undermine it. The following Management in Practice gives an example of a team in trouble, in part because contextual factors did not support it.

Management in practice   **A community mental health team**

The management of a healthcare unit decided to reduce the number of hospital places and increase resources for community care. As part of the change a resource centre was established containing multidisciplinary teams, each with about 30 staff, to provide a 24-hour service for the severely mentally ill in the community. The service would use a team approach with a flattened hierarchy and greater mutual accountability, and this was supported by many team building and similar activities.

It soon became clear that many staff could not cope with the extra responsibility and shared decision making. The job is difficult and sometimes dangerous, since people's lives are at stake. Management therefore changed the system to clarify the role of each member of staff and to give a clearer structure of authority and management. It also recognised that, while team working may be an ideal, it needs to be supported by broader management structures and practices.

Source: Communication from a manager in the service.

How can teams try to manage their context?

Faraj and Yan (2009) observe that many teams operate in uncertain environments where, among other things, their members compete with other units for resources and information. Teams therefore need to perform 'boundary work' to establish and maintain the boundaries, and conduct interactions across them. They need, for example, to acquire information and resources, manage external relations with stakeholders, and protect team resources from competing demands. To assess this empirically Faraj and Yan (2009) developed a questionnaire to assess the extent to which teams engaged in boundary work, and how this affected performance. Examples of the questions illustrate the point:

- **Boundary reinforcement** (e.g.) To what extent has this team tried to create a clear sense of identity and purpose?
- **Boundary buffering** (e.g.) To what extent are outsiders prevented from 'overloading' the team with either too much information or too many requests?
- **Boundary spanning** (e.g.) To what extent does the team encourage its members to solicit information and resources from elsewhere in and/or beyond the division? (p. 611)

> ### Activity 17.6   Critical reflection on teams
>
> Recall some teams of which you have been a member.
>
> - Which of the advantages and disadvantages have you observed?
> - When teams have performed well, or badly, can you relate that to ideas in this chapter, such as the stages of group development, or to Belbin's team roles?

17.10   Integrating themes

Sustainable performance

Building Terminal 5 at London Heathrow provided the airport's owner, BAA, with an opportunity to set new standards in environmental sustainability – and also with a novel way of using teams to deliver the project. Some of the early decisions – such as the requirement only to use timber approved by the Forest Stewardship Council and to avoid using polyvinyl chloride (PVC) – will deliver environmental sustainability to BAA for many years. Early in the process an environmental advisory assessment team was created, composed of environmental experts from across the construction industry. Its purpose was to help the project team to develop tools that would create a robust sustainability framework from the outset, such as to review project design proposals and make recommendations on environmental performance. This included setting challenging sustainability targets for the terminal in areas such as energy, water, pollution control and waste management.

These requirements then became part of the brief of the integrated teams created to deliver the 16 projects, and 147 separate subprojects in this massive project – which they did, on time and in budget, on 27 March 2008 (Wolstenholme *et al.*, 2008). The director of capital projects at BAA attributes much of this success to the system of integrated teams. These were not formed in the conventional way (by gathering representatives of relevant companies or disciplines) but by selecting only individuals with the right skill sets for the activity in hand, irrespective of employer. It was seen as a virtual organisation, using skills from consultants, contractors, suppliers and necessary skills from BAA itself. Their work was supported by a novel form of contract which encouraged teams to focus on delivering their part of the project to the customer and not, as is often the case in construction, trying to blame another company for any difficulties. The achievement of individual team milestones was celebrated, and supported by an award scheme which acknowledged exceptional performance – including those who helped to meet the sustainability targets.

Governance and control

Whatever the structure and form of governance arrangements, these will be directed at monitoring and controlling those responsible for areas of work – frequently members of senior teams. A significant challenge here is that successful groups take on a life of their own, and can become increasingly independent of the organisation that created them. As members learn to work together they generate enthusiasm and commitment – and become harder to control. The team may divert the project to meet goals that they value, rather than those of the sponsor. As experts in the particular issue they can exert great influence over management, by controlling or filtering the flow of information to the organisation as a whole, so that their goals become increasingly hard to challenge.

Chapter 7 (Section 7.7) examines the concept of groupthink, which occurs when members become so attached to a group that they suppress dissenting views so as not to jeopardise their acceptance by the other members. A common feature of groups which have succumbed to this condition is their inability to consider a range of alternatives rationally, or to see the likely consequences of the choice they made. This at the same time makes some external governance arrangement all the more necessary, and also all the more challenging to put into practice.

Internationalisation

A common feature of internationalisation is that companies create multinational or global teams to work on projects or regular activities. Such teams are often 'virtual', in the sense that although they are working on a common task they are physically separated and span different time zones. Their dominant means of communication is usually through computer-based systems such as emails and videoconferencing.

Virtual teams face all the challenges of team performance that face teams which are located in the same place, and in addition they need to overcome the difficulties of working with those from different cultures. Their transitory nature means that members may be part of several such teams simultaneously, limiting their ability to build close relationships with members of any particular one. Finally, virtual meetings lack the physical cues present in face-to-face meetings, which makes it more difficult for members to give and respond to the non-verbal cues that prevent misunderstanding.

Govindarajan and Gupta (2001) surveyed executives from European and US multinationals with experience of virtual teams, and concluding that they face unique challenges:

- **Cultivating trust among team members** Trust between members encourages co-operation and avoids conflict, and is highest when members share similarities, communicate frequently and operate in a common context of norms and values. By their nature, global teams suffer on all these dimensions.
- **Hindrances to communication** Distance hinders face-to-face communication, which technology can still only partially resolve. Language barriers are a further block to communication: even if people are speaking the same language, differences in meaning and usage can obstruct work. Cultural differences (Chapter 4) mean that members bring profound differences in values to the discussions. Those from collectivist cultures place a high value on achieving consensus, and are willing to prolong a meeting to achieve it: this can seem wasteful to those from individualist cultures who place less value on consensus.

Summary

1   **Distinguish the types of teams used by organisations**

- As management faces new expectations about cost and quality, many see teams as a way of using the talents and experience of the organisation more fully to meet these tougher objectives.
- Hackman's typology shows the opportunities and challenges faced by top teams, taskforces, professional support, performing, human service, customer service and production teams respectively.

2   **Use a model to analyse the composition of a teams**

- Belbin identified nine distinct roles within a team and found that the balance of these roles within a team affected performance. The roles are: implementer, co-ordinator, shaper, plant, resource investigator, monitor–evaluator, teamworker, completer and specialist.

3   **Identify the stages of team development and explain how they move between them**

- Forming, storming, norming, performing and adjourning. Note also that these stages occur iteratively as new members join or circumstances change.

4 Identify specific team processes and explain how they affect performance

- Effective teams develop a common approach and working methods, develop skills in several types of communications, and are skilled in observation and review, enabling them to learn from their experience.

5 Evaluate the outcomes of a team for the members and the organisation

- Members benefit from being part of a social group, from meeting performance expectations, from experiencing an effective team, and developing transferable teamwork skills.
- The organisation can benefit from the combination of skills and professions, although the evidence of the links to organisational success are mixed

6 Outline the contextual factors that influence team performance

- Teams are not necessary for all tasks.
- Teams need to be supported by suitable payment systems and by education and training, and by relevant technologies.
- Teams themselves can act to manage their boundaries effectively.

7 Show how ideas from the chapter add to your understanding of the integrating themes

- Designing and constructing Terminal 5 at Heathrow to meet new standards of sustainability is a good example of how well-managed teams from diverse professional and organisational backgrounds can contribute to this central management challenge.
- Teams that are effective face the danger that as their success increases they become resistant to criticism – the members themselves believe their own propaganda. This well-documented feature of teams makes it paradoxically difficult for governance systems to control those teams which, in the wider interest, most need to be controlled.
- Teams working internationally face additional challenges in that they lack the nuances that come from regular face-to-face interaction.

Review questions

1 What are the potential benefits of teamwork to people and performance?

2 Katzenbach and Smith (1993) distinguish between working groups and real teams. Describe the differences, and suggest when each form is appropriate to a task.

3 W.L. Gore and Associates (see Part Case) is beginning to form more distant teams. What management issues are likely to arise in this form of team?

4 How many stages of development do teams go through? Use this model to compare two teams.

5 List the main categories of behaviour that can be identified in observing a group.

6 Compare the meaning of the terms 'task' and 'maintenance' roles.

7 Evaluate Belbin's model of team roles. Which three or four roles are of most importance in an effective team? What is your preferred role?

8 Give examples of the external factors that affect group performance. Compare the model with your experience as a group member.

9 What are the potential disadvantages of teams?

10 Summarise an idea from the chapter that adds to your understanding of the integrating themes.

Concluding critical reflection

Think about your experience of teams, and about the ways in which your organisation uses teams. Review the material in the chapter and then make notes on the following questions:

- Which of the issues discussed in this chapter struck you as being relevant to practice in your organisation?
- Thinking of the teams in which you have worked, which are effective and which ineffective? What happens in the effective teams that does not happen in the less effective ones? What team-building skills do people use, and to what extent are they supported or hindered by wider organisational factors? Are teams supported by specific coaching or guidance? What **assumptions** have people made when creating teams?
- What factors such as the history of the company or your personal experience have shaped the way you use teams? Does your current use of teams appear to be right for your present **context** position and company – or would you use a different approach in other circumstances?
- Have people put forward **alternative** working methods (such as introducing more self-managing teams), based on practice in other companies? If you could find such evidence, how may it affect company practice?
- What **limitations** can you identify in any of these team theories, or in your organisation's approach to using teams? Do people create too many teams or too few?

Further reading

Belbin, R.M. (1993), *Team Roles at Work*, Butterworth/Heinemann, Oxford.

> An account of the experiments that led Belbin to develop his model of team roles.

Druskat, V.U. and Wheeler, J.V. (2004), 'How to lead a self-managing team', *MIT Sloan Management Review*, vol. 45, no. 4, pp. 65–71.

Govindarajan, V. and Gupta, A.K. (2001), 'Building an effective global business team', *MIT Sloan Management Review*, vol. 42, no. 4, pp. 63–72.

> Two contemporary articles based on empirical research in a manufacturing plant and a series of global businesses respectively.

Hackman, J.R. (1990), *Groups that Work (and Those that Don't)*, Jossey-Bass, San Francisco, CA.

Katzenbach, J.R. and Smith, D.K. (1993), *The Wisdom of Teams*, Harvard Business School Press, Boston, MA.

> Both books contain many good examples of the use of teamwork.

Hackman, J. R. and Wageman, R. (2005), 'A theory of team coaching', *Academy of Management Review*, vol. 30, no. 2, pp. 269–287.

> Valuable overview of the development of interest in team processes, and of research into the skills of team development.

Hayes, N. (2002), *Managing Teams*, Thomson Learning, London.

> A lively and well-referenced account of many of the issues covered here.

Weblinks

These websites have appeared in this and other chapters:

www.cisco.com
www.vuitton.com
www.microsoft.com
www.oticon.com
www.bmw.com
www.lilly.co.uk
www.gore.com

Each has tried to develop new approaches to using teams – encouraging staff to share ideas and experience, as well as gaining personal satisfaction from them. Try to gain an impression from the site (perhaps under the careers/working for us section) of what it would be like to work in an organisation in which teams are a prominent feature of working.

 For video case studies, audio summaries, flashcards, exercises and annotated weblinks related to this chapter, visit **www.pearsoned.co.uk/mymanagementlab**

PART 5 CASE

W.L. GORE & ASSOCIATES IN EUROPE

www.gore.com

W.L. Gore & Associates is a remarkable example of a business organised around team principles. While working as a scientist at Dupont Corporation, Bill Gore became convinced of the potential value of polytetrafluoroethylene (PTFE), commonly known as Teflon, as an insulating material for wire. This led him and his wife Vieve to begin W.L. Gore & Associates in Newark, Delaware, in 1958. The company has plants around the world, including three in Scotland – two in Livingston and one in Dundee. In March 2010 it again featured near the top (at number 7) in *The Sunday Times* list of 'Britain's Best 100 Companies to Work For'. The company is owned by the Gore family and the associates (see below).

In 1969 Bill and Vieve Gore's son, Bob, discovered that PTFE could be stretched to form a strong porous material, which enabled the company to broaden the range of its electronics products to include new applications such as medical implants, high-performance fabrics and solutions to environmental pollution. The business is well known for the GORE-TEX® brand, under which many of its products are marketed. GORE-TEX® fabric works in a wide range of temperatures, does not age, is weather durable, porous and strong.

The focus of the business is the development, manufacture and engineering of products and technologies based on PTFE and other fluoroplastics for a wide range of applications. It has four product divisions:

1 **electronic products:** special cables and cable assemblies for the aviation, aerospace, automation, telecommunication, medical and IT industries;
2 **medical products:** vascular grafts, implants, patches and dental implants;
3 **fabrics:** branded high-performance fabrics for sportswear, leisurewear, work and protective wear;
4 **industrial products:** filter media and gaskets in environmental technologies, and in the food, fibre and textile industries.

The company has a tradition of valuing close and direct personal contact among people, which is seen as essential to the success of this kind of innovative business. There are no job titles in the company – all employees are known as 'associates'. Associates are hired for a broad area of work and, with the guidance of their sponsors and a growing understanding of opportunities and team objectives, commit to projects that match their skills. Teams organise around opportunities and leaders emerge based on the needs and priorities of a particular business unit – some would provide technical leadership, others business leadership and so on. Leaders usually emerge naturally by demonstrating special knowledge, skill or experience that is in line with business objectives.

The company has avoided traditional hierarchy, opting instead for a team-based environment that fosters personal initiative, encourages innovation and promotes direct communication. The business philosophy reflects the belief that given the right environment there are no limits to what people can accomplish, provided these are consistent with the business objectives and strategies.

Associates work to four principles:

1 fairness to each other and everyone with whom they come in contact;
2 freedom to encourage, help and allow other associates to grow in knowledge, skill and scope of responsibility;
3 the ability to make one's own commitments and keep them;
4 consultation with other associates before undertaking actions that could affect the reputation of the company – this is known as the waterline principle.

The last principle is intended to balance the risks of innovation: while associates are encouraged to be innovative they are not expected to make significant financial commitments without thorough review and participation by other associates and in line with business objectives.

Selection is rigorous. Would-be associates spend up to eight hours being interviewed, over three days. This careful selection appears to pay off, as more than half of the staff have worked at the company for at least ten years. A new associate is assigned one or more sponsors who help them become acquainted with the company and its ways of working, ensure they receive credit and recognition for their work, and ensure that they are fairly paid.

Courtesy of W.L. Gore & Associates UK Ltd. © 2007 W.L. Gore & Associates

To ensure a fair and effective pay structure, the company asks associates to rank their team members each year in order of contribution to the enterprise. This includes an associate's impact and effectiveness as well as past, present and future contributions. The company ensures that pay is competitive by regularly comparing the pay of Gore associates with their peers at other companies.

The benefit plan consists of core benefits and flexible benefits. Core benefits are provided to all eligible associates and include pay, holidays, sick pay, life insurance and the Associate Stock Option Plan (ASOP). The purpose of ASOP is to provide equity ownership in the company, and through that a degree of financial security in retirement. All associates can acquire a share in the company, in which the Gore family holds a major stake. An associate from the UK commented:

Leadership probably happens in three different ways. We still have the concept of natural leaders emerging through followership. There are then some areas of the business where leaders are appointed, and we probably find that more in this plant where we have a large production operation. We need associates with operational expertise which meets our business needs.

Decisions to take on additional staff are made on a consultative basis. At the moment it's very much project driven in certain areas. So a group would be working on a specific new product development,

and they'll look at the resources they require for that work – and if they haven't got the resources a decision will be taken to go outside. What therefore tends to happen is that people are brought into the business with a specific area of work in mind. Not necessarily a job description but a role description. That would then settle that person into the business. Once that work commitment has finished, they'll then try to seek an alternative role in the business, with another dedicated team.

We have about 140 associates in this plant, organised according to what we call the three-legged principle. The legs consist of sales, product management and manufacture, and these legs are bound together in areas such as marketing, administration, inside sales and vendor support. We also have a position called product specialist, and that person is typically someone with a technical background, who is perhaps working in sales. They are in effect sales people, developing very close links with our customers. They work very closely with our customers on current products, but also to identify customer requirements, and move with them to research and develop new products. And we have a team of them in each plant. All of them take an industry sector. Say, for example, in the fabrics plant, we have a product specialist looking after the fire industry, one looking after police, one military, one ski. Each group covers customers throughout Europe.

Associates tend to be committed to one area of work. So, for example, here in industrial filtration we are working on products for office automation technology – basically photocopiers – and we then assemble a team to develop that product. There'd be some production people, engineers, admin support: somebody will have seen a need, researched the product, brought together a team.

The focus is very much on the R&D. One challenge is to retain the team-working ethos while working globally. There is a danger of duplication if the interests of separate teams in different parts of the world evolve in such a way that they are working on similar products. Yet at the same time we don't want to create structures or processes that stifle creativity. We don't want to say that people should focus on specific areas of research. We need to find ways of sharing expertise globally.

Freedom of choice is not total. People will be asked at some point to go on a work commitment by the leader of the business group. When there is a pressing business objective, someone leading a commitment will find the right person for the job, in a way that is best for them and the company. Leaders might be appointed because people recognise that they have exercised leadership within their function (say, as a chief chemical engineer). It could also be that each plant has an overall business leader. We have a business leader for industrial filtration and, if there was a particular skill needed on an area of work, he may decide to ask somebody to commit to that.

Balance between procedures and guidelines, and human initiative

We do have standard procedures and rules and regulations. The underpinning principle is to keep them to the minimum, and it's about questioning why we need them. If there's a business reason why that is the best way to deal with it then we're not afraid to put in policies and procedures, for example ISO 9000. There is a mentality that people understand the need for processes when there's something tangible. So, in manufacturing, people accept that that is required. Less so in areas like HR, where there is a reluctance to do anything that people would see as a limiting structure. So if people can readily see the need, we put in procedures; but when it's not tangible we are very questioning about whether it's required. We are very flexible in the way we introduce things. If it increases profits, protects health and safety, and if people can see the tangible results, then there really isn't too much of a problem. The buy-in is absolutely essential.

How do you go about securing that buy-in?

You go and speak to key people and influence people, and you make a judgement as to who is key to get this project through, trying to see where opposition might come from, and trying to deal with it before you actually impose the procedure. You don't need everyone fully committed – apart from those who actually have to do something. Commitment in Gore is very much when you personally have to deliver something, so a commitment in Gore is when you commit to doing XYZ on a certain project. It's not in terms of 'you've got my support', it's 'I have to deliver for a certain project'. Buy-in is willingness to accept and to put the effort in on behalf of the team.

In a report accompanying the announcement of the 2007 'Britain's Best 100 Companies' award Karl Williamson, a member of the new product development team, said: 'It's nice to go to the shows and see the garment that you have had a hand in making.' He took a six-week job at the company to kill time after graduating 11 years ago and never left. 'There is something special about it,' he says. There must be – almost half (45 per cent) the workforce have been on the payroll for at least ten years.

Carole-Anne Smith, the firm's European specialist for snow sports, admits that Gore was not initially an easy place to work. 'I hated it when I started,' she says. 'Gore challenges you as an individual more. I had come from a very structured organisation. Here you do not get a job specification, you get set the problem.'

This autonomy empowers workers at the firm, which gets top positive scores for staff believing they can make a difference (89 per cent), feeling fully involved (88 per cent) and finding work stimulating (85 per cent). Staff also say working at the firm is good for their personal growth, giving it a top score of 89 per cent.

Even though how you get the job done is up to you, workers are not left to go it alone. Asking for help is seen as a sign of strength. Each individual chooses a person to help them grow and develop, and people say colleagues go out of their way to help them and care a lot about each other (both 88 per cent) and are fun to work with (87 per cent).

After her initial reservations, Smith is surprised she has been at Gore as long as she has: 'I never imagined I would stay longer than five years,' she says. Smith has travelled around the world with the firm and found it very accommodating when she requested reducing her working week to three days after having her children. 'I have no plans to leave,' she adds.

In 2010 the company employed just over 400 people in the UK, most at the three sites in Scotland and more than half of them (52 per cent) have put in ten or more years' service, while 71 per cent have put in at least five years. Each employee receives 50 hours of formal training a year, and is offered a range of flexible working options including part-time hours, compressed hours and working from home. New mothers receive 26 weeks maternity leave on full pay and 13 at 90 per cent plus 13 weeks unpaid additional leave if they want it. New fathers get two weeks off on full pay. Other benefits include performance and profit-related pay, free private healthcare, dental insurance, critical illness cover, discounted services and a subsidised canteen. There is a generous final salary pension scheme into which the firm contributes 25 per cent of employees' pay.

Sources: Company website; discussion with associates; *Sunday Times*, 11 March 2007, 7 March 2010. Copyrighted material reproduced with the permission of W.L. Gore & Associates. © 2005 W.L. Gore & Associates.

Part case questions

- How does W.L. Gore & Associates influence staff to work on vital projects?

- How do research staff influence each other? Compare the way that people at Gore and at Semco influence other members of the company.

- How is W.L. Gore & Associates balancing personal and institutional sources of power and influence?

- How does management ensure that associates are motivated to work on projects that are important to the company's future prosperity?

- If you were a talented research scientist, what would be the attractions and rewards of working for Gore?

- Which theories of human needs appear to be supported by the reported policies and attitudes at W.L. Gore & Associates?

- In what ways are the associates at Gore empowered?

- Why do teams seem to work so well for Gore? What benefits do you think they bring both to the business and to the individuals? What if teams compete, rather than co-operate?

- What, if any, differences are there between Gore's approach and that used by Cisco?

PART 5
SKILLS DEVELOPMENT

To help you develop your skills, as well as knowledge, this section includes tasks that relate the key themes covered in the Part to your daily life. Working through these will help you to deepen your understanding of the skills and insights that you can use in many situations.

Task 5.1 Acquiring power to influence others

Power is a feature of any group or organisation, and to work effectively people need to acquire and use power – the capacity of individuals to exert their will over others. Chapter 14 identifies personal and organisational sources of power: coercive, reward, expertise and referent. It also shows that a person's position in the organisation can affect his/her access to power. Using some or all of these behaviours, based on the ideas in the book, will help you become more familiar with ways of increasing your power, and hence your ability to influence others.

1 **Use tactics to influence others**
   Draw on the Yukl and Falbe (1990) research to select the right tactics to use when influencing others:
   - Use rational persuasion – logical arguments backed up with convincing information – when influencing your boss.
   - Use exchange, personal appeal and legitimating tactics (e.g. relating your request to organisational policy) when influencing colleagues.
   - Use inspirational appeal and pressure when influencing subordinates.

2 **Gain control over organisational resources**
   - To use the power which comes from being able to offer something to others you want to influence, seek out opportunities that give you control over budgets, information, expertise, facilities – anything which others may value and that you can use in return. The investment and trouble in gaining that control will usually be worthwhile.

3 **Manage your reputation – be visible**
   Try to understand what the culture of your organisation most values in successful staff, and what images it is best to avoid. Do they prefer those who are risk takers or those who play safe? Do the important things get agreed during social occasions or in formal meetings? How are people expected to behave with colleagues? Also:
   - Ensure that your achievements are known about, and that people talk about them.
   - Manage your boss – find out what is important to him/her, and try to help him/her achieve him/her goals – why irritate a person who can affect your career?

4 **Build your network**
   Research clearly shows that networking pays; by giving contacts, sources of information, sources of rewards and so on. Networks take time to develop, so don't waste time before you start. They also need maintaining – do people favours that they will remember when you want something from them.

5 **Develop your expertise**

Ensure that the skills and knowledge you have are relevant to the organisation, and that you keep them up to date. Concentrating on significant new areas of technical or administrative knowledge will soon mean that you are acknowledged as the local expert, so that others seek out your views and opinions.

6 **Be ready to share power with subordinates**

They will probably be more committed to working for you, and more importantly, delegating will give you more time to cultivate the external and senior contacts you need to develop your power.

Task 5.2   Motivating others

Being able to motivate others (colleagues as well as subordinates) will be one of the keys to your performance as a manager. While there is no single answer to this managerial challenge, the theories in Chapter 15 give some clues about the practices and skills you can use.

1 **Recognise individual differences**

Individuals have unique interests and needs, and all motivational theories need to be implemented with these in mind. They help to indicate likely motives and processes, but motivating people depends on recognising their diversity.

2 **Enable people to pursue their goals through their work**

If responsible, informed people are able to do work that satisfies their needs they will be more committed and motivated to it than if it does not satisfy them. People who seek challenge and achievement will thrive in jobs that enable them to set goals, have autonomy in how they do the work and receive feedback on performance.

3 **Use goals imaginatively**

Goal-setting theory includes some clear prescriptions about the motivational effects of goals, such as setting goals that are clear and challenging, but achievable allow staff to participate in setting goals or explain the reasons for them convincingly; and provide feedback on performance. Also try to build and maintain people's self-confidence in their abilities, as this affects how they react to challenging goals.

4 **Ensure that effort will lead to performance**

People will be more motivated if they see a predictable link between effort and performance – which can be done by ensuring they are clear about what is expected, have adequate training opportunities, have competent colleagues, and have adequate facilities and technologies.

5 **Ensure that performance is clearly linked to rewards**

People will also be more motivated if they are confident that performance will be rewarded – so ensure that appraisal and reward schemes are seen to be well designed and fairly administered.

6 **Check for equity**

While equity theory is hard to test empirically, strong anecdotal evidence shows the dangers of inadvertent management action leading to a sense of inequity and therefore a loss of motivation. Ensure that perceived differences in the ratio of inputs to rewards can be justified, and also that people are using appropriate bases of comparison.

7 **Ensure extrinsic rewards are satisfied as well as intrinsic ones**

People value extrinsic rewards as well as intrinsic ones. Money matters to most people, and ensuring that they see their pay is adequate and fair for the work they do, provides an essential basis on which to build other motivational practices.

Task 5.3   Interpersonal communication

Interpersonal communication skills are a vital management skill. This activity helps you develop your awareness and understanding of listening.

Answer *True* or *False* to each of these statements:

1   People's thoughts can interfere with their listening.
2   People may resist listening to others who blame or get angry with them.
3   People are more likely to talk to those with whom they feel safe than to those with whom they do not.
4   People who have something they are keen to say are good at listening.
5   Some people listen too much because they are afraid of revealing themselves.
6   Talking is more important than listening.
7   People who feel very emotional about issues make good listeners.
8   People who are very angry are rarely good listeners.
9   People are less likely to hear messages that agree with their view than messages which challenge those views.
10 Fatigue never affects the quality of people's listening.

How did you score?

The correct answers to the good listening test are:

1 True	2 True	3 True	4 False	5 True
6 False	7 False	8 True	9 False	10 False

Give yourself two points for each correct answer. Most accomplished listeners will score 16 or more. A score under 10 suggests that you can benefit by improving your listening skills, as you are probably missing a lot of useful information.

Task 5.4   Observing a group

A useful skill to develop is that of observing the processes within a group – that is, how the members work together. This can give you a new insight into the successful and unsuccessful group practices, which you can then use to improve future groups.

One method is to observe the behaviours within the group, noting how other members react and how that affects the performance of the team – perhaps using the list in Chapter 17:

Proposing	Putting forward a suggestion, idea or course of action
Supporting	Declaring agreement or support for an individual or their idea
Building	Developing or extending an idea or suggestion from someone else
Disagreeing	Criticising another person's statement
Giving information	Giving or clarifying facts, ideas or opinions
Seeking information	Seeking facts, ideas or opinions from others

Alternatively you could assess how well a team is performing a task by asking, at the end of a meeting:

- What did people do or say that helped or hindered the group's performance?
- What went well during that task that we should try to repeat?
- What did not go well, which we could improve?

Another idea is to rate the team using the following scales – circle the number that best reflects your opinion of the discussion in a group.

1 How effectively did the group obtain and use necessary information?

1	2	3	4	5	6	7
Badly						Well

2 To what extent was the group's organisation suitable for the task?

1	2	3	4	5	6	7
Unsuitable						Suitable

3 To what extent did members really listen to each other?

1	2	3	4	5	6	7
Not at all						All the time

4 How fully were members involved in decision taking?

1	2	3	4	5	6	7
Low involvement						High involvement

5 To what extent did you enjoy working with this group?

1	2	3	4	5	6	7
Not at al						Very much

6 How well was time used?

1	2	3	4	5	6	7
Badly						Well

PART 6
CONTROLLING

Introduction

Any purposeful human activity needs some degree of control if it is to achieve what is intended. From time to time you check where you are in relation to your destination. The sooner you do this, the more confident you are of being on track. Frequent checks ensure that you take corrective action quickly to avoid wasting effort and resources.

An owner-manager can often exercise control by making a personal observation then using experience to make a decision about corrective action; however, as the organisation grows so does its complexity. It becomes increasingly difficult to know the current position as work goes on in many separate places at the same time. Work activity, objectives and measures may differ across the organisation, making it difficult for senior managers to understand what is working well and what is not.

To help them exercise control, managers use a range of systems and techniques. Chapter 18 introduces operations management as a source of control and discusses the concept of controlling the quality of products and services. Chapter 19 explores control in more detail, investigating how organisational performance is monitored and adjusted to ensure that the firm meets it objectives. Chapter 20 investigates finance as a form of control showing the main financial measures that managers use to assess performance.

The Part case is Tesco, Britain's largest retailer, which illustrates many approaches to controlling an ever-expanding business.

CHAPTER 18
MANAGING OPERATIONS AND QUALITY

Aim

To introduce the organisation as a set of linked operational processes working together to deliver a product that conforms to a predefined quality standard.

Objectives

By the end of your work on this chapter you should be able to outline the concepts below in your own terms and:

1 Define the term operations management

2 Describe the transformation process model of operations management

3 Show how operations management can contribute to the competitiveness of the organisation

4 Identify different forms of operational activity

5 Define the term quality in the operational context

6 Show how ideas from the chapter add to your understanding of the integrating themes

Key terms

This chapter introduces the following ideas:

operations management	span of processes
transformation process	break-even analysis
craft system	layout planning
factory production	total quality management
operations strategy	

Each is a term defined within the text, as well as in the Glossary at the end of the book.

Case study   Zara

Amancio Ortega Gaona began working as a delivery boy for a shirt-maker when he was 13 years old. He later managed a tailor's shop where he made night-shirts and pyjamas. In 1963, when still in his 20s, he started 'Confecciones GOA' in La Coruña to manu-facture women's pyjamas (and later lingerie prod-ucts), initially for sale directly to garment wholesalers. In 1975, however, when a German customer can-celled a large order, the firm opened its first Zara retail shop in La Coruña, Spain. The original intent was simply to have an outlet for cancelled orders, but this experience taught Ortega the importance of the 'mar-riage' between the operations of production and retailing. This was a lesson that guided the evolution of the company from then on. As Mr Miguel Diaz, a senior marketing executive reiterated in 2001:

Copyright © Inditex

> **It is critical for us to have five fingers touching the factory and the other five touching the customer.**

The company had six stores by 1979 and estab-lished retail operations in all the major Spanish cities during the 1980s. In 1988 the first international Zara store opened in Porto, Portugal, followed shortly by New York City in 1989 and Paris in 1990. But the real 'step-up' in foreign expansion took place during the 1990s when Zara entered Europe, the Americas and Asia.

Zara is now present across the world, with a net-work of over 1,500 stores. Its international presence shows that national frontiers are no impediment to sharing a single fashion culture. Zara claims to move with society, dressing the ideas, trends and tastes that society itself creates. It is claimed that Zara needs only two weeks to develop a product and get it into stores, in comparison with the industry aver-age of nearly six months. Zara has a large design team and the design process is closely linked to the public. Information travels from the stores to the de-sign teams, transmitting the demands and concerns of the market. The vertical integration of activities – design, production, logistics and sales in the com-pany's own stores – means that Zara is flexible and fast in adapting to the market. Its model is charac-terised by continuous product renovation. Zara pays special attention to the design of its stores, its shop windows and interior decor, and locates them in the best sites of major shopping districts.

Source: Author's own, based on www.zara.com

Case question 18.1

Good operations management is based on process consistency.

- What do you think are the major managerial challenges in setting up an operations system to serve a fast-moving and fickle market such as fashion?

18.1   Introduction

Zara is a fashion company that relies heavily on good operational systems. It is an integrated business in that it does most of the work itself: it designs, manufactures, distributes and sells the products. It relies on quick turnaround times on most products, which it sells in relatively large quantities. Its garments must be available on time to catch the latest fashion trend and must also be of a consistent quality to ensure that customers will return to buy again.

Two factors are critical to Zara's success: the creative ability to catch the mood of the customer with interesting and exciting designs; and the operational capability to design, manufacture and distribute goods quickly and efficiently. Neither factor can exist alone – it needs both good design AND good operational processes.

Good process and practice has always been important in production and manufacturing areas, but many companies in the service sector now use the methods of operations management. The chapter begins by introducing the basic concepts and language that underpin operations management, which you will be able to use in any sector of the economy. It will then discuss what a 'product' is in services and manufacturing respectively. It then shows what operations managers typically do, and concludes by exploring the meaning of quality and how to manage it.

18.2   What is operations management?

System and process

> The Matrix is a system, Neo. That system is our enemy. But when you're inside, you look around, what do you see? Businessmen, teachers, lawyers, carpenters – the very minds of the people we are trying to save . . . Many of them are so inured, so hopelessly dependent on the system, that they will fight to protect it. Source: Morpheos to Neo, *The Matrix.*

Morpheus is attempting to open the mind of his student Neo to the true nature of life in *The Matrix* and show that reality is a fabrication, a virtual world created to enslave the human race. The challenge Morpheus faces is that Neo, like the rest of humanity, is so familiar with the current situation that he cannot imagine another state of being.

Modern societies are similar in that the state of organisation of our everyday lives is so pervasive that it is difficult for most people to imagine a different way. We live in a world of systems, which shape our personal lives, our transport, our security and our work. Our lives are continually 'managed' within the system that is our society. Such systems bring safety and economy by removing many random events, and allowing better use of time and energy. Organisations also benefit from consistency and predictability. Creating effective systems is the central challenge of operations management.

The operations challenge

Operations management is all of the activities, decisions and responsibilities of managing the production and delivery of products and services.

Slack *et al.* (2007) define **operations management** as the activities, decisions and responsibilities of managing the production and delivery of products and services.

The way to do this is to implement systems and processes that are:

- repeatable – can be done over and over again;
- consistent – produce the same result every time;
- reliable – do not break down randomly.

The standard of performance now required against each criterion is growing because of:

- increased competition in cost and quality as a result of globalisation and the development of new technologies, especially in information and communications;
- more complex activities as more sophisticated customers expect more differentiated products with higher functionality;
- tighter environmental regulation to control pollution; and
- legislation on employment and working conditions.

Process therefore needs also to be:

- efficient – producing most output for least input;
- competitive – at least as good as others who are doing the same types of things;
- compliant with the legislation that governs the industrial environment.

Case question 18.2

- Do you think the current tendency towards globalisation will help or hinder Zara's success?

The transformation process

The first step in achieving an efficient, process-based organisation is to understand the work of the organisation as a **transformation process** which turns inputs (or resources) into the outputs that are the product.

Figure 1.1 (slightly adapted here as Figure 18.1) models the transformation process. It shows inputs entering the operational processes of the organisation which transforms them into an output that is the product or service to be sold. There are two types of input:

- **transforming** resources are the elements that carry out the transformation; and
- **transformable** resources are the elements that the process transforms into the product.

The **transformation process** refers to the operational system that takes all of the inputs; raw materials, information, facilities, capital and people and converts them into an output product to be delivered to the market.

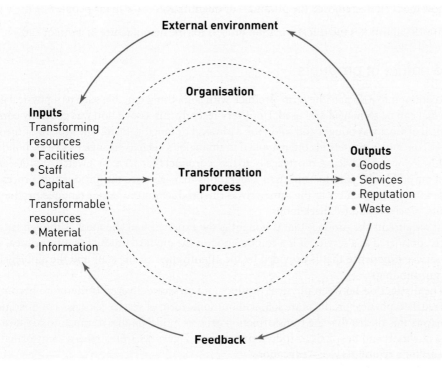

Figure 18.1
The transformation process

Transforming resources are:

- facilities – buildings, equipment/tools and process technology;
- staff – people involved in the transformation process working to complete activities, operate machinery or maintain the equipment;
- capital which is needed to buy materials and pay for the facilities and staff.

Transformable resources are:

- materials such as metal, wood or plastic, which become parts such as nuts and bolts, structures, or printed circuit boards, which can be built into the final product such as cars, buildings or phones. In moving through the transformation process the physical form of input materials will change to create the eventual product;
- information such as design specifications, assembly instructions, scientific concepts or market intelligence. Information is used in two ways. First, it can be used to inform the transformation process, such as design specifications or diagrams. Second, the information itself can become part of the output, such as turning raw financial data into published accounts.

Also included in the transformation process is a feedback system which monitors and captures deviations from the process norms. Feedback is needed to ensure the process performs in a repeatable, reliable and consistent manner. As there are bound to be variations in material quality and in the wear and tear of equipment, monitoring is essential in even the best processes.

There are two broad types of process feedback:

- Feedback that is internal to the transformation process ensures that it results in a consistent product. This feedback is generally quantitative in nature and monitors key aspects of the product or process, e.g. the number of units produced, dimensions such as weight of a chocolate bar or measurements such as the temperature of an oven. Any deviation in the measurements indicates that the process is not performing correctly and requires some remedial action.
- Feedback that is external to the transformation process ensures that the product is accepted by the market and satisfies the customer. This type of feedback can be either qualitative – how the customer enjoyed the product – or quantitative – how many people buy it.

Figure 18.2 illustrates the transformation process for the manufacture of a motor car.

The nature of products

It is common to associate the term 'product' with something tangible such as a physical artifact that can be seen, held and used. Until very recently this association was generally correct as most of what was bought and sold took a physical or tangible form. The growth of the service sector means the term is often applied to intangibles such as financial services, holidays, healthcare or legal advice. A mortgage is no less a product than a car or a watch. It is designed for a purpose, sold, paid for and used. Operations managers see the 'production' process of these intangible products in the same way as the production process of tangible products – inputs, processes and feedback loops.

In restaurants the product that is bought is the experience of the meal. Although eating-out is considered as a service, it is a combination of the physical product that is the meal and the service experience that is provided by the attentiveness of the staff and the ambience of the surroundings.

The distinction between physical product and service delivered is therefore becoming blurred. Few physical products are sold without some form of service package. For operations managers this means that the transformation process model applies as much to restaurants, banks, schools and hospitals as it does to factories. Figure 18.3 illustrates a transformation process for a typical service – education.

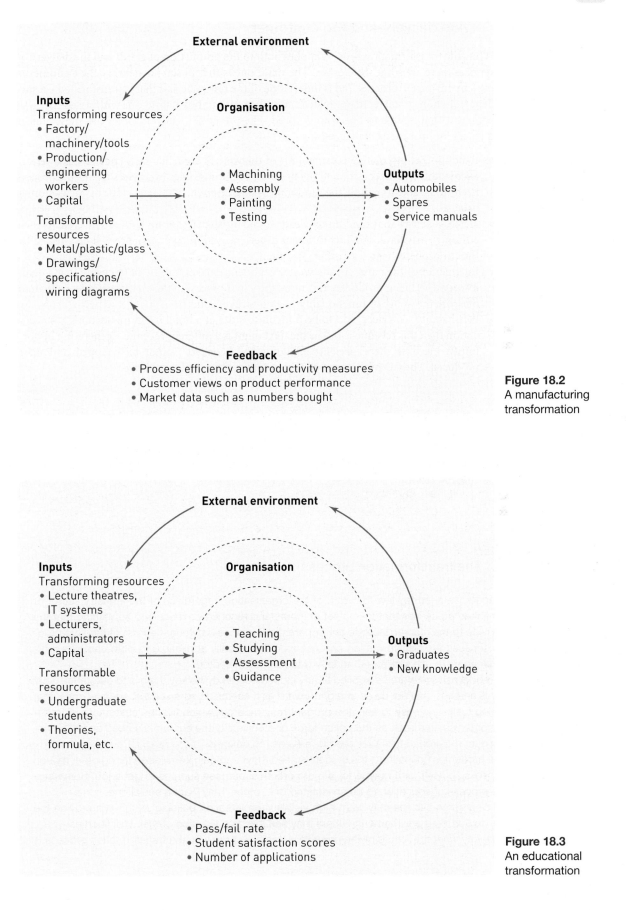

Figure 18.2
A manufacturing transformation

Figure 18.3
An educational transformation

Service delivery and the customer

While the transformation process applies both to the production of goods and the delivery of services there are some differences. The main one is that in service delivery the customer is present during the process, and is indeed one of the raw materials that is transformed – a student from non-graduate to graduate, a customer with untidy hair to one with styled hair or a patient with a disease to one who is cured. The presence of the customer has these consequences for operations managers:

- Randomness – in manufacturing most of the work is done in a factory closed to interference by the eventual customer. The presence of the customer in services means the process needs to be able to handle the randomness that unpredictable behaviour by the customer brings.
- Heterogeneity – that randomness leads to inconsistencies in the service delivered, as each customer may have a slightly different experience: a dining experience will be affected by the atmosphere created by other customers.
- Intangibility – the nature of the service experience makes it difficult to ensure that a quality service is being produced. It is more difficult to measure the service experience than to measure the utility or functionality of a physical product.
- Perishability – services tend to be difficult to store, if a hotel room misses a night's occupation then this revenue is lost as the next night is a different revenue – generating opportunity. Likewise the experience of going to a concert cannot be wrapped and mass produced. The CD of the concert cannot match the actual experience.

Activity 18.1   Service operations

- If you have ever sought legal advice consider, from a customer's perspective, how a lawyer can ensure consistency, reliability and repeatability in the process of delivering legal services.

Key ideas   The transformation process

As operations managers we need to view the work of the organisation, regardless of the industry sector or product, as a set of linked processes that take a set of inputs and reconfigure these into something that the organisation can provide to the market. Despite the apparent differences between the form of tangible products and intangible services the transformation process model is equally applicable to both contexts. This allows operations managers to use similar methods and tools in each sector.

This operational model can therefore be applied to any industry context, the key thing is to determine what the product actually is and this may not be as straightforward as it seems. In some cases, such as consumer goods, the need being fulfilled is easy to see, the product may be a car which fills the customer's need for transport. In service organisations such as the police force or a university the customer's need and therefore the nature of the product required to fulfil that need is less easy to define.

In a university the product is education – the student's need maybe to gain knowledge for no other reason than knowledge possession itself, or it maybe for a more practical purpose such as to get a job. Some students may want the process of education to be an isolated one, others may want a social one.

In relation to policing some citizens may want high visibility, proliferation policing as this will provide the perception of a safe and ordered environment. Others may see this as a violation of their civil liberties.

Understanding exactly what the nature of the product is can affect the way the transformation process is set up.

18.3 The practice of operations management

The birth of process management

When we walk into a McDonald's we enter a process for queuing, are served by someone who is not a trained waiter, and purchase a meal cooked by someone who is not a skilled chef. It has been designed to particular standards of quality; is the product of a process of manufacture; and will be exactly the same way regardless of where or when it is bought. McDonald's is the ultimate in systemisation.

Process design is often associated with Fredrick Winslow Taylor (who we have met previously in Chapter 2) and his five principles of management. In the late nineteenth and early twentieth centuries the US was experiencing rapid industrialisation. Driven by new technologies, more complex forms of organisation were emerging and many of the world's best known companies were being founded – including ESSO, General Motors and Ford. Skilled workers were scarce, even basic language skills were difficult to find. Taylor and his idea of scientific management solved this problem by making the attributes of the worker mostly irrelevant. Taylor and his supporters believed in 'rationalism' or the view that if one understands something one should be able to state it explicitly and write a rule for it. Taylor's objective in applying rules and procedures to work was to replace uncertainty with predictability. By applying this thinking to the process of manufacture then reliability, consistency and repeatability would result.

> The **craft system** refers to a system in which the craft producers do everything. With or without customer involvement, they design, source materials, manufacture, sell and perhaps service. The craft system is based on workers with the embodied knowledge, skill and experience to carry out all necessary activity.

Management in practice   Disney's 'production' of cartoons

At the age of 21, Walter Elias 'Walt' Disney left the midwest, moved to Hollywood and opened his own movie studio. In *The Magic Kingdom* Steven Watts (2001) describes Walt Disney's attempts to apply the techniques of mass production to the art of making cartoons. Disney had great admiration for Henry Ford and his achievements, and introduced an assembly line at the Disney studio. Like all production lines this system employed a rigorous division of labour. Instead of drawing entire scenes, artists were given narrowly defined tasks, meticulously sketching and inking characters while supervisors looked on with stopwatches timing how long it took to complete each activity. During the 1930s this 'production' system resembled that of an automobile plant. Hundreds of young people were trained and fitted into the machine for 'manufacturing' entertainment. While this was labelled the 'Fun Factory' the working conditions on the assembly line were not always fun for the workers, with operations management methods leading to employee dissatisfaction and strikes.

Before Taylor, work was based on the **craft system** where individuals controlled the work process because their skill and knowledge told them what to do and how to do it. However, this left managers and owners who were trying to implement **factory production** with a level of control over the process of manufacture similar to that which a beekeeper has over the productive capacity of a hive of bees. To take full advantage of the possibilities of mechanisation and the factory system, all of the activities within a particular transformation process had to be fully understood by those who controlled the organisation.

> **Factory production** is a process-based system that breaks down the integrated nature of the craft worker's approach and makes it possible to increase the supply of goods by dividing tasks into simple and repetitive processes and sequences which could be done by unskilled workers and machinery on a single site.

Although Taylor carried out the experiments that resulted in his five principles almost exclusively in the steel industry, his ideas have endured to become the basis of operations management today. These ideas were initially developed by Henry Ford into the production line system that came to dominate manufacturing, and have since spread to the service sector.

While the principles of Taylor had a profound and positive effect on efficiency, they also had some negative effects which are worth considering in the context of operations management. The separation of the conception of the work, the planning and organising, from the execution, or doing, of the work coupled with the implementation of detailed process for the worker to follow with no task-related discretion had the effect of deskilling the worker and disrupting the craft system. In Taylor's system the worker was reduced to little more than a pair of hands trained in a very limited way to carry out a small set of repetitive tasks.

This deskilling effect meant that the worker no longer had the knowledge or skill to ensure the manufacture of a quality product. This depended more on the quality of the process of manufacture than on the skill of the workman. With this system the design of the process was paramount as a poorly designed process would produce a poor product.

Activity 18.2 Taylor's processes

- Look around at the organisations that you come into contact with in your daily life. Try to identify the processes that they use. Can you find any that are not underpinned in some way by Taylor's principles?

Management in practice Seeking the best www.sunseeker.com

From modest beginnings in a shed, to a workforce of 2,500, modern shipyards and world-beating technology, Sunseeker is the iconic brand in the supply of super-yachts to the super-rich. While the products are at the cutting edge of quailty and technology, the company remains committed to craftsmanship. Although much of the work in design and manufacturing is done by computers and machinery, Sunseeker claims the basis of its success is the skill of the artisans who form and polish the woods, metals and glass, that produce the work of art that is a Sunseekeer yacht.

The production process is a subtle blend of machine-produced fabication using the best that process management can offer, and hand-assembly and detail finishing where the human influence on product quality cannot be matched.

Sunseeker admits that you can build a quality boat without the traditonal craftsmanship they rely on – but, they say, it wouldn't be Sunseeker . . .

Source: Company website.

Activity 18.3 Craft versus factory

- Consider the manufacture of high-quality products such as a Sunseeker yacht, a Rolls-Royce motor car or a Rolex watch. In each of these products consider which parts of the manufacturing process are best done by machines and which parts are best done by hand.

Operations strategy

Chapter 8 looks at managing strategy as the process of setting an organisation's future direction. As operations is the means by which the company creates and delivers products, a company also needs an **operations strategy**. Slack *et al.* (2007) define operations strategy as the pattern of decisions that shapes the long-term capability of an operation – which is intended to support the corporate strategy. It clarifies the primary purposes and characteristics of the operations processes, and designs the systems to achieve these.

Operations strategy is the pattern of decisions that shapes the long-term capability of the operation.

Management in practice   Linn Products www.linn.co.uk

Linn Products was established in 1972 by Ivor Tiefenbrun. Born in Glasgow, he was passionate about two things – engineering and listening to music. When he couldn't buy a hi-fi good enough to satisfy his needs he decided to make one himself.

In 1972 Linn introduced the Sondek LP12 turntable, the longest-lived hi-fi product still in production anywhere in the world and still the benchmark by which all turntables are judged. The Linn Sondek LP12 turntable revolutionised the hi-fi industry, proving categorically that the source of the music is the most important component in the hi-fi chain. Linn then set out to make the other components in the hi-fi chain as revolutionary as the first, setting new standards for performance over the years with each new product.

Today, Linn is an independent, precision-engineering company uniquely focused on the design, manufacture and sale of complete music and home theatre systems for customers who want the best. Linn systems can be found throughout the world in royal residences and on-board super-yachts.

At Linn operations is an integrated process, from product development through to after-sales service. All aspects of Linn's products are designed in-house and all the key processes are controlled by Linn people. Linn believe that everything can be improved by human interest and attention to detail. So the same person builds, tests and packs a complete product from start to finish. He/she takes all the time necessary to ensure that every detail is correct.

Only then will the person responsible for building the product sign his/her name and pack it for despatch. Every product can be tracked all the way from that individual to the customer, anywhere in the world. Linn systems are sold only by selected specialist retailers which have a similar commitment to quality products and service.

Source: Company website.

Activity 18.4   Searching for excellence

- While most organisations strive for excellence in some way or other, consider the operational challenges in actually becoming and remaining a world leader.

Case study   Zara – the case continues: operations strategy: react rather than predict

What sets Zara apart from many of its competitors is what it has done with its business information and operations processes. Rather than trying to forecast demand and producing to meet that (possible) demand, it concentrates on reacting swiftly to (actual) demand. A typical clothes supplier may take three months to develop the styles for a season's range and the same again to set up the supply chain and manufacturing processes: six months pass before the garments are in the stores. Zara does this in weeks by:

- making decisions faster with better information;
- running design and production processes concurrently;
- holding stocks of fabric that can be used in several lines;
- distributing products more efficiently.

Some criticise Zara for copying designs from more prestigious brands. Customers do not seem to mind, as they buy Zara's affordable garments when they are in fashion. The company's operations strategy is clearly directed at speed – ensuring the shortest time between the design idea and the garment in the stores.

Case question 18.3

- Investigate the operational strategy of another large clothing retailer such as Marks and Spencer. Can you identify any differences?

The 4 Vs of operations

Although all operations systems transform input resources into output products, they differ on four dimensions:

- Volume: how many units are produced of a given type of product. Consumer goods are examples of high-volume production, supported by investment in specialised facilities, equipment and process planning.
- Variety: how many types (or versions) of a product have to be manufactured by the same facility. Fashion houses and custom car makers use more hand tools and highly skilled staff to enable the flexibility required to make a variety of unique products.
- Variation in demand: how the volume of production varies with time. Facilities at holiday resorts have to cope with vast differences in throughput depending on the time of year.
- Visibility: the extent to which customers see manufacturing or delivery process. This applies mainly to the service sector where the presence of the customer is vital to the process.

Management in practice   **Bidding for success** www.ebay.co.uk

Founded in 1995, eBay connects a diverse and passionate community of individual buyers and sellers, as well as small businesses. Its collective impact on e-commerce is staggering, in 2008, the total worth of goods sold on eBay was $60 billion–$2,000 every second.

With more than 88 million active users globally, eBay is the world's largest online marketplace, where any-one can buy and sell almost anything. The website is part car-boot sale, part auction house, part local market, part high street store, with the cost determined by how much people are prepared to pay.

eBay's strategy in recent years has been to move from a bid-only auction site to a site that also sells fixed price goods from other retailers much like other internet-based sellers such as Amazon. However, during the strategic shift this aspiration has not always been matched by eBay's operational capability to deliver. In 2009 the site experienced technical difficulties due to the inabilty of its operational processes and systems to cope with the increased volume and variety of orders that were the result of this strategic move. These difficulties resulted in the site being unavailable for periods of time and a consequent loss of revenue.

Sources: *Financial Times,* 23 November 2009; company website.

18.4   **Operations processes**

The 4 V's are key considerations in defining operations strategy. Before designing the detailed processes, managers decide on the type of operation it will be: what volume, how much variation, how will volume vary with time, and how visible?

Production systems

For production operations these decisions translate into two main considerations: volume of product and flexibility of the operations system – its ability to cope with changes in volume and/or variety. Hayes and Wheelwright (1979) propose that a single manufacturing system cannot efficiently produce different volumes of a variety of products. If a high volume is required consistently and reliably, then the manufacturing system must be arranged to produce only one product. If several products are required then a more flexible system is required to cope with their multiple requirements. Hayes and Wheelwright categorise four types of production operation (see Figure 18.4).

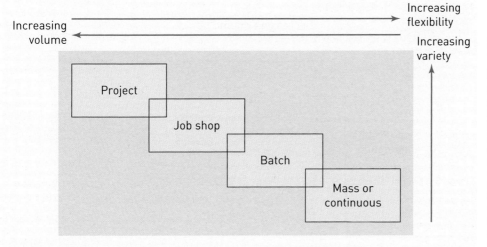

Figure 18.4
The product–process matrix

Source: Adapted and reprinted by permission of Harvard Business Review. Figure adapted from Link Manufacturing Process and Product Lifecycles, *Harvard Business Review*, vol. 57, no. 1, pp. 133–140 by R. H. Hayes and S. C. Wheelwright, Copyright © 1979 Harvard Business School Publishing Corporation; all rights reserved.

Project systems

These exist at the low-volume end of the spectrum and deal with the manufacture of very small numbers of product – often only single units. This entails many interdependent parallel operations of long duration to achieve an output. Examples include construction projects such as oil rigs, dams and skyscrapers, in which thousands of operations accumulate to complete one product over several years. The defining feature of this system is that the product is built in one place with all the resources brought to it and all the activities going on around it. The product will not move until it is complete, and sometimes not at all.

Job-shop systems

These are also relatively low-volume producing special products or services to customer specifications with little likelihood that any product will be repeated often. In a manufacturing context a tool room that makes special tools and fixtures is a classic example, as is a tailor who makes made-to-measure clothes to customer requirements. Such low-volume systems tend to use general-purpose equipment manned by highly skilled personnel. They exhibit a high degree of flexibility but have high unit costs.

Batch operations

These are possibly the most common systems in use today. Many different products are produced at regular or irregular intervals. One of the distinctive features of such systems in comparison to job-shop systems is that, since orders are repeated from time to time, it becomes worthwhile to spend time planning and documenting the sequence of processing operations, employing work study techniques, providing special tooling and perhaps some automation. There will be a mix of skilled, semi-skilled and unskilled labour in this type of system.

Mass production and continuous flow manufacturing

This type is used where demand for a single product is sufficiently high to warrant the installation of specialised automatic production lines. With their high rates of output and low manning levels, unit costs are typically very low. Such systems generally have little flexibility. Where the entities produced are discrete items such as cars or mobile phones, the term 'mass production' is used, where the entity is not discrete such as chemicals like petroleum or other substances such as cement then the term 'continuous production' is used.

Service systems

In service delivery operations, the product–process matrix does not adequately cater for the fourth V – visibility: the presence of the customer in the process and the potential for

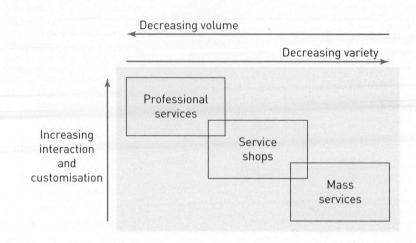

Figure 18.5
Service process
types

diversity and randomness this brings will defeat the best-designed processes. Figure 18.5 shows a similar model which helps in categorising service processes.

Professional services

These are high-contact operations where customers may spend a lot of time in the process. These services provide high levels of customisation and are adaptable to individual customer's needs. As a result the operational system relies on skilled and knowledgeable people rather than high levels of automation. Typical examples of these may be legal services or healthcare.

Service shops

These offer lower levels of customer contact and less customisation to deal with larger volumes of customers with similar needs. Examples include most restaurants and hotels, high street banks and many public services. Essentially the customer is buying a fairly standardised service which maybe slightly customised to the customers' needs. While people are still an integral part of the process they will tend to have limited skills and knowledge and have less discretion while working within a more rigid process.

Mass services

These provide standardised customer transactions, very limited contact time and little or no customisation: the emphasis is on automation and repetition. Staff will be low skilled and follow set procedures much like the staff on a production line, and the processes may be highly automated. Typical mass services include supermarkets, call centres and mass transport systems. For example, in a railway station, staff can sell tickets but have no discretion to offer customised journeys or make decisions beyond the scope of the process.

Activity 18.5   **Cutting up craft skills**

Consider a service such as a surgical operation. Do you think that routine surgery could be carried out by more scientifically managed methods where, for example, the person that performs the operation is not a qualified surgeon, but is trained to carry out a single procedure?

It is important to note that in the service sector 'interaction' (how much the customer can intervene in the process) is not the same as 'contact time'. A lecture to a large number of students is high in 'contact' but comparatively low in 'interaction': so high duration of contact does not always mean a more interactive service.

'Customisation' reflects the degree to which the service provided is tailored to the needs of the customer. Organisations which have a high degree of both interaction and customisation are categorised as professional services, e.g. legal practices. Conversely, organisations which have a low degree of both interaction and customisation are categorised as mass services, e.g. schools. The purpose of such classification of systems is to allow operations managers to decide how systems should be set up to deliver the type of process required.

These classifications exist as a continuum. Using education as an example, most state schools would be positioned near the bottom right-hand corner of the matrix. However a fee-paying school could be positioned more to the top-left due to its lower class sizes, greater provision of support staff and additional extra-curricular activities. Another example would be a specialist clinic dealing with rare and difficult to diagnose and treat conditions, which may operate as a professional service while a hospital that deals with standard operations such as cataracts or hip replacements may be set up more as a service shop. The type of service operation is therefore less about what the service is and more about how it might be provided.

18.5   Process design

Span of processes: make or buy?

When Henry Ford developed his moving assembly-line method of producing the Model T car, he chose to 'own' all stages of production, i.e. the widest possible span of processes. Ford's company owned the rubber plantations that supplied the raw materials for the tyres; the forests that supplied the wood for the wheels; and the iron mines, steel plants, foundries, forges, rolling mills and machine shops that manufactured the engine and other components. Its ownership of the complete span of processes even extended to a shipping line and a railroad to transport materials and product.

Today no car manufacturer tries to manage such a wide **span of processes**, as specialism is the key to efficient operations. Parts require a different set of skills and machinery to produce than those required to assemble them into the car itself – so it is more efficient for a dedicated supplier to make them. Direct control of the operation has been replaced to a great extent by contractual control of the supplier.

> The **span of processes** is the variety of processes that a company chooses to carry out in-house.

This is equally true in the service sector, where in a service such as airline travel, a company may decide to focus on the long-haul flights between hub airports, leaving the feeder flights to and from the hubs to be provided by other airlines. Likewise, the catering service and maintenance activity might be outsourced to specialist suppliers.

Activity 18.6   The supply chain

- Consider a consumer product such as a bicycle – choose a popular model from one of the larger more famous brands and investigate its manufacturing process drawing a supply chain map that includes all of the companies that are involved in the manufacture of this one item.

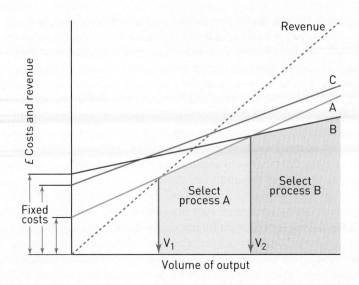

Figure 18.6
Break-even analysis

Process selection

Having identified strategically which type of operation you want to create in relation to the 4Vs, what you want to do within your operation and what you want to buy-in from a specialist supplier, the question then to be answered is what process configuration to implement.

The first thing to consider is the amount of automation to be used in comparison to manpower. Automation, while expensive, is generally very efficient therefore more investment in automation (fixed cost) will result in less need for manpower and therefore lower the variable costs of production. In this case a simple **break-even analysis** may help in making the choice. For each of the process sequences to be compared, the fixed and variable costs are determined. Fixed costs are those, such as special tooling costs, which are required to set up the processes and are independent of the volume of output. Variable costs are those, such as direct labour and material costs, which vary in direct proportion to the volume of output. Figure 18.6 shows how the total costs of three process sequences (A, B and C) change with volume of output, alongside the associated revenue.

A **break-even analysis** is a comparison of fixed versus variable costs that will indicate at which point in volume of output it is financially beneficial to invest in a higher level of infrastructure.

The figure shows that, for quantities below V_1, none of the process sequences recover their costs; for quantities between V_1 and V_2, process sequence A is the most economical; for quantities greater than V_2, process B becomes the least costly. In this example process sequence C is uncompetitive at all levels of output.

Case study   Zara – the case continues: the design centre

Zara designs all its products in-house – about 40,000 items per year from which 10,000 are selected for production. The firm encourages a collegial atmosphere among its designers, who seek inspiration from many sources such as trade fairs, discotheques, catwalks and magazines. Extensive feedback from the stores also contributes to the design process.

The designers for women's, men's and children's wear sit in different halls in a modern building attached to the headquarters. In each of these open spaces the designers occupy one side, the market specialists the middle and the buyers (procurement and production planners) occupy the other side. Designers first draw design sketches by hand and then discuss them with colleagues – not only other designers but also the market specialists and planning and procurement people. This process is crucial in retaining an overall 'Zara style'.

The sketches are then redrawn where further changes and adjustments, for better matching of weaves, textures and colours, are made. Critical decisions are made at this stage, especially regarding the selection of fabric. Before moving further through the process, it is necessary to determine whether the new design could be produced and sold at a profit.

The next step is to make a sample, a step often completed manually by skilled tailors located in the small pattern and sample-making shops co-located with the designers. If there are any questions or problems, the tailors can just walk over to the designers and discuss and resolve them on the spot.

The final decision on what, when and how much to produce is normally made by agreement between the relevant designer, market specialist, and procurement and production planner.

Facility layout

In addition to the sequence of the processes, consideration must also be given to their physical layout in relation with each other. **Layout planning** is an important issue because operational efficiency will be affected by the chosen layout's effects on the following factors:

- amount of inter-process movement of materials and/or customers;
- health and safety of staff and customers;
- levels of congestion and numbers of bottlenecks;
- utilisation of space, labour and equipment;
- levels of work-in-progress inventory required.

Layout planning is the activity that determines the best configuration of resources such as equipment, infrastructure and people that will produce the most efficient process.

In the layout of service operations there may be other factors to consider, as a result of the customers' participation in the processes:

- Maximum product exposure – in the layout of retail stores, basic purchases and check-out stations are often positioned remote from the shop entrance, obliging the customer to walk past displays of other more-profitable products, which they may be enticed to buy.
- The 'ambience' of the physical surroundings – décor, noise levels, music, temperature and lighting may affect the customers' judgement of the service, how long they stay and how much they spend.
- The customers' perception of waiting times.

The reason for the inclusion of the word 'perception' in this last point is best illustrated by an example. An airline operating at Houston airport experienced a high level of complaints from its passengers about the waiting time in the baggage-reclaim area. The airline's solution was to re-direct baggage to the carousel furthest from the arrival gates. Although passengers had to walk further, and the baggage took just as long to arrive, the customers' perceptions were that the waiting time had been reduced.

Layout planning occurs at three levels of detail:

- Layout of departments on the site. For example, in a public house this would concern the sizing and positioning of the public bar, the lounge bar, toilets, kitchen and storeroom within the confines of the building used.
- Layout within departments. Continuing with the bar example, this would address the sizing and positioning of customer seating areas, the drinks counter, the food counter, slot machines, public telephone, passageways, etc.
- Layout of workplaces. For the bar counter this would determine the detailed layout of pumps for draught beers and other drinks, cash registers, sinks, shelves for bottled beers, spirits, wines and soft drinks, etc.

There are four well-established forms of facility layout: fixed position, process, product and cell.

Fixed-position layout

This configuration is typically used for low-volume, project-type operations where the product being produced is massive, and movement of the material from process to process is impossible or impractical. Bridges, oil rigs and office buildings fall into this category, so the processes required come to the site.

In the service sector, football stadiums, theatres, cinemas and lecture rooms are all examples of fixed-position layouts, where the service that is the performance is presented in one place for communal attendance.

Process layout

This form of layout is used when there is no dominant flow pattern, and is particularly appropriate for job shop and small-batch operations. Figure 18.7 is a schematic representation of a process layout, showing three (of many) job process sequences.

By bringing similar process types together in departments, the advantages of flexibility and concentration of process expertise are gained. The disadvantages are: long delivery times; high levels of materials handling and transport; relatively high levels of work-in-progress inventory; low equipment utilisation; and consequent high unit costs. Scheduling of many jobs with different process routes through a process layout while monitoring their progress are among the most challenging tasks for operations managers.

Many service operations adopt the process layout but, instead of material movements, customers move from department to department; common examples include supermarkets, department stores, museums, art galleries and libraries.

Product layout

Where the demand for a single product is sufficiently high to warrant truly continuous operation mass production for discrete items such as, cars mobile phones, ball-point pens and confectionery; and process systems for 'fluids' such as oil products, sugar and cement. It is possible to have an automatic production line specially designed to incorporate not only the sequence of processes, but also an automatic transport system to move the product from process to process, in unison. With such a system there is no need for expensive work-in-progress

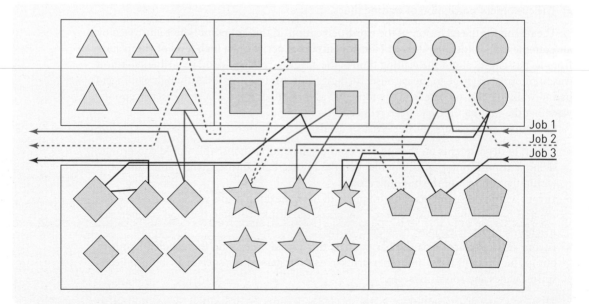

Figure 18.7 Process layout

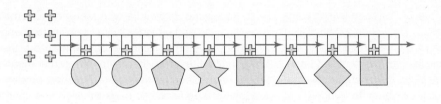

Figure 18.8
Product layout

between processes, less floor space is required, and throughput time for a particular item is very short.

However, although such systems deliver very low unit costs, they are vulnerable because of the absence of work-in-progress buffers: if one process fails, very quickly the whole line comes to a halt. Since only a single product type is produced, the challenge for the operations manager is to balance the level of output with the anticipated level of customer demand. When an imbalance occurs it is often reported in the business press; for example, computer components, such as memory chips, seem to be in a perpetual flux of over-supply and shortage. Automobile companies also are guilty of overproducing then storing cars until they are sold. As a car buyer this is an important consideration as the 'new' car that you buy may not be new at all but may have been 'stored' in a car park for a year or more before it is sold. Applications of the product layout are less common in service operations, but the following display some of its characteristics: self-service cafeteria, student registration, automatic mail sorting and some hospital diagnostic procedures.

Cell or group layout

Cell or group layout is suitable for many small- to medium-batch operations, and is a modified form of product layout. The difference is that whereas the products manufactured in a product layout have identical process sequencing requirements, and are obviously members of a family (e.g. different sizes and colours of a particular style of shoe), the products produced in a cell layout have similar process sequencing requirements, but may otherwise be dissimilar in appearance.

In order to convert a process layout to a cell layout, a study must first be made of the process sequences of all the products made, with a view to identifying clusters that are similar. Service operations which exhibit some of the cell layout's attributes include car tyre/exhaust/battery replacement outlets, and island-layout self-service cafeterias.

Case study   Zara – the case continues: production process

Zara manufactures approximately 50 per cent of its products in its own network of Spanish factories and uses subcontractors for all sewing operations. The other half of its products are procured from outside suppliers. With its relatively large and stable orders, Zara is a preferred customer for almost all its suppliers. This is important as suppliers will therefore prioritise Zara orders and generally be more responsive.

The make/buy decisions are usually made by the procurement and production planners. The key criteria for making these decisions are required levels of

speed and expertise, cost-effectiveness and availability of sufficient capacity. Such decisions are made carefully, paying great attention to minimising the risks associated with achieving the correct workmanship and speed of supply.

For its in-house production, half of all fabrics are purchased un-dyed to allow faster response to mid-season colour changes.

The purchased fabric is then cut by machine. A typical factory has three or four cutting machines with long tables, where typically 30 to 50 layers of fabric are laid out under a top paper layer. The cutting pattern is generated by the CAD system (which automatically minimises fabric waste), checked by skilled operators, and then drawn by the machine onto the top layer (so that cut pieces can be identified later).

After a final visual check by the operator, the machine then cuts the multiple layers into hundreds of different small pieces. Operators then pack each piece into a separate clear plastic bag to be sent to sewing subcontractors.

Zara uses subcontractors for all sewing operations. Subcontractors themselves often collect the bagged-up cut pieces, along with appropriate components (such as buttons and zippers) in small trucks. There are some 500 sewing subcontractors in close proximity to La Coruña and most work exclusively for Zara. Zara closely monitors their operations to ensure quality, compliance with labour laws and adherence to the production schedule. Zara believes that outsourcing a highly labour-intensive operation,

such as sewing, allows its own factories to remain more focused and provides more flexibility to change production volumes quickly. Subcontractors then bring back the sewn items to the same factory, where each piece is inspected. Finished products are then placed in plastic bags, labelled and sent to the distribution centre.

Completed products procured from outside suppliers are also sent directly to the distribution centre and Zara control their quality by sampling batches of these.

Case questions 18.4

- Is Zara a craft or a factory system?
- Review the information about the manufacturing system Zara uses, then list its advantages and disadvantages.

18.6 The main activities of operations

Providing goods and services to a customer depends on five key operations activities, and these provide a useful way of describing and analysing an organisation's operations system (Sprague, 1990). These activities are:

- capacity
- standards
- materials
- scheduling
- control.

None of these activities operate alone but combine to form an operations system.

Capacity

Capacity is the ability to yield an output – it is a statement of the ability of the numerous resources within an organisation to deliver to the customer. Defining capacity depends on identifying the main resources required to deliver a saleable output – staff, machinery, materials and finance. Capacity is limited by whichever resource is in shortest supply – a hospital's capacity to conduct an operation will be determined by some minimum number of specifically competent surgeons, nurses and related professionals. In service organisations all aspects of capacity may be visible to the customer – they can see the quality of staff, and the state of the physical equipment and resources.

Standards

Standards relate to either quality or work performance. Quality standards are embedded in the specification of the product or service delivered to the customer. Work performance standards enable managers to estimate and plan capacity by providing information on the time it takes to do something. One of the advantages which low-cost airlines have established is that the time it takes them to turn around an aircraft between landing and take-off is much lower than for conventional airlines. This enables them to fly more journeys with each aircraft – significantly increasing capacity at little cost.

Materials

A vital aspect of the operations function is to ensure an adequate supply of the many material resources needed to deliver an output. One of the dilemmas is that holding stocks of materials, called inventory, is expensive – it ties up working capital, incurs storage costs and in changing markets there is a risk that stocks become outdated because of a change in model. Too much material can be as problematic as too little. Materials management is particularly important in manufacturing systems where all labour costs are invested in the product itself. In service settings most material is simple and is usually consumed by the customer during the service process.

Scheduling

This is the function of co-ordinating the available resources by time or place – specifying which resources need to be available and when, in order to meet demand. It begins with incoming information about demand and its likely impact on capacity. Service, productivity and profitability depend on matching supply with demand. Capacity management generates supply; scheduling links demand with capacity. It can be carried out over several time periods. Aggregate scheduling is done for the medium term, and is closely associated with planned levels of capacity: as airlines plan their future fleets, which they need to do several years ahead, they make judgements about both their capacity and the likely demand (translated into frequency of flights on particular routes). Master scheduling deals with likely demand (firm or prospective orders) over the next few months, while dispatching is concerned with immediate decisions, for example about which rooms to allocate to which guests in a hotel.

Control

Control is intended to check whether the plans for capacity, scheduling and inventory are actually working. Without control, there is little point in planning, as there is no mechanism then to learn from the experience. There are generally four steps in the control process:

- setting objectives – setting direction and standards;
- measuring – seeing what is happening;
- comparing – relating what is happening to what was expected to happen;
- acting – taking short-term or long-term actions to correct significant deviations.

Only through control can immediate operations be kept moving towards objectives, and lessons learned for future improvements.

Management in practice   **Computing speed** www.dell.com

By redesigning its whole supply chain, Dell has made a virtue out of speed and response to customers in a way that repays the company by efficient use of money. Customers buy online and pay for their product in advance. Dell also tries to manage the elective choices customers make by offering discounts for inventory that is moving too slowly. Its operational control system is such that customers can call into Dell to check progress in the manufacture of their order. By then Dell has the use of their money and some time later will pay its suppliers' bills for the materials they have provided. This system is so responsive that Dell is able to change its pricing structure daily to take advantage of material price fluctuations and to price aggressively for certain markets in ways that its less flexible competitors find difficult to match.

Source: Company website.

Quality

What is quality?

In addition to the factors that govern the design of effective and efficient operations systems, features of the product or service that is being delivered must also be considered – especially price and quality.

For undifferentiated products, such as transport, consumer goods such as cleaning products, or services, such as fast food, the price will be paramount as many customers will reason that cheapest is best. The price the customer is charged is governed largely by the cost the company incurs in producing the product or service. That in turn is largely driven by the efficiency of the operation. Therefore, if low cost is important, the operational processes – how they are sequenced, the automation and tooling, and the people who work within them – must all be designed with low cost in mind. This may mean compromising on the quality of the product by offering a basic service or product as opposed to a more comprehensive or functional one.

Quality appears difficult to quantify as it depends on the product, the application and the subjective views of the person making the assessment. As Crosby (1979) wrote:

> The first erroneous assumption is that quality means goodness, or luxury or shine, or weight. The word 'quality' is used to signify the relative worth of things in such phrases as 'good quality', bad quality . . . Each listener assumes the speaker means what he or she, the listener, means by the phrase . . . This is precisely the reason we must define quality as conformance to requirements if we are to manage it. If a Cadillac conforms to the requirements of a Cadillac then it is a quality car, if a Pinto conforms to the requirements of a Pinto then it is a quality car. Don't talk about poor quality or high quality talk about conformance and non-conformance. (p. 14)

Crosby's proposal moves the definition of quality from a term that is nebulous and difficult to define to a set of more tangible measures.

Key ideas | **Product quality**

The quality of products and services is not absolute but is based on the requirements of the customer. Therefore any product, as long as it does what the customer wants of it, can be considered a quality product. The most important activity is therefore to define and understand precisely what the customer is expecting and set-up operations to deliver exactly that.

Six features help to define quality in terms of what customers expect:

- Functionality – what the product does. Where price is less of a consideration, products that do more may be more attractive. This is especially true with technology-based products such as the iPhone where functionality is the prime consideration in choice: users see a product that does more as being of higher quality than one that does less.
- Performance – how well it does what it is meant to do. This element will feature more strongly in higher value 'statement' products such as a Porsche car, where top-speed and acceleration are considered important. A product that is faster, more economical, stronger or easier to use will be seen as higher quality than others which are not. A higher performance product is seen as a higher quality product.
- Reliability – the consistency of performance over time. Are the promises made to the customer honoured correctly and in the same way over many occasions? A more reliable product is seen as a higher-quality product.

- Durability – how robust it is. This may feature more on products that are used a lot such as tools and equipment or products that operate in a harsh environment. Climbing equipment needs to be resistant to breakage. A more durable product is seen as a higher-quality product.
- Customisation – how well the product fits the need. This is more relevant in products where additional features may be added to the core functions in products, such as a mobile phone or in financial services. The more a product or service fits exactly to a customer's need the higher quality it is seen to be.
- Appearance – how the product looks. This is important not only to convey the correct image such as a well-decorated house or a highly polished car but also where appearance affects the utility of the product such as a website: a clear layout will be a major factor in how easy it is to use. A product that looks good is considered a higher-quality product.

The customer's perception of quality will combine some or all of these factors: each of which can contribute to the quality standard the customer desires.

Case study　　Zara – the case continues: cost and quality

The middle-aged mother buys clothes at Zara because they are cheap, while her teenage daughter buys there because they are in fashion. The matching of both low cost and acceptable quality is a winning combination. Like any other industry low cost in the clothing industry is obtained by having efficient and streamlined operational processes. Quality is more subjective; with garments, quality is defined more by the design or 'look' that the customer wants to be seen wearing rather than the quality of the construction. Most of these garments are destined to have a short life, as they will be discarded or relegated to the back of the wardrobe when fashion changes. This means certain aspects of manufacturing quality such as durability and robustness will be of little importance to the customer so long as a certain standard is reached.

Case question 18.5

- Consider the concept of fashion, what does quality actually mean? Think of specific factors that define the quality of fashion.

Additional dimensions of service quality

All of the elements mentioned apply to both products and services and are commonly labelled the 'tangibles'. In service operations intangible features affect perceptions of quality:

- Responsiveness – willingness to help a customer and provide prompt service. While applicable to all service encounters, this element is most powerful in a less structured service environment where there is more opportunity for the customer to request something at random that may be outwith the normal scope of the operation. A high-class restaurant may be expected to be more responsive than a fast-food outlet where the customer would not think to request an alteration to the meal on offer.
- Assurance – ability of the operation to inspire confidence. This element is most easily illustrated in provision of professional services: in a dental surgery the ambience of the surroundings, the equipment, and the knowledge and expertise of the staff make the customer feel secure.
- Empathy – understanding and attentiveness shown to customers. Here the focus is mainly on the skills of the staff, their awareness of others and ability to communicate effectively. This is most easily seen in relation to the emergency services where empathising with the victim is both a key feature of the service experience and a critical factor in the effective performance of the task.

Order-winning and order-qualifying criteria

A good way to determine the relative importance of each quality element is to distinguish between order winning criteria and order qualifying criteria (Hill, 1993).

- Order-winning criteria are features that the customer regards as the reason to buy the product or service. Improving these will win business.
- Order-qualifying criteria will not win business but may lose it – if they are not met they will disqualify the product or service from consideration.

Quality management

Quality depends on operational systems in place. Theory and techniques about managing quality were developed first in the manufacturing sector, but are now also used in the service sector.

In manufacturing, craftspeople tend to have pride in their work and continuously strive to improve their mastery of the craft. During the evolution of the factory system, the craft system suffered as management subdivided the work process into smaller tasks performed by different people. This had two detrimental effects on quality. First, no single person was responsible for the whole process, so the pride in work that was evident in the craft system and was the basis of quality was removed. Second, craft skills were eroded and the consequence of this was that the capability of the individual to build quality into a product was lost. In essence, process management removed quality assurance from the remit of production staff, in effect taking the responsibility for producing quality products away from manufacturing workers. To remedy this situation attempts were made to 'build' quality into the process with more and more detailed and comprehensive processes used for the manufacture of each product. This, however, had only limited success.

The problem of production quality was not fully grasped until the mid to late twentieth century with pioneers such as Juran (1974), Deming (1988) and Feigenbaum (1993), working to develop philosophies and methods. Although developed initially in the West it was the Japanese who had most success as they applied the lessons widely and conscientiously. They also recognised the fundamental truth of craft production, which is the person who performs the transformation is the best person to ensure quality. The Japanese quality revolution was therefore based on placing the responsibility for quality with the worker. History has thus come full circle, with individuals taking pride in doing quality work and striving to make regular improvements in the production process.

Key ideas **Principles of total quality management (TQM)**

- **Philosophy:** waste reduction through continuous improvement.
- **Leadership:** committed and visible from top to bottom of the organisation.
- **Measurement:** costs involved in quality failures – the cost of quality.
- **Scope:** everyone, everywhere across whole supply chain.
- **Methods:** simple control and improvement techniques implemented by teams.

Total quality management (TQM) is a philosophy of management that is driven by customer needs and expectations and focuses on continually improving work processes.

Although there were many people involved in the search for quality and many systems developed, the principles are best encapsulated in the system of **total quality management** (TQM). This advocates that a constant effort to remove waste adds value. Some of these wastes are obvious – scrapped material and lost time through equipment failure – but other wastes come through bad systems or poor communications, and may be more difficult to find and measure. Progressive, small improvements reduce costs as the operational process uses resources more effectively. Crosby (1979) introduced the idea that 'quality is free': it is getting it wrong that costs money.

In contrast with the scientific management approach, modern writers propose that quality management should not be separated from production: everyone is responsible for contributing to quality. Methods used include team working, brainstorming techniques and simple statistical process controls (Oakland, 1994).

Thinking about quality at the design stage brings important benefits. Choices here should incorporate ideas and information from as many insiders, customers and suppliers as is sensible. Such processes capture the prevention and 'right first time' ideals and create opportunities to save cost and time. Waste minimisation is the goal – waste being the use of resources that does not add value for the customer. Note that customers are not the only stakeholders. Management may be able to justify an activity not directly required by a direct customer – such as environmental and legal obligations.

Quality systems and procedures

While it is relatively simple to understand the elements that make up quality and the philosophy behind it, operationalising it by implementing a system to embed quality into all that the organisation does is a different matter. A quality management system consists of the organisational structure, responsibilities, procedures, processes and resources for implementing quality management. Dale (2007) proposes that:

> The purpose of a quality management system is to establish a framework of reference points to ensure every time a process is performed the same information, methods, skills and controls are used and applied in consistent manner. (p. 280)

The documentation which makes up the quality system has three levels:

1 Company quality manual – a basic document that provides a concise summary of the quality management policy, strategy and system together with how it supports the company objectives and organisational structure.
2 Procedures manual that describes the function, structure and responsibilities of each department.
3 Detail work instructions, specifications, standards and methods which support the processes.

While setting up a quality system is relatively straightforward, achieving its effective implementation requires some additional elements:

- A clear quality strategy that supports the company strategic objectives – this is necessary to provide the direction that keeps the company quality programme in line with operational strategy.
- Top management support – the top management must understand and believe in the benefits of doing things right, promote these at all times, communicate the principles of quality development and maintain a clear idea of what quality means for the operation.
- Team-based approach – these days everyone must work together to achieve the quality goals.
- Investment in training – changes in attitudes, work practice and skills are key, therefore the achievement of quality throughout the organisation is very much reliant on the development of quality people.

18.8   Integrating themes

Sustainable performance

All pollution is caused in some way by an operational failure. Whether it is a poorly designed process producing more waste than necessary or the result of an accident, the cause is an inadequate operations process. Hawken *et al.* (1999) describe the planet Earth in operational terms as a transformation process where resources are constantly input to biological, chemical and geological processes which transform them into other states. They claim that human beings, through production and consumption, have created an industrial metabolism that exists beside, and disrupting, the Earth's natural processes.

The Earth, however, is a closed system: resources cannot be added or taken away, they can only be changed. As the finite resources of the planet are transformed through industrial activity into increasing amounts of waste, the Earth's capacity to sustain life will be compromised. Although operations managers are continually striving to increase the efficiency of industrial processes and reduce waste, on a planetary scale, levels of waste are enormous. Every product has a 'hidden history' of waste: producing 1 ton of paper consumes 98 tons of resources. The point is that while waste at the factory level is being addressed, waste on a planetary scale is only beginning to be understood. Today legislation is being introduced that requires organisations to work in a more sustainable manner. Operations managers need to design and operate the processes of transformation by considering the entire external supply chain and its effect on the planet, not just the internal processes of the factory.

Governance and control

Safety and quality standards are now more prevalent than ever. In addition to umbrella organisations such as the International Standards Organisation (ISO) and the British Standards Institute (BSI) all industries have specific bodies such as the Civil Aviation Authority (CAA) for airline safety and the Food Standards Agency (FSA) which is concerned with food and how it is sold and labelled.

As more standards are introduced and business becomes more highly regulated, it is the responsibility of the operations staff to design processes that are compliant in how they operate. There have been many high-profile cases where industrial accidents such as the Cyanide gas leak in Bhopal caused by Union Carbide or the radiation leak at the Three Mile Island Nuclear Generating facility operated by Metropolitan Edison have led to serious disasters. These examples were the result of process failure. Operations personnel must become aware of the governance regulating all operational activity, as any contravention, while probably not newsworthy, will have some detrimental effect on the business, the customer or the environment.

Internationalisation

Advances in technology and telecommunications mean that few major organisations operate locally – most buy and sell internationally. This expanded context provides both opportunities and challenges. The main challenge is increased competition as geographical barriers are removed and companies from other countries enter global markets. From an operational perspective, the world market for goods and services is not a level paying field, differentials in labour, power and utility costs and availability of natural resources provide some, what could be called 'unfair', advantages. The corresponding opportunity is that all companies have better access to a larger supplier network. Puig *et al.* (2009), from their study of the textiles industry, propose that this means that companies must become more aggressive in their adoption of the appropriate operations strategy, focusing on higher value-adding activities, not relying solely on price as a competitive advantage but also on quality and customer support.

Summary

1 **Define the term operations management**

- Operations management is the activities, decisions and responsibilities of managing the production and delivery of products and services.
- This includes responsibility for people and process and product.

2 Describe the transformation process model of operations management

- Transformation process is the organisational system that takes inputs:
  - facilities
  - staff
  - finance
  - raw materials
  - information

and transforms these into output products – either tangible goods or intangible services – that can be sold in the market.

3 Show how operations management can contribute to the competitiveness of the organisation

- By designing and implementing systems and processes that are repeatable, consistent, reliable, efficient and compliant with the legislation that governs the overall environment.
- By creating an operations system that is aligned with the goals of the organisation in terms of volume of output, variety of product, variation in demand and visibility of process.

4 Identify different forms of operational activity

- Managing the capacity of the transformation process.
- Setting process and product standards to be adhered to within the transformation process.
- Managing the materials pipeline into and through the transformation process.
- Scheduling of the required resources to be used in the transformation process.
- Controlling the activities within the transformation process.

5 Define the term quality and describe features that can be used to quantify it

- Quality means conformance to the requirements of the customer.
- Product or service quality can be described in relation to functionality, performance, reliability, durability, customisation and appearance.

6 Show how ideas from the chapter add to your understanding of the integrating themes

- All waste is the result of an operations failure, so performance depends on changes to operations to reduce waste not just within the immediate process but across the supply chain.
- Operations staff work in an increasingly regulated environment, so need to focus on designing processes that are not only efficient and sustainable, but which also comply with regulatory and control systems.
- The growth of international trade brings challenges for operations managers as they seek to satisfy geographically dispersed customers in conjunction with equally dispersed suppliers.

Review questions

1 Review some consumer goods such as mobile phones, cars and kitchen appliances. Identify the service elements attached to the purchase of these products.

2 Discuss why variation in the inputs to the transformation process is a bad thing. Which of the five inputs is likely to be subject to most variation and which to least?

3 Why is control over quality at source so important?

4 How does service quality differ from manufacturing quality?

5 Why is delivery reliability more important than delivery speed?

6 Describe and discuss the importance of the demand/supply balance.

7 Discuss why it is impossible to have a single production system that is equally efficient at all volumes of throughput.

8 Describe the differences between product, process and cell layouts.

9 Discuss the concepts of order winners and order qualifiers.

10 Summarise an idea from the chapter that adds to your understanding of the integrating themes.

Concluding critical reflection

Think about the ways in which a company you are familiar with deals with operational issues such as capacity, scheduling, quality or cost. Then make notes on the following questions:

- What ideas discussed in this chapter struck you as being relevant to practice in this company?

- To what extent does this company experience external pressures from customers or competitors for increased operational performance?

- Identify the main inputs, outputs and feedback mechanisms used in the company's transformation process.

- Identify the main processes that the company uses and analyse how well they work.

- Describe the relationship between operations and other parts of the organisation.

- Identify the features that are used to define the quality of the product or service that this company provides.

Further reading

Crosby, P. (1979) *Quality is Free,* McGraw Hill, New York.

> A classic text detailing the basics of quality management and showing how it all started.

Lowson, R.H. (2002) *Strategic Operations Management the New Competitive Advantage,* Routledge, London.

> An established comprehensive and authoritative text specialising in operations strategy and its philosophies and techniques.

Slack, N., Chambers, S. and Johnston, R. (2009) *Operations Management,* Prentice Hall, Harlow.

> A large buffet-style bible which covers all of the main topics in operations management today.

Sprague, L. (2007) 'Evolution of the field of operations management,' *Journal of Operations Management,* 25, 219–238.

> A brief but comprehensive summary of the field of operations a management from a historical perspective.

Weblinks

These are the websites that have appeared in this chapter:

www.zara.com
www.sunseeker.com
www.linn.co.uk
www.ebay.co.uk
www.dell.com

Visit two of the websites in the list (or any other company that interests you) and navigate to the pages dealing with the products and services they offer. This is usually the first one you see, but in some it may be further back.

● What messages do they give about the nature of the goods and services they offer? What challenges are they likely to raise for operations in terms of their emphasis on, for example, quality, delivery or cost? What implications might that have for people working in the company?

● See if you can find any information on the site about the operating systems, or how they link with their suppliers.

For video case studies, audio summaries, flashcards, exercises and annotated weblinks related to this chapter, visit
www.pearsoned.co.uk/mymanagementlab

CHAPTER 19

PERFORMANCE MEASUREMENT AND CONTROL

Aim

To show why control is one of the four tasks of managing, and how the design of control and performance measurement systems can support organisations in meeting their goals.

Objectives

By the end of your work on this chapter you should be able to outline the concepts below in your own terms and:

1 Define control and explain why it is an essential activity in managing

2 Describe and give examples of the generic control activities of setting targets, measuring, comparing and correcting

3 Discuss strategies and tactics used to gain and maintain control

4 Explain how the choice of suitable measures of performance can help in managing the organisation

5 Explain why those designing performance measurement and control systems need to take account of human reactions to managerial control

6 Show how ideas from the chapter add to your understanding of the integrating themes.

Key terms

This chapter introduces the following ideas:

control	**efficiency**
control process	**effectiveness**
control system	**key performance indicator**
standard of performance	**balanced scorecard**
range of variation	**management by objectives**
corrective action	**input measures**
process measures	**organisational performance**
output measures	

Each is a term defined within the text, as well as in the Glossary at the end of the book.

Case study   Performance management in the NHS

NHS foundation trusts (often called Foundation hospitals) are at the cutting edge of the Government's commitment to devolution and decentralisation of public services and are at the heart of a patient-led NHS. They are not subject to direction from Whitehall. Instead local managers and staff working with local people have the freedom to develop services tailored to the particular needs of their patients and local communities. *A Short Guide to NHS Foundation Trusts*

Foundation Trusts were announced by Health Secretary Alan Milburn in 2002 and by 2009, 122 Foundation Trusts existed. They have been created to devolve decision making from central government to local communities, so that they are more responsive to the needs and wishes of local people and are an important part of the government's agenda to create a patient-led NHS in England. The introduction of Foundation Trusts represents a milestone in the history of the NHS, for each hospital that achieves Foundation status it brings a significant change to the way it is controlled.

Although Foundation Trusts are still part of the NHS and work to NHS care standards, hospitals that gain Foundation status are accountable locally to a Board of governors and nationally to Monitor (the independent regulator of NHS Foundation Trusts). This form of control should allow each hospital more autonomy to use its income derived from the Primary Care Trusts to provide more relevant care and services for its geographical area. Foundation Trusts are similar to co-operatives where local people, patients and staff can become members and governors.

Hospitals are among the most complex organisations in existence today. They employ a large number of highly skilled staff, utilise very sophisticated technology, operate extremely complex processes and often deal in life or death situations. The issue of their performance has been at the forefront of the

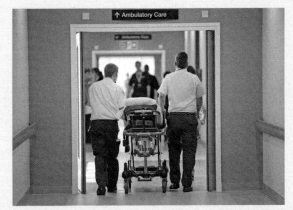

Getty Images

government's agenda for many years. Central to the issue of performance is the issue of control. The creation of Foundation hospitals is representative of a shift in philosophy between centralised, one size fits all, directive control by government to a more decentralised, customised and empowered form of control. This means that hospitals are responsible for managing their own income in an attempt to create a market-like environment, in the hope that empowered managers will be better able to intelligently allocate resources to areas of most need and behave more efficiently.

However, in some cases the changes had undesirable consequences – and accusations of 'third world' hospitals.

Sources: *A Short Guide to NHS Foundation Trusts*, 2005, Department of Health Publications; *The Times*, 18 March 2009.

Case questions 19.1

- Why does control matter in a hospital?
- What will be the main issues in developing control systems in a hospital?

Introduction

Mistakes in organisations are generally the result of a loss of control that leads to the delivery of a sub-optimal product. Chapter 18 discusses how organisations must implement processes that are consistent, repeatable and reliable; for a hospital this means providing a level of care that meets the required quality standards on these criteria – and in this context failure to do so can be devastating.

Controlling a hospital is something that starts at the top, with those to whom hospital managers are responsible. They face strategic issues, such as how to balance central and local control and whether to adopt a mechanistic or organic approach to control. Operational control is then devolved through the management of the hospital and, as discussed in Chapter 10, is visible in the organisational structure through the span of control and scope of responsibility allocated to each manager. Decisions on how to staff the hospital, who is responsible for what, how to design processes and what equipment to buy are all part of ensuring that the hospital operates correctly. This **control** system must then be embodied in a system measuring whether the hospital is performing in the way it should and achieving the quality standards set for it.

> **Control** is the process of monitoring activities to ensure that results are in line with the plan and acting to correct significant deviations.

All managers exercise control as they transform input resources into output products and services. No matter how thoroughly they might plan their objectives and how to meet them, unforeseen internal and external events will intervene. Managers therefore need to supplement the activity of planning with that of controlling – checking that work is going to plan and, if necessary, taking corrective action. The sooner they note deviations, the easier it is to bring performance into line. This applies at all levels – a senior nurse responsible for the flow of patients in the Accident and Emergency department, a consultant responsible for the quality of work in an operating theatre or a general manager responsible for overall hospital performance.

In this sense, control has many positive meanings standing for order, predictability or reliability. If things are under control, employees are clear about what they are expected to do and customers know what standard of product they will receive. Control is therefore an essential part of organisational life: it helps to ensure that the co-operative work of many resources adds value. An absence of such control implies uncertainty, chaos, inefficiency and waste. However, control depends on influencing people, so designing a control system is not purely a technical, rational process, but one that needs to take account of human factors and the context that it operates in.

The chapter begins by describing what managerial control is and the strategies and tactics that can be used to achieve it. It then goes on to discuss how to measure an organisation's performance. The next section analyses types of control suitable for different organisational models. Finally, the last section introduces a human perspective on control and discusses how control and performance measurement affects employees.

> The **control process** is the generic activity of setting performance standards, measuring actual performance, comparing actual performance with the standards, and acting to correct deviations or modify standards.

> A **control system** is the way the elements in the control process are designed and combined in a specific situation.

19.2　What is control and how to achieve it?

The control process

The **control process** is intended to support the achievement of objectives. Managers design specific **control systems** for different organisational activities. Although their degree of formality and explicitness varies, the control process incorporates four elements, as shown in Figure 19.1; setting objectives or targets, measuring actual performance, comparing this against the standard, and taking action to correct any significant gap between the two.

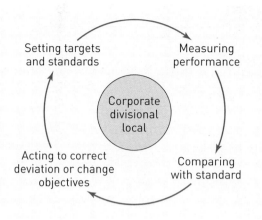

Figure 19.1
The control process

Setting targets

Targets provide direction and a **standard of performance** to aim for. The standard will itself affect achievement – people will ignore standards that are too high as unattainable, or too low as not being worthwhile. Some measures are generic, widely used and relevant to most management situations such as employee satisfaction or absence, costs against budget or sales against target. Managers will also use measures that are unique to their activity and area of responsibility – pages of advertising booked or students recruited.

Some aspects of performance can be measured in objective and quantifiable terms – such as sales, profit or return on assets. Equally important aspects of performance (product innovation, flexibility, company reputation or service quality) are more subjective and here managers look for acceptable qualitative measures.

Standard of performance is the defined level of performance to be achieved against which an operations actual performance is compared.

Measuring – the tools of control

Control requires that performance can be measured against a target. Table 19.1 shows the sources of information people can use to measure performance, and their advantages and disadvantages: combining them gives a more reliable picture of performance than relying on one alone.

Comparing

This step shows the variation between actual and planned performance. There is bound to be some variation from the plan, so before taking action a manager needs to know the acceptable

Table 19.1 Common sources of information for measuring performance

	Advantages	Disadvantages
Personal observation	Gives first-hand knowledge, information is not filtered, shows the manager is interested	Subject to personal bias, time consuming, obtrusive – people see what is happening
Oral reports	Quick way to get information, allows for verbal and non-verbal feedback	Information is filtered, no permanent record
Written reports	Comprehensive, and can show trends and relationships, easy to store and retrieve	Time to prepare, may ignore subjective factors
Online information systems	Rapid feedback, often during the process	Information overload, may be stressful to staff

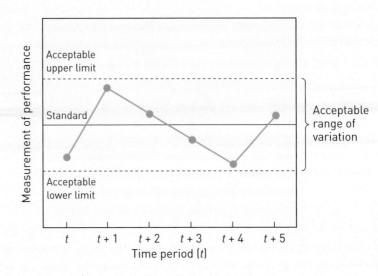

Figure 19.2
Defining the
acceptable range
of variation

The **range of variation** sets the acceptable limits within which performance can vary from standard without requiring remedial action.

range of variation – the acceptable limits of variation between actual and planned performance. Acceptable range of variation is illustrated in Figure 19.2 As long as the variation is within this range, the manager need take no action – but as it goes beyond that range, the case for action becomes stronger, especially if the trend is continuing. This stage also implies searching for the causes of a significant variation, to increase the chances of an appropriate response.

Correcting

Corrective action aims to correct problems to get performance back on track.

The final step is to act on significant variations from the plan – either to correct future performance or to revise the standard. Attempts to bring performance up to the required standard could involve any aspects of the transformation process and involves taking **corrective action** such as redesigning a process or resetting a machine or cutting prices to sell excess stocks. This may mean dealing with longer-term issues of product design, quality or staff skill levels.

Activity 19.1   Assessing control systems

Consider the course you are studying. With your fellow students, analyse how your performance on the course is controlled by answering the following questions:

- What standards of performance are you expected to achieve?
- Who sets the standards?
- Are they clear or ambiguous?

- How is your performance measured?
- Do you know what the criteria are?
- How often is performance measured?

- Who compares your performance with the standard?
- Is this done publicly?
- Is the comparison objective or subjective?

- What happens if your performance is not up to standard?
- What feedback do you get?
- Is it useful?

| Management in practice | Enron – the opposite of control |

The Enron scandal, revealed in October 2001, eventually led to the bankruptcy of the Enron Corporation, an energy company based in Texas, and the dissolution of its auditor, Arthur Andersen, one of the largest accountancy partnerships in the world.

Enron was formed in 1985 after the merger of Houston Natural Gas and InterNorth. By 1992, Enron was the largest merchant of natural gas in North America. In an attempt to achieve further growth, Enron pursued a diversification strategy. By 2001, Enron had become a conglomerate that owned and operated gas pipelines, pulp and paper plants, and electricity and water plants. The corporation also traded in financial markets for products and services. When chief executive Jeffrey Skilling was hired, he developed a staff of executives who were able, by exploiting accounting loopholes and poor financial control, to hide billions in debt from failed deals and projects. The roots of the scandal lay in the accumulation over several years of inappropriate habits and values, which finally spiralled out of control.

From late 1997 until its collapse, the primary motivations for Enron's accounting and financial transactions seem to have been to keep reported income and reported cash flow up, asset values inflated, and liabilities off the books. As a result, in addition to the bankruptcy, many executives at Enron were later sentenced to prison.

However, the loss of control was not limited to accounting, by the mid-1990s Enron had developed a culture that encouraged innovation and risk-taking: short-term performance goals were generously rewarded to the detriment of longer-term sustainability. There were few organisational control mechanisms in place to ensure that managers were performing in a sensible and professional manner.

Source: McLean and Elkind (2003).

Strategies for control – mechanistic or organic?

Managers design a control system using their assumptions about how it will affect behaviour. Rules and procedures can be implemented to give people precise and unambiguous direction on how to perform tasks and deal with unusual events. Alternatively they can be written in broader terms leaving more discretion to staff. Procedures may cover all aspects of work or only a small number of critically important activities. Controls may emphasise conformity or encourage creativity.

If such decisions are made consistently and coherently, this suggests that managers are taking a strategic approach to control, in the sense that they have a clear understanding of its purposes and how to implement it. Two opposing strategies are mechanistic and organic: terms first introduced in Chapter 10.

Mechanistic control involves the extensive use of rules and procedures, top-down authority, written job descriptions and other formal methods of influencing people to act in desirable ways. In contrast, organic control involves the use of flexible authority, relatively loose job descriptions, a greater reliance on self-control and other less formal methods. Both are distinct and will be effective in different situations. Table 19.2 compares the two strategies.

Which strategy to choose?

Chapter 10 contrasts mechanistic and organic structures, and introduces the theory that choice of form reflects one or more contingencies. It also points out that organisations often combine both approaches, using mechanistic forms in stable, predictable operations, and organic for more volatile, uncertain parts of the business. The same thinking can be used in considering the choice of control systems. John Child (2005) proposed contingency factors

Table 19.2 Examples of mechanistic and organic controls

Tools	Mechanistic control	Organic control
Supervision	Stress on following procedures and plans	Stress on encouraging learning and creativity
Organisation structure	Top-down authority, emphasis on position power, detailed job descriptions	Dispersed authority, emphasis on expert power, flexible job descriptions
Rules and procedures	Detailed, on many topics	Broad, on as few topics as practicable
Machinery	Information on performance used by supervisors to check on staff	Information on performance used by staff to learn and improve
Cultural	Encourages conformity, focus is on controlling individuals	Encourages creativity and innovation, promotes freedom

that could affect the choice of control strategy – such as competitive strategy, importance of innovation and employee expertise. Table 19.3 compares these and informs the decision of whether a mechanistic or organic approach would be appropriate.

Being aware of these alternative approaches enables managers to choose an appropriate approach to control that is suitable for the context.

Tactics for control

While defining the overall control strategy is the first step in creating a coherent and consistent control system, this has to be supported by a set of practices that encourage their achievement. Each of the following control mechanisms can contribute in the right

Table 19.3 Contingencies and choice of control strategies

Contingency	When	Control strategy likely to be appropriate
Competitive strategy	Cost leadership	Mechanistic, use of rules and procedures, and machinery to measure quantitative output
	Differentiation	Organic, use of HRM and cultural controls stressing self-managing teams, and qualitative output measures
Importance of innovation	Low	Mechanistic, use of rules and procedures, and machinery to measure quantitative output
	High	Organic, use of HRM and cultural controls stressing self-managing teams, and qualitative output measures
Employee expertise	Low	Mechanistic, use of rules and procedures, and machinery to measure quantitative output
	High	Organic, use of HRM and cultural controls stressing self-managing teams, and qualitative output measures

circumstances. Some, such as management by objectives, are more suited to organic control strategies where workers are given more autonomy in how to do their work than to mechanistic strategies where autonomy is discouraged.

Direct supervision

In small organisations most control is by process and supervision as the owner or the management team can see directly what is happening. They can personally inspect and report on progress, quickly see whether or not it is in line with the plan, and act if necessary. Done with enthusiasm and sensitivity this method is very effective – if people use it clumsily staff will find it intrusive and overbearing.

Organisation structure

Most organisations set out what people are expected to do by giving them job descriptions that allocate the person's tasks and responsibilities. These can be very narrowly and specifically defined, or they can be broad and defined in general terms. They may also establish with whom the job holder is expected to communicate, and the boundaries of his/her responsibility. This is a form of control as it constrains people – by specifying what they can or cannot do, and what output standards they should achieve. Similarly, organisations can be centralised, with control being held at the top, or decentralised with control spread throughout the structure.

Rules and procedures

As organisations become too large for personal control, managers develop rules and procedures to control activities and alert senior people to significant deviations. Rules establish acceptable behaviour and levels of performance, and so are a way of controlling the workforce. They can guide people on how to conduct the business, how to perform the tasks, how to apply for equipment or what to do when a customer places an order.

Management by objectives

Some organisations use a system of **management by objectives** to exercise control. Here managers and throughout the hierarchy agree their goals for the following period. The approach is partly based on goal-setting theory (Chapter 15), which predicts that the level of difficulty of a goal will affect the effort people put into achieving it. The key is that workers should focus on the outcome to be achieved and therefore must be given the latitude to achieve it by a variety of methods as they see fit.

Management by objectives is a system in which managers and staff agree their objectives, and then measure progress towards them periodically.

Control through machinery

In this method, machines or information systems are designed to control, directly or indirectly, what people do. Direct technological controls occur where the machine directs what people do or say. Assembly lines transport the object being made along a moving conveyor, with operators performing a short task to add another piece to the product, with almost no scope to alter the way they work. The speed of work is paced by the machine, the time spent on the task is very short, and there is limited scope for worker interaction. The scripts in a call centre specify the questions to ask, how to respond to customer questions and how to close the conversation; they have a similar controlling effect on the way a person works. In process industries such as brewing, computer sensors capture information on process performance, compare it with set criteria and, if needed, automatically adjust the equipment to keep the process in line with the plan.

Human resource management control

The processes of HRM discussed in Chapter 11 can support the control process. Selection and training procedures ensure that the number and type of recruits fit the profile of attitudes, social skills and technical competence that support wider objectives, and that new staff are trained to follow the company's ways of working. The appraisal and reward system can encourage behaviour that supports business objectives. The behaviour of employees can be controlled by offers of rewards if people comply with management policies and of penalty if they do not.

Key ideas | **Barker on concertive control**

Barker (1993) notes three broad strategies that have evolved as organisations seek to control members' activities. The first is 'simple control', the direct, authoritarian and personal control of work by bosses, best seen in nineteenth-century factories and in small family owned companies today. The second is 'technological control', in which control emerges from the physical technology, such as in the assembly line found in traditional manufacturing. Third and most familiar is bureaucratic control, in which control derives from the hierarchically based social relations of the organisation and the rules that reward compliance and punish non-compliance.

Technological control resulted not only from technological advances but also from worker alienation and dissatisfaction with the despotism too often possible in simple control. But technological control via the assembly line also led to worker dissatisfaction. Bureaucratic control, with its emphasis on rational–legal rules, hierarchical monitoring and rewards for compliance was developed to counter the problems of technological control.

Bureaucracy too has problems: the main one being an inability to respond quickly to changing conditions. Many companies have sought to overcome these problems by introducing a greater degree of self-control, such as the use of self-managing teams. Barker's research in one company showed how team members developed values and norms about good team behaviour, and put pressure on members, especially new members, to follow them. This form of concertive control was not only stronger than many bureaucratic controls, but was also less visible, as team members accepted it as the normal way of doing things.

Source: Barker (1993).

Values and beliefs

Another approach to control aims to ensure that members of the organisation meet management requirements by encouraging internal compliance rather than relying on external constraint. To the extent that a unit develops a strong culture with which staff can identify will help to control their actions. Extensive socialisation and other practices encourage them to act in ways that are consistent with the dominant values and beliefs. This may be positive but can sometimes be oppressive and constraining.

Activity 19.2 | **Examples of control tools**

- From your experience of organisations – a part-time job or the university – identify examples of each of these approaches to control.
- What are their advantages and disadvantages in the situation where they are used?

Case study   NHS – the case continues

The case for control . . .

The introduction of Foundation Trusts has not been without its critics. Some pointed out that they go against the NHS principles. Others doubt whether the Foundation members will be able to control hospital management, which is heavily influenced by powerful medical professionals with a tradition of autonomy and resistance to outside interference with their professional judgements.

A further concern is that Foundation Trusts will quickly copy the US and come to see some conditions as more profitable (or less costly), and concentrate on those at the expense of others. A 2007 World Health Organisation report found that despite US expenditure being almost double that of the UK, the outcomes were no better. A study undertaken by the King's Fund in Homerton University Hospital NHS Foundation Trust found the governors disappointed and disillusioned. One governor said:

> I regret to say that I wouldn't be able to pinpoint a particular point or issue that I have been able to achieve by my being a governor.

Another report found that it is too easy to invite members to sit on sub-committees where they quickly become bogged down in the minutiae of operational planning, while the main decisions are taken elsewhere.

Sources: World Health Statistics, (2007), *The World Health Organisation*. Graphical representation of different outcomes and expenditure, (2007) *World Health Organisation,* Brettingham (2005).

Case questions 19.2

- Why do you think it would be difficult to exercise effective control in the role of hospital governor?
- Why do you think professions such as doctors resist managerial control?

Management in practice   An Apple a day . . .   www.apple.com

All organisations use a mix of control tactics, many combining mechanistic and organic strategies. A simple example of this can be seen in organisations that both design and manufacture products. The Apple iPad was launched on 27 January 2010, the latest in a long line of innovative high-tech products that Apple Inc. has introduced. The company has a creative and flexible culture that allows innovation to flourish. The success of the company is built on the excellence of this design and development capability. Ideas cannot be 'manufactured' by process or thought of 'to order' therefore the control strategy used for RD workers is very organic, with knowledge workers working within a flexible and supportive environment.

However, the products are manufactured using a more mechanistic approach. Each unit must be exactly the same with each manufacturing process designed to be completely consistent and reliable. Control of quality is critical with manufacturing tolerences sometimes specified in microns (millionths of a meter) and process defect rates of less than one in a million. Cleanliness is vital, with clean rooms set up to ensure contaminants are reduced to a minimum.To achieve this workers must fit into the process with no deviation tolerated, as any unplanned activity will lead to a process failure.

Control of cost in volume manufacturing is also critical, with companies such as Apple manufacturing their products in low-wage countries, using many of the principles of scientific management, within a strict control system where reducing cost is the critical target. People doing exactly what they are told is the key to production efficiency in this system.

Sources: Gamble *et al.* (2004); company website.

> ### Activity 19.3 · Control and level of skill
>
> - Many companies use cheap labour overseas. What are the advantages and disadvantages in doing so?
> - Discuss with your fellow students whether, from a manufacturing control point of view, lower skilled and poorly educated workers are better than more highly skilled and better educated workers.
> - Which do you think will be easier to control?

19.3 · How do you know you are in control?

Once the strategy for guiding the control system has been decided and the tactics to be used for controlling the organisation selected, some mechanism for setting standards and monitoring performance must be implemented. This depends on measuring key variables regularly.

Types of performance measurement

In the last chapter we discussed the processes of the organisation and how feedback must be gathered to ensure they are consistently reliable. Feedback is a control mechanism based on measuring defined parameters at the beginning, during or at the end of the process. Figure 19.3 illustrates these in relation to a car journey.

Input measures

An **input measure** is an element of resource that is measured as it is put in to the transformation process.

Think of the journey as a 'process' of travelling from one place to another. Drivers can re-fuel the car before a journey. If they then measure what they put in and what is left at the end, and doing some arithmetic, they can calculate the fuel efficiency of the car. In organisational terms this may mean measuring the amount of material that is input to the process, then working to reduce the waste so that less is needed. A more sophisticated **input measure** may be the skill of the workers, since a better worker may result in a more efficient process.

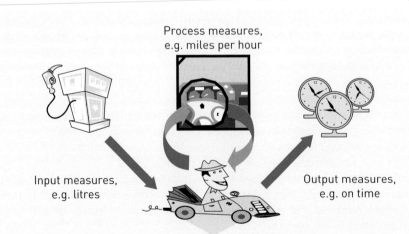

Process measures, e.g. miles per hour

Input measures, e.g. litres

Output measures, e.g. on time

Figure 19.3 Types of performance measure

Process measures

Instruments can measure speed during the journey to tell us whether we are moving fast enough to arrive as planned. Moving too quickly means arriving too soon, with the associated reduction in fuel efficiency; moving too slowly means the danger of being late. In organisational terms, **process measures** may be the heat of an oven, the flow rate of liquid in a pipe or the speed of rotation of a machine. In all cases, deviation from the norm will indicate possible sub-optimal performance. Another process measure is health and safety – the number and type of accidents occurring during a process, against a target of zero.

A **process measure** is a measurement taken during an operational process that provides data on how the process is performing.

Output

This is the activity of measuring the quantity of output for a definable area of work – whether for a unit or the business as a whole. In relation to our car journey this may be the arrival time or total fuel used. In an operational process this may simply be the number of units produced: is it on target or not? It may be a dimension: is a 100 gram bar of chocolate actually 100 grams? If more, then too much chocolate has been given and profit reduced; if less, the customer is receiving less than the advertised amount and the company is in trouble. Other popular **output measures** are financial metrics such as labour and materials cost.

An **output measure** is a measurement taken after an operational process is complete.

The measures taken in our car journey should show us how to alter the process the next time to improve either fuel consumption or on-time performance. The same is true in operational processes. The measures taken should provide information that allows the control system to be adjusted to achieve a better outcome and so optimise efficiency.

Performance measures are required to calculate how efficiently or effectively our organisation is operating. While both these terms are sometimes used interchangeably, in fact they have very different meanings.

Efficiency

Efficiency is often thought of as 'doing things right'. It is a measure of output divided by the inputs needed to produce the output. It is widely used to show how productively a process is working, and how well people have managed it – more output for fewer inputs is better since that implies that value is being added to the resources. A simple measure of output would be sales revenue (number sold × price), while input can be measured by the cost of acquiring and transforming resources into the output. An increase in the ratio of output to input indicates an increase in efficiency. Managers are under constant pressure from shareholders or taxpayers to produce their output more efficiently, by using fewer resources.

Efficiency is a measure of the inputs required for each unit of output.

Effectiveness

Effectiveness is often thought of as 'doing the right things'. It is a measure of how well the outcomes of a process relate to the broader objectives of the unit – that is, how well the process supports the achievement of broader goals. A library can measure the efficiency of its cataloguers by recording the number of volumes catalogued by each employee. That would not measure effectiveness, which would require measures of accuracy, consistency, timeliness or maintenance of the catalogue. A delivery service can measure efficiency (cost of the service) or effectiveness (predictability, frequency of collections or accuracy of deliveries).

Effectiveness is a measure of how well an activity contributes to achieving organisational goals.

Case study   NHS – the case continues

The measurement and target culture

A report analysing the failures of the mid-Stafford-shire NHS Foundation Trust placed some of the blame on the performance measurement system. One performance metric that was criticised was the Accident and Emergency (A&E) four-hour, waiting-time target. Staff told the Healthcare Commission that there was a lot of pressure on them to meet this target. Several doctors recounted occasions where managers had asked them to leave seriously ill patients to treat minor ailments so the target could be met. One had even been asked to leave a heart-attack patient being given life-saving treatment.

Nurses reported leaving meetings in tears after being told their jobs were at risk after breaching the target. And the report concluded that patients were sometimes 'dumped' into wards near A&E with little nursing care so the targets could be met.

The four-hour target, which in simple terms aims to ensure that patients are treated and either admitted or sent home within four hours, at first glance seems straightforward. However, on further consideration it is much more complicated to enforce. Not all patients that come in have the same requirements; indeed doctors had identified that some groups of patients such as those with chest pains, recovering from alcohol or drug overdoses, and those too elderly or vulnerable to be discharged in the middle of the night should be exempt. Some hospitals were getting round the four-hour target with observation wards attached to the A&E which patients could be admitted to. Others refused to accept patients into their A&E departments from the ambulance so that the 'four-hour clock' would not start ticking.

Unthinkingly, trying to meet this simple but ultimately misconceived target seriously damaged patient care.

Source: Learning and Implications from the Mid-Staffordshire NHS Foundation Trust, Monitor-Independent Regulator of NHS Foundation Trusts Final Report – 5 August 2009.

Case questions 19.3

- Do you think it is appropriate to allocate performance measures of any sort in organisations that deal directly with people with potentially life threatening conditions?

- Investigate other performance measures used in the NHS. Try to find some that are misconceived and therefore open to abuse.

19.4   How to measure performance

Choosing performance measures

There are five generic performance objectives – quality, speed, dependability, flexibility and cost. These can be broken down into more detailed measures such as product produced or materials used, or aggregated into composite measures such as a customer satisfaction scores. The composite measures usually have more strategic relevance, indicating such things as how a product is performing in the market. The more detailed measures tend to have more operational relevance such as how a process or person is performing. Detailed measures are usually monitored more closely and more often – in some cases highly mechanised processes are monitored by sensors hundreds of times per second. In practice, companies will utilise a range of measures to build a complete picture of how the company is performing – much like a doctor will check a number of things such as blood pressure, heart rate and cholesterol level rather than relying on any single one for a diagnosis. Table 19.4 shows how detail performance measures can be aggregated into more general composite ones.

There are two problems with devising useful performance measures. The first is the difficulty in achieving a balance between having a few measures on one hand (straightforward and simple but comprehensive enough to be useful) and having too many detailed measures (complex and difficult to manage) on the other. Most often a compromise is reached by

Table 19.4 Aggregating performance measures

Composite measure	Customer satisfaction		Agility		Resilience
Generic measure	Quality	Dependability	Speed	Flexibility	Cost
Detail measure	Defects per unit Customer returns Scrap rate	Mean time between failures Lateness	Delivery time Throughput	Range of functionality Number of options	Raw material cost Labour cost

Source: Adapted from Slack *et al.* (2007).

making sure that there is a clear link between the measures chosen and the strategic objectives of the operation in relation to quality, speed, dependability, flexibility and cost. This means that if good quality is the main reason that customers buy the product or service then more emphasis should be placed on implementing measures that ensure the quality rather than cheapness of the product. The most important measures are called **key performance indicators (KPIs)**.

The second is the problem of setting performance targets that do not create the wrong behaviours as employees try to find ways around them so that the target is met but to the detriment of the overall operation. Here common sense must be applied and the consequences of each target must be thoroughly considered in tandem with the overall control strategy that is in place. In the NHS four-hour case, the key to the successful operation of the A&E is in the skill of the staff, the quality of the support infrastructure and equipment, and providing the front-line doctors and nurses with the flexibility to do their job the best way that they see fit. Instead of using an output measure such as four-hour waiting time, implementing input measures such as skills matrices combined with process measures such as equipment availability will, if used correctly, ensure the best people are supported by the best equipment. This should lead to reduced waiting times and also improved quality of care.

The five indicators are composites of many smaller measures. For example, quality is a composite of many process measures which ensure that the product produced is exactly as it should be. In the same way, speed is an aggregate of how quickly materials are moved between processes, and how effectively machines and staff work to complete each process.

One criticism of performance measures is the tendency to focus on the 'easy to measure' things such as finance and units of output, while avoiding more complex ones such as customer satisfaction and quality of employee. The more difficult to measure aspects are sometimes the most useful. In design and development work, ensuring that employees have the skills and knowledge to do their jobs will do more for effectiveness than measuring the output of a deficient employee. Likewise, measuring customer satisfaction and loyalty will be more useful than measuring revenue, since a satisfied customer will return and so generate more revenue.

> **Key performance indicator (KPIs)** are a summarised set of the most important measures that inform managers how well an operation is achieving organisational goals.

The balanced scorecard

Kaplan and Norton (1992) noted that while

> traditional financial performance measures worked well for the industrial era . . . they are out of step with the skills and competencies companies are trying to master today. (p. 71)

Financial measures are essential but carry the hazard that short-term targets may encourage practices that damage long-run performance – for example by postponing investment in equipment or customer service. They found that senior executives recognised that no single measure could provide a clear performance target or focus attention on the critical areas of the business. Rather, they wanted a balanced presentation of both financial and operational measures. Their research enabled them to devise a **balanced scorecard** – a set

> The **balanced scorecard** is a performance measurement tool that looks at four areas: financial, customer satisfaction, internal processes and innovation, and learning which contribute to organisational performance.

of measures that gives a fast but comprehensive view of the business. It includes financial measures that tell the results of actions taken, and complements these with measures of customer satisfaction, internal processes and innovation – measures which drive future financial performance.

It allows managers to view performance comprehensively, by answering the following questions:

1 How do customers see us? (customer perspective);
2 What must we excel at? (internal perspective);
3 Can we continue to improve and create value? (innovation and learning perspective);
4 How do we look to shareholders? (financial perspective).

The scorecard illustrated in Figure 19.4 brings together in a single management report many elements of a company's agenda, such as the need to be customer oriented, to shorten response time, improve quality or cut the time taken to launch a new product. It also guards against the dangers of working in isolation, as it requires senior managers to consider all the important operational measures together. They can then judge whether improvement in one area may have been achieved at the expense of another.

Kaplan and Norton (1993) advocate that companies spend time identifying, for each of the four measures, the external and internal factors which are important and developing suitable measures of performance. For example, under the customer heading, they may believe that customers are concerned about time, quality, performance, service and cost. They should therefore articulate goals for each factor, and then translate these goals into specific measures. The approach has been widely adopted (Neely and Al Najjar, 2006) but, despite its popularity, Akkermanns and van Oorschot (2005) point out that it should be applied critically by asking:

● Are the selected measures the right ones?
● Should there be more, or fewer?
● At what levels should performance targets be set?

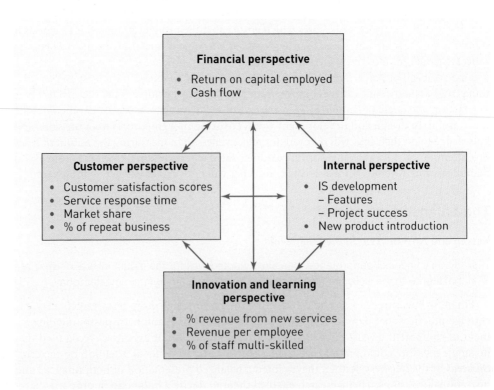

Figure 19.4
The balanced
scorecard

Perspectives in detail

Each perspective of the balanced scorecard can in itself be considered an aggregate measure. It is important to understand what each perspective is there to represent and the detailed measures that could be used in each to provide meaningful information

Innovation and learning perspective

This set of measures should indicate how intangible assets such as people and information are supporting the organisation? The objective is to ensure the company is managing its intangibles in the correct way and it should describe people performance such as skills, talent and know-how with measures such as training logs and attendance, and information performance with measures such as data accuracy and IT fault logging.

Internal perspective

This perspective indicates whether the company is doing the right things in the right way. The objective here is to ensure that the correct processes are being used effectively and efficiently. Measures here maybe productivity, machine down-time or part scrap-rates.

Customer perspective

This perspective indicates whether the customer is getting what they want. The objective is to ensure that the customer is happy with the product or service. The measures therefore represent customer satisfaction such as product in-service performance or number of customer complaints.

Financial perspective

This perspective indicates how well the company is performing financially. Therefore the objective is to represent shareholder value. Here measures can simply be profit, cost or revenue related.

Figure 19.5 illustrates a simple balanced scorecard for an airline. Here they are keen to ensure that the performance of the process for preparing the aircraft for its next flight is as

	Objective	Measurement	Target
Financial	• Increase profit • Grow revenue	• Time aircraft in air • Fuel bill	X% £Y
Customer *(Attract and retain customers)*	• Increase on-time flights • Reduce time on-ground	• Ranking • Repeat custom	1st 100%
Internal *(Fast ground turnaround)*	• Reduce refuelling time • Reduce baggage loading time	• On-time arrival • On-time departure • Loading time • Fuelling time	100% 100% X min Y min
Learning *(Strategic job families e.g., ramp agent)*	• Upskill people • Create IT support system	• Staff availability • Delays due to human error • Data errors	100% 0 0

Figure 19.5
Airline performance measurement

efficient as possible. There are two things worth noting that illustrate the power of this measurement tool. First, if the measures in the learning and growth and the internal perspectives are correct, i.e. the activity is carried out by skilled people and the process is operating as it is supposed to, then there will be less delays so hopefully the customer will be happier with the travel experience. Second, if the turnaround process is carried out efficiently, then the profit should go up as the cost goes down. This illustrates not only the importance of choosing the correct measures but also of how achieving well chosen measures in the learning and growth and internal perspectives should mean that the measures in the customer and the financial perspectives are easier to meet (Kaplan and Norton, 2008).

Activity 19.4   Starting a balanced scorecard

Begin to develop a balanced scorecard for activities within an organisation that you are familiar with.

- Create measures and targets under each of the four headings.
- Comment on the strengths and weaknesses of the balanced scorecard for performance measurement.

Organisational performance is the accumulated results of all the organisation's work processes and activities.

Such measures of **organisational performance** show how well managers have conducted their role of adding value to the resources they have used in their area of responsibility.

Case study   NHS the case continues

The outcome . . .
An inquest into the Mid-Staffordshire Hospital Trust by Monitor found failings in a number of areas. From a performance measurement and control perspective the two most relevant were; 1) a lack of clarity on the standards that should be achieved as the threshold for gaining Foundation status; and 2) that Monitor itself – the regulatory body – must revise its view of what information is required as evidence that performance standards are being achieved.

In addition, among the conclusions drawn by the official independent enquiry chaired by Robert Francis QC, there were two of particular interest to operations and performance management. First, in a conclusion entitled 'Figures preferred to people' the inquiry found that performance data were often given more weight than the opinions of those involved, and that performance systems did not bring to light the serious and systemic failures in the hospital – this despite the sole purpose of performance measurement systems being to do just that.

Second, another conclusion entitled 'A focus on systems not outcomes', indicated that staff were focusing too much on the process and not enough on the care that resulted from the process – again despite the key consideration in designing operational systems being that they produce the correct outcomes.

Source: Learning and Implications from the Mid Staffordshire NHS Foundation Trust, Monitor-Independent Regulator of NHS Foundation Trusts Final Report – 5 August 2009. Independent Inquiry into care provided by Mid-Staffordshire Foundation Trust January 2005–March 2009 chaired by Robert Francis QC – February 2010.

Case question 19.4

- Discuss the difference between a public sector organisation and a private sector company. Do you think that the threat of going out of business tends to make it easier to implement performance measurement systems in a private sector company?

19.5 Situational (contingency) views on performance measures

Different organisations operate using different models and as such the strategies, tactics and tools of control must be matched correctly to ensure an effective fit.

The competing values framework (Quinn *et al.*, 2003) provides a tool for considering how to design a control and performance measurement system. It sets out four models of management, which represent different ways of analysing effectiveness. Although presented as 'competing', Quinn *et al.* also point out that they are parts of a larger whole, in the sense that they focus on different criteria of effectiveness – implying different measures to judge performance. Table 19.5 lists the alternative values, and illustrates performance measures (drawing on Harrison, 2005) consistent with each.

Table 19.5 Performance Standards Based on The Competing Values Framework

Value	Criteria of effectiveness	Examples of performance measures
Rational goal	Attaining goals Output quantity Output quality	Achievement of objectives, task completion, profits Sales, profits, productivity, efficiency Reliability, service, responsiveness, reputation, recognition
Internal process	Efficiency and costs Continuity, smooth workflow	Operating costs, productivity, efficiency Work co-ordination; adequacy, quality and distribution of information
Human relations	Employee satisfaction Interpersonal relations Involvement	Quality of working life, absenteeism, turnover, health and safety Trust, diversity and community relations, conflict resolution Participation in decision making, empowerment
Open systems	Resources: quantity Resources: quality Proactiveness Competitive position Adaptation Innovativeness	Financial resources, physical assets, grants and budgets secured Skills and reputation of staff, knowledge base; quality of clients (student admission grades) Impact on environment – clients, competitors, regulators, suppliers, entry into new markets Standing compared with competitors: reputation for leadership Capacity to cope with external change and uncertainty; flexibility in handling crises, surprises Technological and administrative innovation; implementation of new technologies and practices

Sources: Based on Quinn *et al.* (2003); and Harrison (2005).

19.6 Human considerations in control

Control systems are intended to influence people to act in ways that support the organisational objectives and so reflect the assumptions that those who designed the systems have about the people they are trying to control. The more accurate these assumptions are, the more likely the control system will support business objectives.

People have personal and local objectives that they seek to achieve in addition to, or perhaps in place of, the stated objectives of the organisation. Chapter 15 discussed how people seek to satisfy their human needs at work and how they will evaluate a control system, in part by asking whether it helps or obstructs them in meeting those needs. How they react will reflect their interests and their interpretation of the situation – which may be different from the interests of those establishing the controls.

Control is also a political process in which powerful individuals and groups seek to dominate others. People may oppose a control system not for its intrinsic features, but for what it implies about their loss of power relative to another group, or because they feel it will restrict their ability to use their initiative and experience. Therefore, while there is a clear operational perspective on control or, put another way, a neutral aspect of keeping actions in line with goals, control is also closely tied to ideas about motivation, influence and power.

While effective control depends on suitable control and performance measurement systems, these systems in turn depend on how people see them. Control is only effective when it influences people to act in the way intended by those designing the system, who therefore need to take into account the likely reactions of those being controlled.

Lawler (1976) identified three potential problems with formal control systems. First, management controls lead to 'rigid bureaucratic behaviour'. Most people prefer to act in ways that make them look good to others, so we tend to concentrate on activities that are measured. If the consequences of a poor assessment are severe, then people will tend to focus their efforts on those parts of the job that are assessed, and ignore those which are not. This is exemplified in the NHS case where managers were keen to 'look good' by meeting their assigned targets. The standards tell people what they have to do to perform well and perhaps to gain promotion: these behaviours may not necessarily be in the best interests of the business as a whole. Sales staff in a store who are paid a bonus on the volume of sales may focus on generating sales, perhaps using high-pressure tactics that secure a single sale but discourage the customer from coming again. Or they may focus on sales at the expense of checking stock or maintaining the display areas – especially if these are not assessed as part of the control system. Other examples could be reluctance to work outside one's own area of responsibility, concentrating on meeting sub-unit goals rather than those of the enterprise as a whole, or accepting minimum standards as long as they exceed the target.

Second, controls may encourage people to supply inaccurate information. The more important the measure, the more likely it becomes that people will distort information to enhance recorded performance. The bargaining that surrounds payment by results or a commission payment system is an example. Line managers and employees will have different views about the fairness of a particular piece rate, and the latter will often give invalid data on the complexity of the work or the time it requires to overcome a difficulty, to ensure a more favourable rate.

Third, people may resist a system that they feel threatens their satisfaction or in some way undermines their ability to meet their psychological needs from work. Table 19.6 illustrates this by showing how a control system can have either positive or negative effects on a person's ability to satisfy each of the human needs identified by Maslow (1970) and discussed in Chapter 15. Controls can encourage both positive and negative behaviour – positive by encouraging commitment, enthusiasm and higher ambition, negative if they lead people to be fearful and defensive.

Activity 19.5 Assessing the human effects of a control system

Consider a control system at work, or where you are studying.

- Have they had any effects similar to those that Lawler identified?
- How did that affect the way people reacted to the system?
- How could management have redesigned the controls to avoid those effects?

Table 19.6 Possible Effects of Control Systems on Human Needs

Maslow's categories of human needs	Controls may support satisfaction	Controls may hinder satisfaction
Self-actualisation	Feedback encourages higher performance, accepting new challenges	Controls may limit initiative, autonomy, ability to experiment and discover
Esteem	Publishing successes builds recognition, self-confidence; reputation with colleagues and senior managers	Publishing failure damages esteem, undermines reputation; inaccurate information also damaging
Belongingness	Team-based assessments can support bonding and team development	Individual rewards may breed competition and damage co-operation
Security	Knowledge of how performance is assessed gives certainty	Controls that leave expectations unclear undermine security; information seen as threat
Physiological	Help focus effort and meet performance requirements	Controls highlight poor performance and threaten job

Simons' four levers of control

Another contribution to the human aspects of control systems was made by Robert Simons (1995), who examined the dilemma between control and empowerment:

> How do senior managers protect their companies from control failures when empowered employees are encouraged to redefine how they [do] their jobs? How do [they] ensure that subordinates with an entrepreneurial flair do not put the business at risk? (p. 80)

Simons argued that most managers define control narrowly – as measuring progress against plans to help achieve goals. Such diagnostic control systems are, however, only one ingredient of control. Three other levers are equally important: beliefs systems, boundary systems and interactive control systems.

Diagnostic controls

These enable managers to monitor performance and keep critical variables within preset limits. Most businesses rely on them to help managers track the progress of individuals or units toward targets such as revenue growth and market share, by periodically measuring output and comparing it with preset standards. They are not in themselves enough to ensure performance, since employees pursuing a goal may act in ways that endanger the company.

Beliefs systems

These are concise statements of the core beliefs of the business: how it creates value ('a better type of banking'); the level of performance it strives for ('pursuit of excellence'); and how individuals are expected to manage relationships ('respect for the individual'). Their main purpose is to inspire and promote commitment to the business – in the hope that they will not put personal or local interests above those of the whole.

Boundary systems

These tell people what activities are off-limits – what not to do. Unlike diagnostic controls or beliefs systems, boundary systems are stated in negative terms or as minimum standards.

Pressures to achieve superior results can encourage people to bend the rules, and boundary systems counter this by making it clear what actions are unacceptable – such as not disclosing information to people outside the firm or making improper payments.

Interactive control systems

As organisations grow larger, senior managers have less personal contact with staff, they need to create systems to share emerging information and encourage creativity. They need sensing systems that expose them to new information and help identify patterns of change. Interactive controls are the formal systems that managers use to involve themselves regularly and personally with subordinates, to focus attention on key issues. Simons quotes the example of a major drinks company where senior managers schedule weekly meetings to discuss the latest market and sales information, to challenge subordinates to explain the trends and review their action plans.

Collectively, these four levers of control set in motion powerful forces that reinforce one another. By using the control levers effectively, managers can be confident that the benefits of innovation and creativity are not achieved at the expense of control.

19.7   Integrating themes

Sustainable performance

Many companies now publish formal reports on their environmental policies and performance, seeing it as in their business interests do so. A commitment to measure environmental performance motivates managers to be more analytical and disciplined about their operating processes – less pollution tends to mean a more efficient process. They also believe that the positive public relations gained by socially responsible companies will make the company more attractive to customers and potential employees.

Bebbington (2007) argues that more than just reporting is required: companies should build sustainability into their management control systems so that it can be planned and its performance monitored. Riccabone and Leone (2010) describe the case of Procter and Gamble (P&G) who have built the issue of sustainability into the organisation through four themes:

- delight the customer with sustainable innovations;
- improve the environmental profile of its operations;
- develop social responsibility programmes; and
- equip P&G workers to build sustainability thinking into their everyday work.

They conclude that by doing this the company have gone a long way to making sustainability issues part of the 'business as usual' of the organisation.

Governance and control

Richard Walton (1985) pointed out that managers have to choose between a strategy based on imposing control and one based on eliciting commitment. He argues that the latter is consistent with recognising employees as stakeholders in the organisation, and is likely to lead to higher performance, especially in situations requiring them to use imagination and creativity in an uncertain business environment. He concludes that organisations must develop a culture of commitment if they are to meet customer expectations with respect to quality, delivery and market changes. More recently this type of stakeholder thinking has expanded to include the customer in the organisational performance management system. This is most common in industries such as defence and construction where large and complex projects are carried out and there needs to be a high degree of interaction along the supply chain throughout the duration of the relationship. Here it is important to establish common inter-company performance measures which govern behaviour in-line with commonly accepted objectives.

Internationalisation

Many markets are now international with more companies than ever operating across geographical boundaries. While communications technology can facilitate this type of organisation it has consequences for the control of the organisation. Dispersed companies have all the control issues of local companies but some are amplified.

There is a strategic issue about how much central control to impose, and how much to encourage local autonomy and responsiveness. If part of the reason for success has been the ability of local companies to act entrepreneurially, then implementing a control system that imposes greater central control would be counter-productive.

For reasons of remoteness, head office has comparatively few opportunities to use direct control and supervision, which is often a very effective means. Instead it has to rely more on rules and procedures, and a range of formal financial and output controls. An alternative is to try to develop strong cultural controls, which influence people to act in ways that align with corporate aims, irrespective of their location.

As Chapter 4 shows, countries have developed substantially different management systems, as well as differences of national culture. These factors will affect very significantly how people respond to control systems, as well as raising difficult issues of comparability between the reports for different countries, and the interpretations to be placed upon them.

Summary

1 **Define control and explain why it is an essential activity in managing**

- Control is the counterpart of planning and is the process of monitoring activities to ensure that results are in-line with the plan and taking corrective action if required.
- Organisational control ensures that operational processes remain consistent, repeatable and reliable.

2 **Describe and give examples of the generic control activities of setting targets, measuring, comparing and correcting**

- Setting targets gives direction to an activity and sets standards of acceptable performance.
- Measuring involves deciding what measures to use and how frequently.
- Comparing involves selecting suitable objects for comparison, and the time period over which to do it.
- Correcting aims to rectify a deviation from plan either by altering activities or changing the objectives.

3 **Discuss strategies and tactics used to gain and maintain control**

- Control systems exist on a spectrum where the extremes are mechanistic and organic.
- Mechanistic approaches are likely to be suitable in stable environments or in support of cost leadership strategies.
- Organic approaches are likely to be suitable in unstable environments or in support of differentiation strategies.
- Organisations can use a combination of direct supervision, organisational structure, rules and procedures, management by objectives, machinery, HRM practice and values and beliefs to maintain control.

4 **Explain how the choice of suitable measures of performance can help in managing the organisation**

- Managers can use either input process or output measures to control the organisation.
- The balanced scorecard supplements measures of financial performance with those of customer satisfaction, internal process, and innovation and growth which all play a part in an overall assessment of performance.

- Control systems must be matched to the overall model that the organisation is being managed with in relation to the competing values framework.

5 **Explain why those designing performance measurement and control systems need to take account of human reactions**

- Control depends on influencing people, so is only effective if it takes account of human needs.
- Controls can encourage behaviour that is not in the best interests of the organisation.
- Controls can encourage people to supply the system with inaccurate information.
- People will resist controls that they feel threaten their ability to satisfy their needs from work.

6 **Show how ideas from the chapter add to your understanding of the integrating themes**

- While more companies are reporting on their sustainability record, they will only make a difference when they include sustainability criteria in their routine management control systems, so that it becomes part of 'business as usual' for staff.
- Governance and control systems need to be supported by a culture of commitment if they are to affect behaviour at the operating level.
- Remoteness makes it difficult for international companies to exercise genuine control over distant units, however sophisticated the information technology: cultural controls may be more effective.

Review questions

1 Explain why control is important.
2 Is planning part of the control process?
3 Describe the four steps in the control process.
4 Explain how the balanced scorecard was an improvement on earlier performance measurement systems.
5 Give an original example of a measure in each quadrant of the balanced scorecard.
6 Explain how input, process and output measures differ.
7 Explain why the competing values framework can help in designing a control and performance management system.
8 What are the implications for those designing a control system of Lawler's work on control?
9 Summarise an idea from the chapter that adds to your understanding of the integrating themes.

Concluding critical reflection

Think about the way your company, or one with which you are familiar, seeks to control performance. Review the material in the chapter, and perhaps visit some of the websites identified. Then make notes on the following questions:

- What examples of the themes discussed in this chapter are currently relevant to your company? What types of controls are you most closely involved with? Which of the techniques suggested do you and your colleagues typically use and why? What techniques do you use that are not mentioned here?
- In responding to these issues, what **assumptions** about the nature of control appear to guide your approach? Do the assumptions take account of, say, the competing values framework or the balanced scorecard?
- What factors in the **context** of the company appear to shape your approach to control – is the balance towards a mechanistic or an organic approach, and is that choice suitable for the environment in which you are working?

- What **alternative** approaches to planning have you identified in your work on this chapter? Would any of them possibly make a useful contribution to your organisation?
- Has the chapter highlighted any possible **limitations** in the control systems used in your organisation? Have you considered, for example, if there is too much control, or too little? Have you compared your control processes with those in other companies?

Further reading

Kaplan, R.S. and Norton, D.P. (1992) 'The balanced scorecard: Measures that drive performance', *Harvard Business Review*, vol. 70, no. 1, pp. 71–79.

The original writing on balanced scorecards as performance management tools.

Kaplan, R.S. and Norton, D.P. (2004) *Strategy Maps: Converting intangible assets to tangible outcomes*, Harvard, Boston, MA.

Classic text illustrating how balanced scorecards link performance measurement with operational and corporate strategy showing how a performance management system can ensure both operational and strategic control.

Kaplan, R.S. and Norton, D.P. (2008) *The Execution Premium: Linking strategy to operations for competitive advantage,* Harvard, Boston, MA.

Brings balanced scorecards, performance measurement and management control right up to date, linking them all to show how they can be used to create competitive advantage.

Simons, R. (1995a), 'Control in an age of empowerment', *Harvard Business Review*, vol. 73, no. 2, pp. 80–88.

A review of the range of control strategies which managers can use, showing the range of alternatives.

Weblinks

These websites illustrate the themes of the chapter, and in the Part Case:

www.apple.com
www.tesco.com

Visit any company website and go to the section in which the company reports on its performance:

- What financial measures do they report on most prominently?
- From the chairman's and/or chief executive's reports, what other measures have they been using to assess their performance?

For video case studies, audio summaries, flashcards, exercises and annotated weblinks related to this chapter, visit **www.pearsoned.co.uk/mymanagementlab**

CHAPTER 20

FINANCE AND BUDGETARY CONTROL

Aims

To show why organisations need finance, where it comes from, how its use should be controlled and why financial measures are critical indicators of performance.

Objectives

By the end of your work on this chapter you should be able to outline the concepts below in your own terms and:

1 Describe the role of the finance function in management
2 Interpret basic financial reports
3 Explain the difference between profit and cash
4 Appreciate the importance of financial results in evaluating performance
5 Explain how budgets are important as a management control mechanism
6 Discuss the differences between functional and project-based budgeting
7 Show how ideas from the chapter add to your understanding of the integrating themes.

Key terms

This chapter introduces the following ideas:

capital market
limited liability company
shareholders
cash flow statement
assets
profit and loss statement
balance sheet

fixed assets
current assets
liabilities
shareholders' funds
work breakdown structure
cost breakdown structure

Each is a term defined within the text, as well as in the Glossary at the end of the book.

BASF Group www.basf.com

BASF is one of the world's leading chemical companies, with production sites in 41 countries and customers spread across the world. The head office and main chemical processing complex is located at Lugwigshafen, Germany. The group comprises more than 160 subsidiaries and affiliates. Its main product groups are chemicals, plastics and products for the agricultural industry. It also engages in oil and gas exploration and production.

A main objective of the company is to earn a premium on its cost of capital to ensure profitable growth, thereby giving it a competitive advantage in gaining access to international capital markets. The pursuit of profit has to be achieved while recognising the importance of the principles of sustainable development, combining economic success with environmental protection and social responsibility. BASF's shares are listed in the Dow Jones Sustainability Index. Research and development is at the heart of the group's efforts to retain its competitive position.

BASF has successfully developed highly integrated processing plants to use resources and materials to maximum advantage. Waste and by-products are used as inputs to other processes. Pipe networks facilitate efficient, safe and environmentally friendly transfer of resources. They describe this integration as *Verbund*.

The hazardous nature of the industry demands the highest safety standards. Risk identification, measurement and control are most important. The *Verbund* system minimises undesirable emissions, but also benefits BASF customers. The group maintains close relationships with its customers to find mutually beneficial solutions to their problems. Reward systems for employees are as closely related to corporate objectives as possible, especially by using a measure known as earnings before interest on capital and taxation (EBIT).

© BASF Aktiengesellschaft

A summary of the BASF operating (profit) report for year ended 31 December 2009 is:

	€ millions
Sales	**50,693**
Less cost of sales	36,682
Gross profit on sales	**14,011**
Selling expenses	5,667
General and administrative expenses	1,133
Research and development expenses	1,398
Other items	2,734
Operating profit before tax (EBIT)	**3,079**
Less taxation	1,424
Minority interests	245
Net income	**1,410**

Source: *Company Annual Report*, 2008–2009.

Case questions 20.1

- What was the company's profit in the year to 31 December 2009?
- What proportion of its sales revenue was spent on research and development?

20.1   Introduction

In the financial year that ended on 31 December 2009, BASF made a profit of €1,410 million from its activities. This 'headline' figure is a very crude measure of the effectiveness with which the managers have run the company over the year. The problem for investors is how to assess this performance. Is it consistent with the stated targets of the company? Does the way it has been achieved bode well for the future by, for example, investing in research that will bring returns in later years? Investors will also want to know how these broad summary figures relate to the work of managers and staff within the firm – are they motivated and organised in ways that encourage them to produce good returns in the future?

Similar questions arise about the annual report of any firm. Investors and financial analysts continually evaluate a company's financial performance against its objectives and against comparable businesses. They try to judge its prospects, and how effectively managers are doing their jobs. Much of the information is qualitative and subjective, designed to create a favourable impression and positive expectations.

Chapter 1 describes organisations as aiming to add value to the resources they use. It is crucial to the success of an organisation that it has the appropriate resources and that these are well managed to achieve the results that stakeholders expect. Most companies depend on people in the external environment for the funds they need to grow the business. The main source of information for people outside the business who wish to assess its performance and prospects is the company's annual report to shareholders. This contains a great deal of financial and other data – but is more subjective than at first appears. It is important to know how financial performance is measured, and the assumptions that people make in constructing the figures. It is also important to know how these financial measures relate to the performance of those working within the firm.

The chapter begins by explaining why companies need the capital market and how they communicate with it. A major link in that process is the annual report, so the chapter then explains important parts of that document. The chapter goes on to show how these figures, which are intended mainly for investors outside the organisation, influence and are themselves influenced by processes of internal planning and control. It finishes by looking inside the company at how financial targets are planned for and achieved.

20.2   The world outside the organisation

The pressures on companies to perform

Many people reading this book will be expecting to start a career that they hope will provide an income to support an attractive lifestyle. Few will be thinking about retirement or the need to support themselves after their working lives have ended. This may be a sombre subject to introduce, but it is fundamentally important to understanding the financial environment in which organisations operate.

> **Activity 20.1   Identifying shareholders**
>
> Obtain a copy of the annual report and accounts for Marks & Spencer and Mothercare for the year ended 1 April 2010. What can you discover about the shareholders in the companies?
>
> Reports are available on their websites; **www.marksandspencer.com** and **www.mothercare.com**

Investment companies such as pension funds and life assurance companies expect to pay their investors an acceptable income or lump sum when they retire. The funds can only do this if they invest contributions successfully, and investors naturally expect their premiums to be invested profitably by fund managers. These companies compete with each other, and the rewards for success, and consequent growth in contributions from investors, are high. There is pressure on the fund managers to perform well by identifying good investment opportunities, which is also in the investors' best interests as eventual pensioners. The fund managers will be looking for good investment opportunities in companies that are profitable and well managed. In order to attract money into its business to enable it to expand, management needs to demonstrate to the capital market that it is a profitable and successful business.

The fund managers in the **capital market** expect management to operate their businesses profitably. So this pressure from the external capital market directly affects the organisation and all employees. There may be some periods of low or negative profitability (losses) and the capital markets know that but continual losses will eventually lead to failure, as a company will simply run out of money and fail to meet its financial obligations. So the pressures to perform that managers and employees feel originate outside the organisation. However, as many employees are investors and all are future pensioners dependent on the performance of fund managers, those pressures serve their long-term interests (Coggan, 2002).

> The **capital market** comprises all the individuals and institutions that have money to invest, including banks, life assurance companies and pension funds and, as users of capital, business organisations, individuals and governments.

Within an organisation it is unlikely that managers, apart from those at the top, will feel the direct pressure from outside. Yet, as the chapter shows, this external pressure does affect the expectations that top managers have of those below them. These expectations are gradually transmitted down the organisation, so all staff experience them in some way, even if indirectly. The pressures can be considerable as the senior managers expect to be rewarded with the opportunity to purchase shares in the company at a favourable price at some future time (share or stock options). Sometimes this pressure leads to dubious practices and alleged fraud, designed to enhance the share price, as in the recent cases of Enron and Parmalat. This has brought considerable pressure from regulators to improve corporate governance and the quality of financial reporting.

Raising capital

If you have looked at the annual report of Marks & Spencer or Mothercare you will have discovered that life assurance companies and pension funds are major shareholders. They are just one of the many sources from which large organisations raise capital.

A large public company can raise money by issuing shares to people and institutions that respond to a share issue. The main benefit is to enable companies to finance large-scale activities. The shareholders appoint the directors who are ultimately responsible for managing the company. A shareholder is entitled to vote at general meetings in accordance with the number of shares owned. Once the shareholders have paid for their shares in full they cannot generally be required to pay more money into the company, even if it fails.

The affairs of companies are governed by company law, in some countries administered by a government body such as the Securities and Exchange Commission in the US, and by the body governing the share market, such as the Bourse in France and the Stock Exchange in the UK. Before a company can invite the public to subscribe for shares it has to be registered with the national financial regulators and fulfil a number of requirements. The first step after registration, in order to raise money, is to issue a prospectus which explains the history of the company, what it plans to do as a business, and what it plans to do with the money raised.

If the business is small it will not invite the public to buy shares. The promoters will contribute their own money, most likely in sufficient amount to ensure that they have control (more than 50 per cent of the shares). The amount of capital available to the company in these circumstances will be limited to the money the founders can afford to contribute. They may go to a bank to seek finance, but the willingness of a bank to lend will also depend on the amount subscribed by the shareholders.

Banks, fund managers and investors will contribute only if they believe that it is a sound, well-managed business that is likely to make a profit. The investors have many investment opportunities, they will not invest in a company that will not reward them for the risk they are taking by investing money. The amount of return they expect will be related to the risk – the greater the risk the greater the required return.

Activity 20.2   Borrowing money

- Find out the interest rate at which you could borrow money to (a) buy a car, (b) buy a house or (c) spend on your credit card. Can you explain what you discover?

A **limited liability company** has an identity and existence in its own right as distinct from its owners (shareholders in Europe, stockholders in North America). A shareholder has an ownership right in the company in which the shares are held.

Shareholders are the principal risk takers in a company. They contribute the long-term capital for which they expect to be rewarded in the form of dividends – a distribution from the profit of the business.

A **limited liability company** gives a business access to large amounts of capital, but at the same time allows some protection to the **shareholders**, as they cannot be held liable for the debts of the business in the event of its financial failure. This limited liability means that investors can contribute capital knowing that only their invested capital, and not their private and personal assets, is at risk. This risk is why investors expect a higher return than they would receive if they put their money in a bank or in government securities, where the risk is virtually zero.

20.3   Reporting financial performance externally

Because a company has access to capital in this form there has to be regulation. The Companies Act is the principal instrument of control, with the addition of the Stock Exchange for those listed as public companies within the UK. A most important requirement is to provide information about the performance of the business from time to time (Elliott and Elliott, 2006). The capital markets and indeed anyone that is thinking of investing in a company need to understand how the company is performing and financial measures provide a sort of company 'health check', indicating how well the company is being controlled by the management. This health check is detailed most comprehensively in the company's annual report. Among other things the annual report includes financial information of three distinct types: the cash flow statement, the profit and loss (or income) statement, and the balance sheet.

Activity 20.3   Reading an annual report

Obtain a copy of a company annual report and list the kind of information that you find in it, for example financial, product, people and management.

A **cash flow statement** shows the sources from which cash has been generated and how it has been spent during a period of time.

Cash flow statement

The easiest to understand of the three types of statement is the cash flow, which shows where cash has come from and how it has been spent. The following is a simplified summary of the **cash flow statement** for Marks and Spencer plc for the year ended 28 March 2009.

	£ millions
Net cash inflow from operating activities	1,371.9
Payment of taxation	(81.3)
Net cash inflow from operating activities	1,290.6
Cash flows from investing activities	
Capital expenditure and financial investment	(609.6)
Interest received	12.7
Net cash (outflow) on investing activities	(596.9)
Cash flows from financing activities	
Interest paid	(197.1)
Other debt financing	66.2
Equity dividends paid	(354.6)
Other equity financing	(35.6)
Net cash outflow from financing activities	(521.1)
Net cash inflow from all activities (above)	172.6
Effect of exchange rate changes	7.8
Opening net cash	117.9
Net closing cash	298.3

In the ordinary course of successful business it might be expected that the cash received from trading (selling products or services) should be greater than the cash spent to purchase components, supplies, labour, energy and all the other resources combined to secure the sales. The cash surplus could then be reinvested to help finance expansion and some of it paid to the shareholders as dividend on their investment. Their original contribution remains in the company, however, as part of the continuing capital base. In the case of Marks and Spencer plc there was an increase in cash of £172.6 million after paying dividends, making interest payments and investing in new **assets**.

The idea of a cash surplus being the essential requirement for success is appealing but unfortunately too simplistic. Taking as an example a motor vehicle manufacturer, a car has to be designed and tested, components sourced from suppliers, production lines prepared and cars distributed to dealers before any of the cars can be sold – so there will be very heavy cash outflows before cash starts to come in. This process may take a couple of years. In some industries, such as pharmaceuticals and chemicals, investments in continuing research and development may take ten years or longer before cash begins to flow back, and then only if the research is successful.

> **Assets** are the property, plant and equipment, vehicles, stocks of goods for trading, money owed by customers and cash: in other words, the physical resources of the business.

Much the same thing occurs in new technology based service companies such as eBay as they have to invest heavily in building their website and in advertising to make people aware that they exist before cash begins to flow in. It would be highly unlikely in these conditions for the business to show a cash surplus in periods when it is making such heavy investment.

Activity 20.4   Measuring R&D expenditure

Look at the annual report for BASF (www.basf.com), Siemens (www.siemens.com), Solvay (www.solvay.com) or any large manufacturing business, and find out what it tells you about research and development. List the projects that the report mentions. What does the report say about the length of time before the projects will be profitable?

It is impossible to draw sensible conclusions about the company's financial performance on the basis of cash flow alone. Not only is the annual surplus or deficit influenced by major investment, but other infrequent events, such as a major restructuring exercise following a new strategy, could also distort the impression.

The profit and loss statement

A **profit and loss statement** reflects the benefits derived from the trading activities of the business during a period of time.

The **profit and loss statement** (or income statement) is designed to overcome the limitations of a cash flow statement, although cash has the important characteristic of complete objectivity. Cash flows can be observed, measured and verified. Profit measures are subjective.

The profit after taxation and the profit retained in the business are quite different from the cash surplus reported in the cash flow statement. This is because the profit statement is not based on cash but on business transactions that (a) may result in cash transactions in the future, or (b) reflect cash transactions from previous periods.

Sales may be credit sales that approved customers may pay for later. Cost of goods sold may include the purchase of goods that will be paid for in the next financial year. Operating expenses will include depreciation which, with other terms, is explained below.

Case questions 20.2

Refer to the summary income statement for BASF.

- Calculate the gross profit as a percentage of sales.
- Calculate the operating profit before tax as a percentage of sales.

Activity 20.5   Calculating and comparing profit

Look at the annual report of a company in a similar line of business to M&S.

- Calculate the gross profit in a recent year as a percentage of sales.
- Calculate the profit before tax as a percentage of sales.
- How does the company compare on these measures against M&S?
- Is there a major difference in the items in the profit statements of the two companies?

Depreciation

Depreciation is a major cause of the difference between cash flow and profit. Think about the investments mentioned in relation to motor vehicle production. Apart from occasional modifications, the same basic model may be produced and sold for several years. So the initial investment to develop the design and make the cars should be spread over the life of the investment and will be subtracted from sales revenue in each year. This process is called depreciation. The idea is simple, but there are several estimates required before the annual amount can be measured.

Depreciation is based on the original cost of the investment, including set-up and training, less the expected scrap value at the end of its life. Hence an estimate must be made of the life of the investment, the residual value and the initial cost, which itself is open to conjecture. To make matters worse there are at least four methods of spreading the cost over the lifespan. The simplest is to allocate an equal amount each year. Assets may also be periodically revalued to take account of changes in their fair value (the present value of expected future cash flows, or the expected market price less selling costs if it were to be sold) that then becomes the base for calculating depreciation. In both circumstances, if the fair value is less than the amount already allowed for depreciation, then the difference must be charged as an expense and subtracted from revenue. This reduction in value is described as impairment.

Credit

Most products are not sold for cash but on credit, sometimes for an extended period of time. A retail store might offer generous credit terms in order to promote sales – 'nothing to pay for six months' or 'easy terms over nine months' are familiar promotional devices. Suppose that the company's financial year ends on 31 December and that a customer is buying a personal computer at the end of October on nine months' credit of equal monthly payments. Should the company report the full value of the sale, the three instalments that the customer has paid, or nothing until the PC has been paid for in full? It is usual practice to report the full amount, as the business has a legal contract to force the customer to pay. The idea is fine, but experience shows that not all customers will pay in full. There will be bad debts. An estimate of doubtful debts has to be made before arriving at profit.

Warranty claims

If a problem arises with a product sold under warranty it will be replaced or fixed, but at a cost to the manufacturer. The cost of repairing under warranty has to be estimated because warranty claims may not be made within the same financial year as the sale.

These are simple examples of subjectivity in profit measurement. There are others, but these are sufficient to illustrate that the measure of profit cannot be said to be totally accurate. It is an approximation. Nevertheless, it is the main indication of trading performance measured in financial terms. The question remains, how well does profit reflect good performance? To evaluate this, profit needs to be related to the amount of investment in the business.

Measuring periodic performance

Both the cash flow and the profit statements relate to a period of time – conventionally to a financial or trading year. It is usual for large organisations also to produce brief reports on their performance quarterly or half-yearly.

Just how much profit is desirable has to be considered in relation to the investment in a business. Therefore a measure of investment is needed with which to compare periodic profit. If an investor can invest in risk-free government securities for a guaranteed minimum return, an investment in a risky company that does not offer at least the same expectation of reward would not be considered. So the return, or ratio of profit to investment, would be expected to be higher for a risky than for a risk-free investment. The rate of return required for a particular investment has to be assessed by comparing alternative investment opportunities and their rates of return.

How can the investment base be measured? The obvious base is the amount of the initial investment. If you deposit money in a bank deposit account it will attract interest. At the end of the year you can measure the rate of return by expressing the interest earned for the year as a percentage of the initial investment. If you leave the interest in the account the following year, the investment base would be increased by the amount of interest reinvested. The initial investment plus the interest you earned in the first year now becomes a part of the capital base, as you chose not to withdraw it. The investment base can grow over time. Much the same happens in a business. Profit is generated, some is distributed as a cash dividend and the balance, usually the larger proportion, is retained in the business to finance expansion.

A simple measure of the capital base with which to compare profit appears to be the amount of capital originally contributed plus profit that is retained and added each year to the base.

Another way to look at it, for companies listed on the Stock Exchange, is to relate the profit or earnings per share to the share price. This approach recognises that a successful business will grow and develop a good reputation, reflecting the result of professional management and reliable, high-quality products. If you own shares in such a company you would expect the value of those shares to increase to reflect the success of the business. You would continue to hold the shares only as long as the return, based on the price at which you could sell the shares in the market, is at least equal to that from an alternative investment with similar risk.

A **balance sheet** shows the assets of the business and the sources from which finance has been raised.

The balance sheet

The annual report that shows the capital base of a business is the **balance sheet**. The BASF balance sheet at 31 December 2009 is shown in the next instalment of the case study.

Case study   **BASF Group – the case continues** www.basf.com

Group balance sheet as at 31 December 2009

Assets	€ millions	
Intangible (patents, licences, goodwill)	10,449	
Property, plant and equipment (at cost after depreciation deducted)	16,285	
Financial assets	4,947	
Total long-term assets		31,681
Current assets		
Inventories	6,776	
Accounts receivable from customers and others	7,738	
Other liquid assets (including cash)	5,073	
Current assets		19,587
Total assets		51,268
Shareholders' equity	18,609	
Long-term liabilities	20,979	
Accounts payable and other short-term liabilities	11,680	
Total equity and liabilities		51,268

Fixed (long-term) assets are the physical properties that the company possesses – such as land, buildings, production equipment – which are likely to have a useful life of more than one year. There may also be intangible assets such as patent rights or copyrights.

Current assets can be expected to be cash or to be converted to cash within a year.

The balance sheet reveals two separate but related aspects of the business.

First are the assets categorised as either **long-term (fixed) assets** or **current assets**. These include the physical resources such as property, buildings, machinery, computers, stocks (or inventories) of raw materials, work in progress and completed products, money owed by customers, and cash.

Second are the **liabilities** or the sources of finance that have enabled the business to acquire its assets. Finance (or capital) comes from shareholders by way of contributions for shares when they are first issued, together with retained profits from successful operations as previously explained. This is the shareholders' capital (or **shareholders' funds**). In addition there will usually be money borrowed from a bank and possibly from other sources as well. The sum total of the shareholders' funds and liabilities will equal (or balance with) the amount of assets. The former represents the source from which the finance has been raised. The latter shows the destination or the physical resources in which the capital has been invested. Assets and liabilities are divided into two categories: current, applying to those that are expected to be traded within a year; and non-current, expected to remain in the business longer than a year.

The shareholders are the main risk takers and the profit is attributable to them. Therefore, to measure the efficiency with which the funds are used, it is usual to measure the *rate of return on equity* – the profit after tax divided by shareholders' funds. However, there are many imperfections in the measure, one of which is the fact that goodwill will not usually be included as an asset unless it appears following the purchase of another business. Brands and names such as the title of a newspaper or the name of a consumer product can only be included if they were purchased. They may not be included if internally generated. This apparent inconsistency may be surprising. Accountants argue that newspaper mastheads, or brand names, could be sold separately from the business, whereas goodwill can only be sold with the business as a whole. Goodwill arises when one company is taken over by another for a price greater than the value of the tangible and separately identified intangible assets such as brand names, minus the liabilities (net worth). Further difficulties in measuring a rate of return arise from problems in measuring depreciation and, consequently, asset values, changes in price levels and share values.

> **Liabilities** of a business as reported in the balance sheet are the debts and financial obligations of the business to all those people and institutions that are not shareholders, e.g. a bank or suppliers.
>
> **Shareholders' funds** are the capital contributed by the shareholders plus profits that have not been distributed to the shareholders.

Case question 20.3

- Refer to the summary financial information for BASF. Calculate the rate of return (after tax) on equity (shareholders' funds).

The discussion of the profit statement explained that depreciation in particular is an expense item that was difficult to measure. It represents an attempt to estimate the proportion of the cost of using long-term assets that is attributable to a particular accounting period. Any of the cost that has not already been subtracted in the profit statement remains to be subtracted in the future.

The estimate of doubtful debts subtracted from customers' outstanding accounts (debtors or accounts receivable), estimated warranty claim costs (in a manufacturing company), estimated pension fund liabilities, the value of goodwill, brands or other intangible assets are all highly subjective measures. Furthermore, the accounting policies may well differ between companies even though they are in the same industry. So the aggregate amount shown in the balance sheet for assets is not necessarily a reflection of market values.

Activity 20.6   Comparing accounting policies

Look at the annual reports for two or three companies in the same industry, or in similar industries, and read the section called accounting policies. Make a list of practices that seem to be different.

Share values

While the numbers reflected in the statements discussed are one method of gauging the performance of a company, there is another way of approaching the question of performance measurement. If you were thinking of buying shares in the market through the Stock Exchange, you would consider the likely future returns in relation to the price you would have to pay for the shares. You will therefore be comparing different investment opportunities and will attempt to choose the one that offers the best return for whatever degree of risk you are prepared to accept. The return you expect would be an estimate of future dividends plus the likely growth in the share price, and you would relate this to the price you would have to pay to buy the shares. If the potential investment offered a greater expected return than shares you already hold (assuming the same degree of risk), not only would you be interested in buying the new shares, but you would also be inclined to sell your existing shares to buy new ones to increase your return. It would be rational for all investors in this position to behave in the same way. The consequence of this action should be clear. Selling pressure for the shares of one company would drive the price down to the point at which investors would be indifferent as to which company's shares they purchased, as they would tend to offer the same expected return. This process, known as arbitraging, is likely to happen in a well-organised and efficient market (Ross *et al.*, 2005).

So the measure of performance that shareholders are likely to adopt will not be directly related to the company's financial reports, but more to the financial markets. They will be comparing expected returns with the prices of securities (shares) in the market. This does not mean that financial reports from companies do not serve any useful purpose. They do, because they provide some of the information that helps the traders in shares to assess the likely returns from these companies in the future and, above all, provide information about past performance and recent financial position. While share prices in the market are directly influenced by buying and selling pressure, the expectations that give rise to those pressures come in part from the financial reports.

Companies whose shares do not offer returns consistent with those of competitors are likely to become takeover targets with bids from stronger, more efficient performers. Company directors have to watch their share price, as unexpected movements might signal activity in the market that they ought to know about. For example, if another company is actively buying shares in the market and so raising the price, this might indicate they are planning a takeover bid. If a large shareholder is selling shares, thus pushing the price down, does this mean performance in the company has fallen short of expectations? In both circumstances the directors need to find out what they can about the market activities in order to take defensive action.

The directors and senior managers of a company cannot ignore what is going on in the markets outside their business. They operate in markets, some specific to their own activities, and some general – the capital and labour markets. Their performance is being evaluated all the time and they need to know what the buyers and sellers in the financial markets are thinking. Financial managers will be watching the share price. They have to convert external pressures from the market into pressure for internal action. This is what financial management is about.

20.4 Managing financial performance internally

Gaining financial control of the business

Most managers and employees can do little on their own to influence externally reported performance measures. Nevertheless, everything that happens in the business will have some financial impact. So management needs systems to ensure that the financial consequences of decisions are understood and that the operational plan is adhered to. An organisation cannot wait until the accountant prepares a financial report at the end of the year to see whether it has been profitable or not – by then it is too late. Profit does not just happen. It has to be planned and then controlled to ensure that the plan is executed. (Horngren *et al.*, 2005). The main control mechanism is called budgeting.

Activity 20.7   Preparing a budget

Prepare a simple cash budget for your own finances for next month. You will need to consider the cash you have available from savings in the past, how much cash you expect to receive during the month and what you plan to spend.

The budgeting process usually begins at the top level, when the directors set budgetary targets for business performance. Simple top-level targets may be revenue (sales) and profit. These targets need to be translated into other targets that have meaning at the operating levels.

Management in practice   **Babcock International Group objectives**

This company operates in a range of markets including transport, estates management, defence and energy; therefore the corporate objectives must be relevant to all the divisions to provide an overall direction. A few of its strategic objectives shown are:

- to be top three in the market place;
- to provide a technical service supporting the customer's assets and operations;
- to sustain annual double digit growth at a minimum of 6 percent operating profit;
- to maintain an excellent safety record.

Note the third bullet point – here the top management are setting clear financial targets in relation to growth and profit which will become the basis of the budgeting system as they flow down through the organisation.

Source: Company website.

Budgeting by department

Companies are typically structured into departments such as purchasing, design, production and human resources. Each will be independently managed yet they must be co-ordinated to ensure that all work to achieve the required corporate financial targets. Each function has control over certain parts of the financial jigsaw. Production will have control over the cost of manufacturing activities; purchasing must negotiate prices for supplies of material or components; sales will be responsible for revenue generation; and human resources may be responsible for agreeing salaries. Although managed independently, each depends on the others. The simplest example of this interdependence is in production volumes and the costs associated with economies of scale. Manufacturing costs will vary depending on how well the sales department does its job. More sales mean larger production volumes and so lower costs per unit. Manufacturing budgets will have been based on projected sales, but these are often hard to predict: as with all plans, the outcome may be different.

Management in practice   **The Scottish Parliament**

The Scottish Parliament opened in October 2004 at a cost of £416 million. It was originally budgeted at £40 million, but costs continually rose:

- 17 June 1999 – £109 million: increase by £69 million due to consultancy fees, site costs, demolition, VAT, archaeology work, risk and contingencies.
- 5 April 2000 – £195 million: increase by £86 million for no apparent reason.
- November 2001 – £241 million: increase by £86 million due to design changes resulting from a changed brief.
- December 2002 – £295 million: increase by £54 million due to upgraded security requirement for bombproof cladding.
- July 2003 – £374 million: increase of £79 million partially due to consutancy fees but again unclear.
- September 2003 – £400 million: increase of 26 million due to construction problems in the building interior.
- February 2004 – £416 million: increase of £16 million due to further problems with construction.

Analysis shows a number of reasons for the overspend, the main ones being:

1 Poor budget-setting at the outset due to misunderstanding of what was required and insufficient knowledge of costs.
2 Poor control of spend throughout the project due to lack of understanding of budgeting methods.
3 Lack of a planning and management control system of which cost control was a part.

Sources: *Management of the Holyrood Building Project*, Audit Scotland, June 2004; *House of Commons Research Paper – Building the Scottish Parliament, The Holyrood Project,* House of Commons Library, December 2005.

Without a plan there is no sense of direction or clarity of purpose in the organisation. The process of budget preparation in itself is a useful exercise but it should be done as part of the larger business planning process. Not only does it enable the various parts of an organisation to relate their activities to others, but it is also a valuable co-ordination device helping the various parts of the organisation focus on the same objectives.

The length of the planning cycle depends on the type of product or service being delivered. It may be no more than a couple of months or it could be years. Companies can fail as they grow, simply because the rate of growth outpaces their ability to generate cash. For example, money may be spent purchasing machinery for a production line before any revenue is generated from the sale of the product produced by the machinery.

The simplest budgets are those that are allocated by function, as shown in Table 20.1. In this method, cost is allocated to cover the work carried out within the functional areas.

Some budgets are less specific and need to be spread across the organisation normally as a proportion allocated to each function or area. Examples of these are the:

- **overhead budget** – showing the consumption of resources that cannot be identified with particular functions, e.g. energy and utilities, directors fees; and
- **capital budget** – showing planned spending on new equipment, buildings and acquisitions of other companies.

Once each budget is negotiated and agreed, it becomes part of the operational control system. Each budget will be allocated to a responsible senior manager who will typically distribute it throughout their subordinate managers. A production director may split the budget between machining budget held by the machining manager and the assembly budget by the assembly manager.

Project budgeting

Setting budgets for departments allows an analysis of their costs over a period, but not product and/or activity. A design department may require the production department to build

Table 20.1 Functional budget allocation

Budget	Function	Cost or revenue bearing activities
Sales	Sales and marketing	Sale of product to customer
Materials and parts	Purchasing	Buying parts and material from suppliers
Design and development	Design	Engineering, prototype building, testing, analysis
Manufacturing	Production	Assembly, testing, inspection, packing

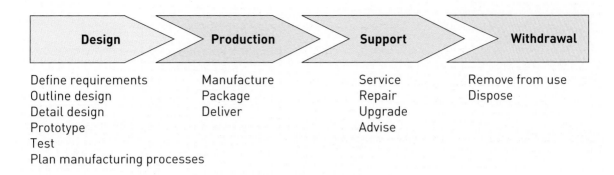

Figure 20.1 A project lifecycle

prototypes or purchasing to buy material for testing. If each department is allocated a yearly budget then it will be difficult to see how much was actually spent on the activities that comprised the design work for a product. Project-based costing tries to overcome this, by using the project lifecycle shown in Figure 20.1.

Each phase must have a budget, but must also have input from other units. This method of budgeting breaks the work into packages that are not necessarily based in one department. This is called a **work breakdown structure** (Gray and Larson, 2008). The mechanism for budgeting and cost collection is called the **cost breakdown structure** and this is based on allocating cost to the packages of work in the work breakdown structure. This means costs can be analysed by work activity rather than by organisational unit.

Project-based costing systems are used by companies that have several products, each following its own lifecycle: a car company will typically have some models in development, some in production, and some no longer made but which still require support and service. Departments will be working on all of these, and allocating their costs not only to the product but to the activity. Figure 20.2 shows a small extract from a cost breakdown structure for an aircraft design and build programme.

Costs will be allocated to the activity rather than the function, and each function will have a budget for work on that activity.

For example, the planning of the production processes may be carried out by production engineering which are part of the production function, but this activity must be done during the development phase of the project because the production processes must be available before the production run begins. Another example is the requirements capture which will be carried out by personnel from across marketing, design and engineering, and production functions, as skills in each area are required to do the job correctly. It is important to understand the cost of each activity so that on completion lessons can be learned for the next product.

While project management methodology, of which cost breakdown structures are a part, is commonly thought of in relation to large products such as buildings and oil rigs, it is useful in any industry where functions 'overlap' on phases of activity. A mobile phone, although small and inexpensive, still has to be designed before it can be produced in volume and the same cross-functional co-operation (and cost management) is needed. Cost breakdown structures are especially useful in very integrated forms of organisation such as matrix structures (Chapter 10) or project teams where the functional distinctions have become almost a secondary feature of the organisation.

The issues of accounting across periods of time (mentioned previously) are also eased with activity-based cost allocation using a cost breakdown structure. It is critical that a budget is set for each phase so that the company knows whether it has overspent or not before moving onto the next phase. Design and development phases are typically all cost, with no income generated. In some cases, especially the design of a unique product for a specific customer, the customer pays instalments towards the cost as the design progresses. In the defence industry the government pays as contractors complete specified stages of work.

A **work breakdown structure** is a system for categorising work activity based on phases or packages of work rather than the unit that is performing the work.

A **cost breakdown structure** is a system for categorising and collecting costs, which allows cost to be attributed and analysed by activity rather than unit.

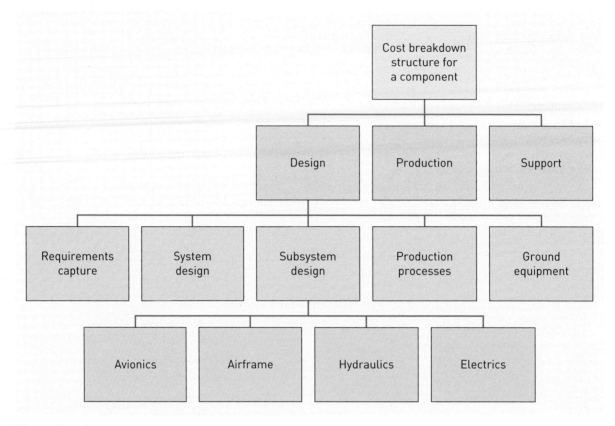

Figure 20.2 Cost breakdown structure

When the product is in full production there is less need for a cost breakdown structure, as costs are generated mainly by the manufacturing function. But, even here, should a problem arise due to a design flaw, design staff must intervene to solve it and the costs of this shown as part of the design cost. An example of this is shown in the following Management in Practice describing the Toyota recall. In this example a design problem was uncovered after many cars had been produced and sold. The cost to rectify is not a production or service cost but is part of the design cost.

Management in practice **Toyota 'brakes' budget**

In early 2010 Toyota announced a product recall across a number of its car types due to a design fault with the anti-lock braking system (ABS).

The ABS, in normal operation, engages and disengages rapidly (many times per second) as the control system senses and reacts to tyre slippage. Some 2010 model year Prius and HS 250h owners had reported experiencing inconsistent brake feel during slow and steady application of brakes on rough or slick road surfaces when the ABS was activated.

Toyota responded to owner concerns with a modification to the design of the ABS system to improve its response time and overall sensitivity to tyre slippage. However, to install this modification all affected cars had to be recalled.

In separate but coincidental issues, Toyota also had to recall vehicles due to problems with the power steering system and the accelerator.

Toyota estimated the cost of these changes in the region of £1.3 billion.

Sources: *The Times* 5 February 2010 an article by R. Lea; Company website.

20.5　Other budgeting considerations

Employee performance

The behaviour of managers can be seriously influenced by the budgeting process in an organisation. If this is authoritarian and unthinking in manner it may lead to suboptimal performance. The pressure to meet budget may be translated into action that is against long-term interests. For example, a salesperson might institute a price increase in the coming month to achieve a short-term sales target.

In some organisations the immediate reaction to employees who fail to achieve budget is negative. Poor budgetary adherence may not be the employees' fault so before taking action it is important to check first whether the budget was intelligently set and if the employees had been given the resources to achieve it. Consistent failure to achieve budget should first lead to a review of the budget to ensure that the targets are fair and achievable. Only then should there be an attempt to take remedial action to improve an activity. The successful use of budgets depends on those affected, managers and staff alike, developing a sense of ownership towards them. As conditions change, the budget should be revised so that it continues to be credible.

A budget is, in essence, short term – usually for no more than one year. Nevertheless it has to be set in a longer-term context and be consistent with the strategy for the future development of the organisation. Long-term investments in research and development, product and market development, new plant and equipment or even the acquisition of other businesses have to be included in the short-term budget, and cash requirements in the cash budget.

Decision making

The one certainty in any organisation is that conditions will change. The budget cannot be revised every time minor changes occur or fresh opportunities arise. An organisation has to be flexible and responsive. Frequently opportunities arise that require prompt action; for example, a special order for a normal product or service that is to be sold at a low promotional price into a new market. In these circumstances the normal measurement of the average cost of producing and delivering the service may be an inappropriate starting point for computing potential profit. Many of the costs will not change as a result of accepting this opportunity: there will be no further research and development, no requirement to increase productive capacity (assuming that capacity is available) and, possibly, little added labour cost. In these conditions consideration need only be given to the costs that will increase directly as a result of choosing to accept this order: delivery, materials or additional resources consumed.

Suppose that Osram has an opportunity to make and sell electric light bulbs to a new retailer. The decision-making process may be as follows:

- Is there enough manufacturing capacity without having to reduce normal production? If so, there is no need to take account of any additional capital costs.
- Are additional employees required or will existing employees have to work longer? If so, the extra costs will be attributable to this order; otherwise there are no added labour costs.
- Do the bulbs need different packaging? In this case there may be design and printing costs as well as costs of packaging material. The set-up costs will have to be included.

The important issue is to identify costs that are directly traceable and attributable to this opportunity. The normal average cost of producing light bulbs may be irrelevant, since that includes the amortised cost of research and development, capital equipment and administrative overheads that will not necessarily increase with this order.

Undoubtedly the retailer is looking for a special price, lower than that which Osram might normally charge. If this price exceeds the identified cost it may be an attractive opportunity. Suppose that the normal selling price is 80 cents and that the usual cost is made up (per unit) as follows:

	Cents
Labour	10
Materials	20
Packaging	5
Delivery	3
Overheads	25
	63
Contribution to profit	17
	80

The retailer wants to buy lamps at 60 cents. If we establish that Osram's overheads will not increase, that labour costs will be 8 cents, materials 20 cents and packaging 10 cents, then the appropriate cost per unit will be 38 cents. If additional delivery is $100 per journey for up to 10,000 light bulbs, the design and set-up costs for printing the packaging are $10,000 and the order is for 100,000 bulbs. Is it acceptable to sell at 60 cents?

		Cents
Unit costs:	Labour	8
	Material	20
	Packaging	10
		38
		$
Cost for 100,000		38,000
Delivery cost		1,000
Design, set-up		10,000
Relevant cost		49,000
Revenue		60,000
Contribution to profit		11,000

This appears to be an acceptable sales opportunity as long as it does not erode Osram's normal market and as long as the existing customers do not expect the normal price to be lowered.

It is the job of the cost or management accountant to process financial information quickly in order to assist managers to take decisions of the kind described above – although many accountants may disagree. Accountants are more likely to be useful if they understand the operational processes of the firm and if the budgeting system is set up with an appropriate cost breakdown structure to produce the correct information.

Routine information for managers

Another aspect of internal financial measurement is more routine. Unlike the system of financial reporting for the organisation as a whole, which is geared to the needs of the capital market, internal information has to be related to the needs of the managers. They will be interested in financial measurements related to their own area of responsibility. For example, a marketing manager will need information about groups of products, brands, customers, regions and marketing areas. In research and development, costs accumulating for each project might be compared with research progress to date. This approach runs right through the value chain, recognising that value can be added from research, development and design, through to distribution and customer service. It is not just the manufacturing process or service delivery process that adds value and requires measurement.

20.6   Integrating themes

Sustainable performance

To understand the environmental impact an organisation has and how it should perform more sustainably, some form of measurement must be made. Environmental accounting and its most evolved form sustainability accounting (Elkington, 1993) have been receiving increasing attention as a vehicle for this (Lamberton, 2005). Gray (1993) identifies three different methods of sustainability accounting:

1   Sustainable cost is a measure of the (hypothetical) cost of restoring the Earth to the state it was in prior to an organisation's impact.
2   Natural capital inventory accounting involves the recording of stocks of natural capital over time, with changes in stock levels used as an indicator of the (declining) quality of the natural environment. There are four types of natural capital: (1) critical – the ozone layer, tropical hardwood, etc.; (2) non-renewable/non substitutable – oil, petroleum and mineral products; (3) non-renewable/substitutable – waste disposal, energy usage; and (4) renewable – plantation timber, fisheries.
3   Input–output analysis which accounts for the physical flow of materials and energy inputs, and product and waste outputs in physical units. It aims to measure all material inputs to the process, and outputs of finished goods, emissions, recycled materials and waste for disposal.

By using a combination of these techniques some attempt can be made by companies to control their operational performance in a sustainable way.

Governance and control

One consequence of competitive conditions is that managers at the top of the organisation feel under great pressure to meet the expectations of stakeholders, especially shareholders in the main financial institutions. These external pressures affect the expectations that top managers have of those below them, and these are gradually transmitted down the organisation, so that all staff experience them in some way, even if indirectly. The pressures can be considerable as the senior managers expect to be rewarded with the opportunity to purchase shares in the company at a favourable price.

Sometimes this pressure leads to dubious practices and alleged fraud designed to enhance the share price, as in the case of Enron (Chapter 19) and Parmalat (Chapter 5). This has brought considerable pressure from regulators to improve corporate governance and the quality of financial reporting.

Internationalisation

Different legal systems, industry financing, taxation systems, structure of the accounting profession, language and traditions mean that financial reporting varies between countries. France, Germany, Portugal, Spain and Japan have historically required compliance with a rigid framework for financial reporting (Alexander and Nobes, 2004). This is now changing as international financial reporting standards (IFRS) are being introduced in more than 90 countries, having started the process in 2005.

IFRS should help to overcome the difficulties of comparing the financial performance of companies in different countries and promote their access to international capital markets. As organisations develop stronger alliances and co-operative arrangements, at both the strategic and operational levels, the role of the accountant is expanded beyond the limits of the organisation within which he/she works. Co-operation in the supply chain can result in improved performance for both organisations involved. To achieve benefits of cost reduction and/or improved profitability through quality improvement, there has to be an open relationship and trust between the organisations. Accountants play a role in this co-operation by advising on the financial consequences for both organisations (Atkinson *et al.*, 2006).

Summary

1 Describe the role of the finance function in management

- It must choose between investment opportunities.
- Shareholders expect management to invest in projects to add shareholder value.
- Management requires adequate financial information.
- The finance function offers a system for assessing the financial consequences of decisions in a relatively objective way.
- Management is required to communicate financial information about the company to actual and prospective shareholders through the financial reports.

2 Interpret basic financial reports

- Operating profit, EBIT and net profit as a proportion of sales is a useful basis for comparing firms in the same industry and for each firm through time.
- All measures of performance based on accounting numbers are subject to the opinions of those who prepare them.

3 Explain the difference between profit and cash

- Profit is based on accounting interpretation of financial data.
- Cash flow measures actual cash transactions and is less subject to opinion than profit.
- In most businesses a financial plan will show expected sales, costs, resources needed to fulfil the plan, a cash forecast and an expected balance sheet.

4 Appreciate the importance of financial results to evaluate performance

- Owners and shareholders, and the capital market generally, exercise significant influence over managers.
- The capital markets' reaction to reports of financial performance affects the ability of the company to raise capital.
- Financial information also helps to measure management performance internally – actual revenue and expenditure can be compared with the budget.
- Financial information can help control the management of projects, to ensure that what is spent corresponds with what has been planned.

5 Explain how budgets are important as a financial control mechanism

- Budgets support the overall operational plan by providing focus and a financial co-ordination mechanism.
- Budgets ensure that the financial targets set at the top level are flowed down through the organisation to allow each manager to understand his/her responsibilities.

6   Discuss the difference between functional and project-based budgeting

- A functional budget is allocated to a functional manager and defines the cost of all the activities that are carried out within that function.
- A project budget is set using a cost breakdown structure that allocates cost to a phase of the project and activity rather than to a function in the management structure.
- The project budget is more flexible, allowing a greater level of analysis to be carried out on cost of each activity and cost over a time period.

7   Show how ideas from the chapter add to your understanding of the integrating themes

- While companies have historically been required by shareholders to report on performance in financial terms, techniques of sustainability accounting are emerging which enable them to report performance on sustainability criteria in an increasingly objective way.
- Pressure from powerful shareholders for high short-term returns on their investments encouraged much of the excessive risk taking which has in turn been the main stimulus for tighter regimes of governance and control.
- To ensure comparability in the financial reports of companies operating in different jurisdictions, each with unique financial reporting requirements, common international financial reporting standards are now emerging.

Review questions

1   Why do companies have to make a profit? Check the website for Marks & Spencer plc (**www.marksandspencer.com**). What do the directors have to say about profit and recent performance?

2   How is profit measured?

3   Explain why profit is different from cash. Look up any company report on **www.carol.co.uk** and see if you can explain the main difference between profit and cash for the company.

4   What does a balance sheet tell us about an organisation? What can you discover about the activities of BASF (**www.basf.com**) from the balance sheet?

5   Can you explain how the external pressures on a company to generate a profit are translated into internal planning systems? Explain how this occurs in M&S. What is the purpose of a budget?

6   How does a budget operate as a control mechanism?

7   Explain why the financial information prepared for external purposes is not necessarily appropriate for managers.

8   Explain the notion of contribution to the profit of a business. What do the directors of M&S and Morrisons (**www.morrisons.co.uk**) have to say in the 2009 annual reports about sources of profit?

Concluding critical reflection

Think about the ways in which your company, or one with which you are familiar, deals with financial reporting and management accounting matters. Then make notes on the following questions:

- What examples of the issues discussed in this chapter struck you as being relevant to practice in your company?
- To what extent do you experience the external pressures from the financial markets for high performance and for frequent and positive financial statements? To what extent do you feel the financial community has a realistic understanding of your business? Has the need to meet short-term financial targets affected long-term performance (e.g. by affecting investment decisions)?

- Is the budget-setting process conducted fairly, and in a reasonably participative way? Are those who must meet the budgets adequately involved in setting them?

- What factors such as the history or current **context** of the company appear to influence the way the company handles these financial and budgeting processes? Does the current approach appear to be right for the company in its context – or would a different view of the context lead to a more effective approach?

- To what extent are people in your organisation aware of the **limitations** of financial measures of performance? Have they acted to take account of this by, for example, considering some kind of balanced scorecard approach?

Further reading

Gray, C.F. and Larson, E.W. (2008), Project Management: The management process, McGraw-Hill/Irwin, New York.

A broad overview of project management and control of costs.

Horngren, C.T., Datar, S.M. and Foster, G. (2007), *Cost Accounting* (12th edn), Financial Times/Prentice Hall, Harlow.

A standard text that covers all areas of the topic in great detail.

Lamberton, G. (2005), 'Sustainability accounting – a brief history and conceptual framework', *Accounting Forum,* vol. 29, no. 1, pp. 7–26.

A summary of the area of sustainability and accounting.

Ross, S., Westerfield, R. and Jordan, B. (2005), *Fundamentals of Corporate Finance* (7th edn) McGraw-Hill/Irwin, New York.

A sound introduction to principles of corporate finance.

Weblinks

These websites contain material relevant to the chapter:

> www.basf.com
> www.marksandspencer.com
> www.mothercare.com
> www.siemens.com
> www.solvay.com
> www.babcock.co.uk
> www.carol.co.uk
> www.morrisons.co.uk

Visit the websites in the list, or for any other company that interests you, and navigate to the pages which include their annual report or investor relations (see also 'recent trading statements'). Sometimes they may include 'presentations to analysts' (who advise fund managers on investment decisions).

- What kind of information do they include in these pages, and what messages are they trying to present to the financial markets? If performance has been poor, what reasons do they give, and what do they promise to do about it? What implications might that have for people working in the company?

- You could keep the most recent trading statement, and then compare it with the next one, which will be issued in a few months.

- Gather information from the media websites (such as **www.ft.com**) that relate to the companies you have chosen. What stories can you find that indicate something about the financial performance of those companies?

 For video case studies, audio summaries, flashcards, exercises and annotated weblinks related to this chapter, visit **www.pearsoned.co.uk/mymanagementlab**

PART 6 CASE

TESCO
www.tesco.com

In 2010 Tesco employed almost 300,000 people in the UK in over 2,000 stores: despite the recession it was continuing to expand by opening new stores and enlarging existing ones. It also has a rapidly growing business overseas.

Jack Cohen founded Tesco in 1919 as a grocery stall, opening the first store in 1929. He was aware that supermarkets had been successful in the US and tried to introduce the idea to the UK. He opened small self-service stores in 1948, followed by his first self-service supermarket in 1956. The company grew rapidly by acquisition during the 1960s, taking advantage of the ending of the Retail Price Maintenance Act. This prohibited retailers from selling goods at prices below the levels agreed with suppliers, and served to prevent the growth of large, efficient stores.

The Act was abolished in 1964, opening the way for Tesco and similar chains to compete with established retailers (mainly small, family-owned local businesses) on price. Tesco's growth enabled it to buy products from food manufacturers much more cheaply than its smaller rivals.

The business continued to grow, but as consumers grew wealthier they became less attracted by the cheapness Tesco offered. In 1985, Ian MacLaurin became the first CEO from outside the Cohen family, and began to reshape the group's operations. He closed many smaller stores, concentrating instead on larger, suburban outlets. He also centralised the distribution system, offered fresh foods, and own-label brands. By 1992 the company was the second largest supermarket chain in the UK, behind Sainsbury's but ahead of Asda and Safeway.

Terry Leahy became CEO in 1997, having previously been marketing director. From this point business growth accelerated in both scale and scope, moving into new geographical areas and product and service markets including:

- Fuel retailing when in 1997 Tesco and Esso forged an alliance that resulted in petrol stations being attached to stores – ten years later there were over 600 Tesco/Esso stores across the UK.

© Tesco plc

- Financial services which began in 1997 when Tesco Personal Finance launched, in partnership with The Royal Bank of Scotland, supplying credit and insurance products to customers. In 2008 Tesco bought the RBS share of the business and plans to offer a wider portfolio of financial products similar to that offered by the established banks.
- Telecommunications when in 2003 the company launched a UK telecoms division, comprising mobile and home phone products. Then in 2004 it purchased the 'C Two-Network' in Japan and launched a broadband service. Then, in 2007, it took part in a joint venture with O2 to form the Tesco Mobile Virtual Network Operator.

Since the mid-1990s the company has been investing in markets overseas, and by 2009 was active in 14 countries outside of the UK. Over half of the group's space is now overseas, and its strategy reflects the lessons learned in developing that business, including:

- Be flexible – each market is unique and requires a different approach.
- Act local – local customers, cultures and suppliers require a local approach: very few members of the Tesco International team are expatriates.
- Keep focus – to be the leading local brand takes years to achieve.

By 2009 the company employed 468,000 people with over 4,300 stores worldwide including 286,000 staff and 2,280 stores in the UK. In Britain stores are in six formats:

1 Tesco Homeplus – larger store for all DIY and home electrical products.
2 Tesco Onestop – small neighbourhood shop.
3 Tesco Express – local stores selling fresh food, wines, beers and spirits.
4 Tesco Metro – larger stores in city centres offering a range of food, including sandwiches and ready–meals.
5 Tesco Superstore – even larger stores offering a wide range of food and non-food products.
6 Tesco Extra – very large, edge-of-town stores offering the widest range of food and non-food items.

In the year to the end of February 2009 the main financial indicators of performance were as shown in the following table.

	2009	2008
Group revenue (£m)	54,327	47,289
Group profit before tax (£m)	2,954	2,803
Profit for the year (m)	2,166	2,130
Earnings per share (p)	28.92	27.02
Dividend per share (p)	11.96	10.9
Group enterprise value	35,907	37,656
Return on capital employed	13%	12.9%

Source: Tesco Annual Report and Accounts 2009, reproduced with permission from Tesco Stores Limited.

To help in controlling such a large and diverse business, Leahy implemented the concept of the balanced scorecard, adapting the idea and calling it the steering wheel. He said:

> If we are to meet our objectives, the Tesco team needs to work together. Because we need to focus on every aspect of what Tesco does, we use a management tool we call the steering wheel to bring together our work in all areas and measure our performance. It helps us manage Tesco in a balanced way, by covering everything we do, and allows us to plan for the future by setting targets for years to come. The steering wheel literally guides us through our daily running of the company, while allowing us to change to meet customers' demands.

The following table shows the balanced scorecard quadrants, with the key performance indicators upon which Tesco focuses.

Tesco steering wheel

Customer	Operations
Earn lifetime loyalty	Shopping is better for customers
The aisles are clear	Working is simpler for staff
I can get what I want	
The processes are good	The way we operate is cheaper for Tesco
I don't queue	
The staff are great	The way we operate is responsible and safe

People	Finance
We trust and respect each other	Grow sales
My manager supports me to do a good job	Maximise profit
My job is interesting	Maximise our investment
I have the opportunity to get on	

Responsibility for delivering the KPIs was delegated to the relevant business unit. Every Tesco store has its own steering wheel with specific deliverables ranging from strategy to day-to-day work. The KPIs are measured regularly and quarterly reports sent to members of the Board for review, so that they can monitor whether or not the business is on track. The summary report for the company is sent to all store managers, and shared with staff. At the end of each year every KPI is reviewed to determine if that aspect of the objectives has been met. The pay of senior management depends on the achievement of these indicators.

The steering wheel is used to communicate strategy across all levels, to align goals and also to manage overall company performance. There is a high-level corporate steering wheel, functional ones, and one for each store. They shape the objectives of all employees so that each works towards achieving the corporate goals. According to one member of Tesco staff: 'The wheel sets the staff targets for areas like customer relations, people, operations and finance. It lets everyone know exactly what we're working on.'

As well as control of the organisation, Tesco attempts to control its customers. In 1994 Tesco launched its Clubcard scheme, which has over 11 million active holders. Shoppers join the scheme by completing a simple form with some personal information about their age and where they live. Their purchases earn vouchers based on the amount they spend. Every purchase they make at Tesco is electronically recorded, and the data analysed to identify their shopping preferences. This is then used to design a package of special offers which are most likely to appeal to that customer, based on an analysis of what they have bought. These offers are mailed to customers with their quarterly vouchers, and each mailing brings a large increase in business.

More broadly, the data are analysed to identify the kind of person each Clubcard holder is – whether they have a new baby, young children, whether they like cooking and so on. Each product is also ascribed a set of attributes – expensive or cheap? An ethnic recipe or a traditional dish? Tesco own-label or an upmarket brand? The information on customers, shopping habits and product attributes is used to support all aspects of the business.

The database is believed to be the largest holding of personal information about named individuals within the UK. In addition to control, this information has also informed a series of strategic decisions, such as the move into smaller store formats, and the launch of the internet shopping site. It also shaped the development and sale of Tesco mobile phones, pet insurance and the Finest food range.

In 2007 Tesco added a fifth section to the steering wheel labelled 'Community', the purpose being to control its performance in areas such as ethics, environment and waste. In 2009 Tesco increased its commitment to sustainable performance by pledging to become a zero-carbon business by 2050. To achieve this it has set performance targets within the Community section measured by KPIs such as a 50 per cent reduction in infrastructure (stores) emissions by 2020 and a reduction in transportation emissions per case by 50 per cent in five years. Tesco managers hope that by taking significant 'green' initiatives like this the company will become more attractive to a wider range of shoppers, and thus benefit not only the environment but also company sales and profits.

Sources: Published information; company website.

Part case questions

- What are the main problems of control in a company of this sort?
- What benefits do you expect the company will have gained from using the steering wheel?
- What other forms of control can you see being used in this account of the company?
- What can you discover about the movement of the Tesco share price over the past year and the reasons for this?
- What are the main operational problems that Tesco management have to deal with in running the UK business?
- What are the main business processes in Tesco that are crucial to satisfying customer requirements?
- Visit the company website and view some of the current stories about its 'green' policies. What examples can you find of the company encouraging consumers to reduce *their* carbon footprint?

PART 6
SKILLS DEVELOPMENT

To help you develop your skills, as well as knowledge, this section includes tasks that relate the key themes covered in the Part to your daily life. Working through these will help you to deepen your understanding of the topic, and develop skills and insights that you can use in many situations.

Task 6.1   Budgeting

Managers typically have fewer resources than they would like, so need to work with budgets – a tool to help them allocate resources between the various tasks they need to carry out. As a planning tool, budgets help identify what activities are important to the wider task, and how much resource to devote to each. Then, as a control tool, they help people to compare how the resources they have actually used compare with what they planned to use. Managers can then take corrective action if needed.

You can develop your skills of budgeting by working on this task.

1   Identify a project that you need to work on over the next few weeks. It could be a major study assignment or dissertation, a piece of research, a charity or student union activity you are taking part in, or an activity at work. The main criteria are that the job is one that matters to you, and will involve using scarce resources, probably of time and money. It could even be a simple personal budget for the next month.
2   List the resources you will need – your time, other people's time, materials, money, information. Think widely, as the more requirements you can anticipate now, the easier it can be to arrange for them to be available in good time. Also think how much of each you will need, being as realistic as possible: it is probably safer to overestimate what you need than to underestimate.
3   Map out when you will need these resources to be available. Do this by listing the tasks down the left-hand side of a sheet, and time (in weeks) across the top. Then work out when you will start and finish each part of the task, to show when you will need a resource. Along the bottom of the sheet you could include a row for money, indicating the total cost, if any, you will be incurring in each week. Alternatively, use that space to summarise the non-financial resources you will be needing that week (such as time).
4   As you work through the task, note regularly what activities you have completed. This is using the budget as a control tool. Compare the resources you planned to use for that with the resources you have actually used.
5   You may also have to act to ensure the budget is in line with what you planned, or take some other action such as trying to secure more resources or changing the objective.
6   Use any deviations as a basis for learning from the experience. If there is a gap, consider why that is, and whether there are any lessons to draw from it (such as being too optimistic or pessimistic, the power of unexpected events, or the influence of other people having different priorities). Use the results and lessons from this task as a starting point for future budgeting activities.

Task 6.2	Analysing a factory operation

Go to the website for the Cameron Balloons' virtual factory, at **www.bized.ac.uk/virtual/cb/**. Do not confuse it with Cameron Balloons' own commercial website (**www.cameronballoons.co.uk**).

The Cameron Balloons' virtual factory site contains background theory and concepts, as well as information about the company's operations.

Write a two-page report analysing the company by using the ideas in Chapter 20, such as:

- What is the business, and what are the main factors upon which the company competes?
- Which represent order winners and which represent order qualifiers?
- What affects the demand for Cameron Balloons' products and services? How variable is the demand likely to be? How can it be forecast?
- What is the main transformation performed in Cameron Balloons?
- Draw a system diagram for the company.
- What workflow systems do you think will be appropriate for the company – line, cell, functional or concentric?
- How do you think Cameron Balloons should manage resources (human, equipment and materials) to deal with variation in demand?
- What quality management philosophies and techniques are appropriate to use in Cameron Balloons?

You could then use the same framework to analyse another company with which you are familiar, or about which you would like to find out more.

GLOSSARY

Administrative management is the use of institutions and order rather than relying on personal qualities to get things done.

The **administrative model of decision making** describes how people make decisions in uncertain, ambiguous situations.

Ambiguity is when people are uncertain about their goals and how best to achieve them.

Arbitrariness (of corruption) is the degree of ambiguity associated with corrupt transactions.

Assessment centres are multi-exercise processes designed to identify the recruitment and promotion potential of personnel.

Assets are the property, plant and equipment, vehicles, stocks of goods for trading, money owed by customers and cash: in other words, the physical resources of the business.

The **balanced scorecard** is a performance measurement tool that looks at four areas: financial, customer satisfaction, internal processes and innovation, which contribute to organisational performance.

A **balance sheet** shows the assets of the business and the sources from which finance has been raised.

Behaviour is something a person does that can be directly observed.

Behaviour modification is a general label for attempts to change behaviour by using appropriate and timely reinforcement.

The **big five** refers to trait clusters that appear consistently to capture main personality traits: openness, conscientiousness, extraversion, agreeableness and neuroticism.

A **blog** is a weblog that allows individuals to post opinions and ideas.

Bounded rationality is behaviour that is rational within a decision process which is limited (bounded) by an individual's ability to process information.

A **break-even analysis** is a comparison of fixed versus variable costs that will indicate at which point in volume of output it is financially beneficial to invest in a higher level of infrastructure.

Bureaucracy is a system in which people are expected to follow precisely defined rules and procedures rather than to use personal judgement.

A **business plan** is a document that sets out the markets the business intends to serve, how it will do so and what finance is required.

The **capital market** comprises all the individuals and institutions that have money to invest, including banks, life assurance companies and pension funds and, as users of capital, business organisations, individuals and governments.

A **cash flow statement** shows the sources from which cash has been generated and how it has been spent during a period of time.

Centralisation is when a relatively large number of decisions are taken by management at the top of the organisation.

Certainty describes the situation when all the information the decision maker needs is available.

A **channel** is the medium of communication between a sender and a receiver.

Co-creation is product or service development that makes intensive use of the contributions of customers.

Collectivism 'describes societies in which people, from birth onwards, are integrated into strong, cohesive in-groups which . . . protect them in exchange for unquestioning loyalty' (Hofstede, 1991, p. 51).

Communication is the exchange of information through written or spoken words, symbols and actions to reach a common understanding.

Competences are the skills and abilities by which resources are deployed effectively – systems, procedures and ways of working.

Competencies (in HRM) refer to knowledge, skills, ability and other personal characteristics required to perform a job well.

A **competitive environment (or context)** is the industry-specific environment comprising the organisation's customers, suppliers and competitors.

Competitive strategy explains how an organisation (or unit within it) intends to achieve competitive advantage in its market.

Complexity theory is concerned with complex dynamic systems that have the capacity to organise themselves spontaneously.

Concertive control is when workers reach a negotiated consensus on how to shape their behaviour according to a set of core values.

Consideration is a pattern of leadership behaviour that demonstrates sensitivity to relationships and to the social needs of employees.

Content is the specific substantive task that the group is undertaking.

Contingencies are factors such as uncertainty, interdependence and size that reflect the situation of the organisation.

Contingency approaches propose that the performance of an organisation depends on having a structure that is appropriate to its environment.

Control is the process of monitoring activities to ensure that results are in line with the plan and acting to correct significant deviations.

The **control process** is the generic activity of setting performance standards, measuring actual performance, comparing actual performance with the standards, and acting to correct deviations or modify standards.

A **control system** is the way the elements in the control process are designed and combined in a specific situation.

Core competences are the activities and processes through which resources are deployed to achieve competitive advantage in ways that others cannot imitate or obtain.

Corporate governance refers to the rules and processes intended to control those responsible for managing an organisation.

Corporate responsibility refers to the awareness, acceptance and management of the wider implications of corporate decisions.

Corrective action aims to correct problems to get performance back on track.

A **cost breakdown structure** is a system for categorising and collecting costs, which allows cost to be attributed and analysed by activity rather than unit.

A **cost leadership strategy** is one in which a firm uses low price as the main competitive weapon.

The **craft system** refers to a system in which the craft producers do everything. With or without customer involvement, they design, source materials, manufacture, sell and perhaps service.

Creativity is the ability to combine ideas in a unique way or to make unusual associations between ideas.

Critical success factors are those aspects of a strategy that *must* be achieved to secure competitive advantage.

Critical thinking identifies the assumptions behind ideas, relates them to their context, imagines alternatives and recognises limitations.

Culture is a pattern of shared basic assumptions that was learned by a group as it solved its problems of external adaptation and internal integration, and that has worked well enough to be considered valid and transmitted to new members (Schein, 2004, p. 17).

Current assets can be expected to be cash or to be converted to cash within a year.

A **customer-centred organisation** is focused upon, and structured around, identifying and satisfying the demands of its consumers.

Customer relationship management (CRM) is a process of creating and maintaining long-term relationships with customers.

Customer satisfaction is the extent a customer perceives that a product matches their expectations.

Customers are individuals, households, organisations, institutions, resellers and governments that purchase products from other organisations.

Data are raw, unanalysed facts, figures and events.

Decentralisation is when a relatively large number of decisions are taken lower down the organisation in the operating units.

A **decision** is a specific commitment to action (usually a commitment of resources).

Decision criteria define the factors that are relevant in making a decision.

Decision making is the process of identifying problems and opportunities and then resolving them.

Decision support systems help people to calculate the consequences of alternatives before they decide which to choose.

A **decision tree** helps someone to make a choice by progressively eliminating options as additional criteria or events are added to the tree.

Decoding is the interpretation of a message into a form with meaning.

Delegation occurs when one person gives another the authority to undertake specific activities or decisions.

Demands are human wants backed by the ability to buy.

Determinism is the view that the business environment determines an organisation's structure.

Differentiation The state of segmentation of the organisation into subsystems, each of which tends to develop particular attributes in response to the particular demands posed by its relevant external environment.

Differentiation strategy consists of offering a product or service that is perceived as unique or distinctive on a basis other than price.

Disintermediation Removing intermediaries such as distributors or brokers that formerly linked a company to its customers.

A **divisional structure** is when tasks are grouped in relation to their outputs, such as products or the needs of different types of customer.

Dynamic capabilities are an organisation's abilities to renew and recreate its strategic capabilities to meet the needs of a changing environment.

e-business refers to the integration, through the internet, of all an organisation's processes from its suppliers through to its customers.

e-commerce refers to the activity of selling goods or service over the internet.

Economies of scale are achieved when producing something in large quantities reduces the cost of each unit.

Effectiveness is a measure of how well an activity contributes to achieving organisational goals.

Efficiency is a measure of the inputs required for each unit of output.

Emergent strategies are those that result from actions taken one by one that converge in time in some sort of consistency pattern.

Encoding is translating information into symbols for communication.

Enlightened self-interest is the practice of acting in a way that is costly or inconvenient at present, but which is believed to be in one's best interest in the long term.

Enterprise resource planning (ERP) is a computer-based planning system which links separate databases to plan the use of all resources within the enterprise.

An **Entrepreneur** is someone with a new venture, project or activity, and is usually associated with creative thinking, driving innovation and championing change.

Equity theory argues that perception of unfairness leads to tension, which then motivates the individual to resolve that unfairness.

Escalating commitment is a bias which leads to increased commitment to a previous decision despite evidence that it may have been wrong.

Ethical audits are the practice of systematically reviewing the extent to which an organisation's actions are consistent with its stated ethical intentions.

Ethical consumers are those who take ethical issues into account in deciding what to purchase.

Ethical decision-making models examine the influence of individual characteristics and organisational policies on ethical decisions.

Ethical investors are people who only invest in businesses that meet specified criteria of ethical behaviour.

Ethical relativism is the principle that ethical judgements cannot be made independently of the culture in which the issue arises.

Exchange is the act of obtaining a desired object from someone by offering something in return.

An **executive information system** provides those at the top of the organisation with easy access to timely and relevant information.

Existence needs reflect a person's requirement for material and energy.

Expectancy theory argues that motivation depends on a person's belief in the probability that effort will lead to good performance, and that good performance will lead to them receiving an outcome they value (valence).

The **external environment (or context)** consists of elements beyond the organisation – it combines the competitive and general environments.

External fit is when there is a close and consistent relationship between an organisation's competitive strategy and its HRM strategy.

An **extranet** is a version of the internet that is restricted to specified people in specified companies – usually customers or suppliers.

Extrinsic rewards are valued outcomes or benefits provided by others, such as promotion, a pay increase or a bigger car.

Factory production is a process-based system that breaks down the integrated nature of the craft worker's approach and makes it possible to increase the supply of goods by dividing tasks into simple and repetitive processes and sequences which could be done by unskilled workers and machinery on a single site.

Feedback (in communication) occurs as the receiver expresses his or her reaction to the sender's message.

Feedback (in systems theory) refers to the provision of information about the effects of an activity.

Femininity pertains to societies in which social gender roles overlap.

Five forces analysis is a technique for identifying and listing those aspects of the five forces most relevant to the profitability of an organisation at that time.

Fixed (long-term) assets are the physical properties that the company possesses – such as land, buildings, production equipment – which are likely to have a useful life of more than one year. There may also be intangible assets such as patent rights or copyrights.

A **focus strategy** is when a company competes by targeting very specific segments of the market.

Foreign direct investment (FDI) is the practice of investing shareholder funds directly in another country, by building or buying physical facilities, or by buying a company.

Formal authority is the right that a person in a specified role has to make decisions, allocate resources or give instructions.

Formalisation is the practice of using written or electronic documents to direct and control employees.

Formal structure consists of guidelines, documents or procedures setting out how the organisation's activities are divided and co-ordinated.

A **formal team** is one that management has deliberately created to perform specific tasks to help meet organisational goals.

Franchising is the practice of extending a business by giving other organisations, in return for a fee, the right to use your brand name, technology or product specifications.

Functional managers are responsible for the performance of an area of technical or professional work.

A **functional structure** is when tasks are grouped into departments based on similar skills and expertise.

The **general environment (or context)** (sometimes known as the macro-environment) includes political, economic, social technological, (natural) environmental and legal factors that affect all organisations.

General managers are responsible for the performance of a distinct unit of the organisation.

Global companies work in many countries, securing resources and finding markets in whichever country is most suitable.

Globalisation refers to the increasing integration of internationally dispersed economic activities.

A **goal (or objective)** is a desired future state for an activity or organisational unit.

Goal-setting theory argues that motivation is influenced by goal difficulty, goal specificity and knowledge of results.

Groupthink is 'a mode of thinking that people engage in when they are deeply involved in a cohesive ingroup, when the members' striving for unanimity overrides their motivation to realistically appraise alternative courses of action' (Janis, 1972).

Growth needs are those that impel people to be creative or to produce an effect on themselves or their environment.

Heuristics Simple rules or mental short cuts that simplify making decisions.

High-context cultures are those in which information is implicit and can only be fully understood by those with shared experiences in the culture.

Horizontal specialisation is the degree to which tasks are divided among separate people or departments.

Human relations approach is a school of management which emphasises the importance of social processes at work.

Human resource management refers to all those activities associated with the management of work and people in organisations.

Hygiene (or maintenance) factors are those aspects surrounding the task which can prevent discontent and dissatisfaction but will not in themselves contribute to psychological growth and hence motivation.

An **ideology** is a set of integrated beliefs, theories and doctrines that helps to direct the actions of a society.

The **illusion of control** is a source of bias resulting from the tendency to overestimate one's ability to control activities and events.

Incremental innovations are small changes in a current product or process which brings a minor improvement.

People use an **incremental model** of decision making when they are uncertain about the consequences. They search for a limited range of options, and policy unfolds from a series of cumulative small decisions.

Individualism pertains to societies in which the ties between individuals are loose.

Influence is the process by which one party attempts to modify the behaviour of others by mobilising power resources.

An **informal group** is one that emerges when people come together and interact regularly.

Informal structure is the undocumented relationships between members of the organisation that emerge as people adapt systems to new conditions, and satisfy personal and group needs.

Information comes from data that have been processed so that they have meaning for the person receiving it.

Information overload arises when the amount of information a person has to deal with exceeds his/her capacity to process it.

Information richness refers to the amount of information that a communication channel can carry, and the extent to which it enables sender and receiver to achieve common understanding.

Information systems management is the planning, acquisition, development and use of these systems.

Initiating structure is a pattern of leadership behaviour that emphasises the performance of the work in hand and the achievement of production or service goals.

Innovation is usually concerned with product or service development.

An **input measure** is an element of resource that is measured as it is put in to the transformation process.

Instrumentality is the perceived probability that good performance will lead to valued rewards, measured on a scale from 0 (no chance) to 1 (certainty).

Intangible resources are non-physical assets such as information, reputation and knowledge.

Integration is the process of achieving unity of effort among the various subsystems in the accomplishment of the organisation's task.

The **interaction model** is a theory of change that stresses the continuing interaction between the internal and external contexts of an organisation, making the outcomes of change hard to predict.

Internal fit is when the various components of the HRM strategy support each other and consistently encourage certain attitudes and behaviour.

International management is the practice of managing business operations in more than one country.

The **internet** is a web of hundreds of thousands of computer networks linked together by telephone lines and satellite links through which data can be carried.

An **intranet** is a version of the internet that only specified people within an organisation can use.

Intrinsic rewards are valued outcomes or benefits that come from the individual, such as feelings of satisfaction, achievement and competence.

Job analysis is the process of determining the characteristics of an area of work according to a prescribed set of dimensions.

Job characteristics theory predicts that the design of a job will affect internal motivation and work outcomes, with the effects being mediated by individual and contextual factors.

A **joint venture** is an alliance in which the partners agree to form a separate, independent organisation for a specific business purpose.

Key performance indicators (KPIs) are a summarised set of the most important measures of performance that inform managers how well an operation is achieving organisational goals.

Knowledge builds on information and embodies a person's prior understanding, experience and learning.

Knowledge management systems are a type of IS intended to support people as they create, store, transfer and apply knowledge.

Layout planning is the activity that determines the best configuration of resources such as equipment, infrastructure and people that will produce the most efficient process.

Leadership refers to the process of influencing the activities of others towards high levels of goal setting and achievement.

A **learning organisation** is one that has developed the capacity to continuously learn, adapt and change.

Liabilities of a business as reported in the balance sheet are the debts and financial obligations of the business to all those people and institutions that are not shareholders, e.g. a bank or suppliers.

Licensing is when one firm gives another firm the right to use assets such as patents or technology in exchange for a fee.

Lifecycle models of change are those that view change as an activity which follows a logical, orderly sequence of activities that can be planned in advance.

A **limited liability company** has an identity and existence in its own right as distinct from its owners (shareholders in Europe, stockholders in North America). A shareholder has an ownership right in the company in which the shares are held.

Line managers are responsible for the performance of activities that directly meet customers' needs.

Low-context cultures are those where people are more psychologically distant so that information needs to be explicit if members are to understand it.

Management is the activity of getting things done with the aid of people and other resources.

Management as a distinct role develops when activities previously embedded in the work itself become the responsibility not of the employee but of owners or their agents.

Management as a universal human activity occurs whenever people take responsibility for an activity and consciously try to shape its progress and outcome.

Management by objectives is a system in which managers and staff agree their objectives, and then measure progress towards them periodically.

A **management information system** provides information and support for managerial decision making.

Management tasks are those of planning, organising, leading and controlling the use of resources to add value to them.

A **manager** is someone who gets things done with the aid of people and other resources.

A **market offering** is the combination of products, services, information or experiences that an enterprise offers to a market to satisfy a need or want.

Market segmentation is the process of dividing markets comprising the heterogeneous needs of many consumers into segments comprising the homogeneous needs of smaller groups.

Marketing is the process by which organisations create value for customers in order to receive value from them in return.

The **marketing environment** consists of the actors and forces outside marketing that affect the marketing manager's ability to develop and maintain successful relationships with its target consumers.

A **marketing information system** is the systematic process for the collection, analysis and distribution of marketing information.

Marketing intelligence is information about developments in the marketing environment.

The **marketing mix** is the set of marketing tools – product, price, promotion and place – that an organisation uses to satisfy consumers' needs.

Marketing orientation refers to an organisational culture that encourages people to behave in ways that offer high-value goods and services to customers.

Masculinity pertains to societies in which social gender roles are clearly distinct.

A **matrix structure** is when those doing a task report both to a functional and a project or divisional boss.

A **mechanistic structure** means there is a high degree of task specialisation, people's responsibility and authority are closely defined and decision making is centralised.

The **message** is what the sender communicates.

A **metaphor** is an image used to signify the essential characteristics of a phenomenon.

Metcalfe's law states that the value of a network increases with the square of the number of users connected to the network.

A **mission statement** is a broad statement of an organisation's scope and purpose, aiming to distinguish it from similar organisations.

A **model (or theory)** represents a complex phenomenon by identifying the major elements and relationships.

Motivation refers to the forces within or beyond a person that arouse and sustain their commitment to a course of action.

Motivator factors are those aspects of the work itself that Herzberg found influenced people to superior performance and effort.

Multinational companies are managed from one country, but have significant production and marketing operations in many others.

Needs are states of felt deprivation, reflecting biological and social influences.

A **network structure** is when tasks required by one company are performed by other companies with expertise in those areas.

Networking refers to behaviours that aim to build, maintain and use informal relationships (internal and external) that may help work-related activities.

Noise is anything that confuses, diminishes or interferes with communication.

Non-linear systems are those in which small changes are amplified through many interactions with other variables so that the eventual effect is unpredictable.

A **non-programmed (unstructured) decision** is a unique decision that requires a custom-made solution when information is lacking or unclear.

Non-receptive contexts are those where the combined effects of features of the organisation (such as culture or technology) appear likely to hinder change.

Non-verbal communication is the process of coding meaning through behaviours such as facial expression, gestures and body postures.

Observation is the activity of concentrating on how a team works rather than taking part in the activity itself.

An **office automation system** uses several systems to create, process, store and distribute information.

An **open system** is one that interacts with its environment.

Operational plans detail how the overall objectives are to be achieved, by specifying what senior management expects from specific departments or functions.

Operational research is a scientific method of providing (managers) with a quantitative basis for decisions regarding the operations under their control.

Operations management is all of the activities, decisions and responsibilities of managing the production and delivery of products and services.

Operations strategy is the pattern of decisions that shapes the long-term capability of the operation.

An **opportunity** is the chance to do something not previously expected.

Optimism bias is a human tendency to see the future in a more positive light than is warranted by experience.

An **organic structure** is one where people are expected to work together and use their initiative to solve problems; job descriptions and rules are few and imprecise.

An **organisation** is a social arrangement for achieving controlled performance towards goals that create value.

An **organisation chart** shows the main departments and senior positions in an organisation and the reporting relations between them.

Organisation structure 'The structure of an organisation [is] the sum total of the ways in which it divides its labour into distinct tasks and then achieves co-ordination among them' (Mintzberg, 1979).

Organisational change is a deliberate attempt to improve organisational performance by changing one or more aspects of the organisation, such as its technology, structure or business processes.

Organisational performance is the accumulated results of all the organisation's work processes and activities.

Organisational readiness refers to the extent to which staff are able to specify objectives, tasks and resource requirements of a plan appropriately, leading to acceptance.

An **output measure** is a measurement taken after an operational process is complete.

Outsourcing (offshoring) is the practice of contracting out defined functions or activities to companies in other countries that can do the work more cost-effectively.

The **participative model** is the belief that if people are able to take part in planning a change they will be more willing to accept and implement the change.

A **perceived performance gap** arises when people believe that the actual performance of a unit or business is out of line with the level they desire.

Perception is the active psychological process in which stimuli are selected and organised into meaningful patterns.

Performance imperatives are aspects of performance that are especially important for an organisation to do well, such as flexibility and innovation.

Performance-related pay involves the explicit link of financial reward to performance and contributions to the achievement of organisational objectives.

A **person culture** is one in which activity is strongly influenced by the wishes of the individuals who are part of the organisation.

A **personality test** is a sample of attributes obtained under standardised conditions that applies specific scoring rules to obtain quantitative information for those attributes that the test is designed to measure.

Pervasiveness (of corruption) represents the extent to which a firm is likely to encounter corruption in the course of normal transactions with state officials.

PESTEL analysis is a technique for identifying and listing the political, economic, social, technological, environmental and legal factors in the general environment most relevant to an organisation.

Philanthropy is the practice of contributing personal wealth to charitable or similar causes.

Planning is the iterative task of setting goals, specifying how to achieve them, implementing the plan and evaluating the results.

A **planning system** refers to the processes by which the members of an organisation produce plans, including their frequency and who takes part in the process.

A **policy** is a guideline that establishes some general principles for making a decision.

Political behaviour is 'the practical domain of power in action, worked out through the use of techniques of influence and other (more or less extreme) tactics' (Buchanan and Badham, 1999).

Political models reflect the view that organisations are made up from groups with separate interests, goals and values, and that these affect how they respond to change.

Political risk is the risk of losing assets, earning power or managerial control due to political events or the actions of host governments.

Power is 'the capacity of individuals to exert their will over others' (Buchanan and Badham, 1999).

A **power culture** is one in which people's activities are strongly influenced by a dominant central figure.

Power distance is the extent to which the less powerful members of organisations within a country expect and accept that power is distributed unevenly.

Preferred team roles are the types of behaviour that people display relatively frequently when they are part of a team.

Prior hypothesis bias results from a tendency to base decisions on strong prior beliefs, even if the evidence shows that they are wrong.

A **problem** is a gap between an existing and a desired state of affairs.

A **procedure** is a series of related steps to deal with a structured problem.

A **process control system** monitors and controls variables describing the state of a physical process.

A **process measure** is a measurement taken during an operational process that provides data on how the process is performing.

The **product lifecycle** suggests that products pass through the stages of introduction, growth, maturity and decline.

A **profit and loss statement** reflects the benefits derived from the trading activities of the business during a period of time.

A **programmed (or structured) decision** is a repetitive decision that can be handled by a routine approach.

Project managers are responsible for managing a project, usually intended to change some element of an organisation or its context.

A **psychological contract** is the set of understandings people have regarding the commitments made between themselves and their organisation.

Radical innovations are large game changing developments that alter the competitive landscape.

The **range of variation** sets the acceptable limits within which performance can vary from standard without requiring remedial action.

The **rational model of decision making** assumes that people make consistent choices to maximise economic value within specified constraints.

Real goals are those to which people give most attention.

Receptive contexts are those where features of the organisation (such as culture or technology) appear likely to help change.

Reintermediation Creating intermediaries between customers and suppliers, providing services such as supplier search and product evaluation.

Relatedness needs involve a desire for relationships with significant other people.

Representativeness bias results from a tendency to generalise inappropriately from a small sample or a single vivid event.

Responsibility refers to a person's duty to meet the expectations others have of them in their role.

Risk refers to situations in which the decision maker is able to estimate the likelihood of the alternative outcomes.

A **role** is the sum of the expectations that other people have of a person occupying a position.

A **role culture** is one in which people's activities are strongly influenced by clear and detailed job descriptions and other formal signals as to what is expected from them.

A **rule** sets out what someone can or cannot do in a given situation.

Satisficing is the acceptance by decision makers of the first solution that is 'good enough'.

Scenario planning is an attempt to create coherent and credible alternative stories about the future.

Scientific management: the school of management called 'scientific' attempted to create a science of factory production.

Selective attention is the ability, often unconscious, to choose from the stream of signals in the environment, concentrating on some and ignoring others.

A **self-managing team** operates without an internal manager and is responsible for a complete area of work.

A **sensitivity analysis** tests the effect on a plan of several alternative values of the key variables.

Shareholders are the principal risk takers in a company. They contribute the long-term capital for which they expect to be rewarded in the form of dividends – a distribution from the profit of the business.

Shareholders' funds are the capital contributed by the shareholders plus profits that have not been distributed to the shareholders.

Situational (contingency) models of leadership attempt to identify the contextual factors that affect when one style will be more effective than another.

The **social contract** consists of the mutual obligations that society and business recognise they have to each other.

Social networking sites use internet technologies which enable people to interact within an online community to share information and ideas.

A **socio-technical system** is one in which outcomes depend on the interaction of both the technical and social subsystems.

A **span of control** is the number of subordinates reporting directly to the person above them in the hierarchy.

The **span of processes** is the variety of processes that a company chooses to carry out in-house.

Staff managers are responsible for the performance of activities that support line managers.

Stakeholders are individuals, groups or organisations with an interest in, or who are affected by, what the organisation does.

Standard of performance is the defined level of performance to be achieved against which an operations actual performance is compared.

Stated goals are those which are prominent in company publications and websites.

Stereotyping is the practice of consigning a person to a category or personality type on the basis of his/her membership of some known group.

A **strategic business unit** consists of a number of closely related products for which it is meaningful to formulate a separate strategy.

Strategic misrepresentation is where competition for resources leads planners to underestimate costs and overestimate benefits, to increase the likelihood that their project gains approval.

A **strategic plan** sets out the overall direction for the business, is broad in scope and covers all the major activities.

Strategy is about how people decide to organise major resources to enhance performance of an enterprise.

Structural choice emphasises the scope which management has to decide the form of structure, irrespective of environmental conditions.

Structure is the regularity in the way a unit or group is organised, such as the roles that are specified.

Subjective probability (in expectancy theory) is a person's estimate of the likelihood that a certain level of effort (E) will produce a level of performance (P) which will then lead to an expected outcome (O).

Subsystems are the separate but related parts that make up the total system.

Sustainable performance refers to economic activities that meet the needs of the present population while preserving the environment for the needs of future generations.

A **SWOT analysis** is a way of summarising the organisation's strengths and weaknesses relative to external opportunities and threats.

A **system** is a set of interrelated parts designed to achieve a purpose.

A **system boundary** separates the system from its environment.

Tangible resources are the physical assets of an organisation such as plant, people and finance.

A **target market** is the segment of the market selected by the organisation as the focus of its activities.

A **task culture** is one in which the focus of activity is towards completing a task or project using whatever means are appropriate.

A **team** is 'a small number of people with complementary skills who are committed to a common purpose, performance goals, and approach for which they hold themselves mutually accountable' (Katzenbach and Smith, 1993).

Team-based rewards are payments or non-financial incentives provided to members of a formally established team that are linked to the performance of the group.

Technology is the knowledge, equipment and activities used to transform inputs into outputs.

The **theory of absolute advantage** is a trade theory which proposes that by specialising in the production of goods and services which they can produce more efficiently than others, nations will increase their economic well-being.

Total quality management (TQM) is a philosophy of management that is driven by customer needs and expectations and focuses on continually improving work processes.

A **trait** is a relatively stable aspect of an individual's personality that influences behaviour in a particular direction.

A **transaction** occurs when two parties exchange things of value to each at a specified time and place.

A **transaction processing system (TPS)** records and processes data from routine transactions such as payroll, sales or purchases.

A **transactional leader** is one who treats leadership as an exchange, giving followers what they want if they do what the leader desires.

The **transformation process** the operational system that takes all of the inputs; raw materials, information, facilities, capital and people and converts them into an output product to be delivered to the market.

A **transformational leader** is a leader who treats leadership as a matter of motivation and commitment, inspiring followers by appealing to higher ideals and moral values.

Transnational companies operate in many countries and delegate many decisions to local managers.

Uncertainty is when people are clear about their goals, but have little information about which course of action is most likely to succeed.

Uncertainty avoidance is the extent to which members of a culture feel threatened by uncertain or unknown situations.

Unique resources are resources that are vital to competitive advantage and which others cannot obtain.

User generated content (UGC) is text, visual or audio material which users create and place on a website for others to view.

Valence is the perceived value or preference that an individual has for a particular outcome.

Validity occurs when there is a statistically significant relationship between a predictor (such as a selection test score) and measures of on-the-job performance.

Value is added to resources when they are transformed into goods or services that are worth more than their original cost plus the cost of transformation.

A **value chain** 'divides a firm into the discrete activities it performs in designing, producing, marketing and distributing its product. It is the basic tool for diagnosing competitive advantage and finding ways to enhance it' (Porter, 1985).

Vertical specialisation refers to the extent to which responsibilities at different levels are defined.

Virtual teams are those in which the members are physically separated, using communications technologies to collaborate across space and time to accomplish their common task.

Wants are the form which human needs take as they are shaped by local culture and individual personality.

Wikinomics describes a business culture in which customers are no longer only consumers but also co-creators and co-producers of the service.

A **work breakdown structure** is a system for categorising work activity based on phases or packages of work rather than the unit that is performing the work.

A **working group** is a collection of individuals who work mainly on their own but interact socially and share information and best practices.

REFERENCES

Abrahamson, E. (2004), *Change Without Pain*, Harvard Business School Press, Boston, MA.

Adair, J. (1997), *Leadership Skills*, Chartered Institute of Personnel and Development, London.

Adams, J.S. (1963), 'Towards an understanding of inequity', *Journal of Abnormal and Social Psychology*, vol. 67, no. 4, pp. 422–436.

Adler, P.S. and Borys, B. (1996), 'Two types of bureaucracy: Enabling and coercive', *Administrative Science Quarterly*, vol. 41, no. 1, pp. 61–89.

Ahearne, M., Jones, E., Rapp, A. and Mathieu, J. (2008), 'High touch through high tech: The impact of salesperson technology usage on sales performance via mediating mechanisms', *Management Science*, vol. 54, no. 4, pp. 671–685.

Akkermanns, H.A. and van Oorschot, K.E. (2005), 'Relevance assumed: A case study of balanced scorecard development using system dynamics', *Journal of the Operational Research Society*, vol. 56, no. 8, pp. 931–941.

Alderfer, C. (1972), *Existence, Relatedness and Growth: Human needs in organizational settings*, Free Press, New York.

Alexander, D. and Nobes, C. (2004), *International Introduction to Financial Accounting*, Financial Times/Prentice Hall, Harlow.

Allen, N.J. and Hecht, T.D. (2004), 'The "romance of teams": Toward an understanding of its psychological underpinnings and implications', *Journal of Occupational & Organizational Psychology*, vol. 77, no. 4, pp. 439–461.

Alvarez, S.A. and Barney, J.B. (2005), 'How do entrepreneurs organize firms under conditions of uncertainty?', *Journal of Management*, vol. 31, no. 5, pp. 776–793.

Alvesson, M. and Billing, Y.D. (2000), 'Questioning the notion of feminine leadership: A critical perspective on the gender-labelling of leadership', *Gender, Work and Organization*, vol. 7, no. 3, pp. 144–157.

Amaral, L.A.N. and Uzzi, B. (2007), 'Complex systems – a new paradigm for the integrative study of management, physical, and technological systems', *Management Science*, vol. 53, no. 7, pp. 1033–1035.

Ambec, S. and Lanoie, P. (2008), 'Does it pay to be green? A systematic overview', *Academy of Management Perspectives*, vol. 22, no. 4, pp. 45–62.

Anand, N. and Conger, J.A. (2007), 'Capabilities of the consummate networker', *Organizational Dynamics*, vol. 36, no. 1, pp. 13–27.

Andersen, T.J. (2000), 'Strategic planning, autonomous actions and corporate performance', *Long Range Planning*, vol. 33, no. 2, pp. 184–200.

Anderson, C., Spataro, S.E. and Flynn, F.J. (2008), 'Personality and organizational culture as determinants of influence', *Journal of Applied Psychology*, vol. 93, no. 3, pp. 702–710.

Anderson, L.W. and Krathwohl, D.R. (2001), *A Taxonomy for Learning, Teaching and Assessing: A revision of Bloom's taxonomy of educational objectives*, Longman, New York, NY.

Ansoff, H.I. (1965), *Corporate Strategy*, Penguin, London.

Argenti, P.A. (2004), 'Collaborating with activists: How Starbucks works with NGOs', *California Management Review*, vol. 47, no. 1, pp. 91–116.

Argenti, P.A., Howell, R.A. and Beck, K.A. (2005), 'The strategic communication imperative', *MIT Sloan Management Review*, vol. 46, no. 3, pp. 83–89.

Argyris, C. (1999), *On Organizational Learning*, (2nd edn) Blackwell, Oxford.

Arnolds, C.A. and Boshoff, C. (2002), 'Compensation, esteem valence and job performance: An empirical assessment of Alderfer's ERG theory', *International Journal of Human Resource Management*, vol. 13, no. 4, pp. 697–719.

Atkinson, A., Kaplan, R. and Young, S. (2006), *Management Accounting* (5th edn), Financial Times/Prentice Hall, Harlow.

Babbage, C. (1835), *On the Economy of Machinery and Manufactures*, Charles Knight, London. Reprinted in 1986 by Augustus Kelly, Fairfield, NJ.

Balogun, J., Gleadle, P., Hailey, V.H. and Willmott, H. (2005), 'Managing change across boundaries: Boundary-shaking practices', *British Journal of Management*, vol. 16, no. 4, pp. 261–278.

Barker, J.R. (1993), 'Tightening the iron cage: Concertive control in self-managing teams', *Administrative Science Quarterly*, vol. 38, no. 3, pp. 408–437.

Barnard, C. (1938), *The Functions of the Executive*, Harvard University Press, Cambridge, MA.

Baron, R.A. and Greenberg, J. (1997), *Behavior in Organizations*, Pearson Education, Upper Saddle River, NJ.

Barrett, S.D. (2009), 'EU/US open skies – competition and change in the world aviation market: the implications for the Irish aviation market', *Journal of Air Transport Management*, vol. 15, no. 2, pp. 78–82.

Barthélemy, J. (2006), 'The experimental roots of revolutionary vision', *MIT Sloan Management Review*, vol. 48, no. 1, pp. 81–84.

Bartlett, C.A. and Ghoshal, S. (2002), *Managing Across Borders: The transnational solution*, Harvard Business School Press, Boston, MA.

Baum, J.R. and Locke, E.A. (2004), 'The relationship of entrepreneurial traits, skill and motivation to subsequent venture growth', *Journal of Applied Psychology*, vol. 89, no. 4, pp. 587–598.

Beall, A.E. (2004), 'Body language speaks: Reading and responding more effectively to hidden communication', *Communication World*, vol. 21, no. 2, pp. 18–20.

Beardwell, J. and Claydon, T. (2007), *Human Resource Management: A contemporary approach*, (5th edn) FT/Prentice Hall, Harlow.

Bebbington, J. (2007), *Accounting for Sustainable Development Performance*, CIMA Publishing, Elsevier, London.

Bechet, T.P. and Maki, W.R. (1987), 'Modelling and forecasting focusing on people as a strategic resource', *Human Resource Planning*, vol. 10, no. 4, pp. 209–217.

Beer, M. and Cannon, M.D. (2004), 'Promise and peril in implementing pay-for-performance', *Human Resource Management*, vol. 43, no. 1, pp. 3–48.

Beer, M., Spector, B., Lawrence, P.R., Quinn Mills, D. and Walton, R.E. (1984), *Managing Human Assets*, Macmillan, New York.

Belbin, R.M. (1981), *Management Teams: Why they succeed or fail*, Butterworth/Heinemann, Oxford.

Belbin, R.M. (1993), *Team Roles at Work*, Butterworth/Heinemann, Oxford.

Benders, J., Delsen., L. and Smits, J. (2006), 'Bikes versus lease cars: The adoption, design and use of cafeteria systems in the Netherlands', *International Journal of Human Resource Management*, vol. 17, no. 6, pp. 1115–1128.

Berle, A.A. and Means, G.C. (1932), *The Modern Corporation and Private Property*, The Macmillan Company, New York.

Berlo, D.K. (1960), *The Process of Communication: An introduction to theory and practice*, Holt, Rinehart & Winston, New York.

Berners-Lee, T. (1999), *Weaving the Web*, Orion, London.

Bernoff, J. and Li, C. (2008), 'Harnessing the power of the oh-so-social web', *MIT Sloan Management Review*, vol. 49, no. 3, pp. 36–42.

Biggs, L. (1996), *The Rational Factory*, The Johns Hopkins University Press, Baltimore, MD.

Bjorn-Andersen, N. and Turner, J. (1994), 'Creating the twenty-first century organization: The metamorphosis of Oticon', in R. Baskerville *et al.*, *Transforming Organizations with Information Technology*, Elsevier Science/North-Holland, Amsterdam.

Blackwell, E. (2004), *How to Prepare a Business Plan* (4th edn), Kogan Page, London.

Blake, R.R. and Mouton, J.S. (1979), *The New Managerial Grid*, Gulf Publishing, Houston, TX.

Blakstad, M. and Cooper, A. (1995), *The Communicating Organization*, Institute of Personnel and Development, London.

Blau, P.M. (1970), 'A formal theory of differentiation in organizations', *American Sociological Review*, vol. 35, no. 2, pp. 201–218.

Bloemhof, M., Haspeslagh, P. and Slagmulder, R. (2004), *Strategy and Performance at DSM*, INSEAD, Fontainebleau (Case 304-067-1, distributed by The European Case Clearing House).

Blowfield, M. and Murray, A. (2008), *Corporate Responsibility: A critical introduction*, Oxford University Press, Oxford.

Boddy, D. (2002), *Managing Projects: Building and leading the team*, Financial Times/Prentice Hall, Harlow.

Boddy, D., Boonstra, A. and Kennedy, G. (2009a), *Managing Information Systems: Strategy and organisation* (3rd edn), Financial Times/Prentice Hall, Harlow.

Boddy, D., King, G., Clark, J.S., Heaney, D. and Mair, F. (2009b), 'The influence of context and process when implementing e-health', *BMC Medical Informatics and Decision Making*, vol. 9, no. 9.

Boddy, D., Macbeth, D.K. and Wagner, B. (2000), 'Implementing collaboration between organisations: an empirical study of supply chain partnering', *Journal of Management Studies*, vol. 37, no. 7, pp. 1003–1017.

Boddy, D. and Paton, R.A. (2005), 'Maintaining alignment over the long-term: Lessons from the evolution of an electronic point of sale system', *Journal of Information Technology*, vol. 20, no. 3, pp. 141–151.

Boezeman, E. and Ellemers, N. (2007), 'Volunteering for charity: pride, respect, and the commitment of volunteers', *Journal of Applied Psychology*, vol. 92, no. 3, pp. 771–785.

Boiral, O. (2007), 'Corporate greening through ISO 14001', *Organization Science*, vol. 18, no. 1, pp. 127–146.

Boisot, M.H. (1998) *Knowledge Assets: Securing competitive advantage in the information economy*, Oxford University Press, Oxford.

Bond, S.D., Carlson, K.A. and Keeney, R.L. (2008), 'Generating objectives: Can decision makers articulate what they want?', *Management Science*, vol. 54, no. 1, pp. 56–70.

Bono, J.E. and Judge, T.A. (2004), 'Personality and transformational and transactional leadership: A meta-analysis', *Journal of Applied Psychology*, vol. 89, no. 5, pp. 901–910.

Boulding, W., Staelin, R. and Ehret, M. (2005), 'A customer relationship management roadmap: What is known, potential pitfalls, and where to go', *Journal of Marketing*, vol. 69, no. 4, pp. 155–166.

Bowen, D.E., Ledford, G.E. and Nathan, B.R. (1996), 'Hiring for the organization, not the job', in J. Billsberry (ed.), *The Effective Manager: Perspectives and illustrations*, Sage, London.

Bowen, D.E., Siehl, C. and Schneider, B. (1989), 'A framework for analyzing customer service orientation in manufacturing', *Academy of Management Review*, vol. 14, no. 1, pp. 75–85.

Bozarth, C. (2006), 'ERP implementation efforts at three firms', *International Journal of Operations & Production Management*, vol. 26, no. 11, pp. 1223–1239.

Brettingham, M. (2005), 'Local control over foundation trusts is "rhetoric"', *British Medical Journal*, vol. 330, p. 1408.

Brews, P.J. and Hunt, M.R. (1999), 'Learning to plan and planning to learn: Resolving the planning school/learning school debate', *Strategic Management Journal*, vol. 20, no. 10, pp. 889–913.

Brewster, C. (1994), 'European HRM: Reflection of, or challenge to, the American concept?' in P. Kirkbride (ed.), *Human Resource Management in Europe*, Routledge, London.

Brookfield, S.D. (1987), *Developing Critical Thinkers*, Open University Press, Milton Keynes.

Buchanan, D. (2001), *The Lived Experience of Strategic Change, A hospital case study,* Leicester Business School Occasional Paper 64.

Buchanan, D. and Badham, R. (1999), *Power, Politics and Organizational Change: Winning the turf game*, Sage, London.

Buchanan, D.A. (2008), 'You stab my back, I'll stab yours: Management experience and perceptions of organization political behaviour', *British Journal of Management*, vol. 19, no. 1, pp. 49–64.

Buchanan, D.A. and Huczynski, A.A. (2010), *Organizational Behaviour* (7th edn), Financial Times/Prentice Hall, Harlow.

Buchanan, L. and O'Connell, A. (2006), 'A brief history of decision making', *Harvard Business Review*, vol. 84, no. 1, pp. 32–41.

Burgers, J.H., Van Den Bosch, F.A.J. and Volberda, H.W. (2008), 'Why new business development projects fail: Coping with the differences of technological versus market knowledge', *Long Range Planning*, vol. 41, no. 1. pp. 55–73.

Burns, J.M. (1978), *Leadership*, Harper & Row, New York.

Burns, T. (1961), 'Micropolitics: mechanisms of organizational change', *Administrative Science Quarterly*, vol. 6, no. 3, pp. 257–281.

Burns, T. and Stalker, G.M. (1961), *The Management of Innovation*, Tavistock, London.

Butt, J. (ed.) (1971), *Robert Owen: Prince of cotton spinners*, David & Charles, Newton Abbott.

Byron, K. (2008), 'Carrying too heavy a load? The communication and miscommunication of emotions by email', *Academy of Management Review*, vol. 33, no. 2, pp. 309–327.

Cadbury, A. (1992), *Report of the Committee on the Financial Aspects of Corporate Governance*, Gee and Co. Ltd, London.

Caldwell, R. (2003), 'The changing roles of personnel managers: Old ambiguities, new uncertainties', *Journal of Management Studies*, vol. 40, no. 4, pp. 983–1004.

Carroll, A.B. (1989), *Business and Society: Ethics and stakeholder management*, South Western, Cincinatti, OH.

Carroll, A.B. (1999), 'Corporate social responsibility', *Business and Society*, vol. 38, no. 3, pp. 268–295.

Catmull, E. (2008), 'How Pixar fosters collective creativity', *Harvard Business Review*, vol. 86, no. 9, pp. 64–72.

Chaffey, D. (ed.) (2003), *Business Information Systems* (2nd edn), Financial Times/Prentice Hall, Harlow.

Chandler, A.D. (1962), *Strategy and Structure*, MIT Press, Cambridge, MA.

Chatterjee, S. (2005), 'Core Objectives: Clarity in Designing Strategy', *California Management Review,* vol. 47, no. 2, pp. 33–49.

Cherns, A. (1987), 'The principles of sociotechnical design revisited', *Human Relations*, vol. 40, no. 3, pp. 153–162.

Child, J. (1972), 'Organizational structure, environment and performance: The role of strategic choice', *Sociology*, vol. 6, pp. 1–27.

Child, J. (1984), *Organisation: A guide to problems and practice* (2nd edn), Harper & Row, London.

Child, J. (2005), *Organization: Contemporary principles and practice*, Blackwell Publishing, Oxford.

Child, J., Chung, L. and Davies, H. (2003), 'The performance of cross-border units in China: A test of natural selection, strategic choice and contingency theories', *Journal of International Business Studies*, vol. 34, no. 3, pp. 242–254.

Child, J. and Tsai, T. (2005), 'The dynamic between firms' environmental strategies and institutional constraints in emerging economies: Evidence from China and Taiwan', *Journal of Management Studies*, vol. 42, no. 1, pp. 95–125.

Chung, M.L. and Bruton, G.D. (2008), 'FDI in China: What we know and what we need to study next', *Academy of Management Perspectives*, vol. 22, no. 4, pp. 30–44.

Cober, R.T., Brown, D.J., Keeping, L.M. and Levy, P.E. (2004), 'Recruitment on the net: How do organizational web site characteristics influence?', *Journal of Management*, vol. 30, no. 5, pp. 623–646.

Coggan, P. (2002), *The Money Machine*, Penguin, Harmondsworth.

Colbert, A. E. and Witt, L. A. (2009), 'The Role of Goal-Focused Leadership in Enabling the Expression of Conscientiousness', *Journal of Applied Psychology*, vol. 94, no. 3, pp.790–796.

Colville, I.D. and Murphy, A.J. (2006), 'Leadership as the enabler of strategizing and organizing', *Long Range Planning*, vol. 39, no. 6, pp. 663–677.

Conger, J.A. and Kanungo, R.N. (1994), 'Charismatic leadership in organizations: Perceived behavioral attributes and their measurement', *Journal of Organizational Behavior*, vol. 15, no. 5, pp. 439–452.

Cooke, S. and Slack, N. (1991), *Making Management Decisions* (2nd edn), Prentice Hall, Hemel Hempstead.

Corfield, R. (2009), *Successful Interview Skills*, Kogan Page, London.

Cornelius, P., Van de Putte, A. and Mattia, R. (2005), 'Three decades of scenario planning at Shell', *California Management Review*, vol. 48, no. 2, pp. 92–109.

Crosby, P. (1979), *Quality is Free*, McGraw-Hill, New York.

Culbertson, S.S. (2009), 'Do satisfied employees mean satisfied customers?', *Academy of Management Perspectives*, vol. 23, no. 1, pp. 76–77.

Currie, G. and Proctor, S.J. (2005), 'The antecedents of middle managers' strategic contribution: The case of a professional bureaucracy', *Journal of Management Studies*, vol. 42, no. 7, pp. 1325–1356.

Cusumano, M. (1997), 'How Microsoft makes large teams work like small teams', *MIT Sloan Management Review*, vol. 39, no. 1, pp. 9–20.

Cyert, R. and March, J.G. (1963), *A Behavioral Theory of the Firm*, Prentice Hall, Englewood Cliffs, NJ.

Czarniawska, B. (2004), *Narratives in Social Science Research*, Sage, London.

Dale, B.G. (2007), 'Quality management systems', in B.G. Dale (ed.) *Managing Quality*, Prentice Hall, Harlow.

Daniels, A., Daniels, J. and Abernathy, B. (2006), 'The leader's role in pay systems and organizational performance', *Compensation and Benefits Review*, vol. 38, no. 3, pp. 56–60.

Davenport, T.H. (1998), 'Putting the enterprise into enterprise systems', *Harvard Business Review*, vol. 76, no. 4, pp. 121–132.

Davenport, T.H. and Harris, J.G. (2005), 'Automated decision making comes of age', *MIT Sloan Management Review*, vol. 46, no. 4, pp. 83–89.

Deal, T.E. and Kennedy, A.A. (1982), *Corporate Culture: The rites and rituals of corporate life*, Addison-Wesley, Reading, MA.

Dearstyne, B.W. (2005), 'BLOGS: The new information revolution?', *Information Management Journal*, vol. 39, no. 5, pp. 38–44.

Deery, S., Iverson, R.D. and Walsh, J.T. (2006), 'Towards a better understanding of psychological contract breach: A study of customer service employees', *Journal of Applied Psychology*, vol. 91, no. 1, pp. 166–175.

De Hoogh, A.H.B., Den Hartog, D.N. and Koopman, P.L. (2005), 'Linking the big five-factors of personality to charismatic and transactional leadership: Perceived dynamic work environment as a moderator', *Journal of Organizational Behavior*, vol. 26, no. 7, pp. 839–865.

Delmar, F. and Shane, S. (2003), 'Does business planning facilitate the development of new ventures?', *Strategic Management Journal*, vol. 24, no. 12, pp. 1165–1185.

Deming, W.E. (1988), *Out of the Crisis*, Cambridge University Press, Cambridge.

Devinney, T.M. (2009), 'Is the socially responsible corporation a myth? The good, the bad, and the ugly of corporate social responsibility', *Academy of Management Perspectives*, vol. 23, no. 2, pp. 44–56.

de Wit, B. and Meyer, R. (2004), *Strategy: Process, content and context, an international perspective*, International Thomson Business, London.

Dimbleby, R. and Burton, G. (2006), *More Than Words: An introduction to communication* (4th edn), Routledge, London.

Doganis, R. (2006), *The Airline Business* (2nd edn), Routledge, London.

Donachie, I. (2000), *Robert Owen: Owen of New Lanark and New Harmony*, Tuckwell Press, East Linton.

Donaldson, L. (1995), *Contingency Theory*, Dartmouth, Aldershot.

Donaldson, L. (1996), *For Positive Organization Theory*, Sage, London.

Donaldson, L. (2001), *The Contingency Theory of Organizations*, Sage, London.

Doz, Y. and Kosonen, M. (2008), 'The dynamics of strategic agility: Nokia's rollercoaster experience', *California Management Review*, vol. 50, no. 3, pp. 95–118.

Drucker, P.F. (1954), *The Practice of Management*, Harper, New York.

Drucker, P.F. (1999), *Innovation and Entrepreneurship* (2nd edn), Butterworth-Heinemann, Oxford.

Drummond, H. (1996), *Escalation in Decision-making*, Oxford University Press, Oxford.

Duncan, R.B. (1972), 'Characteristics of organizational environments and perceived environmental uncertainty', *Administrative Science Quarterly*, vol. 17, no. 3, pp. 313–328.

Echikson, W. (2001), 'When big oil gets connected', *Business Week e-biz*, (3 December), pp. 19–22.

Edvardsson, B. and Enquist, B. (2002), 'The IKEA saga: How service culture drives service strategy', *Services Industries Journal*, vol. 22, no. 4, pp. 153–186.

Elkington, J. (1993), 'Coming clean: The rise and rise of the corporate environmental report', *Business Strategy and the Environment*, vol. 2, no. 2, pp. 42–44.

Elliott, B. and Elliott, J. (2006), *Financial Accounting and Reporting* (7th edn), Financial Times/Prentice Hall, Harlow.

Equal Opportunities Commission (2006), *Facts about Women and Men in Great Britain*, EOC, London.

Faraj, S. and Yan, A. (2009), 'Boundary work in knowledge teams', *Journal of Applied Psychology*, vol. 94, no. 3, pp. 604–617.

Fayol, H. (1949), *General and Industrial Management*, Pitman, London.

Feigenbaum, A.V. (1993), *Total Quality Control*, McGraw-Hill, New York.

Feng, K.C., Chen, E.T. and Liou, W.C. (2004), 'Implementation of knowledge management systems and firm performance: An empirical investigation', *Journal of Computer Information Systems*, vol. 45, no. 2, pp. 92–104.

Fiedler, F.E. and House, R.J. (1994), 'Leadership theory and research: A report of progress', in C.L. Cooper and I.T. Robertson (eds), *Key Reviews of Managerial Psychology*, Wiley, Chichester.

Financial Reporting Council (2006), *The Combined Code on Corporate Governance*, FRC, London.

Finkelstein, S. (2003), *Why Smart Executives Fail: And what you can learn from their mistakes*, Penguin, New York.

Finkelstein, S., Whitehead, J. and Campbell, A. (2009a), 'How inappropriate attachments can drive good leaders to make bad decisions', *Organizational Dynamics*, vol. 38, no. 2, pp. 83–92.

Finkelstein, S., Whitehead, J. and Campbell, A. (2009b), *Think Again: Why good leaders make bad decisions and how to keep it from happening to you*, Harvard Business School Press, Boston, MA.

Fleishman, E.A. (1953), 'The description of supervisory behavior', *Journal of Applied Psychology*, vol. 37, no. 1, pp. 1–6.

Fletcher, M. and Harris, S. (2002), 'Seven aspects of strategy formulation', *International Small Business Journal,* vol. 20, no. 3, pp. 297–314.

Floyd, S.W. and Wooldridge, B. (2000), *Building Strategy from the Middle: Reconceptualizing the Strategy Process*, Sage, Thousand Oaks, CA.

Flyvbjerg, B. (2008), 'Curbing optimism bias and strategic misrepresentation in planning: Reference class forecasting in practice', *European Planning Studies*, vol. 16, no. 1, pp. 3–21.

Follett, M.P. (1920), *The New State: Group organization, the solution of popular government*, Longmans Green, London.

Fombrun, C., Tichy, N.M. and Devanna, M.A. (1984), *Strategic Human Resource Management*, Wiley, New York.

Foss, N.J. (2003), 'Selective intervention and internal hybrids: Interpreting and learning from the rise and decline of the Oticon Spaghetti Organization', *Organization Science*, vol. 14, no. 3, pp. 331–349.

Fox, A. (1974), *Man mismanagement*, Hutchinson, London.

Freeman, R.E. (1984), *Strategic Management: A stakeholder approach*, Pitman, Boston, MA.

French, J. and Raven, B. (1959), 'The bases of social power', in D. Cartwright (ed.), *Studies in Social Power*, Institute for Social Research, Ann Arbor, MI.

Friedman, M. (1962), *Capitalism and Freedom*, University of Chicago Press, Chicago, IL.

Friedman, T. (2005), *The World is Flat: A brief history of the globalized world in the 21st century*, Penguin/Allen Lane, London.

Friedman, R.A. and Currall, S.C. (2003), 'Conflict escalation: Dispute exacerbating elements of e-mail communication', *Human Relations*, vol. 56, no. 11, pp. 1325–1347.

Fu, P.P. and Yukl, G. (2000), 'Perceived effectiveness of influence tactics in the United States and China', *Leadership Quarterly*, vol. 11, no. 2, pp. 252–266.

Furst, S.A., Reeves, M., Rosen, B. and Blackburn, R.S. (2004), 'Managing the life cycle of virtual teams', *Academy of Management Executive*, vol. 18, no. 2, pp. 6–20.

Gabriel, Y. (2005), 'Glass cages and glass palaces: Images of organization in image-conscious times', *Organization*, vol. 12, no. 1, pp. 9–27.

Gamble, J., Morris, J. and Wilkinson, B. (2004), 'Mass production is alive and well: The future of work and organization in east Asia', *International Journal of Human Resource Management*, vol. 15, no. 2, pp. 397–409.

García-Morales, V.J., Lloréns-Montes, F.J. and Verdú-Jover, A.J. (2008), 'The effects of transformational leadership on organizational performance through knowledge and innovation', *British Journal of Management,* vol. 19, no. 4, pp. 299–319.

Gebhardt, G., Carpenter, G.S. and Sherry, J.F. (2007), 'Creating a market orientation: A longitudinal, multifirm, grounded analysis of cultural transformation', *Journal of Marketing,* vol. 70, no. 4, pp. 37–55.

Geerlings, W. and vanVeen, K. (2006), 'The future qualities of workforces: A simulation study of the long-term consequencies of minor selection decisions', *International Journal of Human Resource Management*, vol. 17, no. 7, pp. 1254–1266.

George, S. and Weimerskirch, A. (1998), *Total Quality Management*, Wiley, New York.

Germain, D. and Reed, R. (2009), *a book about innocent*, Penguin, London.

Gilbreth, F.B. (1911), *Motion Study: A method for increasing the efficiency of the workman*, Van Norstrand, New York.

Gilbreth, L.M. (1914), *The Psychology of Management*, Sturgis & Walton, New York.

Giraudeau, M. (2008), 'The drafts of strategy: Opening up plans and their uses', *Long Range Planning*, vol. 41, no. 3, pp. 291–308.

Glaister, S. and Travers, T. (2001), 'Crossing London: Overcoming the obstacles to CrossRail', *Public Money & Management*, vol. 21, no. 4, pp. 11–17.

Glassop, L. (2002), 'The organizational benefits of teams', *Human Relations*, vol. 55, no. 2, pp. 225–249.

Govindarajan, V. and Gupta, A.K. (2001), 'Building an effective global business team', *MIT Sloan Management Review*, vol. 42, no. 4, pp. 63–71.

Graham, P. (1995), *Mary Parker Follett: Prophet of management*, Harvard Business School Press, Boston, MA.

Grant, R.M. (1991), 'The resource-based theory of competitive advantage: Implications for strategy formulation', *California Management Review*, vol. 33, no. 3, pp. 114–135.

Grant, R.M. (2003), 'Strategic planning in a turbulent environment: Evidence from the oil majors', *Strategic Management Journal*, vol. 24, no. 6, pp. 491–517.

Grattan, L. and Erickson, T.J. (2007), '8 ways to build collaborative teams', *Harvard Business Review*, vol. 85, no. 11, pp. 100–109.

Gray, C.F. and Larson, E.W. (2008), *Project Management: The management process*, McGraw-Hill/Irwin, New York.

Gray, R. (1993), *Accounting for the Environment*, Chapman, London.

Greenwood, R.G., Bolton, A.A. and Greenwood, R.A. (1983), 'Hawthorne a half century later: Relay assembly participants remember', *Journal of Management*, vol. 9, Fall/Winter, pp. 217–231.

Greer, C.R. (2001), *Strategic Human Resource Management*, Prentice Hall, Englewood Cliffs, New Jersey.

Gronroos, C. (2007), *Service management and marketing: A customer relationship management approach* (3rd edn), Wiley, Chichester.

Groves, K.S. (2005), 'Linking leader skills, follower attitudes, and contextual variables via an integrated model of charismatic leadership', *Journal of Management,* vol. 31, no. 2, pp. 255–277.

Guest, D.E. (1987), 'Human resource management and industrial relations', *Journal of Management Studies*, vol. 24, no. 5, pp. 502–521.

Guest, D.E. (2004), 'The psychology of the employment relationship: An analysis based on the psychological contract', *Applied Psychology*, vol. 53, no. 4, pp. 541–555.

Guler, I. (2007), 'Throwing good money after bad? Political and institutional influences on sequential decision making in the venture capital industry', *Administrative Science Quarterly*, vol. 52, no. 2, pp. 248–285.

Gupta, A.K. and Govindarajan, V. (2000), 'Knowledge management's social dimension: Lessons from Nucor Steel', *Sloan Management Review*, vol. 42, no. 1, pp. 71–80.

Guthrie, D. (2006), *China and Globalization: The social, economic and political transformation of Chinese society*, Routledge, London.

Hackman, J.R. (1990), *Groups that Work (and Those that Don't)*, Jossey-Bass, San Francisco, CA.

Hackman, J.R. and Oldham, G.R. (1980), *Work Redesign*, Addison-Wesley, Reading, MA.

Hackman, J.R. and Wageman, R. (2005), 'A theory of team coaching', *Academy of Management Review*, vol. 30, no. 2, pp. 269–287.

Hagel, J. and Brown, J.S. (2001), 'Your next IT strategy', *Harvard Business Review*, vol. 79, no. 10, pp. 105–113.

Hales, C. (2001), *Managing through Organization*, Routledge, London.

Hales, C. (2005), 'Rooted in supervision, branching into management: Continuity and change in the role of first-line manager', *Journal of Management Studies*, vol. 42, no. 3, pp. 471–506.

Hales, C. (2006), 'Moving down the line? The shifting boundary between middle and first-line management', *Journal of General Management*, vol. 32, no. 2, pp. 31–55.

Hall, E. (1976), *Beyond Culture*, Random House, New York.

Hamm, S. (2007), *Bangalore Tiger*, McGraw-Hill, New York.

Handy, C. (1988), *Understanding Voluntary Organizations*, Penguin, Harmondsworth.

Handy, C. (1993), *Understanding Organizations* (4th edn), Penguin, Harmondsworth.

Hargie, O.D.W. (1997), *Handbook of Communication Skills*, Routledge, London.

Harrison, E.F. (1999), *The Managerial Decision-making Process* (5th edn), Houghton Mifflin, Boston, MA.

Harrison, M. (2005), *Diagnosing Organizations: Methods, models and processes* (3rd edn), Sage, London.

Hartley, J. (ed.) (2008), *Managing to Improve Public Services*, Cambridge University Press, Cambridge.

Harvey, J.B. (1988), 'The Abilene paradox: The management of agreement', *Organizational Dynamics*, vol. 17, no. 1, pp. 17–43.

Hawken, P., Lovins, A.B. and Lovins, L.H. (1999), *Natural Capitalism: The next industrial revolution*, Earthscan, London.

Hayes, N. (2002), *Managing Teams*, Thomson Learning, London.

Hayes, R.H. and Wheelwright, S.C. (1979), 'Link manufacturing process and product lifecycles', *Harvard Business Review*, vol. 57, no. 1, pp. 133–140.

Helgesen, S. (1995), *The Female Advantage: Women's ways of leadership*, Currency/Doubleday, New York.

Heller, R. (2001), 'Inside Zara', *Forbes Global*, 28 May, pp. 24–25, 28–29.

Herzberg, F. (1959), *The Motivation to Work*, Wiley, New York.

Herzberg, F. (1968), 'One more time: How do you motivate employees?', *Harvard Business Review*, vol. 46, no. 1, pp. 53–62.

Herzberg, F. (1987) 'One more time: How do you motivate employees?', *Harvard Business Review*, vol. 65, no. 5, pp. 109–120.

Hill, C.W.L. and Pickering, J.F. (1986), 'Divisionalization, decentralization and performance of large United Kingdom companies', *Journal of Management Studies*, vol. 23, no. 1, pp. 26–50.

Hill, T. (1993), *Manufacturing Strategy Text and Cases*, Macmillan, London.

Hillman, A.J. (2005), 'Politicians on the board of directors: Do connections affect the bottom line?', *Journal of Management*, vol. 31, no. 3, pp. 464–481.

Hinds, P.J. and Pfeffer, J. (2003), 'Why organizations don't "know what they want": Cognitive and motivational factors affecting the transfer of expertise', in M.S. Ackerman, V. Pipet and V. Wulf (eds), *Sharing Expertise beyond Knowledge Management*, MIT Press, Cambridge, MA.

Hodgkinson, G.P., Sadler-Smith, E., Burke, L.A., Claxton, G. and Sparrow, P.R. (2009), 'Intuition in organizations: Implications for strategic management', *Long Range Planning*, vol. 42, no. 3, pp. 277–297.

Hodgkinson, G.P., Whittington, R., Johnson, G. and Schwarz, M. (2006), 'The role of strategy workshops in strategy development processes: Formality, communication, co-ordination and inclusion', *Long Range Planning*, vol. 39, no. 5, pp. 479–496.

Hofstede, G. (1989), 'Organizing for cultural diversity', *European Management Journal*, vol. 7, no. 4, pp. 390–397.

Hofstede, G. (1991), *Cultures and Organizations: Software of the mind*, McGraw-Hill, London.

Hofstede, G. (2001), *Culture's Consequences: Comparing values, behaviors, institutions and organizations across nations*, Sage, London.

Hofstede, G. and Hofstede, G.J. (2005), *Cultures and organizations: Software of the mind* (2nd edn), McGraw-Hill, New York.

Homburg, C., Jensen, O. and Krohmer, H. (2008), 'Configurations of marketing and sales: A taxonomy', *Journal of Marketing*, vol. 72, no. 2, pp. 133–154.

Hopkins, M.S. (2009), 'What the "Green" consumer wants', *MIT Sloan Management Review*, vol. 50, no. 4, pp. 87–89.

Hopkins, M.S. (2009), 'What executives don't get about sustainability', *MIT Sloan Management Review*, vol. 51, no. 1, pp. 35–40.

Horngren, C.T., Foster, G. and Datar, S.M. (2005), *Cost Accounting* (11th edn), Financial Times/Prentice Hall, Harlow.

House, R.J. (1996), 'Path–goal theory of leadership: Lessons, legacy and a reformulation', *Leadership Quarterly*, vol. 7, no. 3, pp. 323–352.

House, R.J., Hanges, P.J., Javidan, M., Dorfman, P.W. and Gupta, V. (2004), *Culture, Leadership and Organizations: The GLOBE study of 62 societies*, Sage, Thousand Oaks, CA.

House, R.J. and Mitchell, T.R. (1974), 'Path–goal theory of leadership', *Contemporary Business*, vol. 3, no. 2, pp. 81–98.

Huczynski, A.A. (2004), *Influencing Within Organizations* (2nd edn), Routledge, London.

Huczynski, A.A. and Buchanan, D.A. (2007), *Organizational Behaviour* (6th edn), Financial Times/Prentice Hall, Harlow.

Humphrey, S.E., Nahrgang, J.D. and Morgeson, F.P. (2007), 'Integrating motivational, social, and contextual work design features: A meta-analytic summary and theoretical extension of the work design literature', *Journal of Applied Psychology*, vol. 92, no. 5, pp. 1332–1356.

Huselid, M.A. (1995), 'The impact of human resource management practices on turnover, productivity and corporate financial performance', *Academy of Management Journal*, vol. 38, no. 3, pp. 635–672.

Ibbott, C. and O'Keefe, R. (2004), 'Transforming the Vodafone/Ericsson relationship', *Long Range Planning*, vol. 37, no. 3, pp. 219–237.

Imai, M. (1986), *Kaizen – the Key to Japan's Competitive Success*, McGraw-Hill, New York.

Iyengar, S.W. and Lepper, M.R. (2000), 'When choice is demotivating: Can one desire too much of a good thing?', *Journal of Personality and Social Psychology*, vol. 79, no. 6, pp. 995–1006.

Iyer, B. and Davenport, T.H. (2008), 'Reverse engineering Google's innovation machine', *Harvard Business Review*, vol. 86, no. 4, pp. 58–68.

Jager, B., Minnie, C., Jager, J. and Welgemoed, M. (2004), 'Enabling continuous improvement: A case study of implementation', *Journal of Manufacturing Technology Management*, vol. 15, no. 4, pp. 315–331.

Janis, I.L. (1972), *Victims of Groupthink*, Houghton-Mifflin, Boston, MA.

Janis, I.L. (1977), *Decision Making: A psychological analysis of conflict, choice and commitment*, The Free Press, New York.

Jantunen, A. (2005), 'Knowledge processing capabilities and innovative performance: An empirical study', *European Journal of Innovation Management*, vol. 8, no. 3, pp. 336–349.

Jennings, D. (2000), 'PowerGen: The development of corporate planning in a privatized utility', *Long Range Planning*, vol. 33, no. 2, pp. 201–219.

Johns, G. (2006), 'The essential impact of context on organizational behavior', *Academy of Management Review*, vol. 31, no. 2, pp. 386–408.

Johnson, G., Langley, A., Melin, L. and Whittington, R. (2007), *Strategy as Practice: Research directions and resources*, Cambridge University Press, Cambridge.

Johnson, G., Scholes, K. and Whittington, R. (2008), *Exploring Corporate Strategy* (8th edn), Financial Times/Prentice Hall, Harlow.

Johnson, J. and Tellis, G.J. (2008), 'Drivers of success for market entry into China and India', *Journal of Marketing*, vol. 72, no. 1, pp. 1–13.

Jones, O. (2000), 'Scientific management, culture and control: A first-hand account of Taylorism in practice', *Human Relations*, vol. 53, no. 5, pp. 631–653.

Jones, R.A., Jimmieson, N.L. and Griffiths, A. (2005), 'The impact of organizational culture and reshaping capabilities on change implementation success: The mediating role of readiness for change', *Journal of Management Studies,* vol. 42, no. 2, pp. 361–386.

Judge, T.A., Piccolo, R.F. and Ilies, R. (2004), 'The forgotten ones? The validity of consideration and initiating structure in leadership research', *Journal of Applied Psychology*, vol. 89, no. 1, pp. 36–51.

Juran, J. (1974), *Quality Control Handbook*, McGraw-Hill, New York.

Kahay, P.S., Carr, H.H. and Snyder, C.A. (2003), 'Evaluating e-business opportunities. Technology and the decentralization of information systems', *Information Systems Management*, vol. 20, no. 3, pp. 51–60.

Kahneman, D. and Tversky, A. (1974), 'Judgement under uncertainty: Heuristics and biases', *Science*, vol. 185, pp. 1124–1131.

Kalb, K., Cherry, N., Kauzloric, R., Brender, A., Green, K., Miyagawa, L. and Shinoda-Mettler, A. (2006), 'A competency-based approach to public health nursing performance appraisal', *Public Health Nursing*, vol. 23, no. 2, pp. 115–124.

Kanter, R.M. (1979), 'Power failure in management circuits', *Harvard Business Review*, vol. 57, no. 4, pp. 65–75.

Kanter, R.M. (2001), 'The ten deadly mistakes of wanna dots', *Harvard Business Review*, vol. 79, no. 1, pp. 91–100.

Kaplan, R.S. and Norton, D.P. (1992), 'The balanced scorecard – measures that drive performance', *Harvard Business Review*, vol. 70, no. 1, pp. 71–79.

Kaplan, R.S. and Norton, D.P. (1993), 'Putting the balanced scorecard to work', *Harvard Business Review*, vol. 71, no. 5, pp. 134–142.

Kaplan, R.S. and Norton, D.P. (2008), *The Execution Premium: Linking strategy to operations for competitive advantage*, Harvard Business School Press, Boston, MA.

Katzenbach, J.R. and Smith, D.K. (1993), *The Wisdom of Teams*, Harvard Business School Press, Boston, MA.

Kay, J. (1996), *The Business of Economics*, Oxford University Press, Oxford.

Keaveney, P. and Kaufmann, M. (2001), *Marketing for the Voluntary Sector*, Kogan Page, London.

Kelman, H.C. (1961), 'Processes of opinion change', *Public Opinion Quarterly*, vol. 25, no. 1, pp. 57–78.

Kennedy, G., Boddy, D. and Paton, R. (2006), 'Managing the aftermath: Lessons from The Royal Bank of Scotland's acquisition of NatWest', *European Management Journal*, vol. 24, no. 5, pp. 368–379.

Kersley, B., Alpin, C., Forth, J., Bryson, A., Bewley, H., Dix, G. and Oxenbridge, S. (2006), *Inside the Workplace: Findings from the 2004 Workplace Employment Relations Survey*, Routledge, London.

Ketokivi, M. and Castañer, X. (2004), 'Strategic planning as an integrative device', *Administrative Science Quarterly*, vol. 49, no. 3, pp. 337–365.

Kipnis, D., Schmidt, S.M. and Wilkinson, I. (1980), 'Intra-organizational influence tactics: Explorations in getting one's way', *Journal of Applied Psychology*, vol. 65, no. 4, pp. 440–452.

Kirby, M.W. (2003), *Operational Research in War and Peace: The British Experience from the 1930s to the 1970s*, Imperial College Press, London.

Kirca, A.H., Jayachandran, S. and Bearden, W.O. (2005), 'Market orientation: A meta-analytic review and assessment of its antecedents and impact on performance', *Journal of Marketing*, vol. 69, no. 2, pp. 24–41.

Kirkman, B.L., Lowe, K.B. and Gibson, C.B. (2006), 'A quarter century of *Culture's Consequences*: A review of empirical research incorporating Hofstede's cultural values framework', *Journal of International Business Studies*, vol. 37, no. 3, pp. 285–320.

Kirsch, D., Goldfarb, B. and Gera, A. (2009), 'Form or substance: The role of business plans in venture capital decision making', *Strategic Management Journal*, vol. 30, no. 5, pp. 487–515.

Klein, G. (1997), *Sources of Power: How people make decisions*, MIT Press, Cambridge, MA.

Klein, N. (2000), *No logo: Taking aim at the brand bullies*, Flamingo, London.

Kleiner, A. (2003), *Who Really Matters: The core group theory of power, privilege and success*, Doubleday, New York.

Knapp, M.L. and Hall, J.A. (2002), *Non-verbal Communication in Human Interaction*, Thomson Learning, London.

Kochan, T.A. *et al.* (2003), 'The effects of diversity on business performance: Report of the diversity research network', *Human Resource Management*, vol. 42, no. 1, pp. 3–21.

Kolb, D., Rubin, E. and Osland, J. (1991), *Organizational Psychology*, Prentice Hall, Englewood Cliffs, NJ.

Kolk, A. and Pinkse, J. (2005), 'Business responses to climate change: Identifying emergent strategies', *California Management Review*, vol. 47, no. 3, pp. 6–20.

Komaki, J. (2003), 'Reinforcement theory at work: Enhancing and explaining what workers do', in L.W. Porter, G.A. Bigley and R.M. Steers (eds), *Motivation and Work Behavior* (7th edn), Irwin/McGraw-Hill, Burr Ridge, IL.

Komaki, J.L., Coombs, T., Redding, T.P. and Schepman, S. (2000), 'A rich and rigorous examination of applied behavior analysis research in the world of work', in C.L. Cooper and I.T. Robertson (eds), *International Review of Industrial and Organizational Psychology*, Wiley, Chichester, pp. 265–367.

Konzelmann, S., Conway, N., Trenberth, L. and Wilkinson, F. (2006), 'Corporate governance and human resource management', *British Journal of Industrial Relations*, vol. 44, no. 3, pp. 541–567.

Kotler, P., Armstrong, G., Wong, V. and Saunders, J. (2008), *Principles of Marketing* (5th European edn), Financial Times/Prentice Hall, Harlow.

Kotter, J.P. (1982), *The General Managers*, The Free Press, New York.

Kotter, J.P. (1990), *A Force for Change: How leadership differs from management*, The Free Press, New York.

Kotter, J.P. and Heskett, J. (1992), *Corporate Culture and Performance*, Free Press, New York.

Kotter, J.P. and Schlesinger, L.A. (1979), 'Choosing strategies for change', *Harvard Business Review*, vol. 57, no. 3, pp. 106–114.

Krackhardt, D. and Hanson, J.R. (1993), 'Informal networks: The company behind the chart', *Harvard Business Review*, vol. 71, no. 4, pp. 104–111.

Kramer, R.M. (2006), 'The great intimidators', *Harvard Business Review*, vol. 84, no. 2, pp. 88–96.

Kumar, N. (2006), 'Strategies to fight low-cost rivals', *Harvard Business Review*, vol. 84, no. 12, pp. 104–112.

Kumar, V., Venkatesan, R. and Reinartz, W. (2006), 'Knowing what to sell, when, and to whom', *Harvard Business Review*, vol. 84, no. 3, pp. 131–137.

Lamberton, G. (2005), 'Sustainability accounting – a brief history and conceptual framework,' *Accounting Forum*, vol. 29, no. 1, pp. 7–26.

Latham, G.P. and Locke, E.A. (2006), 'Enhancing the benefits and overcoming the pitfalls of goal setting', *Organizational Dynamics*, vol. 35, no. 4, pp. 332–340.

Laudon, K.C. and Laudon, J.P. (2004), *Management Information Systems: Managing the digital firm* (8th edn), Prentice Hall, Upper Saddle River, NJ.

Lawler, E.E. (1976), 'Control systems in organizations', in M.D. Dunnette (ed.), *Handbook of Industrial and Organizational Psychology*, Rand-McNally, Chicago, IL.

Lawler, E. (2008), *Talent*, Jossey-Bass, San Francisco, CA.

Lawrence, P. and Lorsch, J.W. (1967), *Organization and Environment*, Harvard Business School Press, Boston, MA.

Lawson, P. (2000), 'Performance-related pay', in R. Thorpe and G. Homan (eds), *Strategic Reward Systems*, Prentice Hall, Harlow.

Legge, K. (1978), *Power, Innovation and Problem Solving in Personnel Management*, McGraw-Hill, London.

Legge, K. (1995), *Human Resource Management: Rhetorics and realities*, Macmillan, London.

Legge, K. (2005), *Human Resource Management: Rhetorics and realities* (anniversary edn), Macmillan, London.

Leidecker, J.K. and Bruno, A.V. (1984), 'Identifying and using critical success factors' *Long Range Planning*, vol. 17, no. 1, pp. 23–32.

Le Meunier-FitzHugh, K. and Piercy, N.F. (2008), 'The importance of organisational structure for collaboration between sales and marketing', *Journal of General Management*, vol. 34, no. 1, pp. 19–35.

Lengel, R.H. and Daft, R.L. (1988), 'The selection of communication media as an executive skill', *Academy of Management Executive*, vol. 11, no. 3, pp. 225–232.

Levitt, T. (1960), 'Marketing myopia', *Harvard Business Review*, vol. 38, no. 4, pp. 45–56.

Levitt, T. (1983), 'The globalization of markets', *Harvard Business Review*, vol. 61, no. 3, pp. 92–102.

Lewin, K. (1947), 'Frontiers in group dynamics', *Human Relations*, vol. 1, no. 1, pp. 5–41.

Likert, R. (1961), *New Patterns of Management*, McGraw-Hill, New York.

Likert, R. (1967), *The Human Organization: Its Management and Value*, McGraw-Hill, New York.

Lindblom, C.E. (1959), 'The science of muddling through', *Public Administration Review*, vol. 19, no. 2, pp. 79–88.

Linstead, S., Fulop, L. and Lilley, S. (2004), *Management and Organization: A critical text*, Palgrave Macmillan, Basingstoke.

Lister, B. (2008), 'Heathrow Terminal 5: Enhancing environmental sustainability', *Proceedings of the Institution of Civil Engineers – Civil Engineering*, vol. 161, no. 5, pp. 21–24.

Lock, D. (2007), *Project Management* (9th edn), Gower, Aldershot.

Locke, E.A. (1968), 'Towards a theory of task motivation and incentives', *Organizational Behavior and Human Performance*, vol. 3, no. 2, pp. 157–189.

Locke, E.A. and Latham, G.P. (1990), *A Theory of Goal Setting and Task Performance*, Prentice Hall, Englewood Cliffs, NJ.

Locke, E.A. and Latham, G.P. (2002), 'Building a practically useful theory of goal setting and task motivation – A 35-year odyssey', *American Psychologist*, vol. 57, no. 9, pp. 705–717.

Lorsch, J.W. (1986), 'Managing culture: The invisible barrier to strategic change', *California Management Review*, vol. 28, no. 2, pp. 95–109.

Lovallo, D. and Kahneman, D. (2003), 'Delusions of success', *Harvard Business Review*, vol. 81, no. 7, pp. 56–63.

Luthans, F. (1988), 'Successful vs effective real managers', *Academy of Management Executive*, vol. 11, no. 2, pp. 127–132.

Lynch, R. (2003), *Corporate Strategy* (3rd edn), Financial Times/Prentice Hall, Harlow.

Magretta, J. (2002), *What Management Is (and Why it is Everyone's Business)*, Profile Books, London.

Malighetti, P., Paleari, S. and Redondi, R. (2009), 'Pricing strategies of low-cost airlines: the Ryanair case study', *Journal of Air Transport Management*, vol. 15, no. 4, pp. 195–203.

Mallin, C.A. (2007), *Corporate Governance,* (2nd edn) Oxford University Press, Oxford.

March, J.G. (1988), *Decisions and Organizations*, Blackwell, London.

Martin, J. (2002), *Organizational Culture: Mapping the terrain*, Sage, London.

Maslow, A. (1970), *Motivation and Personality* (2nd edn), Harper & Row, New York.

Massey, A.P., Montoya-Weiss, M.M. and Holcom, K. (2001), 'Re-engineering the customer relationship: Leveraging knowledge assets at IBM', *Decision Support Systems*, vol. 32, no. 2, pp. 155–170.

Matten, D. and Moon, J. (2008), '"Implicit" and "explicit" CSR: A conceptual framework for a comparative understanding of corporate social responsibility', *Academy of Management Review*, vol. 33, no. 2, pp. 404–424.

Mattila, A.S. (2009), 'How to handle PR disasters? An examination of the impact of communication response type and failure attributions on consumer perceptions', *Journal of Services Marketing*, vol. 23, no. 4, pp. 211–218.

Mayo, E. (1949), *The Social Problems of an Industrial Civilization,* Routledge and Kegan Paul, London.

McClelland, D. (1961), *The Achieving Society*, Van Nostrand Reinhold, Princeton, NJ.

McCrae, R.R. and John, O.P. (1992), 'An introduction to the five-factor model and its applications', *Journal of Personality*, vol. 60, no. 2, pp. 175–215.

McEntire, L.E., Dailey, L.R., Holly, K. and Mumford, M. (2006), 'Innovations in job analysis: Development and application of metrics to analyze job data', *Human Resource Management Review*, vol. 16, no. 3, pp. 310–323.

McGregor, D. (1960), *The Human Side of Enterprise*, McGraw-Hill, New York.

McKeen, J.D. and Smith, H.A. (2003) *Making IT Happen: Critical issues in IT management*, Wiley, Chichester.

McLaren, D.J. (1990), *David Dale of New Lanark*, Heatherbank Press, Milngavie.

McLean, B and Elkind, P. (2003), *The Smartest Guys in the Room*, Penguin, London.

McMillan, E. and Carlisle, Y. (2007), 'Strategy as order emerging from chaos: A public sector experience', *Long Range Planning*, vol. 40, no. 6, pp. 574–593.

McSweeney, B. (2002), 'Hofstede's model of national cultural differences and consequences: A triumph of faith – failure of analysis', *Human Relations*, vol. 55, no. 1, pp. 89–118.

Melancon, S. and Williams, M. (2006), 'Competency-based assessment center design: A case study', *Advances in Human Resource Management*, vol. 8, no. 2, pp. 283–314.

Micklethwait, J. and Wooldridge, A. (2003), *The Company: A short history of a revolutionary idea*, Weidenfeld and Nicolson, London.

Miller, S., Wilson, D. and Hickson, D. (2004), 'Beyond planning: Strategies for successfully implementing strategic decisions', *Long Range Planning*, vol. 37, no. 3, pp. 201–218.

Mintzberg, H. (1973), *The Nature of Managerial Work*, Harper & Row, New York.

Mintzberg, H. (1979), *The Structuring of Organizations*, Prentice Hall, Englewood Cliffs, NJ.

Mintzberg, H. (1994a), *The Rise and Fall of Strategic Planning*, Prentice Hall International, Hemel Hempstead.

Mintzberg, H. (1994b), 'Rethinking strategic planning. Part I: Pitfalls and fallacies', *Long Range Planning*, vol. 27, no. 3, pp. 12–21.

Mintzberg, H., Raisinghani, D. and Theoret, A. (1976), 'The structure of unstructured decision processes', *Administrative Science Quarterly*, vol. 21, no. 2, pp. 246–275.

Mitroff, I.I. (1983), *Stakeholders of the Organizational Mind*, Jossey-Bass, San Francisco, CA.

Morgan, G. (1997), *Images of Organization*, Sage, London.

Morgan, N.A., Vorhies, D.W. and Mason, C.H. (2009), 'Market orientation, marketing capabilities, and firm performance', *Strategic Management Journal*, vol. 30, no. 8, pp. 909–920.

Moritz, M. (2009), *Return to the Little Kingdom*, Duckworth Overlook, London.

Mowday, R.T. and Colwell, K.A. (2003), 'Employee reactions to unfair outcomes in the workplace: The contribution of Adams' equity theory to understanding work motivation', in L.W. Porter, G.A. Bigley and R.M. Steers (eds), *Motivation and Work Behavior* (7th edn), Irwin/McGraw-Hill, Burr Ridge, IL.

Muthusamy, S.K., Wheeler, J.V. and Simmons, B.L. (2005), 'Self-managing work teams: Enhancing organisational innovativeness', *Organisational Development Journal*, vol. 23, no. 3, pp. 53–67.

Nauta, A. and Sanders, K. (2001), 'Causes and consequences of perceived goal differences between departments within manufacturing organizations', *Journal of Occupational & Organizational Psychology*, vol. 74, no. 3, pp. 321–342.

Neely, A. and Al Najjar, M. (2006), 'Management learning not management control: The true role of performance measurement', *California Management Review*, vol. 48, no. 3, pp. 101–114.

Newell, S. (2006) 'Selection and assessment', in T. Redman and A. Wilkinson (eds) *Contemporary Human Resource Management*, Financial Times/Prentice-Hall, Harlow, pp. 65–98.

Newell, S. and Tansley, C. (2001), 'International uses of selection methods', in C.L. Cooper and I.T. Robertson (eds), *International Review of Industrial and Organizational Psychology*, Wiley, Chichester.

Newman, A.J. and Patel, D. (2004), 'The marketing directions of two fashion retailers', *European Journal of Marketing*, vol. 38, no. 7, pp. 770–789.

Nonaka, I. and Takeuchi, H. (1995), *The Knowledge Creating Company*, Oxford University Press, New York.

Nutt, P.C. (2002), *Why Decisions Fail: Avoiding the blunders and traps that lead to debacles*, Berrett-Koehler, San Francisco, CA.

Nutt, P.C. (2008), 'Investigating the success of decision making processes', *Journal of Management Studies*, vol. 45, no. 2, pp. 425–455.

Oakland, J. (1994), *Total Quality Management*, Butterworth/Heinemann, Oxford.

O'Connell, J.F. and Williams, G. (2005), 'Passengers' perceptions of low cost airlines and full service carriers', *Journal of Air Transport Management*, vol. 11, no. 4, pp. 259–272.

Ogbonna, E. and Harris, L.C. (1998), 'Organizational culture: It's not what you think', *Journal of General Management*, vol. 23, no. 3, pp. 35–48.

Ogbonna, E. and Harris, L.C. (2002), 'Organizational culture: A ten-year, two-phase study of change in the UK food retailing sector', *Journal of Management Studies*, vol. 39, no. 5, pp. 673–706.

O'Gorman, C., Bourke, S. and Murray, J.A. (2005), 'The nature of managerial work in small growth-oriented businesses', *Small Business Economics*, vol. 25, no. 1, pp. 1–16.

Ordanini, A., Rubera, G. and Sala, M. (2008), 'Integrating functional knowledge and embedding learning in new product launches: How project forms helped EMI Music', *Long Range Planning*, vol. 41, no. 1, pp. 17–32.

Orlitzky, M., Schmidt, F. and Rynes, S. (2003), 'Corporate social and financial performance: A meta-analysis', *Organization Studies*, vol. 24, no. 3, pp. 403–441.

Paik, Y. and Choi, D. (2005), 'The shortcomings of a standardized global knowledge management system: The case study of Accenture', *Academy of Management Executive*, vol. 19, no. 2, pp. 81–84.

Pan, S.L. (1999) 'Knowledge management at Buckman Laboratories', in H. Scarbrough and J. Swan (eds) *Case Studies in Knowledge Management,* IPO, London. (1999).

Papke-Shields, K.E., Malhotra, M.K. and Grover, V. (2006), 'Evolution in the strategic manufacturing planning process of organizations', *Journal of Operations Management*, vol. 24, no. 5, pp. 421–439.

Parker, D. and Stacey, R. (1994), *Chaos, Management and Economics: The implications of non-linear thinking*, Hobart Paper 125, Institute of Economic Affairs, London.

Parker, L.D. and Ritson, P.A. (2005), 'Revisiting Fayol: Anticipating contemporary management', *British Journal of Management*, vol. 16, no. 3, pp. 175–194.

Parry, E. and Tyson, S. (2008), 'An analysis of the use and success of online recruitment methods in the UK', *Human Resource Management Journal*, vol. 18, no. 3, pp. 257–274.

Pascale, R. (1990), *Managing on the Edge*, Penguin, London.

Pedler, M., Burgoyne, J. and Boydell, T. (1997), *The Learning Company: A strategy for sustainable development* (2nd edn), McGraw-Hill, London.

Peloza, J. (2006), 'Using corporate social responsibility as insurance for financial performance', *California Management Review*, vol. 48, no. 2, pp. 52–72.

Peters, T.J. and Waterman, D.H. (1982), *In Search of Excellence*, Harper & Row, London.

Pettigrew, A. (1985), *The Awakening Giant: Continuity and change in Imperial Chemical Industries*, Blackwell, Oxford.

Pettigrew, A. (1987), 'Context and action in the transformation of the firm', *Journal of Management Studies*, vol. 24, no. 6, pp. 649–670.

Pettigrew, A., Ferlie, E. and McKee, L. (1992), *Shaping Strategic Change*, Sage, London.

Pfeffer, J. (1992a), *Managing with Power*, Harvard Business School Press, Boston, MA.

Pfeffer, J. (1992b), 'Understanding power in organizations', *California Management Review*, vol. 34, no. 2, pp. 29–50.

Pfeffer, J. (2005), 'Producing sustainable competitive advantage through the effective management of people', *Academy of Management Executive*, vol. 19, no. 4, pp. 95–106.

Pfeffer, J. and Sutton, R.I. (2006), 'Evidence-based management', *Harvard Business Review*, vol. 84, no. 1, pp. 62–74.

Pfeffer, J. and Sutton, R.I. (2006), *Hard Facts, Dangerous Truths and Total Nonsense*, Harvard Business School Press, Boston, MA.

Pierce, J.L. and Gardner, D.G. (2004), 'Self-esteem within the work and organizational context: A review of the organization-based self-esteem literature', *Journal of Management*, vol. 30, no. 5, pp. 591–622.

Pierce, L. and Snyder, J. (2008), 'Ethical spillovers in firms: Evidence from vehicle emissions testing', *Management Science*, vol. 54, no. 11, pp. 1891–1903.

Pinder, J. (2001), *The European Union: A very short introduction*, Oxford University Press, Oxford.

Pinto, J. (1998), 'Understanding the role of politics in successful project management', *International Journal of Project Management*, vol. 18, no. 2, pp. 85–91.

Plakoyiannaki, E., Tzokas, N., Dimitratos, P. and Saren, M. (2008), 'How critical is employee orientation for customer relationship management? Insights from a case study', *Journal of Management Studies*, vol. 45, no. 2, pp. 268–293.

Porter, C.E. and Donthu, N. (2008), 'Cultivating trust and harvesting value in virtual communities', *Management Science*, vol. 54, no. 1, pp. 113–128.

Porter, M.E. (1980a), *Competitive Strategy*, Free Press, New York.

Porter, M.E. (1980b), *Competitive Advantage*, Free Press, New York.

Porter, M.E. (1985), *Competitive Advantage: Creating and sustaining superior performance*, Free Press, New York.

Porter, M.E. (1994), 'Competitive strategy revisited: a view from the 1990s', in P.B. Duffy (ed.), *The Relevance of a Decade,* Harvard Business School Press, Boston, MA.

Porter, M.E. (2008), 'The five competitive forces that shape strategy', *Harvard Business Review*, vol. 86, no. 1, pp. 78–93.

Prastacos, G., Soderquist, K., Spanos, Y. and Van Wassenhove, L. (2002), 'An integrated framework for managing change in the new competitive landscape', *European Management Journal*, vol. 20, no. 1, pp. 55–71.

Pratten, J. and Scoffield, S. (2007), 'The role of the internet in the marketing of independent public houses in the UK', *Service Industries Journal*, vol. 27, no. 1–2, pp. 125–137.

Pugh, D.S. and Hickson, D.J. (1976), *Organization Structure in its Context: The Aston Programme I*, Gower, Aldershot.

Puig, F., Marques, H. and Ghauri, P.N. (2009), 'Globalisation and its impact on operational decisions', *International Journal of Operations and Production Management*, vol. 29, no. 7, pp. 692–719.

Pye, A. (2002) 'Corporate Directing: Governing, strategizing and leading in action', *Corporate Governance – an International Review*, vol. 10, no. 3, pp. 153–162.

Quinn, J.B. (1980), *Strategies for Change: Logical incrementalism*, Irwin, Homewood, IL.

Quinn, R.E., Faerman, S.R., Thompson, M.P. and McGrath, M.R. (2003), *Becoming a Master Manager* (3rd edn), Wiley, New York.

Reiter-Palmon, R., Brown, M., Sandall, D., Bublotz, C. and Nimps, T. (2006), 'Development of an O*Net web-based job analysis and its implementation in the US Navy: Lessons learned', *Human Resource Management Review*, vol. 16, no. 3, pp. 294–309.

Restubog, S.L.D., Bordia, P. and Tang, R.L. (2007), 'Behavioural outcomes of psychological contract breach in a non-western culture: The moderating role of equity sensitivity', *British Journal of Management*, vol. 18, no. 4, pp. 376–386.

Riccabone, A. and Leone, E.L. (2010), 'Implementing strategies through management control systems: The case of sustainability', *International Journal of Productivity and Performance Management*, vol. 59, no. 2, pp. 130–144.

Rivard, S., Bennoit, A.A., Patry, M., Pare, G. and Smith, H.A. (2004), *Information Technology and Organizational Transformation*, Elsevier/Butterworth-Heinemann, Oxford.

Robbins, S.P. and Coulter, M. (2005), *Management* (8th edn), Pearson Education, Upper Saddle River, NJ.

Roberts, P. and Dowling, G. (2002), 'Corporate reputation and sustained superior financial performance', *Strategic Management Journal*, vol. 23, no. 12, pp. 1077–1093.

Roberts, J., McNulty, T. and Stiles, P. (2005), 'Beyond agency conceptions of the work of the non-executive director: Creating accountability in the boardroom', *British Journal of Management*, vol. 16, Supplement 1, pp. S5–S26.

Robertson, I. (1996), 'Personnel selection and assessment', in P. Warr (ed.), *Psychology at Work* (4th edn), Penguin, Harmondsworth.

Robey, D., Schwaig, K.S. and Jin, L. (2003), 'Intertwining material and virtual work', *Information and Organization*, vol. 13, no. 3, pp. 111–129.

Roddick, A. (1991), *Body and Soul*, Ebury Press, London.

Rodriguez, P., Uhlenbruck, K. and Eden, L. (2005), 'Government corruption and the entry strategies of multinationals', *Academy of Management Review*, vol. 30, no. 2, pp. 383–396.

Roethlisberger, F.J. and Dickson, W.J. (1939), *Management and the Worker*, Harvard University Press, Cambridge, MA.

Ronen, S. and Shenkar, O. (1985), 'Clustering countries on attitudinal dimensions – a review and synthesis', *Academy of Management Review*, vol. 10, no. 3, pp. 435–454.

Rosen, S. (1998), 'A lump of clay', *Communication World*, vol. 15, no. 7, p. 58.

Rosener, J.B. (1997), *America's Competitive Secret: Women managers*, Oxford University Press, Oxford.

Ross, S., Westerfield, R. and Jordan, B. (2005), *Fundamentals of Corporate Finance*, McGraw-Hill/Irwin, New York.

Rousseau, D.M. and Schalk, R. (2000), *Psychological Contracts in Employment: Cross-national perspectives*, Sage, London.

Royle, E. (1998), *Robert Owen and the commencement of the millennium: A study of the Harmony community*, Manchester University Press, Manchester.

Rugman, A.M. (2005), *The Regional Multinationals*, Cambridge University Press, Cambridge.

Rugman, A.M. and Hodgetts, R.M. (2003), *International Business*, FT/Prentice Hall, Harlow.

Ryals, L. (2005), 'Making customer relationship management work: The measurement and profitable management of customer relationships', *Journal of Marketing*, vol. 69, no. 4, pp. 252–261.

Sabherwal, R., Hirschheim, R. and Goles, T. (2001), 'The dynamics of alignment: Insights from a punctuated equilibrium', *Organization Science*, vol. 12, no. 2, pp. 179–197.

Sahay, A. (2007), 'How to reap higher profits with dynamic pricing', *MIT Sloan Management Review*, vol. 48, no. 4, pp. 53–60.

Sahlman, W.A. (1997), 'How to write a great business plan', *Harvard Business Review*, vol. 75, no. 4, pp. 98–108.

Saunders, C., Van Slyke, C. and Vogel, D.R. (2004), 'My time or yours? Managing time visions in global virtual teams', *Academy of Management Executive*, vol. 18, no. 1, pp. 19–31.

Scarbrough, H. and Swan, J. (eds) (1999), *Case Studies in Knowledge Management*, IPD, London.

Schaefer, A. (2007), 'Contrasting institutional and performance accounts of environmental management systems: Three case studies in the UK water & sewerage industry', *Journal of Management Studies*, vol. 44, no. 4, pp. 506–535.

Schein, E. (2004), *Organization Culture and Leadership* (3rd edn), Jossey-Bass, San Francisco, CA.

Schwartz, B. (2004), *The Paradox of Choice*, Ecco, New York.

Schwenk, C.R. (1984), 'Cognitive simplification processes in strategic decision making', *Strategic Management Journal*, vol. 5, pp. 111–128.

Senge, P., Smith, B., Kruschwitz, N., Laur, J. and Schley, S. (2008), *The Necessary Revolution: How individuals and organizations are working together to create a sustainable world*, Nicholas Brealey Publishing, London.

Shao, L. and Webber, S. (2006), 'A cross-cultural test of the "five-factor model of personality and transformational leadership"', *Journal of Business Research*, vol. 59, no. 8, pp. 936–944.

Sharp, B. and Dawes, J. (2001), 'What is differentiation and how does it work?', *Journal of Marketing Management*, vol. 17, no. 7/8, pp. 739–759.

Shaw, M.E. (1978), 'Communication networks fourteen years later', in L. Berkowitz (ed.), *Group Processes*, Academic Press, London.

Shaw, W.H. (1991), *Business Ethics*, Wadsworth, Belmont, CA.

Simon, H. (1960), *Administrative Behavior*, Macmillan, New York.

Simons, R. (1995), 'Control in an age of empowerment', *Harvard Business Review*, vol. 73, no. 2, pp. 80–88.

Sine, W.D., Mitsuhashi, H. and Kirsch, D.A. (2006), 'Revisiting Burns and Stalker: Formal structure and new venture performance in emerging economic sectors', *Academy of Management Journal*, vol. 49, no. 1, pp. 121–132.

Skinner, B.F. (1971), *Contingencies of Reinforcement*, Appleton-Century-Crofts, East Norwalk, CT.

Slack, N., Chambers, S. and Johnston, R. (2007), *Operations Management*, FT/Prentice Hall, Harlow.

Smith, A. (1776), *The Wealth of Nations*, ed. with an introduction by Andrew Skinner (1974), Penguin, Harmondsworth.

Smith, A. and Sparks, L. (2009), 'Reward redemption behaviour in retail loyalty schemes', *British Journal of Management*, vol. 20, no. 2, pp. 204–218.

Smith, J.H. (1998), 'The enduring legacy of Elton Mayo', *Human Relations*, vol. 51, no. 3, pp. 221–249.

Smith, M., Busi, M., Ball, P. and Van Der Meer, R. (2008), 'Factors influencing an organisation's ability to manage innovation: A structured literature review and conceptual model', *International Journal of Innovation Management*, vol. 12, no. 4, pp. 655–676.

Sparrow, P., Brewster, C. and Harris, H. (2004), *Globalizing Human Resource Management*, Routledge, London.

Sparrowe, R.T. and Liden, R.C. (2005), 'Two routes to influence: Integrating leader–member exchange and social network perspectives', *Administrative Science Quarterly*, vol. 50, no. 4, pp. 505–535.

Sparrowe, R.T., Liden, R.C., Wayne, S.J. and Kraimer, M.L. (2001), 'Social networks and the performance of individuals and groups', *Academy of Management Journal*, vol. 44, no. 2, pp. 316–325.

Sprague, L. (1990), 'Operations management: Productivity and quality performance', in E.G.C. Collins and M.A. Devanna (eds), *The Portable MBA*, Wiley, New York.

Sprague, L. (2007), 'Evolution of the field of operations management', *Journal of Operations Management*, vol. 25, no. 2, pp. 219–238.

Spriegel, W.R. and Myers, C.E. (eds) (1953), *The Writings of the Gilbreths*, Irwin, Homewood, IL.

Stacey, R. (1994), *Managing the Unknowable*, Jossey Bass, San Francisco, CA.

Stavins, R.N. (1994), 'The challenge of going green', *Harvard Business Review*, vol. 72, no. 4, pp. 38–39.

Steinbock, D. (2001), *The Nokia revolution*, American Management Association, New York.

Stern, N. (2009), *A Blueprint for a Safer Planet: How to manage climate change and create a new era of progress and prosperity*, The Bodley Head, London.

Stewart, R. (1967), *Managers and their Jobs*, Macmillan, London.

Storey, J. (1992), *Developments in the Management of Human Resources*, Blackwell, Oxford.

Stott, P.A. (2010), 'Detection and attribution of climate change: A regional perspective', *Wiley Interdisciplinary Reviews – Climate Change*, vol. 1, no. 2.

Sull, D. (2005), 'Strategy as active waiting', *Harvard Business Review*, vol. 83, no. 9, pp. 120–129.

Sull, D.N. (2007), 'Closing the gap between strategy and execution', *MIT Sloan Management Review*, vol. 48, no. 4, pp. 30–38.

Sull, D.N. and Spinosa, C. (2005), 'Using commitments to manage across units', *MIT Sloan Management Review*, vol. 47, no. 1, pp. 73–81.

Swartz, M. and Watkins, S. (2002), *Power Failure: The rise and fall of Enron*, Aurum, London.

Tannenbaum, R. and Schmidt, W.H. (1973), 'How to choose a leadership pattern: Should a manager be democratic or autocratic – or something in between?', *Harvard Business Review*, vol. 37, no. 2, pp. 95–102.

Tapscott, D. (2009), *Grown Up Digital: How the net generation is changing your world*, McGraw-Hill, New York.

Tapscott, D. and Williams, A.D. (2006), *Wikinomics: How mass collaboration changes everything*, Viking Penguin, New York.

Tayeb, M.H. (1996), *The Management of a Multicultural Workforce*, Wiley, Chichester.

Taylor, F.W. (1917), *The Principles of Scientific Management*, Harper, New York.

Taylor, J.W. (2008), 'A comparison of univariate time series methods for forecasting intraday arrivals at a call center', *Management Science*, vol. 54, no. 2, pp. 253–265.

Thomas, A.B. (2003), *Controversies in Management: Issues, debates and answers* (2nd edn), Routledge, London.

Thompson, J.D. (1967), *Organizations in Action*, McGraw-Hill, New York.

Thompson, M.P.A. and Walsham, G. (2004), 'Placing knowledge management in context', *Journal of Management Studies*, vol. 41, no. 5, pp. 725–747.

Thompson, P. and McHugh, D. (2002), *Work Organizations: A critical introduction*, Palgrave, Basingstoke.

Tidd, J. and Bessant, J. (2009), *Managing Innovation: Integrating technological, market and organisational change*, Wiley, Chichester.

Toffler, B.L. and Reingold, J. (2003), *Final Accounting: Ambition, greed and the fall of Arthur Andersen*, Broadway Books, New York.

Tonnessen, T. (2005), 'Continuous innovation through company-wide employee participation', *The TQM Magazine*, vol. 17, no. 2, pp. 195–207.

Tran, T. and Blackman, M. (2006), 'The dynamics and validity of the group selection interview', *Journal of Social Psychology*, vol. 146, no. 2, pp. 183–201.

Trevino, L.K. (1986), 'Ethical decision-making in organisations: A person–situation interactionist model', *Academy of Management Review*, vol. 11, no. 3, pp. 601–617.

Trevino, L.K. and Weaver, G.R. (2003), *Managing Ethics in Business Organizations: Social scientific perspectives*, Stanford University Press, Stanford, CA.

Trist, E.L. and Bamforth, K.W. (1951), 'Some social and psychological consequences of the longwall method of coal getting', *Human Relations*, vol. 4, no. 1, pp. 3–38.

Trompennaars, F. (1993), *Riding the Waves of Culture: Understanding cultural diversity in business*, The Economist Books, London.

Truss, C. and Gill, J. (2009), 'Managing the HR function: The role of social capital', *Personnel Review*, vol. 38, no. 6, pp. 674–695.

Tuckman, B. and Jensen, N. (1977), 'Stages of small group development revisited', *Group and Organizational Studies*, vol. 2, pp. 419–427.

Turner, M.E. and Pratkanis, A.R. (1998), 'Twenty-five years of groupthink theory and research: Lessons from an evaluation of the theory', *Organizational Behavior and Human Decision Processes*, vol. 73, no. 2, pp. 105–115.

Uhl-Bien, M. and Graen, G.B. (1998), 'Individual self-management: Analysis of professionals' self-managing activities in functional and cross-functional teams', *Academy of Management Journal*, vol. 41, no. 3, pp. 340–350.

Van der Heijden, K. (1996), *Scenarios: The art of strategic conversation*, Wiley, Chichester.

Van der Vegt, G.S. and Bunderson, J.S. (2005), 'Learning and performance in multidisciplinary teams: The importance of collective team identification,' *Academy of Management Journal*, vol. 48, no. 3, pp. 532–547.

Vogel, D. (2005), *The Market for Virtue: The potential and limits of corporate social responsibility*, Brookings Institution Press, Washington, DC.

Vroom, V.H. (1964), *Work and Motivation*, Wiley, New York.

Vroom, V.H. and Yetton, P.W. (1973), *Leadership and Decision-making*, University of Pittsburgh Press, Pittsburgh, PA.

Wall, T.D. and Clegg, C.W. (1981), 'A longitudinal field study of group work redesign', *Journal of Occupational Behaviour*, vol. 2, no. 1, pp. 31–49.

Wall, T.D., Kemp, N.J., Jackson, P.R. and Clegg, C.W. (1986), 'Outcome of autonomous workgroups: A long-term field experiment', *Academy of Management Journal*, vol. 29, no. 2, pp. 280–304.

Walsham, G. (1993), *Interpreting Information Systems in Organisations*, Wiley, Chichester.

Walton, E.J. (2005), 'The Persistence of Bureaucracy: A meta-analysis of Weber's model of bureaucratic control', *Organization Studies*, vol. 26, no. 4, pp. 569–600.

Walton, R.E. (1977), 'Work innovations at Topeka: After six years', *Journal of Applied Behavioral Science*, vol. 13, no. 3, pp. 422–433.

Walton, R.E. (1985), 'From control to commitment in the workplace', *Harvard Business Review*, vol. 63, no. 2, pp. 76–84.

Watts, S. (2001), *The Magic Kingdom: Walt Disney and the American way of life*, Houghton-Mifflin, Boston, MA.

Watson, T.J. (1994), *In Search of Management*, Routledge, London.

Weber, M. (1947), *The Theory of Social and Economic Organization*, Free Press, Glencoe, IL.

Weeks, J. (2004), *Unpopular Culture: The culture of complaint in a British bank*, University of Chicago Press, Chicago, IL.

Weill, P. and Ross, J. (2005), 'A matrixed approach to designing IT governance', *MIT Sloan Management Review*, vol. 46, no. 2, pp. 26–34.

West, M.A., Guthrie, J.P., Dawson, J.F., Borrill, C.S. and Carter, M. (2006), 'Reducing patient mortality in hospitals: The role of human resource management', *Journal of Organizational Behavior*, vol. 27, no. 7, pp. 983–1002.

Westphal, J.D. and Bednar, M.K. (2008), 'The pacification of institutional investors', *Administrative Science Quarterly*, vol. 53, no. 1, pp. 29–72.

Whetten, D.A. and Cameron, K.S. (2002), *Developing Management Skills* (6th edn), Prentice Hall International, Upper Saddle River, NJ.

Whipp, R., Rosenfeld, R. and Pettigrew, A. (1988), 'Understanding strategic change processes: Some preliminary British findings', in A. Pettigrew (ed.), *The Management of Strategic Change*, Blackwell, Oxford.

Whitley, R. (1999), *Divergent Capitalisms: The social structuring and change of business systems*, Oxford University Press, Oxford.

Whitley, R. (2009), 'US capitalism: A tarnished model?', *Academy of Management Perspectives*, vol. 23, no. 2, pp. 11–22.

Whittington, R., Molloy, E., Mayer, M. and Smith, A. (2006), 'Practices of strategising/organising: Broadening strategy work and skills', *Long Range Planning*, vol. 39, no. 6, pp. 615–629.

Wieder, H., Booth, P., Matolcsy, Z.P. and Ossimitz, M.-L. (2006), 'The impact of ERP systems on firm and business process performance', *Journal of Enterprise Information Management*, vol. 19, no. 1, pp. 13–29.

Williams, K., Haslam, C. and Williams, J. (1992), 'Ford vs Fordism: The beginnings of mass production?', *Work, Employment and Society*, vol. 6, no. 4, pp. 517–555.

Willoughby, K.A. and Zappe, C.J. (2006), 'A methodology to optimize foundation seminar assignments', *Journal of the Operational Research Society*, vol. 57, no. 8, pp. 950–956.

Winstanley, D. and Woodall, J. (2000), 'The ethical dimension of human resource management', *Human Resource Management Journal*, vol. 10, no. 2, pp. 5–20.

Woiceshyn, J. (2009), 'Lessons from "Good Minds": How CEOs use intuition, analysis and guiding principles to make strategic decisions', *Long Range Planning*, vol. 42, no. 3, pp. 298–319.

Wolf, A. and Jenkins, A. (2006), 'Explaining greater test use for selection: The role of HR professionals in a world of expanding regulation', *Human Resource Management Journal*, vol. 16, no. 2, pp. 193–213.

Wolff, H.-G. and Moser, K. (2009), 'Effects of networking on career success: A longitudinal study', *Journal of Applied Psychology*, vol. 94, no. 1, pp. 196–206.

Wolstenholme, A., Fugeman, I. and Hammond, F. (2008), 'Heathrow Terminal 5: Delivery strategy', *Proceedings of the Institution of Civil Engineers – Civil Engineering*, vol. 161, no. 5, pp. 10–15.

Womack, J.P. and Jones, D.T. (1996), *Lean Thinking: Banish waste and create wealth in your corporation*, Simon and Schuster, New York.

Woodward, J. (1958), *Management and Technology*, HMSO, London.

Woodward, J. (1965), *Industrial Organization: Theory and practice*, Oxford University Press, Oxford (2nd edn 1980).

Yip, G.S. (2003), *Total Global Strategy II*, Pearson Education, Upper Saddle River, NJ.

Yukl, G.A. (2001), *Leadership in Organizations* (5th edn), Prentice Hall, Upper Saddle River, NJ.

Yukl, G. and Falbe, C.M. (1990), 'Influence tactics in upward, downward and lateral influence attempts', *Journal of Applied Psychology*, vol. 75, no. 2, pp. 132–140.

Yukl, G. and Tracey, J.B. (1992), 'Consequences of influence tactics used with subordinates, peers and the boss', *Journal of Applied Psychology*, vol. 77, no. 4, pp. 525–535.

Zheng, C., Morrison, M. and O'Neill, G. (2006), 'An empirical study of high performance HRM practices in Chinese SMEs', *International Journal of Human Resource Management*, vol. 17, no. 10, pp. 1771–1803.

Zolkiewski, J. (2004), 'Relationships are not ubiquitous in marketing', *European Journal of Marketing*, vol. 38, no. 1/2, pp. 24–29.

INDEX

Note: Bold page numbers indicate chapter extents, glossary definitions, tables, figures and diagrams